THE MELODY
LINGERS ON

Happy Graduation, Michael
Best of Luck in Music
We've enjoyed singing with you!
Barb + Ralph Gibson
May 27, 1990

THE MELODY LINGERS ON

The Great Songwriters and Their Movie Musicals

ROY HEMMING

Newmarket Press
New York

LC 85-061812
ISBN 0-937858-57-9

First Edition

1 2 3 4 5 6 7 8 9 0

TO MY MOTHER AND FATHER,
*who really started all this when they took me to see my first movie musical at the ol'
neighborhood Strand—when I was just a bit younger than the genre*

AND TO DAVID AND JOANNE,
*who helped convince me that a whole younger generation still loved and is touched by the
songs of these composers and their movie musicals*

Contents

Acknowledgments
ix

INTRODUCTION
xi

HAROLD ARLEN
1

IRVING BERLIN
29

GEORGE GERSHWIN
55

JEROME KERN
85

JIMMY MCHUGH
123

COLE PORTER
151

RALPH RAINGER
187

RICHARD RODGERS
211

HARRY WARREN
253

RICHARD WHITING
301

And Not To Be Forgotten:
Nacio Herb Brown, Hoagy Carmichael,
Frank Loesser, Arthur Schwartz,
Jule Styne, James Van Heusen
323

CONTENTS

Academy Award Nominations/Winners
373

Bibliography
376

Index
381

ACKNOWLEDGMENTS

For their guidance or help in locating and verifying information for some of the chapters and/or making useful materials available, the author is especially grateful to David Berk, Larry Carr, Joe Franklin, Morton Gould, Murray Grand, Julie Hirsch, Ethel Reichenthal Kanowith, Edward Jablonski, David Lahm, John Meyer, Lucille Meyers, Constance Rainger, Ken Richards, Leo Robin, Joe Savage, Alfred E. Simon, Kay Swift, Mary Tyler, Margaret Whiting, and Ronny Whyte.

For their helpful comments on parts of the manuscript in progress, the author is deeply grateful to David Hajdu, Edward Jablonski, Genevieve Kazdin, Barbara Lea, Larry O'Leno, Alfred E. Simon, and Michael Wasserman.

Attributions regarding the "dubbers" of various performers' singing voices are based primarily on the pioneering articles on this subject by Larry Carr and Miles Krueger.

Special thanks must go to Esther Margolis, founder and president of Newmarket Press, for suggesting the book as a "sequel" to a Critic's Choice tribute I wrote about Irving Berlin's musicals for *Video Review* on the occasion of Berlin's ninety-fifth birthday; and, most particularly, to Newmarket's Katherine Heintzelman for her crucial and always gracious guidance and nurturing of the manuscript through to its publication.

Introduction

Thanks to movie revival houses, television, and, most recently, videocassettes and videodiscs, the songs and dances of movie musicals are reaching more people today than their creators ever envisioned. What were essentially planned as "passing entertainments" in the 1930s, '40s, and '50s continue to be more popular than ever—and many have become revered classics among critics and cultural historians as well as among legions of film buffs. Many of these entertainments, in other words, have become anything but passing. Their melodies have indeed lingered on.

The great movie musicals of past years have frequently been written about and judged in terms of their star performers—Fred Astaire, Bing Crosby, Alice Faye, Judy Garland, Betty Grable, Gene Kelly, Frank Sinatra, and so on. Sometimes their creative directors have been studied and analyzed too—Busby Berkeley, Arthur Freed, Vincente Minnelli.

But the keystones of musicals are the songwriters, the men and women who compose the music and write the lyrics for the songs, dances, and production numbers. And it's usually the songs that bring viewers back to the old musicals time and time again, or that attract new generations to see and enjoy them for the first time. Yet for many years the Hollywood studios, with few exceptions, treated songwriters far less respectfully than they did their stars or directors. They rarely celebrated their work the way Broadway did.

The public celebrated it, however. Many of these movies' songs have gone far beyond the films they came from, or the radio and TV *Hit Parade,* or sheet-music and best-seller lists of their respective years. They still provide the programming core for radio stations that specialize in so-called "standard pops," and are the basic repertoire for thousands of supper club and cabaret performers in all parts of the country.

I'm not sure I agree with those wags who say that these songs have survived because the producers of bygone years made movies for a wide cross section of adults, in contrast to the youth orientation of so many of today's movies and pop songs. Forgotten in that argument is the fact that most old-time movie producers thought that the average American had the mind of a twelve-year-old. It's more than possible, I suspect, that today's MTV shorts and rock movies will be viewed in 2015 and 2025 with much the same kind of nostalgia that we now witness for the music of the '30s and '40s.

Whatever the case, many of the movie musicals of the past and their songs do indeed survive. This book takes us back to them, through the composers who I believe contributed the most to the so-called "golden age" of movie musicals. It covers both their original work for Hollywood *and* the movie versions of their Broadway shows (which are the way most people continue to know these shows). It also, perhaps, puts an unjust emphasis on the composers at the expense of the lyricists. Of the ten songwriters I've selected, only Irving Berlin and Cole Porter regularly wrote lyrics as well as music. The others are composers who usually worked with different lyricists. But I have scrupulously tried to give proper credit throughout to the respective lyricists of each song, even though my primary focus remains on the composers. After all, Oscar

Hammerstein II's wife, Dorothy, had a point when she properly disputed someone's reference to "Jerome Kern's 'Ol' Man River' " by insisting that "Jerome Kern wrote *da - da - dada*. It was my husband who wrote 'Ol' Man River'!" There are indeed many lyricists who deserve the accolade of "great" just as much as the composers under discussion here. But that's another book.

Each chapter begins with a biographical sketch of the composer, summarizing key facts about his life prior to his movie work, in order to put the films in proper historical perspective. Further biographical material is included as part of the discussion of individual films where appropriate.

The chief focus of each chapter is a series of capsule critiques of the most interesting of each composer's movies and the individual songs within them—including not only his original movie work but also those adapted from Broadway shows and, in some cases, nonmusicals. These critiques are also intended, in part, as a guide for those who may want to collect or anthologize favorite musical sequences for their own home libraries through the use of videocassette recorders. Some of these critiques have been adapted from reviews I have written for *Video Review* and other publications, but in all cases the critiques have involved rewatching the entire movie or its musical sequences from my own extensive collection or other sources.

Finally, at the end of each chapter, there is a complete checklist of each composer's movies and their songs—with an indication as to which ones are available on sound-track LP (audio) recordings, videocassettes, or videodiscs as of mid-1986. The list includes some that have been withdrawn from the active catalogs, but which may still be available in shops that specialize in cut-outs or out-of-print discs or cassettes.

I make no pretentions about the biographical material being exhaustive or comprehensive with regard to any of the composer's lives. Nor are there significantly new revelations about these composers or their work. That has not been my purpose. My primary aim has been to bring together in one volume a wealth of information previously available to musical and movie buffs only from a wide variety of different sources—and to present it in a critical framework centered in movie musicals. A bibliography at the end of this book includes a number of recommended, in-depth composer biographies and other reference studies.

There is also no attempt at a musicological analysis of individual songs, as in Alec Wilder's trailblazing *American Popular Song*. The aim, instead, is to provide movie buffs with an overview of the major songwriters and hundreds of their songs—to enhance the viewing of the movies themselves whenever and wherever they are shown, or, in some cases, to guide you past those that there'll be no loss in your missing.

A few words about the dates given for individual movies: in the listings and in most of the critiques of specific films, I have adhered to the official release date of the picture in the United States. However, a songwriter may have worked on that film during a one or two-year period prior to that date, and sometimes biographical material reflects that difference.

No book about movie musicals, of course, can ever equal the special pleasures of watching the musicals themselves, whether in a theater or on a TV screen, and hearing their songs. It is my hope that the information and commentary in this book will encourage, extend, and heighten those pleasures.

R. H.
New York City, 1986

Harold Arlen in the 1970s.

HAROLD ARLEN

*L*yricist Ira Gershwin once noted that "many Arlen songs take time to catch on." But when they do, he added, they last. Never a standard "32-bar man," Arlen created some of this century's most distinctive and individual songs. Yet of all the major American popular-music composers who worked both on Broadway and in Hollywood, Arlen was probably identified with fewer hit shows and movies than any of the others. Arlen's movie work, moreover, was never identified with one or two particular studios the way that of Berlin, Gershwin, Rainger, and Warren was. Over the years Arlen free-lanced with most of the major studios, and he created some of his best work for what, at the time, were lesser studios and for independent producers.

Yet even if he didn't have a total of twenty-eight movies to his credit, Arlen would be a candidate for any Hollywood songwriters' hall of fame for two scores alone: 1939's *The Wizard of Oz* and 1954's *A Star Is Born.* Each film gave Judy Garland a song with which she will forever be identified: the young, winsome Judy of '39 with "Over the Rainbow," and the mature, belting-her-heart-out Judy of '54 with "The Man That Got Away." Along the way, Arlen would gather nine Academy Award

I

nominations, although only one actual win (for "Over the Rainbow"). And none of his Broadway shows would yield as many song hits as his movies.

Arlen's Broadway output included an antiwar satire (*Hooray for What!*, 1937, with Ed Wynn), a salute to an early feminist (*Bloomer Girl*, 1944, with Celeste Holm), and three musicals that presented blacks in leading roles (*St. Louis Woman*, 1946, with Pearl Bailey and the Nicholas Brothers; *House of Flowers*, 1954, with Pearl Bailey and Diahann Carroll; and *Jamaica*, 1957, with Lena Horne). Perhaps most tellingly of all, none of these Broadway shows was ever turned into a movie musical—not because of their songs, certainly, but because the shows' books were considered too controversial or "ahead of their time" by the studio chieftains then in control of major production. But these shows nonetheless helped to win many admirers for Arlen as a quality songwriter who took chances and didn't always play it safe, especially where race relations are concerned.

Harold Arlen was born Hyman Arluck on February 15, 1905, in Buffalo, New York. He was about seven years old when he began singing in the choir of the synagogue where his father was cantor. As Arlen's musical interests developed, his parents encouraged him to study music seriously and perhaps even become a music teacher—on the theory that he could then pick his own working hours and avoid having to toil on *shabbas,* the Jewish Sabbath.

But young Harold's main musical interests turned out to be jazz and show music, not exactly the sort his parents hoped he'd pursue. He was fifteen when he dropped out of high school to take a job playing piano in a Buffalo silent-movie theater. Within a few years he was playing in Buffalo cafés and had organized his own combo, The Snappy Trio. This expanded to The Southbound Shufflers, which played on Lake Erie steamers. Arlen was then wooed away to join a well-known eleven-piece jazz band, The Buffalodians. Arlen became the band's pianist, arranger, and singer. As he once told an interviewer: "I could always improvise and I loved to invent unconventional turns for the men in the band who couldn't do anything but follow the written melody. I wanted them to get off it and sound like somebody from New York."

Arlen finally decided to take both himself and his arrangements to New York City. Over the next three years Arlen not only sold some arrangements in New York but also began writing his own songs. Then in 1928, at age twenty-three, he was hired to be the pianist and vocalist with Arnold Johnson's well-known dance band—which meant a chance to sing on radio with the band, in addition to its other performance dates. When the Johnson band was signed for *George White's Scandals of 1928,* one of Arlen's jobs was to sing some of the show's songs in the pit during intermission, to stimulate the songs' sheet-music sales. One of the people who heard him and liked him was composer Vincent Youmans (*No, No, Nanette* and *Hit the Deck*).

Youmans hired Arlen as a singer for his 1929 musical *Great Day*. During breaks in rehearsals, Arlen would sometimes noodle with songs of his own. Composer Harry Warren, on a visit to friends in the show, heard Arlen one day and introduced him to a young lyricist, Ted Koehler, with the suggestion that Koehler put words to a tune he'd heard Arlen playing. He did—and the song became "Get Happy."

Arlen and Koehler succeeded in selling "Get Happy" to the producer of *The 9:15 Revue*. The producer gave it to Ruth Etting to sing as the first-act finale. The revue didn't become a hit, but "Get Happy" did. And it convinced Arlen that he should cut back on performing and concentrate more on songwriting. He signed with the Remick publishing company, which helped him win an important assignment: writing songs for the revues at Harlem's fashionable Cotton Club, which presented all-black shows mixing Harlem jazz and popular songs for strictly white audiences.

More than any other white pop composer, Arlen always had a special affinity for black music. According to Arlen biographer Edward Jablonski, the great black singer Ethel Waters once called Arlen "the Negro-ist white man" she had ever known. Arlen traces some of this to his father, who had settled in Louisville, Kentucky, when he first came to the United States from Eastern Europe as a youngster of eleven. In Louisville, Arlen's father picked up some of the musical inflections of American blacks. Arlen once said that he could remember improvisations by his father in *shul* which were remarkably like some of Louis Armstrong's, even though the elder Arlen had never heard Armstrong up to then.

This background, together with an early fascination with jazz, was to be reflected in many of the songs that Harold Arlen would compose—songs that went further than George Gershwin's in treating American popular music as a melting pot of white European styles (with a touch or two of Semitic flavoring) and black African influences (as refocused in the blues and in jazz rhythms).

For eight Cotton Club revues between 1930 and 1934, Arlen wrote hit after hit, among them "I've Got the World on a String," "Between the Devil and the Deep Blue Sea," "I Love a Parade," and "Ill Wind," all with lyrics by Koehler. But the biggest hit of all—the one that shot Arlen overnight into the top rank of '30s composers—was "Stormy Weather."

Arlen and Koehler originally wrote "Stormy Weather" for Cab Calloway, but for various reasons Calloway didn't get to sing it in the Cotton Club revue for which it was intended. Meanwhile, Arlen himself cut a 78-rpm recording of the song with Leo Reisman's popular dance orchestra. It became such a hit that the producer of the Cotton Club revues convinced Ethel Waters, who had just been in two flop Broadway revues in a row, to forgo her threats to retire and sing "Stormy Weather" in the Cotton Club's next revue, backed by the Duke Ellington Orchestra. Waters created a sensation with the song, and for many years thereafter it was closely identified with her—at least until Lena Horne made it hers for another generation with the 1943 movie *Stormy Weather*.

Meanwhile, Arlen was also writing songs to be interpolated into Broadway shows, such as "Sweet and Hot" (lyrics by Jack Yellen) for 1931's *You Said It* and "I Gotta Right to Sing the Blues" (lyrics by Koehler) for *Earl Carroll's Vanities of 1932*. In the *Vanities* cast was a beautiful young Powers model, Anya Taranda, still in her teens. Arlen was soon dating her regularly. He also continued performing—cutting more records as a singer with Leo Reisman's orchestra, and also playing piano for Ethel Merman, Frances Williams, and Lyda Roberti for their club dates and appearances as part of the stage shows at Broadway movie theaters. He also led an act in 1933 at the newly opened Radio City Music Hall, an act built around "Stormy Weather."

Then a one-picture Hollywood invitation came from an unexpected source. Columbia Pictures, which had begun to emerge from Hollywood's "minor leagues" with some well-received Frank Capra and Frank Borzage comedies and dramas, decided to try a couple of original musicals. The result: *One Night of Love* (1934), a mixture of operetta and grand opera with new songs by Victor Schertzinger and Gus Kahn, and starring the Metropolitan Opera's comely Grace Moore; and *Let's Fall in Love* (1934), a musical-comedy spoof of Hollywood's penchant for exotic European actresses in the early '30s, with a score by Hollywood newcomers Arlen and Koehler.

Harold Arlen's Major Movies and Their Songs

Viewed today, *Let's Fall in Love* is little more than an agreeable B-movie, obviously produced on a modest budget. But in 1934 it stood out for the freshness of its approach to movie-making itself, especially for not being afraid to poke fun at some of the behind-the-scenes shams producers are willing to use to boost box-office receipts. In this case, to meet his studio's need for an exotic foreign star in the era of Garbo and Dietrich, a determined young director (played by Edmund Lowe) carefully grooms a Brooklyn lass into his new "Swedish discovery"—until romance rears its head and the director's jealous girlfriend blows the whistle on the charade. It's all spiritedly played by Lowe, Gregory Ratoff (as the harried studio head), and, particularly, by Ann Sothern, making her movie "re-debut" under a new name, having appeared in a few earlier films and on Broadway as Harriette Lake. Sothern, with a charming if slight singing voice that Hollywood has used only intermittently throughout her long movie career, sings the title number several times, and shares the lilting "Love Is Love Anywhere" with handsome crooner (later bandleader) Art Jarrett.

Arlen, with Koehler, wrote five songs for *Let's Fall in Love,* only three of which were used. The title song also took on some very personal meaning for Arlen in relation to Anya Taranda. According to Arlen biographer Edward Jablonski, Arlen's cross-country phone calls to Anya "mounted up" during that first visit to Hollywood—and it was obvious to most people that he was eager to get back to New York.

To the surprise of most of the other Hollywood studios, both *Let's Fall in Love* and *One Night of Love* scored well at the box office—if not well enough to encourage Columbia to make many more original musicals. Moreover, both films' title songs made *Variety*'s list of the country's ten most popular songs, with Arlen's staying on the list for a total of twelve weeks.

Arlen's first stay in Hollywood would be less than half that. He returned to Anya in New York and soon began work on the score for a Shubert revue, *Life Begins at 8:40* (lyrics by Ira Gershwin and E. Y. "Yip" Harburg). The cast was headed by Bert Lahr and Ray Bolger (for whom Arlen would later write some of the songs for *The Wizard of Oz*). The revue's title was a variation on a best-selling book of 1934, *Life Begins at 40,* altered to reflect the then-common starting time for Broadway shows. None of Arlen's songs for the revue became hits, although one came close ("Let's Take a Walk Around the Block") and two others have survived as favorites of cabaret performers ("Fun to Be Fooled" and "You're a Builder-Upper").

But with new productions on Broadway still limited by the pinch of the Depression, Arlen gladly accepted a short-term contract to return to Hollywood—first at the

Samuel Goldwyn Studios and then at Warner Brothers. He and Koehler rented the Hollywood home of Metropolitan Opera baritone Lawrence Tibbett, and Arlen became close friends in Hollywood with two fellow composers, George Gershwin and Harry Warren.

Because his original lyricist, Ted Koehler, had taken a job as a producer at Universal, Arlen composed the score for Samuel Goldwyn's *Strike Me Pink* (1936) with lyricist Lew Brown, best known for his collaborations with Ray Henderson and Buddy DeSylva. *Strike Me Pink* costars Eddie Cantor and Ethel Merman—in one of the worst movies either one of them ever made. Although only four scriptwriters are officially credited, legend has it that fourteen were involved in concocting its limp story about a timid amusement-park entrepreneur (Cantor) beset by racketeers. Originally, Harold Lloyd was to have made the picture, but he apparently had better sense than Cantor.

Arlen's score includes one of the most banal torch songs he ever wrote, "First You Have Me High, Then You Have Me Low," which Merman has the bad luck to have to sing as her first number. Merman's other big number, "Shake It Off With Rhythm," is catchy musically, but it's burdened with some of Brown's least imaginative lyrics. Even more mundane is the seemingly endless "The Lady Dances," which Cantor shares with a pert but shrill-voiced young singer-dancer billed as Rita Rio.

Arlen, according to biographer Jablonski, spent more time hanging around the set of *Strike Me Pink* than composers usually do, but not necessarily to check on the way his songs were being filmed. Anya Taranda had come west and won a small role in *Strike Me Pink* as one of the Goldwyn Girls. She and Arlen would be married after both of them returned to New York in 1937.

But first Arlen would contribute songs to three Warner Brothers musicals, working with lyricist E. Y. "Yip" Harburg. Another alumnus of Earl Carroll's Broadway revues, Harburg was a native New Yorker who had acquired the Yiddish nickname Yipsel (or Squirrel) as a kid on the Lower East Side. Over the years it had been shortened to Yip, the name by which he would thereafter be known. Before teaming with Arlen, Harburg had written lyrics for several major song hits, including "April in Paris" (music by Vernon Duke), and that quintessential Depression anthem, "Brother, Can You Spare a Dime?" (music by Jay Gorney).

Ironically for a composer who, by the mid-'30s, had already acquired a reputation for his skillful melding of black styles with white, Arlen's first assignment at Warner Brothers was a movie starring Al Jolson, the best-known exponent of the kind of stereotyped blackface wailing that has long drawn the ire of blacks. Jolson's *The Singing Kid* (1936) is also weighed down by the creakiest of plots—about a Broadway star who loses his voice and finds it again in the peaceful hinterlands, thanks to a sweet little moppet (Sybil Jason) and a fresh romantic interest (Beverly Roberts). None of the Arlen-Harburg songs are remembered today, although one of them, "You're the Cure for What Ails Me," is an agreeably sunny ballad sung in turn by Jolson, Jason, and two of the 1930s' most familiar "character comedians," Edward Everett Horton and Allen Jenkins. For the picture's finale, Jolson pulls out a medley of his old hits, rather than trusting any new Arlen-Harburg contributions.

Arlen's next assignment, *Gold Diggers of 1937,* wasn't much of an improvement. Despite the cheerful presence of Joan Blondell, Dick Powell, Victor Moore, and Glenda Farrell in leading roles, plus several elaborate production numbers staged by Busby Berkeley, this third edition in Warner's once-popular *Gold Diggers* series faltered badly

Lee Dixon and Rosalind Marquis sing "Let's Put Our Heads Together" in Gold Diggers of 1937 *(1936).*

with a trite script (about insurance manipulation). The movie's disappointing critical and box-office reception resulted in its being the last of the numbered *Gold Diggers* musicals ('33, '35, '37), with the final edition in '38 called *Gold Diggers in Paris.*

For the '37 edition, Arlen and Harburg shared songwriter credits with two veterans of the earlier editions, Harry Warren and Al Dubin. The latter team produced the picture's only hit song, "With Plenty of Money and You." But I must admit being partial to one of the forgotten Arlen-Harburg contributions, the romantically genial "Let's Put Our Heads Together." Although modeled perhaps too obviously on Arlen's '34 hit "Let's Fall in Love," it has an easy-going, ingratiating melody and tongue-in-cheek June-Moon lyrics. In the movie, Dick Powell sings the first chorus to Joan Blondell, with follow-up snatches divided among Farrell, Moore, Rosalind Marquis, Jack Norton (Hollywood's most famous "drunk" bit player of the '30s and '40s), and a half-dozen unidentified players, some of them Busby Berkeley chorines on whose pretty faces Berkeley loved to focus his cameras for two-second close-ups each. The song, regrettably, is abruptly interrupted (and then forgotten) by a reprise of Arlen and Harburg's so-so "Speaking of the Weather," which then provides the basis for a lengthy tap routine by Lee Dixon. "Let's Put Our Heads Together" deserved better.

Soon after Dick Powell and Joan Blondell married each other in real life, they were reteamed by Warner Brothers for *Stage Struck* (no relation to a better-known 1957 picture of the same title with Susan Strasberg and Henry Fonda). Busby Berkeley was again the director, for a none-too-credible backstage mishmash, the umpteenth variation on "the show must go on" formula of *42nd Street*. This time Arlen and Harburg got to write the whole score. But no hits emerged—partly because Warner Brothers was then feuding about broadcast fees with ASCAP (the American Society of Composers and Publishers), and so the songs never got the kind of radio play then essential to creating nationwide pop hits.

Two of *Stage Struck*'s songs are essentially pieces of material for the Yacht Club Boys, a comedy-vocal quartet. That means Harburg's lyrics are what counts, especially for the song sometimes called "The Income Tax" but officially titled "The New Parade," with its swipes at ever-rising taxes. Arlen's two ballads, the up-tempo "Fancy Meeting You" and the dreamier "In Your Own Quiet Way," have long since been forgotten, despite commercial recordings by Powell and by Eddy Duchin's Orchestra. In fact, *Stage Struck* is today the rarest of Busby Berkeley's '30s musicals in terms of television showings or theatrical revivals. The *New York Times*'s film critic Frank S. Nugent aptly summed up the picture's fate when he noted that "we seem to recall reading somewhere that tears were shed at the Powell-Blondell nuptials; it must have been by someone who had seen *Stage Struck*."

When his Warner Brothers contract expired, Arlen decided to freelance and thereafter divided his time between Hollywood and New York. In 1936, at Paramount, Arlen and Harburg contributed a specialty number for trumpeter-vocalist Louis ("Satchmo") Armstrong and comedienne-vocalist Martha Raye to sing in the finale of *Artists and Models* (1936). The movie is one of the studio's sprightliest '30s musicals in terms of both script and musical numbers. Jack Benny stars as the head of a struggling advertising agency trying to ensure that his client's model gets crowned queen of the Artists and Models Ball. Most of the musical numbers are by Burton Lane and Ted Koehler, with one each also by the teams of Victor Schertzinger and Leo Robin, Victor Young and Koehler, and Arlen and Harburg.

Arlen and Harburg's number, "Public Melody No. 1," is a lively, foot-tapping G-man spoof set in Harlem. It features Raye (in black body makeup), Armstrong, and a large corps of mostly black dancers doing little more than *hi-dee-ho'*ing around the principals. It's the sort of number that, from today's perspective, seems hip and even a bit droll on the surface but that, in a broader sense, plays disconcertingly on '30s stereotypes about Harlem blacks, "loose women," and street crime.

Arlen and Harburg worked out the number together with a promising young Broadway director who had been brought to Paramount with great fanfare and then given little to do as the studio kept rejecting idea after idea that he proposed. The young man was Vincente Minnelli, whom Arlen had first met when they worked on *Earl Carroll's Vanities of 1932*. "Public Melody No. 1" would be the only production number that Minnelli conceived that was actually filmed on his first Hollywood go-round. Minnelli, unhappy with the studio's handling of the number, bought out the rest of his Paramount contract and returned to Broadway. Five years later, he would change his mind about Hollywood and accept a contract to work at MGM—and, as the saying goes, the rest is history.

Arlen himself would move on to MGM even sooner for what has become one of the all-time movie classics: the 1939 production of *The Wizard of Oz*. Arlen was tapped after Jerome Kern, MGM's original choice as composer, suffered a heart attack and mild stroke and was forbidden by his doctors from working for a long period. Ironically, Arlen's own health that same year was uncertain. Soon after the death of George Gershwin from a brain tumor, Arlen began suffering from headaches. His doctor at first suspected "sympathetic hypochondria," since Arlen had been a friend and great admirer of Gershwin. But after a series of examinations, it turned out that Arlen had "a cyst of the maxillary antrum pressing on a nerve," to quote biographer Jablonski. Following surgery to remove the cyst, Arlen went to work on *The Wizard of Oz* headache-free—at least as far as his physical health was concerned.

Virtually every movie buff knows that Judy Garland got the role that made her a star only after a deal fell through for MGM to borrow Shirley Temple from Twentieth Century-Fox. Almost as well-known is the fact that the movie's most famous song, the beautifully tender Arlen-Harburg "Over the Rainbow," nearly got cut from the picture after its first preview, because studio executives thought it slowed down the action of the first part of the picture too much. Fortunately, saner heads prevailed and the number stayed.

What is less well-known is that Yip Harburg originally didn't think much of Arlen's melody for "Over the Rainbow" either. According to Arlen, Harburg thought it was something that should be sung by Nelson Eddy with a symphony orchestra behind him, not by a twelve-year-old girl in a Kansas farmyard (even if the twelve-year-old was being played by the sixteen-year-old Garland). Harburg has said that he believes his lyrics "brought the song down" with childlike words.

Whatever doubts Harburg or anyone else may have had about the song, it clicked when the movie was released. It not only won Arlen and Harburg an Academy Award for Best Song, but it also went on to hold the No. 1 spot on radio's *Your Hit Parade* for seven weeks—and then became one of the most beloved of all American pop standards. Judy Garland, in her later years, told Edward Jablonski that "I have sung it dozens of times and it's still the song that is closest to my heart. It is so symbolic of everybody's dream and wish that I am sure that's why people sometimes get tears in their eyes when they hear it. . . . It is very gratifying to have a song that is more or less known as my song, or my theme song, and to have had it written by the fantastic Harold Arlen."

What has become increasingly clear with the annual TV reshowings of *The Wizard of Oz* is how wonderful the rest of the Arlen-Harburg score is. "Ding, Dong, the Witch Is Dead," "Follow the Yellow Brick Road," "We're Off to See the Wizard," and the three-way "If I Only Had a Brain/a Heart/the Nerve" may have all started out as just pieces of incidental, plot-related material, but they're very special, high-quality material indeed. Their melodies are simple enough for kids to remember and sing for weeks after they've seen the movie, and yet warmly appealing to adults as well—especially with Harburg's clever lyrics as sung by Garland as Dorothy, Ray Bolger as the Scarecrow, Bert Lahr as the Cowardly Lion, and Jack Haley as the Tin Man.

Unlike "Over the Rainbow," one other Arlen-Harburg song did get cut from the final picture. It's "The Jitterbug," originally planned for a scene in which Dorothy, the Scarecrow, the Tin Man, and the Cowardly Lion enter the Haunted Forest singing the cheerfully bouncy tune. It was cut to tighten the picture's action and, musically speaking at least, its absence is no major loss. A "reconstruction" of the sequence, put

Jack Haley (as the Tin Man), Ray Bolger (as the Scarecrow), Judy Garland (as Dorothy), and Bert Lahr (as the Cowardly Lion), about to enter the Haunted Forest in The Wizard of Oz *(1939). Harold Arlen and E. Y. Harburg wrote a bouncy song called "The Jitterbug" for this sequence, but it was cut to tighten the film's action.*

together from home movies that Arlen himself made on the set during the picture's shooting, plus Arlen's copy of the original soundtrack recording, was first shown publicly in 1982 as part of the popular "Lyrics and Lyricists" series at New York City's 92nd Street YMHA—and it was later shown on a television program produced by Jack Haley, Jr. Recordings of the song itself by Judy Garland and Betty Hutton have long been available, without making much of an impression even on the Garland cultists —further evidence that the song's omission from *The Wizard of Oz* has not deprived us of some "long-lost gem." "The Jitterbug" is also the sort of topically late-'30s song that could easily have dated the film—something that none of the other songs in the picture do, and something that would have become increasingly noticeable with the passing years. Another brief musical sequence cut from *The Wizard of Oz* surfaced publicly in the 1984 compilation feature *That's Dancing*—a sequence in which Ray Bolger performs a marvelous dance (partly involving trick photography) to the tune of "If I Only Had a Brain." Its omission from the original picture is more to be regretted than that of "The Jitterbug."

Judy Garland got to sing another Harold Arlen song in another 1939 movie when "God's Country" (originally in the 1937 Broadway production of *Hooray for What!*) was interpolated into MGM's *Babes in Arms* to provide a patriotic finale for the film version of that Rodgers and Hart Broadway show (with only a couple of the original Rodgers and Hart songs actually surviving the screen transfer). With World War II having started in Europe shortly before the picture's release, Roger Edens updated some of Yip Harburg's original lyrics to take swipes at "Il Duce" and "Der Fuhrer," as well as to plug a few of MGM's stars among America's great resources. Garland, Mickey Rooney, Douglas MacPhail, Betty Jaynes, and the MGM chorus turn "God's Country" into a wonderfully rousing "be glad you're an American" wrap-up for *Babes in Arms*.

Also at MGM in 1939, Arlen and Harburg created a famous piece of material for Groucho Marx to sing in the Marx Brothers's *At the Circus:* "Lydia, the Tattooed Lady." Since Groucho's singing range was limited, Arlen's tune is not very adventurous —which also serves, of course, to keep attention on Harburg's quip-filled rhymes.

For *At the Circus* Arlen also composed a lovely but forgotten romantic ballad, "Two Blind Loves," using as its starting theme the old nursery song "Three Blind Mice." Kenny Baker and Florence Rice (daughter of the popular sportscaster Grantland Rice) sing it early in the film. Strictly routine is another song that Baker sings just before the picture's madcap finale, "Step Up and Take a Bow."

With Warner Brothers's *Blues in the Night* (1941), Arlen composed what was then considered the most specifically Arlen-like score he'd yet written for the movies. For this melodramatic tale of a small group of jazz musicians trying to piece their lives together from one-night stands, Arlen, working with Johnny Mercer as lyricist, was able to compose more openly in a jazz realm than at any time since he'd left the Cotton Club revues. Regrettably, no real jazzmen were entrusted to depict the story's leading characters, although bandleaders Jimmie Lunceford and Will Bradley make brief appearances as fictionally named bandleaders in a couple of sequences. The roles of the musicians in the story are played by Richard Whorf (as the pianist), Jack Carson (trumpeter), Elia Kazan (clarinetist), Peter Whitney (bassist), and Billy Halop (drummer), with Priscilla Lane as the singer married to Carson.

The title song became a hit almost simultaneously with the picture's release during the Christmas holiday season of 1941—and it has remained a pop classic ever since. It's sung first in *Blues in the Night* as a 12-bar blues lament by William Gillespie in a St. Louis jail cell, and it's later reprised several times by others in more expanded versions. Arlen has said that he tried to write a blues that would sound authentically St. Louis or New Orleans, to fit the movie's principal locales for the song. "Blues in the Night" also earned Arlen his second Academy Award nomination (although it lost to Kern's "The Last Time I Saw Paris" from *Lady Be Good*).

The only other song from *Blues in the Night* that has become a pop standard is "This Time the Dream's on Me," a fairly conventional but appealingly bittersweet ballad, sung by Priscilla Lane. "Hang On to Your Lids, Kids" is a perky tune with jive-talk Mercer lyrics that Lane and her fellow band members toss back and forth as they stowaway in a railway boxcar. One other good Arlen-Mercer song, "Says Who, Says You, Says I," is virtually tossed away during the Will Bradley Orchestra's sequence by the clowning vocal delivery of Mabel Todd, a blonde, buck-toothed, shrill-voiced comedienne who enlivened a number of late-'30s Warner pictures but who did no service to this particular song in this film.

With the United States' entry into World War II, virtually every Hollywood studio put together a patriotically themed movie revue with top stars doing a hodge-podge of musical-comedy numbers—whether or not those stars could sing or dance. Paramount's 1942 entry, *Star-Spangled Rhythm,* surrounded the variety acts with a slim if silly story line about a studio gatekeeper (Victor Moore) who, with the help of a studio phone operator (Betty Hutton), tries to pass himself off as an important studio executive in order to impress the on-leave shipmates of his sailor son (Eddie Bracken). Paramount entrusted all of the musical numbers to Arlen and Mercer, and although the picture is inevitably something of a mishmash, the good numbers are prime Arlen indeed.

The best one is "That Old Black Magic." It's sung by Johnny Johnston, a good-looking, honey-voiced crooner who played in a number of '40s musicals (and later was a popular supper-club performer with Kathryn Grayson, to whom he was then married). The song is then danced by ballerina Vera Zorina, in a solo choreo-graphed by George Balanchine (then her husband) that has little to do with the lyrics Johnston has just sung. But it's a beautiful dance—one of the most elegiac that Balanchine ever created for the movies, with a scantily clad Zorina dancing lyrically amid snowflakes like an out-of-reach will-o'-the-wisp. Paramount, recognizing a sure hit, also picked "That Old Black Magic" as the principal theme to use behind the opening titles of *Star-Spangled Rhythm.*

"Hit the Road to Dreamland" is a frothy, offbeat lullaby sung by Mary Martin and Dick Powell as the last two customers in a train's club car, trying to delay saying goodnight to each other—to the growing frustration of the waiters who want to close up shop for the night. Martin and Powell are wonderfully matched in the number, catching the sly humor of Mercer's lyrics without undercutting the song's essentially romantic mood. A counterpoint bit to the song is a joy in itself, as the Golden Gate Quartette (playing the waiters) rhythmically explain their own situation, and with polite firmness finally get the couple to move on.

"On the Swing Shift" and "Doin' It for Defense" are topical but strictly routine numbers. The first one is introduced by Dona Drake, a performer who apparently had a thing for alliterative stage names, having previously been billed as Rita Rio when she sang Arlen's "The Lady Dances" with Eddie Cantor in *Strike Me Pink* six years earlier. The song is then sung and danced by Marjorie Reynolds and Betty Rhodes as part of a glisteningly unrealistic defense-plant sequence that makes one wonder how we won the war. The second song is screeched out by Betty Hutton as she and the sailors ride around in a jeep.

Glamour gals Paulette Goddard, Dorothy Lamour, and Veronica Lake look as if they're having fun with a bit of special material that spoofs their own movie trade-marks, "A Sweater, a Sarong, and a Peek-a-Boo Bang." Arlen keeps the vocal range of the song simple, since two of the three ladies weren't much as singers. (Actually, Lake is dubbed by Martha Mears.) But they all put across Mercer's lyrics with verve. Less successful is a follow-up chorus, sung in drag by Arthur Treacher, Walter Catlett, and Sterling Holloway. Their version just isn't funny, perhaps because these three "character comedians" aren't as well-known on their own as Goddard, Lamour, and

Paulette Goddard, Dorothy Lamour, and Veronica Lake spoof their movie trademarks in Arlen's and Mercer's "A Sweater, a Sarong, and a Peek-a-Boo Bang," from Paramount's wartime revue Star-Spangled Rhythm *(1942).*

Lake. Perhaps the male part of the number might have worked better with three "name" stars.

Two other numbers in *Star-Spangled Rhythm* are embarrassing by today's standards. Eddie Anderson, the longtime "Rochester" of Jack Benny's radio and TV troupe, sings "Sharp as a Tack" wearing an outlandishly checkered zoot suit, and then dances to the tune with a slinkily dressed Katherine Dunham. The number reflects the sort of racial stereotypes that make some TV stations feel justified in deleting it when the movie is shown on television. Badly dated, too, is the patriotic finale, "Old Glory," which Bing Crosby sings against a flimsy replica of the Presidents' faces on Mount Rushmore. The song lacks both the rousing spirit and honest sentiment of Irving Berlin's "God Bless America" and the "good neighborly" feel of Arlen and Harburg's "God's Country." It settles instead for a series of corny clichés that border on the simplistic and jingoistic.

That same year, MGM's operetta queen Jeanette MacDonald tried to repeat the success she had with *The Firefly* six years earlier, mixing spy story and operetta. But 1942's *Cairo,* set in Egypt in the early days of World War II, bombed with both critics and audiences, and it turned out to be MacDonald's last starring film until a 1947 comeback attempt. Most of the score of *Cairo* (except for some arias and a few concert standbys) is by Arthur Schwartz and Yip Harburg. But when Ethel Waters was added to the cast as MacDonald's maid (a role that so infuriated Lena Horne as demeaning of someone of Waters' Broadway stature that Horne swore *she* would never play a maid in any movie—and never did), Harburg got MGM to interpolate "Buds Won't Bud" into *Cairo.* It's a song that he and Arlen had written for Broadway's *Hooray for What!* but which was dropped from that '37 production. The song provides one of the few musically valid reasons for watching *Cairo* today, and it remains the best example in movies of Waters' light and witty singing style—in contrast to the dramatic pathos for which she became known after *Cabin in the Sky* and the later *Member of the Wedding.*

A year later, for the 1943 film version of the all-black musical fable *Cabin in the Sky,* Arlen and Harburg provided Ethel Waters with one of her all-time classics: "Happiness Is Just a Thing Called Joe." The song was added to *Cabin in the Sky* through an unusual series of circumstances. The original Broadway score for *Cabin in the Sky* had been composed by Vernon Duke, with lyrics by John Latouche. Partly to "open up" the stage action and partly because of a decision to change the character of Georgia Brown from a dancing part (played on Broadway by Katherine Dunham) to a singing role for Lena Horne (making her feature film debut), producer Arthur Freed felt that several new songs were needed. But both Duke and Latouche were in the armed forces and unavailable. So Freed turned to Arlen and Harburg, with whom he had worked on *The Wizard of Oz* and with whom director Vincente Minnelli had worked on Broadway and at Paramount. Arlen's reputation for having a special feeling for black music was also a major factor in the choice.

In addition to the pseudo-spiritual "Li'l Black Sheep," sung in the movie's opening church sequence, Arlen and Harburg wrote a duet for Eddie Anderson and Lena Horne ("Life's Full o' Consequence") and a solo for Horne ("Ain't It de Truth"). During the filming, however, Waters reportedly grew increasingly jealous of the younger and more beautiful Horne and the way the character of Georgia Brown was being enlarged for her. The last straw apparently came when Horne was given a chorus of what had been Waters' show-stopping number on Broadway, "Taking a Chance on Love." Arlen and Harburg helped rebalance the situation with another solo for Waters: "Happiness Is Just a Thing Called Joe." Waters even gets to sing it twice.

Just as "Stormy Weather" is filled with the despairing, negative quality of the blues, so "Happiness Is Just a Thing Called Joe" is filled with the positive glow of human faith in another person. Thanks to Arlen and Harburg, Waters got the best song in the movie—even more of a showstopper than the Broadway number that Hollywood made her share with Horne. Meanwhile, Horne's solo, "Ain't It de Truth," got cut from the final release (although it would later be sung by Horne in Arlen's *Jamaica* on Broadway in 1956). Another song also cut from *Cabin in the Sky,* "I Got a Song," made it to Broadway two years later when Arlen and Harburg used it in *Bloomer Girl.*

Despite its musical merits, *Cabin in the Sky* is unfortunately as full of uncomforta-

Lena Horne as Georgia Brown in Cabin in the Sky *(1943).*

For Ethel Waters in the movie version of Cabin in the Sky, *Arlen and Harburg wrote "Happiness is Just a Thing Called Joe," a song that became closely identified with Waters ever after.*

bly dated racial and religious stereotypes as the earlier and more controversial *The Green Pastures* (1936). Although Waters radiates warmth and sincerity in her role, Eddie Anderson as the hero (Little Joe) rarely rises above his familiar "Rochester" characterization for Jack Benny, and Lena Horne is much too mannered a *femme fatale* as Georgia Brown. Two normally fine performers, Kenneth Spencer and Rex Ingram, ham things up too much as competing agents of heaven and hell, respectively. And in supporting roles, Louis Armstrong, Manton Moreland, Willie Best, Butterfly McQueen, and John W. Bubbles are mostly wasted. For all its once-overpraised folkloristic whimsy, *Cabin in the Sky* today seems more simplistic than simple, more whimpering than whimsical. But it does give us one of the greatest Arlen songs, "Happiness Is Just a Thing Called Joe."

A few months after the release of *Cabin in the Sky,* Twentieth Century-Fox released another musical with an all-black cast, *Stormy Weather,* which took its title and biggest production number from the Arlen-Koehler song hit of 1933. The cast is impressive in terms of black musical talent: Bill Robinson, Lena Horne, Fats Waller, Ada Brown, Dooley *(Casablanca)* Wilson, the Nicholas Brothers, Cab Calloway and his Orchestra, and the Katherine Dunham Dancers. But the film itself is a most uneven affair.

The flimsy plot of *Stormy Weather,* which merely serves as a framework for musical number after musical number, pretends to be a biography of dancer Robinson, best-known to moviegoers for several appearances in Shirley Temple musicals of the

Stormy Weather (1943) featured some of the finest black musical talent ever gathered for one film, including Bill Robinson, Lena Horne, and Cab Calloway.

'30s and as the inspiration for Fred Astaire's now-classic "Bojangles of Harlem" number in *Shall We Dance.* As biography, the picture is as inaccurate as *Night and Day* is as a Cole Porter biography.

Today the musical numbers of *Stormy Weather* have historic value for what they show us, in particular, of Robinson, Brown, and Waller. And the "Stormy Weather" finale is still exciting for its windswept staging and Horne's plaintive singing, in the sultry, "pretty-voiced" style that Horne now disowns as forced on her by Hollywood. She may now sing and feel the song more as a protest number (as she did in her 1981 Broadway show *Lena Horne: A Lady and Her Music,* later a TV special), but there's no denying the impact her original version still has—especially when coupled with the work of Dunham's dancers in one of the best pop ballets any movie musical had presented to that time.

Just as "Happiness Is a Thing Called Joe" has remained a classic even among those of us who find fault overall with *Cabin in the Sky,* so "My Shining Hour" has survived the critical catcalls hurled at the 1943 Fred Astaire movie from which it comes, *The Sky's the Limit.* This Arlen-Mercer ballad provides the musical highlight of an otherwise humdrum wartime romance, about a Flying Tigers ace (Astaire) who is mistaken by a magazine photographer (Joan Leslie) for a wartime shirker. Leslie gets the first chorus of "My Shining Hour" (with her singing voice dubbed by the justly named Sally Sweetland), backed by the neon-outlined instruments of Freddie Slack's Orchestra. Astaire reprises part of the song a bit later with a sillier set of lyrics that have mostly been forgotten over the years by singers of the standard romantic chorus. Still later in the movie, Astaire and Leslie dance a romantic adagio to it—one that's pretty much patterned after some of the Astaire-Rogers and Astaire-Hayworth dances, but with Leslie just not in the same league as those earlier Astaire partners.

The Sky's the Limit also contains a sprightly vocal duet, "I've Got a Lot in Common With You," that's undeserving of the neglect it has suffered since 1943. Part of its obscurity may stem from the way it's used in the movie, with the song's lyrics not really fitting the particular dramatic situation for which they're applied. In that situation, Leslie is set to go on to sing a solo at a serviceman's club, when Astaire joins her onstage and insists on cutting into her act right after she's begun the song. They then proceed to banter lyrics back and forth that could never possibly have been sung by Leslie solo—but which, on their own duet terms, are spunkily challenging to each singer in the style of Frank Loesser's classic "Baby, It's Cold Outside" (for 1949's *Neptune's Daughter*). After two delightful choruses of the song, which include "in" references to Astaire's movies with Hayworth and Leslie's with James Cagney, the couple breaks into a lively if unimaginative tap routine.

Astaire's final song in *The Sky's the Limit* has become an Arlen-Mercer classic and a standby for virtually every saloon singer in the land: "One for My Baby (and One More for the Road)." But Mercer's lyrics are disturbing and jarring in view of what has become an increasingly tragic problem in America. The mixture of drinking and driving has resulted in such carnage on our nation's highways in recent years—prompting many state legislatures to enact tougher drunk-driving laws—that the song has now taken on meaning far beyond what Arlen and Mercer presumably intended when they first wrote it. To compound matters, the way "One for My Baby" is sung and danced by Astaire in *The Sky's the Limit* represents the most flagrant "smash 'em

Fred Astaire and Joan Leslie dance to Arlen's and Mercer's Oscar-nominated "My Shining Hour" (from The Sky's the Limit, *1943).*

up" example in all of that great performer's work of Astaire's occasional penchant for routines that are destructive and violent.

When the Oscar nominations for 1943 came around, Arlen scored a rare triple-play: "My Shining Hour," "That Old Black Magic," and "Happiness Is Just a Thing Called Joe." But as often happens with multinominations for the same person, Arlen lost out altogether. (The winner that year was "You'll Never Know" by Harry Warren and Mack Gordon, from *Hello, Frisco, Hello.*)

Two more Academy Award nominations came out of the next two films for which Arlen wrote new songs. For Samuel Goldwyn's *Up in Arms* (1944), starring Danny Kaye in his feature movie debut, Arlen reteamed with Ted Koehler to write the romantic ballad "Now I Know" (which lost to "Swinging on a Star" by James Van Heusen and Johnny Burke, from *Going My Way*). That song and the wry "Tess's Torch Song" are sung in *Up in Arms* by Dinah Shore, also making her feature film debut, and they are both tailor-made for the jazz-oriented, bluesy style for which Shore was then best known from her work on the radio program "The Chamber Music Society of Lower Basin Street."

For Paramount's *Here Come the Waves* (1945), essentially a wartime tribute to the Navy's women's branch, Arlen and Mercer wrote the Oscar-nominated "Ac-cent-tchu-ate the Positive" (which lost to Rodgers and Hammerstein's "It Might As Well Be Spring" from *State Fair*). It's a bouncy song dedicated to the power of positive thinking, in much more comic terms than Norman Vincent Peale would use on the subject. The song itself is better remembered today than the shabby production number that introduces it in *Here Come the Waves*—an "Amos 'n' Andy"–style blackface number sung by Bing Crosby as a mailman and Sonny Tufts as an apartment-building doorman.

Crosby also gets to sing two fine Arlen-Mercer ballads in *Here Come the Waves:* "I Promise You" and "Let's Take the Long Way Home," the latter an extension of sorts (at least in terms of its lyrics) of "Let's Take a Walk Around the Block" from the Arlen-Harburg *Life Begins at 8:40.* But the movie's most entertaining number is a reprise of Arlen and Mercer's 1942 hit "That Old Black Magic"—with Crosby delightfully spoofing the style of his then–No. 1 rival, Frank Sinatra, amidst the squeals of the bobby-soxers in his audience.

Crosby also abets another Sinatra spoof in 1945's *Out of This World,* for which Arlen and Mercer provided the title tune. In this minor but light-heartedly pleasant musical-comedy, Eddie Bracken plays a skinny telegram messenger who is turned into a radio singing sensation by an enterprising Veronica Lake, with the help of bobby-soxers manipulated to scream and squeal at certain moments. If this sounds like a takeoff on the Sinatra phenomenon of the mid-1940s, it is. But it's made even funnier and the satire broader—at least in mid-'40s terms—by having Bracken sing with Bing Crosby's voice. The title tune made radio's *Your Hit Parade* in July of 1944, just a few months after Sinatra left that program as a regular vocalist. Sinatra never came back on the show to offer his version and, curiously, the song's not listed among the many Arlen tunes Sinatra has sung for recordings, broadcasts, or concerts over the years.

With the end of World War II, the need for escapist movie musicals disappeared from the priority lists of the major Hollywood studios. The economic jitters that afflicted the first postwar years also undercut expensive musical productions. In this atmosphere, Arlen returned to New York to work on *St. Louis Woman,* an all-black show that divided the critics and Broadway audiences and closed after 113 performances, but which some believe contains one of Arlen's best and most regrettably neglected scores. During this period, however, two early-'30s Arlen songs received fine reprises in, of all things, bottom-of-the-barrel B-musicals. In Monogram's *Swing Parade of 1946,* Connie Boswell offers a memorably throaty "Stormy Weather," while in Republic's *Earl Carroll Sketchbook,* Constance Moore once again proves what an underrated singer-actress she was with a sultrily ladylike "I Gotta Right to Sing the Blues" (which had originally been introduced in Carroll's 1932 *Vanities*).

In 1947 Arlen returned to Hollywood to work with lyricist Leo Robin on the score for *Casbah,* a musical version of the 1939 romantic drama *Algiers*—the one in which underworld kingpin Charles Boyer, contrary to what hundreds of radio and TV impersonators think, does *not* lure Hedy Lamarr into the Casbah but, rather, is lured by her into *leaving* the Casbah, whereupon he meets a fatal police bullet. (*Algiers,* in turn, had been based on one of the most popular of all '30s French films, *Pepe le Moko,* with Jean Gabin.) The musical *Casbah* has acquired something of a cult status among many Arlen fans as an underappreciated gem. True, the picture was too quickly dismissed by most critics in 1947, partly because few of them seemed willing to accept singer Tony Martin in any serious role. But *Casbah* is, at best, a most uneven film.

Martin is surprisingly good as a singing Pepe, balancing the character's slick charm and desperate toughness almost as well as Boyer and Gabin before him. And he sings the Arlen songs splendidly. Yvonne De Carlo, as Pepe's jilted girlfriend, and Peter Lorre, as the slimy police investigator, also make fine characterizations out of fairly stereotyped roles. But the key role of the visiting beauty (played by Lamarr in *Algiers*) is so relentlessly boring as played by Marta Toren that Pepe's flipping for her just doesn't ring true. Some of the lesser characters also sabotage credibility by seeming to be refugees from B-movies about Chicago gangsters rather than from French North Africa.

One of Arlen's songs for *Casbah* has deservingly become a pop standard, the buoyant "Hooray for Love." But the best-staged song in the movie itself is the fatalistically romantic "It Was Written in the Stars," which Martin sings with single-minded coolness while the Katherine Dunham Dancers give vent to more surgingly intense passions in the square below Pepe's Casbah quarters. Also most affecting is the plaintive ballad "What's Good About Good-bye," which Martin makes memorable in its one brief chorus.

"What's Good About Good-bye" is similar in style and mood to one of Arlen's all-time great songs, "Last Night When We Were Young," which in 1949 would be cut out of MGM's *In the Good Old Summertime* despite the efforts of Judy Garland to keep it in. Actually, "Last Night . . ." had previously been cut from another movie, 1935's *Metropolitan*. Arlen wrote the song in 1935, when he and Yip Harburg were renting the Hollywood home of baritone Lawrence Tibbett and presented it to Tibbett as a sort of thank-you. Tibbett liked the song so much that he recorded it and then interpolated it into the mostly operatic *Metropolitan*—only to have the studio cut it from the final release.

Garland discovered Tibbett's out-of-print recording in the 1940s, fell in love with the song, and added it to her repertoire. Few singers have ever been able to project the quiet ache of Harburg's lyrics about love's "morning after" and arch their way through Arlen's unusual melody as unforgettably as Judy Garland, especially in her soundtrack recording of the song for *In the Good Old Summertime*. But a decision was made to use only familiar, turn-of-the-century songs in that picture ("Meet Me Tonight in Dreamland," "Put Your Arms Around Me, Honey," "Play That Barber-shop Chord," etc.). And so this charming, winsome musical adaptation of *The Shop Around the Corner* (with its locale shifted from 1930s Budapest to 1900 Chicago) lost the song that might have given it its greatest musical distinction. Arlen's—and Garland's—luck in having "Over the Rainbow" saved for *The Wizard of Oz* was not to be repeated here.

You lose some, you win some. The following year, another Arlen song, 1929's "Get Happy," was interpolated at the last minute into another Garland movie, *Summer Stock*. Shooting had been completed on the picture when producer Joe Pasternak decided that the finale needed strengthening. So nearly two months later, Garland was called back to the studio to rehearse and film the decidedly upbeat "Get Happy," which had always been one of her favorite songs. Since *Summer Stock*'s original choreographer, Nick Castle, was away on another assignment, the picture's director, Charles Walters, himself a former dance director, devised the sequence—presenting Garland in a tuxedolike jacket and a black fedora, dancing snappily with a small male chorus line, against a simple backdrop of painted clouds in a bright orange sky.

Judy Garland in "Get Happy," a 1929 Harold Arlen-Ted Koehler song that was added at the last minute to the 1950 film Summer Stock.

"Get Happy" is one of the most exhilarating numbers Garland ever filmed—and, ironically, the last number she would ever film at MGM. (A few months later, during rehearsals for *Royal Wedding* with Fred Astaire, problems involving Garland's erratic behavior would reach the point where MGM permanently cancelled her contract.) When *Summer Stock* was released, many viewers noticed that Garland was considerably slimmer in the "Get Happy" number than in the rest of the picture. A rumor began spreading that the number had been shot years earlier but not used for Minnelli's *Ziegfeld Follies of 1946.* The truth was that in the two months between the completion of *Summer Stock*'s other footage and the filming of the added "Get Happy," Garland had shed about fifteen pounds.

Between 1950 and 1954, Arlen contributed incidental songs to a number of strictly routine movie musicals, including MGM's *Mr. Imperium* (lyrics by Dorothy Fields), and three for Twentieth Century-Fox: *My Blue Heaven* (lyrics by Ralph Blane), *Down Among the Sheltering Palms* (lyrics by Blane), and *The Farmer Takes a Wife* (lyrics by Dorothy Fields). Not only were all of these movies evidence that Hollywood had run out of fresh ideas for its musicals, but they also showed that Arlen's switches in collaborators weren't enough to spark any major new songs out of him. Even the magisterial voice of former Metropolitan Opera basso Ezio Pinza, fresh from his Broadway triumph in Rodgers and Hammerstein's *South Pacific,* couldn't raise *Mr.*

Imperium's "Let Me Look at You" and "Andiamo" above the routine—nor save a bad picture about a mythical king's ill-fated romance.

The Farmer Takes a Wife is perhaps the biggest disappointment. This remake of a popular 1930s nonmusical movie, set on the Erie Canal of the 1850s (when the world moved at four miles per hour), merely shows that Technicolor, elaborate costumes, and picturesque backgrounds cannot make up for miscasting (city-slick Betty Grable in Janet Gaynor's old role as a homespun lass) or the lack of memorable songs—although one lovely Arlen ballad, "With the Sun Warm Upon Me," never stood much of a chance because of Dale Robertson's ho-hum delivery.

The Country Girl is not normally thought of as a Harold Arlen movie, but it is. Paramount's chilling, hard-hitting 1954 adaptation of Clifford Odets's drama of self-deceit and self-destruction—specifically about an alcoholic actor and the wife who seemingly can't find the strength to leave him—won Grace Kelly an Oscar for her performance as the wife. But it's really Bing Crosby's picture, proving what a good dramatic actor lay beneath all those years of crooning "White Christmas" and trading wisecracks with Bob Hope in *Road* pictures.

Both Crosby and Paramount felt he should play the part as a *singing* actor, and so Arlen and Ira Gershwin were commissioned to write four songs for the movie version of Odets's play. They're all forgotten today, regrettably in two cases: the poorly titled but lovely ballad "The Search Is Through," and the lightly lilting "It's Mine, It's Yours." Crosby recorded both of them commercially, but they got little airplay in those beginning days of the Elvis Presley boom and the rock 'n' roll takeover of the airwaves. Perhaps someday they'll be rediscovered.

A rediscovery of another sort of "lost" Arlen did occur in 1983, involving the 1954 *A Star Is Born.* For that Judy Garland blockbuster—a musical remake of another 1930s Janet Gaynor hit, about the devastating personal price of Hollywood stardom —Arlen, working again with lyricist Ira Gershwin, wrote six songs. But soon after the nearly three-hour movie's premiere in 1954, exhibitor complaints about the picture's length led Warner Brothers to trim it by nearly 30 minutes. Among the cuts were two of Arlen's songs, "Lose That Long Face" and "Here's What I'm Here For." The shortened version of *A Star Is Born* then remained in circulation for the next twenty-nine years, both theatrically and on TV, garnering generous praise as one of the all-time great movie musicals—and establishing one of its remaining songs, "The Man That Got Away," as an Arlen (and Garland) classic.

But some of us who had seen the complete, original version early in its 1954 run kept bemoaning the cuts—not just privately but in various magazine articles. Director George Cukor was known to be so upset over the cut version that he resolutely refused to attend any showings of it up to the time of his death. Meanwhile, Warner Brothers claimed that the trimmed footage had been lost or destroyed during one of several turnovers of studio ownership. After Judy Garland's death, her heirs said they had checked out several other possible leads, all without success.

A few zealots kept persisting in their belief that copies of the missing footage must exist somewhere. Among them was Ron Haber, head of the film department of the Los Angeles County Museum of Art. In 1982, with prodding from Fay Kanin, president of the Academy of Motion Picture Arts and Sciences, Warner Brothers agreed to underwrite a search by Haber through its storage depots and underground warehouses

Judy Garland belts out "The Man That Got Away" in A Star is Born *(1954). The song became as much "hers" as Arlen's earlier "Over the Rainbow."*

on both the East and West Coasts. After six months of searching, Haber found about twenty minutes of the deleted footage, some of it attached to alternate, cut, or unused scenes from other Warner films. Both of the deleted Arlen musical sequences were found. Haber also discovered the complete, original stereo soundtrack and files of black-and-white stills that had been taken on the set as scenes were shot in '54. Studio editors then went to work to match appropriate stills with the soundtrack to piece out the gaps for the six or seven still-missing minutes of actual film footage. A few months later, a "restored" original version of *A Star Is Born* was premiered at New York's Radio City Music Hall to an enthusiastic audience and then put into general distribution theatrically and on videocassette.

The restored version verifies how much *all* of the original Arlen-Gershwin musical numbers contribute to *A Star Is Born.* They are not just well integrated into the plot structure, they also underscore subtle yet important aspects of character and situation as the movie traces the rise of a young singer (Garland) and the simultaneous decline of the actor she loves (James Mason). "Here's What I'm Here For," for example, is pivotal to Mason's marriage proposal to Garland, as they listen to a playback of the song as she's just recorded it, unaware that the whole recording-studio crew is eaves-dropping on their conversation. It's a charming, deliciously funny, and touching scene in one respect, yet also bitterly ironic in what it symbolizes about the personal privacy of performers and what they're really "here for." The song also gives additional poignance to a later musical send-up of Garland's day at the studio, "Somewhere There's a Someone"—a number that takes more than a few digs at some of Garland's own '40s musicals.

"Lose That Long Face," in effect, "sandwiches" one of Garland's most heart-wrenching scenes in *A Star Is Born,* as she pours out to her studio boss her sense of failure in not being able to check Mason's decline and pleads in utter despair for help —and then pulls herself together to go back onto the movie set to belt out a retake of the song and its sunny lyrics. There are few moments in any movie musical that

Garland sings "Lose that Long Face," one of the songs cut from A Star is Born *soon after its 1954 release, but restored in the 1983 "reconstructed version."*

can match the impact of those scenes together. They sum up not only a lot about the character Garland is playing, but also quite a bit about performers' emotional conflicts that audiences rarely see. Without the song, Garland's big dramatic scene loses much of its impact.

But the individually greatest number in *A Star Is Born* remains "The Man That Got Away"—which, unbeknownst to the character Garland is playing, foreshadows what's in store for her. Vocally, it's the finest moment in Garland's adult movie career, as she shapes the complex song from a soft and gentle lament to an all-stops-out torcher.

A Star Is Born's other well-known number, "Born in a Trunk," is a lengthy but brilliant musical-comedy *tour de force* that traces a singer's rise from spotlight-stealing kid to Broadway star. It was not composed by Arlen, however. According to Arlen biographer Edward Jablonski, Arlen and Gershwin had written two songs for that spot ("Green Light Ahead" and "I'm Off the Downbeat"), but both had been rejected by the producers and choreographer. Meanwhile, after a series of production delays and a serious illness, Arlen returned to New York to work on the Broadway show *House of Flowers.* In Arlen's absence, Leonard Gershe put together the "Born in the Trunk" number, incorporating such songs as George Gershwin's "Swanee," Moises Simon's "The Peanut Vendor," Norton and Burnett's "My Melancholy Baby," and several other pop standards.

In most respects, *A Star Is Born* crowns Harold Arlen's career as a movie songwriter. It also marks his last major film musical, but not his last movie work. In 1962, together with Yip Harburg, Arlen contributed four songs to an animated cartoon feature, *Gay Purr-ee,* for which Judy Garland, Robert Goulet, Red Buttons, and Hermione Gingold provided the principal soundtrack voices. A whimsical tale about a provincial French kitten who goes to Paris, *Gay Purr-ee* proved to be too sophisticated for most youngsters and was not a commercial success. But one of its songs, "Little Drops of Rain," is premium Arlen and Harburg—a tender, plaintive ballad with some of the same childlike, searching innocence of "Over the Rainbow." Garland sings it with that unique mixture of restraint and all-out pathos that made her one of the greatest of all-American pop singers, especially when the song was by Harold Arlen.

Garland, in her last movie, would also introduce the last song that Arlen wrote specifically for a movie: the title song for *I Could Go On Singing* (1963). It gets the picture off to an exhilarating start as Garland does a complete chorus as the opening titles roll—and then she reprises it for one of those full-throated, belted-out, exciting finales that make you wish that she could indeed just go on singing and that Arlen could just keep on composing such songs.

But after the death of his wife in 1970, and with recurring problems affecting his own health (including Parkinson's disease), Arlen remained inactive for most of the last two decades of his life. From time to time he would begin a new project—such as a TV musical in 1973 with lyricist Martin Charnin, titled *Clippity-Clop and Clementine* (set in horse-and-buggy days)—only to drop it, unfinished and unproduced. He also composed a few incidental songs with Yip Harburg, Dory Langdon, and Carolyn Leigh. After numerous bouts of illnesses and a cancer operation, Arlen died at his home in New York City on April 23, 1986.

In the only authoritative Arlen biography to date, Edward Jablonski's *Harold Arlen, Happy With the Blues,* music publisher E. H. "Buddy" Morris is quoted as saying: "Anybody can walk in off the street and give you a hit. That doesn't make him a great songwriter. Harold has always been a long-pull composer who expresses himself honestly. His songs last and are, ultimately, more valuable than the off-the-street hit." Harold Arlen has certainly proved that with his movie songs over the years.

HAROLD ARLEN'S MOVIES AND SONGS ON TAPE AND DISC

MANHATTAN PARADE (1932), Warner Brothers. B&W. Directed by Lloyd Bacon. With Smith and Dale (Joe Smith, Charles Dale), Winnie Lightner, Charles Butterworth, Dickie Moore, Luis Alberni. Song: "I Love a Parade" (lyrics, Ted Koehler); plus songs by others.
THE BIG BROADCAST (1932), Paramount. B&W. Directed by Frank Tuttle. With Stuart Erwin, Bing Crosby, Leila Hyams, George Burns, Gracie Allen, Sharon Lynn; Kate Smith, the Boswell Sisters, Cab Calloway and his Orchestra, the Mills Brothers, Donald Novis, Arthur Tracy, Vincent Lopez and his Orchestra. Song: "Kickin' the Gong Around" (lyrics, Ted Koehler); plus songs by others. Soundtrack LP: excerpt included in *The Big Broadcast of 1932,* Soundtrak 101.
TAKE A CHANCE (1933), Paramount. B&W. Directed by Lawrence Schwab and Monte Brice. With Charles "Buddy" Rogers, Lillian Roth, June Knight, James Dunn, Cliff Edwards, Lilian Bond. Song: "It's Only a Paper Moon" (lyrics, Billy Rose and E. Y. Harburg); plus songs by others.

LET'S FALL IN LOVE (1934), Columbia. B&W. Directed by David Burton. With Edmund Lowe, Ann Sothern, Gregory Ratoff, Betty Furness. Songs: "Let's Fall in Love," "Love Is Everywhere," "This Is Only the Beginning" (lyrics, Ted Koehler). Soundtrack LP: Excerpts only, included in *Harold Arlen in Hollywood,* Music Masters JJA 19763. Two songs also included in *Harold Arlen Sings: 1933–1937,* Music Masters JJA 19759.
STRIKE ME PINK (1936), Samuel Goldwyn for United Artists release. B&W. Directed by Norman Taurog. With Eddie Cantor, Ethel Merman, Sally Eilers, William Frawley, Brian Donlevy, Parkyarkarkus, Rita Rio. Songs: "First You Have Me High, Then You Have Me Low," "The Lady Dances," "Calabash Pipe," "Shake It Off With Rhythm," "If I Feel This Way Tomorrow, Then It's Love" (lyrics, Lew Brown). Soundtrack LP: excerpts only, included in *Harold Arlen in Hollywood,* Music Masters JJA 19763. Two songs also included in *Merman in the Movies: 1930–38,* Music Masters Encore ST 101.
THE SINGING KID (1936), Warner Brothers.

B&W. Directed by William Keighley. With Al Jolson, Beverly Roberts, Sybil Jason, Edward Everett Horton, Allen Jenkins, Wini Shaw, Cab Calloway and his Orchestra, the Yacht Club Boys. Songs: "Save Me, Sister," "You're the Cure for What Ails Me," "I Love to Sing-a," "My, How This Country Has Changed," "Here's Looking at You" (lyrics, E. Y. Harburg); plus songs by others. Soundtrack LP: Excerpts only, Caliban 6013 (with excerpts from four other non-Arlen movies).

GOLD DIGGERS OF 1937 (1936), Warner Brothers. B&W. Directed by Lloyd Bacon. With Dick Powell, Joan Blondell, Victor Moore, Glenda Farrell, Lee Dixon, Osgood Perkins. Numbers created and directed by Busby Berkeley. Songs: "Speaking of the Weather," "Life Insurance Song," "Let's Put Our Heads Together," "Hush Ma Mouth" (lyrics, E. Y. Harburg); plus songs by others. Soundtrack LP: excerpts only, included in *Harold Arlen in Hollywood,* Music Masters JJA 19763, and *Hooray for Hollywood,* United Artists LA361H.

STAGE STRUCK (1936), Warner Brothers. B&W. Directed by Busby Berkeley. With Dick Powell, Joan Blondell, Warren William, Jeanne Madden, Frank McHugh, Spring Byington. Songs: "In Your Own Quiet Way," "The New Parade," "Fancy Meeting You," "You're Kinda Grandish" (lyrics, E. Y. Harburg). Soundtrack LP: excerpts only, included in *Harold Arlen in Hollywood,* Music Masters JJA 19763.

ARTISTS AND MODELS (1937), Paramount. B&W. Directed by Raoul Walsh. With Jack Benny, Ida Lupino, Richard Arlen, Gail Patrick, Martha Raye, Connie Boswell, Louis Armstrong, Andre Kostelanetz and his Orchestra. Song: "Public Melody No. 1" (lyrics, E. Y. Harburg); plus songs by others. Soundtrack LP: excerpt only, included in *Harold Arlen in Hollywood,* Music Masters JJA 19763.

MERRY-GO-ROUND OF 1938 (1937), Universal. B&W. Directed by Irving Cummings. With Jimmy Savo, Bert Lahr, Alice Brady, Mischa Auer, Joy Hodges, Louise Fazenda, Dave Apollon and his Orchestra. Song: "The Woodman's Song" (lyrics, E. Y. Harburg); plus songs by others.

THE WIZARD OF OZ (1939), MGM. B&W and Color. Directed by Victor Fleming. With Judy Garland, Frank Morgan, Ray Bolger, Jack Haley, Bert Lahr, Billie Burke, Margaret Hamilton. Songs: "Over the Rainbow," "We're Off to See the Wizard," "Ding, Dong, the Witch Is Dead," "Munchkinland," "In the Merry Old Land of Oz," "If I Only Had a Brain," "If I Only Had a Heart," "If I Only Had the Nerve" (lyrics, E. Y. Harburg). Soundtrack LP: *The Wizard of Oz,* MCA 39046. Videocassette and videodisc: MGM-UA.

BABES IN ARMS (1939), MGM. B&W. Directed by Busby Berkeley. With Mickey Rooney, Judy Garland, Charles Winninger, June Preisser, Guy Kibbee, Grace Hayes, Betty Jaynes, Douglas MacPhail, Margaret Hamilton. Song: "God's Country" (lyrics, E. Y. Harburg, Roger Edens); plus songs by others. Soundtrack LP: Sandy Hook SH2077; also Curtain Calls 100/6–7 (with *Babes on Broadway*). Videocassette: MGM/UA.

AT THE CIRCUS (1939), MGM. B&W. Directed by Mervyn LeRoy. With Groucho, Chico, and Harpo Marx, Kenny Baker, Florence Rice, Eve Arden, Margaret Dumont. Songs: "Two Blind Loves," "Step Up and Take a Bow," "Lydia, the Tattooed Lady," "Swingali" (lyrics, E. Y. Harburg). Soundtrack LP: excerpts only, included in *Harold Arlen in Hollywood,* Music Masters JJA 19763. Videocassette: MGM/UA.

LOVE AFFAIR (1939), RKO Radio. B&W. Directed by Leo McCarey. With Irene Dunne, Charles Boyer, Lee Bowman, Maria Ouspenskaya, Astrid Allwyn, Maurice Moscovitch. Song: "Sing, My Heart" (lyrics, Ted Koehler); plus songs by others.

BLUES IN THE NIGHT (1941), Warner Brothers. B&W. Directed by Anatole Litvak. With Priscilla Lane, Richard Whorf, Betty Field, Jack Carson, Lloyd Nolan, Elia Kazan, Jimmie Lunceford and his Orchestra, Will Bradley and his Orchestra. Songs: "Blues in the Night," "Hang On to Your Lids, Kids," "This Time the Dream's on Me," "Says Who, Says You, Says I" (lyrics, Johnny Mercer). Soundtrack LP: excerpts only, included in *Harold Arlen in Hollywood,* Music Masters JJA 19763.

RIO RITA (1942), MGM. B&W. Directed by S. Sylvan Simon. With Bud Abbott, Lou Costello, Kathryn Grayson, John Carroll, Barry Nelson, Tom Conway. Song: "Long Before You Came Along" (lyrics, E. Y. Harburg); plus songs by others.

CAIRO (1942), MGM. B&W. Directed by W. S. Van Dyke II. With Jeanette MacDonald, Robert Young, Reginald Owen, Ethel Waters, Lionel Atwill, Mona Barrie, Dooley Wilson. Song: "Buds Won't Bud" (lyrics, E. Y. Harburg); plus songs and arias by others. Soundtrack LP: excerpt only, included in *Harold Arlen in Hollywood,* Music Masters JJA 19763.

STAR-SPANGLED RHYTHM (1942), Paramount. B&W. Directed by George Marshall. With Betty Hutton, Eddie Bracken, Victor Moore, Gil Lamb, plus guest appearances by Bing Crosby, Bob Hope, Mary Martin, Dick Powell, Vera Zorina, Paulette Goddard, Veronica Lake, Dorothy Lamour, Alan Ladd, Eddie "Rochester" Anderson, Johnny Johnston, Marjorie Reynolds, and others. Songs: "Hit the

Road to Dreamland," "That Old Black Magic," "Sharp As a Tack," "A Sweater, a Sarong, and Peek-a-Boo Bang," "On the Swing Shift," "I'm Doin' It for Defense," "He Loved Me 'Til the All-Clear Came," "Old Glory" (lyrics, Johnny Mercer). Soundtrack LP: Curtain Calls 100/20.

CAPTAINS OF THE CLOUDS (1942), Warner Brothers. Color. Directed by Michael Curtiz. With James Cagney, Dennis Morgan, Brenda Marshall, Alan Hale, George Tobias. Song: "Captain of the Clouds" (lyrics, Johnny Mercer).

CABIN IN THE SKY (1943), MGM. B&W. Directed by Vincente Minnelli. With Ethel Waters, Eddie "Rochester" Anderson, Lena Horne, Rex Ingram, Kenneth Spencer, Louis Armstrong, Duke Ellington and his Orchestra. Songs: "Happiness Is Just a Thing Called Joe," "Life's Full o' Consequence," "Li'l Black Sheep" (lyrics, E. Y. Harburg); plus songs by others. Soundtrack LP: Hollywood Soundstage 5003; also, excerpts included in *Harold Arlen in Hollywood,* Music Masters JJA 19763. Videocassette: MGM/UA.

STORMY WEATHER (1943), Twentieth Century-Fox. B&W. Directed by Andrew Stone. With Bill Robinson, Lena Horne, Eddie "Rochester" Anderson, Fats Waller, Ada Brown, Katherine Dunham Dancers, Cab Calloway and his Orchestra. Song: "Stormy Weather" (lyrics, Ted Koehler); plus songs by others. Soundtrack LP: Soundtrak 103; also Sandy Hook SH2037.

THE SKY'S THE LIMIT (1943), RKO Radio. B&W. Directed by Edward H. Griffith. With Fred Astaire, Joan Leslie, Robert Benchley, Robert Ryan, Eric Blore, Freddie Slack and his Orchestra. Songs: "My Shining Hour," "A Lot in Common With You," "One More for My Baby (and One More for the Road)" (lyrics, Johnny Mercer); plus songs by others. Soundtrack LP: Curtain Calls 100/19 (with Gershwin's *A Damsel in Distress*).

THANK YOUR LUCKY STARS (1943), Warner Brothers. B&W. Directed by David Butler. With Eddie Cantor, Joan Leslie, Dennis Morgan, Edward Everett Horton, S. Z. Sakall; guest appearances by Bette Davis, Ann Sheridan, Errol Flynn, John Garfield, Olivia de Havilland, Ida Lupino, Alexis Smith, Dinah Shore, Hattie McDaniel, Spike Jones and his Orchestra, Alan Hale, Jack Carson, George Tobias, others. Song: "Blues in the Night" (lyrics, Johnny Mercer); plus songs by others. Soundtrack LP: Curtain Calls CC100/8.

THEY GOT ME COVERED (1943), Samuel Goldwyn for RKO Radio release. B&W. Directed by David Butler. With Bob Hope, Dorothy Lamour, Lenore Aubert, Otto Preminger, Eduardo Ciannelli, Marion Martin, Donald Meek. Song: "Palsy-Walsy" (lyrics, Johnny Mercer).

RIDING HIGH (1943), Paramount. B&W. Directed by George Marshall. With Dorothy Lamour, Dick Powell, Victor Moore, Cass Daley, Gil Lamb, Bill Goodwin, Rod Cameron. Song: "He Loved Me 'Til the All-Clear Came" (lyrics, Johnny Mercer).

UP IN ARMS (1944), Samuel Goldwyn for RKO Radio release. Directed by Elliott Nugent. With Danny Kaye, Dinah Shore, Dana Andrews, Constance Dowling, Louis Calhern, Lyle Talbot, Margaret Dumont, the Goldwyn Girls. Songs: "Now I Know," "Tess's Torch Song," "All Out for Freedom" (lyrics, Ted Koehler); plus songs by others. Soundtrack LP: Soundtrak STK 113.

HERE COME THE WAVES (1944), Paramount. B&W. Directed by Mark Sandrich. With Bing Crosby, Betty Hutton, Sonny Tufts, Ann Doran, Catherine Craig. Songs: "Ac-cent-tchu-ate the Positive," "Let's Take the Long Way Home," "I Promise You," "There's a Fellow Waiting in Poughkeepsie," "That Old Black Magic," "Here Come the Waves," "Join the Navy" (lyrics, Johnny Mercer). Soundtrack LP: excerpts only, included in *Harold Arlen in Hollywood,* Music Masters JJA 19763.

KISMET (1944), MGM. Color. Directed by William Dieterle. With Ronald Colman, Marlene Dietrich, James Craig, Edward Arnold, Florence Bates, Harry Davenport. Songs: "Willow in the Wind," "Tell Me, Tell Me, Evening Star" (lyrics, E. Y. Harburg).

OUT OF THIS WORLD (1945), Paramount. B&W. Directed by Hal Walker. With Veronica Lake, Eddie Bracken, Diana Lynn, Olga San Juan, Parkyarkarkus, Florence Bates, Mabel Paige. Soundtrack dubbed by Bing Crosby. Songs: "June Comes Around Every Year," "Out of This World" (lyrics, Johnny Mercer); plus songs by others.

RADIO STARS ON PARADE (1945), RKO Radio. B&W. Directed by Leslie Goodwins. With Wally Brown, Alan Carney, Ralph Edwards, Frances Langford, Skinnay Ennis and his Orchestra, Rufe Davis, Don Wilson, the Town Criers. Song: "That Old Black Magic" (lyrics, Johnny Mercer); plus songs by others.

SWING PARADE OF 1946 (1945), Monogram. B&W. Directed by Phil Karlson. With Gale Storm, Phil Regan, Connie Boswell, The Three Stooges, Louis Jordan and his Orchestra, Will Osborne and his Orchestra. Song: "Stormy Weather" (lyrics, Ted Koehler); plus songs by others.

EARL CARROLL SKETCHBOOK (1946), Republic. B&W. Directed by Albert S. Rogell. With Constance Moore, William Marshall, Barbara Allen (Vera Vague), Edward Everett Horton, Bill Goodwin. Song: "I Gotta Right to Sing the Blues" (lyrics, Ted Koehler); plus songs by others.

CASBAH (1948), Universal. B&W. Directed by John Berry. With Tony Martin, Yvonne De Carlo, Marta Toren, Peter Lorre, Thomas Gomez, Douglas Dick, Katherine Dunham Dancers. Songs: "Hooray for Love," "It Was Written in the Stars," "For Every Man There's a Woman," "The Monkey Sat in the Cocoanut Tree," "What's Good About Good-bye" (lyrics, Leo Robin). Soundtrack LP: excerpts included in *Harold Arlen in Hollywood,* Music Masters JJA 19763.

ROAD HOUSE (1948). Twentieth Century-Fox. B&W. Directed by Jean Negulesco. With Ida Lupino, Richard Widmark, Cornel Wilde, Celeste Holm. Song: "One More for My Baby (and One More for the Road)" (lyrics, Johnny Mercer); plus songs by others.

SLIGHTLY FRENCH (1949), Columbia. B&W. Directed by Douglas Sirk. With Don Ameche, Dorothy Lamour, Janis Carter, Adele Jergens, Willard Parker. (A remake of 1934's *Let's Fall in Love.*) Song: "Let's Fall in Love" (lyrics, Ted Koehler); plus songs by others.

YOUNG MAN WITH A HORN (1950), Warner Brothers. B&W. Directed by Michael Curtiz. With Kirk Douglas, Lauren Bacall, Doris Day, Juano Hernandez, Mary Beth Hughes, Hoagy Carmichael. Song: "Get Happy" (lyrics, Ted Koehler); plus songs by others.

THE PETTY GIRL (1950), Paramount. B&W. Directed by Henry Levin. With Joan Caulfield, Robert Cummings, Elsa Lanchester, Melville Cooper, Mary Wickes, Frank Jenks. Songs: "Fancy Free," "Ah Loves Ya," "The Petty Girl," "Calypso Song" (lyrics, Johnny Mercer).

MY BLUE HEAVEN (1950), Twentieth Century-Fox. Color. Directed by Henry Koster. With Betty Grable, Dan Dailey, David Wayne, Mitzi Gaynor, Jane Wyatt, Una Merkel, Louise Beavers. Songs: "Friendly Islands," "Live Hard, Work Hard, Love Hard," "It's Deductible," "Halloween," "Don't Rock the Boat, Dear," "What a Man," "Cosmo Cosmetics," "I Love a New Yorker" (lyrics, Ralph Blane); plus songs by others. Soundtrack LP: Titania 503 (with *You Were Meant for Me*).

WHEN YOU'RE SMILING (1950), Columbia. B&W. Directed by Joseph Santley. With Frankie Laine, Billy Daniels, Jerome Courtland, Lola Albright, Bob Crosby, Kay Starr, the Mills Brothers, Jerome Cowan. Song: "That Old Black Magic" (lyrics, Johnny Mercer); plus songs by others.

SUMMER STOCK (1950), MGM. Color. Directed by Charles Walters. With Judy Garland, Gene Kelly, Gloria De Haven, Eddie Bracken,

Phil Silvers, Marjorie Main, Carleton Carpenter, Hans Conried. Song: "Get Happy" (lyrics, Ted Koehler); plus songs by others. Soundtrack LP: MGM (withdrawn). Videocassette: excerpt included in *That's Entertainment,* MGM/UA.

I'LL GET BY (1950), Twentieth Century-Fox. Color. Directed by Richard Sale. With June Haver, William Lundigan, Gloria De Haven, Thelma Ritter, Dennis Day; guest appearances by Jeanne Crain, Dan Dailey, Victor Mature, Reginald Gardiner. Song: "I've Got the World on a String" (lyrics, Ted Koehler); plus songs by others. Soundtrack LP: Titania 504.

SUNNY SIDE OF THE STREET (1951), Columbia. B&W. Directed by Richard Quine. With Frankie Laine, Billy Daniels, Terry Moore, Jerome Courtland, Lynn Bari, Toni Arden, Dick Wesson. Song: "Let's Fall in Love" (lyrics, Ted Koehler); plus songs by others.

MR. IMPERIUM (1951), MGM. B&W. Directed by Don Hartman. With Lana Turner, Ezio Pinza, Marjorie Main, Sir Cedric Hardwicke, Keenan Wynn, Debbie Reynolds, Barry Sullivan. Songs: "Andiamo," "Let Me Look at You," "My Love and My Mule" (lyrics, Dorothy Fields); plus songs by others. Soundtrack LP: excerpt included in *Harold Arlen in Hollywood,* Music Masters JJA 19763; studio recording of some of the songs by Pinza in RCA Victor LM-61 (withdrawn).

MEET DANNY WILSON (1952), Universal. B&W. Directed by Joseph Pevney. With Frank Sinatra, Shelley Winters, Raymond Burr, Alex Nichol. Song: "That Old Black Magic" (lyrics, Johnny Mercer); plus songs by others.

WITH A SONG IN MY HEART (1952), Twentieth Century-Fox. Color. Directed by Walter Lang. With Susan Hayward, Rory Calhoun, David Wayne, Thelma Ritter, Una Merkel, Robert Wagner, Leif Erickson. Song: "Get Happy" (lyrics, Ted Koehler); plus songs by others. Soundtrack LP: excerpt included in *Susan Hayward,* Legends 1000/3.

DOWN AMONG THE SHELTERING PALMS (1953), Twentieth Century-Fox. Color. Directed by Edmund Goulding. With Mitzi Gaynor, William Lundigan, Gloria De Haven, David Wayne, Jane Greer. Songs: "Who Will It Be When the Time Comes?," "I'm the Ruler of the South Sea Island," "The Opposite Sex," "What Make de Difference?" (lyrics, Ralph Blane); plus songs by others.

THE FARMER TAKES A WIFE (1953), Twentieth Century-Fox. Color. Directed by Henry Levin. With Betty Grable, Dale Robertson, Thelma Ritter, Eddie Foy Jr., Gwen Verdon, John Carroll. Songs: "With the Sun Warm Upon Me," "On the Erie Canal," "Today I Love Everybody," "When I Close My Door," "Some-thin' Real Special," "We're in Business," "Can You Spell Schenectady?," "We're Doin' It for the Natives in Jamaica" (lyrics, Dorothy Fields).

THE COUNTRY GIRL (1954), Paramount. B&W. Directed by George Seaton. With Bing Crosby, Grace Kelly, William Holden, Anthony Ross, Gene Reynolds. Songs: "It's Mine, It's Yours," "Dissertation on a State of Bliss," "The Land Around Us," "The Search Is Through" (lyrics, Ira Gershwin). Soundtrack LP: excerpts only, included in *Harold Arlen in Hollywood,* Music Masters JJA 19763.

A STAR IS BORN (1954), Warner Brothers. Color. Directed by George Cukor. With Judy Garland, James Mason, Jack Carson, Charles Bickford, Tommy Noonan, Amanda Blake. Songs: "The Man That Got Away," "Gotta Have You Go With Me," "It's a New World I See," "Here's What I'm Here For," "Lose That Long Face," "Someone at Last (Somewhere There's a Someone)" (lyrics, Ira Gershwin); plus songs by others. Soundtrack LP: CBS Special Products ACS-8740. Videocassette: Warner Home Video 11335A/B (restored version).

YOUNG AT HEART (1955), Warner Brothers. Color. Directed by Gordon Douglas. With Doris Day, Frank Sinatra, Dorothy Malone, Ethel Barrymore, Gig Young. Song: "One for My Baby (and One More for the Road)" (lyrics, Johnny Mercer); plus songs by others. Soundtrack LP: Titania 500 (with *April in Paris*); also studio recording by Day and Sinatra, Columbia CL-6339 (withdrawn).

I'LL CRY TOMORROW (1955), MGM. B&W. Directed by Daniel Mann. With Susan Hayward, Eddie Albert, Margo, Richard Conte, Jo Van Fleet. Song: "Happiness Is Just a Thing Called Joe" (lyrics, E. Y. Harburg); plus songs by others. Soundtrack LP: included in *Susan Hayward,* Legends 1000/3.

INTERRUPTED MELODY (1955), MGM. Color. Directed by Curtis Bernhardt. With Eleanor Parker, Glenn Ford, Roger Moore, Cecil Kellaway, Walter Baldwin. Song: "Over the Rainbow" (lyrics, Ted Koehler); plus songs and arias by others. Soundtrack LP (sung by Eileen Farrell), MGM 3185 (withdrawn).

CHA-CHA-CHA-BOOM (1956), Columbia. B&W. Directed by Fred F. Sears. With Perez Prado, Helen Grayce, Steve Dunne, the Mary Kaye Trio, Luis Arcaraz and his Orchestra, Manny Lopez and his Orchestra, Jose Gonzalez Gonzalez. Song: "Get Happy" (lyrics, Ted Koehler); plus songs by others.

THAT CERTAIN FEELING (1956), Paramount. Color. Directed by Norman Panama. With Bob Hope, Eva Marie Saint, Pearl Bailey, George Sanders. Song: "Hit the Road to Dreamland" (lyrics, Johnny Mercer); plus songs by others.

BUS STOP (1956). Twentieth Century-Fox. Color. Directed by Joshua Logan. With Marilyn Monroe, Don Murray, Betty Field, Arthur O'Connell, Eileen Heckert, Hope Lange. Song: "That Old Black Magic" (lyrics, Johnny Mercer). Videocassette: CBS/Fox.

THE EDDY DUCHIN STORY (1956), Columbia. Color. Directed by George Sidney. With Tyrone Power, Kim Novak, Victoria Shaw, James Whitmore. Song: "Let's Fall in Love" (lyrics, Ted Koehler); plus songs by others. LP: MCA 37088 (with Carmen Cavallaro, who dubbed the soundtrack piano).

PEPE (1960), Columbia. Color. Directed by George Sidney. With Cantinflas, Shirley Jones, Dan Dailey, Edward G. Robinson, Maurice Chevalier, Bing Crosby, Frank Sinatra, Jimmy Durante, Zsa Zsa Gabor, Debbie Reynolds, Bobby Darin, Andre Previn, other guest stars. Song: "Let's Fall in Love" (lyrics, Ted Koehler); plus songs by others. Soundtrack LP: Colpix 507 (withdrawn).

GAY PURR-EE (1962), UPA animated cartoon feature for Warner Brothers release. Color. Directed by Abe Levitow. With the voices of Judy Garland, Robert Goulet, Hermione Gingold, Red Buttons, Mel Blanc. Songs: "Paris Is a Lonely Town," "Take My Hand, Paree," "Roses Red, Violets Blue," "The Money Cat," "Little Drops of Rain," "Mewsette," "Bubbles," "The Horse Won't Talk." Soundtrack LP: Warner Brothers B-1479.

I COULD GO ON SINGING (1962), Barbican for United Artists release. Color. Directed by Ronald Neame. With Judy Garland, Dirk Bogarde, Jack Klugman, Gregory Phillips, Aline MacMahon. Song: "I Could Go On Singing" (lyrics, E. Y. Harburg); plus songs by others. Soundtrack LP: Capitol SW-1861.

PAPER MOON (1973), Paramount. B&W. Directed by Peter Bogdanovich. With Ryan O'Neal, Tatum O'Neal, Madeline Kahn, John Hillerman. Song: "It's Only a Paper Moon" (lyrics, E. Y. Harburg); plus songs by others. Soundtrack LP: Paramount PAS-1012 (withdrawn).

FUNNY LADY (1975), Columbia-Warner Brothers. Color. Directed by Herbert Ross. With Barbara Streisand, James Caan, Omar Sharif, Roddy McDowall, Ben Vereen. Song: "It's Only a Paper Moon" (lyrics, E. Y. Harburg); plus songs by others. Soundtrack LP: Arista 9004.

THAT'S DANCING (1985). MGM. Color. Compilation feature directed by Jack Haley, Jr. With Gene Kelly, Mikhail Baryshnikov, Ray Bolger, Liza Minnelli, Sammy Davis, Jr. Song: "If I Only Had a Heart"; plus songs by others. Videocassette: MGM/UA.

Irving Berlin rehearses with some of the cast of 1938's Alexander's Ragtime Band: *Alice Faye, Tyrone Power, and Don Ameche.*

IRVING BERLIN

*I*rving Berlin has no place in American music. He *is* American music." That's how Jerome Kern, himself no slouch as a composer, once described the man who has written more hit songs over more decades than any other American.

For a good part of the 1930s and 1940s, it also looked as if Irving Berlin were writing more songs for movie musicals than anyone else. The ads for some of those movies even played up Berlin's name as big as the picture's stars—and that included such box-office blockbusters of the day as Fred Astaire, Ginger Rogers, Bing Crosby, Alice Faye, Judy Garland, and Ethel Merman, among others. Sometimes his name was placed before the title *or* the stars'. Very few movie songwriters got that kind of treatment—then or now.

Berlin can rightfully be called the man who, more than anyone else, "invented" the kind of popular song that dominated movie musicals for their first few decades. Its roots go back to the jazz-influenced Broadway show tunes that Berlin wrote in the decades just before and after World War I—songs that veered sharply away from European operetta traditions and set a simpler, more "natural" pop style.

From the first days that movies found their musical voice, Irving Berlin was very much a part of it. The first successful "talkie" feature, 1927's history-making *The Jazz Singer,* included an Irving Berlin song. Al Jolson, in carefully choosing his music for *The Jazz Singer,* felt he had to have a song by Berlin, then America's best-known pop composer. Jolson chose "Blue Skies," a 1926 hit that had been included in the Broadway show *Betsy.* The song's title was to prove as prophetic for Berlin's movie future as it had been for much of Berlin's career as a songwriter.

Berlin was born Israel Baline, on May 11, 1888, in Temun, in Russian Siberia. He was the youngest of eight children of a poor village cantor who, when Israel was four, bundled up the family and fled a Russian czarist pogrom. They reached the United States with only the most meager of belongings and settled on New York City's Lower East Side. At age eight, soon after his father's death, Israel went to work as a newsboy to help support the family. Later he held odd jobs as a singing waiter in barrooms and restaurants, and as a song plugger at Tony Pastor's Music Hall in Union Square. Those were the days before radio, movies, and recordings changed the way Americans got to hear new songs. Song publishers would use "pluggers" to push their tunes, hoping that listeners liked what they heard enough to buy the sheet music, take it home, and place it on their parlor pianos.

In his early twenties, Israel changed his name to the more American Irving Berlin. He also taught himself to play the piano, only moderately well, as he himself would insist throughout his lifetime. More important, he began writing his own songs—just lyrics at first for others' songs, and then both words and music. He succeeded in getting Florenz Ziegfeld to use several of them in the *Ziegfeld Follies* of 1910 and 1911.

In true showbiz style, Berlin's first big hit came suddenly—in 1911, when he was twenty-three. The song: "Alexander's Ragtime Band." It stopped the show when Emma Carus, a popular performer of the period, sang it in a Chicago vaudeville house. Within weeks, the song was being heard in vaudeville houses from coast to coast. It not only literally swept across the nation, but also across the Atlantic to London, Paris, and other Continental capitals.

Although ragtime certainly wasn't new, Berlin's song stirred up the first nation-wide ragtime craze, with publisher after publisher turning out rags as fast as they could find them. Cashing in on the fad he had started, Berlin wrote "That Mysterious Rag," "Ragtime Violin," "Ragtime Mocking Bird" and "Everybody's Doin' It," among others. He was soon one of the best-known composers in America.

Then tragedy struck. In 1913, Berlin had courted and married Dorothy Goetz, sister of a well-known songwriter, Ray Goetz. Soon after returning from their honeymoon in Cuba, Berlin's bride fell ill with typhoid and died. Berlin, in despair, was unable to write for some time. Finally he turned his emotions into an intimately personal ballad, "When I Lost You." When the song was published, its public acceptance convinced Berlin that there was more to songwriting than instigating popular fads. From then on, simple, direct ballads became more and more a key part of his output.

Berlin wrote his first complete Broadway score in 1914, for *Watch Your Step,* starring the era's most popular dance team, Vernon and Irene Castle. Although the Castles made Berlin's ragtime "Syncopated Walk" the show's most elaborate number, the biggest hit turned out to be "Play a Simple Melody"—a tune that's remained a pop standard ever since.

During World War I, Berlin joined the Army as a private, and talked the Army into letting him produce an all-soldier show, *Yip-Yip Yaphank,* as a morale booster for his fellow servicemen. Through Berlin's maneuvering, it ended up as a fund-raiser scheduled to run on Broadway for eight performances. It ran for six weeks, closing just a few weeks before the war ended. And one of the songs it introduced, "Oh, How I Hate to Get Up in the Morning," joined George M. Cohan's "Over There" and Richard Whiting's "Till We Meet Again" as one of the most popular songs to come out of the wartime period.

After the armistice, Berlin returned to Broadway as a regular contributor to new editions of Ziegfeld's *Follies* and other shows. As his success grew, so did his royalties and his personal fortune. He decided to open his own music publishing business and, together with Sam Harris, built the Music Box Theater just off Times Square as a showcase for his own musical revues.

Berlin also made newspaper headlines with his tumultuous courtship of Ellin Mackay—writing love songs such as "Always" and "All Alone" for several shows whose audiences assumed the songs were intended for her and relished them as such. Ellin was the daughter of a wealthy Catholic businessman (president of Postal Telegraph) who opposed a match with Berlin for both religious and social reasons. Berlin, after all, was the son of poor Jewish immigrants, had no formal education, and had made his mark in areas of show business that were not then considered quite "respectable." When Ellin Mackay defied her father and married Berlin in 1926, Mackay disinherited her. Ironically, just a few years later, following the stock market crash of 1929, it would be *nouveau riche* Irving Berlin who would help rescue his wife's father from financial ruin. Mackay not only swallowed his pride for a reconciliation with his daughter, but remained cordial to Berlin for the rest of his life. And, in 1931, Mackay himself married a performer who had risen to stardom from a modest background, opera singer Anna Case.

The Depression that followed the '29 crash dried up funds for Broadway shows, but not for Hollywood movies. As often happens in hard times, people wanted escape —and the excitement of a new medium, talking pictures, at very modest prices, caught on. As America's most famous composer, Irving Berlin was soon in demand for movies.

Irving Berlin's Major Movies and Their Songs

After *The Jazz Singer* revolutionized the motion picture industry and sounded the death knell for both vaudeville and silent movies, Berlin was invited to write the theme songs for several popular movies, including Vilma Banky's *The Awakening* (1928) and Mary Pickford's *Coquette* (1929). Although he had reservations about the sonic qualities of the first soundtracks, he also wrote songs for Al Jolson's *Mammy* (1930) and Harry Richman's *Puttin' on the Ritz* (1930).

But by 1931, disillusion with Hollywood set in—particularly after only one of the songs he had written for Douglas Fairbanks, Sr.'s *Reaching for the Moon* ended up being used. That song, "No Lowdown Lower Than That," is sung in the movie by Bing Crosby, making his film debut in little more than a walk-on role. It remains one of the few interesting parts of the movie, which still turns up occasionally on TV.

Four years would pass before Berlin could be convinced of two things: first, that sound-recording techniques had markedly improved from the earliest film musicals and, second, that the right Hollywood studio with the right producer would treat his music and lyrics with the same respect to which he was accustomed on Broadway. The movie that won him over was the fourth Fred Astaire-Ginger Rogers musical, *Top Hat,* produced in 1935 by Pandro S. Berman for RKO Radio.

As director Mark Sandrich once told an interviewer: "Irving Berlin sat in on all story conferences (for *Top Hat*), with the result that all the songs grew out of the scene structure itself." This was a process that differed markedly from the way most other Hollywood composers worked at other studios. Inevitably, some of these others became not too silently jealous of Berlin.

Top Hat remains arguably the best of all the Fred Astaire–Ginger Rogers musicals —and, for me at least, the best of all the 1930s original musical comedies. Its shamelessly contrived romantic escapism, bright dialogue, Art Deco designs, and wonderful, spontaneous-*looking* dances combine seamlessly with one of Berlin's all-time great scores.

"Cheek to Cheek" and "Isn't This a Lovely Day to Be Caught in the Rain?" have been popular standards since the movie's release, and they're both served up in unforgettably intimate production numbers that put the focus directly on the developing relationship between the characters played by Rogers and Astaire. In contrast to the spectacular production numbers designed by Busby Berkeley for his '30s movies, which took audiences *out* of this world, Astaire and Rogers put their audiences very much into the realm of everyday lovers. And nowhere is this accomplished more adroitly than in *Top Hat*'s "Cheek to Cheek" number.

For all the romantic enchantment of that number, its filming caused no end of problems because of Rogers's feathery costume, which shed rather copiously with each twist and turn, causing more than the usual number of retakes. As Astaire reports in his autobiography, *Steps in Time:* "I had feathers in my eyes, my ears, my mouth, all over the front of my suit. . . . It got to be funny after a while. The news went all over the lot that there was a blizzard on the *Top Hat* set."

Of all the songs by dozens of composers that Fred Astaire has introduced in his movies, the one with which he is still most instantaneously identified is "Top Hat, White Tie and Tails." It was written by Berlin when Astaire wanted a number in *Top Hat* that would rework a dance idea he had tried in a 1930 Ziegfeld show on Broadway, *Smiles.* The show had flopped, but Astaire liked the idea of the number —in which he danced with a line of top-hatted men whom he eliminated one by one, in shooting-gallery style, using his cane as his "gun." Berlin obliged with a rhythmically catchy tune that's become Astaire's signature song ever since.

Top Hat's finale, "The Piccolino," is one of those grandiose production numbers that so many '30s musicals felt they had to have—with dozens of couples spinning and tapping merrily away. This one is briefer and less intricate than "The Carioca," which Fred and Ginger had filmed for *Flying Down to Rio* (1933), or "The Continental" for

Walter Plunkett's feathery costume for Ginger Rogers in the "Cheek to Cheek" number gave Fred Astaire all sorts of problems in Top Hat *(1935). But both movie and song survived.*

The Gay Divorcee (1934). But it's made just as memorable not only by the way Astaire and Rogers dance its climactic solo, but also by Berlin's deliberately self-mocking lyrics.

One other song in *Top Hat* has been virtually forgotten over the years—unfairly, I think. It's a delightful elegy to the single life, "No Strings (I'm Fancy Free)." Astaire sings it early on to buddy Edward Everett Horton and then dances to it exuberantly. In fact, it's the song that really sets the plot in motion, when Astaire's dancing wakes up Rogers, sleeping in a room below. But even as a song on its own, it remains a marvelous and refreshing antidote to all those pop songs that equate romance with wedding bells.

A year after *Top Hat*'s smash success, RKO Radio reteamed Astaire and Rogers with Berlin and director Mark Sandrich for a very different musical, *Follow the Fleet*. It's different not only in locale and style, but also in the way Berlin's songs are used. Instead of being plot motivated, most of the songs seem more arbitrarily inserted and are sometimes even out of joint with the script. "I'd Rather Lead a Band," for example, has lyrics that make it clear the great dream of the singer (Astaire) is to lead a band —yet the whole number centers on tap dancing, *not* leading a band. Similarly, "Let Yourself Go" and "Let's Face the Music and Dance," wonderful as both numbers are, could be placed differently in the picture itself without affecting the storyline.

Fred Astaire extolls the single life to Edward Everett Horton in Top Hat's "No Strings (I'm Fancy Free)."

Below. Fred Astaire (center) explains, "I'd Rather Lead a Band" to his shipmates in Follow the Fleet (1936).

Instead of the Continental elegance and sophistication of *Top Hat, Follow the Fleet* is a more homespun romp about a couple of sailors (Astaire, Randolph Scott) and the two San Francisco sisters (Rogers, Harriet Hilliard) with whom they get romantically involved. At one point in the pre-production planning, RKO considered having Ginger Rogers play both sisters—one a saucy dance-hall hostess, the other a mousy schoolteacher who gets converted into a glamour girl. (Maurice Chevalier had recently played a dual role in the '35 musical *Folies Bergere,* and the technology for simultaneous split-screen images of the same performer was to lure Elisabeth Bergner, Bette Davis, Olivia de Havilland, and others into dual roles in succeeding years.) But the idea fell through as far as *Follow the Fleet* was concerned, and only the dancer role went to Rogers, the schoolteacher role to Hilliard (soon to marry bandleader Ozzie Nelson and later to become his costar in the popular radio and TV series *Ozzie and Harriet*).

Hilliard gets two songs in *Follow the Fleet:* "But Where Are You," a dreamy-type ballad about forsaken love that could fit into any girl-loses-boy sequence, and "Get Thee Behind Me, Satan," originally written for *Top Hat* and inserted here as a soliloquy for Hilliard to sing as she's waiting for Scott to get his hat. The latter song could just as constructively have been cut from this movie too, without injury to either the picture or Berlin's reputation. The lyrics are far from inspired, and it's also surprisingly Victorian in some of its references, equating romantic temptation with the Devil, no less. It's certainly a far cry in spirit from *Top Hat*'s "No Strings."

More up-to-date in philosophy and also catchy in terms of both lyrics and music is "Let Yourself Go." It's sung first by Rogers, whose personality and dancing skills usually helped cover her limited singing ability, and then it's danced by Rogers and Astaire as they take part in a lively dance competition (guess who wins?). What some viewers may find more interesting than Ginger's rather colorless rendition of the song is the backup trio that joins her for the second chorus. In the center of that trio is a pre-star Betty Grable. (The other two singers: Joy Hodges and Jeanne Gray, who graduated only to B-movies.) Another very blonde starlet, Lucille Ball, also turns up in *Follow the Fleet* as one of Rogers wisecracking dance-hall chums, and the future superstar can also be seen briefly in the final production number, "Let's Face the Music and Dance."

"I'm Putting All My Eggs in One Basket" provides one of the picture's highlights —not so much for its cute but irrelevant lyrics as for the dance that Astaire and Rogers do to it. It's the only gagged-up dance routine they ever did, with Ginger particularly funny.

The finale, "Let's Face the Music and Dance," remains one of the best songs Irving Berlin has written for any movie. But the number itself has long divided Astaire-Rogers fans. Its style varies sharply from the movie's middle-brow tone up to that point. It restores the smart evening clothes and Continental elegance of earlier Astaire-Rogers movies, but within a more gravely dramatic, pseudo-ballet-style framework. The number, set in a gambling casino, finds Astaire, who has just lost all his money, saving Rogers from a suicide leap—and then dancing with her through a fairly lengthy routine in which they both keep stone faces, before exiting theatrically "into the future" together. Some people consider it one of the best "serious" dances Astaire and Rogers ever did. That may be so, strictly in terms of dance technique. But some of it is just too pretentious and self-consciously arty for this particular movie, and completely at odds with the type of characters Fred and Ginger have been playing for

Fred Astaire tells Ginger Rogers that "I'm Putting All My Eggs in One Basket" in Follow the Fleet.

the previous one hundred minutes or so. But the song itself—it's great on any level you want to take it.

In 1937, Berlin accepted a bid from Darryl F. Zanuck to write the songs for one of the biggest-budgeted musicals the two-year-old Twentieth Century-Fox studios had attempted to that time: *On the Avenue*. Zanuck, while production chief at Warner Brothers in 1933, had produced the history-making *42nd Street*. At Twentieth Century-Fox he continued to put his personal stamp on several major musicals each year, and for *On the Avenue* he borrowed from Warner Brothers the singer whom *42nd Street* had made a star, Dick Powell.

On the Avenue gave a fresh twist (for its time) to the backstage musical, while repeating one of the Depression era's quintessential romantic fantasies: rich and poor learning they can work things out together (the same theme that is put forth, in different ways, by *It Happened One Night* and *My Man Godfrey,* among others). Dick Powell is cast as a Broadway writer and performer who includes a sketch in a new show that lampoons the richest girl in America (Madeleine Carroll). She sees it and, furious, threatens a lawsuit. Then, changing tactics, she invites Powell to dinner to prove she can be a good sport. Sure enough, they start to fall in love. He rewrites the sketch to flatter her, but his jealous partner (Alice Faye) turns it all around even more outrageously than before. After several more plot twists, everything, of course, ends up with a clinch between Carroll and Powell, while Faye settles for Carroll's millionaire father.

Alice Faye may not get the leading man, but she does get all the best Berlin songs in *On the Avenue,* some of them in duets with Powell. Two ballads, "I've Got My Love to Keep Me Warm" and "This Year's Crop of Kisses," became major pop hits of 1937, remaining on radio's *Your Hit Parade* for several months after the picture's release. Two other songs also got a lot of '37 radio play and even made *Your Hit Parade*'s Top 10 for one week each: "You're Laughing at Me" and "Slummin' on Park Avenue." The latter song also provides the Ritz Brothers with one of the most hilarious "drag" routines of any '30s movie.

Three songs that Berlin wrote for *On the Avenue,* including the title song, got dropped from the picture. But Berlin got even, in a way. One of the songs that *was* used, "You're Laughing at Me," had actually been written by Berlin in 1927 and just filed away. He decided it would work in *On the Avenue* and so, as he told biographer Michael Freedland, "I peddled it to Mr. Zanuck for a great deal of money."

Zanuck knew there were dozens of other Berlin songs—some well-known, others forgotten—that had never been used in the movies. He negotiated to use them for a movie that would trace the romantic ups and downs of a bandleader from the years just before World War I through the late 1930s. Those, of course, were years in which Berlin had been America's No. 1 songwriter—so there was a plentiful supply to choose from. And so, in 1938, *Alexander's Ragtime Band* was produced by Zanuck, using twenty-three Berlin songs. For the first time, a songwriter's name appeared above the picture's title or any of the stars' names in the opening credits.

Twenty of the songs were vintage Berlin, including "All Alone," "What'll I Do," "Everybody's Doin' It," "When the Midnight Choo-Choo Leaves for Alabam'," "The International Rag," and "Easter Parade." But Berlin also wrote three new songs—one of which, "Now It Can Be Told," won that year's Academy Award for Best Song. The movie itself turned out to be one of the biggest musical hits of the entire 1930s.

Some people have mistaken *Alexander's Ragtime Band* for a biography of Berlin. It never was intended as that, and varies too much from the well-known facts of Berlin's life. Actually, the script is a pretty hackneyed affair, along the lines of boy-meets-girl, boy-loses-girl, boy-regains-girl—told this time in terms of a bandleader (Tyrone Power) and a singer (Alice Faye). It merely provides the sketchiest framework for an almost constant parade of Berlin songs. And it's all those songs, and the nostalgic way in which they're presented, that have kept *Alexander's Ragtime Band* a popular TV movie staple over the years.

Once again, Alice Faye gets the lion's share of the songs, and sings them beautifully. But Ethel Merman, in a supporting role, also gets a good batch too—including choruses of "Say It With Music" and "A Pretty Girl Is Like a Melody," which proves that Merman could sing as softly and sweetly as anyone. But she also belts out, in more typically Merman fashion, "Blue Skies," "Steppin' Around," "Hand Me Down My Walking Stick," "Heat Wave," and, best of all, "Pack Up Your Sins and Go to the Devil." Most of the numbers are staged in a straightforward way, as they would be on a stage in the era in which they're supposedly taking place within the story. There are no Busby Berkeley-style overhead angles or complex dance patterns—just an unadorned emphasis on the songs and on the singers.

Perhaps more than any other major musical of the '30s, *Alexander's Ragtime Band* reaffirms music as the great bringer-together, the common bond that can help anybody —not only Alice Faye and Tyrone Power, but anyone in the audience—overcome any problem life may throw at them.

That same year, 1938, Berlin also wrote his third score for a Fred Astaire–Ginger Rogers musical, *Carefree*. This has one of the cleverest and most original musical-comedy plots for its time, predating *Lady in the Dark* in its use of the psychological probing of behavior for the plot's basis. But the picture was beset with problems from the start. The RKO Radio studios were financially troubled and the last two Astaire-Rogers musicals (*Swing Time* and *Shall We Dance*) had not done as well at the box office as their earlier ones. Moreover, Rogers, independently of Astaire, had made a couple of very successful straight comedies (*Vivacious Lady* and *Having Wonderful Time*). So RKO tightened the budget on *Carefree*'s musical numbers and put the picture's emphasis on more purely comic scenes, most of them spotlighting Ginger. *Carefree* is thus pretty much Rogers's picture—and she's delightful in it. The dances and musical numbers, on the other hand, are just not up to the best Astaire-Rogers level.

It's not Irving Berlin's fault. One especially lovely ballad, "The Night Is Filled With Music," got dropped from the final film except for its use as orchestral background music in one scene. Another song, "I Used to Be Color-Blind," was supposed to be the basis for a dream sequence in Technicolor (just as RKO Radio's version of *Irene* with Anna Neagle uses "Alice Blue Gown" as a color sequence in an otherwise black-and-white film). But, for budgetary reasons, "I Used to Be Color-Blind" ended up in black and white, undercutting Berlin's playful lyrics. The sequence itself is still fairly ingenious for its time, in the way in which Astaire and dance director Hermes Pan make imaginative use of slow-motion techniques to heighten the scene's subtle eroticism.

"Change Partners" is a cleverly plot-integrated song that's gone on to become a pop standard. It's the movie's best song. Ironically, Berlin didn't write it for *Carefree*. During the shooting of *Follow the Fleet* two years earlier, Berlin had sensed that Rogers was beginning to chafe at being identified only as Astaire's partner, and that Astaire himself was questioning the wisdom of working with just one dancer in picture after picture. So Berlin wrote "Change Partners" and stored it away, just in case. Out it came when it fit the plot situation in *Carefree,* though a year premature in terms of its original intent.

There is no big dance production number in *Carefree* on the order of *Top Hat*'s "The Piccolino." But there is "The Yam." It's a lively, "everybody-join-in" number that Astaire and Rogers lead at a country club dance. At about the time *Carefree* was being made, Berlin had been quoted in the press—both in the United States and

Alexander's Ragtime Band *(1938): Jack Haley (on drums), Alice Faye, Don Ameche (at the piano), Tyrone Power (on violin).*

on a trip to London—for taking pot shots at the swing-music craze sweeping the country and making superstars of such bandleaders as Benny Goodman, Jimmie Lunceford, and Artie Shaw. "Swing music isn't music," Berlin said. "It's just a way of playing it. It's a fad. It'll die." And so some interpreted "The Yam" as Berlin's attempt to come up with a nonswing popular dance tune on the order of Britain's 1938 hit "The Lambeth Walk"—but something as American as apple pie or, well, yams. Neither the tune nor the dance step that Astaire and Hermes Pan created for it caught on. "The Yam" was soon forgotten.

So, too, were most of the six songs that Berlin wrote the following year for Twentieth Century-Fox's *Second Fiddle,* starring ice-skating queen Sonja Henie and the studio's reigning matinee idol, Tyrone Power. More than one critic applied the picture's title to Berlin's score—unfairly, I'd argue. The number one problem was with the picture's script, which started out with a potentially good idea and then buried it in subroutine situations and dialogue. The idea: to spoof the much-publicized search by David O. Selznick to find an actress to play Scarlett O'Hara in *Gone With the Wind.*

In *Second Fiddle,* a movie company has been searching for two years for someone to play the heroine in its great epic, *Girl of the North.* The company finally decides to take a chance on Candidate No. 436—a Minnesota schoolteacher-skater (Henie) who's been discovered by the studio's press agent (Power). She's brought to Hollywood with great ballyhoo. But then *Second Fiddle* falls apart when the agent fixes up a phony romance for her with another of the studio's stars (Rudy Vallee), even though he's fallen in love with her himself. It takes too many scenes before true love wins out. But along the way there are some pleasing Berlin songs—especially one that the frustrated press agent writes (courtesy of Irving Berlin, of course) for Vallee to sing to Henie, "I Poured My Heart Into a Song." It remains one of Berlin's most under-appreciated ballads among all his movie songs.

Vallee also gets to sing "When Winter Comes," a spirited tribute to the cuddling that cold weather inspires. Mary Healy (playing Vallee's girlfriend) torches her way through "I'm Sorry for Myself," a so-so tune that may have been forty years ahead of its time with its self-pitying, "miserable me" lyrics. There's also "Back to Back," a tongue-in-cheek, up-tempo musical antonym to Berlin's own "Cheek to Cheek." "Back to Back" would seem to be tailor-made for a late-'30s swing hit, and in fact was recorded in an appropriately swinging arrangement in England by Carroll Gibbons's Orchestra. Perhaps American bandleaders rejected the tune because of Berlin's verbal jabs at swing music. If so, they missed a good one.

Rudy Vallee (at top) sings "An Old-Fashioned Song is Always New" in a production number from Irving Berlin's Second Fiddle *(1939).*

In one of his rare song-and-dance turns, Clark Gable led six MGM chorines through Berlin's "Puttin' on the Ritz" in the 1939 anti-war satire Idiot's Delight.

MGM, meanwhile, was not about to miss a chance in 1939 to give its Number One male star, Clark Gable, a chance to kick up his heels in a musical number—when they cast him as the brash, cynical vaudeville hoofer in Robert E. Sherwood's own adaptation of his sardonic antiwar play, *Idiot's Delight.* Gable had previously had roles in four musicals, but his co-stars and others had done all the singing and dancing in them, not him. This time (for the only time in his movie career), Gable both sings and dances—in a deliberately hackneyed and deliciously funny routine to Berlin's 1930 hit, "Puttin' on the Ritz." It remains the highlight of a still-interesting if dated and sometimes simplistic indictment of both warmongers and pacificists. And by using Berlin's "Puttin' on the Ritz" for the movie's key musical number (not part of the original Broadway play with Lunt and Fontanne), Sherwood fittingly reinforces his script's send-up of the social and political phonies victimizing each other as they move the world toward another war (which would, indeed, begin just seven months after the movie's premiere).

Berlin was also the victim during this period of professional sniping, which some attribute to "sour grapes" among songwriters jealous of Berlin's ability to turn out hit after hit—and also of his way of working out better financial deals for himself than most others ever won. Rumors, dating back to the late '20s, began recirculating that Berlin may not have written all the songs credited to him—that, instead, he may have bought songs from unknowns and had his publishing company issue them under his name. Berlin not only vigorously denied such charges, but also won several lawsuits growing out of them. Still, innuendos resurfaced with a 1940 movie, *Rhythm on the River,* starring Bing Crosby and Mary Martin. Its plot centers on a showbiz entrepreneur (played by Basil Rathbone), described early in the movie as "America's most popular songwriter," who secretly buys music from Crosby and lyrics from Martin and passes the songs off as his own—until Crosby and Martin rebel. When Rathbone "explains" his practice at one point, he notes that his own creative juices had dried up when his wife died. That led some people to draw a parallel to Berlin's personal crisis after the death of his first wife in 1913. But others dismissed the parallel, pointing out that the elegant Rathbone character in *Rhythm on the River* was completely unlike Berlin in style and appearance and that if the character was, in fact, based on anyone, it certainly wasn't Berlin. Producers, directors, and others came forward saying they could document example after example of Berlin's turning out—even sweating out—his own songs. Berlin has been accepted without challenge *as* Berlin ever since.

Two years later, one of Bing Crosby's biggest movie successes at the same studio, Paramount, would be in an Irving Berlin musical: *Holiday Inn*. Berlin composed twelve songs for this one, but eleven got overshadowed by the one that became the all-time record and sheet-music bestseller, "White Christmas." Crosby introduces it in the picture in a disarmingly simple and straightforward way, as he sits at a piano and croons it to Marjorie Reynolds, who then joins in for a chorus (with Reynolds's singing voice dubbed by Martha Mears).

Although *Holiday Inn* has been identified ever since its release with the Christmas season because of "White Christmas," it's actually a tribute to eight holidays year-round—with "Let's Start the New Year Right," "Be Careful It's My Heart" (for Valentine's Day), and "Easter Parade" (the only vintage Berlin song in the movie), the best remembered. Most forgettable is the wartime-inspired but banal "Song of Freedom" (for the Fourth of July), certainly no match for Berlin's classic "God Bless America," which had been introduced four years previously on a radio broadcast by Kate Smith and would be used in three later '40s movies.

The plot of *Holiday Inn* is one of those slight, escapist confections about two performers (Bing Crosby, Fred Astaire) in love with the same girl (Marjorie Reynolds), with most of the action set in a country inn that's open to the public only on holidays. But the story rarely gets in the way of an almost steady parade of songs and dances, which Paramount's wartime austerity forced to be filmed fairly modestly with stagebound sets.

Crosby gets most of the songs—and the girl. But Berlin obviously had Astaire in mind when he wrote "You're Easy to Dance With," and Astaire makes the words seem completely appropriate as he spins around the dance floor with Virginia Dale. Astaire also uses one of the movie's least memorable songs, "Say It With Firecrackers" (a second Fourth of July entry), for a snappy tap routine that is reputedly the fastest precision dance that he or anyone else ever filmed.

While *Holiday Inn* was providing warmly sentimental fare in wartime movie theaters, Berlin was hard at work putting together an all-soldier revue on Broadway, as a tribute to America's fighting men and women. *This Is the Army* was modeled on Berlin's *Yip-Yip Yaphank* of World War I, but bigger and better—and it was even more of a smash hit. Berlin set up a special company (This Is the Army Inc.) so that all profits from the show and its 1943 movie version went to the Army Relief Fund. The Army, for its part, "loaned" some 350 soldiers for the production.

Berlin's patriotic gesture did not sit well with everyone, however. The president of the American Federation of Radio Artists protested that a scheduled series of broadcasts featuring members of the show was providing unfair competition to professional radio personalities. For a short period, songs from *This Is the Army* were banned on the radio. Berlin went on the counterattack, with public support from fellow

George Murphy rehearses fellow soldiers in Berlin's wartime This Is the Army (1943).

songwriter Cole Porter and such major Broadway stars as Helen Hayes. The federation yielded. Two of *This Is the Army*'s songs, "I Left My Heart at the Stage Door Canteen" and "I'm Getting Tired So I Can Sleep" promptly went on to become *Hit Parade* entries.

Warner Brothers bought the movie rights to *This Is the Army* and assigned Michael Curtiz, fresh from winning an Oscar for *Casablanca,* to direct the transfer to the screen. Curtiz and associate producer Hal Wallis worked without salaries, and key crew members, including the cameramen, donated their salaries to the Army Relief Fund.

The movie added a story that begins in World War I, when a dancer (George Murphy) joins the Army and produces an all-soldier show called, not so coincidentally, *Yip-Yip Yaphank.* After the war, he resumes his career until World War II breaks out. At a concert at which Kate Smith sings "God Bless America," he is moved to volunteer to produce a new all-soldier revue—and from there on, the musical is much as it had been presented on Broadway. The addition of "God Bless America" created a few problems, however. Since 1938, Berlin had assigned all royalties to that song, in perpetuity, to the Girl Scouts and Boy Scouts of America. A formula had to be worked out for a percentage of the movie's profits to go to the Scouts as well as to the Army Relief Fund.

The movie version of *This Is the Army* is a rousing, colorful, patriotic variety show. Its unabashed flag waving is tempered by the good humor and honest sentiment of Berlin's song lyrics—as in "This Is the Army, Mr. Jones," "Poor Me, on K.P.," "How About a Cheer for the Navy?" and "I Left My Heart at the Stage Door Canteen." But the most memorable moment comes when Irving Berlin himself appears to recap the song hit he'd written twenty-five years earlier for *Yip-Yip Yaphank,* "Oh, How I Hate to Get Up in the Morning." Cast as a reluctant World War I soldier, Berlin sings it with a raspy but perfectly in-tune voice—giving the all-time serviceman's lament its definitive delivery.

Berlin himself used to love telling the story about a studio crew member who heard Berlin recording the number for the soundtrack and said to a colleague: "If the guy who wrote this song could hear the way *this* guy is singing it, he'd turn over in his grave!"

Berlin, at fifty-seven in 1945, was still far from written out. His first postwar movie, *Blue Skies,* is a mixture of old and new Berlin songs—seventeen in all. Bing Crosby and Fred Astaire are cast once again, this time in Technicolor and with the musical numbers staged more elaborately than in the wartime *Holiday Inn.* And once again Bing Crosby gets the girl and the best songs, including the new "You Keep Coming Back Like a Song," and the vintage "Blue Skies" and "All By Myself."

But Astaire, in top hat and tails, steals the picture with another oldie, "Puttin' on the Ritz," with as imaginative a piece of tap-dance mastery and split-screen cinematography as Astaire ever filmed. After debonairly singing the lyrics of the Berlin song (which he had recorded as early as 1930), Astaire ends up precision-dancing with ten images of himself. It's a spectacular routine—and, for a while, it looked as if it might be Astaire's last. Just before the picture's release, Astaire announced that he was retiring from the movies at age forty-seven.

Berlin would be at least partly responsible for that retirement lasting only about two years. So was Gene Kelly. He and Judy Garland were at work in the pre-production stages of 1948's *Easter Parade,* a 1910 "period musical" for which Berlin had written half a dozen new songs to supplement the well-known title song and other vintage tunes the picture planned to use. But then Kelly suffered an ankle injury that forced his withdrawal from the picture. Kelly joined MGM in pleading with Astaire to replace him. The twin prospects of working with Garland in a musical with a Berlin score proved irresistible to Astaire, and he accepted. *Easter Parade* not only turned out to be one of Astaire's best and most successful movies, but also led him to shelve his retirement from movie musicals for at least another decade.

Berlin himself made movie history with *Easter Parade,* not for his songs but for his financial deal for the picture. He reportedly got half a million dollars plus a percentage of the profits—the latter something other songwriters had unsuccessfully sought for years from other studios. Producer Arthur Freed also has reported that Berlin was especially attracted to the picture by the opportunity to work with Judy Garland, who had been singing many of Berlin's songs for years on radio.

Whether it was the deal, or Garland and Astaire, or MGM's track record for quality '40s musicals, or whatever, Berlin's new songs for *Easter Parade* are among the best he's ever written for the movies. One ballad, "It Only Happens When I Dance With You," made the *Hit Parade.* The genial "A Fella With an Umbrella" even manages to survive the rather feeble singing of Peter Lawford (as a young Englishman who tries to pick up Garland during a rainstorm) before Garland chimes in. One comedy number has become a classic: "We're a Couple of Swells," with Garland and Astaire cavorting in tramp costumes, blackened teeth, and smudgy makeup, as they send up the elegant airs of the Park Avenue elite. Here Berlin's lyrics are more teasing and less nose thumbing than those he'd written for "Slummin' on Park Avenue" in 1937's *On the Avenue.* Berlin also provides Astaire with songs for two show-stopping dances: "Drum Crazy," set in a toy shop, and the rollicking, swinging "Stepping Out With My Baby." For the latter, Astaire again makes imaginative use of film technique for a slow-motion dance in the foreground, in counterpoint to a fast-stepping, fast-clapping chorus line in the background.

Most of the vintage Berlin songs in *Easter Parade* perfectly fit the 1910 period setting of the story, which traces the efforts of a successful dancer (Astaire) to act as

For "We're a Couple of Swells," Fred Astaire and Judy Garland cavorted in tramp costumes and blackened teeth in Easter Parade *(1948).*

a Pygmalion for a neophyte (Garland) when his partner (Ann Miller) quits the act. Garland gets to sing "I Wanna Go Back to Michigan" and "I Love a Piano," and, with Astaire, "Snooky Ookums" and "When That Midnight Choo-Choo Leaves for Alabam'." In a dance to "Beautiful Faces Need Beautiful Clothes," Garland and Astaire also get to spoof—none too subtly but hilariously—the trouble that Astaire had with Ginger Rogers's feathery costume for *Top Hat.* And Ann Miller turns Berlin's 1927 "Shaking the Blues Away" into one of the snappiest, show-stopping routines she's ever done.

Berlin was reportedly delighted when MGM, in 1948, bought the movie rights to his Broadway hit *Annie Get Your Gun*—specifically for Judy Garland and at the unprecedented sum of $700,000. *Annie Get Your Gun* had been Berlin's first postwar Broadway show, and a personal smash for Ethel Merman in the title role of the legendary Western sharpshooter Annie Oakley. But MGM considered Merman not bankable enough "box office" nationwide and, at forty, too old for the part in terms of movie closeups. However, Garland, at the age of twenty-six, was beginning to have

45

serious health problems, partly the result of years of overwork and dieting, and the pills prescribed for both. (In *Easter Parade,* for example, there are evident fluctuations in Garland's weight from scene to scene.) Soon after *Easter Parade,* Garland, on the brink of exhaustion, had to withdraw from a planned reteaming with Astaire in *The Barkleys of Broadway.* After a rest period and one other picture (*In the Good Old Summertime*), Garland reported to work to begin *Annie Get Your Gun.*

She recorded the songs for the soundtrack and started shooting several of the musical numbers under Busby Berkeley's direction. But after about six weeks of Garland's repeated lateness or not showing up at all, MGM concluded that she was not up to finishing the film—that she was, in fact, on the brink of a complete breakdown. Garland was replaced by Betty Hutton, and what might have been a great movie musical had to settle for being just a good one.

Garland was not the only replacement *Annie Get Your Gun* faced before filming was complete. Frank Morgan, originally cast as Buffalo Bill, died suddenly and his role was taken by Louis Calhern. First Busby Berkeley and then Charles Walters were replaced as the director, with the more prosaic George Sidney finally getting the job.

The raucous Betty Hutton brings plenty of vitality and spunk to the movie version of *Annie Get Your Gun,* but little of the clarion brightness of Merman or the warmth and special magic that Garland might have shown. Yet the movie remains much more faithful to its Broadway original than most film adaptations to that time —even while opening up the action to the real outdoors, sometimes spectacularly. Virtually all of the show's songs are kept, including two that had made the *Hit Parade* in 1946, "They Say That Falling in Love Is Wonderful" and "Doin' What Comes

Betty Hutton in "I'm an Indian, Too," from Berlin's Annie Get Your Gun *(1950).*

Naturally," plus "I've Got the Sun in the Morning," "The Girl That I Marry," "You Can't Get a Man With a Gun," "Anything You Can Do (I Can Do Better)," "I'm an Indian, Too," and "There's No Business Like Show Business." Several of the show's songs did get cut, however, including the genially hillbilly "Moonshine Lullaby" and the chipper "Who Do You Love, I Hope." One song that had been cut from the Broadway show, the wonderfully wistful "Let's Go West Again," was set to be reinserted in the movie and was accordingly recorded by Garland and the MGM chorus, but then was cut from the Hutton version.

In 1952 another of Berlin's big Broadway hits was fairly faithfully transferred to the screen: *Call Me Madam.* And this time Hollywood finally did right by Ethel Merman, when Twentieth Century-Fox decided to star her in the role she had made her own on Broadway. After all, it had been written specifically for her by Howard Lindsay and Russel Crouse (coauthors of *Life With Father*) and Berlin, and this time the character's age was ambiguous enough.

Call Me Madam is a lively, lighthearted spoof of President Harry Truman's sending Washington hostess Perle Mesta to be ambassador to the tiny principality of Liechtenstein (fictionalized here as Lichtenburg). Mesta, in the years immediately following World War II, had become the most famous party giver in Washington —parties which brought together influential people in and out of government. There were rumors that Truman's wife was not all that happy about Mesta's influence and had "ordered" her husband to get her out of Washington. As the ambassador to Liechtenstein, Mesta continued to make headlines by her refreshingly democratic way of getting around old-fashioned governmental protocol. It was a situation tailor-made for a musical comedy. And in the "good sport" tradition, Perle Mesta and Bess Truman themselves went to see the show and then went backstage to tell Merman how much they had enjoyed it.

The movie version of *Call Me Madam* is as much a '50s period piece as *Top Hat* is a '30s one. Its dialogue is filled with fast-flying jabs at everything from contemporary fads and politics to Margaret Truman's singing. Berlin's songs spur much of the spoofing spirit along, beginning with Merman's belting out of "I'm the Hostess With the Mostes' on the Ball" to "Can You Use Any Money Today?," a musical swipe at Uncle Sam's foreign-aid programs. But it's Berlin's ballads that hit the mark best of all—and remain just as up-to-date today. They include "The Best Thing for You Would Be Me," "Marrying for Love," and "It's a Lovely Day Today," even if the first two are marred a bit by George Sanders's singing them with the overly phony foreign accent he adopted for the role.

"It's a Lovely Day Today" is also used to prove the power of American pop music in winning a royal heart, when Lichtenburg's princess (Vera-Ellen) hears the song in a music shop and decides to acquire the sheet music—which, just so coincidentally, prominently displays Irving Berlin's picture on its cover. Berlin also gets an on-screen mention at the Lichtenburg ball, when Merman asks the bandleader if he has anything "hot, up-to-date." The bandleader, after a moment of hesitation, comes up with a score, saying: "Here it is—an American song. Irving Berlin." The song turns out to be the 1913 "International Rag," which Merman proceeds to belt out in her inimitably zesty, brassy style.

Merman again stops the show, this time with Donald O'Connor's help, with one of Berlin's greatest duets, "You're Just in Love." The song gets two outings—first when

Ethel Merman sings "Can You Use Any Money Today?" to George Sanders in the 1953 film version of Irving Berlin's Call Me Madam.

Merman tries to shake O'Connor (playing her press attaché) out of the doldrums over the seemingly ill-fated course of his romance with the princess, and then later when Merman and O'Connor reverse roles, with him trying to cheer her up. Either way, it's the sort of optimistic, "you-can-take-it" song that Berlin has always done better than anyone else.

Two of the Broadway show's songs were not used in the movie. "They Like Ike," about the then-uncertain political candidacy of war hero Dwight Eisenhower, had been made passé by the 1952 Presidential election. The other song, a ballad for the press attaché, "Once Upon a Time Today," was replaced by an even better Berlin tune, "What Chance Have I With Love?" The unhappy-in-love O'Connor sings it amiably and then dances a letting-off-steam number that smacks a little too much at its end of Astaire's destructive "One for My Baby" in 1943's *The Sky's the Limit.* O'Connor's dancing skills come off much more agreeably in a duet with Vera-Ellen to "Something to Dance About."

With several hit movies having taken their titles from Berlin songs (*Alexander's Ragtime Band, Blue Skies, Easter Parade*), it was probably inevitable that one would eventually appropriate the 1942 song hit "White Christmas" as the title for a Bing Crosby movie—and that's exactly what happened in 1954. For *White Christmas,* Crosby was costarred with Danny Kaye in a musical that took a little bit from *Holiday Inn,* a little bit from *Blue Skies,* and then reshuffled everything with nine new Berlin songs and seven vintage ones.

Crosby and Kaye play two Army buddies who become song-and-dance stars after the war. While on a vacation in New England with two showgirls (Rosemary Clooney and Vera-Ellen), they get involved with helping their former general (Dean Jagger) save from bankruptcy the ski resort he owns. But the plot rarely gets in the way of the songs—and one of them, "Count Your Blessings Instead of Sheep," ended

Donald O'Connor in "What Chance Have I with Love," one of the two new songs written by Berlin for the film version of Call Me Madam.

up on the *Hit Parade* for sixteen weeks and gave pop singer Eddie Fisher one of his biggest-selling record hits of the '50s. *White Christmas* itself turned into the top money-making film of 1954.

Still, *White Christmas* doesn't hold up as well today as either *Blue Skies* or *Holiday Inn,* partly because Crosby and Kaye don't play off each other as well as did Crosby and Astaire. Kaye has only one really clever solo, "Instead of Dance, It's Choreography," a spoof of the arty trend in '50s dance routines. Clooney's smooth way with a melody almost makes you overlook the lyrics of "Love, You Didn't Do Right by Me." Clooney and Vera-Ellen fare better with "Sisters," which Crosby and Kaye then mime amusingly to the ladies' voices. All four join voices for a routine minstrel number (using Berlin's "Mandy," of course) and, saving the best for the last, the title-song finale.

Berlin's last big movie musical to date has been 1954's *There's No Business Like Show Business*—which again takes a title from a Berlin song hit. Just as Berlin's "God Bless America" has become something of an unofficial alternate national anthem, so "There's No Business Like Show Business" has become the unofficial anthem of the whole world of popular entertainment.

The movie of that title is the most extravagantly produced of all the Berlin song parades, in the splashiest Twentieth Century-Fox color and in CinemaScope (which frequently ends up in unfortunate frame croppings on TV). Of the thirteen Berlin songs, only two were written for the picture. Once again Irving Berlin's name is listed before the title in the opening credits.

This time the plot follows a family of song-and-dance performers over a quarter of a century between the two World Wars. Ethel Merman and Dan Dailey, Jr., are Mama and Papa, and their offspring grow up to be Donald O'Connor, Mitzi Gaynor, and Johnny Ray. Merman, fresh from scoring a hit in the movie version of *Call Me*

Third-billed Marilyn Monroe steals the show in 1954's There's No Business Like Show Business *(shown here in the "After You Get What You Wanted" number).*

Madam, gets top billing and the lion's share of the songs—and a script characterization that allows her to come up with more than the wisecracks of most of her previous films. Even so, the picture is stolen by third-billed Marilyn Monroe, as a showgirl with whom O'Connor (second-billed) falls in love. This, incidentally, would be the last picture in which Monroe would not be top-billed, other than her final, *The Misfits,* in which she yielded the top line to her longtime idol, Clark Gable.

Monroe, in her most seductive manner, purrs the lyrics to "After You Get What You Wanted," dressed in a form-fitting, partly see-through white gown that looks as if she'd been poured into it. The song itself is atypically Berlin—a bit on the cynical side. But Monroe delivers it with a comic irony that softens its pettish edge.

Even better is the sizzling Monroe version of "Heat Wave," arguably the most exhibitionistically provocative number she ever filmed. Still, it's filled with a contagious sense of fun. Less effective is Monroe's overmannered version of "Lazy," which especially suffers in comparison with a similar number, Cole Porter's "The Laziest Gal in Town," which Marlene Dietrich sang more coolly yet more seductively in Alfred Hitchcock's *Stage Fright* (1950).

Berlin's two new songs for *There's No Business Like Show Business* are strictly routine: "A Man Chases a Girl (Until She Catches Him)," which provides O'Connor with an excuse for an exuberant dance; and "A Sailor's Not a Sailor (Until a Sailor Is Tattooed)," which does nothing for either the sailor-suited Merman or Gaynor—least of all for Merman who is sporting a mustache. Everyone fares much better with the old songs, which they sing and dance to a terrific turn. Among them: "Play a Simple Melody," "When That Midnight Choo-Choo Leaves for Alabam'," "A Pretty Girl Is Like a Melody," "Let's Have Another Cup of Coffee," "Remember," and, of course, the song that first made Berlin's name synonymous with American popular music, "Alexander's Ragtime Band."

However threatened Berlin may have felt back in the late '30s by the swing music craze and the rise of the big bands as the hit-makers of the day, he kept right on composing for Broadway and Hollywood in his own way—and kept right on being a regular on *Your Hit Parade.* But the arrival of rock 'n' roll in the mid-'50s was another matter. It left him completely alienated. By the time the TV edition of *Your Hit Parade* folded in 1959—or, as some critics have phrased it, surrendered to rock and the Top 40—Irving Berlin had already gone into retirement. Aside from the theme song for the 1957 movie *Sayonara* (starring Marlon Brando and Red Buttons), Berlin has not added anything to his movie output in the last twenty-nine years.

But what an incredible output it remains. As Cole Porter so aptly put it in rhyme in one of his own hit songs, "You're the Top" (from *Anything Goes*): *"You're the top, you're a Berlin ballad."*

IRVING BERLIN'S MOVIES AND SONGS ON TAPE AND DISC

THE JAZZ SINGER (1927), Warner Brothers. B&W. Directed by Alan Crosland. With Al Jolson, May McAvoy, Warner Oland, Eugenie Besserer, Myrna Loy. Song: "Blue Skies"; plus songs by others. Soundtrack LP: Soundtrak 102. Videocassette: CBS/Fox.

THE AWAKENING (1928), United Artists. B&W. Directed by Victor Fleming. With Vilma Banky. Song: "Marie."

LADY OF THE PAVEMENTS (1929), United Artists. B&W. Directed by D. W. Griffith. With Lupe Velez, William Boyd, Jetta Goudal. Song: "Where Is That Song of Songs for Me?"

COQUETTE (1929), United Artists. B&W. Directed by Sam Taylor. With Mary Pickford, George Irving, Johnny Mack Brown, Louise Beavers, William Janning. Song: "Coquette."

HALLELUJAH (1929), MGM. B&W. Directed by King Vidor. With Daniel L. Haynes, Nina Mae McKinney, Harry Gray, William Fontaine. Songs: "Waiting at the End of the Road," "Swanee Shuffle"; plus traditional spirituals.

THE COCOANUTS (1929), Paramount. B&W. Directed by Joseph Santley and Robert Florey. With Groucho, Chico, Harpo, Zeppo Marx, Mary Eaton, Oscar Shaw, Kay Francis, Margaret Dumont. Songs: "When My Dreams Come True," "Monkey Doodle-Doo," "Florida by the Sea," "Tale of the Shirt." Soundtrack LP: Soundtrak 108.

THE TIME, THE PLACE AND THE GIRL (1929), Warner Brothers. B&W. Directed by Howard Bretherton. With Betty Compson, James Kirkwood, Grant Withers, Vivian Oakland. Song: "How Many Times?"; plus songs by others.

GLORIFYING THE AMERICAN GIRL (1929), Paramount. B&W and color. Directed by Millard Webb. With Mary Eaton, Dan Healy,

Helen Morgan, Rudy Vallee, Eddie Cantor, plus walk-on by Irving Berlin. Production "under the personal supervision of" Florenz Ziegfeld. Song: "Blue Skies"; plus songs by others. Soundtrack LP: Helen Morgan excerpt included in *The Torch Singer and the Mountie* on Trisklog 4. Videocassette: Discount Video.

MAMMY (1930), Warner Brothers. B&W. Directed by Michael Curtiz. With Al Jolson, Louise Dresser, Lois Moran, Lowell Sherman. Songs: "Let Me Sing and I'm Happy," "Across the Breakfast Table Looking at You," "To My Mammy," "Knights of the Road." Soundtrack LP: Milloball TMSM-34031 (with *20 Million Sweethearts*); excerpts included in *Irving Berlin 1909–1939*, Music Masters JJA 19747.

PUTTIN' ON THE RITZ (1930), United Artists. B&W. Directed by Edward H. Sloman. With Harry Richman, Joan Bennett, Lilyan Tashman, James Gleason. Songs: "With You," "Puttin' on the Ritz," "Alice in Wonderland"; plus songs by others. Soundtrack LP: Meet-Patti Discs PRW-1930; excerpts included in *Irving Berlin 1909–1939*, Music Masters JJA 19744.

REACHING FOR THE MOON (1931), United Artists. B&W. Directed by Edmund Goulding. With Douglas Fairbanks, Bebe Daniels, June Clyde, Edward Everett Horton, Bing Crosby. Song: "When the Folks High Up Do the New Lowdown." Soundtrack LP: Excerpt included in *Where the Blue of the Night Meets the Gold of the Day*, Biograph BLP-M1. Videocassette: Thunderbird; also Penguin.

KID MILLIONS (1934), Samuel Goldwyn for United Artists release. B&W and color. Directed by Roy Del Ruth. With Eddie Cantor, Ann Sothern, Ethel Merman, George Murphy. Song: "Mandy"; plus songs by others. Soundtrack LP: Classic International Filmusicals CIF-3007.

TOP HAT (1935), RKO Radio. B&W. Directed by Mark Sandrich. With Fred Astaire, Ginger Rogers, Edward Everett Horton, Helen Broderick, Erik Rhodes, Eric Blore. Songs: "No Strings," "Top Hat, White Tie and Tails," "Isn't This a Lovely Day to Be Caught in the Rain," "Cheek to Cheek," "The Piccolino." Soundtrack LP: EMI Pathe Marconi 2-C184-95807/8 (import); also, excerpts included in *Hollywood Story*, Festival F214. Videocassette: Nostalgia Merchant; also RKO Home Video.

FOLLOW THE FLEET (1936), RKO Radio. B&W. Directed by Mark Sandrich. With Fred Astaire, Ginger Rogers, Randolph Scott, Harriet Hilliard, Lucille Ball, Betty Grable, Astrid Allwyn. Songs: "We Saw the Sea," "Let Yourself Go," "Get Thee Behind Me, Satan," "I'd Rather Lead a Band," "But Where Are You?," "I'm Putting All My Eggs in One Basket," "Let's Face the Music and Dance." Soundtrack LP: Sandy Hook SH2099. Videocassette: Nostalgia Merchant; also RKO Home Video.

THE GREAT ZIEGFELD (1936), MGM. B&W. Directed by Robert Z. Leonard. With William Powell, Luise Rainer, Myrna Loy, Virginia Bruce, Frank Morgan, Fanny Brice. Song: "A Pretty Girl Is Like a Melody"; plus songs by others. Soundtrack LP: Classic International Filmusicals CIF-3005. Videocassette: excerpt included in *That's Entertainment*, MGM/UA.

ON THE AVENUE (1937), Twentieth Century-Fox. B&W. Directed by Roy Del Ruth. With Dick Powell, Madeleine Carroll, Alice Faye, the Ritz Brothers, Joan Davis, Lynn Bari. Songs: "He Ain't Got Rhythm," "The Girl on the Police Gazette," "You're Laughing at Me," "This Year's Crop of Kisses," "I've Got My Love to Keep Me Warm," "Slummin' on Park Avenue." Soundtrack LP: Hollywood Soundstage 401.

ALEXANDER'S RAGTIME BAND (1938), Twentieth Century-Fox. B&W. Directed by Henry King. With Tyrone Power, Alice Faye, Don Ameche, Ethel Merman, Jack Haley, John Carradine. Songs: "Now It Can Be Told," "My Walking Stick," "I'm Marching Along With Time," "Blue Skies," "Heat Wave," "Say It With Music," "Pack Up Your Sins (and Go to the Devil)," "What'll I Do," "Remember," "International Rag," "When That Midnight Choo-Choo Leaves for Alabam'," "Ragtime Violin," "Everybody's Doin' It," "Oh, How I Hate to Get Up in the Morning," "We're on Our Way to France," "Easter Parade," "All Alone," "For Your Country and My Country," "Alexander's Ragtime Band." Soundtrack LP: Hollywood Soundstage 406; also, excerpts included in *Merman in the Movies: 1930–38*, Music Masters Encore ST101.

CAREFREE (1938), RKO Radio. B&W. Directed by Mark Sandrich. With Fred Astaire, Ginger Rogers, Luella Gear, Ralph Bellamy, Jack Carson. Songs: "They Turned Loch Lomond Into Swing," "The Night Is Filled With Music," "I Used to Be Color-Blind," "Change Partners," "The Yam." Soundtrack LP: Sandy Hook SH2010; also Classic International CIF-3004 (with *Flying Down to Rio*). Videocassette: Nostalgia Merchant; also RKO Home Video.

THE STORY OF VERNON AND IRENE CASTLE (1939), RKO Radio. B&W. Directed by Henry C. Potter. With Fred Astaire, Ginger Rogers, Walter Brennan, Edna May Oliver, Lew Fields. Song: "Syncopated Walk"; plus songs by others. Soundtrack LP: Caliban 6000 (with *Daddy Long Legs*). Videocassette: Nostalgia Merchant.

SECOND FIDDLE (1939), Twentieth Century-Fox. B&W. Directed by Sidney Lanfield. With Tyrone Power, Sonja Henie, Rudy Vallee, Edna May Oliver, Mary Healy. Songs: "I Poured My Heart Into a Song," "When Winter Comes," "I'm Sorry for Myself," "An Old-Fashioned Song Is Always New," "Back to Back," "Song of the Metronome."

IDIOT'S DELIGHT (1939), MGM. B&W. Directed by Clarence Brown. With Norma Shearer, Clark Gable, Edward Arnold, Joseph Schildkraut, Burgess Meredith, Charles Coburn. Song: "Puttin' on the Ritz"; plus songs by others. Videocassette: MGM/UA; also included in *That's Entertainment,* MGM/UA.

LOUISIANA PURCHASE (1942), Paramount. Color. Directed by Irving Cummings. With Bob Hope, Vera Zorina, Victor Moore, Irene Bordoni, Dona Drake. Songs: "Take a Letter to Paramount Pictures," "Before the Picture Starts," "You're Lonely and I'm Lonely," "Louisiana Purchase," "Dance With Me (at the Mardi Gras)."

HOLIDAY INN (1942), Paramount. B&W. Directed by Mark Sandrich. With Bing Crosby, Fred Astaire, Marjorie Reynolds, Virginia Dale, Walter Abel. Songs: "Happy Holiday," "Holiday Inn," "Let's Start the New Year Right," "Be Careful, It's My Heart," "You're Easy to Dance With," "Abraham," "I Can't Tell a Lie," "Easter Parade," "Let's Say It With Firecrackers," "Song of Freedom," "I'll Capture Your Heart Singing," "Plenty to Be Thankful For," "White Christmas." Soundtrack LP: Soundtrak 112. Videocassette: MCA.

HELLO, FRISCO, HELLO (1943), Twentieth Century-Fox. Color. Directed by H. Bruce Humberstone. With Alice Faye, John Payne, Jack Oakie, June Havoc, Lynn Bari. Song: "Doin' the Grizzly Bear"; plus songs by others. Soundtrack LP: Caliban 605 (with *Spring Parade*); also, excerpt included in *Alice Faye,* Scarce Rarities 5502.

POWERS GIRL (1943), United Artists. B&W. With Anne Shirley, George Murphy, Carole Landis, Dennis Day, Benny Goodman Orchestra. Song: "A Pretty Girl Is Like a Melody"; plus songs by others.

HERS TO HOLD (1943), Universal. B&W. Directed by Frank Ryan. With Deanna Durbin, Joseph Cotten, Charles Winninger. Song: "God Bless America"; plus songs by others.

THIS IS THE ARMY (1943), Warner Brothers. Color. Directed by Michael Curtiz. With George Murphy, Joan Leslie, Ronald Reagan, Charles Butterworth, Alan Hale, Rosemary De Camp, Dolores Costello, Una Merkel, Ruth Donnelly, Kate Smith, Frances Langford, Gertrude Niesen, Irving Berlin. Songs: "This Is the Army, Mr. Jones," "I Left My Heart at the Stage Door Canteen," "The Army's Made a Man Out of Me," "I'm Getting Tired So I Can Sleep," "Your Country and My Country," "God Bless America," "Oh, How I Hate to Get Up in the Morning," "The Well-Dressed Man in Harlem," "Poor Little Me, I'm on K.P.," "With My Head in the Clouds," "How About a Cheer for the Navy," "We're on Our Way to France," "American Eagles," "Ladies of the Chorus," "Mandy," "My Sweetie," "What Does He Look Like?," "This Time Is the Last Time." Soundtrack LP: Hollywood Soundstage 408; also Sandy Hook SH2035. Videocassette: Video Images (Video Yesteryear); Discount Video; Budget Video; Sheik Video.

CHRISTMAS HOLIDAY (1944), Universal. B&W. Directed by Robert Siodmak. With Deanna Durbin, Gene Kelly, Gladys George, Gale Sondergaard. Song: "Always"; plus songs by others.

THE JOLSON STORY (1946), Columbia. Color. Directed by Alfred E. Green. With Larry Parks, Evelyn Keyes, William Demarest, Bill Goodwin, Scotty Beckett. Song: "Let Me Sing and I'm Happy"; plus songs by others. Soundtrack LP: Pelican 129; also Take Two 103 (includes alternate takes and out-takes).

BLUE SKIES (1946), Paramount. Color. Directed by Stuart Heisler. With Bing Crosby, Fred Astaire, Joan Caulfield, Olga San Juan, Billy DeWolfe. Songs: "You Keep Coming Back Like a Song," "Serenade to an Old-Fashioned Girl," "A Couple of Song and Dance Men," "Gettin' Nowhere," "My Captain's Working for Me Now," "You'd Be Surprised," "I'll See You in C-u-b-a," "The Little Things in Life," "Always," "A Pretty Girl Is Like a Melody," "How Deep Is the Ocean," "Not for All the Rice in China," "White Christmas," "Puttin' on the Ritz," "This Is the Army, Mr. Jones," "Any Bonds Today?" Soundtrack LP: Soundtrak STK104; also Sandy Hook SH2095; Videocassette: MCA.

BIG CITY (1947), MGM. B&W. Directed by Norman Taurog. With Margaret O'Brien, Robert Preston, George Murphy, Danny Thomas, Betty Garrett, Lotte Lehmann. Song: "God Bless America"; plus songs by others.

THE FABULOUS DORSEYS (1947), United Artists. B&W. Directed by Alfred W. Green. With Tommy Dorsey, Jimmy Dorsey, Janet Blair, William Lundigan, Paul Whiteman, Helen O'Connell, Bob Eberle, Henry Busse, Charlie Barnet, Ziggy Elman, Art Tatum. Songs: "Marie," "Everybody's Doin' It"; plus songs by others. Videocassette: Republic; Budget Video; Video Images (Video Yesteryear).

EASTER PARADE (1948), MGM. Color. Directed by Charles Walters. With Judy Garland, Fred Astaire, Ann Miller, Peter Lawford. Songs: "It Only Happens When I Dance With You," "Steppin' Out With My Baby," "A Fella With an Umbrella," "A Couple of Swells," "Better Luck Next Time," "Drum Crazy," "Beautiful Faces Need Beautiful Clothes," "The Girl on the Magazine Cover," "When That Midnight Choo-Choo Leaves for Alabam'," "Snooky Oookums," "Ragtime Piano," "I Love a Piano,"

"Everybody's Doin' It," "I Wanna Go Back to Michigan," "Happy Easter," "Easter Parade." Soundtrack LP: MGM SES-40 (withdrawn). Videocassette: MGM/UA.

JOLSON SINGS AGAIN (1949), Columbia. Color. Directed by Henry Levin. With Larry Parks, Barbara Hale, William Demarest, Bill Goodwin. Song: "Let Me Sing and I'm Happy"; plus songs by others.

ANNIE GET YOUR GUN (1950), MGM. Color. Directed by George Sidney. With Betty Hutton, Howard Keel, Keenan Wynn, Louis Calhern, Edward Arnold, J. Carrol Naish. Songs: "Colonel Buffalo Bill," "I've Got the Sun in the Morning," "I'm an Indian, Too," "You Can't Get a Man With a Gun," "My Defenses Are Down," "They Say That Falling in Love Is Wonderful," "Doin' What Comes Naturally," "The Girl That I Marry," "Anything You Can Do (I Can Do Better)," "There's No Business Like Show Business." Soundtrack LP: MGM 509 (withdrawn); also, soundtrack of uncompleted version with Judy Garland, Sound Stage 2302; excerpt included in *That's Entertainment, Part 2,* MCA 2-11002. Videocassette: excerpt included in *That's Entertainment, Part 2,* MGM/UA.

MEET DANNY WILSON (1952), Universal. B&W. Directed by Joseph Pevney. With Frank Sinatra, Shelley Winters, Raymond Burr, Alex Nichol. Song: "How Deep Is the Ocean"; plus songs by others.

CALL ME MADAM (1953), Twentieth Century-Fox. Color. Directed by Walter Lang. With Ethel Merman, Donald O'Connor, Vera-Ellen, George Sanders, Billy De Wolfe. Songs: "The Hostess With the Mostes' on the Ball," "Can You Use Any Money Today?," "International Rag," "The Ocarina," "What Chance Have I With Love?," "Something to Dance About," "The Best Thing for You Would Be Me," "It's a Lovely Day Today," "Marrying for Love," "You're Just in Love." Soundtrack LP: DRG-Stet DS25001 (with *Guys and Dolls*).

SO THIS IS LOVE (1953), Warner Brothers. Color. Directed by Gordon Douglas. With Kathryn Grayson, Merv Griffin, Walter Abel, Jeff Donnell, Rosemary DeCamp. Song: "Remember"; plus songs by others.

WHITE CHRISTMAS (1954), Paramount. Color. Directed by Michael Curtiz. With Bing Crosby, Danny Kaye, Rosemary Clooney, Vera-Ellen, Dean Jagger. Songs: "The Best Things Happen While You're Dancing," "Count Your Blessings," "Sisters," "I Wish I Was Back in the Army," "Snow," "Love, You Didn't Do Right by Me," "I'd Rather See a Minstrel Show," "Mandy," "The Old Man," "What Can You Do With a General?," "Let Me Sing and I'm Happy," "Abraham," "Blue Skies," "Heat Wave," "Choreography," "White Christmas." Videocassette: Paramount.

THERE'S NO BUSINESS LIKE SHOW BUSINESS (1954), Twentieth Century-Fox. Color. Directed by Walter Lang. With Ethel Merman, Donald O'Connor, Marilyn Monroe, Dan Dailey, Mitzi Gaynor, Johnny Ray. Songs: "Play a Simple Melody," "Remember," "When That Midnight Choo-Choo Leaves for Alabam'," "Let's Have Another Cup of Coffee," "A Pretty Girl Is Like a Melody," "Heat Wave," "Alexander's Ragtime Band," "A Man Chases a Girl (Until She Catches Him)," "You'd Be Surprised," "A Sailor's Not a Sailor (Until a Sailor's Tattooed)," "After You Get What You Wanted," "There's No Business Like Show Business." Soundtrack LP: Decca 8091 (withdrawn); excerpts included in *The Unforgettable Marilyn Monroe,* Movietone 72016 (withdrawn); also *Monroe: La Voce, Le Musiche e I Films,* RCA Italiana TPL1-7025 (import).

LOVE ME OR LEAVE ME (1955), MGM. Color. Directed by Charles Vidor. With James Cagney, Doris Day, Cameron Mitchell, Robert Keith. Song: "Shaking the Blues Away"; plus songs by others. Soundtrack LP: CBS Special Products ACS-8773.

SAYONARA (1957), Warner Brothers. Directed by Joshua Logan. With Marlon Brando, Red Buttons, Ricardo Montalban, Miyoshi Umeki, Miiko Taka, Martha Scott, James Garner. Song: "Sayonara."

THAT'S ENTERTAINMENT (1974), MGM. B&W and color. All-star compilation feature directed by Jack Haley, Jr. Songs: "A Pretty Girl Is Like a Melody," "Puttin' on the Ritz"; plus songs by others. Soundtrack LP: MCA2-11002. Videocassette: MGM/UA.

YOUNG FRANKENSTEIN (1974), Twentieth Century-Fox. B&W. Directed by Mel Brooks. With Gene Wilder, Madeline Kahn, Peter Boyle, Marty Feldman, Teri Garr, Cloris Leachman. Song: "Puttin' on the Ritz." Videocassette: CBS/Fox.

THAT'S ENTERTAINMENT, PART 2 (1976), MGM, B&W and color. All-star compilation feature directed by Jack Haley, Jr. Songs: "Easter Parade," "Stepping Out With My Baby," "A Couple of Swells"; plus songs by others. Soundtrack LP: MCA MG1-5301. Videocassette: MGM/UA.

PENNIES FROM HEAVEN (1981). MGM. Directed by Herbert Ross. With Steve Martin, Bernadette Peters, Christopher Walken, Tommy Rall, John McMartin. Song: "Let's Face the Music and Dance"; plus songs by others. Videocassette: MGM/UA.

Fred Astaire, George Gershwin and Ira Gershwin going over a tune for Shall We Dance *in July of 1937.*

GEORGE GERSHWIN

When George Gershwin arrived in Hollywood in 1930, he was one of the hottest names in American music—with a string of Broadway successes behind him and a growing reputation as a "serious" composer for the concert hall. He was also well-known as an enthusiastic party-goer. So it wasn't surprising that some of the movie colony went out of its way to wine and dine him. One persistent legend has it that a gossip columnist, unable to attend the first big party, decided to write it up anyway. Her readers learned the next day that Hollywood had given a warm welcome to "the great composer George Gershwin and his lovely wife Ira." (A similar story has been attributed to a London reporter, but Kay Swift, a close friend of Gershwin's, told me she always understood that it indeed happened in Hollywood.)

George and Ira Gershwin may have had a marriage of sorts, but it wasn't, of course, as husband and wife. As this century's most successful team of songwriting brothers, the Gershwins actually worked together for only nineteen years—from 1918 to 1937. George died tragically young at age thirty-eight, while working in Hollywood. Ira, his brother's senior by two years, continued to write lyrics for the songs of other composers for another seventeen years. But the songs that George and Ira wrote together remain in a class by themselves—and have provided movie musicals with some of their greatest and most enduring song treasures.

George Gershwin was born in Brooklyn, New York, on September 26, 1898. The family name was then spelled Gershvin, and George's first name was listed on his birth certificate as Jacob. But according to brother Ira, he was known from the beginning within the family as George. When George was not quite a year old, his father moved the family to the Lower East Side of Manhattan, where George then spent the rest of his boyhood and teen years.

Contrary to the film biography *Rhapsody in Blue* (1946), Gershwin did not grow up in poverty. His father was a middle-class businessman who provided modestly well for his family, including music lessons for his son. George was about twelve when, with his parents' encouragement, he began taking formal piano lessons. His teacher reported mixed emotions to the Gershwin family about their son's talent. On the one hand, George showed more interest in learning and practicing than did most other students. At the same time, his chief intertest was clearly in the popular music of the day, not the classics his teacher thought he should be studying. The composer that young George most idolized at this time: Irving Berlin.

By age fifteen, Gershwin had not only started writing songs of his own, he had also become the youngest staff pianist working for the Tin Pan Alley publishing firm of Remick, earning fifteen dollars a week. At Remick he soon acquired a reputation as a better-than-average pianist, and he got to meet Berlin and another early idol, Jerome Kern. He also met several young lyricists, including Irving Caesar and Murray Roth, with whom he began collaborating on songs.

Gershwin and Roth succeeded in getting one of their songs interpolated into *The Passing Show* of 1916. But among that show's fourteen songs by different songwriters, it attracted little attention. And it reportedly netted Gershwin a mere seven dollars. But it was enough to encourage him to continue writing.

The following year, Gershwin became a rehearsal pianist for *Miss 1917,* a Broadway show on which Jerome Kern was collaborating with Victor Herbert and whose cast was headed by Vivienne Segal, Lew Fields, and Marion Davies. The show lasted only a month on Broadway. But during rehearsal breaks, Gershwin sometimes entertained the cast with improvisations and some of his songs. One who was especially impressed was Vivienne Segal. At a Sunday night concert that some of the cast members of *Miss 1917* gave soon after the show closed, Segal introduced Gershwin and Caesar's "There's More to a Kiss than X-X-X" and "You-oo, Just You." Among those who liked the songs was Max Dreyfus, head of the Harms music-publishing firm. He offered Gershwin a job at the same money he was then making at Remick (thirty-five dollars a week). But instead of being a pianist and song plugger for the work of others, Gershwin would be required only to compose his own songs. He was nineteen.

Over the next two years, Gershwin, mostly with Irving Caesar as lyricist, turned out a number of songs that were interpolated into Broadway revues or introduced by vaudeville performers such as Nora Bayes. Only one of them became a hit—but a gigantic one. It was "Swanee," which Al Jolson sang in the revue *Sinbad.* "Swanee" became the biggest sheet-music and record best-seller Gershwin would know in his lifetime.

In 1919 Gershwin composed his first full Broadway score, for a bedroom farce called *La La Lucille.* It enjoyed a respectable three-month run, and it produced a modest hit in "Nobody But You," with lyrics by Buddy DeSylva (one of four lyricists with whom Gershwin collaborated on the show's fourteen songs).

That same year, George White, who had been a dancer in *Miss 1917,* entered the ranks of Broadway's producers with the first of what would be an almost-annual series of successful musical-comedy revues. He asked Gershwin to write the score for *George White's Scandals of 1920*—and then, in succession, for the *Scandals* of 1921, 1922, 1923, and 1924. More than anything else, these revues catapulted Gershwin to the front rank of Broadway composers of the 1920s. Among his *Scandals* songs (with a variety of lyricists) were "Somebody Loves Me," "I'll Build a Stairway to Paradise," and "Drifting Along With the Tide."

For the *Scandals* of 1922, Gershwin also wrote a twenty-five-minute production number that was, in effect, a one-act jazz opera. Titled *Blue Monday,* it had a somber libretto by Buddy DeSylva—about a Harlem woman who is prodded by a romantic rival to kill her lover in the mistaken belief that he is going out of town to see another woman. The "other woman" turns out to be his mother. The number was performed by whites in blackface and went over well during the *Scandals* of '22's New Haven tryout. But the New York opening-night critics were not so kind. Charles Darnton of the *World,* for example, called it "the most dismal, stupid, and incredible blackface sketch that has probably ever been perpetrated." Charles Pike Sawyer of the *Post* compared it to a mixture of *La Bohème* and *Tristan and Isolde,* "burlesqued almost beyond recognition." George White, who had been doubtful about the merits of the number from the beginning, promptly dropped *Blue Monday* after the opening-night performance, contending that it was too grim for a revue.

Paul Whiteman thought otherwise. His orchestra was in the '22 *Scandals* and Whiteman liked the "jazz opera" enough to commission Gershwin to write an extended work for orchestra that would be part of a concert of "serious jazz" that Whiteman planned to present at New York's Aeolian Hall on February 12, 1924. Gershwin agreed. As he later put it: "There had been so much chatter about the limitations of jazz, not to speak of manifest misunderstandings of its function, that I resolved, if possible, to kill that misconception." But then Gershwin got so involved in the production of a London show (*The Rainbow*) and another Broadway musical (*Sweet Little Devil*) that he notified Whiteman just before Christmas that he couldn't possibly complete an extended piece by early February. Whiteman, not to be put off, insisted that all he needed was a piano score—that his band's arranger, Ferdie Grofé, could complete the orchestration from there. And so Gershwin went to work on the piece, composing some of it on trains between New York and Boston (where *Sweet Little Devil* was in tryout). Ira gave the composition its name: *Rhapsody in Blue.*

The premiere, at which Gershwin himself was the piano soloist, was a tremendous success—with most of the audience if not with all of the music critics. Several major reviewers dismissed the *Rhapsody in Blue* as "trite and feeble," "sentimental and vapid," "empty and meaningless." But the critic for *The New York Times* called Gershwin "an extraordinary talent, a young composer with aims that go far beyond those of his ilk." And a critic for *Musical America* went so far as to hail the *Rhapsody* as "greater than Stravinsky's *The Rite of Spring.*"

The enthusiastic response led Whiteman to repeat the concert twice in the next two months, once again at Aeolian Hall and then at the larger Carnegie Hall. Whiteman's orchestra also recorded the *Rhapsody in Blue* with Gershwin as the piano soloist

—and it soon became a best-seller. By the end of 1924 Gershwin was the most talked-about composer in America. Unlike most other songwriters of the time, he would from then on pursue a dual career—with one foot planted in musical comedy, the other in the concert hall.

In 1925 Gershwin and Grofé revised and expanded the *Rhapsody in Blue* for symphony orchestra, and it entered the repertoire of a number of major orchestras. Its success as a concert work led to Gershwin's being commissioned to write several other instrumental concert works. Meanwhile, the *Rhapsody in Blue* would, in effect, launch Gershwin's movie career, when it was played in its entirety in a spectacularly staged sequence of the early talkie revue, *King of Jazz,* in 1930. Gershwin would also be paid ten thousand dollars for a two-week appearance at one of New York City's most popular movie-and-stage-show palaces, the Roxy, playing the *Rhapsody* with Paul Whiteman's orchestra in conjunction with *King of Jazz*'s premiere.

While the *Rhapsody in Blue* was making Gershwin a wealthy man, he continued to turn out songs for such Broadway and London musical comedies as 1926's *Oh, Kay!* and *Tip-Toes,* 1927's *Funny Face* and *Rosalie,* 1929's *Strike Up the Band,* and 1930's *Girl Crazy.* Among their songs that went on to become pop standards: "That Certain Feeling," "Do, Do, Do," "Someone to Watch Over Me," "Sweet and Lowdown," "'S Wonderful," "How Long Has This Been Going On?," "Soon," "Strike Up the Band," "But Not for Me," "Embraceable You," "Bidin' My Time," and "I Got Rhythm."

Most significantly, beginning in 1924, Gershwin began collaborating almost exclusively with his brother Ira as lyricist. The collaboration had begun surreptitiously a few years earlier, with Ira contributing lyrics to a number of shows under the pseudonym of Arthur Francis. As critic John S. Wilson has written in *The Gershwins:* "George and Ira were as dissimilar as two brothers could be. And yet the various pluses and minuses of these two very distinct and individually creative men were so complementary, fitting together as snugly as the parts of a cleanly cut jigsaw puzzle, that, together, they formed a remarkable complete whole."

Whereas George was egotistical, socially gregarious, a lover of the spotlight, and full of nervous energy, Ira was basically shy, even tempered, slower moving, and methodical. George remained a bachelor all of his life (with any number of reputed romantic attachments), whereas Ira settled down to married life when he was twenty-nine.

Usually George composed a melody first, to which Ira would then set lyrics. Occasionally Ira would come up first with the idea for a title or even a brief, catchy rhyme scheme, which George would then develop into a song. Although George's melodies were harmonically more sophisticated than most other popular songs of the '20s and '30s, Ira's lyrics remained spare and down-to-earth. Even his titles were full of average-person colloquialisms ("I've Got a Crush on You," "Bidin' My Time," "Nice Work If You Can Get It," "Let's Call the Whole Thing Off"). There was also a droll sense of humor to many of Ira's lyrics, and a literacy that never insulted the listener's intelligence. As for the Gershwins' love ballads—from 1924's "The Man I Love" to 1937's "Love Walked In"—they remain distinguished by their straightforward avoidance of oversweet sentimentality. Where others' songs were sticky or outright yucky, the Gershwins' were affectionate and touching.

The stock market crash of 1929 drastically undercut the Gershwins' Broadway bonanza—along with that of many other songwriters and show folk, of course. In fact, the Gershwins had to wait months to get any of their royalties and fees from the crash-devastated Florenz Ziegfeld for the ill-fated '29 production of *Show Girl,* which starred Ruby Keeler, Jimmy Durante, Duke Ellington's Orchestra, and ballerina Harriet Hoctor (in a ballet version of Gershwin's *An American in Paris*). That same year, another Ziegfeld production, *Ming Toy* (based on the popular play *East Is West*), for which the Gershwins had written seven songs, including "Embraceable You," was completely aborted.

The movie industry, however, was in a relatively healthier condition—particularly after talkies caught on in 1927. Almost anyone with good Broadway credentials was in demand by Hollywood. So, in 1929, George and Ira signed contracts to write the score for a motion picture to be made at the Fox Studios sometime the following year. As George told an interviewer at the time: "I go to work for the talkies like any other amateur, for I know little about them."

As on Broadway, he learned fast.

George Gershwin's Major Movies and Their Songs

Contrary to many reports, George Gershwin did not make his movie debut in 1930's *King of Jazz.* In fact, he does not appear in the picture at all. But he steals it anyway—musically. For one of the longest sequences in this early Technicolor revue is devoted to a complete performance of the original version of Gershwin's *Rhapsody in Blue* by Paul Whiteman's Orchestra. The piano soloist in that sequence has been misidentified over the years by some reviewers as Gershwin himself. And, indeed, from some angles the performer looks a bit like Gershwin. But he is actually the Whiteman Orchestra's longtime pianist, Roy Bargy, as confirmed to me by Bargy's daughter Jeanne.

King of Jazz was Universal Pictures's spectacular entry among the array of all-star musical-comedy revues that virtually every major studio turned out in the early talkie years of 1929 and 1930. It mixes straightforward song-and-comedy vaudeville turns with lavish musical production numbers in the style of Broadway's *Ziegfeld Follies*—all directed by a Ziegfeld veteran, John Murray Anderson. Most of the movie is stagebound and only rarely cinematic. But it boasts some incredibly extravagant sets and moving stages that have, even to this day, rarely been equaled.

The *Rhapsody in Blue* number has one of the most eye-boggling sets of all. The sequence starts with a wildly plumed solo dancer spotlighted atop a mammoth drum, with his shadow dramatically dominating the scene. Then it cuts to five pianists playing (or going through the motions of playing) the giant keyboard of the most grandiose baby-blue piano you're ever likely to see. Suddenly, at the command of a clarinet-

The Paul Whiteman orchestra performing the extravagantly staged "Rhapsody in Blue" in King of Jazz *(1930).*

playing magician, the giant piano's lid starts to open slowly—and, from *within* the piano, rises the whole Whiteman orchestra. As the *Rhapsody* progresses, the camera moves back and forth between the players and an elegantly attired group of models (all in blue) posing around the giant piano—and then to top-hatted chorines (in blue tights and tails) who dance up and down a series of ramps leading to the piano! What all this has to do with the *Rhapsody in Blue* I've never been able to figure out. But it's a visually mesmerizing number in a bold, glittery, surreal style that few movies have ever attempted on such a scale.

The rest of *King of Jazz* is as uneven as most revues of this period. But at least it has one virtue over MGM's *Hollywood Revue of 1929* or Warner Brothers's *Show of Shows,* in that most of its performers seem to *belong* in a musical-comedy revue—and not, as musicals historian and critic Ethan Mordden has put it about some of these other revues, looking "not unlike an audition." In other words, the studio's players are not assigned to song-and-dance numbers they really can't do, but instead to comedy sketches, most of them short and snappy. That leaves most of the musical numbers to the Whiteman aggregation and a fast-stepping dozen or more chorines.

Bing Crosby, in his movie debut, sings one song behind the movie's opening titles and then appears on-screen a bit later as one of Whiteman's Rhythm Boys (the others: Harry Barris and Al Rinker) to sing several other tunes. John Boles, Jeannie Lang, the Brox Sisters, the Sisters G, jazz violinist Joe Venuti, and guitarist Eddie Lang are also featured in other musical numbers—all by songwriters other than Gershwin. The best of these numbers are the toe-tapping "Happy Feet" (by Jack Yellen and Milton Ager) and the extravagant finale, "The Melting Pot of Jazz," which purports to show how all of Europe's musical traditions have combined to produce American jazz. Amazingly, no African cultures are shown—pointing up the very limited definition of jazz that was prevalent in pop-music circles in the late '20s and early '30s. The movie's title, in fact, is considerably misleading from today's viewpoint, since Whiteman's nickname as "The King of Jazz" was based only on his dominance among white, jazz-influenced popular bandleaders. His other nickname, "Pops" Whiteman, was much more accurate.

King of Jazz was filmed in a relatively primitive, two-strip Technicolor process, which most of the Hollywood studios abandoned in the early '30s as too expensive and not good enough. (Beginning in the late '30s, a three-strip process came into wide use.) For the movie's recent release on videodisc and videocassette, the color has been electronically doctored to compensate for the original's lack of good blue hues.

Color was also one of the original attractions of another 1930 movie with Gershwin music, *The Song of the Flame.* It was adapted from a 1925 Broadway musical on which Gershwin had collaborated with Herbert Stothart, Otto Harbach, and Oscar Hammerstein II. At one point, the picture even opened up in a pioneer wide-screen format. But neither such technical inventiveness nor the hitless Gershwin score could save the movie from its already outdated, operettalike libretto about a Russian peasant girl who saves the life of a prince by sacrificing her virginity to a fellow revolutionary leader. Bernice Claire, who adorned several of Warner Brothers's early talkie operettas, had the thankless starring role.

The Fox movie that had brought the Gershwin brothers to Hollywood didn't get made until early 1931. *Delicious,* starring Fox's then-popular romantic team of Janet Gaynor and Charles Farrell, turned out to be a delectable if slight musical about an illegal Scottish immigrant (Gaynor), the Long Island playboy with whom she falls in love, and the various social and legal complications they have to overcome before the final clinch.

Delicious was only a modest hit and none of its songs went on to become hits on their own. One Gershwin biographer, Charles Schwartz, charges that Gershwin was so busy being wined and dined by the film colony that he didn't have time to work —and so most of the film's tunes "were taken from his grab bag of previously written material or were discards from other musicals merely fitted with appropriate [new] lyrics by Ira to match the screenplay." Another Gershwin biographer, Edward Jablonski, disputes that. Although one song, "Blah-Blah-Blah," was taken "out of the trunk," Gershwin worked hard on the others, Jablonski says—especially on the extended instrumental piece, "New York Rhapsody."

The score's most under-appreciated ballad, "Somebody From Somewhere," suffers from being sung in the movie by a nonsinger (Gaynor). It's an unusually lovely, wistful ballad of the "longing-for-Mr.-Right" variety which, to my knowledge, only Ella Fitzgerald among later pop singers has recorded. "Blah-Blah-Blah," meanwhile, gives a delightful going-over to Tin Pan Alley composers of the "June-moon-spoon-tune" type, with lyrics that spoof the basic ingredients of so many late '20s and early '30s pop songs. Unfortunately, it's also sung by a nonsinger, Swedish-accented comedian El Brendel, so that it comes across more as an incidental piece of comic material

Janet Gaynor was the heroine in Delicious *(1931), the first film for which George Gershwin composed an original score.*

than as a song. Later-day cabaret singers, including Diahann Carroll and Barbara Lea, have shown what a good song it really is—and it became one of the highlights of the 1983 Broadway musical *My One and Only,* whose entire score used both familiar and unfamiliar Gershwin songs, though often in situations unrelated to the original intent of the lyrics (as, especially, with "Blah-Blah-Blah").

The "New York Rhapsody" accompanies a seven-minute dream sequence in *Delicious* in which the lass played by Gaynor tries to escape from her problems by fleeing into the New York night. The sequence is photographed from eccentric, German Expressionist–like angles, with the city's lights creating ominously dramatic shadows on the stylized sets. The city's sounds, dominated by the rhythm of riveting, grows wilder and wilder, leading Gaynor to almost throw herself into the river. It's one of the most imaginative and adventurous musical sequences of any movie to that time, even though Fox cut some of it after the premiere from fears that it was too "arty" for general audiences. Soon after the release of *Delicious,* Gershwin reworked the "New York Rhapsody" (which he had originally sketched as "Rhapsody in Rivets") into a concert work for piano and orchestra, finally calling it simply *Second Rhapsody.* Its concert premiere was given in 1932 by the Boston Symphony Orchestra, with Gershwin as the piano soloist. Most critics found it more assured in technique and more rhythmically inventive than the earlier *Rhapsody in Blue,* but less inspired overall. The *Second Rhapsody* has survived as an occasional concert piece, mostly on pops-concert programs.

After the lukewarm reception for *Delicious,* George and Ira returned to Broadway. Over the next four years, they created some of their most adventurous stage works, beginning with 1931's spoof of Presidential politics, *Of Thee I Sing,* the first musical comedy to win a Pulitzer Prize. This was followed in 1933 by an unsuccessful sequel, *Let 'Em Eat Cake,* in which blue-shirted revolutionaries overthrow the U.S. government and establish a dictatorship—a subject that most of the people who could afford theater tickets in the midst of the Depression weren't too ready to laugh at, even if accompanied by a likeable Gershwin score.

Then, in 1933, Gershwin decided that the time had come to write the American opera that, on and off, he'd thought about ever since *Blue Monday.* As early as 1930, the Metropolitan Opera had offered Gershwin a contract to compose an opera. But he had kept putting off such a project for lack of what he felt was a suitable subject. For a while, he considered an opera based on the ancient Hebrew legend of the Dybbuk. Then he turned to DuBose Heyward's novel *Porgy* and the 1927 play that Heyward wrote with his wife, Dorothy, and entered into tentative correspondence with Heyward about collaborating on a "folk opera" version. Heyward, meanwhile, had been approached by Jerome Kern and Oscar Hammerstein II (fresh from their success with *Show Boat*) for permission to adapt *Porgy* into a musical. Heyward finally gave Gershwin the nod. They spent most of 1934 and 1935 working on *Porgy and Bess,* with Ira acting as editor of the libretto and writing some of the lyrics.

Although the Metropolitan Opera at first expressed interest in an opera on the *Porgy* story, Gershwin decided against an arrangement with the Met. He told friends that he didn't want to spend several years composing an opera that would be performed once or twice a week for three or four weeks and then "put into mothballs," as had been the case with other American operas produced by the Met. He also felt that a Broadway theatrical production would permit the all-black cast he envisioned. And so he signed with the Theatre Guild to produce *Porgy and Bess* on Broadway.

The production met a mixed reception when it opened in October of 1935. It survived only 124 performances to noncapacity houses. Still, as critic John S. Wilson has noted, that was "far more than it might ever have received at the Metropolitan Opera House."

With his most recent stage efforts not having won the kind of enthusiastic audiences or critical acclaim that he had hoped for, Gershwin accepted an offer from RKO Radio to return to Hollywood. Fred Astaire, with whom George and Ira had worked on Broadway's 1924 *Lady, Be Good!* and 1927's *Funny Face,* was eager to do a movie musical with a Gershwin score. George, for his part, hoped to show that he had not lost his touch for light-hearted, popular musical comedy. And so he and Ira signed with RKO for *Shall We Dance,* the seventh musical to costar Astaire with Ginger Rogers (who had first attracted Hollywood's attention as one of the stars of Gershwin's 1930 Broadway musical, *Girl Crazy*).

Yet George had misgivings. Astaire and Rogers had hit it big with two Irving Berlin–scored films in succession, and then with one by Jerome Kern that had included the 1936 Academy Award winner for Best Song ("The Way You Look Tonight"). Gershwin was convinced that any subsequent Astaire-Rogers vehicles, and anything he might write for them, could only be viewed as anticlimactic. But with Irving Berlin's encouragement, he decided to chance it.

His fears were at least partly warranted. *Shall We Dance,* despite lavish praise from most of the critics, fell below previous Astaire-Rogers musicals in box-office receipts. Part of the problem was similar to what had undercut Gershwin's Broadway popularity while winning him artistic kudos—for, in an effort to avoid repeating past formulas,

Shall We Dance *(1937): Fred Astaire and Harriet Hoctor in the ballet section of the film's title number.*

Astaire and Rogers had gone highbrow, or at least had given that impression. Instead of playing a hoofer or a sailor, this time Astaire was a ballet dancer. And Rogers, too, had assumed the more sophisticated and elegant manner of a musical star. It worked for the characters they play in *Shall We Dance* and stretched their acting abilities, but it lost them some of their fans in the process, at least temporarily.

Shall We Dance contains some of Astaire and Rogers's most pretentious material —but, happily, some of their best as well. Part of the movie slyly spoofs the 1936 Broadway hit *On Your Toes* (music and lyrics by Rodgers and Hart), which had mixed classical ballet with pop and jazz beats. Astaire would mix these ingredients more adroitly in some of his later '40s and '50s movies than he does here. In fact, his *pas de deux* with the extremely limited Harriet Hoctor (just before the movie's finale) consists mostly of repetitious turns and poses. And Gershwin's music for this sequence is boring—sounding like an endless "vamp" until he can cut loose with a more traditional song. Which is exactly what finally happens after Rogers enters the scene and the movie's lively title song takes over.

Except for that sequence and some other incidental moments when he's trying to be "arty" for the film's ballet scenes, Gershwin has provided *Shall We Dance* with the best score he ever did for a movie. Astaire's first solo is especially bright and jazzy —"Slap That Bass," in which Astaire joins a group of black workers in the engine room of an ocean liner, with the chugs of the ship's engines and other machinery supplying a unique rhythm section. Ira's lyrics, meanwhile, help set the stage for the developing plot's conflict between popular music and the classics.

Another highlight: the "Walking the Dog" pantomime sequence, set to a perky Gershwin instrumental (which was later published as an orchestral piece, titled simply *Promenade*). Astaire, trying to find a way to get together with fellow ship passenger Rogers, discovers her walking her dog on the ship's kennel deck. He borrows a dog from a steward so that he can promenade too—first behind Rogers, then alongside her. It's a charming sequence, partly stolen by the expressions of the dogs—and ending up with Astaire and Rogers arm in arm, keeping time to Gershwin's melody as the dogs watch from the sidelines.

The promenade sequence leads directly into a song by Astaire to Rogers, "I've Got Beginner's Luck," whose lyrics express Astaire's delight in finding that *"the first time I fall in love, I'm in love with you."* The song, however, is thrown away in one brief chorus. Much the same happens with "They Can't Take That Away From Me," one of Gershwin's all-time great ballads, which gets a single chorus as Fred and Ginger ride a fog-enshrouded ferry boat—although it then reappears briefly as a theme during Astaire's pre-finale ballet with Hoctor. Gershwin himself was known to be upset about this "short shrift" treatment when the picture was released. In *The Gershwin Years* by Edward Jablonski and Lawrence D. Stewart, George is quoted as saying that "the picture doesn't take advantage of the songs as well as it should." In these two cases, at least, he was certainly right.

Two other songs get more fully-scaled treatments: "They All Laughed" and "Let's Call the Whole Thing Off." Rogers sings the first number in a nightclub setting and then gets tricked into an impromptu dance with Astaire—the first dance they have done together in the movie even though the picture is already half over! Once they get beyond the extended and silly "will-this-be-ballet-or-pop?" introduction, they launch into one of the most wonderfully spirited tap routines they ever did—alternately teasing and challenging each other with dance steps, and then swirling merrily around the dance floor before ending atop a set of white grand pianos. It's the only really archetypal "old style" Astaire-Rogers routine in the whole picture—and it's a wonderful one.

Most *un*typical is the gimmicky dance on roller skates that they do to "Let's Call the Whole Thing Off," a number that predates roller disco by at least forty years. Astaire and Rogers reportedly spent four days and a total of thirty "takes" shooting this one number, which lasts on-screen less than three minutes. Yet neither Astaire nor Rogers looks at ease or completely comfortable as they glide and tap away on their skates. The song itself is another matter. It comes across as the catchiest and cleverest song in the movie, thanks especially to the fun that Ira's lyrics poke at any number of words in the English language that some people pronounce one way, others another —such as either, neither, potato, tomato, pajamas, and oysters. "Let's Call the Whole Thing Off" was the first Gershwin movie song to make radio's *Your Hit Parade,*

Ginger Rogers and Fred Astaire donned roller skates to perform "Let's Call the Whole Thing Off" in Shall We Dance—*a number that required four days and thirty "takes" to shoot.*

although "They Can't Take That Away From Me" followed quickly and lasted six weeks longer.

George and Ira stayed on at RKO Radio to write the songs for another Astaire musical of 1937, *A Damsel in Distress.* Some critical wags promptly retagged it *A Dancer in Distress,* since it marked Astaire's first movie since 1933 without Rogers. Astaire had felt for some time that a temporary splitting up of the team would be desirable for both of them—"to keep us from falling into a rut," as he has put it in his autobiography. Rogers also wanted to do more nonmusical films, so that she would not be typed unfairly as just the uncreative half of a dance team. But RKO could not come up with another worthy dance partner for Astaire. At first, Ruby Keeler was considered for *A Damsel in Distress.* But it was decided that, with her distinctive American twang, Keeler could never pass muster as the plot's English aristocrat's daughter. Also considered was British dancing star Jessie Matthews (of the 1936 movie version of Rodgers and Hart's *Evergreen*), until it turned out that she was taller than Astaire.

The part finally went to nondancer Joan Fontaine, then a promising B-movie ingenue. One theory at the studio was that if a nondancer played opposite Astaire, she would avoid *any* comparisons with Rogers. The choice, however, undercut whatever chance the movie might have had with audiences curious to see Astaire work with another major partner—and virtually assured a critical lambasting when Fontaine's gracious attempt at dancing turned out to be feeble indeed.

That was (and remains) a shame—for *A Damsel in Distress* is, otherwise, a better-than-average musical comedy with a good Gershwin score. The picture starts off breezily with "I Can't Be Bothered Now," sung by Astaire after being prodded into a song and dance by some London street buskers. The song is marvelously tailored to Astaire's debonair style, but it is regrettably cut short after just a single chorus. (It got much more of a play in the previously mentioned 1983 Broadway musical, *My One and Only*.) The romantic "A Foggy Day (in London Town)" gets just a chorus and a half, but in a beautifully photographed sequence as Astaire wanders not through London but through the fog-blanketed English countryside, singing the number as a reminiscence of his earlier meeting of Fontaine. Surprisingly, there's no dance. (Astaire would make up for that by using a similarly misty background for one of the most effective dances in a later movie, 1957's *Funny Face*, which also has a Gershwin score.)

The countryside further provides the locale for "Things Are Looking Up," a romantic ballad that Astaire sings to Fontaine right after she admits she's fallen in love with him. But then the song's title takes on an unfortunate countermeaning as Fontaine and Astaire start to dance to it. By photographing the number in an outdoor setting, however, the cameramen are able to disguise Fontaine's limited dance abilities by having trees, fences, gates, and bushes conveniently cut her off while the main focus is kept on Astaire.

The surprise of *A Damsel in Distress* is how well two other leading performers, comedians George Burns and Gracie Allen, dance—a carryover, undoubtedly, from

The show-stopping amusement park sequence in A Damsel in Distress *(1937) teamed Fred Astaire with comics (and former vaudeville hoofers) Gracie Allen and George Burns.*

their days in vaudeville. Early on, they team up with Astaire for some lively, old-fashioned hoofing to Gershwin's "Put Me to the Test." Ira wrote lyrics to the song but they got cut from the movie. (He saved the lyrics and later gave them to Jerome Kern, who wrote a partly new melody to go with them for 1944's *Cover Girl*.)

Burns and Allen also team with Astaire for the movie's show-stopping "fun house" production number. It begins with Gracie's charming singing of "Stiff Upper Lip," with its lyrics full of such Britishisms as "pip-pip," "stout fellow," and "toodle-oo." Then follows an extended dance by the threesome through an amusement park's revolving barrels, chutes, and moving platforms. They end up with a visually imaginative dance in front of giant convex and concave mirrors. It's one of the 1930s' most clever and entertaining production numbers—with Gracie a particular standout.

Gershwin also provided several English folklike songs, "The Jolly Tar and the Milkmaid" and "Sing of Spring," for the plot's so-called Madrigal Singers to do in a mock-stuffy manner. Much more memorably, three amusingly mismatched ladies among the Madrigal Singers—Jan Duggan, Mary Dean, and Pearl Amatore—also get to join Astaire in introducing "Nice Work If You Can Get It," the only one of the songs in *A Damsel in Distress* to go on to *Your Hit Parade* (for ten weeks). "Nice Work" also provides the music for Astaire's drum dance finale, in which he uses drumsticks and his feet for a virtuosic but eventually tiresome display of thump-thump-thumping. (Astaire would do a similar but more inventive routine to Irving Berlin's "Drum Crazy," in 1948's *Easter Parade*.)

The supporting cast of *A Damsel in Distress* also includes Ray Noble, the great English bandleader whose early '30s recordings (including many movie songs) remain among the best dance-band arrangements still in circulation. But Noble makes no musical contributions to the film, playing a strictly comic role as a rather dim-witted Englishman, mostly as a foil to some of Gracie Allen's sillier lines. Nonsinger Reginald Gardiner, cast as a butler at Fontaine's castle, gets one musical number, however—and he pulls it off hilariously, as a frustrated opera singer who sneaks out into the garden to belt out *"Ah, che a voi perdoni iddio"* from Flotow's opera *Martha*. Gardiner's singing voice in this scene was dubbed by tenor Mario Berini, who went on to a Metropolitan Opera career in the '40s.

From *A Damsel in Distress,* George and Ira went directly to work on the score for *The Goldwyn Follies,* a lavish, musical-comedy revue in the still fairly new three-strip Technicolor process. The production blends ballet sequences featuring Vera Zorina, opera excerpts with Met singers Helen Jepson and Charles Kullmann, pop songs by Ella Logan and Kenny Baker, and comedy routines by the Ritz Brothers, Bobby Clark, and Edgar Bergen and Charlie McCarthy. With this multimillion-dollar mishmash, producer Samuel Goldwyn hoped to establish himself as Hollywood's equivalent to Broadway's Ziegfeld. He didn't. On the contrary, some critics thought the movie was titled all too accurately.

By the time the picture went into production, Gershwin had begun to cut back on the rounds of parties, dinners, and social functions that he had previously enjoyed so much. His associates found him moodier and more and more irritable. A love affair with actress Paulette Goddard reportedly ran out of steam when she declined to leave husband Charles Chaplin for Gershwin. Then, during a concert performance with the Los Angeles Philharmonic in February of 1937, Gershwin momentarily blacked out in the middle of a performance of his *Concerto in F.* A medical examination could find nothing physically wrong with him, and the incident was attributed to nerves and overwork. When he suffered another similar blackout a few months later, plus a series of blinding headaches, hospital tests still turned up nothing other than nervous tension. It was suggested that Gershwin needed a psychoanalyst, not medical treatment. Some of Gershwin's friends even concluded that he was just unhappy working within Hollywood's often-frustrating studio system, and that his health would clear up if and when he returned to Broadway, where he had more "say" as to how his songs would be used.

But Gershwin's condition worsened seriously in late June and early July of 1937. On July 9, he was rushed to Los Angeles's Cedars of Lebanon Hospital in a coma. Doctors there finally diagnosed the problem as a cystic brain tumor. An exploratory operation the next day revealed that the tumor was inoperable. Gershwin died the following morning without regaining consciousness.

The news of his death stunned a nation which still considered Gershwin, for all of his popular successes, its most promising young composer, with his best yet to come. Over the next few weeks, memorial concerts and radio broadcasts brought tributes from Irving Berlin, Jerome Kern, Cole Porter, Richard Rodgers, Hoagy Carmichael, George M. Cohan, Walter Damrosch, Leopold Stokowski, Arnold Schoenberg, Jascha Heifetz, Lily Pons, Fred Astaire, Al Jolson, and dozens of other personalities from all parts of the vast musical spectrum that George Gershwin had come to represent.

At his death, Gershwin had completed only part of the projected score for *The Goldwyn Follies.* Vernon Duke, whom Gershwin had known since the early 1920s, was selected to complete the score with Oscar Levant and lyricist Ira. This included the music for an extended ballet sequence that George Balanchine was choreographing for Vera Zorina. Originally, Balanchine and Gershwin had planned to use Gershwin's 1928 concert piece *An American in Paris.* Ira even prepared a scenario for the ballet. But producer Goldwyn vetoed it as too highbrow after watching a partial run-through that Balanchine had prepared after three weeks of work. "The miners in Harrisburg won't understand it," Goldwyn complained. The furious choreographer, according to Bernard Taper's biography, *Balanchine,* shot back: "There are no miners in Harrisburg. I know because I've been there!" But Goldwyn could not be swayed. The ballet to *An American in Paris* was out. (Gene Kelly, of course, would later prove how wrong Goldwyn was by using the score for the ballet finale of his popular, Oscar-winning 1952 musical, *An American in Paris.*)

If Gershwin had been upset that some of his songs for *Shall We Dance* and *A Damsel in Distress* got short shrift, then he would surely have been bothered by the way Goldwyn literally threw away the very last song Gershwin composed before his illness completely incapacitated him: "Our Love Is Here to Stay" (actually titled and published as "Love Is Here to Stay," but now more widely known with the prefatory "Our" of its lyric.) In *The Goldwyn Follies,* Kenny Baker sings it while his girlfriend (Andrea Leeds) and the studio boss (Adolphe Menjou) listen to him on the radio, and part of Baker's performance is covered by dialogue between Menjou and Leeds. The song would not become a pop standard until after 1952, when Gene Kelly used it for one of the musical highlights of *An American in Paris.*

On the other hand, another ballad, "Love Walked In," gets plenty of mileage in *The Goldwyn Follies*. It's sung several times in the movie by Kenny Baker, then used as background music in a couple of sequences, and is reprised during the finale by Baker, Helen Jepson, and Andrea Leeds (with Leeds's singing voice dubbed by Virginia Verrill). It's a lovely, airily confident romantic ballad that stayed on *Your Hit Parade* for fourteen weeks in 1938.

Three years after Gershwin's death, MGM would make a movie musical bearing the title of one of Gershwin's late '20s Broadway hits, *Strike Up the Band*. But other than using the title song for the picture's finale, the film would bear no relation to the Broadway show, either in plot or musical content. Whereas the Broadway show was a satiric jab at war and international politics (with a book by George S. Kaufman and Morrie Ryskind), the movie was another "hey-kids-let's-put-on-a-show" exercise for Mickey Rooney and Judy Garland, as directed by Busby Berkeley. The "Strike Up the Band" number is the basis for a spirited Berkeley finale, with what looks like half of Central Casting's available teenagers singing, dancing, or going through the motions of playing orchestral instruments—as an eighteen-year-old Judy Garland belts out the song with that bright-eyed, upbeat effervescence of hers that knew no equal in early '40s Hollywood.

The following year, MGM similarly took the title of another '20s Gershwin show, *Lady, Be Good!*, plus two of that show's Gershwin songs, and then wrapped a completely different story around them—throwing in three numbers by other song-writers (Kern-Hammerstein and Edens-Freed) as well. The movie also altered the punctuation of the original Broadway title, eliminating the comma and exclamation point, making the movie just *Lady Be Good*.

The title wasn't all that got defanged, for the story that MGM's scriptwriters came up with has to be the most excruciatingly dull and dim-witted account ever about songwriting itself. Ann Sothern and Robert Young play a songwriting team whose lives seem to be a revolving door of marriage and divorce, in between laughably corny sequences of how they go about "creating" hit songs. Fortunately, most of the musical numbers come off well, as sung by Sothern (long underrated by Hollywood as a musical performer), John Carroll, Connie Russell, and Virginia O'Brien. One of Sothern's non-Gershwin songs, Kern and Oscar Hammerstein's "The Last Time I Saw Paris," would even win the 1941 Academy Award for Best Song.

The top-billed Eleanor Powell, playing essentially a supporting role as a dancer-friend of Sothern's, manages to steer clear of most of the script's inanities and steals the picture with her spectacular tap dancing to Gershwin's "Oh, Lady, Be Good!" and "Fascinating Rhythm." Busby Berkeley stages the latter song for the film's finale in his most ostentatious manner—with eight grand pianos on a series of five-foot-high moving platforms, and with one hundred male dancers in white tie, tails, and canes accompanying a top-hatted Powell. The dancers eventually toss Powell back and forth pendulum-style, in one of the most intricate and breathtaking numbers that Powell ever filmed.

When it came to 1943's *Girl Crazy*, MGM was much more faithful to the original stage version of that 1930 show than it had been with either *Strike Up the Band* or *Lady Be Good*. And it was certainly more faithful than RKO's 1932 movie version, which had altered the book drastically to suit the vaudeville-based talents of comedians Robert Woolsey and Bert Wheeler, and had kept only five of the Broadway show's twelve Gershwin songs (with a new one added by the Gershwins, "You've Got What

Gets Me"), all of them unevenly handled by such performers as Dixie Lee, Kitty Kelly, Eddie Quillan, and a twelve-year-old Mitzi Green.

MGM's version was in more expert hands all around—including Arthur Freed as producer, Roger Edens as musical coordinator, Hugh Martin and Ralph Blane in charge of the vocal arrangements (later that same year they would write the score for *Meet Me in St. Louis*), and a cast headed by Mickey Rooney and Judy Garland. Busby Berkeley was to have been the director, but he got fired soon after the picture's start because of disagreements with Freed, Edens, and Garland—although he remained in charge of some of the dance numbers.

MGM kept almost all of the Broadway show's original songs (using two of them, however, as strictly instrumental backgrounds), and interpolated "Fascinating Rhythm" (originally from *Lady, Be Good!*) as a swing number for Tommy Dorsey and his orchestra, with Mickey Rooney at the piano. Most hearteningly (and most unusually for '40s Hollywood), MGM also kept all of Ira's wonderful lead-in verses to the songs.

The picture starts off with a rousing performance, set in a New York nightclub, of "Treat Me Rough" by June Allyson. She appears only in this one sequence and, at the time, was simultaneously filming her official debut role on the MGM lot in *Best Foot Forward*. Contrary to the ultra-sweet, "nice girl" image she would soon establish in most of her '40s movies, Allyson lunges into the song in the rough-and-tumble manner of Betty Hutton. It's a lusty performance, made even more fascinating by its contrast with Allyson's usual style. Rooney, playing a spoiled young New York playboy, wraps up the sequence with an energetic Apache dance with one of the club's chorines.

The scene then changes, as Rooney gets shipped off to the wide, open spaces of Arizona, to an all-male college that's as far from New York and its showgirl distractions as his father can get him. And the next musical number, to underline the difference in locale, provides as sharp a contrast as you can get to the opening "Treat Me Rough" —as Garland and a group of the college lads drawl their way lazily (and marvelously) through "Bidin' My Time." The sequence ends with a spirited square-dance routine, in which Rooney turns up in the most outrageous of dude-cowboy outfits.

The picture then moves into high gear with Rooney and Garland's nonpareil performance of "Could You Use Me?" In it, Garland (as the dean's daughter), coolly keeps the wolfish, overeager Rooney at bay as they trade Ira's mixture of romantic pleas and put-downs. Among all the numbers that Garland and Rooney did in a total of nine pictures, this one, perhaps best of all, shows the special rapport that existed between them and made them such a popular team. (It's challenged only by their version of Rodgers and Hart's "I Wish We Were in Love Again" in 1948's *Words and Music*.)

Garland also shines with "Embraceable You" and "But Not for Me," which she sings beautifully in an unusually light and (for her) most delicate style. (Her dance partner for "Embraceable You," incidentally, is Charles Walters, later to be her director for *Easter Parade* and *Summer Stock*.) For the finale, Garland more typically belts out "I Got Rhythm" as the prelude for dozens upon dozens of Busby Berkeley dancers taking over for a mammoth, swinging jamboree. Curiously, for this number Berkeley, perhaps miffed at having been relieved as director of the whole picture, merely reuses a number of ideas from his famous "Lullaby of Broadway" sequence in

Mickey Rooney, Judy Garland, and Tommy Dorsey cut loose in the "I Got Rhythm" finale to Girl Crazy *(1943).*

Gold Diggers of 1935, only slightly camouflaging them with the cowboy costumes and props.

If MGM's *Girl Crazy* proved that a major Hollywood studio could do right by a Gershwin show, Warner Brothers's *Rhapsody in Blue* proved that Hollywood, in 1945, was still not ready to make honest biographies about major musical personalities. Most of the well-intended but dreadful screenplay was the figment of the imaginations of Howard Koch (one of the coscripters of 1942's Oscar-winning *Casablanca*), Elliot Paul (author of the novel *The Last Time I Saw Paris*), and Sonya Levien (a later Oscar-winner for the script of '55's *Interrupted Melody*)—and it's an embarrassment all around. The screenplay supposedly follows Gershwin's life from East Side poverty (untrue) on to Park Avenue and Beverly Hills riches and a successful but lonely life at the top (only partly true). Fictitious are two big, cliché-ridden romantic attachments, one to an expatriate American socialite in Paris (played by Alexis Smith), the other to a singer (Joan Leslie) who loves him from the sidelines from his song-plugging days to the end. Gershwin's parents are presented as stereotypical, Old World Jewish types by Morris Carnovsky and Rosemary DeCamp, and Ira and his wife are one-dimensionally portrayed by Herbert Rudley and Julie Bishop. (Gershwin's other brother, Arthur, and his sister, Frances, are not even mentioned.) As Gershwin, Robert Alda at least looks a bit like the composer, and he tries his best to create a believably human portrait out of the script's banalities—but he loses the battle.

Good musical numbers might have helped override these shortcomings, but the production falls down badly there, too. Warner Brothers either couldn't or didn't want to feature non-Warner stars who had been associated historically with various Gershwin shows (such as Fred Astaire, Ginger Rogers, Ethel Merman, Vivienne Segal, Gertrude Lawrence, or Victor Moore). And so only Al Jolson (singing "Swanee"), Anne Brown (the original Bess, singing "Summertime" from *Porgy and Bess*), and Paul Whiteman (for the *Rhapsody in Blue* and several other sequences) re-create a few of their real-life musical numbers. The rest of the time we have to settle for Gershwin's great show tunes being unimaginatively presented by jazz pianist-singer Hazel Scott in a nightclub setting or by the fictitious Joan Leslie character (whose singing voice was dubbed by Louanne Hogan).

Oscar Levant is also on hand, mostly for wisecracking repartee—although he also gets to play part of the *Concerto in F* and the *Rhapsody in Blue*. The concerto excerpt is marred by one of the movie's most unbelievable scenes. As Levant is playing the concerto's final movement in an NBC broadcast, the actor playing conductor Walter Damrosch is handed a piece of paper and stops the performance just before the end of the movement to announce that Gershwin has just died. Then Levant and the orchestra, bravely and stirringly, pick up where they'd left off and finish the final two minutes of the concerto. Dramatic it may be, but not very likely in any concert—and untrue in this case.

As with so many '40s musicals, there is also no resemblance whatsoever in that

The none-too-accurate 1945 film biography Rhapsody in Blue *starred Robert Alda as Gershwin and Alexis Smith as a fictional patroness.*

scene, nor in the two *Rhapsody in Blue* sequences, to normal symphony stage-seating arrangements. Not only is the conductor half a block away from his players, but the orchestral groupings that Hollywood's designers apparently thought "looked" better would probably also create some bizarre sounds and imbalances in most concert halls, as well as creating serious problems for one part of the orchestra in hearing the other part. Moreover, the overly arty camera angles and boring visual presentation of the final *Rhapsody in Blue* sequence (supposedly taking place at New York's Lewissohn Stadium) make one realize how far the camerawork for today's concert telecasts has come since 1945.

There are, however, a couple of interesting musical surprises in *Rhapsody in Blue*. Tom Patricola, who introduced "Somebody Loves Me" in *George White's Scandals of 1924*, appears briefly to sing (with Leslie) part of that song in a scratchy but still serviceable voice. And two excerpts from the ill-fated *Blue Monday* are presented with Whiteman conducting—and were to remain for many years the only decently filmed sample of that operatic curiosity until a Swiss performance was telecast in Europe and the United States in 1981.

The biggest Gershwin surprise of all came in 1947, when Twentieth Century-Fox released a "new" Gershwin musical, *The Shocking Miss Pilgrim*, starring Betty Grable and Dick Haymes. The score was put together for the movie from unpublished songs and sketches that Gershwin had left at his death. For years it had been known that Gershwin had written dozens of songs that had been cut out of various productions or that hadn't gotten into them at all. It was also known that one of his closest friends and fellow songwriters, Kay Swift (composer of "Can't We Be Friends" for Libby Holman), had not only helped Gershwin edit some of his manuscripts but also had helped him for years to write down song ideas for possible future use. And so Kay Swift and Ira Gershwin were commissioned to come up with ten previously unused Gershwin songs as the basis for the score of *The Shocking Miss Pilgrim*. Ira rewrote the lyrics for some of them to fit the movie's story.

These efforts merely indicated that there weren't that many neglected Gershwin gems lurking around waiting to be discovered. Two romantic ballads, "Guess I'll Be Changing My Tune" and "For You, for Me, for Evermore," proved pleasant enough —and the latter song even went on to two weeks on *Your Hit Parade*. But the rest of the score turned out to be serviceable at best, at least as presented in the context of the movie.

When *The Shocking Miss Pilgrim* did only so-so business at the box office, Gershwin wasn't blamed but rather Twentieth Century-Fox's casting of popular "pin-up girl" Betty Grable in a costume role that gave her no chance to show off her legs. Grable plays a young suffragette in 1874 Boston, fighting for women's rights as office workers, and falling in love with her boss (Dick Haymes) in the process. The idea for the story is better than the screenplay that finally emerged. The picture is also stuffily directed by George Seaton, with the musical numbers staged routinely—especially a big, heavy-handed waltz sequence that never gives Gershwin's lilting "One, Two, Three" much of a chance.

However disappointing the "new" Gershwin musical of 1947 may have been, MGM's recycling of "old" Gershwin for 1951's *An American in Paris* resulted in one of the best musicals of all time—and the 1951 Academy Award winner for Best Picture (plus six other Oscars). The story is slight, about an American GI (Gene Kelly) who stays on in Paris after World War II to study painting and falls in love with a shopgirl (Leslie Caron), but not without complications. What counts most is the way Gershwin's songs—half of them already familiar standards by '51—are worked logically into the story and then sung and danced with exuberance and panache by Kelly and his costars. The view of Parisian bohemia may be strictly Hollywood and unrealistically sentimental, but there's an infectious *joie de vivre* about *An American in Paris* that few American movie musicals have ever sustained so completely throughout nearly two hours' running time—a *joie de vivre* that comes as much out of its Gershwin score as it does from its screenplay or performances.

In major ways, *An American in Paris* might be said finally to do justice to both the title number and a song that were respectively eliminated or slighted in the last movie that Gershwin actually worked on, 1938's *The Goldwyn Follies*. Not only is the symphonic poem *An American in Paris* used for an extended ballet finale, but "Our Love Is Here to Stay" becomes *the* romantic ballad of the picture. Gene Kelly sings the song to Leslie Caron at a much more leisurely and expressive tempo than Kenny Baker used in the earlier film, and then dances a haunting *pas de deux* to it with Caron in a handsomely photographed scene along the moonlit banks of the Seine.

Several lesser-known Gershwin songs also get memorable treatment. French music-hall star Georges Guétary (in his only American film appearance) sings "I'll Build a Stairway to Paradise" (from *George White's Scandals of 1922*) as it might be staged at the Folies Bergère, with beautifully plumed chorines descending a vast staircase, the steps of which light up as Guétary's feet touch them. Earlier, Kelly, Guétary, and Oscar Levant team up for "By Strauss" (from 1936's *The Show Is On*), cavorting at first playfully and then campily to its mock-schmaltziness, before ending with a charming dance between Kelly and septuagenarian Mary Jones. Kelly and Levant (who plays Kelly's struggling pianist buddy) also clown merrily to "Tra-la-la" (from 1922's *For Goodness Sake*), with Kelly wrapping up the number with one of those casual tap dances at which he was always so masterful.

Among the better-known songs, Kelly does a delightfully unorthodox "I Got Rhythm," partly in French and partly in English, with a bunch of Parisian kids as his song-and-dance partners. Kelly and Guétary also do a buoyant duet to "'S Wonderful," as each of them happily describes the girl he's in love with, not realizing they're singing about the same girl.

Levant also gets the ego trip of a lifetime for his performance of the final section of Gershwin's *Concerto in F*. Not only is he the piano soloist but also the conductor, four of the principal violinists, the xylophonist, the tympanist, and the gong player. It's a much less reverential treatment than Levant gave the same *Concerto in F* excerpt in *Rhapsody in Blue* a few years earlier, but much more enjoyable as movie fare.

For the final ballet, Gershwin's original score was considerably reorchestrated by Conrad Salinger and Johnny Green, partly to accommodate the ballet's scenario, partly to bring the music closer to the splashy, distinctive "MGM sound" of the '50s. The ballet is one of the longest uninterrupted dance sequences of any Hollywood movie to 1951, lasting just under eighteen minutes. Visually, it's a colorful, innovative blockbuster, viewing Paris through the colors and designs of some of the most famous painters—and made even more stunning because it is preceded by a Beaux Arts Bal sequence whose basic color scheme is black and white. The ballet blends classical, jazz, and pop dance styles with imaginative decor and costumes based on the paintings of

"I'll Build a Stairway to Paradise," from An American in Paris *(1951), featured French music-hall star Georges Guétary in his only American film appearance.*

Dufy (for the Place de la Concorde), Van Gogh (for the Place de l'Opéra), Utrillo (for a Montmartre street), Manet (for a flower market), Rousseau (for a street fair), and Toulouse-Lautrec (for the Moulin Rouge). The ballet remains designer-director Vincente Minnelli's and choreographer-star Kelly's finest contribution among many to musical films.

The last major Gershwin musical comedy to be adapted to the screen to date has been 1957's *Funny Face.* Actually, it takes only the title of a 1927 Broadway show and four of George and Ira's songs from that show, and then appends some other songs and a completely different, contemporary '50s story. But it does so with a visual style that's bold and stunning, with the most striking color images since *An American in Paris* and with imaginative use of split-screen techniques, frame freezing, color spotting, and other techniques. Although made at Paramount, the picture has the look, sound, and overall style of one of the great MGM musical classics, which isn't surprising since producer Roger Edens and director Stanley Donen transported key members of MGM's unique "Freed Unit" to work on the picture at Paramount.

The story is a variation on *Pygmalion,* set in the glamorous world of high-fashion

Leslie Caron and Gene Kelly in a scene from the final ballet sequence of the Oscar-winning An American in Paris.

magazines. Fred Astaire plays a Richard Avedon–type photographer who transforms a gaminesque bookworm (Audrey Hepburn) into a top fashion model, with help from a jet-propelled editor (Kay Thompson). The picture almost gets bogged down midway by a lengthy, mockingly anti-intellectual section about the model's fascination with a trendy Existentialist-type philosopher (Michel Auclair), but even that part is saved by the ingratiating performances of the principals and some pungent, tongue-in-cheek jabs at the followers of "in" movements.

Almost all of the musical numbers are outstanding. Audrey Hepburn proves herself a most adept dance partner with Astaire in the dreamy "He Loves and She Loves," filmed in an idyllic country setting by a pond, complete with swans and ducks. It is one of the most romantic duets Astaire ever did with any partner. The same setting is also used for the movie's finale, as the reunited couple appropriately sings "'S Wonderful." Hepburn also gets to sing "How Long Has This Been Going On?" (dropped from the original '27 stage production and later used in '28's *Rosalie*). She sings it in a slow, effectively introspective way—using her own voice, by the way, in contrast to her being dubbed for most of the songs in '64's *My Fair Lady*. "How

Fashion photographer Fred Astaire shows editor Kay Thompson and her staff the photo he hopes will convince them to hire Audrey Hepburn as his model, in Funny Face *(1957).*

Long Has This Been Going On?" also serves as the music for a jazzy dance by Hepburn with two unidentified male dancers in a smokey Paris bistro.

Astaire sings the warm and genial title song to Hepburn in the magazine's red-lit dark room as he develops photographic enlargements of her. When she accidentally gets in his way at one point, he merely reaches out and they begin one of those romantic dances that Astaire and his partners always made look so casual and easy but which, choreographically, were assuredly anything but.

The fourth song from the original stage production is the almost-forgotten "Let's Kiss and Make Up," which Astaire sings to Hepburn after a disagreement. The song is fine, but the dance that Astaire then does to it in the street below Hepburn's hotel room is not one of Astaire's more inspired—and not very Parisian with its mock-matador climax.

"Clap Yo' Hands" (from '26's *Oh, Kay!*) is interpolated for Astaire and the marvelous Kay Thompson to sing and dance during a scene in which they crash an Existentialist bash. Thompson also shines in the non-Gershwin opening song, "Think Pink" (by Leonard Gershe and Roger Edens) and joins Astaire and Hepburn in the jaunty "Bonjour, Paris" (also by Gershe and Eden), in which the trio sings and dances its way around some of Paris's most photogenic sites.

The only other major Gershwin film since 1957 remains Samuel Goldwyn's 1959 production of *Porgy and Bess*. If one accepts George, Ira, and DuBose Heyward's classification of that work as a folk opera and not a musical, then it falls outside the scope of this volume. In any case, it was a controversial production, plagued with problems. The original director, Rouben Mamoulian, who had staged the 1935 Broadway production, quit after disagreements with Goldwyn, and was replaced by Otto Preminger, who proceeded to direct the picture in a heavy-handed, sometimes even creaky style. Worst of all, the movie openly reflects outdated stereotypes of blacks as mostly lazy, whoring, gambling, and drug-addicted people—and did so at a time when the civil rights movement was making significant headway throughout the entire U.S. in battling such demeaning images.

Even if one attempts to bypass the stereotypes of the libretto as just those of a flawed or unenlightened "period piece" and focuses, instead, on Gershwin's unquestionably great score, the film version of *Porgy and Bess* gets more minuses than pluses. Musically, it's not as strong as it could have been—beginning with Andre Previn's flaccid musical direction (which others obviously liked well enough to award him an Oscar for it) and continuing into many of the performances. Most regrettably, the singing voices of most of the principal roles are dubbed—by Robert McFerrin for Sidney Poitier as Porgy, Adele Addison for Dorothy Dandridge as Bess, Loulie Jean Norman for Diahann Carroll as Clara, and Inez Matthews for Ruth Attaway as Serena. Only Pearl Bailey as Maria and Sammy Davis, Jr., as Sportin' Life come through with their own voices. The Gershwin estate was reportedly so unhappy with this movie version that it exercised its option to buy back the music rights, which has effectively prevented the rerelease of the film either theatrically or on video.

A number of other '40s and '50s musicals include Gershwin songs in performances that deserve at least a mention. In *Ziegfeld Follies of 1946,* the best of the all-star revues Hollywood has turned out, Fred Astaire and Gene Kelly teamed for the first time, sparring through song and dance to Gershwin's "The Babbit and the Bromide," which Astaire and his sister Adele had introduced in Broadway's original *Funny Face.*

In the movie that reunited Astaire and Ginger Rogers after ten years' separation, *The Barkleys of Broadway* (1949), Hollywood's most popular dance team finally got to perform to Gershwin's "They Can't Take That Away From Me," which Astaire had merely sung to Rogers in *Shall We Dance.* It was worth the wait, turning out to be one of their finest romantic adagios together, and with the benefit of Technicolor (which none of their '30s movies had).

Audrey Hepburn sings "How Long Has This Been Going On?" in Funny Face. *The song was dropped from the original 1927 Broadway version.*

In Judy Garland's musical version of *A Star Is Born* (1954), the most extended production number, "Born in a Trunk," comes to a smashing climax with as thrilling a version of Gershwin's "Swanee" as anyone has ever belted out. The song thereafter became closely identified with Garland, who sang it continually in concert appearances and on television.

As for *When the Boys Meet the Girls,* a 1965 "update" by MGM of *Girl Crazy,* with "Bidin' My Time" entrusted to Herman's Hermits and "I Got Rhythm" and "But Not for Me" to Connie Francis and Harve Presnell, the less said the better.

George Gershwin's life may have been tragically short, yet the songs he left us continue to rank among the century's best—if not *the* best—as so many movie musicals make clear. One of the finest tributes ever paid that contribution comes from songwriter Harold Arlen, who once told John S. Wilson that "anyone who knows George's work, knows George. The humor, the satire, the playfulness of most of his melodic phrases were the natural expression of the man."

Fred Astaire and Gene Kelly sing and dance Gershwin's "The Babbitt and the Bromide" in Ziegfeld Follies of 1946—*the first time the movies' two most popular and innovative dancers ever danced together on-screen.*

KING OF JAZZ (1930), Universal. Color. Directed by John Murray Anderson. With Paul Whiteman and his Orchestra, Laura La Plante, John Boles, the Rhythm Boys, the Brox Sisters, Joe Venuti, Eddie Lang. Music: "Rhapsody in Blue"; plus songs by others. Videocassette: MCA

SONG OF THE FLAME (1930), First National. Color and partly wide-screen. Directed by Alan Crossland. With Bernice Claire, Alexander Gray, Noah Beery. Songs: "Song of the Flame," "Cossack Love Song" (in collaboration with Herbert Stothart, Otto Harbach, Oscar Hammerstein II); plus songs by others.

DELICIOUS (1931), Fox. B&W. Directed by David Butler. With Janet Gaynor, Charles Farrell, El Brendel, Raul Roulien, Manya Roberti, Virginia Cherrill, Mischa Auer. Songs: "Somebody From Somewhere," "Delishious," "Blah-Blah-Blah," "Katinkitschka," "Welcome to the Melting Pot," "You Started It" (lyrics, Ira Gershwin). Music: "The New York Rhapsody." Soundtrack LP: excerpts included in *The Gershwins in Hollywood,* Music Masters JJA-19773.

GIRL CRAZY (1932), RKO. B&W. Directed by William A. Seiter. With Robert Woolsey, Bert Wheeler, Mitzi Green, Eddie Quillan, Kitty Kelly, Arline Judge. Songs: "Could You Use Me?," "Embraceable You," "Sam and Delilah," "But Not for Me," "I Got Rhythm," "You've Got What Gets Me" (lyrics, Ira Gershwin). Soundtrack LP: excerpts included in *The Gershwins in Hollywood,* Music Masters JJA-19773.

THE GREAT ZIEGFELD (1936), MGM. B&W. Directed by Robert Z. Leonard. With William Powell, Myrna Loy, Luise Rainer, Fanny Brice, Virginia Bruce, Frank Morgan. Music: "Rhapsody in Blue" (part); plus songs by others. Soundtrack LP: Classical International CIF-3005.

SHALL WE DANCE (1937), RKO Radio. B&W. Directed by Mark Sandrich. With Fred Astaire, Ginger Rogers, Edward Everett Horton, Ketti Gallian, Eric Blore, Harriet Hoctor. Songs: "Slap That Bass," "Let's Call the Whole Thing Off," "They Can't Take That Away From Me," "They All Laughed," "I've Got Beginner's Luck," "Shall We Dance" (lyrics, Ira Gershwin). Music: "Walking the Dog (Promenade)." Soundtrack LP: Soundtrak STK-106; also EMI Pathe Marconi 2C-184-95807/8 (import). Videocassette: RKO Home Video; also Nostalgia Merchant.

A DAMSEL IN DISTRESS (1937), RKO Radio. B&W. Directed by George Stevens. With Fred Astaire, Joan Fontaine, George Burns, Gracie Allen, Ray Noble, Reginald Gardiner, Constance Collier, Jan Duggan. Songs: "I Can't Be Bothered Now," "The Jolly Tar and the Milkmaid," "Stiff Upper Lip," "Things Are Looking Up," "A Foggy Day (in London Town)," "Nice Work If You Can Get It," "Put Me to the Test" (lyrics, Ira Gershwin). Soundtrack LP: Curtain Calls 100/19 (with *The Sky's the Limit*); also, excerpts on Scarce Rarities 5505 (with *Follow the Fleet*). Videocassette: RKO Home Video; also Nostalgia Merchant.

THE GOLDWYN FOLLIES (1938), Samuel Goldwyn for United Artists release. Color. Directed by George Marshall. With Adolphe Menjou, Andrea Leeds, Kenny Baker, Vera Zorina, the Ritz Brothers, Phil Baker, Ella Logan, Bobby Clark, Helen Jepson, Charles Kullmann. Songs: "Love Walked In," "Our Love Is Here to Stay," "I Was Doing Alright," "I Love to Rhyme" (lyrics, Ira Gershwin); plus songs and ballet music by others. Soundtrack LP: excerpts included in *The Gershwins in Hollywood,* Music Masters JJA-19773. Videocassette: Embassy.

STRIKE UP THE BAND (1940), MGM. B&W. Directed by Busby Berkeley. With Mickey Rooney, Judy Garland, William Tracy, June Preisser, Paul Whiteman and his Orchestra. Song: "Strike Up the Band" (lyrics, Ira Gershwin). Soundtrack LP: Curtain Calls 100-9/10 (with *Girl Crazy,* '43 version). Videocassette: MGM/UA.

LADY BE GOOD (1941), MGM. B&W. Directed by Norman Z. McLeod. (Finale directed by Busby Berkeley). With Eleanor Powell, Ann Sothern, Robert Young, Red Skelton, Lionel Barrymore, John Carroll, Dan Dailey, Connie Russell, the Berry Brothers. Songs: "Fascinating Rhythm," "Hang On to Me," "Oh, Lady Be Good" (lyrics, Ira Gershwin); plus songs by others. Soundtrack LP: Hollywood Soundstage HS5010; also Caliban 6010 (with *Going Places*); also, excerpts included in *The Gershwins in Hollywood,* Music Masters JJA-19773. Videocassette: excerpt included in *That's Entertainment, Part 2,* MGM/UA

GIRL CRAZY (1943), MGM. B&W. Directed by Norman Taurog and Busby Berkeley. With Mickey Rooney, Judy Garland, Nancy Walker, June Allyson, Rags Ragland, Tommy Dorsey and his Orchestra. Songs: "Embraceable You," "Could You Use Me," "Bidin' My Time," "But Not for Me," "Treat Me Rough," "Sam and Delilah," "Fascinating Rhythm," "Bronco Busters," "Cactus Time in Arizona," "I Got Rhythm" (lyrics, Ira Gershwin); plus songs by others. Soundtrack LP: Hollywood Soundstage

HS-5008; also Curtain Calls 100/9–10 (with *Strike Up the Band*).

BROADWAY RHYTHM (1943), MGM. B&W. Directed by Roy Del Ruth. With George Murphy, Ginny Simms, Gloria DeHaven, Nancy Walker, Charles Winninger, Lena Horne, Ben Blue, Eddie "Rochester" Anderson. Song: "Somebody Loves Me" (lyrics, Buddy DeSylva, Ballard MacDonald); plus songs by others.

RHAPSODY IN BLUE (1945), Warner Brothers. B&W. Directed by Irving Rapper. With Robert Alda, Joan Leslie, Alexis Smith, Oscar Levant, Hazel Scott, Charles Coburn, Julie Bishop, Paul Whiteman, Al Jolson, Anne Brown. Songs: "Somebody Loves Me" (lyrics, Buddy DeSylva, Ballard MacDonald); "Swanee" (lyrics, Irving Caesar); "Yankee Doodle Blues" (lyrics, Buddy DeSylva, Irving Caesar); "Liza" (lyrics, Gus Kahn, Ira Gershwin); "Do It Again," "Blue Monday Blues," (lyrics, Buddy DeSylva); "I'll Build a Stairway to Paradise" (lyrics, Buddy DeSylva, Arthur Francis/Ira Gershwin); "Summertime," "I Got Plenty o' Nuthin'" (lyrics, DeBose Heyward, Ira Gershwin); "Fascinating Rhythm," "The Man I Love," "Delischious," "Mine," "Oh, Lady, Be Good!" "Bidin' My Time," "Clap Yo Hands," "Love Walked In," "Someone to Watch Over Me," "Embraceable You," "I Got Rhythm," " 'S Wonderful" (lyrics, Ira Gershwin). Music: "Cuban Overture," "An American in Paris," "Rhapsody in Blue" (parts). Soundtrack LP: Titania 512; excerpts included in *The Gershwins in Hollywood,* Music Masters JJA-19773.

GEORGE WHITE'S SCANDALS OF 1945 (1945), RKO Radio. B&W. Directed by Felix Feist. With Joan Davis, Jack Haley, Philip Terry, Martha Holliday, Gene Krupa and his Orchestra, Ethel Smith, Margaret Hamilton. Song: "Liza" (lyrics, Gus Kahn, Ira Gershwin); plus songs by others.

ZIEGFELD FOLLIES (1946), MGM. Color. Directed by Vincente Minnelli. With Fred Astaire, Gene Kelly, Judy Garland, Lena Horne, Lucille Ball, Lucille Bremer, Kathryn Grayson, Fanny Brice, Red Skelton, Cyd Charisse, Esther Williams, James Melton, Marion Bell, Virginia O'Brien, Keenan Wynn. Song: "The Babbitt and the Bromide" (lyrics, Ira Gershwin); plus songs by others. Soundtrack LP: Curtain Calls 100/15–16. Videocassette: excerpt included in *That's Entertainment,* MGM/UA

THE JOLSON STORY (1946), Columbia. Color. Directed by Alfred E. Green. With Larry Parks, Evelyn Keyes, William Demarest, Bill Goodwin. Song: "Swanee" (lyrics, Irving Caesar); plus songs by others. Soundtrack LP: Pelican 129.

THE SHOCKING MISS PILGRIM (1947), Twentieth Century-Fox. Color. Directed by George Seaton. With Betty Grable, Dick Haymes, Anne Revere, Allyn Joslyn, Gene Lockhart. Songs (collated from unpublished Gershwin manuscripts by Kay Swift and Ira Gershwin): "Aren't You Kinda Glad We Did?," "For You, For Me, Forevermore," "But Not in Boston," "Back Bay Polka," "(Guess I'll Be) Changing My Tune," "One, Two, Three," "Stand Up and Fight," "Sweet Packard," "Waltzing Is Better Sitting Down," "Waltz Me No Waltzes," "Demon Rum" (lyrics, Ira Gershwin). Soundtrack LP: Classic International CIF-3008 (with *Mother Wore Tights*).

YOU WERE MEANT FOR ME (1948), Twentieth Century-Fox. B&W. Directed by Lloyd Bacon. With Jeanne Crain, Dan Dailey, Oscar Levant, Barbara Lawrence, Percy Kilbride. Music: "Concerto in F" (part); plus songs by others.

LOOK FOR THE SILVER LINING (1949), Warner Brothers. Color. Directed by David Butler. With June Haver, Ray Bolger, Gordon MacRae, Charles Ruggles, Rosemary DeCamp, S. Z. Sakall. Song: "Oh Gee, Oh Joy" (lyrics, P. G. Wodehouse, Ira Gershwin); plus songs by others. Soundtrack LP: Titania 504 (with *I'll Get By*).

THE BARKLEYS OF BROADWAY (1949), MGM. Color. Directed by Charles Walters. With Fred Astaire, Ginger Rogers, Oscar Levant, Gale Robbins, Jacques Francois, Billie Burke, George Zucco. Song: "They Can't Take That Away From Me" (lyrics, Ira Gershwin). Music: "Concerto in F" (part); plus songs by others. Soundtrack LP: Soundtrak STS-116; Videocassette: MGM/UA

JOLSON SINGS AGAIN (1949), Columbia. Color. Directed by Henry Levin. With Larry Parks, Barbara Hale, William Demarest, Bill Goodwin. Song: "Swanee" (lyrics, Irving Caesar); plus songs by others.

ALWAYS LEAVE THEM LAUGHING (1949), Warner Brothers. B&W. Directed by Roy Del Ruth. With Milton Berle, Virginia Mayo, Ruth Roman, Bert Lahr, Alan Hale. Song: "Embraceable You" (lyrics, Ira Gershwin).

YOUNG MAN WITH A HORN (1950), Warner Brothers. B&W. Directed by Michael Curtiz. With Kirk Douglas, Lauren Bacall, Doris Day, Juano Hernandez, Mary Beth Hughes, Hoagy Carmichael. Song: "The Man I Love" (lyrics, Ira Gershwin); plus songs by others.

TEA FOR TWO (1950), Warner Brothers. Color. Directed by David Butler. With Doris Day, Gordon MacRae, Gene Nelson, Eve Arden, Patrice Wymore, Billy DeWolfe, S. Z. Sakall, Virginia Gibson. Song: "Do Do Do" (lyrics, Ira Gershwin); plus songs by others.

I'LL GET BY (1950), Twentieth Century-Fox.

Color. Directed by Richard Sale. With June Haver, William Lundigan, Gloria DeHaven, Thelma Ritter, Harry James and his Orchestra, Dennis Day, Jeanne Crain, Victor Mature, Dan Dailey, Reginald Gardiner. Song: "Yankee Doodle Blues" (lyrics, Buddy DeSylva, Irving Caesar); plus songs by others.

LULLABY OF BROADWAY (1951), Warner Brothers. Color. Directed by Roy Del Ruth. With Doris Day, Gene Nelson, Gladys George, Billy DeWolfe, S. Z. Sakall, Anne Triola. Song: "Somebody Loves Me" (lyrics, Buddy DeSylva, Ballard MacDonald); plus songs by others. Soundtrack LP: Caliban 6008.

AN AMERICAN IN PARIS (1951), MGM. Color. Directed by Vincente Minnelli. With Gene Kelly, Leslie Caron, Oscar Levant, Nina Foch, Georges Guétary, Mary Jones. Songs: "I Got Rhythm," " 'S Wonderful," "Our Love Is Here to Stay," "Nice Work If You Can Get It," "I Don't Think I'll Fall in Love Today," "Tra-la-la," "By Strauss" (lyrics, Ira Gershwin); "I'll Build a Stairway to Paradise" (lyrics, Buddy DeSylva, Ray Goetz). Music: "An American in Paris," "Concerto in F" (parts). Soundtrack LP: MGM 93 (withdrawn); also, excerpts included in *That's Entertainment*, MCA 2-11002, and in *The Gershwins in Hollywood*, Music Masters JJA-19773. Videocassette: MGM/UA; also, excerpts in *That's Entertainment*, MGM/UA, and *That's Entertainment, Part 2*, MGM/UA. Videodisc: MGM/UA.

MEET DANNY WILSON (1952), Universal. B&W. Directed by Joseph Pevney. With Frank Sinatra, Shelley Winters, Raymond Burr, Alex Nichol. Song: "I've Got a Crush on You" (lyrics, Ira Gershwin); plus songs by others.

STARLIFT (1952), Warner Brothers. B&W. Directed by Roy Del Ruth. With Janice Rule, Dick Wesson, Ron Hagerty, Doris Day, Gordon MacRae, Virginia Mayo, Gene Nelson, James Cagney, Gary Cooper, Lucille Norman, Phil Harris, Jane Wyman, Randolph Scott, Ruth Roman, Louella Parsons. Songs: "Liza" (lyrics, Gus Kahn, Ira Gershwin); " 'S Wonderful" (lyrics, Ira Gershwin); plus songs by others. Soundtrack LP: Titania 510 (with *Call Me Mister*).

WITH A SONG IN MY HEART (1952), Twentieth Century-Fox. Color. Directed by Walter Lang. With Susan Hayward, Rory Calhoun, David Wayne, Thelma Ritter, Una Merkel, Robert Wagner, Leif Erickson. Song: "Embraceable You" (lyrics, Ira Gershwin); plus songs by others. Soundtrack LP: excerpts included in *Susan Hayward*, Legends 1000/3; also, studio-recorded excerpts in *Jane Froman: With a Song in My Heart*, Capitol T-309 (withdrawn).

SOMEBODY LOVES ME (1952), Paramount. Color. Directed by Irving Brecher. With Betty Hutton, Ralph Meeker, Adele Jergens, Robert Keith. Song: "Somebody Loves Me" (lyrics, Buddy DeSylva, Ballard MacDonald); plus songs by others.

I'LL SEE YOU IN MY DREAMS (1952), Warner Brothers. Color. Directed by Michael Curtiz. With Doris Day, Danny Thomas, Patrice Wymore, Frank Lovejoy, Mary Wickes, Jim Backus. Song: "Liza" (lyrics, Gus Kahn, Ira Gershwin); plus songs by others. Soundtrack LP: Caliban 6008 (with *Lullaby of Broadway*).

THE GLENN MILLER STORY (1954), Universal. Color. Directed by Anthony Mann. With James Stewart, June Allyson, Charles Drake, George Tobias, Frances Langford, Count Basie, Gene Krupa, Ben Pollack, the Modernaires. Song: "Bidin' My Time" (lyrics, Ira Gershwin); plus songs by others. Soundtrack LP: MCA 1624.

A STAR IS BORN (1954), Warner Brothers. Color. Directed by George Cukor. With Judy Garland, James Mason, Jack Carson, Tom Noonan, Amanda Blake. Song: "Swanee" (lyrics, Irving Caesar); plus songs by others. Soundtrack LP: CBS Special Products ACS-8740. Videocassette: Warner Home Video 11335A/B (restored version).

YOUNG AT HEART (1955), Warner Brothers. Color. Directed by Gordon Douglas. With Doris Day, Frank Sinatra, Dorothy Malone, Ethel Barrymore, Gig Young. Song: "Someone to Watch Over Me" (lyrics, Ira Gershwin); plus songs by others. Soundtrack LP: Titania 500 (with *April in Paris*); also studio recording by Day and Sinatra, Columbia CL-6339 (withdrawn).

THREE FOR THE SHOW (1955), Columbia. Color. CinemaScope. Directed by H. C. Potter. With Betty Grable, Jack Lemmon, Marge and Gower Champion, Myron McCormick. Song: "I've Got a Crush on You," "Someone to Watch Over Me," (lyrics, Ira Gershwin); plus songs by others. Soundtrack LP: Mercury 25204 (withdrawn); also, excerpt in *The Gershwins in Hollywood*, Music Masters JJA-19773.

SINCERELY YOURS (1955), Warner Brothers. Color. Directed by Gordon Douglas. With Liberace, Dorothy Malone, Joanne Dru, Alex Nichol, Lori Nelson, William Demarest. Music: "Rhapsody in Blue" (part), plus medley of "Embraceable You," "The Man I Love," "Liza," "I Got Rhythm."

THAT CERTAIN FEELING (1956), Paramount. Color. Directed by Norman Panama. With Bob Hope, Eva Marie Saint, Pearl Bailey, George Sanders. Song: "That Certain Feeling" (lyrics, Ira Gershwin), plus songs by others.

THE EDDY DUCHIN STORY (1957), Columbia. Color. Directed by George Sidney. With Tyrone Power, Kim Novak, Victoria Shaw, James Whitmore, Larry Keating. Song: "The Man I Love" (lyrics, Ira Gershwin); plus songs by others. LP: MCA VIM-7215. (featuring

Carmen Cavallero, who dubbed the soundtrack).

FUNNY FACE (1957), Paramount. Color. Directed by Stanley Donen. With Audrey Hepburn, Fred Astaire, Kay Thompson, Michel Auclair, Suzy Parker, Virginia Gibson. Songs: "Funny Face," "How Long Has This Been Going On?," "He Loves and She Loves," "Kiss and Make Up," "Clap Yo' Hands," " 'S Wonderful" (lyrics, Ira Gershwin); plus songs by others. Soundtrack LP: DRG-Stet DS-15001.

BEAU JAMES (1957), Paramount. Color. Directed by Melville Shavelson. With Bob Hope, Vera Miles, Alexis Smith, Paul Douglas, Darren McGavin, Jimmy Durante, George Jessel, Sammy Cahn. Song: "Someone to Watch Over Me" (lyrics, Ira Gershwin); plus songs by others.

THE HELEN MORGAN STORY (1957), Warner Brothers. B&W. Directed by Michael Curtiz. With Ann Blyth, Paul Newman, Richard Carlson, Alan King. Songs: "Someone to Watch Over Me," "I've Got a Crush on You," "Do Do Do" (lyrics, Ira Gershwin). Soundtrack LP: RCA LOC-1030.

PORGY AND BESS (1959), Samuel Goldwyn for Columbia release. Color. Todd-AO. Directed by Otto Preminger. With Sidney Poitier, Dorothy Dandridge, Diahann Carroll, Pearl Bailey, Clarence Muse, Sammy Davis, Jr., Brock Peters. Songs: "Summertime," "Crap Game," "A Woman Is a Sometime Thing," "Honey Man's Call," "Yo' Mammy's Gone," "Gone, Gone, Gone," "Porgy's Prayer," "They Pass by Singing," "My Man's Gone Now," "The Train Is at the Station," "I Got Plenty o' Nuthin'," "Bess, You Is My Woman Now," "I Can't Sit Down," "I Ain't Got No Shame," "It Ain't Necessarily So," "What You Want wid Bess?," "It Takes a Long Pull to Get There," "De Police Put Me In," "Time and Time Again," "Strawberry Woman's Call," "Crab Man's Call," "A Red-Headed Woman," "Dere's a Boat Dat's Leavin' Soon for New York," "Good Mornin' Sistuh," "Bess, Oh Where's My Bess?," "I'm on My Way" (lyrics, DuBose Heyward, Ira Gershwin). Soundtrack LP: CBS OS2016.

KISS ME STUPID (1964), Mirisch/Phalanx for Lopert/United Artists release. Color. Directed by William Wyler. With Dean Martin, Kim Novak, Ray Walston, Felicia Farr, Mel Blanc. Songs: "Sophia," "I'm a Poached Egg," "All the Living Day" (lyrics, Ira Gershwin).

WHEN THE BOYS MEET THE GIRLS (1965), MGM. Color. Directed by Alvin Ganzer. With Connie Francis, Harve Presnell, Herman's Hermits, Louis Armstrong, Liberace, Sam the Sham and the Pharoahs. Songs: "But Not for Me," "Treat Me Rough," "Bidin' My Time," "I Got Rhythm," "Embraceable You" (lyrics, Ira

Gershwin); plus songs by others. Soundtrack LP: MGM 4334 (withdrawn).

THOROUGHLY MODERN MILLIE (1967), Universal. Color. Directed by George Hill Roy. With Julie Andrews, Mary Tyler Moore, Carol Channing, John Gavin, James Fox, Beatrice Lillie, Jack Soo. Song: "Do It Again" (lyrics, Ira Gershwin); plus songs by others. Soundtrack LP: MCA DL1500. Videocassette: MCA.

STAR! (1968), Twentieth Century-Fox. Color. Todd-AO. Directed by Robert Wise. With Julie Andrews, Daniel Massey, Michael Craig, Richard Crenna, Robert Reed, Beryl Reid. Songs: "Dear Little Boy," "Do Do Do," "Someone to Watch Over Me" (lyrics, Ira Gershwin); plus songs by others. Soundtrack LP: Twentieth Century-Fox 5102 (withdrawn).

LADY SINGS THE BLUES (1972), Paramount. Color. Directed by Sidney J. Furie. With Diana Ross, Billy Dee Williams, Richard Pryor, James Callahan, Sid Melton. Songs: "The Man I Love," "Our Love Is Here to Stay" (lyrics, Ira Gershwin); plus songs by others. Soundtrack LP: Motown 7-758D. Videocassette and videodisc: Paramount.

NEW YORK, NEW YORK (1977). United Artists. Color. Directed by Martin Scorsese. With Liza Minnelli, Robert DeNiro, Mary Kay Place, Georgie Auld, Lionel Stander. Song: "The Man I Love" (lyrics, Ira Gershwin); plus songs by others. Soundtrack LP: Liberty LKBL-00750. Videocassette and videodisc: CBS/Fox (restored version)

MANHATTAN (1979). MGM. Color. Directed by Woody Allen. With Woody Allen, Diane Keaton, Michael Murphy, Meryl Streep, Mariel Hemingway. Background score of instrumental versions of Gershwin songs played by the New York Philharmonic (Zubin Mehta) and others. Soundtrack LP: CBS JS360020. Videocassette: MGM/UA.

Jerome Kern in his pre-Hollywood days.

JEROME KERN

*I*f Irving Berlin set the patterns for much of this century's popular American song styles, then Jerome Kern was the man who turned those styles into an art form—first on the Broadway stage and then in the movies.

Physically, Kern was a small man (about 5′6″ tall). But in terms of his musical influence, he was—and remains—a giant. He was also, by his own admission, a first-class snob and the possessor of a volatile temper that got him into trouble with virtually every collaborator with whom he worked over the years. He had a counterbalancing and impish sense of humor that made most colleagues forgive his finickiness, however. The 1946 movie biography *Till the Clouds Roll By* is not very accurate in presenting Kern as the quiet-spoken, even-tempered character Robert Walker plays, or in the way it dramatizes other aspects of his life.

But Kern often used his snobbism and short temper for the distinct benefit of the productions on which he worked. He demanded the best not only of himself but of everyone else working on a show or movie. He believed that musical standards on Broadway and in Hollywood were not always as high as they should (and could) be —and, most important, that the public could be educated to appreciate higher standards. His point is proved by the status today of "The Way You Look Tonight" and "Long Ago and Far Away" (written for movies) or "Smoke Gets in Your Eyes," "All the Things You Are," and "Ol' Man River" (written for Broadway but used in major films)—to name just a few of the Kern songs that rank among the all-time greats.

Jerome David Kern was born in New York City on January 27, 1885, the youngest son of a middle-class stabler (in those horse-and-buggy days) of Czech and German-Jewish background. Jerry, as he was known throughout his life, was the youngest of nine children, of whom only three survived childhood. His mother, an amateur pianist, gave Jerry his first piano lessons when he was about five years old. But an event of even greater impact occurred on his tenth birthday, when his mother took him to see a Broadway musical. He quickly became a fan, attending as many as his family could afford. He would then entertain friends by playing the songs from the latest musicals he'd seen by Victor Herbert, Reginald DeKoven, and Ivan Caryll.

When Kern was twelve, his family moved to Newark, where his father went to work for a small department store (eventually becoming the firm's executive vice president). Throughout his high-school years, Jerry often played piano at school functions and wrote his first songs for school plays. Despite pressure from his father to enter the business world, Jerry—with support from his mother—held out for a career in music. In 1902 he enrolled at the New York College of Music (later to be absorbed into New York University).

At the same time he took a low-level job at the Lyceum music publishing firm. Somewhere along the way, Kern made an impression on Max Dreyfus, who had taken over as head of the T. B. Harms publishing house. Dreyfus hired Kern to be a rehearsal pianist for various vaudeville acts and Broadway musicals in which Harms had an interest. Dreyfus also encouraged Kern as a composer and placed two of his songs in a 1904 Weber and Fields revue, *An English Daisy*. Not one of New York's critics noted Kern's contributions in their reviews.

Discouraged, Kern took off for Europe to hear and absorb whatever music he could in Germany and England. For several months he studied in a small town near Heidelberg—but never, as some accounts of Kern's life erroneously state, at Heidelberg University.

London made the biggest impression on Kern—particularly its West End theater and music-hall attractions, which he found more to his taste than the Viennese-style operettas that dominated Broadway's musical theater at that time. Over the next few years, Kern made several trips back to London and became an enthusiastic Anglophile. Charles Frohman, an American who had become a major London producer, hired Kern to write incidental songs for some of his productions—among them a song called "The Canoe," which was introduced by Billie Burke (later to become Mrs. Florenz Ziegfeld and a popular movie comedienne, best remembered as the Good Witch in *The Wizard of Oz*). Kern also met P. G. Wodehouse, then a young journalist on the London *Globe* and an aspiring lyricist with whom Kern began collaborating.

On a side trip to the small Thames village of Walton in 1909, Kern also met Eva Leale, daughter of the manager of the local inn at which Kern stayed. Kern and Eva fell in love. They were married a year later.

Kern's fascination with and his growing knowledge of English musicals led to his being hired to help adapt a number of them for Broadway. In the process, Kern sometimes rewrote the songs to improve their chances of going over with American audiences. He also saw to it that some of his own songs were interpolated into the productions. Between 1904 and 1914, more than one hundred Kern songs were to be heard in some thirty Broadway musicals, although only one of them ("How'd You Like to Spoon With Me") became a major song hit. At the same time, Kern's gradually improving economic situation enabled him to buy into the Harms publishing firm—just a few shares at first but gradually increasing over the years, so that by the 1930s Kern owned 25 percent of the Harms stock.

Kern's big Broadway breakthrough came in 1914 with *The Girl From Utah.* Of the eight songs that Kern wrote for it, the tender, exquisite "They Didn't Believe Me" became the show's biggest hit. It also helped revolutionize the style of American show songs for decades to come, replacing the European operetta-inflected style of Romberg and Herbert with a more lyrically long-lined, ballad style. *The Girl From Utah* is also a classic example of the right show at the right time. The outbreak of World War I in Europe had dampened the enthusiasm of many theater-goers for the German and Viennese imports that had dominated Broadway for decades.

Between 1915 and 1918, Kern furthered his reputation as a musical revolutionary when he became composer-in-residence for the Princess Theater, just down the block from the location at that time of the Metropolitan Opera House in New York. The intimate size of the house (299 seats) required modest productions in terms of casts, sets, chorus, and orchestral players. The Louis XV–style of the house also gave it an elitist aura, on which the management capitalized to present productions that eschewed the low-brow comedians and vaudevillelike acts then a staple of most Broadway musicals. For the Princess Theater, Kern, working mostly with Guy Bolton as play-wright and P. G. Wodehouse as lyricist, composed such shows as *Very Good Eddie, Nobody Home,* and *Oh, Boy!*

What made these shows different from most others was the way Kern's songs were integrated into the plot. Instead of a musical number stopping the action, it usually helped advance it. In a 1917 interview for the *Dramatic Mirror,* Kern expressed it this way: "It is my opinion that the musical numbers should carry on the action of the play, and should be representative of the personalities of the characters who sing them."

Meanwhile, Kern continued to write songs for other Broadway shows and, as soon as the war ended, he again shuttled between New York and London almost annually. His postwar Broadway shows included a few flops but mostly hits, such as *Sally* (1920) and *Sunny* (1925), both starring the popular Marilyn Miller. The Ziegfeld-produced *Sally,* in fact, became the biggest-grossing Broadway hit up to its time.

Yet none of Kern's successes equaled the critical and popular acclaim he received with the opening of *Show Boat* (also produced by Ziegfeld) in 1927. Kern had read Edna Ferber's sprawling novel about a turn-of-the-century Mississippi showboat family soon after the book came out in 1926. Before he even finished reading it, he began talking with his *Sunny* collaborator, Oscar Hammerstein II, about adapting Ferber's novel into a musical. Ferber was uncertain at first about giving permission. But Kern and Hammerstein convinced her they wanted to create a genuine "musical play," not a musical comedy with a chorus line of scantily-clad showgirls or with comics who interjected unrelated gags or specialty routines. It would adhere, they insisted, to Kern's long-expressed but sometimes-compromised belief in a musical in which the songs would evolve naturally from situations and dialogue to enhance characterization while advancing the plot.

Show Boat did that like no other American musical had ever done before. It was more than a combination of drama, comedy, and Americana with music, for Show Boat also dared to include an interracial theme as a key dramatic element—and to give a major role as well as the song that expresses the play's basic *leitmotif*, "Ol' Man River," to a black performer (the noted bass-baritone Jules Bledsoe). However, another major supporting role, that of the showboat's black cook, Queenie, would be played in the original production by a white in blackface—Tess Gardella, famous in vaudeville and on radio for her impersonation of a comedy character named "Aunt Jemima."

For the important mulatto character, Julie, the Ziegfeld production cast the popular white nightclub singer Helen Morgan, then twenty-seven—providing Morgan with her most famous role and a lasting identification with Kern's songs. Morgan had made her Broadway debut in Kern's 1920 *Sally,* as a chorus girl. Over the next few years, she became a popular nightclub singer of torch songs, usually perched atop a piano. Morgan also began to win notoriety for her drinking and her involvement with underworld characters who controlled most of the Prohibition-era clubs. But Kern had liked Morgan in the 1924 revue *Americana,* and he felt that the worn, dissipated quality that her voice had taken on made her perfect for the gentle, troubled Julie. (In 1931, Kern also announced plans for a musical version of *Camille* to star Morgan, but nothing ever came of the project.)

In *Show Boat,* Kern gave Morgan two show-stopping songs: "Can't Help Lovin' That Man" and "Bill." The latter actually wasn't written for *Show Boat,* but for one of the Princess Theater shows, 1918's *Oh, Lady! Lady!!,* from which it had been dropped before the New York opening. A year later, it was interpolated into *Zip Goes a Million,* which folded during its pre-Broadway tryout. Although Hammerstein altered some sixteen bars of P. G. Wodehouse's original lyrics for *Show Boat,* Hammerstein insisted throughout his life that the lyrics for "Bill" be fully credited to Wodehouse in all programs and on all recordings.

Kern's entire score for *Show Boat* was enthusiastically acclaimed from the start as the most inventive and most immediately appealing of his career. Critic after critic declared that, with *Show Boat,* the American musical theater had come of age. Kern was even approached by the Metropolitan Opera about writing an American opera for that house. He declined, insisting that his technical abilities for opera were too limited. He preferred to continue working within the framework of musical theater—and to keep raising its range, scope, and standards.

With the success of *Show Boat,* Kern's pioneering work in integrating songs and text became an accepted axiom of more and more musicals. Kern's example also helped pave the way for more serious musical plots, involving real, multi-dimensional characters instead of the one-dimensional, mythical "Ruritanians" who inhabited so many other composers' musicals up to the early '30s.

Ironically, soon after *Show Boat* pointed the new direction for American musical theater, the economics of Broadway took a nosedive with the 1929 stock market crash. Integrated book musicals became riskier and riskier to produce. Besides, Hollywood was beginning to do them better, with its greater flexibility for scene changes. Inevitably, the movies beckoned to Jerome Kern—first for adaptations of some of his stage hits and then for original film scores.

Jerome Kern's Major Movies and Their Songs

With *Show Boat*'s history-making success on Broadway in '27 and '28, followed by hit productions in London in '28 and in Paris and Australia in '29, it was not surprising that it would be the first Kern musical to be made into a movie.

Just a few months after the publication of Ferber's book in 1926, Universal Pictures purchased the film rights to *Show Boat,* intending to produce a straight, silent-picture drama. Then, over the next year, two things happened almost simultaneously. First, there was the success of the Kern-Hammerstein musical version on Broadway. Second was Warner Brothers's unexpected success with its first talkies—setting off Hollywood's sound revolution. With other studios quickly getting into the act with talkies and part-talkies, Universal decided that dialogue and music would have to be added to the almost-completed, silent *Show Boat.*

At first, the studio settled on adding only some Negro spirituals and work songs, and on having the heroine, Magnolia, sing "Carry Me Back to Ol' Virginny" in one sequence. But as the reputation of the Broadway musical spread through sheet-music sales and radio, Universal worried that its Kern-less version would face unfavorable comparisons. Production was stopped as the studio began several months of negotiations with Ziegfeld, Kern, Hammerstein, and the music publishers T. B. Harms for rights to the Broadway version. In January of 1929, contracts were finally signed. The sale price: a then-record $100,000.

In order to salvage as much of the completed footage as possible and to make the revisions quickly, Universal's founder and production chief Carl Laemmle decided to add only two of Kern's best-known songs to the film: "Ol' Man River" and "Can't Help Lovin' That Man" (the latter actually published as "Can't Help Lovin' Dat Man," but with "That" now more widely if unauthentically used). But contrary to the way they were used in the original, both would be sung by the leading lady, Magnolia—played by Laura La Plante, but with her singing voice dubbed by Eva Olivotti. The first song replaced "Carry Me Back to Ol' Virginny" in a cabaret sequence, and the second was placed in a concert sequence near the end of the picture. "Ol' Man River" and some of Kern's other themes would also be heard as instrumental background themes.

But then Laemmle went a step further. He added a two-reel prologue, in which he and Florenz Ziegfeld introduce musical highlights from the Broadway production, sung by members of the original cast. These include Helen Morgan singing "Bill" and "Can't Help Loving That Man," Tess Gardella singing "C'mon Folks" and "Hey, Feller!" and Jules Bledsoe and the chorus singing "Ol' Man River."

With the prologue and the two-hour-and-ten-minutes part-talkie film proper, the first movie version of *Show Boat* ran nearly three hours with an intermission. I have never seen this version and, according to *Show Boat* historian Miles Kreuger, no sound print of the 1929 version is known to have survived. But reviews do—and most of them are not kind. For example, Richard Watts in the New York *Herald-Tribune* wrote that the film is "a long, tedious, and only occasionally attractive exhibit."

Creighton Peet of the New York *Post* wrote that "not all of the picture talks, which is fortunate, for the recording is pretty bad."

Two of Kern's other Broadway successes, *Sally* and *Sunny,* were transferred to the screen as full-fledged talkies in 1929 and 1930, respectively, by Warner Brothers/ First National, with both shows' original star, Marilyn Miller. Despite lavish productions, neither picture was the movie hit Warners had hoped for—and Miller's star faded rapidly before her death in 1936, at age thirty-seven. I have never seen *Sally* but I have seen *Sunny* and also Miller's non-Kern *Her Majesty Love* (1931), and it's easy to tell why she didn't click in movies. Though pert, blonde, and personable, she had a rather flat speaking voice and didn't always read her lines convincingly. As for her singing voice, it was smallish and sometimes not quite on pitch. Like Gertrude Lawrence, Miller was apparently one of those stage stars who projected much better across the footlights of a theater than in front of the cameras—especially when playing ingenue-type roles in her thirties.

In *Sunny* she seems far too mature for the adolescent romantic shenanigans she has to go through—as an English circus bareback rider who stows away on an ocean liner in order to follow back to America the soldier she loves (but who's committed to another). The far-too-complicated plot is not always believable, and there's too much of it in the movie version. Only part of Kern's original Broadway score is used and most of that comes in the first half hour of the picture, with spirited performances of the title song, of "Who?" (by Miller), and of "Two Little Blue Birds" (by subplot romancers Joe Donahue and Inez Courtney). The transitions into the songs are often arbitrary (especially the shipboard "I Was Alone") and not in keeping with Kern's reputation for integrating songs and plot. But there is more orchestral underscoring throughout the picture (all to Kern themes) than is usual in movies of the 1929–31 period.

Although Kern had not been encouraged by Hollywood's treatment of his scores in 1929 and 1930, he agreed to go to Hollywood himself in July of 1930 to write an original score with Otto Harbach for a First National film to be called *Stolen Dreams.* It was planned as a musical adventure film, about a French spy (Irene Delroy) and an American aviator with whom she falls in love (Jack Whiting). After writing six songs and watching some of the early filming, Kern returned to New York. Several weeks later, First National had a change of heart about the movie. After the initial excitement over "all-singing, all-dancing" talkies, a decline seemed to set in at the box office. Rip-roaring action pictures, meanwhile, were doing well—particularly aviation films, following the success of Howard Hughes's *Hell's Angels.* And so First National decided to drop the Kern-Harbach songs and turned the picture into a straight "actioner." Retitled *Men of the Sky,* it was released in 1931 to a lukewarm critical and box-office reception, and was soon forgotten—as were Kern's songs, which were never reused.

But Hollywood was not about to forget Kern himself. In 1934, no fewer than three Kern stage musicals reached the screen: Warner Brothers's *Sweet Adeline,* MGM's *The Cat and the Fiddle,* and Fox's *Music in the Air.* All three met mixed receptions. Despite many wonderful Kern songs well-integrated into their plots, the three were burdened with operetta-ish scripts that have grown more and more dated with the passing years, even if, in their time, they offered some offbeat twists.

In *Sweet Adeline,* set in the 1890s, the heroine is the daughter of a Hoboken beer-garden owner who falls in love with a struggling young composer. There's also

Irene Dunne as a 1890s Hoboken barmaid who becomes a musical star in Sweet Adeline *(1934).*

a melodramatic subplot about Spanish-American War spies. The almost too robustly healthy Irene Dunne has the title role originally written for the more gently fragile Helen Morgan (and played on Broadway by Morgan as her first starring show following *Show Boat*). Dunne especially lacks the special pathos that Morgan brings to the recordings she made of "Why Was I Born?" and "Don't Ever Leave Me," though she fares well with the elegant "Here Am I" and "Lonely Feet," the latter interpolated into the movie from an unsuccessful 1934 London production of the Kern-Hammerstein *Three Sisters*. During a rehearsal sequence, Winifred Shaw gets to sing the one new song Kern wrote for the movie, "We Were So Young," but it's lost behind Shaw's phony Spanish accent as a Mata Hari–type character. Shaw, however, does get to feed the movie's funniest line to Hugh Herbert (typecast as a dim-witted theatrical producer) when, in response to her ultradramatic pronouncement that "the show must go on!" he looks her straight in the eye and asks, "Why?"

The Cat and the Fiddle is a more sophisticated, Continental-style romance, but also essentially old-fashioned for all of its sly and witty trimmings. Ramon Novarro plays a struggling young composer living in Brussels and Jeanette MacDonald is a newly arrived American songwriter with whom he promptly falls in love. They run off to Paris together after he helps her write a song that becomes a big hit, "The Night Was Made for Love." But career problems drive them apart. She takes up with a doting and not-too-doddering impresario (Frank Morgan), but not for long. On the day of the premiere of Novarro's first operetta, the leading lady gargles with too much rum and can't go on. Guess who shows up to replace her (without even a hint of a rehearsal!) and saves the show? Clever dialogue, spirited performances, and, most of all, a delightful Kern-Harbach score—left more intact than any previous Kern screen transfer— keep it all breezily entertaining. The operetta finale was also one of the first musical sequences to be photographed in the new three-strip Technicolor process, which would become the standard color system for the movie industry within a few years.

MGM had hoped that *The Cat and the Fiddle* would boost the sagging career of former silent-film matinee idol Novarro, who, it turned out, had a small but pleasant singing voice. But the picture failed to arrest Novarro's decline. Instead, it did much more for Jeanette MacDonald, reinforcing her image as a blithe, classy heroine of slightly risqué musical comedies—an image that MGM chief Louis B. Mayer would soon alter in his determination to make his studio's pictures the most wholesome in the industry, particularly after the 1934 crackdown against "movie immorality" by the Hays Office and by various other local and national censorship groups.

Mayer also took a more personal interest in MacDonald's career than in most of his other stars of the time. He is usually held responsible for Vivienne Segal's role in *The Cat and the Fiddle* (as a would-be star of Novarro's operetta) being cut to ribbons so as to keep the focus on MacDonald. Segal, with a light lyric soprano similar in some ways to that of MacDonald, had starred on Broadway in Kern's *Oh, Lady! Lady!!* as well as in Rodgers and Hart's *A Connecticut Yankee,* plus a few early Warner musicals at about the same time that MacDonald was beginning her career at Paramount. But Segal gets only about three scenes in the release print of *The Cat and the Fiddle,* with just one song, the so-so "One Moment Alone." She became so disenchanted with Hollywood because of this experience that she never again made another film—to Hollywood's distinct loss, judging by her delightful performance in the movie *Viennese Nights* (1929) and in later Broadway musicals.

MacDonald gets the lion's share of Kern's songs in *The Cat and the Fiddle* and does them well, including not only the exceptionally lovely "The Night Was Made for Love" but also the bittersweet "Try to Forget" and the wryly teasing "She Didn't Say Yes (She Didn't Say No)." Musically, at least, the picture still has its charms, however dated the story itself now seems.

Just as *The Cat and the Fiddle* didn't do much to further Ramon Novarro's transition from silents to talkies, *Music in the Air* failed in a similar goal for Gloria Swanson. For her first and last all-out movie musical (in contrast to a few talkie dramas in which she sang incidental songs), Swanson plays a temperamental prima donna with just a few too many outdated silent-movie gestures and with a merely serviceable soprano singing voice. The weak casting of the rest of the movie further undercut whatever success Kern and Hammerstein's '32 Broadway hit might have had in its screen transition.

Anyone seeing the movie version of *Music in the Air* for the first time today may be startled by the striking similarity of its opening to that of the much more recent *The Sound of Music* (1965), also to a Hammerstein libretto—as the camera pans down from the sky to a long shot of an Alpine village. Of course, the earlier *Music in the Air* is photographed in black and white and the village is obviously a Hollywood-studio set, in contrast to the later movie's sweeping color vistas of the real Alps.

The plot of *Music in the Air* is a thin but clever switch on old-fashioned Bavarian operetta librettos, with a pretty young Alpine village lass (June Lang) being taken under the wing of a monocled Munich operetta composer (John Boles) who has quarreled with his prima donna (Swanson). The unexpected twist is that the newcomer turns out to be dreadful as a performer. In a key scene, the script gives the Munich music director (Joseph Cawthorne) a line to the effect that amateurs have the conceit to think they can start at the top of the ladder and then blame everybody else when they fall—a line that surely reflected some of the ultraprofessional Kern's attitudes about show business in general. But there's still a happy ending, as the girl and her schoolteacher boyfriend (Douglass Montgomery), also disillusioned by his experiences in "the big time" (including a fling with Swanson), return wiser and contentedly, like Dorothy from Oz, to their simpler home-sweet-home in the Alps.

Although the picture's message may have been more pertinent to Depression audiences than most early '30s musicals, *Music in the Air* sinks under the weight of the heavy-handed direction of Joe May (best-known for his German-made '20s thrillers and a few later Hollywood B-movies) as well as the much-too-flamboyant, often whining performances by its stars. The performers also fail to do justice to one of Kern's finest scores. The enchanting "I've Told Every Little Star" gets several outings—most appealingly near the beginning with Lang and Montgomery (dubbed by Betty Hiestand and James O'Brien), following a lively scene that also, in part, delightfully spoofs village choristers. The waltz "One More Dance" becomes the basis for an amusingly overplayed vocal battle between Boles and Swanson, but she's much too arch with another lighthearted waltz, "I Am So Eager." The catchy "We Belong Together" is thrown away almost off-handedly in the finale by the four principals. Unfortunately —or perhaps fortunately, considering the film's vocal talent—a delightful third waltz, "And Love Was Born," and one of the original show's best and most enduring ballads, "The Song Is You," were dropped from the movie.

Cavalier treatment of Broadway scores was common in '30s Hollywood, and the 1935 RKO Radio version of Kern's *Roberta* was no exception. The movie dropped both "The Touch of Your Hand" and "You're Devastating" (though it kept them as instrumental background music for a fashion-show sequence). Even so, *Roberta* is, arguably, the first movie adaptation of a Broadway musical that turned out better than the original. This time the casting deserves much of the credit. But it's still the Kern-Harbach musical numbers that keep this *Roberta* the film classic it is.

First, there's Irene Dunne singing "Yesterdays" as elegantly and touchingly as anyone has ever sung it, and then, a bit later, making "Smoke Gets in Your Eyes" one of the great, unforgettably poignant moments in any '30s musical. Second, there's Fred Astaire and Ginger Rogers dancing two of their all-time best numbers: one a spirited, spontaneous-looking "hoofing" routine in practice slacks to "I'll Be Hard to Handle," the other a wistfully elegant adagio to "Smoke Gets in Your Eyes." Dance critic Arlene Croce, in her definitive book analyzing all the Astaire-Rogers films, calls "I'll Be Hard to Handle" a pivotal sequence in the history of the Astaire-Rogers team. "The wonderful secret they seemed to share in 'The Continental' [in their previous film, *The Gay Divorcee*] becomes here a magical rapport that is sustained throughout three minutes of what looks like sheerest improvisation. . . . It's like a moment of *cinema verité* bursting through the surface of a polished commercial film."

Roberta's story is a slight one, about an ex-football player (Randolph Scott) who inherits his aunt's Parisian couturier business. He falls in love (not without complications, of course) with the couturier's manager (Irene Dunne), unaware that she is a refugee Russian princess. Much more interesting is a subplot about a member of a traveling American band (Fred Astaire) and a singer posing as a phony Polish countess

Fred Astaire and Ginger Rogers dance an unforgettable, wistfully romantic adagio to Kern's "Smoke Gets In Your Eyes" in the first film version of Roberta *(1935).*

(Ginger Rogers). As the Comtesse Scharwenka, Rogers slyly spoofs the accent and mannerisms of Lyda Roberti, the Polish-born "blonde bombshell" who played the role on Broadway—and she almost steals the picture.

Some of the topical '30s references, particularly those involving real and phony royalty in Parisian social circles, have lost their effect with the passing years. But the big fashion show near the end, which should presumably have dated the most easily, remains a fascinating bit of elegantly filmed fashion history. And if you look closely, one of the first models to appear after Astaire sings "Lovely to Look At" is a very blonde Lucille Ball—who, some twenty years later as a TV star and executive, would buy the same RKO studios where *Roberta* was filmed.

"Lovely to Look At" is Kern's major addition to the movie version of *Roberta*. It also marked his first collaboration with lyricist Dorothy Fields, daughter of vaudevillian Lew Fields (who had been one of the stars of the first show ever to include a Kern song, 1904's *An English Daisy*). The two were brought together by RKO Radio producer Pandro S. Berman, who at twenty-nine, was then one of Hollywood's youngest production dynamos. But according to Kern biographer Gerald Bordman, Kern did not actually meet Dorothy Fields until *after* Berman had asked her and Jimmy McHugh to write lyrics to a melody that Kern had given him for the fashion sequence. What's more, Berman had even gone ahead and used the song without Kern's prior permission. As a result, there was some trepidation around the studio when Kern was first shown the sequence. Kern not only liked the song, "Lovely to Look At," but also Dorothy Fields. They became friends and active collaborators.

Two other songs in *Roberta* also have somewhat unusual backgrounds. The lyrics for "I'll Be Hard to Handle" were written for the original Broadway production not by the show's lyricist Otto Harbach, but by his nephew, Bernard Dougall. Kern had come up with the melody during the show's Philadelphia tryout, when the producers felt another lively number was needed. But Harbach was busy with other rewriting and suggested giving a chance to his nephew, who had show-business aspirations. Kern agreed, and the song entered the show credited to both Harbach and Dougall. (It remains Dougall's only well-known song.)

"I Won't Dance," which Astaire and Rogers playfully sing in *Roberta* and which is followed by one of Astaire's most free-wheeling tap dances, started out as a song in the ill-fated 1934 Kern-Hammerstein London musical, *Three Sisters*. When Kern realized that a Broadway production of that show was unlikely, he let Hollywood use some of its songs in other productions. Thus "Lonely Feet" ended up in *Sweet Adeline* and "I Won't Dance" in *Roberta*, with some additional lyrics for the latter by Dorothy Fields, including a reference to Astaire and Rogers's Oscar-winning "The Continental" of the previous year.

In 1935, MGM commissioned Kern and Hammerstein to write the score for a projected original musical titled *Champagne and Orchids*, teaming Jeanette MacDonald and Nelson Eddy, fresh from their success in *Naughty Marietta*. At least three songs

Roberta's "I'll Be Hard to Handle," one of the most spontaneous-looking dance routines in any of the ten Astaire-Rogers films.

95

were completed before the project was dropped by MGM in favor of an adaptation of Friml's more traditional operetta *Rose Marie.* In the meantime, Kern stayed at MGM long enough to contribute (with Hammerstein and Roger Edens) the strictly routine title song of a popular Jean Harlow-William Powell film *Reckless* (in which Harlow's ill-matched singing voice is dubbed by Virginia Verrill), and about five or six minutes of unmemorable background music for a routine dramatic programmer, *The Flame Within* (with Ann Harding and Herbert Marshall).

When soprano Grace Moore scored a success combining operatic arias with pop songs in Columbia's 1934 surprise hit *One Night of Love,* other studios decided to sign up photogenic opera stars. And so Gladys Swarthout, Helen Jepson, Lily Pons, Nino Martini, James Melton, and a few others began shuttling between the Metropolitan Opera and Hollywood's sound stages. RKO Radio put its money on petite French coloratura Lily Pons and commissioned Kern and Dorothy Fields to write the score for her movie debut.

I Dream Too Much turned out to be a modest box-office winner despite a run-of-the-mill script, set in Paris, about a struggling young American composer (Henry Fonda) whose singer-wife achieves success before he does, creating all sorts of marital problems. In the end, it's she who proves that musical comedy is as artistically important and satisfying as grand opera—a recurring theme in quite a few Kern musicals. Pons comes across as cute, personable, and bubbly in an innocent '30s manner. But anyone who grew up in later years knowing the television work of comedienne Imogene Coca may find an unnerving resemblance between Pons and Coca—with wisecracks and pratfalls expected at any given moment instead of serious singing. Still, Pons's singing remains delightful—and there's plenty of it in *I Dream Too Much.*

Her operatic arias include a staged sequence from Delibes' *Lakme,* spotlighting its interminable "Bell Song," a Pons specialty in which she exposes a bare midriff that few opera stars in any generation would even attempt. But Pons's attempt to give the Kern-Fields "I Got Love" a lowdown, jazzy quality comes off awkwardly at best, not that the tune is that interesting to begin with. Pons and Kern are both in better form with three more elegant songs through which Pons lets her soprano float seemingly effortlessly: the romantically genial title song, the operetta-ish "I'm the Echo (You're the Song)," and, especially, the lilting "Jockey on the Carousel," the last one charmingly staged on a children's merry-go-round. The title song also provides the movie's big finale, in which an elegant Parisian fashion show (longer than the one in *Roberta*) follows Pons's first chorus and is, in turn, followed by such an unimaginative dance sequence that it is hard to believe comes from the same studio that made the Astaire-Rogers films.

RKO Radio reunited Kern with Astaire and Rogers in 1936—this time for a film original, not a Broadway adaptation, and featuring the best score that Kern would write in Hollywood. The picture was originally set to be titled *I Won't Dance,* after one of the Kern songs Astaire and Rogers had performed in *Roberta.* Then it was changed to *Never Gonna Dance,* with a song of that title appropriately penned by Kern and Fields for the finale. Finally, just before the picture's release, the title was changed again to the much less negative but not exactly accurate *Swing Time.* Neither the picture nor the score "swings" in the true sense of the era's swing-music craze. But Kern's score is, overall, his most unabashedly and buoyantly pop-oriented. It's the key to making *Swing Time* the best Astaire-Rogers film after Berlin's *Top Hat.*

Metropolitan Opera star Lily Pons croons Kern's "I Got Love" in a lowdown blues style in I Dream Too Much *(1935).*

All of the songs are especially well integrated into a slight but clever plot that has Astaire and Rogers spending most of the footage singing and dancing into and out of romantic complications. The fun begins when Astaire tries to pick up dance-teacher Rogers by pretending he can't dance. She literally has to teach him (via Kern and Fields) to overcome his clutziness to "Pick Yourself Up (and Start All Over Again)." Fields's lyrics also have implications that go well beyond the movie's plot for Depression Era audiences.

Swing Time's most eloquent love song, "The Way You Look Tonight," even manages to poke lighthearted fun at itself, or at least at Fields's romantic lyrics. Astaire sings the song to Rogers, who is in another room and, unknown to him, is washing her hair. His singing brings her out of her room, her head full of shampoo lather— as he dreamily croons on without noticing her.

As Ginger gently touches Fred's shoulder at the end of the song, he slowly turns around on the piano bench and, for the first time, both of them realize the state of her appearance. It's a golden moment in the film—and typical of the way that both Kern and Astaire, in their individual work, so often maintained an essentially elegant, sophisticated "atmosphere" even in a comic situation. The song not only went on to fourteen weeks on radio's *Your Hit Parade* (six of them in the No. 1 spot), but also won Kern and Fields the 1936 Academy Award for Best Song.

Swing Time's "A Fine Romance" also went on to the *Hit Parade,* for seven weeks. Kern and Fields call it "a sarcastic love song" on the published sheet music—and it is just that, in a kidding way, as Astaire and Rogers mutually complain about the hands-off treatment that circumstances have forced on their relationship at that point in the story.

"Waltz in Swingtime" is Kern's attempt to blend the classy past with the jazzy present, and it's only partly successful. Perhaps this is not surprising from a composer who, less than a decade earlier, had publicly complained about some of the jazzed-up dance-band arrangements of his songs. The tune itself is neither an easily hummable waltz nor a rhythmically grabbing swinger. But the dance that Astaire and Rogers do to it is another matter. Dance critic Arlene Croce has aptly called it "the most rapturously sustained, endlessly reseeable of all their dances. . . . It just flies—it's the *brio* of romance."

"Bojangles of Harlem" is Astaire's solo-dance highlight in *Swing Time* and an ostensible tribute to the great stage and movie dancer Bill Robinson. Actually, it's the first distinctively Astaire "pop ballet" to blend trick cinematography and ingenious tap choreography—and it goes well beyond Robinson's style in complexity. It's also the only blackface number that Astaire ever did in the movies. But, unlike Al Jolson or Eddie Cantor in *their* movies, Astaire manages to keep it inoffensive by today's standards, with no eye rolling or racially stereotyped "minstrel days" gestures.

"Never Gonna Dance" may well be the best torch song ever written for a man to sing. It's a plaintive ballad expressing Astaire's despair at what he believes is the end of his affair with Rogers. As the two of them say a regretful good-bye in a deserted nightclub, Astaire sings the lyrics with quiet poignancy. Then he and Rogers begin walking silently side-by-side around the dance floor, trying to keep their emotions in check. Finally, and inevitably, they yield to a dance that eventually brings in some of the romantic strains of "The Way You Look Tonight" and the sportiveness of "Waltz in Springtime" before a melancholy ending, as Rogers walks off leaving Astaire alone. It's a number that "achieves the staggering feat of recapitulating their entire relationship in five minutes of dance," as Stephen Harvey so pertinently points out in his critical biography, *Fred Astaire*.

Of course, everything works out for a happy ending—appropriately on top of the world, as represented by a New York skyscraper. In perhaps the most felicitous example of Kern's ingenuity in the songs for *Swing Time,* Fred and Ginger are able to sing, in counterpoint, "The Way You Look Tonight" and "A Fine Romance" (the latter with new, more upbeat lyrics).

Nineteen hundred thirty-six turned out to be a peak movie year for Kern not only because of *Swing Time* but also because of Universal's remake of *Show Boat.* As produced by Carl Laemmle, Jr., it remains one of the genuine musical classics. The '36 version was out of circulation for most of the '40s, '50s, and '60s, after MGM bought all screen rights in 1938 from a financially hard-pressed Universal and withdrew the '36 version pending its own remake. But the '36 *Show Boat* has been reissued theatrically in recent years and, beginning in 1983, it has been shown on a number of TV channels too.

The '36 *Show Boat* has an almost perfect cast. Charles Winninger, the original Cap'n Andy of the '27 Broadway production and Ziegfeld's '32 revival, repeats that role—with just the right mixture of sparkle and solidness. Helen Morgan, in her last film appearance, re-creates her original Julie, in an unforgettable acting and singing performance. Paul Robeson, who had scored a personal triumph as Joe in the '28 London production and then in the '32 Broadway revival, repeats that triumph in the

Helen Morgan as Julie and Irene Dunne as Magnolia, in the classic 1936 film version of Kern's and Hammerstein's Show Boat.

'36 movie. Irene Dunne, who had succeeded Broadway's original Magnolia (Norma Terris) for the '29 national tour, makes a splendid Magnolia—giving one of the finest performances of her distinguished career. The difficult role of Ravenal, the weak gambler whom Magnolia loves and marries, is well played by Allan Jones, who had sung Ravenal in a St. Louis Municipal Opera summer production in 1934. (Universal originally announced popular radio singer Russ Columbo for the role in 1933, but Columbo died in a shooting accident the following year.) For Cap'n Andy's wife, Parthenia, Universal tried to sign Edna May Oliver, who had created the role on Broadway. But Oliver declined in preference to playing the nurse in MGM's version of Shakespeare's *Romeo and Juliet,* whose shooting schedule conflicted with that of *Show Boat,* and so the role of Parthenia went to Helen Westley, fresh from a memorable performance in the screen version of Kern's *Roberta.* Hattie McDaniel, later to become the first black actress to win an Oscar (for *Gone With the Wind*), re-creates the role of Queenie, the showboat's cook, which she had played in *Show Boat*'s first West Coast production in 1932. Other *Show Boat* stage veterans include Sammy White (as Frank, one of the showboat performers) and Francis X. Mahoney (as Rubber Face, one of the backstage hands).

The combination of this outstanding cast with James Whale's tight, atmospheric direction results in a *Show Boat* that moves along briskly yet warmly, and that smoothly integrates the Kern-Hammerstein score into Ferber's bittersweet story of the ups and downs of Cap'n Andy's showboat family—with the ever-present motif of the Mississippi River as a sometimes cruel, sometimes amiable life force. There are, to be sure, production weaknesses, particularly in the '30s studio look of many of the sequences. But even some of these take on a period charm.

Most important, Kern's music flows right from the trumpet flourishes that introduce the opening titles. The movie's big romance is set up quickly yet firmly through song, in a scene obviously modeled on the balcony scene from *Romeo and Juliet.* Jones (on the levee level) joins Dunne (on the deck of the *Cotton Blossom* above) for the duet, "Make Believe."

Fifteen minutes into *Show Boat,* Paul Robeson stops the show with "Ol' Man River." Against a relatively simple montage sequence, Robeson sings the number in a deeply expressive but unexpectedly subdued interpretation. It's unexpected in relation to Robeson's reputation for having a huge bass voice that easily filled the biggest concert halls—not to mention the all-stops-out versions we've heard from so many other singers over the years. Robeson proves the old saying that sometimes less is more.

Almost immediately there's another showstopper, as Helen Morgan (as Julie) sings "Can't Help Lovin' That Man." Contrary to the way many other torch singers have done the song over the years, Morgan sings it in a relatively bouncy "up" tempo. By 1936 there was a worn quality to Morgan's light soprano voice, but a delicate, subtle one that gave her singing a poignance and believability few other torch singers of her generation could match. Morgan is joined for a second chorus of "Can't Help Lovin' That Man" by Robeson and Hattie McDaniel, while Irene Dunne goes into a mock shuffle dance that remains the comedy highlight of the picture—and a wonderful reminder of how Dunne could shift from eloquent drama to lowbrow comedy more quickly and naturally than virtually any other singing star of the '30s.

In fact, soon after the "shuffle" sequence, Dunne is elegantly singing "You Are Love" with Jones on the showboat's moonlit deck—in the score's most operetta-ish but still most romantically appealing song. Then she's soon back to kicking up her heels in "Gallavantin' Around," which Kern and Hammerstein wrote especially for the '36 movie, to be performed as one of the showboat's song-and-dance acts. Dunne does the number in blackface, rolling her eyes around in the Jolson-Cantor tradition and generally carrying on in a pickaninny manner that comes across today as racially stereotyped and offensive, although historically accurate in terms of the showboat era's numbers. The song reappears at the movie's end, sung and danced in a much more elegant manner by Magnolia's grown daughter, Kim, as part of the 1920's Broadway show in which she's debuting. The contrast between the two versions is obviously meant to show how the black-inspired routines of the old showboats had influenced —and been reshaped by—American musical theater.

Kern's and Hammerstein's two other new songs for the '36 *Show Boat* are both routine. "I Have the Room Above Her" is sung by Ravenal soon after he joins the showboat troupe and finds that his room is directly above Magnolia's. It serves a functional purpose in spurring a secret and beautifully photographed nocturnal rendezvous between the budding lovers. "Ah Still Suits Me" gives Robeson an extra song, which he shares in part with Hattie McDaniel. Though apparently designed to provide a light interlude between surrounding dramatic scenes, the lyrics, unfortunately, depict Joe (the Robeson character) as something of a lazy, shiftless "Tom."

To make room for these additions, several of the original show's better songs were cut. The lovely, romantic "Why Do I Love You?", according to *Show Boat* historian Miles Kreuger, was recorded and filmed by Dunne and Jones for a scene in which they drive around Chicago in a new "horseless carriage"—but it was cut "only days before the film's opening" to tighten the running time. Part of the song is still heard instrumentally in the background during the little that's left of the scene in the automobile. Also deleted: "Life Upon the Wicked Stage," a much more wryly amusing commentary on "showbiz folks" than "Ah Still Suits Me" is on black domestic relations.

The "horseless carriage" scene, in which Allan Jones and Irene Dunne sing "Why Do I Love You?," was cut from the '36 Show Boat *before its release.*

But, happily, remaining as the movie's unequivocally No. 1 showstopper is Helen Morgan's "Bill." Morgan sings it standing simply by a piano (being played by Harry Barris, one of the original Rhythm Boys trio with which Bing Crosby got his start). Morgan sings it with such quiet feeling and pathos that it becomes one of the picture's most unforgettable musical scenes—challenged only by Robeson's "Ol' Man River." Morgan is in only about twenty minutes of the nearly two-hour movie, but she comes close to stealing the whole picture.

As superb as most of the '36 *Show Boat* is, it falls apart badly in its final segments, as it tries to condense too much of Ferber's plot and too many passing years into too short a time. The movie's ending is particularly arbitrary—reuniting Magnolia and Ravenal accidentally at their grown daughter Kim's Broadway opening night, and then joining them in a fervent, tear-filled reprise of "You Are Love" from their theater box. But then the original Broadway ending has long had its critics, too (Cap'n Andy bumps into Ravenal at Fort Adams, and arranges individually for both Ravenal and Magnolia to rejoin him on the *Cotton Blossom* where everyone kisses and presumably makes up). Still, these final blemishes cannot take away from the sweep, grandeur, and human warmth of the '36 *Show Boat* overall. It remains one of the all-time great movie musicals.

With the smash box-office success of both *Show Boat* and *Swing Time,* Kern and his wife decided to build a new, permanent home in Beverly Hills and to sell the Bronxville, New York, home they had maintained through their first years in Hollywood. Kern also determined to free-lance among the various Hollywood studios, and so signed one-picture contracts with Columbia, Paramount, and Universal.

Columbia hoped that Kern and Fields could do for Grace Moore what they had done for Lily Pons with *I Dream Too Much.* But their score for *When You're in Love* (1937), and the picture itself, turned out to be a disappointment. In this one, Moore plays an Australian prima donna who can't get back into the United States because of a visa infraction—until her aides hit upon the idea of her marrying an American and entering as his wife. Since the man turns out to be Cary Grant, it's pretty obvious that

Opera diva Grace Moore runs the gamut from Schubert and Puccini to Kern and hi-de-ho in When You're in Love *(1937), in which she co-stars with Cary Grant.*

the rest of the picture will center on changing the platonic marriage of convenience into a hot romance. But the plot is developed without much wit or cleverness, and the staging of the big musical finale is almost a parody of over-arty pretentiousness.

Moore sings "In the Gloaming," "Siboney," Schubert's "Serenade," and "Vissi d'arte" from Puccini's *Tosca*—and she even makes a painfully arch stab at *hi-dee-ho*-ing Cab Calloway's "Minnie the Moocher" that is even less successful than Pons's "I Got a Song" (in *I Dream Too Much*) in trying to prove she's a "regular gal." Kern's contributions are limited to two songs. "The Whistling Boy" is a mildly charming waltz that Moore sings to a group of music-school moppets who've come to hear her rehearse. Not only is the sequence overly precious in execution, but Moore has difficulty enunciating all the lyrics understandably for adults in the audience, let along the kids she's supposedly singing to. She does much better with a lovely, more typical Kern ballad, the unimaginatively titled "Our Song." This one's presented in the most ultraromantic of Hollywood back-lot styles, as Moore and Grant loll in a gloriously fake, misty woodland setting. But whatever mood Kern and Moore may have hoped to set with the song is unintentionally broken (at least for today's viewers) when, at the song's end, Grant turns to Moore and says straight-facedly what has become, through so many '30s movies, a camp cliché: "Thanks, that was swell!"

Paramount's *High, Wide and Handsome* turned out better all around—not the least for the warmly spirited performance of Irene Dunne in her fourth Kern musical, although it's the first written specifically for the movies, with a script (as well as lyrics) by Oscar Hammerstein II. The picture also reunites Dunne with her *Roberta* leading man, Randolph Scott, in a brawny, colorful, and quite unusual story for a movie musical—about oil drillers in 1850s Pennsylvania. In light of recent international oil crises, the story now seems outright prehistoric, but it still works entertainingly, thanks to Rouben Mamoulian's vigorous direction and the way the fine Kern-Hammerstein songs are worked in. In some ways, the picture is a modest precursor of Rodgers and Hammerstein's *Oklahoma!* as a blend of melody and western period piece (even if only western Pennsylvania). Interestingly, Mamoulian would also direct Broadway's *Oklahoma!* in 1943.

High, Wide and Handsome begins brightly with the rollicking title song, sung by Dunne's character as part of a traveling "medicine show" run by her father (Raymond Walburn). In a more romantic mood are two splendid ballads, "Can I Forget You?" and "The Folks Who Live on the Hill," both of which Dunne sings beautifully. Dunne also lets loose convincingly with a lowdown "Allegheny Al," which she shares amusingly with Dorothy Lamour (in one of Lamour's earliest non-sarong roles). There are also such serviceable tunes as "Will You Marry Me Tomorrow, Maria?" for a barn dance sequence, and "A Simple Maid," for Dunne to warble to some farmyard animals.

For a projected 1937 Universal picture titled *Riviera,* Kern wrote several songs to lyrics by Dorothy Fields, only to have the production "scratched" before filming began, because of Universal's financial difficulties and a change of top management. Undeterred, Kern signed a contract with RKO Radio to compose the score for a new, modern-dress Irene Dunne musical comedy, *Joy of Living,* based on a story by Dorothy Fields and her brother Herbert. But while working on it, on March 21, 1937, Kern suffered a heart attack, complicated by a mild stroke. It was July before his doctors would even consider letting him resume work. In the meantime, RKO debated about going ahead with *Joy of Living* as a straight comedy, similar to such recent Dunne hits as *The Awful Truth* and *Theodora Goes Wild.* But by the time filming was ready to start, Kern was able to deliver at least some of the songs he had originally planned.

Joy of Living thus comes across less as a musical comedy than as a romantic farce with incidental songs—and it's generally uneven whatever its form. Dunne plays a musical-comedy star romantically pursued by playboy Douglas Fairbanks, Jr., in those crazy ways that could happen only in screwball comedies of the '30s. Fairbanks wants to rescue Dunne from the band of overprotective relatives who are sponging off her and preventing her from having any fun. Some of the scripting is clever and funny; some of it is just plain silly. Of the four Kern songs, only "(Tell Me) What's Good About Goodnight" is top-drawer Kern—and it gets the movie's one lavish production number right after the opening titles. Dunne later reprises it in one of the picture's funniest sequences, in which she tries to hurry a radio conductor through the song so that she can make a hasty retreat from the studio. As the conductor, Franklin Pangborn is hilarious in what looks like a deliberately wicked takeoff on the then-popular (and often pretentious) André Kostelanetz.

"Just Let Me Look at You" and "A Heavenly Party" are amiable enough, at least as sung by Dunne, but they get lost in the overall comic situations of which they're

Irene Dunne (left), and Lucille Ball (right), with Guy Kibbee, Alice Brady, and Jean Dixon, in Joy of Living *(1937)—which lost part of its planned score because of Kern's heart attactk.*

a part. And "You Couldn't Be Cuter" is just too cloyingly cutesy in the type of "moppet serenade" number that one would have thought Kern and Fields wouldn't try again after Grace Moore's "Whistling Boy" in *When You're in Love*.

Joy of Living would mark Irene Dunne's last movie musical (or, perhaps more accurately, semi-musical), although a few of her later comedies and dramas would include an incidental song or two. All of Dunne's major musicals, in fact, had been Kern musicals. More than any other star, she came to epitomize in both voice and manner the type of lyrical loveliness and elegance, even classiness, for which Kern is best known. Yet, like Kern himself, she also had a delightfully impish sense of down-to-earth fun that made her stand out from other '30s sopranos and which lent itself perfectly to Kern's own efforts to deflate the artiness that sometimes crept into his work.

Kern's slow recovery from his heart attack caused him to turn down an offer from MGM to write the score for *The Wizard of Oz*. But in 1938 he agreed to collaborate with both Hammerstein and Harbach on a new Broadway-bound musical that would first be tried out during the popular summer season of the St. Louis Municipal Opera. *Gentlemen Unafraid* told a story about two lovers separated by the Civil War. Although Kern's score won generally favorable reviews, the show itself didn't—and never made

The Kern-Fields classic "Remind Me" was first introduced by Peggy Moran (shown with Robert Cummings) in One Night in the Tropics *(1940).*

Broadway. But one of its songs, "Your Dream Is the Same As My Dream," ended up in a movie two years later.

The movie was Universal's *One Night in the Tropics.* The rest of the score was the one Kern had written for the unproduced *Riviera* more than two years earlier. Kern agreed to let the studio interpolate the songs into a completely different story, based on the book *Love Insurance* by Earl Derr Biggers. The picture, which has the look of a slightly glossier version of the B musicals at which Universal excelled in the '40s, is essentially a silly four-way romantic comedy involving Allan Jones, Nancy Kelly, Robert Cummings, and Peggy Moran. But it's best remembered today as the movie that introduced comics Bud Abbott and Lou Costello. They wander in and out of the action in strictly supporting roles, but completely steal the show with such routines as their classic "Who's on First?"

"Your Dream Is the Same as My Dream" gets Universal's dressiest, moonlit treatment at a key point in the picture, and it is well sung by Allan Jones and whoever dubbed for Nancy Kelly, but it never caught on. However, another song that's virtually thrown away in an early scene has gone on to become a Kern classic: "Remind Me." The late, great song stylist Mabel Mercer rescued this one from oblivion in the late '40s and made it a part of her permanent repertoire, turning it into a cult favorite at first, and then, eventually, an accepted Kern standard. In the movie, it's sung routinely, partly to a rhumba beat, by Peggy Moran (playing a nightclub singer). Allan Jones also sings "You and Your Kiss," a pleasant but undistinguished ballad, and the lively "Farañdola" provides a merry background for the movie's madcap finale.

THE MELODY LINGERS ON

With *One Night in the Tropics* and *Joy of Living,* the feeling grew in Hollywood that Kern was in decline since his heart attack. That attitude was only partly abated when Kern and Hammerstein wrote a new Broadway musical deliberately reminiscent of the intimate Princess Theater plays: *Very Warm for May.* It received a lukewarm reception and closed after fifty-nine performances. But one of its songs went on to eleven weeks on *Your Hit Parade* and has since come to rank as one of Kern's masterpieces: the tender and warm-hearted "All the Things You Are." One other song from that show, "All in Fun," eventually became a supper-club standard, too.

Three years later, in 1944, MGM would ostensibly adapt *Very Warm for May* for a movie, retitled *Broadway Rhythm.* But it kept only a hint of the original plot (about the problems of a Broadway producer) and just slightly more than a hint of the original score. Ginny Simms sings "All the Things You Are" in her ultrasmooth, crooning style, and George Murphy (never as good a singer as he was a dancer) gets a medley that includes a bit of "All in Fun" and "That Lucky Fellow." The rest of the picture features interpolated songs by other songwriters, such as "Pretty Baby" (for Gloria DeHaven and Charles Winninger), "Milkman, Keep Those Bottles Quiet" (for Nancy Walker and Ben Blue), and "Brazilian Boogie" (for Lena Horne, in perhaps the most embarrassingly garish sequence Horne ever got stuck with)—all of them far from Kern's league.

In the meantime, a tepid 1941 movie remake of *Sunny* by RKO Radio, starring British actress-singer Anna Neagle and Broadway's Ray Bolger, also fared badly. Neagle had come to the United States at the outbreak of World War II, hoping to duplicate the success she had enjoyed in London in light musicals. But critics and audiences alike found *Sunny* too old-fashioned and the film's direction by Herbert Wilcox (Neagle's husband) lackluster. Neagle herself comes across charmingly, especially in her dance numbers with Bolger. Regrettably, Neagle also failed to click in an RKO remake of Harry Tierney's *Irene,* and thereafter stuck to nonmusicals until her postwar return to Britain.

Just when Kern's fortunes seemed to be at a low point on both Broadway and in Hollywood, Kern won his second Academy Award for Best Song in 1941. But it wasn't for a song he'd written for the movies. A year earlier, Oscar Hammerstein had sent Kern lyrics that he'd written following the fall of Paris to the Nazis in June of 1940. Kern composed to them the poignant, nostalgic "The Last Time I Saw Paris," with the specific instructions on the score that it be sung "not sadly." Supper-club and radio chanteuse Hildegarde soon popularized the song, and also made a 78-rpm recording which Kern himself supervised. Then MGM arranged to include "The Last Time I Saw Paris" in its 1941 film *Lady Be Good*—even though the picture's title and most of the rest of the score came from the Gershwins. Kern's song, movingly sung by Ann Sothern, provided one of the film's best moments, and went on to win the Oscar. There was an uproar about its nomination, however, since the song had not been written specifically *for* a film. Kern, to the surprise of many, agreed with the objections and helped to lobby for changes in the Academy's rules. But, in the meantime, he graciously accepted the Oscar.

Next, in one of those ironies of which show business is so full, Oscar Hammerstein approached Kern about a musical adaptation of a play by Lynn Riggs, *Green Grow the Lilacs.* According to biographer Gerald Bordman: "Kern reminded Hammerstein that the 1931 production had been a failure. Turning a hit play into a musical was difficult enough; musicalizing a flop loaded the dice against the writers." Richard Rodgers felt otherwise. Since his usual collaborator, Lorenz Hart, was ailing, Rodgers went to work with Hammerstein. The musical opened in New Haven in 1943 as *Away We Go!* A week later, in Boston, the title was changed to *Oklahoma!* And the rest, as they say, is history.

Kern did accept an invitation to work with Johnny Mercer on the score for a 1942 Columbia movie, *You Were Never Lovelier,* costarring Fred Astaire and Rita Hayworth, who had clicked as a team a year earlier in Cole Porter's *You'll Never Get Rich.* The plot is strictly a piece of wartime romantic escapism, set in Buenos Aires instead of Paris, Venice, or other prewar locales—partly because the war had eliminated overseas markets for U.S. films except throughout Latin America. Wartime conditions also limited the film's budget and the staging of the musical numbers. As a result, there is too much plot—and a complicated one at that, involving the Latin tradition of daughters within a family marrying in the sequence of their ages. Hayworth plays the eldest daughter, who's in no hurry to get married, to the chagrin of her sisters, their fiancés, and their parents. Hayworth's father (Adolphe Menjou) hatches a plot to hurry things along, but a mix-up gets an out-of-work American hoofer (Astaire) into the act—with complication following complication until the inevitable happy ending.

Along the way, the movie is made enjoyable by Kern's best score since *Swing Time,* plus the charismatic interplay between Hayworth and Astaire. Hayworth is so breathtakingly beautiful in this one that Astaire seems guilty of understatement when he sings Kern and Mercer's title song to her. Astaire and Hayworth (whose singing voice was dubbed here by Nan Wynn) also get to sing the ultraromantic "Dearly Beloved"—and that's the song that went on to become the movie's big hit, settling down on *Your Hit Parade* for seventeen weeks.

Another enduring Kern standard (even if it never made *Your Hit Parade*) is "I'm Old-Fashioned," which Hayworth/Wynn sing as the prelude to a two-and-a-half-minute Hayworth-Astaire dance that is a marvel of romantic charm and snappy footwork. The entire number was made a part of a hit multimedia ballet by Jerome Robbins for the New York City Ballet in 1983—with the original film sequence first projected on a huge screen, followed by Robbins's 20-minute set of live variations on the movie's original routine, danced by the ballet company (to music based on Kern's melody by Morton Gould), and ending with the live dancers performing together with the projected Astaire-Hayworth images. The success of Robbins's ballet certainly says much about the artistic value and durability of what some people once looked upon as just "passing" movie entertainment.

In addition to these three Kern ballads (all of them, incidentally, given Latin beats at some point within the film), *You Were Never Lovelier* also boasts one of Kern's few forays into a jitterbug number, "The Shorty George," featuring sprightly Mercer lyrics. It's a much more down-to-earth tune than the more self-consciously hybrid "Waltz in Swingtime" (for *Swing Time*), and Astaire and Hayworth turn it into a showstopping tap sequence.

One other song deserves a mention, the wonderfully hummable "These Orchids If You Please," even though it's virtually thrown away in two brief, plot-related uses. The score's only clinker is "Wedding in the Spring," sung by Cugat vocalist Lina

Above: Rita Hayworth and Fred Astaire dance to Kern's "I'm Old-Fashioned" in You Were Never Lovelier *(1942).*

Right: "The Shorty George," one of Kern's few jitterbug numbers, is breezily performed by Hayworth and Astaire in You Were Never Lovelier.

Romay—a song that owes more to Middle European operetta than to anything Latin American.

Rita Hayworth is also the star of 1944's *Cover Girl,* one of the most popular of all World War II-era movie musicals and Kern's only collaboration with Ira Gershwin as lyricist. The plot mixes a trite backstage romance with a fresher (for '44) look at the world of glamorous magazine models—all in vivid Technicolor. *Cover Girl* holds up better than most musicals of its time, not only in the way it integrates its songs and dances into the plot (a reflection of Kern's presence and influence) but also in the way Gene Kelly's choreography advances the storyline. Kelly and Hayworth also bring to the dances and musical numbers an overall *joie de vivre* that few others have ever matched, before or since.

"Put Me to the Test," in particular, shows how much lively, unison dancing can be done in a cramped space (representing the tiny stage of the scene's Brooklyn club), as Hayworth and Kelly maneuver gracefully and spiritedly up and down the set's few platforms, steps, and ramp. The song itself has an interesting history. George and Ira Gershwin wrote a song with the same title in 1937 for Fred Astaire's *A Damsel in Distress,* but it ended up being used only instrumentally behind a dance by Astaire with George Burns and Gracie Allen. Ira, however, remained fond of the unused lyrics and so he gave them to Kern while they were working on *Cover Girl* and suggested that he write a new tune to go with them. Musically, both tunes begin almost identically, but then they go on their very independent ways, with Kern's tune being much sprightlier than Gershwin's (at least as arranged in the respective movies).

Gene Kelly and Rita Hayworth look on as agent Eve Arden trades quips with showgirl Leslie Brooks in Cover Girl *(1944).*

The rollicking "Make Way for Tomorrow," in which Hayworth and Kelly are joined by Silvers (playing Kelly's sidekick), has an almost Sousa-march spirit, as the threesome romps through empty early-morning streets engaging in some lively precision dancing. Later, the song is transformed effectively into a lilting waltz tempo for a brief solo dance by Hayworth.

The hauntingly beautiful "Long Ago and Far Away" became the movie's big song hit (with twenty weeks on *Your Hit Parade*), even though it's the most routinely presented of all the Kern songs in the picture. Hayworth (dubbed here by Martha Mears) and Kelly sing it to each other backstage following a spat, and then dance just a few simple steps before she falls into his arms and they amble off, hand-in-hand.

According to a story related by biographer Gerald Bordman, Kern had difficulty getting Gershwin, well-known for his slow work habits, to come up with the lyrics for "Long Ago and Far Away." So after what Kern thought was a generous waiting period, he composed his own lyric and sent it off to Gershwin. It began, "Watching little Alice pee. . . ." Ira, says Bordman, was both amused and ashamed—and promptly went to work on a serious lyric for the song that would eventually bring him more royalties than any single lyric he ever wrote with his brother George. "Long Ago and Far Away" won an Academy Award nomination for Best Song in 1944 (but lost to Van Heusen and Burke's "Swinging on a Star" from *Going My Way*).

"Long Ago and Far Away" and "Make Way for Tomorrow" provide the major themes for *Cover Girl*'s technically trailblazing and innovative "Alter Ego" jazz ballet, in which Kelly, through double-image synchronization, dances with himself—or, rather, dances with two representations of his psyche. Much less imaginative, musically and visually, is the lengthy title number. It begins with fourteen cover girls (representing such magazines as *Vogue, McCall's, Cosmopolitan, Harper's Bazaar, Redbook,* and *Woman's Home Companion*) all posing prettily but statically for a series of split-screen images, while Kern's song gushes from a chorus on the soundtrack in syrupy mood-music style.

After Rodgers and Hammerstein's *Oklahoma!* became the blockbuster Broadway hit of '43 and '44, it was inevitable that some Hollywood studio would come up quickly with a musical version of a similar "pioneer spirit" Americana tale. And that's exactly what Universal did in '44 for its leading musical star, Deanna Durbin—turning the novel *The Girl of the Overland Trail* into the movie musical *Can't Help Singing*. And who better to handle the score than the composer of *Show Boat* and *High, Wide and Handsome* (and almost *Oklahoma!*)? Kern was agreeable to the project, but Oscar Hammerstein was committed to other projects with Richard Rodgers and was unavailable. The movie's producer, Felix Jackson (who would marry Durbin in 1945), suggested lyricist E. Y. "Yip" Harburg, who, until then, had collaborated mostly with Harold Arlen.

Kern and Harburg's *Can't Help Singing* emerged as no rival to *Oklahoma!*, but it's a generally entertaining if uneven "outdoors" musical, beautifully photographed in Technicolor. Durbin plays a spunky young lady who disobeys her father in 1847 and runs off to join a wagon train heading west. Her intention: to catch up with the young Army lieutenant she wants to marry (David Bruce). But enroute she falls in love with a handsome young card shark on the wagon train (Robert Paige), and decides to settle down with him when they all reach California. The story line came in for some wartime criticism, for its implied approval of its heroine's "dumping" the soldier who'd gone off to do his duty and her taking up with someone else. Of course, the fact that the soldier (as played by Bruce) is such a bland character didn't make the choice seem all that debatable within the context of the picture—not that Paige, as the gambler, was any great shakes as a hero himself. In fact, it is the weak casting of the male roles that most undercuts the total impact of the picture.

With "More and More," Kern gave Deanna Durbin the best song she ever got to introduce in any of her movies. Durbin sings it to Paige in a beautifully subdued, caressing way, in a romantic, moonlit setting. Harburg's directly simple lyrics make the song all the more appealing. The song went on to fifteen weeks on *Your Hit Parade* —the last Kern song to become a popular hit in his lifetime.

Another ballad, "Any Moment Now," works cleverly on two plot-related levels, as Durbin breathes in the beauty of the wide-open spaces, simultaneously realizing that she's fallen in love with Paige. As she sings the line "Suddenly the world becomes a wonderland," the camera pans to one of the movie's most breathtaking canyon vistas. The double entendre may not be subtle (Universal's pictures rarely were), but it's visually spectacular.

The movie's title song is more memorable for its staging than for the song itself. Durbin sings it in a huge, old, round, wooden bathtub, up to her shoulders in suds. Paige joins in on the other side of the wall as he, too, sits in a different-style tub. It's a happy tune whose lyrics end up slyly spoofing the need for singers to always keep singing. "Cal-i-for-ni-ay" is perhaps too obvious a parallel song for "Oklahoma!", and not half as rousing. In fact, Kern makes it a waltz—which seems inappropriate for the state either within or outside the context of the movie itself.

Centennial Summer, set during Philadelphia's Centennial Exposition in 1876, would be the last movie for which Kern would write an original score. Like *Can't Help Singing,* the movie sought to cash in on another success—in this case, MGM's 1943 hit *Meet Me in St. Louis* (set during the St. Louis Exposition of 1903). But, again, the

Cornel Wilde, Jeanne Crain, Dorothy Gish, Walter Brennan, Linda Darnell, and William Eythe were among the nonsingers cast in singing roles for Centennial Summer *(1946).*

copycat was uneven. The biggest problem was Twentieth Century-Fox's decision to cast no fewer than seven nonsingers in the major singing roles. Dubbing the singing voice of one performer for another had become fairly common movie practice by the '40s, but not to the all-out extent of *Centennial Summer.* At a time when musicals were undergoing a major resurgence on Broadway following *Oklahoma!,* movie musicals seemed to be moving in a curious direction away from using, at least on-screen, the abundant musical talent available to them. (In fairness to one of the cast members, it should be noted that Constance Bennett did indeed occasionally sing, undubbed, in films, including '34's *Moulin Rouge,* but her range was limited and its quality modest.)

Another problem arose because of Kern's impatience with his new collaborator, Leo Robin. Knowing Kern's reputation as a perfectionist and also as a hothead when he didn't like something, Robin (with a long list of hits behind him with Richard Whiting and Ralph Rainger) took extra pains, and time, with *Centennial Summer's* lyrics. But Kern wanted to get back to New York to oversee the 1946 Broadway revival of *Show Boat.* (Also in the offing: a new Broadway musical that Hammerstein wanted to do with Kern, *Annie Get Your Gun.*) Continual nudging on Kern's part apparently could not speed up Robin's work. Finally, Kern took several unused songs that he had previously written with other lyricists and submitted them to the studio together with the few songs that he and Robin had completed. Then Kern took off for New York. Robin was understandably miffed, especially when the studio decided to go ahead and use Kern's mixed package.

Kern's score, whatever its origins or collaborators, succeeds in keeping at least some of *Centennial Summer* bearable. Certainly the routine "family story" doesn't. Like *Meet Me in St. Louis,* it focuses on a couple of sisters and their romantic entanglements at the time of a major exposition. Jeanne Crain (dubbed by Louanne Hogan) gets to sing the plaintive "In Love in Vain" and the more roseate "The Right Romance." Larry Stevens introduces the buoyantly romantic "All Through the Day" (lyrics by Hammerstein), and Avon Long (who had played Sportin' Life in Gershwin's *Porgy and Bess*) makes the catchy "Cinderella Sue" (lyrics by Yip Harburg) one of the movie's musical highlights. That cheerful paean to early risers, "Up With the Lark" (lyrics by Robin), involves virtually the whole cast—and their dubbers.

Despite critical brickbats and weak box office returns for *Centennial Summer,* two of Kern's songs went on to *Your Hit Parade:* "In Love in Vain" for thirteen weeks and "All Through the Day" for twenty weeks. But Kern never knew of their success. In early November of 1945, soon after returning to New York and while *Centennial Summer* was still shooting, he collapsed as he was walking alone on a New York City street. The patrolman who saw him fall summoned an ambulance. But Kern, despite his long history of heart disease, carried no identification specifying whom to contact in a medical emergency. He was rushed to a ward in the City Hospital on Welfare Island before proper identification could be made and his personal physician contacted. Two days later, Kern briefly regained consciousness and was moved to a private room in Doctors' Hospital in Manhattan. But soon after the transfer, he lapsed into a coma and died on November 11, 1945. The official cause of death was attributed to a cerebral hemorrhage.

Radio broadcasts and memorial concerts over the following weeks paid nation-wide tribute to Kern, with most of them unequivocally hailing him as America's foremost composer at the time of his death. The Broadway revival of *Show Boat* (for which Kern and Hammerstein had written a new song, "Nobody Else But Me"), proceeded to open on schedule on January 5, 1946—and to run for more than four hundred performances. And music from *Show Boat* began to appear increasingly in America's concert halls.

The most grandiose tribute to Kern following his death came from MGM, in the form of a long (137 minutes), lavish movie biography, *Till the Clouds Roll By*. Actually, the film had been planned before Kern's death—and with his begrudging cooperation. Producer Arthur Freed, a longtime Kern admirer, had convinced MGM chief Louis B. Mayer to let him plan an all-star musical around Kern's life and works, even before the box-office success of Warner Brothers's movies about Gershwin and Porter. Freed's staff then spent more than two years clearing the complicated rights to some one hundred Kern songs that might be used, some of them just in background instrumentals.

Kern, who had always kept his private life as private as he could, insisted that the story line be nominal and that the emphasis be on the musical numbers. Guy Bolton, who had collaborated on the books of many Kern shows dating back to the Princess Theater thirty years earlier, was assigned to draft the screenplay. Just as Kern's music had previously survived quite a few mediocre Broadway and Hollywood librettos, so too it survived the genteel, slow-moving script that Bolton finally fashioned for *Till the Clouds Roll By*—as well as several changes in directors, from Busby Berkeley to Henry Koster to Richard Whorf.

The tall, handsome, easy-going Robert Walker was cast as the short, fastidious, basically aloof, and often quick-tempered Kern. His transatlantic wooing of his English bride (played by Dorothy Patrick), his missing of the sailing of the ill-fated *Lusitania*, and a few incidents involving the ups and downs of some of his productions were the only remotely factual elements of the screenplay. More dramatic but fictional is a sequence supposedly involving his best friend's spoiled, star-struck daughter, who walks out of a show when Kern gives a song he'd promised her to the show's star—with the girl later redeeming herself by "going it alone" in the boondocks without "Uncle" Jerry's help. Lucille Bremer seems to be sleepwalking through the role of the girl, and Van Heflin got stuck with the dull part of the father.

Happily, the plentiful musical numbers are lively and colorful, if occasionally overorchestrated in the big, mushy MGM style of the '40s. They begin with an extended, fifteen-minute series of excerpts from act 1 of *Show Boat* as it would be performed on a stage. The sequence is a sort of tryout for the Technicolor remake of *Show Boat* that MGM had been planning ever since buying the film rights from Universal in 1938. Although Jeanette MacDonald and Nelson Eddy had originally been mentioned for the leading roles, their box-office popularity had faded by the mid-'40s, and so newcomer Kathryn Grayson was cast as Magnolia and Tony Martin as Ravenal. They sing "Make Believe" most touchingly, but without surpassing Irene Dunne and Allan Jones in the '36 version. The strong-voiced Caleb Peterson similarly fails to supplant memories of Paul Robeson with his otherwise impressive version of "Ol' Man River." In a logical (but, in '45, still daring) piece of casting, Freed assigned Lena Horne to the mulatto role of Julie. But Horne's singing of "Can't Help Lovin' That Man" is much too dreamy eyed and "pretty" (in a style Horne herself has since derided as

For the extended Show Boat *sequence in the Kern movie biography,* Till the Clouds Roll By *(1946), Virginia O'Brien (center) and Tony Martin perform "Life Upon a Wicked Stage," a number that was cut from the 1936 version of the musical.*

inflicted upon her by Hollywood), and it's certainly disappointing in comparison with Helen Morgan's '36 version. Virginia O'Brien, in the minor role of Ellie (one of the showboat entertainers), leads a group of showgirls in a delightfully deadpanned "Life Upon the Wicked Stage," a song which had been cut from the '36 film. The sequence also includes a rousing chorus of "Cotton Blossom," with William Halligan making a brief (and forgettable) appearance as Cap'n Andy.

The best of *Till the Clouds Roll By*'s subsequent sequences include Angela Lansbury's wryly flirtatious "How'd You Like to Spoon With Me?" (from 1905's *The Earl and the Girl*), June Allyson and Ray MacDonald's splashing through the rain as they sing and dance to "Till the Clouds Roll By" (from 1917's *Oh, Boy!*), Allyson's cutting up with a chorus of singers and dancers for "Cleopatterer" (from 1917's *Leave It to Jane*), Lena Horne's ultratorchy "Why Was I Born?" (from 1929's *Sweet Adeline*), and Dinah Shore's warmly moving "The Last Time I Saw Paris" (from 1941's *Lady Be Good*), sung as Kern had specified ("not sadly").

Best of all are two Judy Garland numbers, directed (at Garland's insistence) by her then-husband, Vincente Minnelli, and in both of which a lighter-haired-than-usual Garland portrays blonde Marilyn Miller. One is a wistful version of "Look for the Silver Lining" (from 1920's *Sally*), and the other is a medley from *Sunny* (1925) comprising a spectacularly staged circus potpourri (including gilt-painted elephants) climaxed by the movie's most elegantly high-stepping song-and-dance number to

"Who?" In this number, Garland deftly "covers" her limited movements, necessitated by her being pregnant at the time.

Much less effective are Dinah Shore's overly mushy "They Didn't Believe Me" (from 1914's *The Girl From Utah*), Van Johnson and Lucille Bremer's stilted "I Won't Dance" (from 1935's *Roberta*), Kathryn Grayson's overly quivering "Long Ago and Far Away" (from 1944's *Cover Girl*), and, worst of all, the outlandishly overdone finale of "Ol' Man River" (directed by George Sidney), with Frank Sinatra, in a white tuxedo, singing his heart out as he stands awkwardly atop a Grecian-like column, surrounded by the MGM chorus and orchestra on a series of ascending platforms leading up to more columns on which some of the movie's other MGM stars are perched. It's as silly and pretentious a finale as any movie of any era—and just about as far from Kern's taste and style as possible.

Surprisingly, *Till the Clouds Roll By* makes no use of a number of performers then under contract to MGM (or available to the studio) who had been prominently associated with past Kern productions—such as Irene Dunne, Fred Astaire, Gene Kelly, Jan Clayton, and Eve Arden. MGM, like Warner Brothers with its Gershwin and Porter "biopics," was obviously more interested in promoting certain of the studio's own '40s favorites than in presenting a genuine biographical retrospective.

Kern's music would play a prominent role in yet another biopic, at Warner Brothers in 1949, *Look for the Silver Lining*. This time the subject was Broadway star Marilyn Miller, who had created Kern's *Sunny* and *Sally*. Unfortunately, the cute but vapid June Haver couldn't carry the movie, despite a fairly close physical resemblance to Miller. Haver also faced an extra hurdle in bucking comparison with Judy Garland's vivid if brief portrayal of Miller in *Till the Clouds Roll By*. There was an attempt to re-create a fairly lengthy scene from the original Broadway production of *Sally* (with Haver, S. Z. Sakall, and Walter Catlett), leading to Haver's singing the title song. But the movie's only bright spots are a wonderful tap routine to Kern's "Who?" by Ray Bolger (playing vaudevillian Jack Donohue), and the colorful final production medley of Kern's "Wild Rose" and "Look for the Silver Lining."

If overproduction afflicted much of *Till the Clouds Roll By*, it almost sinks MGM's 1951 Technicolor remake of *Show Boat*. The sets, costumes, and overall production design are far more spectacular than Universal's '36 version—and MGM claimed at the time that the showboat itself was the largest movable prop ever made for a motion picture. What got lost, however, was the spirit and human warmth of the earlier version—for which George Sidney's listless direction must share some of the blame with a thoroughly rewritten and virtually humorless script by John Lee Mahin, a much-respected MGM veteran who had never previously written a musical.

Mahin compressed the story line to keep it all within the late 19th century and to reunite Magnolia and Ravenal while their daughter Kim is still a youngster. As Miles Kreuger so rightly concludes in his definitive history of *Show Boat:* "Although this alteration serves well to tighten the love story, it shifts the emphasis away from the more heroic theme of the river as a life force and the character of Magnolia as a woman who learns to triumph over adversity. The emphasis is placed upon domesticity rather than majesty."

The casting of Kathryn Grayson as Magnolia and Howard Keel as Ravenal also significantly shifts the balance of the story away from Magnolia. Keel, in the best

performance he's ever given, makes Ravenal a much stronger, more interesting character than the prosaic, fluttery-voiced Grayson does with Magnolia (especially in comparison with Irene Dunne's earlier performance).

But it's Ava Gardner, as Julie, who steals the '51 *Show Boat*. Although Lena Horne
was first mentioned for the role (and had, in effect, "auditioned" for it in the *Show
Boat* excerpts included in *Till the Clouds Roll By*), MGM decided that not all parts
of the country were ready in 1951 for a black woman playing a mulatto married to
a white man. Judy Garland was then announced for the role, but her succession of
illnesses, walkouts, and suspensions reached their climax in 1950 with her final dismissal
from MGM. Gardner (ironically, one of Lena Horne's best friends in Hollywood) got
the role—and made the most of it. She is marvelously sensual and life affirming in the
early scenes, and then heartbreakingly lost and drink sodden in the later sequences.
Scriptwriter Mahan, in one of his more positive contributions, also added a key scene
for Julie at the picture's end—making Julie responsible for Ravenal's returning to the
showboat and to Magnolia, and giving Julie (unseen by the other principals) the final
and emotionally heart-tugging closeup as the showboat moves down the river to the
strains of "Ol' Man River." It's all a bit hokey, but it's much more effective than the
ending of the '36 version—and Gardner makes it especially memorable.

Gardner is less successful with Julie's songs, through no fault of her own. She
originally recorded both "Can't Help Lovin' That Man" and "Bill" for the soundtrack,
in a half-singing, half-speaking style. But studio executives were divided about the
result and, just before the picture's release, they decided to have Annette Warren, a
professional singer, overdub both songs. However, the soundtrack album of the movie
had already been pressed and so, curiously, it's Gardner's own voice you hear on the
album and Warren's in the film itself. Warren's versions are indeed musically smoother,
but Gardner's are more intimate and expressive, and more consistent with the character
of Julie. Gardner herself summed up her feelings about the change to biographer Judith
M. Kass: "I wanted to sing those songs—hell, I've still got a Southern accent—and
I really thought Julie should sound a little like a Negro since she's supposed to have
Negro blood. . . . Those songs like 'Bill' shouldn't sound like an opera. [But] they
substituted [Warren's] voice for mine, and now in the movie my Southern twang stops
talking and her soprano starts singing—hell, what a mess."

Well, not exactly a mess—but it *is* typical of the overslickness and synthetic aura
of the whole '51 *Show Boat*. The Gardner/Warren version of "Can't Help Lovin' That
Man" is even slower and more languid than Lena Horne's '46 version—and simply
no match for Helen Morgan's '36 version.

MGM's '51 version eliminates all three of the new songs Kern wrote especially
for the '36 film ("I Have the Room Above Her," "Ah Still Suits Me," and "Gallivantin'
Around"), but it restores four of the original show's songs omitted in '36 ("Why Do
I Love You?" "Where's the Mate for Me?" "I Might Fall Back on You," and "Life
Upon the Wicked Stage"). Except for Julie's two songs and the Keel-Grayson duets
("Make Believe," "You Are Love," "Why Do I Love You?"), the other musical
highlights belong to Marge and Gower Champion. Their lively, athletic "Life Upon
the Wicked Stage" is cleverly staged so that the camera "stays" on Marge as she moves
around, but in such a way that Gower keeps popping up alongside her in different
costumes without a break in continuity. Whether it's trick photography or superfast
changes out of camera range (or a combination of both), the number restores at least

The showboat Cotton Blossom, *built for the 1951 film version of* Show Boat. *Among the actors in this scene are Ava Gardner, Marge and Gower Champion, and Joe E. Brown.*

some of the fun that the '51 screenplay and Sidney's stolid direction have wrung out of much of the picture.

As Cap'n Andy, Joe E. Brown is wonderfully cast, but the role has been so cut back that he's in less of the picture than the Champions are as the showboat dance team. Still, Brown projects what's left of Cap'n Andy with great flair and warmth—in a very different style from Charles Winninger in '36. Similarly, the role of the black ship's hand, Joe, is severely truncated, and the role of Queenie, his wife, virtually eliminated. But Joe still gets to sing "Ol' Man River"—and, as performed by William Warfield, it's one of the movie's few genuinely moving, great moments.

Warfield's version of "Ol' Man River" is slower and more outwardly sorrowful than Paul Robeson's in '36. The sequence is beautifully photographed through an atmospheric, nighttime mist, intercut with scenes of Julie and her husband leaving the

Marge Champion, Kathryn Grayson, and Ann Miller in the 1952 color remake of Roberta, *retitled* Lovely to Look At.

showboat. This whole sequence was directed by Roger Edens during an illness of George Sidney, and makes one wish that Edens had directed more of the picture.

With all its shortcomings, the '51 *Show Boat* still has Kern's magnificent score to keep it sailing. And it has color—for a musical that cries out for color. Yet, overall, it is no match for the black-and-white '36 version.

The last major remake to date of a Kern musical has been the 1954 MGM version of *Roberta,* retitled *Lovely to Look At* (from the song Kern added to the '35 film version). Unfortunately, neither the addition of Technicolor nor the inclusion of more of Kern's original Broadway songs could compensate for the feeble and increasingly outdated story. The Russian expatriate angle is eliminated altogether, and this time it's an American comedian (Red Skelton) who inherits the Parisian dress shop, now run by two sisters (Kathryn Grayson and Marge Champion). The comedian comes to Paris with two showbiz buddies (Howard Keel and Gower Champion), hoping to cash in on the inheritance and put the money into a Broadway show. But, first, they must get the business back on its feet. Predictably, romantic entanglements arise—with the Kern songs interspersed along the way. Unfortunately, none of the songs are presented as memorably as in the '35 version. Ann Miller comes closest with a sizzling tap routine to "I'll Be Hard to Handle." But neither Grayson's simpering versions of "Yesterdays" and "Smoke Gets in Your Eyes," nor her mannered duets with Howard Keel on "The Touch of Your Hand" and "You're Devastating," catch fire. And Marge and Gower Champion's gimmicked-up "I Won't Dance" (with fashion dummies) is simply no match for the classic '35 dance that Astaire and Rogers did just in practice clothes.

In all, Jerome Kern composed the scores for some nine original film musicals, and there were another eleven movies between 1929 and 1952 that were adaptations of Kern stage productions. Their songs unquestionably constitute some of the finest ever to come from any composer. The grace of Kern's ballads, the inventiveness of his rhythmic numbers, and the subtle ways he sought to stretch the formulas and styles of his day provide a legacy that seems to grow richer with the passing years—as songs that have always been widely liked rise further and further above "the herd." Through it all, Kern never lost his popular touch—nor his belief that good popular music could also be a durable art form.

JEROME KERN'S MOVIES AND SONGS ON TAPE AND DISC

SHOW BOAT (1929), Universal. B&W. Directed by Harry Pollard. With Laura LaPlante, Joseph Schildkraut, Otis Harlan, Alma Rubens, Emily Fitzroy, Stepin Fetchit. Songs: "Ol' Man River," "Can't Help Lovin' Dat Man" (lyrics, Oscar Hammerstein II); plus, in separate prologue, "Bill" (lyrics, P. G. Wodehouse); plus songs by others.

SALLY (1929), Warner Brothers/First National. B&W. Directed by John Francis Dillon. With Marilyn Miller, Alexander Gray, Joe E. Brown, Pert Kelton, T. Roy Barnes. Songs: "Sally" (lyrics, Al Dubin, Joe Burke); "Look for the Silver Lining" (lyrics, Buddy DeSylva); "Wild Rose" (lyrics, Clifford Grey); plus songs by others. Soundtrack LP: excerpts included in *Legends of the Musical Stage*, Take Two 104.

SUNNY (1930), First National. B&W. Directed by William A. Seiter. With Marilyn Miller, Lawrence Gray, O. P. Heggie, Inez Courtney. Songs: "Who?," "D'ya Love Me?," "Two Little Blue Birds," "I Was Alone," "Sunny" (lyrics, Otto Harbach, Oscar Hammerstein II).

THE CAT AND THE FIDDLE (1934), MGM. B&W and Color. Directed by William K. Howard. With Ramon Navarro, Jeanette MacDonald, Frank Morgan, Jean Hersholt, Charles Butterworth, Vivienne Segal. Songs: "The Night Was Made for Love," "She Didn't Say Yes," "Try to Forget," "A New Love Is Old," "Don't Ask Me Not to Sing," "One Moment Alone," "The Breeze Kissed Your Hair," "Poor Pierrot," "I Watch the Love Parade," "The Crystal Candelabra," "Ha Cha Cha," "Impressions in a Harlem Flat." Soundtrack LP: Caliban 6049; also, excerpt included in *A Tribute to Jeanette MacDonald*, OASI 594.

MUSIC IN THE AIR (1934), Fox. B&W. Directed by Joe May. With Gloria Swanson, Douglass Montgomery, John Boles, Al Shean, Reginald Owen, June Lang, Marjorie Main, Fuzzy Knight. Songs: "I've Told Every Little Star," "One More Dance," "I Am So Eager," "We Belong Together," "Music in the Air," "There's a Hill Beyond a Hill" (lyrics, Oscar Hammerstein II). Soundtrack LP: excerpts included in *Jerome Kern in Hollywood*, Music Masters JJA-19747.

SWEET ADELINE (1934), Warner Brothers. B&W. Directed by Mervyn Leroy. With Irene Dunne, Donald Woods, Dorothy Dare, Hugh Herbert, Wini Shaw, Hugh Herbert, Louis Calhern, Phil Regan. Songs: "Here Am I," "Why Was I Born?," "Don't Ever Leave Me," "'Twas Not So Long Ago," "Molly O'Donahue," "We Were So Very Young," "Out of the Blue," "Down Where the Wurtzburger Flows," "Lonely Feet" (lyrics, Oscar Hammerstein II). Soundtrack LP: Titania 506 (with *High, Wide and Handsome*).

ROBERTA (1935), RKO Radio. B&W. Directed by William A. Seiter. With Irene Dunne, Fred Astaire, Ginger Rogers, Randolph Scott, Helen Westley, Claire Dodd. Songs: "Let's Begin," "Yesterdays," "Smoke Gets in Your Eyes" (lyrics, Otto Harbach); "I'll Be Hard to Handle" (lyrics, Otto Harbach, Oscar Hammerstein II, Bernard Dougall); "I Won't Dance" (lyrics, Oscar Hammerstein II, Dorothy Fields); "Lovely to Look At" (collaboration by Kern, Jimmy McHugh, Dorothy Fields); plus songs by others. Soundtrack LP: Sandy Hook/Radiola SH2061; also Classic International CFI-3011; also excerpts included in *Jerome Kern in Hollywood*, Music Masters JJA-19747.

RECKLESS (1935), MGM. B&W. Directed by Victor Fleming. With Jean Harlow, William Powell, Franchot Tone, May Robson, Rosalind

Russell, Mickey Rooney, Allan Jones, Ted Healy. Song: "Reckless" (lyrics, Oscar Hammerstein II, Roger Edens); plus songs by others. Soundtrack LP: excerpt only, included in *That's Entertainment,* MCA 2-11002. Videocassette: excerpt only, included in *That's Entertainment,* MGM/UA.

I DREAM TOO MUCH (1935), RKO Radio. B&W. Directed by John Cromwell. With Lily Pons, Henry Fonda, Osgood Perkins, Eric Blore, Lucille Ball, Scotty Beckett. Songs: "I Dream Too Much," "I'm the Echo, You're the Song," "I Got Love" (lyrics, Dorothy Fields); "Jockey on the Carousel" (collaboration with Jimmy McHugh, Dorothy Fields). Soundtrack LP: Grapon 15 (with *One Night of Love*). Videocassette: Budget Video.

SWING TIME (1936), RKO Radio. B&W. Directed by George Stevens. With Fred Astaire, Ginger Rogers, Victor Moore, Helen Broderick, Eric Blore, George Metaxa, Betty Furness. Songs: "Pick Yourself Up," "The Way You Look Tonight," "Bojangles of Harlem," "A Fine Romance," "Never Gonna Dance," "Waltz in Swingtime," "It's Not in the Cards" (lyrics, Dorothy Fields). Soundtrack LP: Soundtrak STK-106; also Sandy Hook SH-2028. Videocassette: RKO Home Video; Nostalgia Merchant.

SHOW BOAT (1936), Universal. B&W. Directed by James Whale. With Irene Dunne, Allan Jones, Charles Winninger, Helen Morgan, Paul Robeson, Hattie McDaniel, Helen Westley, Donald Cook, Charles Middleton, Francis X. Mahoney. Songs: "Cotton Blossom," "Cap'n Andy's Ballyhoo," "Where's the Mate for Me?," "Make Believe," "Ol' Man River," "Can't Help Lovin' Dat Man," "Ah Still Suits Me," "Gallivantin' Around," "I Have the Room Above Her," "Mis-ry's Comin' Around," "You Are Love" (lyrics, Oscar Hammerstein II); "Bill" (lyrics P. G. Wodehouse); plus songs by others. Soundtrack LP: Xeno 251.

HIGH, WIDE AND HANDSOME (1937), Paramount. B&W. Directed by Rouben Mamoulian. With Irene Dunne, Randolph Scott, Dorothy Lamour, Charles Bickford, Akim Tamiroff, Elizabeth Patterson. Songs: "I Can't Forget You," "High, Wide and Handsome," "The Folks Who Live on the Hill," "Can You Marry Me Tomorrow, Maria?," "The Things I Want," "Allegheny Al" (lyrics, Oscar Hammerstein II). Soundtrack LP: excerpts, Titania 506 (with *Sweet Adeline*).

WHEN YOU'RE IN LOVE (1937), Columbia. B&W. Directed by Robert Riskin. With Grace Moore, Cary Grant, Aline MacMahon, Thomas Mitchell, Henry Stephenson. Songs: "Our Song," "The Whistling Boy" (lyrics, Dorothy Fields); plus songs by others. LP:

studio recordings of Kern score included in *Grace Moore Sings,* Decca 9593 (withdrawn).

JOY OF LIVING (1938), RKO Radio. B&W. Directed by Tay Garnett. With Irene Dunne, Douglas Fairbanks Jr., Alice Brady, Jean Dixon, Lucille Ball, Eric Blore, Franklin Pangborn, Guy Kibbee. Songs: "You Couldn't Be Cuter," "Just Let Me Look at You," "What's Good About Goodnight," "A Heavenly Party" (lyrics, Dorothy Fields). Soundtrack LP: excerpts included in *Jerome Kern in Hollywood,* Music Masters JJA-19747.

THE STORY OF VERNON AND IRENE CASTLE (1939), RKO Radio. B&W. Directed by H. C. Potter. With Fred Astaire, Ginger Rogers, Walter Brennan, Edna May Oliver, Lew Fields. Song: "You're Here and I'm Here" (lyrics, Harry B. Smith); plus songs by others. Soundtrack LP: Caliban 6000 (with *Daddy Long Legs*). Videocassette: Nostalgia Merchant.

ONE NIGHT IN THE TROPICS (1940), Universal. B&W. Directed by A. Edward Sutherland. With Allan Jones, Nancy Kelly, Robert Cummings, Bud Abbott, Lou Costello, Mary Boland, Peggy Moran, Leo Carillo, William Frawley. Songs: "Remind Me," "Back in My Shell," "You and Your Kiss" (lyrics, Dorothy Fields); "Your Dream Is the Same as My Dream" (lyrics, Otto Harbach, Oscar Hammerstein II).

SUNNY (1941), RKO Radio. B&W. Directed by Herbert Wilcox. With Anna Neagle, Ray Bolger, John Carroll, Edward Everett Horton, Grace Hartman, Paul Hartman, Helen Westley. Songs: "Who?," "D'ya Love Me?," "Two Little Blue Birds," "Sunny" (lyrics, Otto Harbach, Oscar Hammerstein II).

LADY BE GOOD (1941), MGM. B&W. Directed by Norman Z. McLeod. (Finale directed by Busby Berkeley.) With Eleanor Powell, Ann Sothern, Robert Young, Red Skelton, Lionel Barrymore, John Carroll, Dan Dailey, Connie Russell, the Berry Brothers. Song: "The Last Time I Saw Paris" (lyrics, Oscar Hammerstein II); plus songs by others. Soundtrack LP: Hollywood Soundstage HS5010.

YOU WERE NEVER LOVELIER (1942), Columbia. B&W. Directed by William A. Seiter. With Fred Astaire, Rita Hayworth, Adolphe Menjou, Leslie Brooks, Adele Mara, Larry Parks, Xavier Cugat and his Orchestra. Songs: "Dearly Beloved," "The Shorty George," "Wedding in the Spring," "These Orchids," "You Were Never Lovelier," "I'm Old-Fashioned" (lyrics, Johnny Mercer); plus songs by others. Soundtrack LP: Curtain Calls 100/24 (with *Cover Girl*). Videocassette: RCA/Columbia.

COVER GIRL (1944), Columbia. Color. Directed by Charles Vidor. With Rita Hayworth,

Gene Kelly, Phil Silvers, Eve Arden, Lee Bowman, Otto Kruger, Jinx Falkenburg. Songs: "The Show Must Go On," "Who's Complaining?," "Put Me to the Test," "Long Ago and Far Away," "Sure Thing," "That's the Best of All" (lyrics, Ira Gershwin); "Make Way for Tomorrow" (lyrics, Ira Gershwin, E. Y. Harburg); plus songs by others. Soundtrack LP: Curtain Calls 100/24 (with *You Were Never Lovelier*).

BROADWAY RHYTHM (1944), MGM. B&W. Directed by Roy Del Ruth. With George Murphy, Ginny Simms, Gloria DeHaven, Nancy Walker, Charles Winninger, Lena Horne, Ben Blue, Eddie "Rochester" Anderson. Based in part on *Very Warm for May*. Songs: "All the Things You Are," "That Lucky Fellow," "All in Fun," "In Other Words," "Seventeen" (lyrics, Oscar Hammerstein II); plus songs by others.

CAN'T HELP SINGING (1944), Universal. Color. Directed by Frank Ryan. With Deanna Durbin, Robert Paige, Akim Tamiroff, David Bruce, June Vincent, Ray Collins. Songs: "Can't Help Singing," "More and More," "Elbow Room," "Cal-i-for-ni-ay," "Swing Your Sweetheart," "Any Moment Now" (lyrics, E. Y. Harburg). Soundtrack LP: Titania 509 (with *DuBarry Was a Lady*); also, studio-recorded excerpts by Durbin included in Ace of Hearts E-60 (English import).

CENTENNIAL SUMMER (1946), Twentieth Century-Fox. Color. Directed by Otto Preminger. With Jeanne Crain, Cornel Wilde, Linda Darnell, Constance Bennett, Dorothy Gish, Walter Brennan, William Eythe, Barbara Whiting, Avon Long. Songs: "In Love in Vain," "Up With the Lark," "The Right Romance," "Railroad Song" (lyrics, Leo Robin); "All Through the Day" (lyrics, Oscar Hammerstein II); "Cinderella Sue" (lyrics, E. Y. Harburg). Soundtrack LP: Classic International CIF-3009 (with *State Fair*); also, excerpts included in *Jerome Kern in Hollywood, Vol. 2*, Music Masters JJA-19784.

TILL THE CLOUDS ROLL BY (1946), MGM. Color. Directed by Richard Whorf, with sequences directed by George Sidney, Vincente Minnelli. With Robert Walker, Van Heflin, Lucille Bremer, Dorothy Patrick; Judy Garland, Kathryn Grayson, Tony Martin, Lena Horne, June Allyson, Angela Lansbury, Dinah Shore, Van Johnson, Cyd Charisse, Frank Sinatra, other guest stars. Songs: "Cotton Blossom," "Make Believe," "Can't Help Lovin' Dat Man," "Ol' Man River," "Life Upon the Wicked Stage," "Who Cares If My Boat Goes Upstream?," "The Last Time I Saw Paris," "Why Was I Born?," "One More Dance," "All the Things You Are" (lyrics, Oscar Hammerstein II); "Till the Clouds Roll By," "Cleopatterer," "Leave It to Jane"

(lyrics, P. G. Wodehouse); "They Didn't Believe Me" (lyrics, Herbert Reynolds); "How d'Ya Like to Spoon With Me?" (lyrics, Edward Laska); "I Won't Dance" (lyrics, Otto Harbach, Oscar Hammerstein II, Dorothy Fields); "Smoke Gets in Your Eyes," "Yesterdays," "She Didn't Say Yes" (lyrics, Otto Harbach); "Sunny," "Who?" (lyrics, Otto Harbach, Oscar Hammerstein II); "Look for the Silver Lining" (lyrics, Buddy DeSylva); "A Fine Romance" (lyrics, Dorothy Fields); "Long Ago and Far Away" (lyrics, Ira Gershwin). Soundtrack LP: Soundtrak 115; also, Sandy Hook SH-2080; also deleted numbers included in *Cut! Outtakes from Hollywood's Greatest Musicals,* Out Take Records 2. Videocassette: MGM/UA.

LOOK FOR THE SILVER LINING (1949), Warner Brothers. Color. Directed by David Butler. With June Haver, Ray Bolger, Gordon MacRae, Charles Ruggles, S. Z. Sakall. Songs: "Who?," "Sunny" (lyrics, Otto Harbach, Oscar Hammerstein II); "Look for the Silver Lining," "Whip-Poor-Will" (lyrics, Buddy DeSylva); "Wild Rose" (lyrics, Clifford Grey); plus songs by others. Soundtrack LP: Titania 504 (with *I'll Get By*).

THAT MIDNIGHT KISS (1949), MGM. Color. Directed by Norman Taurog. With Mario Lanza, Kathryn Grayson, Ethel Barrymore, Jose Iturbi, Keenan Wynn, Marjorie Reynolds, Arthur Treacher. Song: "They Didn't Believe Me" (lyrics, Herbert Reynolds); plus songs and arias by others.

SHOW BOAT (1951), MGM. Color. Directed by George Sidney. With Kathryn Grayson, Howard Keel, Ava Gardner, Joe E. Brown, Marge and Gower Champion, William Warfield, Agnes Moorehead, Robert Sterling. Songs: "Cotton Blossom," "Where's the Mate for Me?," "Make Believe," "Can't Help Lovin' Dat Man," "Mis'ry's Comin' Around," "Ol' Man River," "You Are Love," "Why Do I Love You" (lyrics, Oscar Hammerstein II); "Bill" (lyrics, P. G. Wodehouse); plus song by others. Soundtrack LP: MGM 559 (withdrawn); also, excerpts included in *That's Entertainment,* MCA 2-11002. Videocassette: MGM/UA; also excerpts included in *That's Entertainment,* MGM/UA.

BECAUSE YOU'RE MINE (1952), MGM. Color. Directed by Alexander Hall. With Mario Lanza, Doretta Morrow, James Whitmore, Dean Miller, Jeff Donnell, Spring Byington. Song: "All the Things You Are" (lyrics, Oscar Hammerstein II); plus songs and arias by others.

LOVELY TO LOOK AT (1952), MGM. Color. Directed by Mervyn LeRoy. With Kathryn Grayson, Red Skelton, Howard Keel, Ann Miller, Marge and Gower Champion, Zsa Zsa Gabor. A remake of *Roberta*. Songs: "Smoke

Gets in Your Eyes," "Yesterdays," "The Touch of Your Hand" (lyrics, Otto Harbach); "I Won't Dance" (lyrics, Otto Harbach, Oscar Hammerstein II, Dorothy Fields); "You're Devastating," "The Most Exciting Night" (lyrics, Otto Harbach, Dorothy Fields); "I'll Be Hard to Handle" (lyrics, Oscar Hammerstein II, Dorothy Fields, Berard Dougall); "Lafayette" (lyrics, Dorothy Fields); "Lovely to Look At" (collaboration with Jimmy McHugh, Dorothy Fields); plus song by others. Soundtrack LP: MGM 150 (withdrawn); also, excerpt included in *That's Entertainment, Part 2,* MCA MGI-5301. Videocassette: excerpt only, included in *That's Entertainment, Part 2,* MGM/UA.

THE LAST TIME I SAW PARIS (1954), MGM. Color. Directed by Richard Brooks. With Elizabeth Taylor, Van Johnson, Donna Reed, Walter Pidgeon. Song: "The Last Time I Saw Paris" (lyrics, Oscar Hammerstein II).

THE HELEN MORGAN STORY (1957), Warner Brothers. B&W. Directed by Michael Curtiz. With Ann Blyth, Paul Newman, Richard Carlson, Alan King. Songs: "Bill" (lyrics, P. G. Wodehouse); "Why Was I Born?," "Don't Ever Leave Me," "Can't Help Lovin' Dat Man" (lyrics, Oscar Hammerstein II). Soundtrack LP: RCA LOC-1030.

Jimmy McHugh in the 1950s.

*M*ention Jimmy McHugh to lovers of movie musicals and you're likely to get instant recognition for the name of one of the top songwriters of the past fifty years. Ask about some of the songs that McHugh wrote for movies and you'll probably get such correct titles as "I Feel a Song Coming On," "I Couldn't Sleep a Wink Last Night," "I'm in the Mood for Love," "This Is a Lovely Way to Spend an Evening," and "You're a Sweetheart." But then ask what movies those songs were written for—and you're likely to get more blank stares than answers.

Between 1929 and 1960, Jimmy McHugh probably wrote more great songs for more mediocre, easily forgettable movies than any other well-known composer. Among the films: *Every Night at Eight, That Certain Age, Top of the Town, You'll Find Out, Buck Benny Rides Again, Hers to Hold, Doll Face, Higher and Higher,* and *A Date With Judy.* Yet among that less-than-classic list are four that won·Academy Award nominations for McHugh. And they all helped to make him the most successful Irish-American composer since Victor Herbert, and one of America's all-time great love-song composers—in or out of the movies.

Jimmy McHugh was born into an Irish Catholic family of modest means in

Boston, Massachusetts, on July 10, 1895. His father was a plumber who loved music and his mother was an accomplished pianist who gave her son his first piano lessons. In his teen years, Jimmy studied at Saint Paul's Preparatory School and then worked briefly as an apprentice to his father before deciding that he wanted music as a career.

While enrolled at Staley College in Boston, McHugh got a job as an office boy at the Boston Opera House. He soon acquired a reputation around the house as a talented performer of piano improvisations on opera arias and, through this skill, became a favorite of some top singers and conductors. Before many months had passed, the young office boy had become a rehearsal pianist. Through one of the opera's supporters, McHugh was offered a scholarship to the New England Conservatory of Music. But he turned it down. The eccentricities and artistic temperaments to which he had been exposed at the opera house made him uncertain whether he wanted to continue in classical music.

At the same time, McHugh had also become more and more attracted to the popular music of Irving Berlin and Jerome Kern, and he had begun writing songs modeled after some of their hits. McHugh became convinced that if America were going to produce a great composer, he would come from theater music, not from the concert hall or the opera house. So in 1917, despite the misgivings of his mother and his friends at the Boston Opera, McHugh took a job with the Boston office of Irving Berlin's publishing company. He became one of the office's twenty-two pianists and singers who peddled on bicycles around Boston and its suburbs to plug songs in the Berlin catalog in local stores and vaudeville houses. Berlin provided the bicycle and a salary of eight dollars a week. To some it seemed a step down from the world of opera. But not to McHugh.

In 1921, he decided that if he was ever going to get any of his own songs published, it would more likely be in New York than Boston. So he and his young bride moved to New York, where he went to work for another major music publisher, Mills. Within a year Mills had not only published McHugh's "Emaline," but had also made him one of its professional managers.

One of the most important contacts McHugh made in New York was with the Cotton Club, convincing the popular Harlem nightclub to use some of his songs in its revues. Although the Cotton Club featured the best black performers in the country and was located in the heart of Harlem, the club's shows were designed for white tastes —specifically for the Blue Book socialites, showbiz celebrities, and gangland bosses to whom the Roaring '20s symbolized reveling in jazz music, flaunting Prohibition, and rubbing elbows at establishments such as the Cotton Club. With his tall, powerful physique, the handsome though prematurely bald McHugh fit into that scene more easily than some other well-known songwriters of the era might have.

Between 1922 and 1930, McHugh contributed songs to nine different Cotton Club shows, including several that went on to become major hits: "When My Sugar Walks Down the Street" (lyrics by Irving Caesar and Gene Austin), "I Can't Believe That You're in Love With Me" (lyrics by Clarence Gaskill), and "The Lonesomest Girl in Town" (lyrics by Al Dubin).

McHugh's first contact with the film industry came in 1925, when he was asked by MGM's New York office to write a song to help promote the now-classic war movie *The Big Parade,* starring John Gilbert. "My Dream of the Big Parade" helped sell tickets to the silent picture but was soon forgotten. So, too, was a song that

McHugh wrote a year later to commemorate the death of Rudolph Valentino: "There's a New Star in Heaven Tonight."

In 1927, through another Mills songwriter, J. Fred Coots (composer of such hits as "You Go to My Head" and "Santa Claus Is Coming to Town"), McHugh met a twenty-two-year-old schoolteacher, Dorothy Fields, daughter of Lew Fields, one-half of the famous vaudeville team of Weber and Fields and also a successful Broadway producer. McHugh liked Dorothy Fields and some of her ideas about lyrics, and put her to work with him on one of the Cotton Club revues—the first one, in fact, in which Duke Ellington's Orchestra was featured. Their songs, however, were not the hits of the show.

Nor was a song that McHugh and Fields wrote late in 1927 for a Broadway revue titled *Delmar's Revels.* The two songwriters had gotten the idea for the number one night as they walked down New York City's Fifth Avenue and overheard a young, poorly dressed couple admiring the jewelry on display in a window of Tiffany's. They heard the young man tell his girl how he could never afford "a sparkler like that"— that all he could give her was "nothin' but love." Within the hour McHugh and Fields had begun writing "I Can't Give You Anything But Love, Baby." Producer Harry Delmar gave the song to Bert Lahr and Patsy Kelly to sing in his *Revels* as they sat on a cellar stoop in rags. Perhaps it was too much of a contrast with the elegance and glamour of the surrounding numbers, for the song didn't go over. Delmar dropped it from the show after a few days of previews, telling Fields (as she later recalled to author Max Wilk) that it was "a lousy song."

McHugh, for one, didn't agree. When he and Fields were asked to write songs for a new floor show at the New York club Les Ambassadeurs, they included "I Can't Give You Anything But Love, Baby"—with quite different results. The song not only became a big hit but also catapulted McHugh and Fields into the big time.

The producer of the Ambassadeurs revue was Lew Leslie, who had hired McHugh and Fields because of their Cotton Club work. A few years earlier Leslie had introduced an all-black revue to London called *Blackbirds.* For the next two seasons he shuttled between London and Paris producing various editions of the *Blackbirds* with such performers as Mabel Mercer, Florence Mills, and Elisabeth Welch. The Ambassadeurs show of 1927 marked Leslie's first attempt to stage a similar show in New York. It was such a success that Leslie decided to expand the revue on Broadway—with McHugh and Fields in charge of the entire score.

When *Blackbirds of 1928* opened at the Liberty Theater on 42nd Street on May 9, 1928, it quickly became one of that season's smash hits, especially after Leslie started midnight performances on Thursdays. The Thursday performances attracted the stars of other Broadway shows at an hour they could get to a show, which, in turn, attracted people who wanted to see *Blackbirds* as part of a celebrity-filled audience. The show ran until the summer of 1929, tallying 518 performances, a record to that time for an all-black show.

Virtually overnight, *Blackbirds of 1928* turned Jimmy McHugh and Dorothy Fields into two of America's most celebrated songwriters. In addition to "I Can't Give You Anything But Love, Baby" (sung in the show by Adelaide Hall), their score introduced three other songs that became well-known: "Diga Diga Do," "Doin' the New Low Down," and "I Must Have That Man." There was also another song that never caught on with the general public but became a favorite of blues singers for many years: "Porgy," written seven years before Gershwin's *Porgy and Bess* and inspired by the same DuBose Heyward play (which had opened on Broadway in 1927).

McHugh and Fields weren't so lucky the following year with *Hello Daddy,* starring Dorothy's father, Lew Fields. It failed to produce any hits. Neither did any of their songs for another show produced by Lew Fields in 1930, *The Vanderbilt Revue.* But a few further offers to compose songs for movies began to come in. For Warner Brothers's *The Time, the Place and the Girl* (1929), one of the first of the '30s college-campus musicals, McHugh and Fields wrote "Collegiana." But it didn't make as much of an impression on moviegoers as another song in the picture, J. Fred Coots's and Herb Magidson's "Doin' the Raccoon." That same year McHugh also teamed briefly with Al Dubin, Irving Mills, and Irwin Dash to write "What's Become of Hinky Dinky Parlay Voo?" for Fox's *The Cockeyed World,* a popular (if critically roasted) talkie sequel to the '26 silent comedy classic *What Price Glory?,* with Victor McLaglen and Edmund Lowe again portraying the volatile Captain Flagg and Sergeant Quirk.

The tide turned again on Broadway for McHugh and Fields with Lew Leslie's lavish *International Revue* (1930), featuring Gertrude Lawrence, Harry Richman, and Jack "Baron Munchausen" Pearl. "On the Sunny Side of the Street" and "Exactly Like You" quickly became major hits (and have remained popular standards ever since), even if the revue itself folded after a brief run in the first year of the Depression.

Meanwhile, the stock market crash of 1929 had completely wiped out all of the investments McHugh had made with his '20s earnings. He was broke and living in a one-room, fourth-floor walk-up when he ran into George Gershwin one day on a New York street. Gershwin inquired as to why he hadn't seen McHugh around for a while. When McHugh explained his plight, Gershwin asked if there was anything he could do to help. McHugh at first declined, saying that some royalties were beginning to come in again and that he hoped he'd soon be financially back on his feet. But then, as a sort of lighthearted afterthought, McHugh said, "Of course, I could use a piano." To his surprise and astonishment, a gray upright piano arrived at his apartment a few days later, as a gift from Gershwin. McHugh treasured that piano for the rest of his life.

A devout Catholic throughout his life, even after he separated permanently from his wife, McHugh was bothered by the fact that many of his fellow Catholics in show business had given up going to church. He not only helped to found Saint Malachy's, the so-called actors' church just off Times Square, but also served as one of its organists in the late '20s.

With the Depression making the Broadway scene more insecure than ever, McHugh and Fields were happy to accept a contract from MGM in 1930, and they headed west. Beginning with five now-forgotten songs for a romantic comedy about a golfer, *Love in the Rough* (with Robert Montgomery and Dorothy Jordan), they spent the next few years shuttling from coast to coast, combining their work for MGM with writing songs for occasional New York and Chicago nightclub revues and for another Lew Leslie show, *Clowns in Clover* (which introduced the hit "Don't Blame Me"). In 1933 they also wrote songs for—and appeared in—the opening stage show at New York's Radio City Music Hall.

But, for the most part, after 1930 Jimmy McHugh would be a movie composer.

Jimmy McHugh's Major Movies and Their Songs

Between 1930 and 1934, McHugh wrote songs for eight MGM films—most of them not musicals but rather comedies or dramas with incidental songs. What's more, for the few musicals with which he *was* involved, he was a decidedly lesser contributor.

In 1931's *Cuban Love Song,* starring the Metropolitan Opera's Lawrence Tibbett with Lupe Velez in a story borrowed from *Madame Butterfly* (this time it's a U.S. Marine who fathers a child while stationed in Cuba), two now-forgotten McHugh-Fields songs took a backseat to "The Peanut Vendor" (by Moises Simon, L. Wolfe Gilbert, and Marion Sunshine) and some operatic arias. For the '31 film version of the Broadway hit *Flying High,* MGM dropped all but one of the original DeSylva-Brown-Henderson songs, but the four new McHugh-Fields replacements given to stars Bert Lahr, Charlotte Greenwood, and Kathryn Crawford were forgotten as quickly as the picture. And although McHugh and Fields wrote the title song for '33's successful *Dancing Lady* (with Joan Crawford, Clark Gable, Franchot Tone, and, in minor roles, Fred Astaire and Nelson Eddy), that one was obscured by several songs by Burton Lane and Harold Adamson, including the picture's big hit, "Everything I Have Is Yours." Even one of McHugh's biggest non-MGM hits of the period was primarily a lyrics-only collaboration with Dorothy Fields on "Lovely to Look At," to a melody Jerome Kern had written for a fashion-show sequence in RKO Radio's *Roberta* (1934). Fields and McHugh also worked together expanding Oscar Hammerstein II's original lyrics for Kern's "I Won't Dance" for the same picture.

McHugh finally came into his own as the composer of a complete score for a movie musical with Paramount's *Every Night at Eight* (1935). It was only a modestly budgeted, seventy-eight-minute feature, about the ups and downs of a singing trio (Alice Faye, Frances Langford, Patsy Kelly) who team up with a bandleader (George Raft) and try to make it as radio stars. Although one major reviewer dismissed it as "a photographed radio program," two major song hits emerged: "I Feel a Song Coming On" and "I'm in the Mood for Love," both with lyrics by Dorothy Fields. The latter song became McHugh's first for a movie to make radio's *Your Hit Parade* (for twelve weeks).

Although Raft and Faye get top billing in *Every Night at Eight,* the leading role really belongs to fourth-billed Langford, then an up-and-coming radio singer of twenty-one, making her movie debut. She not only wins Raft in the final reel but also gets two vocal solos to Faye's one. Faye, at age twenty, was still pretty much an up-and-comer herself, but she got the better billing as part of the terms by which she had been loaned to Paramount (then short of female singing talent) by her ailing home studio, Fox. Faye's solo, moreover, is most untypical of the ladylike sort of singing with which she would soon become identified as a star of later 1930s musicals. With "I Feel a Song Coming On," a platinum blonde, saucy Faye seems to be modeling herself on Jean Harlow (as in the '34 *George White Scandals* for Fox), but this time with a touch of Mae West thrown in. Langford plays her role more sweetly, especially when she sings McHugh and Field's romantic "I'm in the Mood for Love." Three other amiable McHugh-Fields songs, "Take It Easy," "Speaking Confidentially," and "Every Night at Eight," get just brief trio performances by Faye, Langford, and Kelly—and are all upstaged by Florence Gill's show-stopping impersonation of Disney's Clara Cluck (a chicken cartoon character) singing Arditi's classic aria "Il Bacio."

Shortly before the release of *Every Night at Eight* and the popular success of two of its songs, Dorothy Fields decided she liked Broadway better than Hollywood and returned to New York. McHugh remained in Hollywood and signed a short-term contract with Darryl F. Zanuck at the newly merged Twentieth Century-Fox. Zanuck, in a bold move, had decided to stake the studio's future on building new stars. His four top choices: seven-year-old Shirley Temple, Norwegian ice-skating star and Olympic champ Sonja Henie, handsome Tyrone Power, and singer Alice Faye.

For Faye's first starring vehicle under the new studio set up, Zanuck chose *King of Burlesque,* with music by McHugh, lyrics by Ted Koehler. *King of Burlesque* is in some ways reminiscent of *42nd Street,* which Zanuck had produced at Warner Brothers in 1932. That earlier hit's star, Warner Baxter, is again cast as a Broadway producer —this time, however, a successful burlesque impresario who wants to go "legit." He does all right at first with a series of lively revues featuring a young singer (Faye), who loves him but gets only stage directions from him in return. Then he meets and falls for a Park Avenue widow (Mona Barrie) who convinces him that his shows aren't classy enough and leads him—you guessed it—into an arty flop and financial disaster. When the society lady walks out on him, the producer takes to the bottle, until Faye cooks up a plot that helps him wind up back on top with an old-style show and in her arms for the final clinch. The story line may be tried and trite, but Zanuck dressed it up with sharp, often-funny dialogue, brisk, uncomplicated production numbers, and some good McHugh songs.

The bright and spunky "I'm Shooting High" not only symbolized Zanuck's hopes for his new studio and for Faye (who sings the song in the picture) but also caught the mood of a public beginning to feel that it had weathered the worst of the Depression and that high hopes were no longer unreasonable. The song moved onto *Your Hit Parade* for six weeks. Although Faye doesn't sing the movie's best ballad, "Lovely Lady," she is the appropriate point of the song as it is sung to her by young radio tenor Kenny Baker—and it, too, went on to *Your Hit Parade.* The now-legendary Fats Waller also makes a brief appearance in *King of Burlesque,* as an elevator operator who gets a spot in the big show at the picture's end, singing McHugh's and Koehler's "I've Got My Fingers Crossed."

McHugh, with Koehler as lyricist, stayed at Twentieth Century-Fox long enough to write four songs for one of 1936's biggest hits with the Zanuck "star bet" who had zoomed to the top fastest of all: Shirley Temple. *Dimples* (originally called *The Bowery Princess*) borrows elements from both *Cinderella* and *Oliver Twist,* to tell a shamelessly sentimental tale of a New York urchin (Temple) who sings and dances as a street entertainer in the Bowery of 1850 while her pickpocket grandfather (Frank Morgan) fleeces unsuspecting onlookers. By the picture's end, they've reformed, of course, and a wealthy dowager (Helen Westley) has made it possible for Shirley to star in a minstrel show in which she dampens everyone's eyes with her performance as Little Eva.

For all of Temple's charms, the blackface finale dates the movie badly today, and none of McHugh's songs prove as interesting or memorable as some of those that

Clark Gable tries to take Joan Crawford's mind off her aching feet in Dancing Lady *(1933), for which Jimmy McHugh and Dorothy Fields wrote the title song.*

In McHugh's Every Night at Eight *(1935), Frances Langford, Alice Faye, and Patsy Kelly play a vocal trio trying to make it in network radio, with George Raft's help.*

Shirley Temple sings several McHugh songs as a street urchin in Dimples *(1936).*

Richard Whiting or Harry Revel wrote for other Temple films of this period. In fact, one *Dimples* song that Temple sings with her arms wrapped around Morgan, "Picture Me Without You," is so overdone in terms of tearjerker bathos that even unabashed weepers are likely to squirm through it.

With Shirley Temple bringing millions to theater box offices, RKO Radio hoped to hit pay dirt with another child star—an eight-year-old boy soprano, Bobby Breen, who had scored a big hit on Eddie Cantor's network radio show. McHugh was assigned to Breen's debut movie, *Let's Sing Again* ('36), which received only a lukewarm reception. Though Breen turned out to be a cute, curly-headed kid with a surprisingly mature singing voice, he wasn't ingratiating enough to overcome audience apathy to the picture's trite, mawkish plot (about a runaway orphan traveling with a small-time circus) nor to the thrown-together look of the production. In addition to musical numbers ranging from "Oy, Marie" to "La donna e mobile" (from Verdi's *Rigoletto*), Breen sings with gusto the title song that McHugh provided (with lyricist Gus Kahn)—a happily outgoing, optimistic ballad that managed to make one week on *Your Hit Parade* in the No. 10 spot, spurred as much by Breen's radio appearances as by the movie.

After bouncing around for a year between RKO, Paramount, and MGM writing incidental (and long since forgotten) songs for movies that often ended up on the bottom half of double-feature bills, McHugh decided to accept a term contract with Universal. Actually, it was with New Universal, as the studio now called itself following the stockholders' ouster of founder Carl Laemmle and his son, and the installation of a new management team. Since one of the studio's biggest hits of 1936 had been the Laemmle-produced *Show Boat,* the new management decided to follow through with a few more musicals, but on a much more modestly budgeted scale. Among the first were three in '37 with scores by Jimmy McHugh: *Top of the Town, You're a Sweetheart,* and *Merry-Go-Round of 1938.* His lyricist for all three: thirty-year-old Harold Adamson, a North Carolinian who had started writing lyrics for college shows at the University of Kansas and then at Harvard before heading for Hollywood.

Top of the Town is an interesting film, but far from a good one. It's one of the few movies to feature two singers who had major Broadway and nightclub careers in the '30s and '40s, Ella Logan and Gertrude Niesen. And though it is essentially just another backstage musical, set in a swank nightclub atop a New York skyscraper, it has a few unusual twists for its time. Chief among them: The leading lady, played by nonsinger Doris Nolan, is an heiress with Communist sympathies. She dresses smartly and lives on Park Avenue, but she goes around calling people "comrade" and making cracks about the way her father and his business associates exploit the working class. More to the point of the plot, she's even been to Russia and has come back determined to bring "proletarian art" to her fashionable friends. The show that she produces turns out to be the dullest, weirdest, and most unproletarian mixture of ballet and a Shakespearean soliloquy from *Hamlet* (butchered by comedian Mischa Auer), with a blackface chorus thrown in! The bored audience starts walking out, until the bandleader (George Murphy), with whom the heiress has a love-hate relationship, saves everything by converting her show into a swing jamboree—convincing her in the process that modern American popular music is for all the people and a better way to break down class barriers. It's an offbeat framework for a musical, especially in 1937, though no less silly and superficial than more conventional backstage stories.

McHugh's pleasant title song is cleverly used to introduce the film's stars and featured characters, with each one singing a line or two of the lyrics in succession as they're identified by the opening credits. It's a useful technique when most of the performers are not well-known (as is the case here), and one that Warner Brothers sometimes used with a few of its mid-'30s musicals, too.

Gertrude Niesen, at this stage of her career concentrating on tearful torch songs, introduces one of McHugh and Adamson's torchiest ballads, "Where Are You?" Niesen sings it in her sultriest, lump-in-the-throat style, in a fairly straightforward, candlelit club setting. It's easily the best representation on film of Niesen the torch singer, and the song itself went on to seven weeks on radio's *Your Hit Parade.* Niesen, with a wry gleam in her eye, also sings "Blame It on the Rhumba," an easy-going lament in which Adamson's lyrics make a sly reference to "The Peanut Vendor," the rhumba by other songwriters that had overshadowed all of McHugh's songs in 1931's *Cuban Love Song.*

The pixie-ish, Glasgow-born Ella Logan (most famous for Broadway's *Finian's Rainbow*) pours an excess of vocal energy into "That Foolish Feeling" and "You're the One for Me," but she can't raise either song to more than passing interest. Logan also gets stuck sharing the latter song with the tiresome vaudeville antics of a trio called The Three Sailors, who wander in and out of too much of the film. Logan and Niesen also add some spirited licks to the long (eleven minutes) but fast-stepping final

In one of the weirdest production numbers of any '30s' musical, Top of the Town *(1938) combines a modern dance routine with a blackface chorus, while Mischa Auer recites the soliloquy from Shakespeare's* Hamlet.

"Jamboree" sequence, which includes a tap dance by Murphy and ten-year-old Peggy Ryan (who would later costar with Donald O'Connor in many Universal musicals of the '40s). All in all, McHugh's songs can't raise *Top of the Town* much above a longer-than-usual B musical with some entertaining numbers here and there—a level at which most of Universal's musicals (with other songwriters as well as McHugh) were to settle over the next decade.

You're a Sweetheart is pretty much in the same category, as it tells a dull, complicated tale about a press agent's efforts to save a financially troubled Broadway show. For this one, McHugh was reunited with Alice Faye, on loan-out from Twentieth Century-Fox, and she helped make the cheerful title song a pop hit (including eleven weeks on *Your Hit Parade*). Faye also dances more than in most of her pictures, including a somewhat nerve-wracking routine to the title tune on the ledges on a theater balcony with costar George Murphy. She also manages to keep a straight face

Gertrude Niesen has one of her few movie roles in Top of the Town *(1937), in which she introduced several McHugh and Adamson songs.*

as she sits wearing a ridiculous, feathery costume, straddling an oversize tree branch while she sings "My Fine Feathered Friend"—although the number quickly deteriorates from perky to jerky as Faye joins the Novelle Brothers for a chirpy bird-call routine that's not half as funny as one that Clara Cluck (Florence Gill) did in Faye's earlier *Every Night at Eight.*

Alice Faye, out on a limb for McHugh's "My Fine-Feathered Friend" in You're a Sweetheart *(1937).*

Another production number in *You're a Sweetheart* was promoted at the time of the picture's release as "The Swing Murder Case." For this one, McHugh and Adamson adapted the old song "When You and I Were Young Maggie" (by J. A. Butterfield and George W. Johnson) for a mock courtroom scene in which Faye, as Maggie, is brought to trial for having murdered the old song with a swing arrangement. The idea's not bad but the number itself is routinely written and staged, and Faye goes through it as if she's not sure whether she's spoofing the original song or the swing version. There's also a maudlin tribute to Will Rogers (who had died a year earlier in a plane crash), built around the McHugh-Adamson song "Oh, Oh, Oklahoma." The song isn't much, but it's a historical curiosity in that it predates Rodgers and Hammerstein's title song for *Oklahoma!* by six years and ends with Adamson's lines, *"Oklahoma, you're O.K! Yip-yip-yipee-I-ay!"*

Universal hoped that *Merry-Go-Round of 1938* might lead to a nearly annual series of revues such as Paramount's *Big Broadcast* or MGM's *Broadway Melody* musicals. But, like the merry-go-round in a popular '30s song, Universal's first edition broke down as far as both critics and audiences were concerned, and the first one became the last. Much of the blame rests with a labored story about four vaudevillians (including Bert Lahr and Jimmy Savo) acting as foster parents for the orphaned daughter (Joy Hodges) of a former colleague. None of the six McHugh-Adamson songs help much, either. In fact, the only bright spots in a dreary picture come from songs by other songwriters interpolated by Lahr and Savo from previous Broadway shows—especially "The Woodman's Song" (by Harold Arlen and Yip Harburg), which Lahr had sung in '36's *The Show Is On.*

The discouraging results of its 1937 musicals, excepting those starring Deanna Durbin, led New Universal away from further A-feature musicals over the next few years. Instead, the studio began to concentrate on hour-long B musicals, which many exhibitors throughout the country liked to run on double-feature programs to balance a main feature that was a heavy-going drama or melodrama. And so McHugh found himself being assigned to write songs for some half-dozen B musicals that have long ago disappeared from theatrical circulation and that rarely show up on TV because they're slightly too long for an hour program (with commercials) and not long enough for most present-day feature-movie slots.

Mixed in with these Bs, however, were two 1938 Deanna Durbin As. The teenaged soprano had scored a major hit in early '37 with an unpretentious, sentimental comedy with music, *Three Smart Girls,* in which Durbin's "Little Miss Fixit" spunkiness hit a responsive chord with late-Depression audiences who never lost faith in "a future for our kids." Durbin had followed it up with the even more successful *One Hundred Men and a Girl,* in which she charms conductor Leopold Stokowski into coming to the rescue of a group of jobless musicians. Just as Shirley Temple had become Twentieth Century-Fox's No. 1 box-office champ, so Durbin suddenly became Universal's and, almost single-handedly, saved Universal from bankruptcy in its first post-Laemmle years.

For Durbin's *Mad About Music*—about a fatherless American girl who invents a father to impress her Swiss schoolmates, only to have the "invention" backfire—McHugh and Adamson composed three songs. Best among them is the ingratiating "I Love to Whistle," which Durbin sings while bicycling through the Swiss countryside.

You're a Sweetheart's *tribute to Will Rogers, built around the McHugh-Adamson song "Oh, Oh, Oklahoma," which predates Rodgers and Hammerstein by six years.*

Once again, the song predates a similarly titled—and this time rhythmically similar —tune by Rodgers and Hammerstein from the much later (1950) *The King and I,* "I Whistle a Happy Tune," raising some curious thoughts about the similitude of the creative process among songwriters when dealing with certain situations. McHugh's whistling song had the bad luck to be introduced in *Mad About Music* just a few months after "Whistle While You Work" (by Frank Churchill and Larry Morey, for Walt Disney's phenomenally successful *Snow White and the Seven Dwarfs*) became a major song hit, including twelve weeks on radio's *Your Hit Parade.* Even so, McHugh's "I Love to Whistle" caught on well enough to go into *Your Hit Parade* just two weeks after the Disney song went off. But the public, by then, was obviously tiring of whistling songs, and McHugh's lasted only two weeks—and has been pretty much forgotten since then. The other McHugh-Adamson songs for *Mad About Music* are even more forgettable, especially the cloyingly pious "Chapel Bells" and the affectedly saccharine "A Serenade to the Stars."

McHugh and Adamson's best song for Deanna Durbin came later that same year with "My Own" for *That Certain Age.* The picture marked Durbin's graduation to a partly romantic role (she gets a crush on foreign correspondent Melvyn Douglas, but ends up happily with teenager Jackie Cooper), and "My Own" provides a liltingly appropriate ballad for her to express her romantic dreams in song.

The picture's popularity, plus a Durbin recording, helped "My Own" move quickly onto *Your Hit Parade,* but for only three weeks. It also won an Academy Award nomination in 1938, but lost out to Rainger and Robin's "Thanks for the Memory" (from *The Big Broadcast of 1938*). While "My Own" has never quite become a popular standard, it has remained one of those songs that many people recognize (and like) whenever they hear it, without always knowing its exact title or its origins.

135

Deanna Durbin and Jackie Cooper in That Certain Age *(1938), which introduced McHugh's "My Own."*

With the expiration of his Universal contract, McHugh returned to New York in mid-1939 to write songs for a Broadway revue with another Hollywood songwriter disillusioned with the studio system, lyricist Al Dubin (Harry Warren's chief collaborator between 1932 and 1938). The revue, *The Streets of New York,* was planned to appeal to New York World's Fair tourists as well as to Broadway regulars, and after a year on Broadway it was literally transferred to the World's Fair grounds (with a partly changed cast). Longtime Broadway comic Bobby Clark headlined the show with newcomers Bud Abbott and Lou Costello (in their only Broadway show before they went to Hollywood). But it was another newcomer who stole the show: the "Brazilian bombshell" Carmen Miranda. Wearing outrageously flamboyant costumes, six-inch heels, and towering headgear adorned with flowers and fruit, Miranda stopped the show night after night with McHugh and Dubin's "The South American Way"—an easy-going samba in which she insinuatingly recounted, in fractured English, the pleasures of the tropics. The song accompanied Miranda to Hollywood when she was signed by Twentieth Century-Fox and is included in her first movie, *Down Argentine Way* (1940).

McHugh returned to Hollywood in 1940, but strictly as a free-lancer. By that time, Universal was turning out more B musicals than any other studio, and hit upon the gimmick of titling some of them after well-known songs, such as *Ma, He's Making Eyes at Me* and *I'm Nobody's Sweetheart Now.* One of the silliest took its title from the 1928 McHugh-Fields song hit, "I Can't Give You Anything But Love, Baby," as it tells a none-too-believable story about a gangster (Broderick Crawford) who kidnaps a young songwriter (Johnny Downs) in an effort to reach his long-lost sweetheart through song. Although McHugh had no objections to the use of the title (or the song itself) and the royalties it would bring him, he declined to write any additional songs for the picture. That hapless assignment fell to Frank Skinner and Paul G. Smith. When *I Can't Give You Anything But Love, Baby* was released during the summer of 1940 (mostly on the bottom-half of double-feature bills), McHugh's title song—spiritedly if undistinctively sung by Peggy Moran—had no difficulty standing out in comparison with the picture's "The Tomato Juice Song" and "Sweetheart of Public School 59."

At Paramount in 1940, McHugh teamed up with one of that studio's best-known lyricists, Frank Loesser (later to become a top composer as well), for *Buck Benny Rides Again*. In most ways this comedy with incidental songs and dances is even more of a photographed radio program than was *Every Night at Eight*. It's pegged to a cowboy character that Jack Benny had developed on his popular weekly radio show, and some of Benny's radio regulars are in the cast: Eddie "Rochester" Anderson, Phil Harris, Dennis Day, and Don Wilson, with the voice of Fred Allen (with whom Benny was supposedly feuding on the air) breaking in now and then to goad Benny.

In between all the fast-paced antics in which Benny gets involved at a dude ranch, the McHugh-Loesser songs turn out to be better than those of most other Benny pictures of the era. One of them, the cheery ballad "Say It (Over and Over Again)," became the film's hit song, going on to seven weeks on *Your Hit Parade*. Lillian Cornell, a rich and sultry-voiced contralto who made only a few early-'40s movies, makes a dramatic showpiece out of the pulsating "Drums in the Night," and Eddie Anderson has fun with a slight piece of musical material built around Rochester's frequent wail of "My! My!" Despite its patriotic-sounding title, "My Kind of Country" is not a wartime flag-waver but a genial cowboy song (the country of the title referring to sagebrush country), which Cornell sings as the lead-in for a Benny spoof of the-deer-and-the-antelope type of cowboy song.

Another popular radio program was the source for half the cast of RKO Radio's *You'll Find Out* (1940), the first movie to team McHugh with lyricist Johnny Mercer. Bandleader Kay Kyser, stronger on showmanship than on musicianship, had parlayed a mixture of music and quiz show into a broadcasting hit called "The Kollege of Musical Knowledge," and then into a surprise movie hit in 1939, *That's Right, You're Wrong*, featuring the members of Kyser's orchestra and very little plot. RKO lost little time putting together a follow-up which would give plenty of songs to Kyser's personable, good-looking vocalists, Harry Babbitt and Ginny Simms, as well as to the band itself. Only this time it was decided to add some chills to the proceedings, through

As Jack Benny looks on, Eddie ("Rochester") Anderson and Theresa Harris kick up their heels to Jimmy McHugh's and Frank Loesser's "My! My!" in Buck Benny Rides Again *(1940).*

a mystery plot involving no less than Boris Karloff, Bela Lugosi, and Peter Lorre (in their only joint appearance in a movie). The result was another moneymaker for RKO, if not too good a picture.

The sketchy mystery plot of *You'll Find Out* is dopier than some of Kyser's comedy antics (and *they're* pretty dopey), and the constant parade of orchestra numbers dissipates whatever suspense there might have been. Fortunately, the songs are good ones—mostly on the catchy, lighthearted side that the Kyser orchestra specialized in, and with lively Mercer lyrics. One romantic ballad that's fetchingly sung by Ginny Simms, "I'd Know You Anywhere," went on to win an Academy Award nomination for 1940 (losing out to Ned Washington and Leigh Harline's "When You Wish Upon a Star" from Disney's *Pinocchio*). Just as appealing is "You've Got Me This Way (Crazy for You)," which Harry Babbitt croons pleasingly in an easy-going, late-'30s band style. Popular in its day but not holding up over the years is "The Bad Humor Man," a novelty tune about a grouchy ice-cream vendor (Ish Kabibble) that spoofs the neighborhood hysteria that results among the small fry at the sound of Good Humor ting-a-lings. The number now looks and sounds more childish than kid-ish.

Radio shows continued to be a major ingredient of yet another RKO Radio film on which McHugh worked in 1942, again with Frank Loesser as lyricist. This time, the programs *Truth and Consequences* and *The Court of Missing Heirs* were worked into the thin, silly plot line of *Seven Days Leave*—about an Army enlistee (Victor Mature) who has seven days to convince a socialite (Lucille Ball) to marry him under the terms of an inheritance. For musical interludes, there were the orchestras of Freddy Martin and Les Brown, plus songstress Ginny Simms (recently separated from the Kyser band and now on her own). Only one of the score's songs is first-rate McHugh—in fact, one of my own favorites among all his compositions: "Can't Get Out of This Mood." It's a much more contemplative ballad than most of McHugh's movie songs, yet with a directly appealing and simple melodic line. Simms sings it silkily, backed by the Martin orchestra.

In the midst of World War II, in 1943, McHugh wrote two sentimental but heartfelt songs that were to catch the feelings of millions of Americans in that period: "Comin' In on a Wing and a Prayer" (lyrics by Adamson) and "Say a Prayer for the Boys Over There" (lyrics by Herb Magidson). The first was introduced on a radio program and went on to twenty-one weeks on *Your Hit Parade*. Deanna Durbin introduced the second song in a wartime tearjerker, *Hers to Hold*, in which she plays an aircraft-factory worker in love with a pilot (Joseph Cotten). "Say a Prayer for the Boys Over There" won McHugh his fourth Academy Award nomination, but again he lost (this time to Harry Warren and Mack Gordon's "You'll Never Know" from *Hello, Frisco, Hello*). In addition to donating his royalties from the two songs to war relief agencies, McHugh wrote two songs that the U.S. Treasury Department used as theme songs for war bond drives in 1944 and 1945: "Buy, Buy, Buy a Bond" and "We've Got Another Bond to Buy." Bing Crosby sang the latter in a specially filmed short subject designed to help sell war bonds in movie theaters throughout the country. McHugh also produced a bond-rally aquacade in Beverly Hills in 1945 that sold twenty-eight-million-dollars' worth of bonds in a single night—the largest single sale of bonds ever recorded in the United States. For such activities, President Harry S Truman awarded McHugh the Presidential Citation soon after the war ended.

Bela Lugosi, as a fake Swami, prepares a seance as bandleader Kay Kyser, vocalist Ginny Simms (standing), and others look on in 1940's You'll Find Out.

For most of the war years, McHugh shuttled back and forth between different studios, working on a wide variety of productions, most of them modestly budgeted films designed strictly as wartime escapist fare. Only a few of them produced any songs that survived the original runs of the pictures themselves.

Paramount's *Happy-Go-Lucky* (1943) was one of the luckiest in that respect. The picture itself is a strictly routine, working-girl-chases-rich-man escapade, sparked by its McHugh-Loesser score and a better-than-average cast headed by Mary Martin, Dick Powell, Betty Hutton, Eddie Bracken, and Rudy Vallee. Martin and Hutton each introduce novelty tunes from which they got years of personal mileage on radio shows —Martin with the catchily nostalgic "Ta-Ra-Ra-Boom-De-Ay" and Hutton with the jive-ily frantic "Murder, He Says!" Martin and Powell also sing the dreamily romantic "Let's Get Lost," which went on to twelve weeks on *Your Hit Parade*.

RKO Radio's *Higher and Higher* (1943) started out as a Broadway show with songs by Rodgers and Hart. But the studio dropped all but one of the original songs in its screen adaptation (the survivor being, surprisingly, one of the show's lesser numbers, "Disgustingly Rich"). Although some critics bemoaned the loss of Rodgers and Hart's "It Never Entered My Mind," "You Are From Another World," and "Nothing But You," most of them had to admit that the replacement songs by McHugh and Adamson were good ones.

Two of them are romantic ballads introduced in the picture by Frank Sinatra, playing his first major movie role at a time when his recordings were seriously challenging Bing Crosby's decade-old position as the country's top pop singer. "This Is a Lovely Way to Spend an Evening" and "I Couldn't Sleep a Wink Last Night" both became Sinatra recording hits and quickly moved onto radio's *Your Hit Parade* (for eight and thirteen weeks, respectively). The latter song also won an Oscar nomination, losing out to a song introduced by Crosby in *Going My Way,* Van Heusen and Burke's "Swinging on a Star." One other Sinatra-sung ballad, "The Music Stopped," didn't catch on quite as well, although it did get considerable radio play and has survived as a favorite of some jazz musicians.

Young Sinatra's dreamy-eyed crooning is the only reason for watching *Higher and Higher* today. The picture's story, about a scullery maid (Michele Morgan) who poses as a debutante in hopes of snaring a rich husband, is mostly pointless and wastes such normally good performers as Morgan, Jack Haley, Leon Errol, Victor Borge, Dooley Wilson, Mary Wickes, Barbara Hale, and, in his feature film debut, a nineteen-year-old Mel Tormé.

With Twentieth Century-Fox's *Something for the Boys* (1944), Cole Porter became the victim of having most of his Broadway songs dumped in the show's transition to a movie. Porter had tailored much of the original score for Ethel Merman. So when Fox cast Carmen Miranda in the role, it was decided that new songs would better serve her as well as costars Perry Como (in his first feature movie) and Vivian Blaine. Porter's Broadway score had not been one of his best, but the McHugh-Adamson replacements are mostly routine too. An exception: an especially attractive ballad that Como sings, "I Wish I Didn't Have to Say Goodnight," which doesn't deserve the obscurity into which it's fallen.

Two equally likable ballads that McHugh and Adamson contributed to *Four Jills in a Jeep* (1944) fared better with the public: "How Many Times Do I Have to Tell You?" and "How Blue the Night?" Dick Haymes sings both songs in this hastily put-together Twentieth Century-Fox recounting of an actual USO tour undertaken in 1943 by Kay Francis, Martha Raye, Carole Landis, and Mitzi Mayfair to entertain the troops in England and North Africa. Haymes plays a GI smitten with Mayfair in a fictionalized part of the movie. Another romantic subplot involves Landis and a pilot she meets, paralleling a real-life event for Landis on one of her tours. In fact, the publicity Landis got when she married the pilot is what led to the movie—as a way to dramatize the personal involvement of those Hollywood performers who were taking risks and roughing it in very un-Hollywood style to entertain troops overseas. But there were complaints from friends of other Hollywood stars who felt they had done as much or more than Francis, Raye, Landis, and Mayfair. They charged that the movie unfairly played up a relatively minor USO tour in relation to some that other stars had undertaken with less publicity. Whatever the case, *Four Jills in a Jeep* was helped at the box office by its inclusion of Betty Grable, Alice Faye, and Carmen Miranda as guest stars, in a sequence dealing with special broadcasts to servicemen and

For Frank Sinatra's feature film debut in Higher and Higher *(1943), most of the Rodgers and Hart Broadway score was dropped. Sinatra got new McHugh-Adamson songs to sing, including "I Couldn't Sleep a Wink Last Night." Here he's with Michele Morgan and Marcy McGuire.*

servicewomen overseas. Each guest star reprised a song she had introduced in an earlier Twentieth Century-Fox movie—all of them by composers other than McHugh. Yet even against this competition, it was McHugh's "How Blue the Night?" that became the movie's hit song, including two weeks on *Your Hit Parade.*

Twentieth Century-Fox's *Doll Face* (1945) also took its cue from some real-life events, this time in the life of burlesque star Gypsy Rose Lee (who had appeared in a number of late '30s Fox films under her real name, Louise Hovick). Pert Vivian Blaine plays a stripper who wants to become a Broadway actress, but that's the only new wrinkle in what is otherwise an ordinary backstage saga with music. Two McHugh-Adamson songs became moderate hits: "Here Comes Heaven Again," a romantic ballad soothingly crooned in the film by Perry Como, and "Hubba-Hubba-Hubba (Dig You Later)," a lively rhythmic number in which Como and songstress Martha Stewart playfully toss around some of the era's jazz slang. In a supporting role, Carmen Miranda, suffering from the picture's absence of color photography, gets to sing and dance "Chico Chico (from Puerto Rico)," a servicably catchy rhumba that failed to repeat the success Miranda had enjoyed earlier in her career with McHugh's "The South American Way."

Quite a few other earlier McHugh hits showed up in movies during the war years, bringing McHugh additional royalties but not being staged in a way to displace previous versions. Among them: "I Feel a Song Coming On," danced by Vera Zorina, backed by a corps of top-hatted male dancers including George Raft, in *Follow the Boys* (1944), a Universal revue that paid tribute, in a broader and more fictionalized way than *Four Jills in a Jeep,* to stars who entertained the troops overseas. In Paramount's army-camp comedy *True to the Army* (1942), Judy Canova tones down her normally strident hillbilly wails to sing a fairly ladylike version of "I Can't Give You Anything But Love, Baby." The same song gets more elegant treatment from Lena Horne as part of a big production number with Bill Robinson in Twentieth Century-Fox's *Stormy Weather* (1943). Horne also sings a jivey "Diga Diga Doo" in *Stormy Weather,* as part of a hot "jungle beat" number in which she wears a costume that would look more appropriate on Carmen Miranda.

After the war, McHugh returned to Broadway for a spell to write songs for the Mike Todd revue *As the Girls Go,* which introduced "You Say the Nicest Things, Baby" and "Nobody's Heart But Mine." As postwar Hollywood turned away from escapist musicals, McHugh found his talents being sought mainly for just another string of mediocre B musicals at RKO Radio and Republic.

One exception was MGM's *A Date With Judy,* a bright, fast-moving if formula "family" comedy-with-music, starring Wallace Beery and Carmen Miranda, but focusing on the rivalry between two teenagers, the studio's up-and-coming Jane Powell and Elizabeth Taylor, for the same beau, Robert Stack. The score is a hodgepodge by different composers, with McHugh and Adamson's "It's a Most Unusual Day" emerging as the picture's No. 2 song hit, after Gabriel Ruiz and Ray Gilbert's "Cuanto la Gusta" (which became one of Miranda's biggest movie hits and a *Hit Parade* entry). "It's a Most Unusual Day" is one of McHugh's most cheerful waltzes, and it provides a festive finale to *A Date With Judy,* as virtually the entire cast joins Jane Powell in singing it. A part of the number is included in MGM's popular '74 compilation feature excerpting its best musicals, *That's Entertainment.*

In addition to providing the finale for *A Date With Judy,* "It's a Most Unusual Day" also, in effect, marked the finale to McHugh's career as a movie-musical composer. He would continue to write incidental songs for a few other films through the 1950s, but they would mostly be for dramas and comedies, not musicals in the traditional sense.

A number of major movie musicals, however, would continue to interpolate earlier McHugh hits. Among them: "I Can't Give You Anything But Love, Baby," which turned up in Universal's *So This Is Paris?* (1954), teasingly sung in French by Gloria DeHaven, as well as in Warner Brothers's *The Helen Morgan Story* (1957), sung more torchily by Gogi Grant, who dubbed most of the songs for Ann Blyth in the title role. McHugh even makes an appearance in *The Helen Morgan Story,* playing himself and accompanying Blyth at the piano for the song.

During the 1950s McHugh also organized a nightclub act made up of eight attractive "singing starlets" with himself as pianist. They toured the country and also performed on television—in a show devoted exclusively to the music of Jimmy

McHugh. There was no shortage of well-known hits to chose from, even if the titles of the movies or shows from which the songs came were usually not so familiar. For Jimmy McHugh, more than any of America's other great songwriters, had proved that good songs could find their way out of mediocre movies as well as outstanding ones —and survive as standards.

Though he cut back on songwriting in his later years, McHugh remained active with other interests. He served two terms as president of the Beverly Hills Chamber of Commerce in the 1950s and he was elected a vice-president of ASCAP in 1962. He also continued to be an enthusiastic sponsor of sports events, especially amateur swimming, through the Amateur Athletic Union of America. His charitable work included organizing the Jimmy McHugh Polio Foundation in 1951 to help Los Angeles hospitals buy the first junior-size respirators for young victims of infantile paralysis, and the foundation sponsored annual balls for many years to raise funds to help fight other diseases as well. An avid art lover and collector, McHugh also loaned many of the French Impressionist paintings he owned to colleges and museums so that others could share in their enjoyment.

McHugh also eagerly fulfilled a commission from President Dwight Eisenhower to write the official song for Radio Free Europe, titled "Crusade for Freedom." A few years later, on his own, he composed "The First Lady Waltz" for Jacqueline Kennedy, and he was among those in attendance at a White House Press Correspondents' dinner honoring President John F. Kennedy and Britain's Prime Minister Harold Macmillan when "The First Lady Waltz" was performed by the U.S. Navy Band and Glee Club. McHugh also wrote the official Massachusetts state song.

He never remarried after separating from his wife early in his career, although he continued to date a succession of younger, attractive models. He was also a frequent escort of columnist Louella Parsons to Hollywood events for many years. George Eels, in *Louella and Hedda,* indicates that Parsons, on her part, developed a serious romantic attachment to McHugh, but that he carefully and skillfully kept from getting too entangled. Perhaps because of his friendship with Parsons and also because of his personal popularity, he was never a target for the public gossip that seems to be part and parcel of Hollywood bachelors' private lives. At the time of his death, a *New York Times* obituary mentioned that he was survived by a son, three grandchildren, and a great-grandchild.

When he died of a heart attack in Beverly Hills on May 23, 1969, at the age of seventy-four, McHugh had still never won an Academy Award despite five nominations. But then Cole Porter and George Gershwin never won Oscars either. That hasn't stopped their songs, nor McHugh's, from finding more secure and lasting places in the Songwriters' Hall of Fame, and in the public's hearts, than some actual Oscar winners. Obviously, Britain's Queen Elizabeth was speaking for more than herself when she told McHugh, at a Royal Command Performance in London in 1951: "Mr. McHugh, you seem to have written all my favorite songs."

THE TIME, THE PLACE AND THE GIRL (1929), Warner Brothers. B&W. Directed by Howard Bretherton. With Betty Compson, Grant Withers, James Kirkwood, Vivian Oakland, Gretchen Hartman. Song: "Collegiana" (lyrics, Dorothy Fields); plus songs by others.

THE COCKEYED WORLD (1929), Fox. B&W. Directed by Raoul Walsh. With Victor McLaglen, Edmund Lowe, Lily Damita, El Brendel, Joe Brown, Stuart Erwin, Bob Burns, Jeanette Dagna, Lelia Karnelly. Song: "What's Become of Hinky Dinky Parlay Voo" (collaboration with Al Dubin, Irving Mills, Irwin Dash); plus songs by others.

LOVE IN THE ROUGH (1930), MGM. B&W. Directed by Charles F. Reisner. With Dorothy Jordan, Robert Montgomery, J. C. Nugent, Dorothy McNulty (Penny Singleton), Benny Rubin, Allan Lane. Songs: "Go Home and Tell Your Mother," "Learning a Lot From You," "One More Waltz," "I'm Doin' That Thing," "Like Kelly Can" (lyrics, Dorothy Fields).

CUBAN LOVE SONG (1931), MGM. B&W. Directed by W. S. Van Dyke. With Lawrence Tibbett, Lupe Velez, Jimmy Durante, Karen Morley, Ernest Torrence, Louise Fazenda, Hale Hamilton. Songs: "Cuban Love Song," "Tramps at Sea" (lyrics, Dorothy Fields); plus songs and arias by others. Studio recording from period: included in *Lawrence Tibbett*, Empire 804.

FLYING HIGH (1931), MGM. B&W. Directed by Charles F. Reisner. With Bert Lahr, Charlotte Greenwood, Pat O'Brien, Charles Winninger, Kathryn Crawford, Guy Kibbee, Hedda Hopper. Songs: "Happy Landing," "We'll Dance Until the Dawn" (lyrics, Dorothy Fields); plus songs by others. Soundtrack LP: excerpt included in *Bert Lahr on Stage, Screen and Radio*, Music Masters JJA-19765.

THE BIG BROADCAST (1932), Paramount. B&W. Directed by Frank Tuttle. With Stuart Erwin, Bing Crosby, Leila Hyams, George Burns, Gracie Allen, Sharon Lynn, Kate Smith, the Boswell Sisters, Cab Calloway and his Orchestra, the Mills Brothers, Donald Novis, Arthur Tracy, Vincent Lopez and his Orchestra. Song: "Goodbye Blues" (lyrics, Arnold Johnson); plus songs by others. Soundtrack LP: Soundtrak 101.

RED-HEADED WOMAN (1932), MGM. B&W. Directed by Jack Conway. With Jean Harlow, Chester Morris, Lewis Stone, Leila Hyams, Una Merkel, Henry Stephenson. Song: "We'll Dance Until the Dawn" (lyrics, Dorothy Fields); plus songs by others.

MEET THE BARON (1932), MGM. B&W. Directed by Walter Lang. With Jack Pearl, Jimmy Durante, ZaSu Pitts. Song: "Clean as a Whistle" (lyrics, Dorothy Fields).

DANCING LADY (1933), MGM. B&W. Directed by Robert Z. Leonard. With Joan Crawford, Clark Gable, Franchot Tone, May Robson, Ted Healy, Fred Astaire, Robert Benchley, Eunice Quedens (Eve Arden), Nelson Eddy, the Three Stooges. Song: "My Dancing Lady" (lyrics, Dorothy Fields).

THE PRIZE-FIGHTER AND THE LADY (1933), MGM. B&W. Directed by W. S. Van Dyke. With Max Baer, Myrna Loy, Walter Huston, Jack Dempsey, Primo Carnera, James J. Jeffreys, Otto Kruger, Jess Willard. Song: "Lucky Fella" (lyrics, Dorothy Fields); plus songs by others.

FUGITIVE LOVERS (1934), MGM. B&W. Directed by Richard Boleslavsky. With Robert Montgomery, Madge Evans, Ted Healy, C. Henry Gordon, Nat Pendleton, Ruth Selwyn. Song: "I'm Full of the Devil" (lyrics, Dorothy Fields).

HAVE A HEART (1934), MGM. B&W. Directed by David Butler. With James Dunn, Jean Parker, Stuart Erwin, Una Merkel. Songs: "Lost in a Fog," "Thank You for a Lovely Evening" (lyrics, Dorothy Fields).

ROBERTA (1935), RKO Radio. B&W. Directed by William A. Seiter. With Irene Dunne, Fred Astaire, Ginger Rogers, Randolph Scott, Helen Westley, Claire Dodd. Songs: "Lovely to Look At" (collaboration by McHugh, Dorothy Fields, Jerome Kern); plus songs by others. Soundtrack LP: Classic International CIF 3011; Sandy Hook SH2061; also, excerpts included in *Jerome Kern in Hollywood*, Music Masters JJA-19747.

HOORAY FOR LOVE (1935), RKO Radio. B&W. Directed by Walter Lang. With Ann Sothern, Gene Raymond, Bill Robinson, Fats Waller, Jeni LeGon, Pert Kelton, Lionel Stander, Georgia Kane. Songs: "Hooray for Love," "I'm in Love All Over Again," "You're an Angel," "Livin' in a Great Big Way," "Palsy Walsy," "Gotta Snap in My Fingers" (lyrics, Dorothy Fields).

I DREAM TOO MUCH (1935), RKO Radio. B&W. Directed by John Cromwell. With Lily Pons, Henry Fonda, Osgood Perkins, Eric Blore, Lucille Ball, Scotty Beckett. Song: "Jockey on the Carousel" (collaboration with Dorothy Fields, Jerome Kern). Soundtrack LP: Grapon 15 (with *One Night of Love*). Videocassette: Budget Video.

EVERY NIGHT AT EIGHT (1935), Paramount. B&W. Directed by Raoul Walsh. With George Raft, Alice Faye, Frances Langford, Patsy Kelly, Harry Barris, Florence Gill (Clara Cluck). Songs: "I'm in the Mood for Love," "It's Great to Be in Love Again," "Speaking Confidentially," "Take It Easy" (lyrics, Dorothy Fields); "I Feel a Song Coming On" (lyrics, Dorothy Fields, George Oppenheimer); plus songs by others. Soundtrack LP: *The Classic Movie Musicals of Jimmy McHugh,* Music Masters JJA-19825.

KING OF BURLESQUE (1935), Twentieth Century-Fox. B&W. Directed by Sidney Lanfield. With Warner Baxter, Alice Faye, Jack Oakie, Arline Judge, Dixie Dunbar, Fats Waller, Nick Long Jr., Kenny Baker, Charles Quigley, Gregory Ratoff, the Paxton Sisters. Songs: "I'm Shooting High," "Lovely Lady," "Spreading Rhythm Around," "Whose Big Baby Are You?" (lyrics, Ted Koehler); plus songs by others. Soundtrack LP: excerpts included in *The Classic Movie Musicals of Jimmy McHugh,* Music Masters JJA-19825.

NITWITS (1935), RKO Radio. B&W. Directed by George Stevens. With Robert Woolsey, Bert Wheeler, Evelyn Brent, Betty Grable, Hale Hamilton, Erik Rhodes. Song: "Music in My Heart" (lyrics, Dorothy Fields); plus songs by others.

DIMPLES (1936), Twentieth Century-Fox. B&W. Directed by William A. Seiter. With Shirley Temple, Frank Morgan, Helen Westley, Bill Robinson, Robert Kent, John Carradine, Stepin Fetchit, Astrid Allwyn, the Hall Johnson Choir. Songs: "Oh, Mister Man Up in the Moon," "What Did the Bluebird Say?," "He Was a Dandy," "Picture Me Without You" (lyrics, Ted Koehler). Soundtrack LP: excerpts included in *The Classic Movie Musicals of Jimmy McHugh,* Music Masters JJA-19825.

LET'S SING AGAIN (1936), RKO Radio. B&W. Directed by Kurt Neumann. With Bobby Breen, Henry Armetta, Vivienne Osborne, George Houston, Grant Withers, Inez Courtney. Song: "Let's Sing Again" (lyrics, Gus Kahn); plus song by others.

HER MASTER'S VOICE (1936), Paramount. B&W. Directed by Joseph Santley. With Edward Everett Horton, Peggy Conklin, Laura Hope Crews, Elizabeth Patterson, Grant Mitchell. Song: "With All My Heart" (lyrics, Gus Kahn).

THE VOICE OF BUGLE ANN (1936), MGM. B&W. Directed by Richard Thorpe.

With Lionel Barrymore, Maureen O'Sullivan, Eric Linden, Dudley Digges, Spring Byington. Songs: "There's a Home in the Mountains," "There's No Two Ways About It" (lyrics, Harold Adamson).

BANJO ON MY KNEE (1936), Twentieth Century-Fox. B&W. Directed by John Cromwell. With Barbara Stanwyck, Joel McCrea, Walter Brennan, Helen Westley, Buddy Ebsen, Tony Martin, the Hall Johnson Choir. Songs: "With My Banjo on My Knee," "Where the Lazy River Goes By," "There's Something in the Air" (lyrics, Harold Adamson).

PALM SPRINGS (1936), Paramount. B&W. Directed by Aubrey Scotto. With Frances Langford, Smith Ballew, Sir Guy Standing, David Niven, E. E. Clive, Spring Byington, Sterling Holloway, Grady Sutton. Song: "I'm in the Mood for Love" (lyrics, Dorothy Fields); plus songs by others.

TOP OF THE TOWN (1937), Universal. B&W. Directed by Ralph Murphy. With George Murphy, Doris Nolan, Ella Logan, Hugh Herbert, Gertrude Niesen, Peggy Ryan, Gregory Ratoff, the Four Esquires, the Californian Collegians. Songs: "Top of the Town," "Where Are You?," "Blame It on the Rhumba," "Jamboree," "That Foolish Feeling," "Fireman, Fireman, Save My Child," "Post Office (I've Got to Be Kissed)" (lyrics, Harold Adamson). Soundtrack LP: excerpts included in *The Classic Movie Musicals of Jimmy McHugh,* Music Masters JJA-19825.

YOU'RE A SWEETHEART (1937), Universal. B&W. Directed by David Butler. With Alice Faye, George Murphy, Charles Winninger, Ken Murray, Andy Devine, the Four Playboys, the Noville Brothers. Songs: "You're a Sweetheart," "My Fine Feathered Friend," "Broadway Jamboree," "Who Killed Maggie? (Swing Murder Case)," "Oh, Oh, Oklahoma" (lyrics, Harold Adamson); plus song by others. Soundtrack LP: excerpts included in *The Classic Movie Musicals of Jimmy McHugh,* Music Masters JJA-19825.

MERRY-GO-ROUND OF 1938 (1937), Universal. B&W. Directed by Irving Cummings. With Bert Lahr, Jimmy Savo, Billy House, Alice Brady, Joy Hodges, Mischa Auer, Louise Fazenda, John King, Barbara Read, Dave Apollon and his Orchestra. Songs: "You're My Dish," "I'm in My Glory," "More Power to You," "Six of One, Half Dozen of the Other," "The Grand Street Comedy Four" (lyrics, Harold Adamson).

WHEN LOVE IS YOUNG (1937), Universal. B&W. Directed by Hal Mohr. With Virginia Bruce, Kent Taylor, Walter Brennan, Greta Meyer, Jean Rogers, Nydia Westman, Sterling Holloway. Songs: "When Love Is Young," "Did

Anyone Ever Tell You?" (lyrics, Harold Adamson).

HITTING A NEW HIGH (1937), RKO Radio. B&W. Directed by Raoul Walsh. With Lily Pons, Jack Oakie, John Howard, Edward Everett Horton, Eric Blore, Eduardo Ciannelli. Song: "This Never Happened Before" (lyrics, Harold Adamson); plus songs by others.

BREEZING HOME (1937), Universal. B&W. Directed by Milton Carruth. With Binnie Barnes, William Gargan, Wendy Barrie, Raymond Walburn, Alma Kruger, Alan Baxter, Willie Best, Elisha Cook, Jr. Songs: "You're in My Heart Again," "I'm Hitting the High Spots" (lyrics, Harold Adamson).

THE DEVIL'S PARTY (1938), Universal. B&W. Directed by Ray McCarey. With Victor McLaglen, William Gargan, Paul Kelly, Beatrice Roberts, Frank Jenks, Ed Gargan, Juanita Quigley. Song: "Things Are Coming My Way" (lyrics, Harold Adamson).

MAD ABOUT MUSIC (1938), Universal. B&W. Directed by Norman Taurog. With Deanna Durbin, Herbert Marshall, Gail Patrick, Arthur Treacher, Jackie Moran, Helen Parrish, William Frawley, Marcia Mae Jones, Franklin Pangborn. Songs: "I Love to Whistle," "Chapel Bells," "Serenade to the Stars," "There Isn't a Day Goes By" (lyrics, Harold Adamson); plus songs and arias by others.

THAT CERTAIN AGE (1938), Universal. B&W. Directed by Edward Ludwig. With Deanna Durbin, Melvyn Douglas, Jackie Cooper, Irene Rich, Nancy Carroll, John Halliday, Juanita Quigley, Jackie Searl. Songs: "That Certain Age," "My Own," "You're As Pretty As a Picture," "Has Anyone Ever Told You Before?," "Be a Good Scout" (lyrics, Harold Adamson); plus songs and arias by others. Soundtrack LP: excerpt included in *The Classic Movie Musicals of Jimmy McHugh,* Music Masters JJA-19825.

YOUTH TAKES A FLING (1938), Universal. B&W. Directed by Archie Mayo. With Joel McCrea, Andrea Leeds, Dorothea Kent, Frank Jenks, Virginia Grey, Isabel Jeans, Marion Martin, Willie Best. Songs: "For the First Time," "Heigh-Ho the Merry-O" (lyrics, Harold Adamson).

RECKLESS LIVING (1938), Universal. B&W. Directed by Frank McDonald. With Robert Wilcox, Nan Grey, Jimmy Savo, Frank Jenks, William Lundigan, Constance Moore, Eleanor Hanson, Mary Brodel. Song: "When the Stars Go to Sleep" (lyrics, Harold Adamson).

THE ROAD TO RENO (1938), Universal. B&W. Directed by S. Sylvan Simon. With Hope Hampton, Randolph Scott, Glenda Farrell, Helen Broderick, Alan Marshall, Samuel S. Hinds. Songs: "Tonight Is the Night," "Riding

Home," "I Gave My Heart Away."

THE FAMILY NEXT DOOR (1939), Universal. B&W. Directed by Joseph Santley. With Hugh Herbert, Joy Hodges, Eddie Quillan, Ruth Donnelly, Juanita Quigley, Cecil Cunningham. Song: "It's a Dog's Life" (lyrics, Harold Adamson).

RIO (1939), Universal. B&W. Directed by John Brahm. With Basil Rathbone, Sigrid Gurie, Victor McLaglen, Robert Cummings, Leo Carillo, Billy Gilbert. Song: "Love Opened My Eyes" (lyrics, Ralph Freed); plus songs by others.

BUCK BENNY RIDES AGAIN (1940), Paramount. B&W. Directed by Mark Sandrich. With Jack Benny, Ellen Drew, Virginia Dale, Lillian Cornell, Eddie "Rochester" Anderson, Phil Harris, Andy Devine, Theresa Harris, Kay Linaker. Songs: "Drums in the Night," "Say It (Over and Over Again)," "My Kind of Country," "My! My!" (lyrics, Frank Loesser). Soundtrack LP: excerpts included in *The Classic Movie Musicals of Jimmy McHugh,* Music Masters JJA-19825.

I CAN'T GIVE YOU ANYTHING BUT LOVE (1940), Universal. B&W. Directed by Albert S. Rogell. With Broderick Crawford, Peggy Moran, Johnny Downs, Warren Hymer, Gertrude Michael, John Sutton, Jessie Ralph, Horace MacMahon. Song: "I Can't Give You Anything But Love, Baby" (lyrics, Dorothy Fields); plus songs by others.

DOWN ARGENTINE WAY (1940), Twentieth Century-Fox. Color. Directed by Irving Cummings. With Don Ameche, Betty Grable, Carmen Miranda, Charlotte Greenwood, the Nicholas Brothers. Song: "The South American Way" (lyrics, Al Dubin); plus songs by others. Soundtrack LP: Caliban 6003 (with *Tin Pan Alley*).

YOU'LL FIND OUT (1940), RKO Radio. B&W. Directed by David Butler. With Kay Kyser, Boris Karloff, Peter Lorre, Bela Lugosi, Helen Parrish, Ginny Simms, Harry Babbitt, Ish Kabibble, Sully Mason, Alma Kruger. Songs: "I'd Know You Anywhere," "You've Got Me This Way," "I've Got a One-Track Mind," "Don't Think It Ain't Been Charming," "Like the Feller Once Said," "(Ting-a-Ling) The Bad Humor Man" (lyrics, Johnny Mercer). (Studio recordings of some songs by Kay Kyser and his Orchestra, for Columbia, long out of print.) Videocassette: Budget video.

YOU'RE THE ONE (1941), Paramount. B&W. Directed by Ralph Murphy. With Orrin Tucker, Bonnie Baker, Lillian Cornell, Jerry Colonna, Albert Dekker, Edward Everett Horton. Songs: "You're the One for Me," "Strawberry Lane," "I Could Kiss You for That," "The Yogi (Who Lost His Will Power)," "Gee, I Wish I'd Listened to My Mother," "My Resistance Is Low" (lyrics, Johnny Mercer); plus songs by others.

SEVEN DAYS LEAVE (1942), RKO Radio. B&W. Directed by Tim Whelan. With Lucille Ball, Victor Mature, Ginny Simms, Harold Peary, Peter Lind Hayes, Ralph Edwards, Arnold Stang, Freddy Martin and his Orchestra, Les Brown and his Orchestra. Songs: "Can't Get Out of This Mood," "Soft-hearted," "Please, Won't You Leave My Girl Alone?," "I Get the Neck of the Chicken," "Puerto Rico," "You Speak My Language" (lyrics, Frank Loesser).

TRUE TO THE ARMY (1942), Paramount. B&W. Directed by Albert S. Rogell. With Judy Canova, Allan Jones, Ann Miller, Jerry Colonna, Clarence Kolb, Rod Cameron. Song: "I Can't Give You Anything But Love, Baby" (lyrics, Dorothy Fields); plus songs by others.

STRICTLY IN THE GROOVE (1942), Universal. B&W. Directed by Vernon Keays. With Leon Errol, Mary Healy, Richard Davies, Ozzie Nelson and his Orchestra, Grace McDonald, Tim Ryan, Charles Lang, Franklin Pangborn, Martha Tilton, Jimmy Wakely Trio, the Dinning Sisters. Song: "Ridin' Home" (lyrics, Harold Adamson); plus songs by others.

IS EVERYBODY HAPPY? (1943), Columbia. B&W. Directed by Charles Barton. With Ted Lewis, Bob Haymes, Nan Wynn, Larry Parks, Lynn Merrick. Song: "On the Sunny Side of the Street" (lyrics, Dorothy Fields); plus songs by others.

HAPPY GO LUCKY (1943), Paramount. B&W. Directed by Curtis Bernhardt. With Dick Powell, Mary Martin, Betty Hutton, Eddie Bracken, Rudy Vallee, Mabel Paige, Clem Bevans. Songs: "Happy Go Lucky," "Murder, He Says," "Let's Get Lost," "Fuddy-Duddy Watchmaker," "Sing a Tropical Song" (lyrics, Frank Loesser); plus song by others. Soundtrack LP: excerpts included in *The Classic Movie Musicals of Jimmy McHugh,* Music Masters JJA-19825.

STORMY WEATHER (1943), Twentieth Century-Fox. B&W. Directed by Andrew Stone. With Bill Robinson, Lena Horne, Eddie "Rochester" Anderson, Fats Waller, Ada Brown, Katherine Dunham dancers, Cab Calloway and his Orchestra. Song: "Diga Diga Doo" (lyrics, Dorothy Fields); plus songs by others.

HERS TO HOLD (1943), Universal. B&W. Directed by Frank Ryan. With Deanna Durbin, Joseph Cotten, Charles Winninger, Evelyn Ankers, Nella Walker. Song: "Say a Prayer for the Boys Over There" (lyrics, Herb Magidson); plus songs and arias by others.

NOBODY'S DARLING (1943), Republic. B&W. Directed by Anthony Mann. With Mary Lee, Gladys George, Louis Calhern, Jackie Moran, Lee Patrick, Marcia Mae Jones. Song: "On the Sunny Side of the Street" (lyrics, Doro-

thy Fields); plus songs by others.

AROUND THE WORLD (1943), RKO Radio. B&W. Directed by Allan Dwan. With Kay Kyser, Joan Davis, Mischa Auer, Harry Babbitt, Georgia Carroll, Ish Kabibble, Sully Mason, Marcy McGuire. Songs: "Don't Believe Everything You Dream," "Candlelight and Wine," "They Chopped Down the Old Apple Tree," "He's Got a Secret Weapon," "Great News in the Making," "Roodle-de-Doo," "A Moke from Shamokin" (lyrics, Harold Adamson).

HIGHER AND HIGHER (1943), RKO Radio. B&W. Directed by Tim Whelan. With Michele Morgan, Jack Haley, Frank Sinatra, Leon Errol, Marcy McGuire, Mel Tormé, Victor Borge, Mary Wickes, Paul and Grace Hartman, Dooley Wilson. Songs: "I Couldn't Sleep a Wink Last Night," "A Lovely Way to Spend an Evening," "The Music Stopped," "It's a Most Important Affair," "Higher and Higher," "You're on Your Own," "Minuet in Boogie," "I Saw You First," "Today I'm a Debutante" (lyrics, Harold Adamson); plus songs by others. Soundtrack LP: Hollywood Soundstage 411. Videocassette: Blackhawk.

MOON OVER LAS VEGAS (1944), Universal. B&W. Directed by Jean Yarbrough. With Anne Gwynne, David Bruce, Barbara Jo Allen (Vera Vague), Connie Haines, Lillian Cornell, the Sportsmen, Gene Austin, Vivian Austin. Song: "A Touch of Texas" (lyrics, Frank Loesser); plus songs by others.

TWO GIRLS AND A SAILOR (1944), MGM. B&W. Directed by Richard Thorp. With Van Johnson, June Allyson, Gloria DeHaven, Jose Iturbi, Jimmy Durante, Lena Horne, Gracie Allen, Ben Blue, Virginia O'Brien, Harry James and his Orchestra with Helen Forrest, Xavier Cugat and his Orchestra with Lina Romay. Songs: "My Mother Told Me," "In a Moment of Madness" (lyrics, Ralph Freed); plus songs by others. Soundtrack LP: excerpt included in *The Classic Movie Musicals of Jimmy McHugh,* Music Masters JJA-19825.

FOUR JILLS IN A JEEP (1944), Twentieth Century-Fox. B&W. Directed by William A. Seiter. With Kay Francis, Martha Raye, Carole Landis, Mitzi Mayfair, Dick Haymes, Phil Silvers, Jimmy Dorsey and his Orchestra, Betty Grable, Carmen Miranda, Alice Faye, George Jessel. Songs: "How Blue the Night," "You Send Me," "Crazy Me," "Ohio," "How Many Times Do I Have to Tell You?," "It's the Old Army Game," "You Never Miss a Trick," "Heil Heel Hitler" (lyrics, Harold Adamson); plus songs by others. Soundtrack LP: Hollywood Soundstage 407.

JAM SESSION (1944), Columbia. B&W. Directed by Charles Barton. With Ann Miller, Jess Barker, Alvino Rey and his Orchestra, Jan

Garber and his Orchestra, Teddy Powell and his Orchestra, Glen Gray and his Casa Loma Orchestra, the Pied Pipers with Jo Stafford, Louis Armstrong and his Orchestra, Charlie Barnet and his Orchestra. Song: "Murder, He Says" (lyrics, Frank Loesser); plus songs by others. Soundtrack LP: Hollywood Soundstage 5014 (with *Reveille with Beverly*).

FOLLOW THE BOYS (1944), Universal. B&W. Directed by Edward Sutherland. With George Raft, Vera Zorina, Grace McDonald, Regis Toomey; Dinah Shore, Jeanette MacDonald, Sophie Tucker, the Andrews Sisters, Marlene Dietrich, Orson Welles, Artur Rubinstein, W. C. Fields, other guest stars. Song: "I Feel a Song Coming On" (lyrics, Dorothy Fields, George Oppenheimer); plus songs by others. Soundtrack LP: Hollywood Soundstage HS-5015.

SOMETHING FOR THE BOYS (1944), Twentieth Century-Fox. Color. Directed by Lewis Seiler. With Carmen Miranda, Vivian Blaine, Michael O'Shea, Phil Silvers, Perry Como, Sheila Ryan, Glenn Langan, Judy Holliday (in a bit role). Songs: "In the Middle of Nowhere," "I Wish We Didn't Have to Say Goodnight," "Wouldn't It Be Nice?," "80 Miles Outside Atlanta," "Samba Boogie," "Boom Brachee" (lyrics, Harold Adamson); plus song by others. Soundtrack LP: excerpts included in *The Classic Movie Musicals of Jimmy McHugh*, Music Masters JJA-19825.

BETWEEN TWO WOMEN (1944), MGM. B&W. Directed by Willis Goldbeck. With Van Johnson, Lionel Barrymore, Gloria DeHaven, Marilyn Maxwell, Keenan Wynn, Keye Luke. Song: "I'm in the Mood for Love" (lyrics, Dorothy Fields).

THE PRINCESS AND THE PIRATE (1944), RKO Radio. Color. Directed by David Butler. With Danny Kaye, Virginia Mayo, Victor McLaglen, Walter Brennan, Walter Slezak. Song: "How'd You Like to Kiss Me in the Moonlight?" (lyrics, Harold Adamson). Videocassette: Embassy.

HER LUCKY NIGHT (1945), Universal. B&W. Directed by Edward Lilley. With the Andrews Sisters, Martha O'Driscoll, Noah Beery Jr., Grady Sutton, Eddie Acuff. Song: "Sing a Tropical Song" (lyrics, Frank Loesser); plus songs by others.

NOB HILL (1945), Twentieth Century-Fox. Color. Directed by Henry Hathaway. With George Raft, Joan Bennett, Vivian Blaine, Peggy Ann Garner, B. S. Pully, Rory Calhoun, the Three Swifts. Songs: "I Walked In (With My Eyes Wide Open)," "I Don't Care Who Knows It," "Touring San Francisco," "Parts of the U.S.A." (lyrics, Harold Adamson). Soundtrack LP: excerpt included in *The Classic Movie*

Musicals of Jimmy McHugh, Music Masters JJA-19825.

RADIO STARS ON PARADE (1945), RKO Radio. B&W. Directed by Leslie Goodwins. With Wally Brown, Alan Carney, Ralph Edwards, Frances Langford, Skinnay Ennis and his Orchestra, Rufe Davis, Don Wilson, the Town Criers. Song: "I Couldn't Sleep a Wink Last Night" (lyrics, Harold Adamson); plus songs by others.

BRING ON THE GIRLS (1945), Paramount. Color. Directed by Sidney Lanfield. With Veronica Lake, Eddie Bracken, Sonny Tufts, Marjorie Reynolds, Alan Mowbray, Johnny Coy, Yvonne de Carlo (in a bit role), Spike Jones and his Orchestra. Songs: "Bring on the Girls," "It Could Happen to Me," "How Would You Like to Take My Picture?," "Uncle Sammy Hit Miami," "You Moved Right In," "I'm Gonna Hate Myself in the Morning" (lyrics, Harold Adamson); plus songs by others.

DOLL FACE (1945), Twentieth Century-Fox. B&W. Directed by Lewis Seiler. With Vivian Blaine, Carmen Miranda, Perry Como, Dennis O'Keefe, Martha Stewart. Songs: "Hubba, Hubba, Hubba (Dig You Later)," "Here Comes Heaven Again," "Someone Is Walking in My Dream," "Chico Chico," "Red, Hot and Beautiful" (lyrics, Harold Adamson). Soundtrack LP: excerpts included in *The Classic Movie Musicals of Jimmy McHugh*, Music Masters JJA-19825.

SWING PARADE OF 1946 (1945), Monogram. B&W. Directed by Phil Karlson. With Gale Storm, Phil Regan, Connie Boswell, the Three Stooges, Will Osborne and his Orchestra, Louis Jordan and his Orchestra. Song: "On the Sunny Side of the Street" (lyrics, Dorothy Fields); plus songs by others.

FREDDIE STEPS OUT (1946), Monogram. B&W. Directed by Arthur Dreifuss. With Freddie Stewart, June Preisser, Frankie Darro, Jackie Moran, Ann Rooney, Noel Neill. Song: "Don't Blame Me" (lyrics, Dorothy Fields); plus songs by others.

DO YOU LOVE ME? (1946), Twentieth Century-Fox. Color. Directed by Gregory Ratoff. With Maureen O'Hara, Dick Haymes, Harry James and his Orchestra, Reginald Gardiner, B. S. Pully, Chick Chandler; Betty Grable (in a guest bit). Song: "I Didn't Mean a Word I Said" (lyrics, Harold Adamson); plus songs by others.

PEOPLE ARE FUNNY (1946), Paramount. B&W. Directed by Sam White. With Jack Haley, Helen Walker, Rudy Vallee, Ozzie Nelson, Art Linkletter, Frances Langford, the Vagabonds. Song: "I'm in the Mood for Love" (lyrics, Dorothy Fields); plus songs by others.

CALENDAR GIRL (1947), Republic. B&W. Directed by Allan Dwan. With Jane Frazee, William Marshall, Kenny Baker, Victor

McLaglen, Gail Patrick, Irene Rich, Franklin Pangborn. Songs: "A Lovely Night to Go Dreaming," "Calendar Girl," "Have I Told You Lately?," "New York's a Nice Place to Visit," "Let's Have Some Pretzels and Beer," "A Bluebird Is Singing to Me," "At the Fireman's Ball" (lyrics, Harold Adamson).

HIT PARADE OF 1947 (1947), Republic. B&W. Directed by Frank McDonald. With Eddie Albert, Constance Moore, Joan Edwards, Gil Lamb, Woody Herman and his Orchestra, Bob Nolan and the Sons of the Pioneers; Roy Rogers and Trigger. Songs: "I Guess I'll Have That Dream Right Away," "Couldn't Be More in Love," "The Customer Is Always Wrong," "Chiquita from Santa Anita," "Is There Anyone Here from Texas?," "The Cats Are Going to the Dogs" (lyrics, Harold Adamson); plus songs by others.

TWO BLONDES AND A REDHEAD (1947), Columbia. B&W. Jean Porter, Jimmy Lloyd, Judy Clark, June Preisser, Tony Pastor and his Orchestra. Song: "On the Sunny Side of the Street" (lyrics, Dorothy Fields); plus songs by others.

SMASH-UP (1947), Universal. B&W. Directed by Stuart Heisler. With Susan Hayward, Lee Bowman, Marsha Hunt, Eddie Albert, Carleton Young. Songs: "Life Can Be Beautiful," "Hush-a-Bye Island," "I Miss That Feeling" (lyrics, Harold Adamson). Soundtrack LP: excerpt included in *The Classic Movie Musicals of Jimmy McHugh*, JJA-19825; also two excerpts included in *Susan Hayward*, Legends 1000/3.

IF YOU KNEW SUZIE (1948), RKO Radio. B&W. Directed by Gordon M. Douglas. With Eddie Cantor, Joan Davis, Bobby Driscoll, Allyn Joslyn, Sheldon Leonard, Charles Dingle. Songs: "Livin' the Life of Love," "My How the Time Goes By," "What Do I Want With Money?" (lyrics, Harold Adamson).

BIG CITY (1948), MGM. B&W. Directed by Norman Taurog. Directed by Alfred W. Green. With Margaret O'Brien, Robert Preston, George Murphy, Danny Thomas, Betty Garrett, Lotte Lehmann. Song: "Don't Blame Me" (lyrics, Dorothy Fields); plus songs by others.

A DATE WITH JUDY (1948), MGM. Color. Directed by Richard Thorpe. With Wallace Beery, Jane Powell, Elizabeth Taylor, Carmen Miranda, Robert Stack, Leon Ames, Scotty Beckett, Xavier Cugat and his Orchestra. Song: "It's a Most Unusual Day" (lyrics, Harold Adamson); plus songs by others.

MAKE-BELIEVE BALLROOM (1949), Columbia. B&W. Directed by Joseph Santley. With Frankie Laine, Nat King Cole, Jerome Courtland, Ruth Warrick, Virginia Welles, Adele Jurgens, Kay Starr, Toni Harper, the Sportsmen, Jimmy Dorsey and his Orchestra,

Gene Krupa and his Orchestra, Jan Garber and his Orchestra, Charlie Barnet and his Orchestra. Song: "On the Sunny Side of the Street" (lyrics, Dorothy Fields); plus songs by others.

ON THE SUNNY SIDE OF THE STREET (1951), Columbia. B&W. Directed by Richard Quine. With Frankie Laine, Terry Moore, Billy Daniels, Audrey Long, Jerome Courtland, Toni Arden, Dick Wesson, Lynn Bari, William Tracy. Song: "On the Sunny Side of the Street" (lyrics, Dorothy Fields); plus songs by others.

HIS KIND OF WOMAN (1951), RKO Radio. B&W. Directed by John Farrow. With Robert Mitchum, Jane Russell, Vincent Price, Tim Holt, Marjorie Reynolds. Song: "You'll Know" (lyrics, Harold Adamson); plus songs by others.

THE STRIP (1951), MGM. B&W. Directed by Leslie Kardos. With Mickey Rooney, Sally Forrest, James Craig, Vic Damone, Monica Lewis, William Demarest, Louis Armstrong and his Orchestra, Earl "Fatha" Hines and his Orchestra, Jack Teagarden and his Orchestra. Song: "Don't Blame Me" (lyrics, Dorothy Fields); plus songs by others.

THE BLUE VEIL (1951), RKO Radio. B&W. Directed by Curtis Bernhardt. With Jane Wyman, Charles Laughton, Joan Blondell, Richard Carlson, Agnes Moorehead. Song: "I Couldn't Sleep a Wink Last Night" (lyrics, Harold Adamson); plus songs by others.

THE RACKET (1951), RKO Radio. B&W. Directed by John Cromwell. With Robert Mitchum, Lizabeth Scott, Robert Ryan, William Talman, Joyce MacKenzie, Robert Hutton, William Conrad. Song: "A Lovely Way to Spend an Evening" (lyrics, Harold Adamson).

THAT'S MY BOY (1951), Paramount. B&W. Directed by Hal Walker. With Dean Martin, Jerry Lewis, Marion Marshall, Polly Bergen, Ruth Hussey, Eddie Mayehoff. Song: "I'm in the Mood for Love" (lyrics, Dorothy Fields); plus songs by others.

MEET DANNY WILSON (1952), Universal. B&W. Directed by Joseph Pevney. With Frank Sinatra, Shelley Winters, Raymond Burr, Alex Nichol, Tony Curtis (in a bit role). Song: "You're a Sweetheart" (lyrics, Harold Adamson); plus songs by others.

LOVELY TO LOOK AT (1952), MGM. Color. Directed by Mervyn Leroy. With Kathryn Grayson, Red Skelton, Howard Keel, Ann Miller, Marge and Gower Champion, Zsa Zsa Gabor. Songs: "Lovely to Look At" (collaboration with Dorothy Fields, Jerome Kern); plus songs by others.

SO THIS IS PARIS? (1954), Universal. Color. Directed by Richard Quine. With Tony Curtis, Gloria DeHaven, Gene Nelson, Corrine Calvet, Paul Gilbert, Allison Hayes. Song: "I Can't Give

You Anything But Love, Baby" (lyrics, Dorothy Fields); plus songs by others.

BRING YOUR SMILE ALONG (1955), Columbia. B&W. Directed by Blake Edwards. With Constance Towers, Frankie Laine, Keefe Brasselle, William Leslie, Mario Siletti. Song: "Don't Blame Me" (lyrics, Dorothy Fields); plus songs by others.

THE BENNY GOODMAN STORY (1955), Universal. B&W. Directed by Valentine Davies. With Steve Allen, Donna Reed, Berta Gersten, Herbert Anderson, Sammy Davis Jr., Harry James, Martha Tilton, Gene Krupa, Lionel Hampton, Ziggy Elman, Ben Pollack, Teddy Wilson, Edward "Kid" Ory. Song: "On the Sunny Side of the Street" (lyrics, Dorothy Fields); plus songs by others. Soundtrack LP: Decca 8252-3 (withdrawn).

THE EDDY DUCHIN STORY (1956), Columbia. Color. Directed by George Sidney. With Tyrone Power, Kim Novak, Victoria Shaw, James Whitmore. Song: "Exactly Like You" (lyrics, Dorothy Fields); plus songs by others. LP: MCA VIM-7215 (with Carmen Cavallaro, who dubbed the soundtrack piano).

HOME BEFORE DARK (1958), Warner Brothers. B&W. Directed by Mervyn Leroy. With Jean Simmons, Dan O'Herlihy, Rhonda Fleming, Efrem Zimbalist Jr. Song: "Home Before Dark" (lyrics, Sammy Cahn).

THE HELEN MORGAN STORY (1957), Warner Brothers. B&W. Directed by Michael Curtiz. With Ann Blyth, Paul Newman, Richard Carlson, Alan King. Songs: "I Can't Give You Anything But Love, Baby," "On the Sunny Side of the Street" (lyrics, Dorothy Fields); plus songs by others.

ASK ANY GIRL (1959), MGM. Color. Directed by Charles Walters. With Shirley MacLaine, David Niven, Rod Taylor, Gig Young, Jim Backus. Song: "I'm in the Mood for Love" (lyrics, Dorothy Fields); plus songs by others.

A PRIVATE'S AFFAIR (1959), Twentieth Century-Fox. Color. Directed by Raoul Walsh. With Sal Mineo, Christine Carere, Barbara Eden, Gary Crosby, Terry Moore, Jim Backus. Songs: "Warm and Willing," "The Same Old Army" (collaboration: McHugh, Jay Livingston, Ray Evans); plus songs by others.

JACK THE RIPPER (1959), Embassy. B&W. Directed by Robert Baker. With Monty Berman, Lee Patterson, Eddie Byrne, George Rose. McHugh composed entire musical score, plus title song with Pete Ruggolo. Filmed in Britain.

LET NO MAN WRITE MY EPITAPH (1960), Columbia. B&W. Directed by Philip Leacock. With Burl Ives, Shelley Winters, James Darren, Jean Seberg, Ella Fitzgerald, Ricardo Montalban. Songs: "I Can't Give You Anything But Love, Baby" (lyrics, Dorothy Fields); "Reach for Tomorrow" (lyrics, Ned Washington).

THE GENE KRUPA STORY (1960), Columbia. B&W. Directed by Don Weis. With Sal Mineo, Susan Kohner, James Darren, Susan Oliver, Yvonne Craig, Red Nichols, Buddy Lester. Songs: "On the Sunny Side of the Street," "Exactly Like You" (lyrics, Dorothy Fields); plus songs by others.

WHERE THE HOT WIND BLOWS (1960), Embassy-MGM. Directed by Jules Dassin. With Gina Lollobrigida, Pierre Brasseur, Marcello Mastroianni, Melina Mercouri, Yves Montand, Paola Stoppa. Title song. (Filmed in Italy. TV title: *The Law*).

THOROUGHLY MODERN MILLIE (1967), Universal. Color. Directed by George Roy Hill. With Julie Andrews, Mary Tyler Moore, Carol Channing, James Fox, James Gavin, Beatrice Lillie, Jack Soo, Anthony Dexter, Mae Clarke. Song: "I Can't Believe That You're in Love With Me" (lyrics, Clarence Gaskill); plus songs by others. Soundtrack LP: MCA DL-71500. Videocassette: MCA.

Cole Porter in the 1950s.

COLE PORTER

*F*or several generations Cole Porter has represented the epitome of sophisticated, witty, clever, sometimes risqué American songwriting. Between 1930 and 1960, he pretty much divided his time, professionally, between Broadway and Hollywood. His movie musicals were far less provocative than his Broadway ones—partly to conform with the demands of movie censorship in the '30s, '40s, and '50s. That's not to say, however, that Porter's movie songs lack vitality, pungency, charm, and sometimes sauciness. Among the now-standard pop hits that Porter wrote specifically for films are "I've Got My Eyes on You," "You'd Be So Nice to Come Home To," "In the Still of the Night," "True Love," "I Concentrate on You," and "Don't Fence Me In."

Contrary to the modest roots of many other famous songwriters, Cole Porter was born wealthy and remained socially prominent throughout his life. He also took pleasure in being the best known of America's WASP songwriters—even though he once told Richard Rodgers that the secret of his (Porter's) success was that he knew how to "write Jewish tunes," with a reliance on minor-key melodies typical of the Jewish musical traditions that he believed formed the basis of pre-rock American pop music.

Cole Albert Porter was born in the small, predominantly farming community of Peru, Indiana, on June 9, 1893. His maternal great-grandfather had settled in the town a few years after the War of 1812 and built up a sizable estate through farming and merchandising. His son (Cole's grandfather), J. O. Cole, left Indiana temporarily while in his twenties to make his own fortune during the California Gold Rush. J. O. did just that, parlaying a small general store near Maryville, California, into other profitable business investments. J. O. returned to Peru, Indiana, in the 1850s, where he opened a brewery and a cold-storage company. His fortune grew steadily from their profits and from investments in midwestern timberland and West Virginian coal and gas. By the time J. O.'s very independent-minded daughter Kate married Samuel Fenwick Porter, a Peru druggist of limited means, the Coles were one of the wealthiest and most powerful families in Indiana.

Cole Porter would be the only child of Kate and Samuel Porter. Because of this, and also because of fragile health as an infant, he was overindulged by both his mother and grandfather. At an early age, he not only had private tutors but began music lessons. Although the self-made, crusty J. O. frowned on men indulging the arts, Cole's mother insisted on his studying them in line with her notion of upper-class refinement. Cole was about age ten when he wrote a brief piano piece titled "Song of the Birds" and dedicated it to his mother. A year later his mother paid for the publishing of another piano piece, "Bobolink Waltz," and happily distributed some one hundred copies to friends and relatives.

Cole's mother also balked at J. O.'s plans to "toughen up" her son by sending him to a military school. Instead, he was sent to the prestigious Eastern prep school Worcester Academy, in Massachusetts. Porter quickly became one of the academy's most popular students—in large part because he was the owner of an upright piano in his living quarters, on which he loved to play and sing popular tunes for his classmates' entertainment.

From Worcester, Porter went to Yale. Though he did not do as well academically during his four years at Yale as he had at prep school, he was a star socially and musically. He became a football cheerleader and a member of such clubs and organizations as The Whiffenpoofs, the Glee Club, the Pundits, the Dramatic Association, the Corinthian Yacht Club, and the Grill Room Grizzlies. As a sophomore he pledged one of the top fraternities on campus (Delta Kappa Epsilon), and as a junior he was tapped for the most socially prestigious of Yale's influential secret societies, Scroll and Key. His personal charm and wit enabled him to overcome both a lisp and short height (5′ 6″), to become a "big man on campus" in just about every respect except the academic.

In the fall of his sophomore year at Yale, Porter submitted an entry in a football-song competition. His "Bingo Eli Yale" not only won the contest, but also became the rage of the campus. He followed it up with another ("Bulldog, Bulldog, Eli Yale"), which also became a Yale classic. Porter was soon being invited to write and help produce college shows. Among his classmates performing in some of them: E. Montillion Woolley, who, as Monty Woolley, later became a Broadway and Hollywood star as well as a lifelong friend of Porter's.

New Haven was not quite a two hours' train ride from New York, and so Porter took in as many Broadway shows as he could, especially the musicals. In the process, he also widened the number of society friends he knew in New York and Long Island.

Following his graduation from Yale, Porter, at his grandfather's insistence, enrolled in the Harvard Law School. But an invitation from some of his former Yale buddies to write another show for the Yale Dramatic Association brought an abrupt end to his law studies. That show's success also encouraged one of Porter's New York society friends to introduce him to composers Jerome Kern and Sigmund Romberg, with an eye toward getting him launched on Broadway. In 1915 a Porter song, "Esmeralda," was used in a Romberg show, *Hands Up.* A few months later another Porter song, "Two Big Eyes," was similarly interpolated into Kern's *Miss Information.* Neither show ran long on Broadway, but the experience was enough to convince Porter that he wanted a future in musical comedy, not the law.

With his former Harvard roommate, T. Lawrason Riggs, Porter wrote both the music and lyrics for a show called *America First,* which spoofed the flag-waving musicals of George M. Cohan. Through wealthy friends, they were able to get it produced, but it was roundly panned by most of the New York critics when it opened on March 27, 1916. A few reviews singled out some of Porter's lyrics for praise, plus the performances of Clifton Webb and a few other cast members. But otherwise the critics made it clear that the type of show with which Porter had been delighting college audiences and alumni groups wasn't good enough for Broadway.

The disastrous reception of *America First* affected Porter and coauthor Riggs differently. Riggs foreswore ever again working on Broadway; he later converted to Roman Catholicism and became a priest (including a period as Yale's Catholic chaplain). As for Porter, for years he encouraged stories (picked up in numerous biographies and profiles) that he fled to Paris and from there joined the French Foreign Legion in North Africa. But one Porter biographer, Charles Schwartz, discredits the Foreign Legion tale. "It was entirely fabricated," says Schwartz—part of "an unmistakably maudlin and overdramatic streak" that Schwartz cites as "particularly noticeable in some of his more sentimental lyrics as well as in his (lifelong) need to make exaggerated claims." There *is* evidence, however, that in Paris during this period Porter was associated with an organization, founded by an American socialite, that helped distribute food supplies in wartime France.

Toward the end of the war, Porter met Linda Lee Thomas, the wealthy former wife of a socially prominent American publisher. She was eight years older than Porter, beautiful, sophisticated, and chic. Although Porter's homosexual preferences were no secret among his friends, Linda and Porter became inseparable and they were married soon after the war's end. To quote biographer Schwartz again: "It would be naive to think that Linda was not aware of Cole's sexual leanings. Since both were highly liberated people ahead of their times in terms of sexual mores, one must assume that Linda essentially accepted Cole on his own terms, though both were discreet enough not to make a big issue of it."

Although Porter and his wife were each wealthy enough just to lead a lavishly comfortable, predominantly social life shuttling between Europe and the United States, Linda is generally credited with being the driving force in keeping his musical career going. She not only encouraged him to take lessons with the French composer Vincent d'Indy at the Schola Cantorum in Paris, but also arranged for leading lights in the theatrical and musical worlds to perform at the sumptuous parties she and Porter hosted in Paris, Venice, and on the Riviera. Among their guests: Noel Coward, Beatrice Lillie, Cecil Beaton, Tallulah Bankhead, Mary Garden, Igor Stravinsky, and Artur Rubinstein —in addition, occasionally, to such world figures as the Aga Khan and England's Prince of Wales (later King Edward VIII, who abdicated and became the Duke of Windsor).

In 1923, Porter was invited by the director of the Ballet Suédoise (Swedish Ballet) to compose the score for a ballet, *Within the Quota,* that the company could take on an American tour. The ballet was well received in Paris, but it was overshadowed by Darius Milhaud's strongly jazz-influenced *The Creation of the World,* which premiered on the same program and which has gone on to become Milhaud's best-known work. The American critics, some weeks later, were rough on Porter's score at its New York premiere on November 28, 1923—just two months before the premiere of Gershwin's *Rhapsody in Blue.*

After the mixed reception for *Within the Quota,* in contrast to the sensational success of Gershwin's *Rhapsody,* Porter never again wrote a "serious" instrumental work—although he occasionally expressed unabashed envy of a number of serious composers with whom he came into social or professional contact. Instead, Porter decided to concentrate on his first love: Broadway musical comedy.

Porter's big Broadway breakthrough came in 1928 with *Paris* (with Irene Bordoni). That show's biggest hit, "Let's Do It (Let's Fall in Love)," became almost the archetypal Cole Porter song for the next several decades—clever, smart, witty, risqué, and melodically appealing. In short order, *Paris* was followed in 1929 by *Fifty Million Frenchmen* (directed by Monty Woolley) and *Wake Up and Dream.* Among their songs: "What Is This Thing Called Love?" "I Loved Him But He Didn't Love Me," "You Do Something to Me," "You've Got That Thing," and "Find Me a Primitive Man."

As Porter's fame and stature skyrocketed on Broadway, he received a call from Walter Wanger, then production supervisor at the Astoria (Long Island) studios of Paramount. Wanger had been a production assistant for Porter's ill-fated *America First* in 1916. He now wanted Porter to write several songs for a movie that Paramount was filming in Astoria, *The Battle of Paris.* Porter eagerly accepted. For the rest of his life, his work would be divided between Broadway and Hollywood musicals, although he would not actually work *in* Hollywood for a substantial period each year until after 1935.

Cole Porter's Major Movies and Their Songs

Porter's first movie venture was not particularly encouraging. *The Battle of Paris* (1929) starred Gertrude Lawrence, then the toast of both Broadway and London, in a piece of romantic fluff that cast her as the partner of a Parisian pickpocket (Charles Ruggles). Complications arise when she falls for one of the pickpocket's victims, a handsome young artist (Walter Petrie). The production was plagued with problems from the start. The initial public rage for talkies had so overtaxed the Astoria facilities that most of the picture had to be shot late at night. On top of that, the director (Robert Florey) and the scriptwriter (Gene Markey) disagreed to such an extent that the crew wanted to change the title to *The Battle of Astoria*. Things got so bad that the director tried to resign from the picture but was held to his contract by Paramount.

Not surprisingly, *The Battle of Paris* ended up a mess. Porter wrote two songs for Lawrence to sing: the perky "Here Comes the Bandwagon" and the insinuating "They All Fall in Love." Neither one made much of an impression on the public, although the latter has survived among those lesser-known Porter songs that remain favorites of some cabaret performers.

Nonetheless, Porter's initiation into moviemaking intrigued him enough to want to do more. His second movie experience, however, would be even less encouraging than his first. Warner Brothers, in adapting *Fifty Million Frenchmen* to the screen in 1931, dropped all the Porter songs, although some of Porter's themes were kept as instrumental background. William Gaxton and Helen Broderick repeated their original Broadway roles, but the focus of the movie was shifted to slapstick comedians Olsen and Johnson. The result was not greeted kindly by either critics or audiences.

However, four of Porter's songs from *Fifty Million Frenchmen* made it to the screen in a 1934 two-reel condensation titled *Paree, Paree,* filmed at Warner's Vitaphone studios in Brooklyn by Sam Sax. The fifteen-minute short subject—one of several made by Vitaphone in the mid-'30s pegged to the songs and plots of Broadway musicals—marked Bob Hope's movie debut, and gave him two songs, "You Do Something to Me" and "You've Got That Thing."

In 1931 one of Porter's Broadway songs not only raised a number of critical eyebrows but also ran into nationwide censorship problems. "Love for Sale" was featured in *The New Yorkers,* an only moderately successful show directed by Monty Woolley and starring Jimmy Durante, Hope Williams, and Fred Waring's Orchestra. In the show, Kathryn Crawford originally sang the song as a white streetwalker. When one major theater critic took issue with both the song and its presentation as being in questionable taste, the producers altered the number to make it more acceptable— placing it in a Harlem-nightclub setting, performed by a black singer, which tells something about the theater's racial attitudes in that era. The radio networks, meanwhile, banned the song outright from the airwaves—a ban that was to stand for many years. The ban merely boosted sales of a recording made shortly after the show's premiere by Fred Waring's Orchestra. "Love for Sale" soon became one of Porter's biggest hits. It has long been a pop standard, but for many decades it was used only as an instrumental in the movies.

Porter's next two Broadway shows further reinforced his reputation for irreverent, risqué, sexually oriented yet sophisticatedly handled material—and also for ignoring the hard times of the Depression as he continued to write about the smart life of society's upper crust. *The Gay Divorce* (1932), starring Fred Astaire and Claire Luce, openly spoofed the rigging of corespondents in divorce cases, and *Nymph Errant* (1933), with Gertrude Lawrence and Elisabeth Welch, centered on an uninhibited young lady determined to lose her virginity. As Hollywood increasingly buckled under to local and national censorship groups concerned with movie morality in the early 1930s, it began to look as if Cole Porter's future would never be as bright in Hollywood as it was on Broadway.

When *The Gay Divorce* was turned into a movie in 1934, the impact of the censors was clearly evident. First, the title was changed to *The Gay Divorcée*—to satisfy church arguments that there was nothing gay about a divorce (in the traditional sense of that adjective). Much of the original show's racy satire was toned down, so that the film became essentially a silly confection about romantic misunderstandings.

Perhaps most arbitrary of all, all but one of Porter's Broadway songs were dumped from *The Gay Divorcée*—not for censorship reasons but because the movie's producer didn't like them and preferred to use new songs and dance numbers by other songwriters under contract to the studio. Among the dropped songs that have survived as Porter standards: "I've Got You on My Mind" and "After You, Who?" The one Porter song used in the movie: "Night and Day." It had become a hit soon after *The Gay Divorce* opened on Broadway in late 1932, and it lasted eighteen weeks on *Variety*'s list of the nation's top ten songs, including five weeks in the No. 1 spot.

With all its changes and modifications, *The Gay Divorcée* was a smash hit—thanks to Fred Astaire and Ginger Rogers in their first costarring leads. Audiences that had loved the duo's only dance (to Vincent Youmans's "The Carioca") in 1933's *Flying Down to Rio,* in which they played secondary roles, found their two dances in *The Gay Divorcée* even better. One of these, to Herb Magidson and Con Conrad's "The Continental," is not only uncommonly long for its time (seventeen minutes) but it is also the picture's most elaborate sequence, including lively Busby Berkeley–like variations by some thirty other dancers. "The Continental" won the first Academy Award ever given for Best Song.

But it's the other Astaire-Rogers dance in *The Gay Divorcée*—to Porter's "Night and Day"—that has made the most significant and longest-lasting impact. More than any previous dance number in a movie, "Night and Day" showed how a song and dance could be more than a plot interruption or aside, how it could instead advance the action and express important aspects of character. As dance critic Arlene Croce has written in her definitive *The Fred Astaire and Ginger Rogers Book,* the "Night and Day" sequence emerges as "an incomparable dance of seduction," since it's the number in which Rogers (in the movie's plot) "gives in" to the pursuing Astaire and begins to fall in love with him. Taking that image a step further, "Night and Day" can be called the number by which Fred Astaire and Ginger Rogers, together, really seduced the moviegoing public with the magic of their dancing and established the screen persona that was to remain basic to their partnership for the rest of the decade. Ironically, Astaire and Rogers would never again appear together in a Cole Porter musical (although Astaire would, with other partners).

The same year that Astaire and Rogers were making movie history with *The Gay Divorcée*—and, in the process, helping to save RKO Radio from bankruptcy in those Depression-plagued years—Porter wrote six songs for a movie that Fox Studios planned to make in 1935, *Adios Argentina.* But before shooting could start, Fox's financial problems caused the picture to be cancelled. (Founder William Fox, under investigation on stock-manipulation charges, had been ousted from the studio and negotiations had begun for the merger of Fox with Darryl F. Zanuck's Twentieth Century Pictures, which became official on May 29, 1935.)

All but one of the songs Porter wrote for *Adios Argentina* remain unpublished. The exception is "Don't Fence Me In." The film's projected producer, Lou Brock, liked a poem of that title by a Montana cowboy, Bob Fletcher, and suggested that Porter set it to music for the film. Although Porter customarily wrote both words and music for all his songs, he agreed that the poem was appropriate for the picture's cowboy story and went ahead and acquired the rights from Fletcher for a modest $200. After *Adios Argentina* was scrapped, Porter forgot about "Don't Fence Me In" until 1944, when another producer (Walter Gottlieb) needed a song for Roy Rogers in a guest spot in the all-star wartime revue *Hollywood Canteen.* "Don't Fence Me In" not only filled that bill but also went on to become one of Porter's biggest moneymaking song hits—even though its homespun western lyrics make it just about the most unrepresentative of all the songs the urbane socialite Porter ever wrote.

More typical of Porter's style are the songs that managed to make the transition from Broadway's *Anything Goes* of 1935 to the Paramount film version of 1936—the first of two versions the studio would make (and the one inanely retitled *Tops Is the Limit* for TV showings, to avoid confusion with the later, 1956 version). This time Porter's original score fared better than that of *The Gay Divorce,* but only marginally. Of the show's twelve songs, three are used in their entirety ("I Get a Kick Out of You," "You're the Top," "There'll Always Be a Lady Fair"), one partially (the title song), and one as an instrumental background theme ("All Through the Night"). To these were added six songs of varying quality by three sets of songwriters under contract to the studio at the time (including Richard Whiting, Hoagy Carmichael, and Frederick Hollander).

Although Hollywood's Production Code required considerable laundering of the double entendres of Porter's lyrics and of Lindsay and Crouse's book for *Anything Goes,* much of the saucy spirit of the original show still manages to come through the '36 film version, thanks especially to Ethel Merman. She repeats the role of the brassy nightclub singer Reno Sweeney that she'd played on Broadway—although this time she doesn't get the leading man at the end. With Bing Crosby in William Gaxton's original role as a Wall Street broker, Paramount shifted the character's romantic interest to a prettier ingenue (played by an eighteen-year-old and very blonde Ida Lupino). But otherwise the framework of the show's story was kept—involving the shipboard misadventures of Merman and Crosby when they get entangled with a meek, superstitious conman who's become public enemy No. 13 (Charles Ruggles, in the role played on Broadway by Victor Moore). Since the conman (who is called Moonface Martin) is masquerading on board ship as a clergyman named the Reverend Dr. Moon, some of the movie's lines take on a different kind of satiric edge in the '80s than they had in the '30s.

Musically, the '36 *Anything Goes* begins with Merman singing the first two lines of Porter's title song as she romps past a line of primly costumed chorines. The music then smoothly segues into a strictly instrumental "All Through the Night" as the chorines begin to open a series of doors over which the film's opening titles are superimposed, with the costumes of the door-openers becoming progressively more glamorous and revealing. For the TV release, there's an eleven-second interruption in this visual sequence (but not in the soundtrack) as the title *Tops Is the Limit* is inserted, incongruously superimposed on a dance sequence from the movie's finale. Surprisingly, nothing further is heard of the title song except for a few instrumental bars mixed in with Frederick Hollander and Leo Robin's "Shanghai-Dee-Ho" (an almost excruciating exercise in stereotypical, "slant-eye" clichés) for the picture's finale.

Merman sings all of "I Get a Kick Out of You" in a nightclub setting that is pure '30s Hollywood. She sits perched in a ring-shaped carrier suspended from the ceiling on a series of cables that enable her to glide above the club's audience as she sings. As critic and theater chronicler Ethan Mordden has aptly put it, it's "somebody's very strange anticipation of high-tech camp." Merman croons the song in a more subdued, plaintive manner than usual, with a few modifications of the original lyrics along the way (such as changing references to sniffing cocaine to sniffing "perfume from Spain").

Much later in the movie, Merman and Crosby make a lively duet of Porter's catchy "You're the Top"—but with considerably altered lyrics from the original. These changes have long puzzled me, since the original lyrics are neither suggestive nor off-color. In a few cases, references to Mickey Mouse, "Garbo's salary," "the nimble feet of Fred Astaire," or "the nose on the great Durante" were presumably cut so as not to plug personalities under contract to other movie studios. But all of the song's well-known references to the Colosseum, the Louvre, a Shakespeare sonnet, the tower of Pisa, and the Mona Lisa were scrapped too—to be replaced by cleverly rhymed but not necessarily better (or better-known) references to a V-8 flivver, "Einstein's noodle," a flight in an autogyro, a Gershwin ditty, and the "curves of Dizzy Dean."

Porter finally got a whole movie score to himself with MGM's *Born to Dance* —a lavish musical comedy that more than one reviewer has said should have been titled *Broadway Melody of 1937* because of its similarity in style and content to other productions in that MGM series. Ironically, considering Porter's reputation for slyly risqué, wittily daring material, it would be MGM, the most aristocratic (some would say squarest) of Hollywood's studios, that was the first to use a complete film score by Porter. He responded with a lively, melodically appealing score with (for him) fairly tame lyrics. Only one song's lyrics could possibly be accused of harboring any double entendres for anyone looking for them: "I've Got You Under My Skin," especially as sultrily cooed by the plot's "heavy," Virginia Bruce. But most clean-minded audiences took the lyrics innocently enough, as just an expression of the singer's infatuation, and "I've Got You Under My Skin" quickly became the first of the songs from *Born to Dance* to go onto radio's *Your Hit Parade,* where it lasted twelve weeks.

Another *Born to Dance* ballad, "Easy to Love," followed on *Your Hit Parade* about four weeks later, lasting only five weeks, but surviving well beyond that as a Porter standard. The song had been written originally for *Anything Goes,* but was discarded in favor of "All Through the Night." In *Born to Dance* it's introduced by James Stewart, whose singing voice is feeble indeed, though he manages to put the song over ingratiatingly in the shy, easy-going manner that was, at the time, turning him into a popular MGM star.

In *Born to Dance,* Stewart plays a sailor who meets a young dancer, Eleanor Powell, at a lonely-hearts club. Their romance not only undergoes the usual ups and downs of such stories, but also ends with Stewart maneuvering a *42nd Street*–style Broadway break for Powell to replace the temperamental star (Bruce) of a big musical. Along the way, Powell gets several chances to show off her dazzling tap-dancing skills, if also her one-dimensional acting ability. For two of her dances, Porter provided likeably snappy songs that never became popular but that fit their sequences perfectly: "Rap-Tap on Wood" and "Swingin' the Jinx Away." The latter is the basis for the spectacular finale, in which Powell and dozens of glitteringly costumed dancers tap up,

In Born to Dance, *(1936), one of his few musicals, rising young star James Stewart sang Cole Porter's "Easy to Love" in an easy-going manner to Eleanor Powell.*

Eleanor Powell in "Swingin' the Jinx Away," the finale to Born to Dance. *This sequence was lifted intact and reused in the 1943 film* I Dood It, *as a wartime "economy move."*

down, and across the decks of a glistening white battleship that could have been designed only by an art director whose heart was into Art Deco more than naval realism.

Radio songstress Frances Langford, who had made only a so-so mark in leading roles in two 1935 Paramount musicals *(Every Night at Eight* and *Palm Springs)* plays fourth fiddle in *Born to Dance* to Powell, Bruce, and comedienne Una Merkel, but does the best singing in the picture. Langford gets the opening chorus of "Swingin' the Jinx

Away," a reprise of "Easy to Love," and joins most of the principals in "Hey, Babe, Hey," a cheerfully *oompah*-ed variation on the traditional "East Side, West Side." The able supporting cast also includes Buddy Ebsen and the movie's coscriptwriter Sid Silvers as sailor buddies of Stewart's, and Raymond Walburn as a navy captain straight out of Gilbert and Sullivan.

MGM chieftain Louis B. Mayer was so pleased with *Born to Dance* after its first previews that he promptly signed Porter for another original movie musical—for the then-extraordinary fee of $100,000. Porter first returned to Broadway, however, for *Red, Hot and Blue,* with Ethel Merman, Jimmy Durante, Bob Hope, and Vivian Vance. It introduced "It's Delovely" and "Riding High" to the ranks of Porter hits. But then it was back to Hollywood and MGM.

By now, Porter had come to love the Hollywood life—with its balmy climate and gracious living, its swimming pools and lavish dinner parties, and, not least of all, its busy (though hidden from public view) gay subculture. As biographer Charles Schwartz notes, Porter "made a practice of returning to the movie colony for approximately four to six months a year for the rest of his life—even when he was not involved in film work." But whatever his personal social life, Porter was not one to let it color the songs he wrote for movies. Recognizing the strict censorship standards followed by all the major studios after 1934, he avoided or toned down the risqué elements (usually sexually "straight") that had long colored his Broadway work.

Porter's second MGM musical, *Rosalie* (1937), was an unequivocally clean adaptation of a 1928 Ziegfeld Broadway musical that starred Marilyn Miller, with songs by Sigmund Romberg and George Gershwin. Bafflingly, Louis B. Mayer opted to dump the original score but kept the already outdated book (by Guy Bolton and William Anthony McGuire)—about a princess from a mythical Balkan kingdom who falls in love with a West Point football star. Mayer also assigned coauthor McGuire to produce the movie version, and asked him to interpolate as much salvagable footage as he could from an aborted 1930 filming of the story planned for Marion Davies.

Then MGM incongruously cast Eleanor Powell, a superb dancer but obviously homespun American in manner and personality, as the princess, and Nelson Eddy, an excellent baritone but not even remotely an athletic performer, as the football-hero cadet. At least a few of the supporting players made more sense, including Frank Morgan (who had been in the original Broadway show) and Edna May Oliver as the king and queen of Romanza, and Ray Bolger as a cadet buddy of Eddy's.

The film that finally emerged remains one of the dullest, drippiest, most overproduced spectacles that MGM or anyone else made in the '30s. The plot and the songs are overwhelmed by grandiose, pretentious production numbers—particularly the title number, which one critic described as employing "acres of Hollywood singers, dancers, and extras." (Actually, two thousand were used.)

Behind the scenes, the title song caused Porter no end of grief. He wrote six versions before coming up with one he felt was right—only to have it rejected by Mayer as too highbrow. Exasperated, Porter went home determined to write the corniest seventh version he could. Mayer loved that one and okayed its use. Among his friends, Porter kept disowning the song even after it went on to twelve weeks on *Your Hit Parade*—until Irving Berlin convinced him to "never hate a song that's sold half a million copies."

Rosalie *(1937) used more singers, dancers, and extras than any musical to its time. Here is Eleanor Powell with just a portion of them in the big production number to Porter's title song.*

There were also problems at first with the movie's other eventual song hit, "In the Still of the Night." Nelson Eddy didn't like its long, unorthodox, 72-measure refrain, and complained that it didn't fall comfortably for his voice. This time Porter fought back and sought out Mayer's help to keep the song in the film—and won. Eddy not only sings "In the Still of the Night" beautifully in *Rosalie,* but also made it part of his concert and radio repertoire for many years thereafter. A few weeks after the movie's release, the song made the No. 10 spot on *Your Hit Parade,* but for just one week before it disappeared completely from the list. Yet over the years "In the Still of the Night" has held its own as a Porter standard—certainly remaining much more popular than "Rosalie" itself.

If Mozart, Beethoven, and Wagner could reuse the themes of one work in another, Porter saw no reason why he couldn't quote from himself too. He does just that in *Rosalie*'s "I've a Strange New Rhythm in My Heart," which openly incorporates part of "Night and Day." Eleanor Powell sings and dances the catchy number with her usual flair. The rest of the score, however, is strictly routine, including "Spring Love Is in the Air" (sung by the beautiful Hungarian mezzo-soprano Ilona Massey, in her film debut), "To Love or Not to Love" (sung by Eddy), and "Why Should I Care?" (sung by Frank Morgan).

The discord that plagued much of the production of *Rosalie* spread to Porter's home life in 1937. His wife, Linda, became increasingly alienated by Porter's extracurricular escapades and left suddenly for their Paris home without him. Several months passed before Porter completed his work on *Rosalie* and sailed for Paris to join her. But relations between them remained cool, as Porter spent most of the summer of 1937 on a walking tour of Germany, Austria, Italy, and Yugoslavia with other friends. In October he returned to New York, without Linda, to start work on a new Broadway musical, *You Never Know* (starring Clifton Webb and Libby Holman).

A few weeks after returning to New York, Porter suffered an accident that was to affect the rest of his life. As he was horseback riding on Long Island, his horse stumbled and fell, crushing both of Porter's legs. For a time doctors feared that the nerve tissue was so damaged that the legs would have to be amputated. But Porter's wife, reached by transatlantic phone, convinced the doctors to hold off any such extreme action until she could return from Paris. Once back in New York, she fought to have the doctors save Porter's legs—arguing that, for anyone so concerned with his appearance, an amputation would destroy his will to live. The doctors warned both Porter and his wife that the alternative would be a painful process of numerous operations to try to rebuild his legs—with very iffy chances for success. Porter decided to take that chance. For the next twenty years, he would continue to turn out Broadway and Hollywood scores despite frequent bouts of pain and serious disability. Meanwhile, Porter reminded friends that the accident had its bright side—that it had reunited him with his wife. She would remain with him through the best and worst of the next seventeen years, until her death in 1954.

In 1938 Porter resumed his career from his hospital bed, completing the score for *You Never Know*—which flopped, but which did produce one hit song, "At Long Last Love." A few months later, Porter began work on another Broadway show, *Leave It to Me,* a spoof about an American diplomat in Moscow, starring Victor Moore, William Gaxton, and Sophie Tucker, with then-unknowns Mary Martin and Gene Kelly in lesser roles. This one was a hit—and it made a star of Mary Martin. Playing a young lady stranded in a Siberian railroad station wearing only a fur coat, Martin stopped the show nightly with her teasing, mock-striptease rendition of "My Heart Belongs to Daddy." It was a song that, for the first time since his accident, proved that Porter was still at the top of his form with clever, witty, slyly suggestive songwriting.

Martin went on to Hollywood the following year, and got to sing "My Heart Belongs to Daddy" in two different movies over the next six years. In the first, Paramount's *Love Thy Neighbor* (1940), starring Jack Benny and Fred Allen, the song is made part of a stage revue within the movie. Martin is shown getting out of a limousine to enter a nightclub, dressed in a shortie fur coat (similar to the white chinchilla she wore in *Leave It to Me*), but this time covering a sequined evening gown. She sings two choruses of the song in a perky but fairly conventional, high-class–gold digger style, as she brushes off one after another black-tied suitors. In Warner Brothers's *Night and Day* (1946), the Porter biopic (to be further discussed on page 169), Martin appears in a similar white fur coat and hat, but this time in Technicolor, and bare legged as she sits atop a huge cake of ice, surrounded by fur-hooded Eskimos. She sings only one chorus of the song, with much more slyly insinuating inflections than in *Love Thy Neighbor,* and in a more swinging arrangement. Toward the end, she sheds her fur muff and finally her coat, to reveal herself in a pale green swimsuit that causes the lineup of Eskimos to faint dead away. The *Night and Day* version, though less complete than the one in *Love Thy Neighbor,* remains the best movie example of the early, saucy Mary Martin—before she became the prim and proper TV hostess of the PBS *Over Easy* series that she has recently been.

By mid-1939, Porter was again getting around fairly actively, albeit painfully, with the help of leg braces and a cane—dividing his time between New York, Hollywood, and Europe, with occasional forays to the Caribbean and South America. For his return to MGM in '39, he composed the score for *Broadway Melody of 1940,* the first and only movie to team Hollywood's two greatest dancing stars of the '30s, Fred Astaire and Eleanor Powell. Some of the dance sequences only emphasize their discordant dance styles, and the plot is as hackneyed as they come—about two hoofers (Astaire and George Murphy) in love with the same dancing star (Powell), and how their friendship takes some nasty bumps in the process. Porter's score helps considerably to gloss over these weaknesses, with two new songs, "I've Got My Eyes on You" and "I Concentrate on You," becoming popular hits. But it is the recycled "Begin the Beguine" with which *Broadway Melody of 1940* reaches its most memorable moments.

"Begin the Beguine" had made only a modest impression in the 1935 Broadway money-loser *Jubilee* (a production that had been heavily financed by MGM). Three years later the song had unexpectedly become a pop hit through a swing arrangement for the orchestra of twenty-eight-year-old Artie Shaw. For *Broadway Melody of 1940,* Roger Edens and Bobby Connolly devised an elaborate, nine-minute, four-part production number, filmed in the most elegantly glittering MGM manner. The song is introduced with a gently swaying beat against a starry, tropical setting by sultry-voiced Lois Hudnett, with an offstage chorus behind her. As the song unfolds, several dozen long-gowned dancers go through undulations that look like a cross between a Martha Graham–type dance and a Hawaiian hula—certainly not very "beguine-ish" (a beguine being a sort of kissing cousin to the rhumba and Caribbean in origin). Powell joins the dancers and, for a minute or so, it looks as if we're in for some more pretentious posturing, arm flailing, and a few high kicks—until Astaire appears from the far recesses of the vast set and joins Powell as the other dancers disappear. Astaire and Powell ease into a stunningly executed, very beguine-flavored dance across an enormous, black-mirrored floor that reflects the stars above as well as the two dancers' images in some of the era's most unforgettably dazzling, crisp, black-and-white cinematography.

The magic of the sequence is suddenly interrupted by an interlude of sheer camp, as a quartet (listed in the picture's credits as the Mood Maids) enter in gaudy costumes and chirp a chorus of the song in a jazzier style, *à la* the Andrews Sisters. They exit and Astaire and Powell reappear in casual, all-white, modern dress. As the soundtrack shifts into a swing version of "Begin the Beguine" dominated by a clarinet solo (clearly modeled after the Shaw recording), Astaire and Powell begin the sharpest, fast-stepping, show-stopping tap dance any duo has ever put on film. (This last section of the four-part number also provides one of the highlights of MGM's 1972 compilation feature, *That's Entertainment.*)

The rest of *Broadway Melody of 1940* never matches the peaks of the "Begin the

In their only movie together, Broadway Melody of 1940 *(1939), Fred Astaire and Eleanor Powell do one of the sharpest, fastest-stepping tap dances any duo has put on film, to Porter's "Begin the Beguine."*

Mary Martin, in costume for her first (and most sedate) movie version of Porter's "My Heart Belongs to Daddy," in Love Thy Neighbor *(1940).*

Beguine" sequence. Astaire and Murphy, in top hat, white tie, and tails, sing and dance "Please Don't Monkey With Broadway," a catchy number that boosts Broadway as the best part of New York City while taking a few swipes at Brooklyn, Harlem, Yorkville, and other areas. The number ends with Astaire and Murphy using their canes as dueling sabers—in a sort of symbolic forecast of the rivalry that the plot has in store for them.

After singing a chorus of Porter's "I Am the Captain" (based on the traditional "Locked in the Cradle of the Deep"), Powell does another of her military drill-like solos, backed by a corps of sailor-suited dancers who help maneuver her through some snappy acrobatic paces. Astaire's less exciting solo-turn comes with "I've Got My Eyes on You." He sings it to a photo of Powell on a piece of sheet music, while Powell, unseen by Astaire, watches from the sidelines. The song is the only one from the picture that made *Your Hit Parade* (for five weeks).

Another Astaire-Powell dance duet is performed to one of Porter's most "up" romantic ballads, "I Concentrate on You." It's well sung by baritone Douglas MacPhail (in a harlequin costume), but Powell (in a blonde wig and wearing toe shoes) whips halfheartedly through a balletlike routine in which she too obviously avoids going up *en pointe* for more than a second or two. Astaire looks similarly out of place when he joins her for the last part of the dance, as the MGM orchestra and chorus swell up lushly on the soundtrack, adding far more aural than choreographic drama to the number.

Porter's next movie score would also be for Fred Astaire: *You'll Never Get Rich,* the first of two modestly budgeted Columbia musicals costarring Astaire with Rita Hayworth. (The second would have a score by Jerome Kern and Johnny Mercer.) Released just a few months before Pearl Harbor in 1941, it was one of the first major musicals to have a home-front, wartime-preparedness background—with Astaire playing a Broadway dance director who joins the army, thus shifting the strictly routine backstage story to an army camp, with the big, final production number part of an army show.

You'll Never Get Rich gets off to a snappy start with Porter's "Boogie Barcarolle," an instrumental which shifts from a brief, balladlike introduction into a fast-stepping dance by Astaire and several dozen chorines, including Hayworth, to a boogie-woogie beat. The spirited number shows how sharply both Astaire and Porter were attuned to the changing beats of the early '40s.

Of the two first-rate ballads that Porter wrote for *You'll Never Get Rich,* only "So Near and Yet So Far" gets first-rate treatment. Astaire first sings the beguine-flavored song to Hayworth, and then they dance a ballroom-style duet to it. The dance makes artful use of Hayworth's Spanish-dance background, and, for the first time in several movie years, teams Astaire with a versatile partner who could genuinely rival

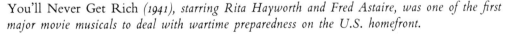

You'll Never Get Rich *(1941), starring Rita Hayworth and Fred Astaire, was one of the first major movie musicals to deal with wartime preparedness on the U.S. homefront.*

Ginger Rogers. The other ballad, "Dream Dancing," is one of Porter's most regrettably neglected gems, a much more buoyant and cheery song than most of those written about dreams. It was cut from the movie, except for use as background music in a scene in which Astaire and Hayworth go dancing in a nightclub. However, an Astaire recording of the song was issued at the time of the picture's release (and is still on several Astaire LPs). Even if "Dream Dancing" had been left in the picture, it would probably have had as little chance of catching on with the public as "So Near and Yet So Far," or any other song from *You'll Never Get Rich,* because broadcast possibilities were then minimal. The film was released during the months when the songs of all ASCAP composers were prohibited from broadcast in a contract dispute between ASCAP (of which Porter was a member) and the broadcasters. And in those days all pop songs, including those from movies, depended on broadcast play and replay to advance their popularity.

The remaining songs of *You'll Never Get Rich* are routine, functional numbers that probably wouldn't have gone very far even without the radio ban. "Shooting the Works for Uncle Sam" is one of those patriotic, march-tempo numbers in which World War II musicals overindulged. As for "The Wedding Cake Cakewalk" finale, it's introduced by Martha Tilton, a former vocalist with Benny Goodman's Orchestra, singing some clever, topical (for '41) Porter lyrics to a so-so melody that ends up quoting from "Night and Day." Then comes an embarrassingly *kitsch-* y dance sequence in which Astaire and Hayworth smile and tap along with a corps of eighty dancers through just about every imaginable B-musical cliché, ending with the stars boogie-woogie-ing atop a giant wedding cake made in the shape of an army tank!

The early '40s also saw movie versions of three of Porter's then-recent Broadway hits: *Panama Hattie* (MGM, 1941), *DuBarry Was a Lady* (MGM, 1943), and *Let's Face It* (Paramount, 1943). None of them bore much resemblance to the high-spirited, often-rowdy originals other than in title and the use of a few Porter songs.

In *Panama Hattie,* Ann Sothern has the role that Ethel Merman played on Broadway, as a brassy nightclub owner who helps foil a spy plot to blow up the Panama Canal. In one of her few disappointing musical-movie appearances, Sothern not only softens the contours of the role, but also takes most of the bite out of it. Although she offers a spirited version of Porter's "I've Still Got My Health" (whose jaunty lyrics fit the show's title-character if not Porter himself at that time), she is much too bland in the duet "Let's Be Buddies," with moppet Jackie Horner. Sothern also recorded an even blander "Make It Another Old-Fashioned, Please," one of Porter's most sophisticated torch songs, but the number (perhaps wisely) got cut out of the final release. Deadpan singer-comedienne Virginia O'Brien, in the principal supporting role that Betty Hutton played on Broadway, does little more than race drably through "Fresh As a Daisy."

The best musical moment in the movie version of *Panama Hattie* comes with an interpolated Porter song, "Just One of Those Things" (from the ill-fated *Jubilee* of 1935). It is sung by Lena Horne, making her MGM debut in one of those musical numbers that, in the 1940s, could be excised (without damage to the plot) in Southern theaters unwilling to present racially mixed entertainment. More deserving of excision, in all parts of the country, were six mostly inferior songs by other songwriters that MGM substituted for the ten Porter songs it cut from the Broadway score for *Panama*

Ann Sothern sings Porter's "Let's Be Buddies" to moppet Jackie Horner in Panama Hattie *(1941).*

Hattie. Most expendable: a rah-rah patriotic number by Burton Lane and Yip Harburg titled "The Son of a Gun Who Picks on Uncle Sam" that even wartime jingoism can't excuse.

Porter's Broadway score for *DuBarry Was a Lady* received even shoddier treatment from MGM, with only three of the show's seventeen songs making the movie version of 1943. This time Merman's original Broadway role went to Lucille Ball, Bert Lahr's to Red Skelton, and, most incongruously of all, Betty Grable's to Virginia O'Brien. The production marked the first Porter musical to be filmed in color. But neither the glitzy production nor some lively musical numbers (most of them by other songwriters) could salvage an essentially boring rewrite of the two-level story—about a nightclub checkroom attendant (Skelton) who accidentally drinks a Mickey Finn and dreams he's Louis XV and that the nightclub owner with whom he's in love (Ball) is Madame DuBarry. Gene Kelly, playing a dancer also in love with Ball, does nicely with the lyrics of Porter's romantic "Do I Love You, Do I?" and the dance that follows it. Later, in the dream, Kelly becomes a revolutionary named The Black Arrow—in a non-Porter sequence that has more than a few anticipations of Kelly's role five years later in Porter's *The Pirate.*

Porter's "Katie Went to Haiti" becomes a swinging number for Tommy Dorsey's Orchestra, with Dick Haymes, Jo Stafford, and the Pied Pipers bouncing the lyrics back and forth in the best early-'40s big-band style. Porter's mock-hillbilly patter song "Friendship," the showstopper of the Broadway production, brings the picture to a spirited close as the principals take turns with the lyrics' jesting rhymes about camaraderie and the value of good friends—a theme with lots of appeal during the war years.

Despite a ridiculous costume, Lena Horne contributed the best musical moment in Panama Hattie *when she sang "Just One of Those Things."*

On Broadway, the wartime *Let's Face It* had been Porter's longest-running show up to that time (547 performances, compared to 420 for runner-up *Anything Goes*). But its success owed more to Danny Kaye's madcap performance than to Porter's music or lyrics. So it wasn't surprising that the '43 movie version kept only two of the show's fifteen songs. The saucy book—about three middle-aged wives who pick up three GIs and go on a spree with them to teach their own philandering husbands a lesson—also got toned down considerably for the movie, even though the roles of the wives were well-cast, with Eve Arden (of the Broadway cast), ZaSu Pitts, and Phyllis Povah. With Bob Hope in the Kaye role, injecting Hope-style topical wartime jokes, there's still a wild and zany flavor to most of the proceedings. But the irrepressible Betty Hutton gets the expanded part of Hope's girlfriend and sails through Porter's "Let's Not Talk About Love" in a rip-roaring fashion that, in contrast to Kaye's way with the song, leaves some of the lyrics completely unintelligible.

While Paramount and MGM were reprocessing (and butchering) his recent Broadway work, Porter wrote an original score for another modestly budgeted Columbia musical that remains among the most misnamed films of the '40s: *Something to Shout About.* Not that there isn't plenty of shouting *in* the picture. Don Ameche, Jack Oakie, William Gaxton, Cobina Wright, Jr., and Veda Ann Borg all apparently took the title literally and actually scream their way through most of the banal dialogue that goes with its backstage plot about Gaxton's attempts to mount a Broadway show. Only Janet Blair, at the time a recent graduate from Hal Kemp's Orchestra, speaks and sings at a bearable decibel level.

Something to Shout About produced one major Porter song hit: "You'd Be So Nice to Come Home To." It's an openly sentimental ballad that hit the bull's-eye with wartime audiences and ended up on radio's *Your Hit Parade* for eighteen weeks in 1943. It's the first song in the movie, and it's tenderly sung by Blair. But the rest of the score goes downhill—although Blair does her best to put across another amiable ballad, "I Always Knew." The opening credits, incidentally, say "Songs by Cole Porter"— perhaps to disassociate Porter from the otherwise uncredited and mundane music that goes beyond the initial melody of two production numbers, "Lotus Blossom" and "Hasta la Vista."

Wartime Hollywood, meanwhile, was also making more profitable use of what might be called recycled Porter. For MGM's *I Dood It* (1943), a whole production number to Porter's "Swinging the Jinx Away" was lifted out of 1936's *Born to Dance* and reused for the later picture's finale. The '40s, of course, were a time when movie revival houses were virtually nonexistent and when TV had not yet come on the scene to run and rerun old movies. So MGM assumed that few moviegoers would notice its wartime "economy move"—since both pictures starred Eleanor Powell, who always seemed to be dancing on the deck of a battleship anyway. MGM's editors even skillfully intercut a few new shots of *I Dood It*'s costar Red Skelton supposedly watching Powell dance the spectacular number.

For Warner Brothers's *Hollywood Canteen* (1944), Porter recycled "Don't Fence Me In" (from the aborted *Adios Argentina* of 1935), this time as a number for cowboy star Roy Rogers. When the song became a big '44 hit, Rogers got Porter's permission to cash in on its popularity by titling one of Rogers's 1945 B westerns for Republic after it—and reprising the song within it. The picture was a hit, helping Rogers keep his place (for the third year in a row) as the No. 1 cowboy star at the box office, and also winning him a place (for the first time) within the top ten moneymaking stars of the year. Porter, of course, benefited handsomely too from the picture's royalties.

With Warner Brothers's *Night and Day* (1946), Cole Porter became another modern American songwriter to be the subject of a movie biography—from the same studio that a year earlier had produced a Gershwin biopic, *Rhapsody in Blue.* As with Gershwin, the relationship to the composer's real life turned out to be strictly coincidental. The idea for a movie about Porter's life reportedly originated with Irving Berlin—not merely as a way to create a movie musical filled with Porter hits, but also as an inspirational story of how Porter had struggled to overcome the terrible injuries to his legs and continued his career. Berlin believed that Porter's spirit in surmounting his accident would have particular application to many wounded or disabled war veterans.

Porter willingly gave his permission for the film, on the condition that he had final script approval. Warners, in turn, paid him $300,000 for the film rights to his life and assigned songwriter-turned-producer Arthur Schwartz as the movie's producer. Porter heartily approved the casting of Cary Grant in the lead, even though any physical resemblance between the two men (particularly in height) was negligible. But, as others have noted, Porter was not the first man to fantasize about having Cary Grant play his life story. Linda Porter also approved the choice of elegant Alexis Smith to portray her. A prominent role was also worked in for Porter's Yale classmate and longtime buddy, Monty Woolley, who, by the 1940s, had become a film star in his own right after Warner's *The Man Who Came to Dinner.*

Porter and Schwartz at first agreed that *Night and Day* should include such performers as Fred Astaire, Ethel Merman, Danny Kaye, Jimmy Durante, Bert Lahr, and Mary Martin doing numbers they had introduced in various Porter musicals. But negotiations for their services bogged down in case after case, sometimes because of conflicting contractual obligations, sometimes because of disagreement over what Warners considered a "reasonable" fee for a guest appearance. The only Porter-requested guest star to sign was Mary Martin, for the previously discussed sequence (page 162) in which she sings "My Heart Belongs to Daddy." In place of the others, several fictionalized composite characters were worked into the script, to be played by Jane Wyman, Eve Arden, Ginny Simms, and several unidentified singers.

The musical numbers they perform in *Night and Day* are, with few exceptions, disappointing in staging and vocal execution. Moreover, the script cavalierly introduces some of Porter's songs with little regard for actual compositional sequence, mixing them up in completely wrong periods of Porter's life. The script goes even further in whitewashing or fictionalizing Porter's private life, particularly a sequence in which he's depicted as a World War I hero. The silliest moment, at least in terms of movie-style clichés, comes when Grant is shown having difficulties composing "Night and Day" and gets help from his adoring Linda (as a wartime nurse) to the nearby "tick, tick, tock of the stately clock" and the "drip, drip, drip of the raindrops" gently sounding on the windowpanes near them. Grant is finally reduced to: "Wait a minute —I think I've got it!" So much for Hollywood's view of the creative processes in songwriting.

Aside from Mary Martin's "My Heart Belongs to Daddy," the only even halfway memorable musical sequences include Monty Woolley's half-sung, half-recited version of part of "Miss Otis Regrets," Eve Arden's teasing way (despite a none-too-convincing French accent) with "I'm Unlucky in Love," and Ginny Simms's velvety crooning of "I've Got You Under My Skin." There's also a spirited Simms-Grant duet of part of "You're the Top" that's memorable as one of the few times Grant sang (and decently, too) in the movies. "Begin the Beguine" gets the biggest production number near the movie's end, featuring Mexican baritone Carlos Ramirez, but its unimaginative Technicolor treatment is no match for the black-and-white magic of MGM's version with Astaire and Powell in *Broadway Melody of 1940*.

Although *Night and Day* was a box-office hit and Porter publicly complimented its makers on several occasions, biographer Charles Schwartz says that Porter privately had many reservations about it. "When the film began to be shown on television years after it had first been released," Schwartz writes, "Cole would watch it at every opportunity so that he could have a good time laughing at the many plot absurdities. . . . Yet considering the numerous fibs about himself that Cole had foisted on an unsuspecting public for decades, one could hardly expect a Hollywood film biography to come any closer to the truth. But then, when you get down to it, Cole wouldn't have wanted the truth told anyway."

If *Night and Day* proved that a mediocre production could be turned into a box-office hit, the next movie for which Porter wrote an original score proved that brilliance on virtually all levels—score, direction, design, casting—could not guarantee a hit at all. When MGM's *The Pirate* did only moderately well on its release in 1948, the MGM brass wrote it off as too sophisticated and arty. Earlier, Louis B. Mayer

Cary Grant was cast as Cole Porter in the 1946 film biography Night and Day. *A prominent role was also created for Porter's Yale classmate and longtime Broadway collaborator, Monty Woolley (center).*

himself reportedly insisted on cutting part of its "Pirate Ballet" as too erotic. Some Southern theaters also cut a dance number by Gene Kelly and the Nicholas Brothers because it featured two blacks dancing as equals with a white man. Little wonder that producer Arthur Freed once called *The Pirate* twenty years ahead of its time. And, indeed, the picture has grown steadily in both critical esteem and popularity in the years since then.

Essentially, *The Pirate* is a fantasy-parody of old-time movie swashbucklers, with one of the wittiest scores Porter ever wrote for the screen, plus some of the most lavish, colorful, imaginative dance routines that either Gene Kelly or MGM had attempted to that time. Kelly plays an itinerant actor-acrobat who decides to woo a maiden (Judy Garland) in a small, nineteenth-century Caribbean town by impersonating the notorious pirate Macoco ("Mack the Black"), with whose exploits she's become romantically fascinated. In the process, Kelly comes up against the real pirate—and saves himself and wins the girl in a climax that could happen only in the movies.

Director Vincente Minnelli not only keeps the sly, ironic story (by S. N. Behrman) moving along brightly, but also does things with color and design that have rarely been equalled. *The Pirate* also marks Judy Garland's transition from the winsome, innocent youngster of earlier pictures to a full-fledged, sophisticated singer-comedienne —even though, in a few scenes, signs of the illnesses that eventually were to disrupt her career are beginning to show in her appearance. But where it really counts, the unique Garland energy and charm are fully there—with many droll, tongue-in-cheek touches of the sort she rarely again got a chance to display so well. Kelly, too, has rarely been better, deliberately caricaturing the flamboyance of such silent-film swashbucklers as Douglas Fairbanks and John Barrymore without ever making his character ridiculous or unlikeable.

Although none of Porter's songs for *The Pirate* became popular hits, the score as a whole is top drawer all the way. "Nina" gets the movie off to a nimble start, as Kelly wanders through the town square flirting with every pretty girl in town, calling them all Nina (because "it's easier that way"). The song leads into a marvelously inventive dance in which Porter and the MGM orchestrators slyly satirize Ravel's *Bolero*. "Mack the Black" is belted out by Garland as a romantic paean to the exploits of Macoco, and a bit later it becomes the basis for the movie's splashy (if no longer erotic) "Pirate Ballet." Garland also gets to sing two gentler ballads which provide the highlights of the score: the wistful "You Can Do No Wrong" and the fervent "Love of My Life" (which understandably provokes the real Macoco into revealing himself). Kelly and Garland bring the movie to a rousing close with a knockabout performance of "Be a Clown," a breezy tribute to the power of comedy both on and off the stage. The number may well be as close as Porter ever came to a philosophy of life in any of his movie songs. (Kelly and Fred Astaire later used "Be a Clown," with additional lyrics by Saul Chaplin, to introduce some sequences in MGM's 1976 compilation feature *That's Entertainment—Part 2*.)

The same year that *The Pirate* was receiving only a lukewarm reception at movie box offices, Broadway audiences were cheering Porter's *Kiss Me, Kate*—the musical comedy now generally rated his greatest single work and certainly his longest-running Broadway hit (1,077 performances). The movie version that came from MGM five years later (minus the comma in the title) was also a big hit. Moreover, it was the first major musical to be filmed in the 3-D process, for which viewers had to wear special glasses, provided by the theaters, in order to get the three-dimensional effect. The 3-D process gave some of the dance movements extra punch, and the tossing of handkerchiefs and other props directly into the camera made some viewers "duck" during some scenes. But the discomfort many felt at having to wear the 3-D glasses for a whole picture doomed the fad fairly quickly, and MGM soon pulled the 3-D *Kiss Me Kate* from circulation and reissued it in a standard version.

Aside from the silliness of all those scenes in which someone throws something into the camera, *Kiss Me Kate* is a knockout of a movie musical—and the most faithful movie adaptation in content, wit, and spirit of all of Porter's Broadway shows. The movie's beginning, however, is completely new. In it, an egotistical actor (Howard Keel) enlists none other than Cole Porter (played, not very realistically, by Ron Randell) to convince the actor's ex-wife (Kathryn Grayson) to join him in Porter's new musical version of Shakespeare's *The Taming of the Shrew*. From then on, the movie generally parallels the show, though sometimes in rearranged continuity, as it deftly weaves two stories—one the backstage battles of the actor and his ex-wife on opening night, the other a condensation (with quite a few liberties) of the Shakespearean comedy they are performing.

Fourteen of the seventeen songs that Porter wrote for *Kiss Me, Kate* are kept, a record among film adaptations of Porter shows—and one number cut from an earlier Porter show is added ("From This Moment On," originally written for 1950's *Out of*

Gene Kelly and Judy Garland sing Porter's "Be a Clown" in the knockabout finale of The Pirate *(1948).*

Kiss Me Kate *(1953) featured one of Porter's best scores and exceptionally spirited performances, not only from Kathryn Grayson and Howard Keel (foreground), but also from (momentarily subdued in the background) Kurt Kazner, Bob Fosse, Bobby Van, Ann Miller, and Tommy Rall.*

This World). Perhaps most surprisingly of all, only a few of the songs' lyrics have been cleaned up for the movie, with any number of typically Porter double entendres coming through.

Kiss Me Kate has more showstopping numbers than almost any other musical from MGM's so-called golden age. Ann Miller has four of them—first flashing her famous legs and some five hundred taps a minute to "Too Darn Hot," then joining Tommy Rall (fresh from American Ballet Theatre) for a stunning duet to "Why Can't You Behave," and, best of all, cavorting heartily with Rall, Bob Fosse, and Bobby Van through "Tom, Dick, and Harry." Miller also holds her own together with Fosse, Rall, Van, Carol Haney, and Jeanne Coyne in the breathtakingly danced "From This Moment On," although that number is really stolen by Fosse and Haney's sizzling middle-section duet. Keenan Wynn and James Whitmore (playing two small-time gangsters trying to collect a gambling debt from Keel) also make the most of one of Porter's most literate (for all its malapropisms) and cleverest songs, "Brush Up Your Shakespeare."

Although not originally written for the screen, *Kiss Me Kate* is still *the* classic Cole Porter movie above all others. Sharing significantly in making everything click are the costumes by Walter Plunkett, the sets of Cedric Gibbons and Urie McCleary, the choreography of Hermes Pan, the music direction of André Previn and Saul Chaplin, and, unexpectedly in light of his uneven track record with musicals, director George Sidney.

In the years between the Broadway and Hollywood versions of *Kiss Me, Kate*, Porter delved into his trunk of unused material to provide incidental songs for several major films. For the MGM comedy *Adam's Rib* (1949), starring Spencer Tracy and Porter's longtime friend Katharine Hepburn, he wrote "Farewell, Amanda"—reworking it from a song written on a 1940 trip to the South Seas and titled "So Long, Samoa." He should have said so long to the tune itself, for it is a decidedly undistinctive addition to the Porter catalog and did nothing for *Adam's Rib*. But the song at least symbolizes Porter's philanthropic bent, for he specified that any profits from it should go to the Damon Runyon Cancer Fund. Hepburn, meanwhile, would work another Porter song into a later Tracy-Hepburn comedy, *The Desk Set* (1957)—this time singing part of "Night and Day" during a party sequence in that picture.

For another longtime friend, Marlene Dietrich, Porter dug out an unused 1927 tune, "The Laziest Gal in Town," for her to perform in *Stage Fright,* a 1950 Alfred Hitchcock melodrama filmed in Britain. Dietrich, lounging elegantly, sings the song as part of a show in which she's appearing within the film's plot—and it remains one of the most deliciously sensual and sultry musical interludes of any of her movies. Dietrich continued to make the song part of her stage appearances for several decades throughout the United States and Europe.

Exactly twenty years after Paramount had produced its first version of *Anything Goes,* the studio released another movie with the same title, one of the same stars (Bing Crosby), and some of Porter's songs. That's as far as any similarity goes between the two versions. The plot of the '56 *Anything Goes* is completely altered to focus on a showbiz team (Crosby, Donald O'Connor) separately signing up a leading lady for a new show, and then trying to untangle the situation as well as their separate romantic involvements. It's all made palatable by some unusually crisp, energetic musical numbers, filmed in Technicolor and VistaVision (Paramount's then-new wide-screen pro-

Marlene Dietrich sings Porter's "The Laziest Gal in Town" in a key scene in Alfred Hitchcock's 1950 melodrama Stage Fright.

cess). As staged alternately by Nick Castle, Ernie Flatt, and Roland Petit, and sung and danced by the two leading ladies, Renée "Zizi" Jeanmaire and Mitzi Gaynor, plus Crosby and O'Connor, the numbers smack more often of the brightness and brassiness of '50s Broadway than of Hollywood.

Although the '56 version of *Anything Goes* uses a few more of Porter's songs than the '36 version, it still mixes them in with songs by others (in this case, James Van Heusen and Sammy Cahn). Best of the numbers to Porter songs is Jeanmaire's "I Get a Kick Out of You," which she sings and dances with infectious flair and zest. There's a wonderful moment in the routine when Buzz Miller and the other dancers surround Jeanmaire and sing out "Cole! Cole! Cole! Cool! Cool! Cool!" in appropriate tribute to the adaptability of Porter's song to the hard-driving, sizzling rhythm of this particular version.

Mitzi Gaynor fares less well with the laundered lyrics of "Anything Goes." Among many other modifications, the line about four-letter words is changed to three-letter words—indicating that mid-'50s Hollywood (*Kiss Me Kate* to the contrary) was still far from letting "anything" go. But Gaynor cuts loose marvelously in the dance part of the number. Crosby, looking paunchier than ever in his last Paramount musical, sings "All Through the Night" (to Jeanmaire) in the romantic, crooning style of which he was still the unchallenged master, though the Roland Petit ballet that Jeanmaire then dances to the song is a bit long-winded and pretentious. O'Connor and Gaynor toss in a breezy "It's Delovely" (originally written for 1936's *Red, Hot and Blue* on Broadway), and all four stars join in with a large corps of dancers for a finger-snapping "Blow, Gabriel, Blow"—perhaps the swinging-est finale that has graced any of Porter's movie musicals.

A year later, in 1957, another lavish Technicolor remake boasted another Porter score—but this time the score was brand-new. What's more, the socially prominent

Porter seemed a natural for it: MGM's *High Society,* a musical version of the 1940 romantic comedy *The Philadelphia Story.* The remake teamed Bing Crosby and Frank Sinatra in a movie for the first time (the two had appeared together many times, however, in radio broadcasts and on TV). For the role of the Philadelphia socialite originally played by Katharine Hepburn both on Broadway and in the first film version, MGM cast a Philadelphia blue blood, Grace Kelly (in her last Hollywood film before marrying Prince Ranier of Monaco). But then MGM switched the story's locale from Philadelphia to Newport—partly to relate the remake's musical side to Newport's reputation as the locale of a major jazz festival in the 1950s.

The plot of *High Society* revolves around a divorced heiress (Kelly) on the eve of her marriage to a socially prominent stuffed shirt (John Lund), and the disruptions caused by the arrival on the scene of her ex-husband (Crosby) and a newspaper reporter (Sinatra) assigned to cover the wedding. Unfortunately, most of the bite of Philip Barry's original dialogue gets muted in Charles Walters's too-genial direction, and in the bland performances of Kelly and Crosby compared to Hepburn and Cary Grant in the original. Disappointingly, Porter's songs don't always compensate for this letdown. Instead of the witty, lyrical, pungent sock of so many earlier Porter scores, *High Society* finds Porter in a generally mellow mood. Apparently, at age sixty-five, Porter no longer had as puckish an attitude about the upper crust as he had at twenty-five or even forty-five.

Crosby's "I Love You, Samantha" and Sinatra's "Mind If I Make Love to You" and "You're Sensational" are pleasant but quickly forgettable ballads. So, too, is the title song that opens the movie, sung to a calypso beat by Louis "Satchmo" Armstrong as a busload of jazz musicians drive into Newport. "Who Wants to Be a Millionaire?" sung by Sinatra and reporter-girlfriend Celeste Holm, has one of the score's catchiest melodies, but its lyrics are uninspired.

But the score for *High Society* is far from a washout. "Now You Has Jazz" provides a bright, lightly swinging interlude for Crosby and Armstrong to sing a jazz-flavored, easy-going duet of the type that Crosby did so well on many of his radio broadcasts but rarely did in the movies. "Well, Did You Evah! (What a Swell Party This Is)," originally written for Broadway's *DuBarry Was a Lady,* also provides a late-in-the-movie, showstopping duet for Crosby and Sinatra, with lyrics revised by Porter to include references to the two baritones' offscreen status as friendly rivals. It's too bad a few equally spirited Crosby-Sinatra duets weren't included earlier.

High Society's greatest plus, however, is "True Love," which became Porter's biggest all-time movie song hit. An openly sentimental ballad, it's sung in a flashback sequence by Crosby and Kelly—and beautifully captures the sort of straightforward romantic simplicity that distinguishes more of Irving Berlin's ballads ("Always," "Remember?") than Porter's. MGM originally planned to have Kelly's singing voice dubbed by a professional vocalist, but Crosby convinced the studio that Kelly had a good enough voice to do it herself—and, indeed, her duet with Crosby adds a special warmth and charm to the sequence. "True Love" not only became the first Porter song to "go gold" with a soundtrack recording (selling more than a million records), but also lasted an impressive twenty-two weeks on *Your Hit Parade* (even though it never went above the No. 2 spot)—doing so in the first years that Elvis Presley and other rock 'n' roll performers were pushing older-style songs off the list.

Zizi Jeanmaire, Bing Crosby, Mitzi Gaynor, and Donald O'Connor in "Blow, Gabriel, Blow," the finale to the 1956 Anything Goes.

"You're Sensational!" sings Frank Sinatra to Grace Kelly in High Society *(1957).*

Porter revamped the lyrics to his '30s "Well, Did You Evah! (What a Swell Party This Is)" for a Frank Sinatra-Bing Crosby duet in High Society.

The smash success of "True Love" and the box-office popularity (despite mixed reviews) of *High Society* marked a significant upturn in Porter's personal fortunes in the '50s. Three of his Broadway shows in a row—*Out of This World* (1950), *Can-Can* (1953), and *Silk Stockings* (1955)—had received decidedly mixed reviews and produced few song hits. At the same time, a series of personal tragedies disrupted his life. First, his mother, to whom he had remained close all his life, suffered a stroke at age 90 and died in August of 1952. Almost simultaneously, the health of Porter's wife, Linda, deteriorated because of emphysema and she too died, in May of 1954. A year later, one of Porter's closest friends of many years, Howard Sturges, died suddenly of a heart attack. Porter's own health also underwent sharp ups and downs—first from a chronic catarrh that caused recurring headaches, then from an intestinal ulcer, and finally from a progressive and painful deterioration of his right leg. Throughout much of this period, Porter threw himself into his work as a means of fighting recurring depression.

But his personal dispirit began to show increasingly in his work, too—perhaps most of all in the last original movie score he would write, for MGM's *Les Girls* (1957). This movie would also mark Gene Kelly's last starring MGM musical, amid signs that the golden age of Hollywood musicals was drawing to a close as the popularity of rock 'n' roll swept the country.

Porter's score for *Les Girls* fails to match the sophisticated charm or cleverness of the script (by John Patrick) and of Kelly's staging of the musical numbers—as three former showgirls (Kay Kendall, Mitzi Gaynor, Taina Elg) recount their experiences with their boss (Kelly) for a libel case growing out of Kendall's memoirs. Only one song, the romantic ballad "Ça, C'est L'Amour" (breathily sung by Elg), reflects Porter even in moderately good form—though its French title may have been too sophisticated for general audiences and kept it from becoming as well-known as it should. "You're Just Too, Too" gets a spirited rendition from Kelly and Kendall (the latter partly dubbed by Betty Wand), but it's really a weak-sister variation on "You're the Top" (from *Anything Goes*). As for "Why Am I So Gone About That Gal?" (sung by Kelly and then danced by him with Gaynor), it neatly spoofs Marlon Brando's leather-jacketed *The Wild Ones* (1953), but does not hold up well outside the context of the sequence. Both the title song, "Les Girls," and "Ladies in Waiting" have little merit in or out of the picture.

The same year as *Les Girls,* Porter wrote two new songs for the MGM film version of his last Broadway show, *Silk Stockings.* Next to *Kiss Me Kate,* it is the most faithful screen transfer of a Porter show, keeping eleven of the original thirteen songs, plus the two new ones. Based on a 1939 MGM movie comedy, *Ninotchka* (which starred Greta Garbo and Melvyn Douglas), *Silk Stockings* focuses on an austere Soviet emissary (Cyd Charisse) who is sent to Paris to check up on a wayward Soviet composer and ends up shedding both Communist ideology and her drab Moscow tunics for Parisian fashions and an American movie producer (Fred Astaire) with whom she falls in love. Their *detente* is advanced through some of the most attractive of Porter's late romantic ballads, including "All of You," "Without Love," and, particularly, "Paris Loves Lovers" (which boasts some of the cleverest of topical Porter rhymes in many years).

Charisse inevitably faced comparisons with Garbo's indelible performance as the original *Ninotchka,* as well as with the admirable Broadway portrayal of Hildegard Knef (sometimes billed in America as Hildegarde Neff)—with Charisse generally coming off third-best, at least in the movie's nonmusical portions. Her singing voice, moreover, is dubbed (by Carol Richards). But when it comes to the dances, Charisse is in a class by herself—bringing them an élan and electricity that makes her performance possibly the best-*danced* leading role anyone has done in a Hollywood musical. Charisse is especially memorable in the romantic duets with Astaire to "Fated to Be Mated" (one of the two new songs) and "All of Me," as well as in the rousing, showstopping "Red Blues" with a corps of fast-moving dancers supporting her.

Astaire, at fifty-eight, shows his age in some of the closeups but not in the spirit or style of his singing and dancing. His dances in *Silk Stockings* with Charisse, in fact, remain among the best of his entire MGM career. With the other new song, "The Ritz Roll and Rock," however, both Astaire and Porter prove less adept at adapting (or even spoofing) rock beats than they had been in earlier movies with jazz, jive, and boogie-woogie. Credit them, at least, with *trying* to keep up with the times.

Some of Porter's lyrics are deftly on-target in poking fun at East-West political attitudes of the '50s—even to working into the countermelody to "Paris Loves Lovers" such terms as imperialistic, militaristic, atheistic, sensualistic, and bourgeois propaganda. Few, indeed, are the songwriters who could use those terms so divertingly—and explicitly. The lyrics to "Siberia" and "Too Bad (We Can't Go Back to Moscow)" even more broadly spoof the Soviet system, and are engagingly sung by a most unlikely trio of Soviet commissars: Peter Lorre, Joseph Buloff, and Jules Munshin. Among the "party girls" during their first rendition of "Too Bad," incidentally, is Barrie Chase, who, the following year, would become Astaire's dancing partner for the first of a series of prize-winning television specials.

"Too Bad (We Can't Go Back to Moscow)" draws some not-too-unhappy reactions from Joseph Buloff, Jules Munshin, and Peter Lorre as a trio of wayward Soviet commissars in Silk Stockings *(1957).*

Not all the satire in *Silk Stockings* is political. Janis Paige, playing a Hollywood swimming star (who keeps trying to shake the water out of her ear when not chasing after the plot's Soviet composer), belts out "Stereophonic Sound," a deliciously funny takeoff on Hollywood's preoccupation in the mid-'50s with such technical innovations as CinemaScope, VistaVision, 3-D, and stereo.

Silk Stockings is far from the classic the original *Ninotchka* is, but its songs and dances give it a vitality and sparkle that keep it above average as musical-comedy entertainment. That is certainly not the case with the songs and dances for the next movie adaptation of a '50s Porter show, Twentieth Century-Fox's *Can-Can* (1960). This lavish, Technicolor production is burdened by a relentlessly unimaginative book (by Abe Burrows)—about how an 1890s Parisian cafe's introduction of can-can dancers scandalized the era's proper folk. Not even such usually personable performers as Frank Sinatra, Shirley MacLaine, Maurice Chevalier, and Louis Jourdan succeed in breathing life into the picture or its songs for more than isolated moments.

Only seven of Porter's fourteen songs for the Broadway show are used. They include such pleasing Porter ballads as "It's All Right With Me" and "C'est Magnifique" (both affably sung by Sinatra), and what is surely Porter's greatest tribute to the French city in which he maintained a part-time home for most of his life, "I Love Paris." The studio also insisted on interpolating three older, better-known Porter standards—"You Do Something to Me," "Let's Do It," "Just One of Those Things" —to bolster a score that had won only modest popularity during its 1953 Broadway run. ("C'est Magnifique" made *Your Hit Parade* in '53 for one brief week as No. 9; "I Love Paris" made it for nine weeks, but never rose above the No. 7 spot.) Porter's music for the dance sequences, especially a rowdy but too-stagey Apache number by MacLaine and three male dancers, is uninspired. But the can-can numbers, staged by

In Silk Stockings *(1959) Fred Astaire and Janis Paige cavort through Porter's "Stereophonic Sound," a spoof of Hollywood's preoccupation with technical innovations in the mid-'50s.*

Hermes Pan and led by Juliet Prowse, give the movie a few zesty moments.

In the three years between Porter's writing the additional songs for *Silk Stockings* and the filming of *Can-Can,* Porter's health deteriorated drastically. In April of 1958 he lost his twenty-year battle with the damage to his legs and his badly infected right leg had to be amputated. This proved to be a psychological blow from which Porter never fully recovered. He began drinking more heavily. In addition to severe depression, he also suffered in the early '60s from kidney stones and a hip fracture, which kept him in and out of several hospitals. In August of 1963 he fell asleep while smoking in bed and had to be hospitalized for burns. A year later, while undergoing treatment for bladder infection, Porter developed pneumonia and died in Saint John's Hospital in Santa Monica, California, on October 15, 1964. He was seventy-one. The official autopsy listed the cause of death as severe bronchopneumonia, but also noted advanced arteriosclerosis, degeneration of the kidneys, and hardening of the arteries.

Porter was buried in his hometown of Peru, Indiana, alongside the grave of his wife. Despite years of lavish spending, he left an estate of nearly six million dollars —most of it from the earnings on his songs.

Though Porter had lived stylishly in a limited social sphere, his songs had reached, entertained, and touched people of all backgrounds and social levels. And those songs, despite the physical pain Porter himself endured for a full third of his life, continued to reflect a lively, outgoing, up-to-date view of the world and the people in it. So it's not surprising that his music has remained popular in the years since his death— with some of his lesser-known songs even receiving new leases on life through such Off-Broadway revues as *The Decline and Fall of the Entire World As Seen Through the Eyes of Cole Porter* (1965) and through renewed championing by a growing number of performers.

But one 1975 movie that started out as a nostalgic tribute to Porter and the '30s

Shirley MacLaine and Juliet Prowse in the "Adam and Eve" dance sequence from Porter's Can-Can *(1960)*.

style of sophisticated musical comedy with which he was most identified ended up receiving critical catcalls worse than any that had greeted any Porter flop during his lifetime. Peter Bogdanovich's superbly photographed *At Long Last Love* not only got bogged down by a silly, boring book but also by a cast of performers who didn't sing all that well—including Burt Reynolds as a handsome playboy, Cybill Shepherd as a ditsy debutante, and Madeline Kahn as a Broadway star—yet were expected to carry the majority of the film's sixteen Porter songs. As for the dancing, it was mostly of the clod hopper variety.

Some critics went so far as to say that *At Long Last Love* merely confirmed that Hollywood was never as good as Broadway in putting across Cole Porter. Perhaps so. But there's no denying that some of the best songs to come out of movie soundtracks since 1930 are Porter songs—whether written originally for Hollywood or Broadway. And they continue to reveal to audiences throughout the world the special characteristics that Yale's provost, Norman S. Buck, so aptly summarized in conferring an

Eileen Brennan, Cybill Shepherd, and Madeline Kahn kick up their heels in At Long Last Love *(1975), intended as a nostalgic tribute to Cole Porter but roundly panned by most critics.*

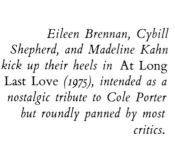

honorary doctorate on Porter in 1960: "Master of the deft phrase, the delectable rhyme, the distinctive melody, you are, in your own words and your own field, the top. . . . Your graceful, impudent, inimitable songs will be played and sung as long as footlights burn and curtains go up." To which we must add: and as long as films and videotapes spin onto theater and television screens.

COLE PORTER'S MOVIES AND SONGS ON TAPE AND DISC

THE BATTLE OF PARIS (1929), Paramount. B&W. Directed by Robert Florey. With Gertrude Lawrence, Charles Ruggles, Walter Petrie, Arthur Treacher, Gladys DuBois, Joe King. Songs: "They All Fall in Love," "Here Comes the Bandwagon"; plus songs by others. Soundtrack LP: included in *Cole Porter in Hollywood,* Music Masters JJA 19767.

FIFTY MILLION FRENCHMEN (1931), Warner Brothers, B&W. Directed by Lloyd Bacon. With Chic Johnson, Ole Olson, William Gaxton, Helen Broderick, Claudia Dell, John Halliday, Bela Lugosi, Vera Gordon. Some of the songs from Porter's score for the original 1929 Broadway production used as instrumental background only. However, a 1934 two-reel Vitaphone short subject, *Paree-Paree,* directed by Sam Sax, with Bob Hope and Dorothy Stone, offered the following songs: "Paree," "You Do Something to Me," "Find Me a Primitive Man," "You've Got That Thing."

THE GAY DIVORCEE (1934), RKO Radio. B&W. Directed by Mark Sandrich. With Fred Astaire, Ginger Rogers, Alice Brady, Edward Everett Horton, Erik Rhodes, Eric Blore, Lillian Miles, Betty Grable. Song: "Night and Day"; plus songs by others. Soundtrack LP: included in *Fred Astaire and Ginger Rogers,* EMI Pathe Marconi 2C184-95807/8 (English import). Videocassette: RKO Home Video; also Nostalgia Merchant.

ANYTHING GOES (1936), TV title: *Tops Is the Limit.* Paramount. B&W. Directed by Lewis Milestone. With Bing Crosby, Ethel Merman, Ida Lupino, Charles Ruggles, Arthur Treacher. Songs: "Anything Goes," "You're the Top," "There'll Always Be a Lady Fair," "Blow, Gabriel, Blow," "All Through the Night"; plus songs by others. Soundtrack LP: excerpts included in *Cole Porter in Hollywood,* Music Masters JJA 19767.

BORN TO DANCE (1936), MGM. B&W. Directed by Roy Del Ruth. With Eleanor Powell, James Stewart, Virginia Bruce, Una Merkel, Sid Silvers, Buddy Ebsen, Frances Langford, Reginald Gardiner. Songs: "I've Got You Under My Skin," "Easy to Love," "Rap-Tap on Wood," "Swingin' the Jinx Away," "Love Me, Love My Pekinese," "Hey, Babe, Hey (I'm Nuts About You)," "Rolling Home." Soundtrack LP: Clas-

sics International Filmusicals CIF-3001; excerpts included in *Cole Porter in Hollywood,* Music Masters JJA 19767.

THE SINGING MARINE (1937), Warner Bros. B&W. Directed by Ray Enright. With Dick Powell, Doris Weston, Lee Dixon, Jane Darwell, Larry Adler. Song: "Night and Day"; plus songs by others.

ROSALIE (1937), MGM. B&W. Directed by W. S. Van Dyke. With Eleanor Powell, Nelson Eddy, Ilona Massey, Ray Bolger, Frank Morgan, Virginia Grey, Edna May Oliver, Reginald Owen, William Demarest, Jerry Colonna. Songs: "In the Still of the Night," "I've a Strange New Rhythm in My Heart," "Rosalie," "Why Should I Care?," "Spring Love Is in the Air," "It's All Over But the Shouting," "To Be or Not to Be in Love," "Who Knows?"; plus songs and arias by others. Soundtrack LP: included in *Cole Porter in Hollywood,* Music Masters JJA 19767. Videocassette: MGM/UA; also, excerpt included in *That's Entertainment,* MGM/UA.

BREAK THE NEWS (1937), General Films/ Monogram. B&W. Directed by Rene Clair. With Maurice Chevalier, Jack Buchanan, June Knight, Marta Labarr, Gertrude Musgrove, Felix Aylmer, Charles Lefeaux. Song: "It All Belongs to You"; plus songs by others.

BROADWAY MELODY OF 1940 (1939), MGM. B&W. Directed by Norman Taurog. With Eleanor Powell, Fred Astaire, George Murphy, Frank Morgan, Ian Hunter, Florence Rice, Lynne Carver. Songs: "Begin the Beguine," "I Concentrate on You," "Please Don't Monkey With Broadway," "Between You and Me," "I've Got My Eyes on You," "I Am the Captain." Soundtrack LP: Classic International Filmusicals CIF-3002. Videocassette: excerpt included in *That's Entertainment,* MGM/UA.

LOVE THY NEIGHBOR (1940), Paramount. B&W. Directed by Mark Sandrich. With Jack Benny, Fred Allen, Mary Martin, Virginia Dale, Veree Teasdale, Eddie "Rochester" Anderson, Theresa Anderson, the Merry Macs, the Merriel Abbott Dancers. Song: "My Heart Belongs to Daddy"; plus songs by others.

YOU'LL NEVER GET RICH (1941), Columbia. B&W. Directed by Sidney Lanfield. With Fred Astaire, Rita Hayworth, Robert Benchley, Osa Massen, Frieda Inescourt, John

Hubbard, Martha Tilton, the Delta Rhythm Boys, Chico Hamilton, Red Mack, Buddy Collette, Joe Comfort. Songs: "Boogie Barcarolle," "So Near and Yet So Far," "Dream Dancing," "Shootin' the Works for Uncle Sam," "Since I Kissed My Baby Goodbye," "Wedding Cake Cakewalk." Soundtrack LP: Hollywood Soundstage 5001 (with *Yolanda and the Thief*). Videocassette: RCA/Columbia VH-10574.

ANDY HARDY'S PRIVATE SECRETARY (1941), MGM. B&W. Directed by George B. Seitz. With Mickey Rooney, Lewis Stone, Ann Rutherford, Kathryn Grayson, Ian Hunter, Fay Holden, Sara Haden. Song: "I've Got My Eyes on You."

PANAMA HATTIE (1942), MGM. B&W. Directed by Norman Z. McLeod (with sequences directed by Roy Del Ruth and Vincente Minnelli). With Ann Sothern, Red Skelton, Virginia O'Brien, Dan Dailey Jr., Lena Horne, Marsha Hunt, Rags Ragland, Ben Blue, Jackie Horner. Songs: "Let's Be Buddies," "I've Still Got My Health," "Just One of Those Things," "Fresh As a Daisy," "Make It Another Old-Fashioned, Please"; plus songs by others. Soundtrack LP: included in *Cole Porter in Hollywood*, Music Masters JJA 19767.

REVEILLE WITH BEVERLY (1943), Columbia. B&W. Directed by Charles Barton. With Ann Miller, Bob Crosby, Duke Ellington and his Orchestra, Count Basie and his Orchestra, Frank Sinatra, the Mills Brothers, Freddie Slack and his Orchestra with Ella Mae Morse, William Wright, Larry Parks, Franklin Pangborn. Song: "Night and Day"; plus songs by others. Soundtrack LP: Hollywood Soundstage 5014 (with *Jam Session*).

SOMETHING TO SHOUT ABOUT (1943), Columbia. B&W. Directed by Gregory Ratoff. With Don Ameche, Janet Blair, William Gaxton, Jack Oakie, Hazel Scott, Teddy Wilson and his Orchestra, Cobina Wright Jr., Lily Norwood (Cyd Charisse), the Bricklayers. Songs: "You'd Be So Nice to Come Home To," "I Always Knew," "Hasta Luego," "Lotus Blossom," "Something to Shout About," "Through Thick and Thin," "It Might Have Been," "Glide, Glider, Glide," "Sailors of the Sky." Soundtrack LP: included in *Cole Porter in Hollywood*, Music Masters JJA 19767.

HERS TO HOLD (1943), Universal. B&W. Directed by Frank Ryan. With Deanna Durbin, Joseph Cotten, Charles Winninger, Evelyn Ankers, Nella Walker, Gus Schilling. Song: "Begin the Beguine"; plus songs by others.

LET'S FACE IT (1943), Paramount. B&W. Directed by Sidney Lanfield. With Bob Hope, Betty Hutton, Eve Arden, ZaSu Pitts, Phyllis Povah, Dona Drake, Marjorie Weaver. Songs: "Let's Not Talk About Love," "Let's Face It";

plus songs by others. Soundtrack LP: included in *Cole Porter in Hollywood*, Music Masters JJA 19767.

DUBARRY WAS A LADY (1943), MGM. B&W. Directed by Roy Del Ruth. With Red Skelton, Lucille Ball, Gene Kelly, Virginia O'Brien, Tommy Dorsey and his Orchestra with Dick Haymes and Jo Stafford, Rags Ragland, Zero Mostel, George Givot, Louise Beavers. Songs: "Do I Love You," "Katie Went to Haiti," "Friendship"; plus songs by others. Soundtrack LP: Titania 509 (with *Can't Help Singing*); also included in *Cole Porter in Hollywood*, Music Masters JJA 19767.

I DOOD IT (1943), MGM. B&W. Directed by Vincente Minnelli. With Red Skelton, Eleanor Powell, Patricia Dane, Richard Ainley, Lena Horne, John Hodiak, Hazel Scott, Jimmy Dorsey and his Orchestra with Helen O'Connell and Bob Eberly. Song: "Swingin' the Jinx Away"; plus songs by others.

SOMETHING FOR THE BOYS (1944), Twentieth Century-Fox. Color. Directed by Lewis Seiler. With Carmen Miranda, Vivian Blaine, Michael O'Shea, Phil Silvers, Perry Como, Sheila Ryan, Glenn Langan, Judy Holliday (in a bit role). Song: "Something for the Boys"; plus songs by others. Soundtrack LP: included in *Cole Porter in Hollywood*, Music Masters JJA 19767.

HOLLYWOOD CANTEEN (1944), Warner Brothers. B&W. Directed by Delmar Daves. With Joan Leslie, Robert Hutton, Dane Clark; guest stars Bette Davis, Joan Crawford, John Garfield, Ida Lupino, Barbara Stanwyck, Jane Wyman, Jack Benny, Joseph Szigeti, the Andrews Sisters, Roy Rogers, Dennis Morgan, Eleanor Parker, Alexis Smith, Kitty Carlisle, Joe E. Brown, Eddie Cantor, Peter Lorre, Sydney Greenstreet, Paul Henreid, Joan McCracken, Irene Manning, Efrem Zimbalist, Carmen Cavallaro and his Orchestra, Jimmy Dorsey and his Orchestra, others. Song: "Don't Fence Me In"; plus songs by others. Soundtrack LP: Curtain Calls 100/11-12 (with *Stage Door Canteen*).

LADY ON A TRAIN (1945), Universal. B&W. Directed by Charles Davis. With Deanna Durbin, Ralph Bellamy, Edward Everett Horton, David Bruce, George Coulouris, Allen Jenkins, Patricia Morrison, Dan Duryea. Song: "Night and Day"; plus songs by others.

DON'T FENCE ME IN (1945), Republic. B&W. Directed by John English. With Roy Rogers, Dale Evans, Gabby Hayes, Lucille Gleason, Bob Nolan and the Sons of the Pioneers. Song: "Don't Fence Me In"; plus songs by others. Videocassette: Nostalgia Merchant.

NIGHT AND DAY (1946), Warner Brothers. Color. Directed by Michael Curtiz. With Cary Grant, Alexis Smith, Monty Woolley, Ginny

Simms, Jane Wyman, Mary Martin, Eve Arden, Alan Hale, Victor Francen, Carlos Ramirez, Estelle Sloan, Milady Mladova, Georges Zoritch. Songs: "Night and Day," "I've Got You Under My Skin," "What Is This Thing Called Love?," "You're the Top," "In the Still of the Night," "I'm in Love Again," "An Old-Fashioned Garden," "Let's Do It," "You've Got That Thing," "You Do Something to Me," "I'm Unlucky in Love," "Miss Otis Regrets," "I Wonder What Became of Sally," "Just One of Those Things," "I Get a Kick Out of You," "My Heart Belongs to Daddy," "Don't Fence Me In," "Begin the Beguine," "Easy to Love," "Anything Goes," "Bulldog Song." Soundtrack LP: excerpts included in *Cole Porter in Hollywood,* Music Masters JJA 19767. Videocassette: Key/CBS-Fox.

THIS TIME FOR KEEPS (1947), MGM. Color. Directed by Richard Thorpe. With Esther Williams, Jimmy Durante, Lauritz Melchior, Johnny Johnston, Dame May Whitty, Tommy Wonder, Xavier Cugat and his Orchestra. Song: "Easy to Love"; plus songs by others.

THE PIRATE (1948), MGM. Color. Directed by Vincente Minnelli. With Judy Garland, Gene Kelly, Walter Slezak, Gladys Cooper, the Nicholas Brothers, George Zucco, Reginald Owen. Songs: "Love of My Life," "Be a Clown," "Nina," "You Can Do No Wrong," "Mack the Black." Soundtrack LP: MGM 2SES-43ST (withdrawn). Videocassette: MGM-UA; also, excerpts included in *That's Entertainment,* MGM/UA.

LUXURY LINER (1948), MGM. Color. Directed by Richard Whorf. With Jane Powell, Lauritz Melchior, George Brent, Frances Gifford, Marina Koshetz, Xavier Cugat and his Orchestra. Song: "I've Got You Under My Skin"; plus songs by others.

ADAM'S RIB (1949), MGM. B&W. Directed by George Cukor. With Spencer Tracy, Katharine Hepburn, Judy Holliday, David Wayne, Tom Ewell, Jean Hagen, Polly Moran. Song: "Farewell, Amanda." Soundtrack LP: included in *Cole Porter in Hollywood,* Music Masters JJA 19767.

LULLABY OF BROADWAY (1951), Warner Brothers. Color. Directed by David Butler. With Doris Day, Gene Nelson, Billy DeWolfe, S. Z. Sakall, Gladys George, Florence Bates. Song: "Just One of Those Things"; plus songs by others. Soundtrack LP: Caliban 6008 (with *I'll See You in My Dreams*).

STAGE FRIGHT (1950), Warner Brothers. B&W. Directed by Alfred Hitchcock. With Marlene Dietrich, Jane Wyman, Michael Wilding, Richard Todd, Joyce Grenfell, Alistair Sim, Kay Walsh. Song: "The Laziest Gal in Town." Studio recording: included in *The Legendary Marlene Dietrich* (CBS/CSP/Murray Hill P3-

14689); also in several other Dietrich LPs.

SUNNY SIDE OF THE STREET (1951), Columbia. Color. Directed by Richard Quine. With Frankie Laine, Terry Moore, Jerome Courtland, Audrey Long, Toni Arden, Dick Wesson, Lynn Bari, William Tracy. Song: "I Get a Kick Out of You"; plus songs by others.

STARLIFT (1951), Warner Brothers. B&W. Directed by Roy Del Ruth. With Janice Rule, Dick Wesson, Ron Hagerty, Doris Day, Gordon MacRae, Virginia Mayo, Gene Nelson, James Cagney, Gary Cooper, Lucille Norman, Phil Harris, Jane Wyman, Randolph Scott, Ruth Roman, Louella Parsons. Songs: "You Do Something to Me," "What Is This Thing Called Love?"; plus songs by others. Soundtrack LP: Titania 510 (with *Call Me Mister*).

BECAUSE YOU'RE MINE (1952), MGM. Color. Directed by Alexander Hall. With Mario Lanza, Doretta Morrow, James Whitmore, Dean Miller, Jeff Donnell, Spring Byington. Song: "You Do Something to Me"; plus songs and arias by others.

THE JAZZ SINGER (1953), Warner Brothers. Color. Directed by Michael Curtiz. With Danny Thomas, Peggy Lee, Mildred Dunnock, Eduard Franz. Song: "Just One of Those Things"; plus songs by others.

KISS ME KATE (1953), MGM. Color. Directed by George Sidney. With Kathryn Grayson, Howard Keel, Ann Miller, Bobby Van, Keenan Wynn, Bob Fosse, James Whitmore, Tommy Rall, Carol Haney, Jeannie Coyne. Songs: "So in Love," "Wunderbar," "Were Thine That Special Face," "Always True to You in My Fashion," "Too Darn Hot," "Every Tom, Dick, and Harry," "I Hate Men," "I've Come to Wive It Wealthily in Padua," "Where Is the Life That Late I Led?," "We Open in Venice," "Brush Up Your Shakespeare," "Why Can't You Behave?," "Kiss Me Kate," "From This Moment On." Soundtrack LP: MGM 3077 (withdrawn). Videocassette: MGM/UA; also, excerpt included in *That's Entertainment, Part 2* (MGM/UA)

EASY TO LOVE (1953), MGM. Color. Directed by Charles Walters. Finale created by Busby Berkeley. With Esther Williams, Van Johnson, Tony Martin, Carroll Baker, John Bromfield, Cyd Charisse, King Donovan, Edna Skinner. Song: "Easy to Love"; plus songs by others.

YOUNG AT HEART (1955), Warner Brothers. Color. Directed by Gordon Douglas. With Doris Day, Frank Sinatra, Dorothy Malone, Ethel Barrymore, Gig Young, Elizabeth Fraser. Song: "Just One of Those Things"; plus songs by others. Soundtrack LP: Titania 500 (with *April in Paris*).

I'LL CRY TOMORROW (1955), MGM,

B&W. Directed by Daniel Mann. With Susan Hayward, Richard Conte, Jo Van Fleet, Eddie Albert, Margo. Song: "Just One of Those Things"; plus songs by others. Soundtrack LP: included in *Susan Hayward*, Legends 1000/3.

HIGH SOCIETY (1956), MGM. Color. Directed by Charles Walters. With Bing Crosby, Grace Kelly, Frank Sinatra, Celeste Holm, Louis Armstrong, Louis Calhern, Sidney Blackmer, Margalo Gilmore. Songs: "True Love," "Who Wants to Be a Millionaire?," "Now You Has Jazz," "High Society Calypso," "I Love You, Samantha," "Little One," "You're Sensational," "Well, Did You Evah!," "Mind If I Make Love to You?" Soundtrack LP: Capitol SN12235. Videocassette and videodisc: MGM/UA.

ANYTHING GOES (1956), Paramount. Color. Directed by Robert Lewis. With Bing Crosby, Mitzi Gaynor, Zizi Jeanmaire, Donald O'Connor, Phil Harris, Roland Petit. Songs: "Anything Goes," "You're the Top," "All Through the Night," "I Get a Kick Out of You," "It's DeLovely," "Blow, Gabriel, Blow"; plus songs by others. Soundtrack LP: Decca 8318 (withdrawn).

THE EDDY DUCHIN STORY (1957), Columbia. Color. Directed by George Sidney. With Tyrone Power, Kim Novak, Victoria Shaw, James Whitmore, Larry Keating. Song: "What Is This Thing Called Love?"; plus songs by others. LP: MCA VIM-7215 (featuring Carmen Cavallaro, who dubbed the soundtrack).

THIS COULD BE THE NIGHT (1957), MGM. CinemaScope. B&W. Directed by Robert Wise. With Jean Simmons, Paul Douglas, Tony Franciosa, Joan Blondell, ZaSu Pitts, Neile Adams, J. Carrol Naish, Murvyn Vye, Julie Wilson, Rafael Compos. Song: "Dream Dancing"; plus songs by others.

THE DESK SET (1957), Twentieth Century-Fox. Color. Directed by Walter Lang. With Spencer Tracy, Katharine Hepburn, Joan Blondell, Dina Merrill, Gig Young. Song: "Begin the Beguine."

SILK STOCKINGS (1957), MGM. Color. Directed by Rouben Mamoulian. With Fred Astaire, Cyd Charisse, Janis Paige, Peter Lorre, George Tobias, Jules Munshin, Joseph Buloff, Wim Sonneveld, Barrie Chase. Songs: "All of Me," "Without Love," "Paris Loves Lovers," "Too Bad," "It's a Chemical Reaction," "Stereophonic Sound," "Silk and Satin," "Silk Stockings," "Fated to Be Mated," "The Ritz Roll and Rock," "The Red Blues," "Josephine," "Siberia." Soundtrack LP: MCA 39074; also, excerpt included in *That's Entertainment, Part 2*, MCA-1-5301. Videocassette: MGM/UA; also, excerpt included in *That's Entertainment, Part 2*, MGM/UA.

LES GIRLS (1957), MGM. Color. Directed by George Cukor. With Gene Kelly, Kay Kendall, Mitzi Gaynor, Taina Elg, Jacques Bergerac, Henry Daniell, Patrick MacNee. Songs: "Ça, C'est L'Amour," "Les Girls," "Ladies in Waiting," "Why Am I So Gone About That Gal?," "You're Just Too, Too!," "Genie's Theme." Soundtrack LP: MGM 3590 (withdrawn). Videocassette: MGM/UA.

CAN-CAN (1960), Twentieth Century-Fox. Todd-AO. Color. Directed by Walter Lang. With Frank Sinatra, Shirley MacLaine, Louis Jourdan, Maurice Chevalier, Marcel Dalio, Juliet Prowse. Songs: "I Love Paris, "C'est Magnifique," "It's All Right With Me," "Come Along With Me," "Live and Let Live," "Maidens Typical of France," "Montmartre," "Let's Do It," "Just One of Those Things," "You Do Something to Me," "Apache Dance." Soundtrack LP: Capitol SM-01301.

LET'S MAKE LOVE (1960), Twentieth Century-Fox. CinemaScope. Color. Directed by George Cukor. With Marilyn Monroe, Yves Montand, Frankie Vaughan, Tony Randall, Wilfred Hyde-Whyte, David Burns, Dennis King Jr., Bing Crosby, Gene Kelly, Milton Berle. Song: "My Heart Belongs to Daddy"; plus songs by others. Soundtrack LP: CBS Special Products ACS-8327.

STAR! (1968), Twentieth Century-Fox. Todd-AO. Color. Directed by Robert Wise. With Julie Andrews, Daniel Massey, Michael Craig, Richard Crenna, Robert Reed, Beryl Reid. Song: "The Physician"; plus songs by others. Soundtrack LP: Twentieth Century-Fox 5102 (withdrawn).

AT LONG LAST LOVE (1975), Twentieth Century-Fox. Color. Directed by Peter Bogdanovich. With Burt Reynolds, Cybill Shepherd, Madeline Kahn, Eileen Brennan, Duilio Del Prete, John Hillerman, Mildred Natwick. Songs: "At Long Last Love," "I Get a Kick Out of You," "Just One of Those Things," "You're the Top," "Find Me a Primitive Man," "Friendship," "But in the Morning, No," "Well, Did You Evah?," "Let's Misbehave," "It's DeLovely," "Most Gentlemen Don't Like Love," "A Picture of You Without Me," "From Alpha to Omega," "Which," "I Loved Him (But He Didn't Love Me);" "Poor Young Millionaire" (music, Peter Bogdanovich, Artie Butler, lyrics, Porter). Soundtrack LP: RCA ABL-2-0967 (withdrawn).

PENNIES FROM HEAVEN (1981), MGM. Directed by Herbert Ross. With Steve Martin, Bernadette Peters, Christopher Walken, Tommy Rall, John McMartin. Song: "Let's Misbehave"; plus songs by others. Videocassette: MGM/UA.

Ralph Rainger in the late 1930s.

$f$ew movie composers were considered classier throughout the 1930s and the early
'40s than Ralph Rainger. Or more versatile. As the chief composer-in-residence
at Paramount and then briefly at Twentieth Century-Fox, Rainger wrote romantic
ballads for Bing Crosby, Continental *chansons* for Maurice Chevalier, provocative
numbers for Marlene Dietrich, insinuating ditties for Mae West, bouncy tunes for
Martha Raye, and love songs for Betty Grable, Don Ameche, and others.

Yet, like Harry Warren in those same years, Rainger never became a "household
name." Even today his name is more likely to bring a response of "Ralph *who?*" than
a glimmer of recognition as the composer of "Thanks for the Memory," "I Wished
on the Moon," "June in January," "Love in Bloom," "Moanin' Low," and dozens of
other songs that have become familiar standards. Like George Gershwin and Richard
Whiting, Rainger died young. But he left a wealth of songs that many longer-lived
songwriters have never equaled in quality—and which, in combination with Leo
Robin's lyrics, say reams about human relationships then and now.

Rainger was born Ralph Reichenthal, in New York City on October 7, 1901,
and grew up in Newark, New Jersey. He began studying piano at about age seven,
at his parents' urging. While still in high school, he dug into music theory and

composition on his own. Although his direction seemed to be toward classical music, he liked ragtime and other popular music enough to play piano for school dances. From high school, he won a scholarship to New York's Institute of Musical Arts, then headed by New York Symphony conductor Walter Damrosch.

But Rainger's father was unhappy with the prospect of a starving musician in the family. So he persuaded his son to quit the institute to study law. Rainger worked his way through law school with odd jobs as a truck driver, a door-to-door salesman and, occasionally, as a piano accompanist for vaudeville hopefuls. Soon after graduation, he married his college sweetheart, Elizabeth (Betty).

In the early 1920s, Rainger became a law clerk in a respected New York law firm. He hated the job. He sought escape by getting a night job as a piano player in a speakeasy—whose owner probably didn't mind having a lawyer around in the guise of a pianist. Then, in 1926, he was offered a job as the pit pianist in a Broadway theater. He took it—and quit law for good.

Soon Rainger was teamed with Edgar Fairchild to become part of a much-admired duo-piano-team playing in Broadway musicals and vaudeville. One of the acts for which they played was that of singer-dancers Clifton Webb and Mary Hay (long before Webb would become a popular movie star in *Laura* and the *Mr. Belvedere* series). When Webb was signed to costar with Fred Allen in the 1929 Broadway revue, *The Little Show,* he saw to it that Rainger came along as pianist in the pit orchestra.

During rehearsals, Webb asked for a number in which he could play a "sweet-back," or pimp, while the revue's leading lady, Libby Holman, sang a "lowdown" blues. Lyricist Howard Dietz liked the idea. Dietz had been responsible for bringing Holman into the show (they'd worked together the year before in a revue called *Merry-Go-Round*). He had also written most of the songs for *The Little Show* with composer Arthur Schwartz. As Dietz later related it in his autobiography, *Dancing in the Dark:*

> "Schwartz and I tried to come up with something appropriate for Libby's husky voice. We listened to a lot of jazz records for some kind of inspiration, but nothing seemed to work. Then one day, during a rehearsal break, I happened to hear our featured pianist, Ralph Rainger, playing something that sounded just right. I brought Schwartz over and he agreed. With his blessings, I wrote the lyric to Ralph's melody. It became 'Moanin' Low.' The whole thing took us half an hour."

"Moanin' Low" became one of the hits of the show and Rainger's first published song. It also made Libby Holman a star—and, ironically, saved *her* from a law career too. Holman's father, a lawyer, had wanted his daughter to go to law school. But when she was graduated from the University of Cincinnati at the age of eighteen, she found she could not enter law school until she was twenty-one. So her father agreed to let her try her luck in the theater—with the proviso that if, after three years, she wasn't successful, she'd return to Cincinnati and enter law school. After a series of shows that didn't make the hit lists, Holman was about ready to give up on Broadway when Dietz signed her for *The Little Show.* It ran for almost two years and Holman, like Rainger, forgot about a law career.

Late in 1930, Rainger also came to the rescue of another Dietz–Holman–Webb-

Allen revue, *Three's a Crowd*. A problem had arisen during the Philadelphia tryouts with one of Holman's solos, with a song about which she wasn't all that wild to begin with: "Body and Soul" (by Johnny Green, Edward Heyman and Robert Sour). The song had already been pulled out of another Broadway-bound revue and was on the verge of being yanked from this one. Green rearranged it several times, but nothing seemed to work. Holman was getting so upset that she warned Dietz that the show might have to be retitled *Two's a Crowd*.

As Broadway musical chronicler Stanley Green has related it in his book *Ring Bells! Sing Songs!:* "The song was finally saved when Howard Dietz, in New York one day, was dashing through Pennsylvania Station. Suddenly he spotted Ralph Rainger. Though Rainger was headed in the opposite direction, Dietz spun him around and, despite Rainger's protests, practically shanghaied him onto the train to Philadelphia." Dietz, in his autobiography, takes the story from there: "Rainger had a special feeling for this type of dark number. Libby, coached by Rainger, experimented with all types of delivery, but it was not until the last night in Philadelphia that they hit on a way to present the song. When the show opened on Broadway in October, 1930, 'Body and Soul' was a showstopper."

The success of "Moanin' Low" led Fanny Brice to ask United Artists to hire Rainger to write a torch song for her to sing in the 1930 movie *Be Yourself*. To lyrics by Brice's husband, Broadway producer and sometime songwriter Billy Rose, Rainger composed "When a Woman Loves a Man." Neither the movie nor the song was a hit. But it led to Rainger's being offered a job as a staff composer at Paramount. And in the Depression year of 1930, a steady job with a busy Hollywood studio had a lot more going for it than the more unpredictable and economically hard-pressed Broadway scene. Never mind that some of his first assignments were for incidental and long-forgotten songs for talkie programmers that quickly faded into oblivion. He was twenty-nine, eating regularly, and gaining a reputation around the studio as a versatile, easy-to-work-with composer.

Ralph Rainger's Major Movies and Their Songs

Soon after his signing, Paramount teamed Rainger with lyricist Leo Robin. Just a year older than Rainger, the Pittsburgh-born Robin had worked with composer Richard Whiting on some of Paramount's first musicals of 1929 and 1930, before the Fox Studios snared Whiting away from Paramount.

Robin and Rainger's first songs together at Paramount were written for Bing Crosby to sing in *The Big Broadcast* (1932). This multistar movie was the first in an almost annual series of Paramount musicals featuring popular radio personalities (many making their screen debuts) in movies that had a minimum of plot surrounding a succession of variety acts. Crosby had rapidly become the nation's hottest radio crooner, and in 1931 and '32 he had made a series of musical shorts for Mack Sennett. But now Paramount was looking to *The Big Broadcast* to see just how much appeal young Crosby would have in a feature film. Crosby not only got billing in *The Big Broadcast* ahead of such other radio stars as George Burns and Gracie Allen, Kate Smith, Cab Calloway, the Boswell Sisters, the Mills Brothers, and Arthur Tracy (the "Street Singer"), but he also became the pivot around which the minimal plot hinged. (He did not, however, get top billing. That went to comedian Stuart Erwin.)

Rainger and Robin tailored their two *The Big Broadcast* songs specifically for Crosby's easy-going, generally low-key style of singing—a style that had already begun to revolutionize pop singing in the late '20s and early '30s, by veering sharply away from the overly mannered, operetta-derived style of most Broadway tenors and baritones (with their rolled "r's" and oily vibratos). Instead, it put the emphasis on a more jazz-oriented, unpretentiously "natural" way of delivering both the melodic line and the lyrics of a song. Crosby, to be sure, had not invented the style. But it would be his voice and personality that made the most impact with it—certainly the most lasting impact.

Since Rainger's reputation thus far was for torch songs, it was perhaps inevitable that the first Rainger and Robin song Crosby sings in *The Big Broadcast* would be a torcher, "Here Lies Love" (also sung in the movie by Arthur Tracy). It went on to thirteen weeks in *Variety*'s listing of the nation's top song hits and might well have typecast Rainger if his other song for the picture, completely different in style, hadn't become an even bigger hit—with 22 weeks in the Top 10, including five weeks in the No. 1 spot. That other song is "Please," an unabashedly romantic plea to "tell me that you love me too," and distinguished among pop songs of the era by *beginning* with the song's highest note. Crosby first sings "Please" in *The Big Broadcast* in a rehearsal scene, accompanied only by jazz great Eddie Lang, who sits with his back to the camera strumming a guitar as Bing faces the camera. In his typically nonchalant style, Bing has no sooner sung the first two lines of the lyric than he turns to Lang and says, "Well, I think I know it"—whereupon he proceeds to skip over most of the remaining lyrics by "da-dee-da-dee-dah-ing" and "boo-boo-boo-ing" the melody. It's the sort of treatment which ensured that audiences would leave the theater humming or whistling the tune, especially after Crosby reprises it in the finale.

The Big Broadcast was a hit and Crosby's movie future was assured. And when "Please" turned into one of 1932's biggest song hits, Rainger's identification with just torch songs was ended. He and Robin were both offered long-term contracts by Paramount.

They were put to work, though not with each other, on 1932's *Blonde Venus,* starring Marlene Dietrich at her sultriest in a Josef von Sternberg tearjerker. While Robin was writing "You Little So-and-So" with Richard Whiting for the picture, Rainger, with Sam Coslow, wrote the tom-tomish "Hot Voodoo." It's neither torrid nor particularly memorable as far as its music or lyrics go, but it's staged by Sternberg in such a way as to make it as suggestive a number as Dietrich got away with in the year before Hollywood's censors began to clamp down seriously with the restrictive Production Code. Clad in a gorilla suit, which she partly sheds along the way so she can sing the song, Dietrich romps around the nightclub setting with gestures and

Right: Bing Crosby, late 1930s. He introduced quite a few Rainger-Robin songs, beginning with 1932's The Big Broadcast, *through 1939's* Paris Honeymoon.

Below: The cool and sultry Marlene Dietrich in the "Hot Voodoo" number from Blonde Venus *(1932).*

movements that can serve as the basis for a whole evening's discussion of the Dietrich-Sternberg brand of psychosexual innuendo.

After writing both words and music for incidental (and forgettable) songs for two 1932 nonmusicals, *Big City Blues* and *Million Dollar Legs,* Rainger was reteamed with Robin for a charming 1933 comedy-with-music, *A Bedtime Story,* starring one of Paramount's biggest money-makers, Maurice Chevalier. In this one, Chevalier plays a Parisian playboy who discovers an abandoned baby that wins his heart and helps change his rakish ways. The three songs Rainger and Robin wrote for Chevalier to sing—"In the Park in Paree," "Monsieur Baby," and "Home-Made Heaven"—are serviceable at best and certainly not as memorable as the songs that Rodgers and Hart had written a year earlier for Chevalier's *Love Me Tonight.* Much more interesting is the movie's only non-Chevalier song, "Look What I've Got," which is sung by featured player Leah Ray, cast as one of Chevalier's ex-flames. Through recordings by Paul Whiteman's Orchestra and other pop bands of the day, the bubbly, happy-go-lucky song went on to become a modest hit—as much for Robin's look-on-the-bright-side-of-life lyrics as for Rainger's melody.

Rainger's next was 1933's *Torch Singer,* a "confessions" type of women's picture popular with '30s matinee audiences. Essentially a drama with songs appropriate to the title-character's career, it stars Claudette Colbert—doing her own singing, most credibly, in songs that Rainger tailored to her limited range. Colbert plays an unwed mother who gives up her child when she can't find work to support it. Four years later, she's become a mildly notorious nightclub singer who, through a fluke, substitutes on a radio broadcast for a stricken children's-program hostess and becomes a big hit in that role. The broadcasts (or, rather, the outrageously contrived script) lead her to her abandoned child and a reunion with the father. The script is a bit vague on just how notorious the singer is—although Colbert's first Rainger and Robin song, "It's a Long, Dark Night," gives a significant hint ("I won't struggle if you want to snuggle"). The perky song is cleverly used through three juxtaposed settings to trace the singer's transition from awkward beginner to chic chanteuse. And if you look quickly at the conclusion of that song, the accompanist who gets up from the piano behind Colbert is Rainger himself. The picture's two other songs (the ballad "Don't Cry, Cry Baby" and the almost-marchlike torch song "Give Me Liberty or Give Me Love") are unmemorable —although the latter is amusing for the way Colbert sings it in a style somewhere between Dietrich and Mae West.

Continuing to "write to order" for specific Paramount stars, Rainger contributed one of Mae West's best-known songs for her second movie, *She Done Him Wrong* (an adaptation of West's own hit '20s play, *Diamond Lil*). It's "A Guy What Takes His Time." Rainger is also credited with the lyrics, although West reportedly contributed the idea and a few of the rhymes. Rainger also adapted an old jazz ballad, "Easy Rider" (by Shelton Brooks) for West to sing in *She Done Him Wrong*—and both songs continued to be part of her nightclub repertoire up to her retirement.

She Done Him Wrong made history on two fronts (besides West's own). First, it became such a box-office bonanza that it literally saved Paramount from bankruptcy —a plight into which the studio had seemed headed earlier in 1933. Second, the film's risqué dialogue and blatant sexuality spurred self-proclaimed protectors of morality around the country into pressuring Hollywood's censorship organization, the Hays

Cary Grant and Mae West starred in She Done Him Wrong *(1933), in which West sang Rainger's "A Guy What Takes His Time."*

Office, into stricter enforcement of the Production Code that had been adopted by all the major studios several years earlier but which, until then, was only casually enforced.

If Rainger's versatility needed any further testing at this point, it came with his next assignment. After writing suggestive ditties for Mae West, torchy ballads for Claudette Colbert, and sultry exotica for Marlene Dietrich, Rainger was assigned to write a song for a child performer to sing in *International House.* The singer: Baby Rose Marie, who eventually dropped the "Baby" when she grew up to be the adult singer now well-known to nightclub, Broadway, and TV audiences. As a child performer, Baby Rose Marie was more in the "plain Jane" Withers mold than the "adorably cute" Shirley Temple mold—but with a distinct comic edge. And at age eight, she could belt out a tune with lung power like few youngsters before Judy Garland.

Rainger's song for her in *International House,* with lyrics by Robin, is the parodistic "My Bluebird's Singing the Blues." Robin's tongue-in-cheek words combine with Rainger's irrepressibly "up" tune for a delicious putdown of so many icky kids' songs from vaudeville. And Baby Rose Marie sings it with an alternately sweet-voiced innocence and a surprisingly (for a youngster) "dirty blues" innuendo. It's one of the funniest parts of a movie that has many other funny sequences, with W. C. Fields, Franklin Pangborn, and George Burns and Gracie Allen.

There are two other Rainger-Robin songs in *International House,* a comedy about an experimental television broadcast from (don't ask why!) a hotel in Shanghai. Rudy Vallee, then a major pop crooner, gets to sing "Thank Heaven for You"—a pleasant enough tune that Vallee self-mockingly sings to his megaphone (then one of his trademark props). But the tune failed to do for Vallee what "Please" had done a year earlier for Crosby, possibly because Vallee's rendition gets interrupted by one-liners from Fields. Uninterrupted, although it would have benefited from some trimming, is the *kitsch*-y "She Was a China Teacup and He Was Just a Mug," an Oriental-flavored number in which lumbering Sterling Holloway cavorts with a group of teacup-costumed chorines, in the sort of routine that Busby Berkeley would surely have handled more imaginatively than the Paramount dance director who supervised this one.

An earlier Rainger tune, "Look What I've Got" (from Chevalier's *A Bedtime Story*), also turns up in *International House,* uncredited, as background music during a clever, pantomimed sequence in which W. C. Fields and Peggy Hopkins Joyce use the same bathroom facilities without being aware of the other's presence. Such re-use of tunes written by studio composers, in movies other than the ones for which they were written, was a common '30s practice—and sometimes helped to keep these songs before the public to boost sheet-music sales and radio airplays. (Rainger, incidentally, had nothing to do with another song for which *International House* is somewhat famous: Cab Calloway's "Reefer Man," by Andy Razaf and J. Russell Robinson. Its drug-drenched lyrics are the cause of the number sometimes being cut from TV showings of the movie.)

Paramount kept Rainger and Robin busy churning out song after song for both major productions and B-pictures in 1933 and 1934. They included the title songs for *Midnight Club,* a dull George Raft crime melodrama, and *Cradle Song,* with German star Dorothea Wieck (of '31's *Maedchen in Uniform*) making an unsuccessful American debut. For another Raft programmer, *The Trumpet Blows,* about an aspiring Mexican matador with *bandito* family links, Rainger composed several Latin-flavored songs that did little to advance President Franklin Roosevelt's then much-touted Good Neighbor Policy toward Latin America.

Two Bing Crosby musicals also figured among Rainger's 1934 Paramount assignments. The first, *She Loves Me Not,* costarring Crosby with Kitty Carlisle and Miriam Hopkins, spawned "Love in Bloom." It has remained one of Rainger and Robin's best known songs—thanks not so much to the movie itself nor even to Crosby's once-popular recording of the ballad, but to Jack Benny's butchering of it as a running gag about his violin-playing on hundreds of radio and TV programs, as well as in several movies (including 1936's *College Holiday*). "Love in Bloom" also won for Rainger and

Robin an Academy Award nomination. (They lost to Con Conrad and Herb Magidson's "The Continental" from Astaire and Rogers's *The Gay Divorcée*.)

Rainger's second 1934 Crosby movie was *Here Is My Heart,* again featuring Kitty Carlisle as Bing's leading lady. Its big Rainger-Robin hit—tallying ten weeks on *Variety*'s top hits list—is "June in January," which has remained a pop standard for many seasons. According to Leo Robin, the title came first, contrary to his usual way of working with Rainger. As Robin told me: "Rainger's first reaction was, 'June in January? You're crazy.' Then he reconsidered, and sat down at the piano to work out a melody to go with it." The title, of course, has long since joined the vernacular to describe any period when winter weather turns unseasonably warm, even though the song's romantic lyrics are only partly concerned with the weather as such.

Robin was particularly renowned for his clever titles, but he always insisted that he wrote his lyrics to fit Rainger's melodies—not the other way around. "Sometimes a phrase just came out of the air," Robin said, "and sometimes the rhythm of Ralph's original tune would suggest an idea for a lyric. Ralph always liked a lyric that wasn't too conventional in style. He encouraged me to dig for distinctive titles."

Bing Crosby became partial to another Rainger and Robin song in *Here Is My Heart:* an elegant ballad titled "(I Dream of You) With Every Breath I Take." He promoted it as much as he could on his weekly radio show and even revived it a couple of times in the '40s, but it never caught on. Perry Como also added it to his broadcast repertory in the '40s, and both Frank Sinatra and Marlene Ver Plank recorded it even later—without any wider acceptance than Bing. I've long wished its fate were otherwise, for "With Every Breath I Take" is an uncommonly worthy song and remains a personal favorite of mine among Rainger's compositions.

For one of 1934's surprise hits, *Little Miss Marker,* based on a Damon Runyon story about racetrack gamblers, Rainger and Robin contributed two memorable songs. One of them, the cynically wistful "Lowdown Lullaby," is heart wrenchingly sung by sultry-voiced Dorothy Dell, whom Paramount was hoping to build into a major star but who was killed in an auto crash soon after the picture's release. Good as Dell is, the picture is stolen by the fourth-billed, five-year-old tot borrowed from Fox to play the title role: Shirley Temple, in the picture that made her a star. Temple and Dell both make the most of the bright, Depression-chasing duet "Laugh, You Son-of-a-Gun." But Dell can't do much with the weak torch song "I'm a Black Sheep Who's Blue," for which neither Robin's penchant for "play-on-words" lyrics nor Rainger's "torcher" reputation comes through this time.

They did come through delightfully, however, in tailoring a song for nonsinger Cary Grant to half-speak, half-sing to his leading lady, Helen Mack, in 1934's *Kiss and Make Up,* a romantic comedy about the cosmetics business. Grant handles the catchy "Love Divided by Two" most creditably, but it still didn't open up a career in musicals for Grant—unlike the case of another leading romantic star of the '30s, Tyrone Power, who ended up in several major musicals without singing a note.

Although his name is not included in the picture's credits, Rainger contributed part of the score to one of 1934's biggest hits, *Bolero.* For it, Paramount secured screen rights to Maurice Ravel's then fairly new (1928) concert piece and used a much-abridged version for the picture's climax, as danced by stars George Raft and Carole

George Raft and Carole Lombard danced to Rainger's "The Rhythm of the Rumba" in Rumba *(1935).*

Lombard (and, as is only too clear in parts of the number, their doubles). Earlier in the picture, Raft dances to a sultry tango, "The Raftero." Rainger not only wrote it, but he's also the pianist (barely seen) in the orchestra in the background. But Paramount played up only Ravel's name in *Bolero*'s credits.

The success of *Bolero* led to a sequel of sorts for Raft and Lombard, mixing a similar melodrama with another type of dance beat: 1935's *Rumba* (with the "h" dropped for reasons the studio never made clear, although one story, possibly apocryphal, says that someone who wasn't a spelling whiz filled out the studio's copyright application). Like so many Hollywood attempts to cash in quickly on one winner, *Rumba* was a flop. But, for it, Rainger composed a fairly long (eleven minutes) orchestral piece titled "The Rhythm of the Rhumba"—developing a simple melody through a number of concert variations, all with a rhumba beat. Rainger hoped the piece would show off his more "serious" musical talent (as had "An American in Paris" for Gershwin) and perhaps even find a place in the concert hall. But "The Rhythm of the Rhumba" failed to make even a fraction of the impact on audiences that Ravel's "Bolero" had made—and Rainger never again attempted a concert-like orchestral score for the movies. (According to his daughter, he did, however, compose an unpublished orchestral suite in 1940—titled *Newspaper Suite,* with movements subtitled "Front Page," "Sports Page," "Society Page," "Comic Strip," etc.)

For the next several years, Rainger contented himself with going back to writing more conventional songs with Robin for a continuous string of Paramount pictures. Although only a few from this mid-'30s period have become pop standards, most of them left '30s audiences pleased at the time. Among the songs: "I Don't Want to Make History (I Just Want to Make Love)," which radio singer Frances Langford sang in her first leading movie role, in *Palm Springs;* "A Rhyme for Love" and "I Adore You" for one of a seemingly endless string of collegiate musicals, this one *College Holiday;* the lovely "Long Ago and Far Away" (no relation to the more famous Jerome Kern-Ira Gershwin song of the same title for '43's *Cover Girl*) for a B musical, *Three Cheers for Love;* and "What Have You Got That Gets Me?" which Jack Benny sings (yes, *sings*) to Joan Bennett in *Artists and Models Abroad.* Ironically, one of Rainger's finest songs, the exceptionally touching "If I Should Lose You," would come from one of Paramount's worst 1936 pictures: *Rose of the Rancho,* a relocated, pop-oriented variation on the old operetta *The Desert Song,* with the mysterious vigilante this time turning out to be a woman, opera and radio star Gladys Swarthout in her movie debut. Happily, both Swarthout and "If I Should Lose You" survived the picture.

In between there were Paramount's almost-annual *Big Broadcast* series. For the *Big Broadcast of 1936,* Rainger teamed for the first and only time with Dorothy Parker, then working on scripts at Paramount. Together they wrote the easy-going, sentimental "I Wished on the Moon" for Bing Crosby. It became the first Rainger song to make radio's then five-month-old *Your Hit Parade.*

For the *Big Broadcast of 1937,* Rainger, reteamed with Leo Robin, wasn't so lucky. In that edition they were upstaged by Leopold Stokowski leading a symphony orchestra in a Bach transcription and at the other extreme, by Martha Raye singing a swing version of "Here Comes the Bride." But one new Robin-Rainger ballad still managed to stand out amid all the usual variety turns: "I'm Talking Through My Heart," as introduced by Shirley Ross, one of the '30s richest-voiced movie thrushes, who had the picture's leading romantic role (her first) opposite Ray Milland.

Shirley Ross would get to sing more Rainger and Robin songs in her next picture, this time with Bing Crosby as her co-star in one of his most popular '30s musicals, *Waikiki Wedding* (1937). Set in the Hawaiian Islands (actually the Paramount back lot), with hundreds of grass-skirted chorines decorating scene after scene, *Waikiki Wedding*, in part, spoofs '30s advertising promotions built around beauty contests (in this case "Miss Pineapple"). The spirited playing of the cast (including Martha Raye and Bob Burns) keep it all amiably diverting—as do the songs. According to Leo Robin, Rainger expected the sunny ballad "Sweet Is the Word for You" to be the picture's big hit (he had written it the night of the birth of his daughter, Constance, and dedicated it to her). But it made only one week on *Your Hit Parade,* in contrast to six for the dreamier "Blue Hawaii." And it would be a non-Rainger-Robin song that became the movie's biggest hit (with twelve *Hit Parade* weeks): "Sweet Leilani," by Hawaiian bandleader Harry Owens, a song Crosby had asked Rainger to let him add to the score as a favor to his friend, Owens.

That same year, Carole Lombard, whose box-office popularity was soaring following '36's *My Man Godfrey,* got stuck with what is arguably Rainger and Robin's worst song, "If It Isn't Pain, Then It Isn't Love." The song had been written originally for Marlene Dietrich to sing in '35's *The Devil Is a Woman* (about a heartlessly sadistic *femme fatale*). But Dietrich had the good sense to reject it. It was then foisted on Lombard to sing in '37's *Swing High, Swing Low* (a revamped version of the Broadway play *Burlesque* and the '29 movie *Dance of Life*). Lombard, doing her own singing (actually half-singing, half-speaking), looks appropriately pained throughout the song.

By 1937, however, Rainger's reputation in Hollywood was as solid within the industry as that of Harry Warren (working at Warner Brothers), Richard Whiting (then switching from Twentieth Century-Fox to Warner Brothers), or Nacio Herb Brown (at MGM). But Paramount's reputation for musicals was not in the same league as the other major studios, except for the *Big Broadcast* series. Sometimes it seemed as if musical numbers were literally tossed into productions that didn't need them, just because the studio had a music department for which it was paying salaries. Scripts would be rewritten so there would be a nightclub sequence requiring one or two songs, or one of the secondary characters would be made a singer (or would-be singer), who'd naturally have to sing a song or two somewhere along the way. Thus Rainger's mid-'30s credits include songs for such nonmusicals as *Four Hours to Kill, Come on Marines, Hideaway Girl, The Texans, Ebb Tide,* and *Easy Living.*

At about the same time, in an effort to give at least a few of its musicals a special distinctiveness, Paramount experimented with an innovative style of down-to-earth "pop opera." That meant that all the dialogue for certain sequences would be sung, but in a strictly popular-music style. For one such attempt, a 1938 melodrama, *You and Me* (with George Raft and Sylvia Sidney), producer Boris Morros and director Fritz Lang brought to Hollywood for the first time Kurt Weill and Bertolt Brecht, who had won fame in pre-Hitler Berlin for *The Three-Penny Opera* and other works that were closer to popular '20s music than to traditional opera. But Weill, unhappy with the studio system and the power exercised by musically illiterate executives, walked out on the production less than halfway through to return to Broadway. (Frederick Hollander completed the assignment).

Less publicized a year earlier was an attempt at a similar pop-opera style by Frank Loesser and Manning Sherwin for *Blossoms on Broadway,* starring Edward Arnold and Shirley Ross in a trite story about con artists. Even though most of the vocalized dialogue was kept to the last part of the picture and presented in a tongue-in-cheek way, nervous Paramount executives decided that the picture needed at least one "sure-fire" hit-type song up front. And so Rainger and Robin were brought in to write a title song, an attractive, easily-remembered ballad. As sung by Ross, it became the only really likable part of a movie whose experimental, hybrid style pleased neither critics nor audiences. The *New York Times* reviewer, Frank S. Nugent, for example, aptly dismissed *Blossoms on Broadway* as "breaking down into song rather than breaking out into it." The picture ended up on the bottom half of double-feature bills in most of the country. (Loesser, of course, would continue to experiment with the idea of a "popular-music opera," finally culminating in his 1956 stage production *The Most Happy Fella,* which has since entered the repertoires of several opera companies.)

Shirley Ross would also play a major part in Rainger's biggest hit of the late '30s—one that, interestingly enough in light of the fiasco of *Blossoms on Broadway,* came about because director Mitchell Leisen wanted to attempt an extended scene that would explain, through just words and music, the past relationship of two of the major characters in *The Big Broadcast of 1938.* Leisen had gone through six different script

Shirley Ross, who had one of the best singing voices in Hollywood in the 1930s, introduced Rainger songs in five films—including "Thanks for the Memory" and "Blossoms on Broadway."

rewrites trying to get the relationship explained in dialogue before he hit on the idea of doing it through song. He wanted to make it clear that the two characters, a formerly married couple who meet accidentally on an ocean liner, are still in love with each other but are unwilling to say so. To complicate matters, the man is being played by a comedian (Bob Hope), so there should be a few laughs in the scene despite its underlying seriousness.

When Leisen first approached Rainger and Robin about the song, Robin—as he later told Max Wilk for his book *They're Playing Our Song*—responded, "It's not easy to say 'I love you' without *saying* it. Most songs come right out and hit it on the nose. But we'll see what we can do." Rainger then suggested that, contrary to their usual work method, Robin write the lyrics first, and then he'd set them to music. Three weeks later, Rainger and Robin were finally ready to play their song for Leisen. They both felt it was short on laughs, though most of the lines had a light touch. It would be a duet, sung by the couple over a drink in the ship's bar as they reminisced about their married days. The title: "Thanks for the Memory." The couple: Bob Hope and Shirley Ross. Among its unforgettable lines:

HE: *"Thanks for the memory . . . of motor trips and burning lips, and burning toast and prunes.*

SHE: *"Thanks for the memory, of candlelight and wine, and castles on the Rhine—*

HE: *"And moments on the Hudson River Line . . .*

SHE *"We said goodbye with a highball,*

HE: *"And I got as high as a steeple. But we were intelligent people—*

SHE: *"No tears, no fuss.*

HE: *"Hooray for us. . . .*

As Robin sang the song to director Leisen, with Rainger at the piano, the songwriters got worried about halfway through when they saw Leisen pull out his handkerchief and start to wipe an eye. As Robin recalled the scene to Max Wilk: "I thought, 'What's this? It's supposed to be funny, and the guy's going to weep.' Well, we finished the song and Leisen said, sniffing, 'No, it's not funny—but I'll take it.'"

Robin still wasn't sure about the song. But Rainger was. He bet Robin ten dollars it would be a hit. "You're crazy," Robin told his partner. "It's not a song, it's a piece of material."

Rainger won the bet when the song went on to ten weeks on radio's *Your Hit Parade*—including three weeks in the No. 1 spot. He also had the honor, with Robin, of accepting an Academy Award statuette that year for Best Song—winning over two Irving Berlin nominations ("Now It Can Be Told" from *Alexander's Ragtime Band* and "Change Partners" from *Carefree*), Harry Warren and Johnny Mercer's "Jeepers Creepers" (from *Going Places*), and Jimmy McHugh and Harold Adamson's "My Own" (from Deanna Durbin's *That Certain Age*).

Although originally written as a duet, "Thanks for the Memory" became primarily identified with Bob Hope alone after he chose it as the theme song for his radio show, which began broadcasting on NBC just a few months after the release of *The Big Broadcast of 1938*. Hope has amended the lyrics many times over the years and he has changed the basic tone of the song from one of sophisticated romantic reminiscence to more straight-faced nostalgia. But, through Hope, Rainger's melody has become one of the most widely recognized pop standards of all time. People who know the song only as Hope's theme rarely fail to be surprised—and moved—when they first see *The Big Broadcast of 1938* on TV or in a movie revival house and hear how marvelously the original duet version holds up, and how touching both Hope and Ross are in the sequence. The song is not just "a piece of material," as Robin first feared, but a genuine "pop aria" that manages to tell more about two characters' feelings for each other than any lines of dialogue could in the same three or four minutes. Few songs written for any movie over the past fifty years can equal it in that respect.

Later in 1938, Paramount tried to cash in on the song's popularity by reteaming Bob Hope and Shirley Ross in a modest-budget domestic comedy titled (surprise!) *Thanks for the Memory*—one of the first times a movie song had an entire movie for an encore. Rainger and Robin were not assigned to write any new songs for the picture, although their title song does get a big play for the battling couple's reconciliation in the last reel. The only new song, "Two Sleepy People," was contributed by Hoagy Carmichael and Frank Loesser, and became a modest hit—as did the routinely scripted picture itself.

Rainger and Robin would keep their duet momentum going in 1939 with another good if less-inspired romantic duet—this time for Shirley Ross to sing with Bing Crosby in *Paris Honeymoon*. The song, "I Have Eyes," lasted seven weeks on *Your Hit Parade* (peaking at the No. 4 spot) and then pretty much disappeared. So too, unfortunately, did Shirley Ross. Though not "Hollywood pretty" in the way '30s producers (and audiences) generally preferred, she was warmly personable and had one of the best singing voices in Hollywood in those years. Rainger knew his ballads were in good hands with Ross and he wrote some of his best for her. After *Paris Honeymoon*, in which Ross lost Crosby to pert Franciska Gaal (a Sonja Henie lookalike who couldn't skate or sing or do more than look cutesy), Ross returned to Broadway for the lead in Rodgers and Hart's *Higher and Higher,* an only so-so hit of 1940. She then retired, except for occasional radio and B-movie work. Her major claim to movie-musical immortality remains the Rainger and Robin song that she, as much as Bob Hope, put over so unforgettably in *The Big Broadcast of 1938.*

Meanwhile, as Bob Hope's popularity soared, more from his radio show than from his early movie roles, Paramount teamed him with other leading ladies—two, in fact, for *Give Me a Sailor:* Martha Raye and Betty Grable (the latter still in the starlet category but just a year or so away from breaking into star status, first on Broadway, then at another studio). For all of Raye's energetic slapstick clowning and Hope's wisecrack slinging, *Give Me a Sailor* is doomed by its convoluted plot, involving two Navy officer brothers (Hope and Jack Whiting) in love with the same girl (Grable). Lost in the jumble are two lovely Rainger and Robin songs. Raye gets to sing one of them twice, in contrasting styles. "Just a Kiss at Twilight" is first offered as a wistful, sentimental ballad as Raye dreamily fries an egg into a heart shape (and sings in the sincere ballad style that Hollywood rarely let her do—and which she did so well). For the film's finale, she half swings, half scats the lyrics in an uptempo version that makes the lyrics unintentionally self-mocking. Much better all around is the ballad "What Goes on Here in My Heart?" that Grable sings as she flirts, in succession, with Whiting, John Hubbard, and other Navy officers at a dance.

As the popularity of Paramount's musicals plummeted, the studio assigned Rainger and Robin to a major project for which it had high hopes: *Gulliver's Travels,* a feature-length animated cartoon by Max and Dave Fleischer. Paramount hoped it would repeat the phenomenal box-office and critical success of Walt Disney's 1938 *Snow White and the Seven Dwarfs* (for RKO Radio). The Fleischer brothers had created Paramount's long-popular Betty Boop and Popeye series in the early '30s. From the beginning, the Fleischers had built many of their cartoon shorts around songs. In fact, some of the earliest Betty Boops were released as part of Paramount's bouncing-ball *Screen Song* series and featured on the soundtrack the voices of Cab Calloway, Louis Armstrong, Ethel Merman, Maurice Chevalier, and others under contract to the studio. When, in 1938, two of *Snow White*'s songs quickly soared into the Top Ten ("Whistle While You Work" and "Heigh Ho," by Frank Churchill and Larry Morey), there was little doubt that the Fleischers' first animated feature would also be built around music.

In freely adapting Jonathan Swift's classic Gulliver stories into a screen fairy tale aimed at children, the Fleischers eliminated most of Swift's bitter, often-savage satire, added stereotypically cartoonish characters, and centered their plot on a silly war that erupts because two kings cannot agree on which song shall be sung at the wedding of Princess Glory to Prince David. One king wants his nation's song, "Faithful," whereas the other king wants his nation's "Forever." Gulliver resolves the conflict and brings about a happy ending by combining the two songs into a new one, "Faithful Forever." Rainger met the plot's musical challenge adroitly, with the combined song emerging as one of his most elegant and touchingly romantic ballads—making *Your Hit Parade* for nine weeks. Kids flocked to see *Gulliver's Travels* (released during the '39 Christmas season), but the critics were lukewarm. The "which song?" basis of the movie's antiwar satire seemed particularly silly and naive in the face of what Hitler's Nazis and Japan's militarists were then doing in the real world. For a while, Rainger entertained hopes that "Faithful Forever" might emerge as a new standard for weddings and anniversaries (much like Carrie Jacob Bond's "I Love You Truly" or Reginald DeKoven's "O Promise Me"), but the publisher failed to promote it as such and the song faded after its brief popularity.

Rainger and Robin wrote their last song for Paramount in 1939: "Love With a Capital U," for *$1,000 a Touchdown.* This one teamed wide-mouthed comedienne Martha Raye with even wider-mouthed comedian Joe E. Brown in the most minor of Paramount's long string of collegiate musical comedies *(College Holiday, College Humor, College Rhythm, College Swing).* The song has an amiable Rainger melody and cute Robin lyrics, saying that Love isn't spelled with a capital L but with a capital U which "just suits me to a capital T." But, like the movie itself, the song never caught on. Perhaps most tellingly of all, it was the only song in the movie—indicating just how much Paramount was downgrading music in favor of straight comedy within a formerly popular genre.

With Paramount obviously less and less interested in producing major musicals, both Rainger and Robin were ready to move on when their contracts expired. Rainger moved back to New York with his family for nearly a year, in hopes of landing a Broadway show for himself and Leo Robin (who stayed in Hollywood). Among the projects that got as far as the discussion stage: a musical set in Sun Valley, with the chorus made up of ice-skaters instead of dancers; a musical for Fred Astaire, who had just ended his seven-year movie partnership with Ginger Rogers and was looking to get away from Hollywood for a year; and a musical version of Anita Loos's *Gentlemen Prefer Blondes,* about which Rainger was not enthusiastic, although Robin was. None of these projects ever worked out. At one point, Rainger even wrote bitterly to Leo Robin that unless your name was Rodgers and Hart, you didn't stand a chance of getting serious backing for a Broadway musical in 1940. (A decade later, it would be Jule Styne who would team with Leo Robin when *Gentlemen Prefer Blondes* finally did reach Broadway, and later Hollywood, as a musical.)

With feelers reaching both Rainger and Robin from MGM and Twentieth Century-Fox, Rainger decided to move back to Hollywood late in 1940. As he told a colleague at the time, he felt that the only way movie musicals stood a chance of "coming back" was through the discovery of new personalities or the development of fresh approaches. He and Robin finally decided that Darryl F. Zanuck, the studio chief at Twentieth Century-Fox, offered the best chance of achieving those objectives. And Zanuck was eager to have Rainger and Robin.

After the first flurry of movie musical hits had sagged disastrously at the box office in the early '30s, Zanuck had spearheaded the rebirth of the movie musical with *42nd Street* in 1932. Now he was convinced he could do it again with a more razzle-dazzle style of musical focusing on exotic locales, usually photographed in Technicolor. Zanuck had already signed Harry Warren after his Warner contract expired in 1939, and adding Rainger and Robin would give him the cream of Hollywood's own studio-nurtured songwriting teams.

For their first Twentieth Century-Fox assignment, Rainger and Robin drew *Moon Over Miami,* with Betty Grable (newly established as a star after Fox's *Down Argentine Way* and *Tin-Pan Alley*), Don Ameche, Carole Landis, and Robert Cummings. It's a handsome, Technicolor remake of one of the studio's most serviceable and

Moon Over Miami *(1941) starred Betty Grable, shown here dancing to Rainger's "Kindergarten Conga" with veteran dance director Hermes Pan.*

often-used scripts about a trio of modern gold diggers. (It was previously filmed in 1937, without music, as *Three Blind Mice,* and then revamped again in 1946 with a different musical score as *Three Little Girls in Blue.*)

The chief pluses of *Moon Over Miami* are its vivid use of Technicolor (Twentieth Century-Fox, in the early '40s, favored the splashiest use of bright, unsubtle colors in its musicals) and its above-average Rainger-Robin score. The movie's fast pace is clearly abetted by such lively songs as "Me-Oh-My Miami," "I've Got You All to Myself," "Is That Good?" and "The Kindergarten Conga," and, most especially, by the cheery ballad "You Started Something." Unfortunately, "Loveliness and Love," one of Rainger's most beautifully tender melodies, gets bogged down not only in Don Ameche's unctuous vocal delivery but also in some untypically drippy Robin lyrics that even the Miami publicity bureau would probably not try to get away with.

Assignments at Twentieth Century-Fox between 1940 and 1942 involved, just as they had at Paramount, sometimes writing incidental (and forgettable) songs for nonmusicals that needed a song or two, including *A Yank in the R.A.F., Tall, Dark and Handsome, Cadet Girl,* and *Tales of Manhattan.* There was even another collegiate comedy, *Rise and Shine,* for which the songs were as shopworn as the plot. But, mostly, Zanuck kept the team busy on musicals which did very well at the box office as strictly escapist fare during the early days of World War II. Zanuck had indeed, once again, outguessed the competition.

One of 1942's biggest hits was *My Gal Sal,* a musical set in the Gay '90s that pretended to be a biography of songwriter Paul Dresser ("On the Banks of the Wabash," "My Gal Sal") and which used many of his songs. But at least half the score of the picture isn't by Dresser at all, but by Rainger and Robin, imitating Dresser's style at least in part. Alice Faye had originally been announced for the lead and Rainger wrote the melody for one of his all-time loveliest ballads, "Here You Are," with Faye's sultry voice in mind. But as shooting neared, Faye balked at making another "period

Betty Grable, the No. 1 pin-up girl of the American armed forces during World War II, and Jane Wyman starred in Footlight Serenade *(1942).*

costumer" (after *In Old Chicago, Rose of Washington Square,* and *Lillian Russell*). Before the issue could be resolved, Faye (married to band leader Phil Harris) reported she was pregnant. She was replaced in *My Gal Sal* by rising star Rita Hayworth, whose looks, personality, and dancing ability made her a natural for musicals, but whose singing voice left much to be desired. So radio singer and B-movie player Nan Wynn was called in to dub Hayworth's singing voice (as she would later do for several other films). In addition to putting over "Here You Are" beautifully, Hayworth/Wynn do nicely by Rainger and Robin's "Oh, the Pity of It All" and "Me and My Fella and a Big Umbrella," all deliberately designed to match Dresser's style. Leading man Victor Mature's singing voice in the picture is also dubbed, by Ben Gage.

Rainger and Robin wrote some ten songs for two wartime musicals starring Betty Grable, at a time when Grable was the No. 1 Pinup girl of the men in the American armed forces. *Footlight Serenade* (1942), with a contemporary-Broadway backstage plot, and *Coney Island* (1943), another backstager but set at the turn of the century, were both box-office successes although they produced no *Hit Parade* song hits from their plentiful scores. That, however, was partly the result of a ban on radio performances during that period by songwriters affiliated with ASCAP (the American Society of Composers and Publishers)—and Rainger was an ASCAP composer. (The controversial ban came about when ASCAP and the radio networks could not come to terms on a royalty contract for playing the music of ASCAP composers, and for many months only songs in the public domain or by members of other associations could be performed on the air.) One song that might otherwise have become a major hit for Rainger was *Coney Island*'s "(I Love You) Take It From There," an engaging romantic ballad that Grable sings in one of the most elegant, picture-frame settings of any of her '40s musicals.

Despite the radio ban, one song for *Footlight Serenade* got extra mileage because of its wartime theme: "I'll Be Marching to a Love Song." It turned up in a number of shorts produced to help sell war bonds in movie theaters and to publicize what Hollywood stars were doing for the war effort.

In October of 1942, Rainger and Robin were invited to a meeting of film executives in New York to discuss plans for upcoming productions. Rainger, wishing a few extra days at home with his wife and children, decided to fly to New York instead of making the three-day transcontinental train trip with Leo Robin, who was nervous about flying. Rainger's plane never reached New York. On the night of October 24, soon after takeoff, the plane was involved in a midair collision with a military craft near Palm Springs, California. All aboard were killed. Just a few weeks earlier, Rainger had celebrated his forty-first birthday with his wife, Betty, and their three children after only recently moving into his newly acquired "dream home" in Beverly Hills.

In fourteen years, Rainger had composed just under two hundred songs for some sixty-five movies. In the process, he not only created some our most enduring pop standards but also *set* a standard for quality melodies in the first decade of the movie musical's Golden Age. His chief collaborator Leo Robin had aptly called those melodies "classy." Even after working in later years with such composers as Kern, Arlen, Warren, Schwartz, and Styne, Robin continued to say that Rainger took second place to none of them in musical taste. Rainger was probably closest to Jerome Kern in the elegance of his ballads, if not always in his musical inventiveness. But whereas Kern brought much of his musical gifts to Hollywood, Rainger found his *in* Hollywood.

RALPH RAINGER'S MOVIES AND SONGS ON TAPE AND DISC

BE YOURSELF (1930), United Artists. B&W. Directed by Thornton Freeland. With Fanny Brice, Robert Armstrong, Harry Green, Gertrude Astor, Babe Kane. Song: "When a Woman Loves a Man" (lyrics, Billy Rose); plus songs by others. Soundtrack LP: excerpts included in *Three of a Kind,* Fannett 146; also, *The Classic Movie Musicals of Ralph Rainger,* Music Masters JJA-19811.

QUEEN HIGH (1930), Paramount. B&W. Directed by Fred Newmeyer. With Frank Morgan, Charles Ruggles, Ginger Rogers, Stanley Smith, Tom Brown, Betty Garde. Songs: "Seems to Me" (lyrics, Dick Howard), "Brother, Just Laugh It Off," "I'm Afraid of You" (collaboration with Arthur Schwartz, Edward Eliscu); plus songs by others.

FOLLOW THE LEADER (1930), Paramount. B&W. Directed by Norman Taurog. With Ed Wynn, Ginger Rogers, Ethel Merman, Lou Holtz, Stanley Smith. Song: "Just Laugh It Off" (collaboration with Arthur Schwartz, E. Y. Harburg); plus songs by others.

SEA LEGS (1930), Paramount. B&W. Directed by Victor Herman. With Jack Oakie, Lillian Roth, Harry Green, Eugene Pallette. Song: "This Must Be Illegal" (collaboration with W. Frank Harling, George Marion, Jr.); plus songs by others. Soundtrack LP: excerpt included in *The Classic Movie Musicals of Ralph Rainger,* Music Masters JJA-19811.

ALONG CAME YOUTH (1931), Paramount. B&W. Directed by Lloyd Corrigan and Norman McLeod. With Charles Buddy Rogers, Frances Dee, Stuart Erwin. Song: "I Look at You and a Song Is Born" (lyrics, George Marion, Jr.); plus songs by others.

THE BIG BROADCAST (1932), Paramount. B&W. Directed by Frank Tuttle. With Stuart Erwin, Bing Crosby, Leila Hyams, George Burns, Gracie Allen, Sharon Lynn, Kate Smith, the Boswell Sisters, Cab Calloway and his Orchestra, the Mills Brothers, Donald Novis, Arthur Tracy, Vincent Lopez and his Orchestra. Songs: "Please," "Here Lies Love" (lyrics, Leo Robin); plus songs by others. Soundtrak LP: Soundtrak 101.

BLONDE VENUS (1932), Paramount. B&W. Directed by Josef von Sternberg. With Marlene Dietrich, Herbert Marshall, Cary Grant, Sidney Toler, Dickie Moore. Song: "Hot Voodoo" (lyrics, Sam Coslow); plus songs by others. Soundtrack LP: excerpt included in *The Classic Movie Musicals of Ralph Rainger,* Music Masters JJA-19811.

THIS IS THE NIGHT (1932), Paramount. B&W. Directed by Frank Tuttle. With Lili Damita, Charles Ruggles, Roland Young, Thelma Todd. Song: "This Is the Night" (lyrics, Sam Coslow).

BIG CITY BLUES (1932), Warner Brothers. B&W. Directed by Mervyn LeRoy. With Joan Blondell, Eric Linden, Evelyn Knapp, Ned Sparks, Guy Kibbee, Lyle Talbot, Inez Courtney, Humphrey Bogart, Jobyna Howland. Song: "I'm in Love With a Tune" (lyrics, Rainger); plus songs by others.

MILLION DOLLAR LEGS (1932), Paramount. B&W. Directed by Edward Cline. With W. C. Fields, Jack Oakie, Andy Clyde, Ben Turpin, Lyda Roberti, Dickie Moore. Song: "It's Terrific" (lyrics, Rainger).

A BEDTIME STORY (1933), Paramount. B&W. Directed by Norman Taurog. With Maurice Chevalier, Helen Twelvetrees, Edward Everett Horton, Baby LeRoy, Adrienne Ames, Gertrude Michael. Songs: "Monsieur Baby," "In a Park in Paree," "Look What I've Got," "Home-Made Heaven" (lyrics, Leo Robin). Soundtrack LP: excerpts included in *The Classic Movie Musicals of Ralph Rainger,* Music Masters JJA-19811.

TORCH SINGER (1933), Paramount. B&W. Directed by Alexander Hall and George Somnes. With Claudette Colbert, Ricardo Cortez, David Manners, Lyda Roberti, Baby LeRoy. Songs: "Don't Be a Cry Baby," "Give Me Liberty or Give Me Love," "It's a Long, Dark Night," "The Torch Singer" (lyrics, Leo Robin). Soundtrack LP: excerpt included in *Hollywood Party,* Pelican 130.

SHE DONE HIM WRONG (1933), Paramount. B&W. Directed by Lowell Sherman. With Mae West, Owen Moore, Cary Grant, Gilbert Roland, Noah Beery, Rochelle Hudson, Rafaela Ottiano, David Landau. Songs: "A Guy What Takes His Time," "Haven't Got No Peace of Mind" (lyrics, Leo Robin); plus songs by others. Soundtrack LP: excerpt included in *The Classic Movie Musicals of Ralph Rainger,* Music Masters JJA-19811.

INTERNATIONAL HOUSE (1933), Paramount. B&W. Directed by Edward Sutherland. With W. C. Fields, Peggy Hopkins Joyce, Stuart Erwin, George Burns, Gracie Allen, Bela Lugosi, Franklin Pangborn, Rudy Vallee, Baby Rose Marie, Cab Calloway and his Orchestra. Songs: "My Bluebird's Singing the Blues," "Thank Heaven for You," "She Was a China Teacup and He Was Just a Mug," "Look What I've Got" (lyrics, Leo Robin); plus songs by others. Soundtrack LP: excerpt included in *The Classic Movie Musicals of Ralph Rainger,* Music Masters JJA-19811.

THE WAY TO LOVE (1933), Paramount. B&W. Directed by Norman Taurog. With Maurice Chevalier, Ann Dvorak, Edward Everett Horton, Minna Gombell, Blanche Frederici, Sidney Toler. Songs: "I'm a Lover of Paree," "It's Oh, It's Ah, It's Wonderful," "In a One-Room Flat," "There's a Lucky Guy" (lyrics, Leo Robin); plus songs by others. Soundtrack LP: Caliban 6013 (with *Playboy of Paris,* others).

CRADLE SONG (1933), Paramount. B&W. Directed by Mitchell Leisen. With Dorothea Wieck, Sir Guy Standing, Evelyn Venable, Louise Dresser, Dickie Moore. Songs: "Cradle Song," "Lonely Little Senorita" (lyrics, Leo Robin).

MIDNIGHT CLUB (1933), Paramount. B&W. Directed by Alexander Hall and George Somnes. With George Raft, Clive Brook, Helen Vinson, Alison Skipworth, Sir Guy Standing. Song: "In a Midnight Club" (lyrics, Leo Robin).

THREE-CORNERED MOON (1933), Paramount. B&W. Directed by Elliott Nugent. With Claudette Colbert, Richard Arlen, Mary Boland, Lyda Roberti, Wallace Ford, Hardie Albright. Song: "Three-Cornered Moon" (lyrics, Leo Robin), cut from final release.

LITTLE MISS MARKER (1934), Paramount. B&W. Directed by Alexander Hall. With Adolphe Menjou, Dorothy Dell, Charles Bickford, Shirley Temple, Lynne Overman, Willie Best. Songs: "Lowdown Lullaby," "I'm a Black Sheep Who's Blue," "Laugh You Son-of-a-Gun" (lyrics, Leo Robin). Soundtrack LP: excerpts included in *The Classic Movie Musicals of Ralph Rainger,* Music Masters JJA-19811.

SHOOT THE WORKS (1934), Paramount. B&W. Directed by Wesley Ruggles. With Jack Oakie, Dorothy Dell, Arline Judge, Alison Skipworth, Ben Bernie, Lew Cody, William Frawley. Songs: "Take a Lesson From the Lark," "Do I Love You?" (lyrics, Leo Robin); plus songs by others.

SHE LOVES ME NOT (1934), Paramount. B&W. Directed by Elliott Nugent. With Bing Crosby, Miriam Hopkins, Kitty Carlisle, Henry Stephenson, Lynne Overman. Song: "Love in

Bloom" (lyrics, Leo Robin); plus songs by others.

THE TRUMPET BLOWS (1934), Paramount. B&W. Directed by Stephen Roberts. With George Raft, Adolphe Menjou, Frances Drake, Sidney Toler. Songs: "This Night My Heart Does the Rhumba," "Pancho," "The Red Cape" (lyrics, Leo Robin).

BOLERO (1934), Paramount. B&W. Directed by Wesley Ruggles. With George Raft, Carole Lombard, Sally Rand, Ray Milland, William Frawley. Music: "The Raftero" and other incidental music by Rainger; plus music by others. Soundtrack LP: excerpt included in *The Classic Movie Musicals of Ralph Rainger,* Music Masters JJA-19811.

HERE IS MY HEART (1934), Paramount. B&W. Directed by Frank Tuttle. With Bing Crosby, Kitty Carlisle, Alison Skipworth, Roland Young, Reginald Owen. Songs: "With Every Breath I Take," "June in January," "Here Is My Heart," "You Can't Make a Monkey of the Moon" (lyrics, Leo Robin). Soundtrack LP: excerpts included in *The Classic Movie Musicals of Ralph Rainger,* Music Masters JJA-19811.

COME ON MARINES (1934), Paramount. B&W. Directed by Henry Hathaway. With Richard Arlen, Ida Lupino, Grace Bradley, Roscoe Karns, Toby Wing, Clara Lou (Ann) Sheridan, Fuzzy Knight. Songs: "Hula Holiday," "Tequila," "Oh Baby, Obey" (lyrics, Leo Robin).

WHARF ANGEL (1934), Paramount. B&W. Directed by William C. Menzies and George Somnes. With Victor McLaglen, Dorothy Dell, Preston Foster. Song: "Down Home" (lyrics, Leo Robin); plus songs by others.

KISS AND MAKE UP (1934), Paramount. B&W. Directed by Harlan Thompson. With Helen Mack, Cary Grant, Genevieve Tobin, Edward Everett Horton. Songs: "Love Divided by Two," "Corned Beef and Cabbage, I Love You," "Mirror Song" (lyrics, Leo Robin). Soundtrack LP: excerpts included in *The Classic Movie Musicals of Ralph Rainger,* Music Masters JJA-19811.

RUMBA (1935), Paramount. B&W. Directed by Marion Gering and Monroe Owsley. With George Raft, Carole Lombard, Margo, Lynne Overman, Gail Patrick. Songs: "I'm Yours for Tonight," "The Magic of You," "Your Eyes Have Said," "If I Knew," "The Rhythm of the Rhumba" (lyrics, Leo Robin). Soundtrack LP: excerpt included in *The Classic Movie Musicals of Ralph Rainger,* Music Masters JJA-19811.

THE BIG BROADCAST OF 1936 (1935), Paramount. B&W. Directed by Norman Taurog. With Jack Oakie, George Burns, Gracie Allen, Lyda Roberti, Wendy Barrie, Bing Crosby, Ethel Merman, Bill Robinson, Ray Noble and his Orchestra, the Nicholas Brothers. Songs: "Double Trouble," "Why Dream" (music-lyrics, Rainger, Richard Whiting, Leo Robin); "I Wished on the Moon" (lyrics, Dorothy Parker); plus songs by others. Soundtrack LP: excerpt included in *The Classic Movie Musicals of Ralph Rainger,* Music Masters JJA-19811.

FOUR HOURS TO KILL (1935), Paramount. B&W. Directed by Mitchell Leisen. With Richard Barthelmess, Helen Mack, Joe Morrison, Ray Milland, Henry Travers. Songs: "Let's Make a Night of It," "Hate to Talk About Myself," "Walking the Floor" (lyrics, Leo Robin).

MILLIONS IN THE AIR (1935), Paramount. B&W. Directed by Ray McCarey. With Willie Howard, Robert Cummings, Eleanore Whitney, John Howard, Joan Davis, Inez Courtney, Wendy Barrie, Benny Baker, Dave Chasen. Songs: "Laughing at the Weather Man," "A Penny in My Pocket" (lyrics, Leo Robin); plus songs by others.

ROSE OF THE RANCHO (1936), Paramount. B&W. Directed by Marion Gering. With Gladys Swarthout, John Boles, Charles Bickford, Willie Howard, Grace Bradley, H. B. Warner. Songs: "If I Should Lose You," "Thunder Over Paradise," "Little Rose of the Rancho," "There's Gold in Monterey," "Got a Girl in Cal-i-for-n-i-a," "Where Is My Love," "The Padre and the Bride" (lyrics, Leo Robin).

PALM SPRINGS (1936), Paramount. B&W. Directed by Aubrey Scotto. With Smith Ballew, Frances Langford, Sir Guy Standing, David Niven, Spring Byington, E. E. Clive, Grady Sutton, Sterling Holloway. Songs: "I Don't Want to Make History (I Just Want to Make Love)," "The Hills of Old Wyoming," "Dreaming Out Loud," "Palm Springs" (lyrics, Leo Robin); plus songs by others. Soundtrack LP: excerpt included in *The Classic Movie Musicals of Ralph Rainger,* Music Masters JJA-19811.

COLLEGE HOLIDAY (1936), Paramount. B&W. Directed by Frank Tuttle. With Jack Benny, George Burns, Gracie Allen, Martha Raye, Johnny Downs, Eleanore Whitney, Marsha Hunt, Leif Erickson, Mary Boland, Ben Blue, Olympe Bradna. Songs: "A Rhyme for Love," "I Adore You," "So What?" (lyrics, Leo Robin); plus songs by others. Soundtrack LP: excerpt included in *Martha Raye,* Legends 1000/5–6.

THREE CHEERS FOR LOVE (1936), Paramount. B&W. Directed by Ray McCarey. With Robert Cummings, Eleanore Whitney, Grace Bradley, John Halliday, Olympe Bradna, Veda Ann Borg, Elizabeth Patterson. Songs: "Where Is My Heart?," "Long Ago and Far Away," "The Swing Tap," "Tap Your Feet" (lyrics, Leo

Robin). Soundtrack LP: excerpt included in *The Classic Movie Musicals of Ralph Rainger,* Music Masters JJA-19811.

POPPY (1936), Paramount. B&W. Directed by A. Edward Sutherland. With W. C. Fields, Richard Cromwell, Rochelle Hudson, Lynne Overman, Catherine Doucet. Song: "A Rendezvous With a Dream" (lyrics, Leo Robin); plus songs by others.

THE BIG BROADCAST OF 1937 (1936), Paramount. B&W. Directed by Mitchell Leisen. With Jack Benny, George Burns, Gracie Allen, Shirley Ross, Ray Milland, Martha Raye, Bob Burns, Eleanore Whitney, Leopold Stokowski, Benny Goodman and his Orchestra, Larry Adler, Benny Fields. Songs: "I'm Talking Through My Heart," "You Came to My Rescue," "Here's Love in Your Eye," "Hi-Ho the Radio," "La Bomba," "Vote for Mr. Rhythm," "Night in Manhattan" (lyrics, Leo Robin); plus songs by others. Soundtrack LP: excerpt included in *The Classic Movie Musicals of Ralph Rainger,* Music Masters JJA-19811; also studio recording of one song included in *The Complete Benny Goodman, Vol. III 1936,* RCA Bluebird AXM2-5532.

RHYTHM ON THE RANGE (1936), Paramount. B&W. Directed by Norman Taurog. With Bing Crosby, Frances Farmer, Martha Raye, Bob Burns, Lucille Gleason. Song: "Drink It Down" (lyrics, Leo Robin); plus songs by others.

HIDEAWAY GIRL (1937), Paramount. B&W. Directed by George Archainbaud. With Martha Raye, Shirley Ross, Robert Cummings, Louis DaPron, Monroe Owsley. Song: "What Is Love?" (music-lyrics, Rainger, Victor Young, Leo Robin); plus songs by others.

WAIKIKI WEDDING (1937), Paramount. B&W. Directed by Frank Tuttle. With Bing Crosby, Shirley Ross, Martha Raye, Bob Burns, Leif Erickson, Grady Sutton, Anthony Quinn. Songs: "Blue Hawaii," "Sweet Is the Word for You," "In a Little Hula Heaven," "Okolehao," "Nani Ona Pua" (lyrics, Leo Robin); plus songs by others. LP: studio recording of songs by Crosby included in *Pocketful of Dreams,* Decca 4252 (withdrawn); also one excerpt included in *The Classic Movie Musicals of Ralph Rainger,* Music Masters JJA-19811.

ARTISTS AND MODELS (1937), Paramount. B&W. Directed by Raoul Walsh. With Jack Benny, Ida Lupino, Richard Arlen, Gail Patrick, Ben Blue, Martha Raye, Louis Armstrong, Judy Canova, Connie Boswell, Andre Kostelanetz and his Orchestra, the Yacht Club Boys, Russell Patterson's Puppets. Song: "I Have Eyes" (lyrics, Leo Robin); plus songs by others.

BLOSSOMS ON BROADWAY (1937), Paramount. B&W. Directed by Richard Wallace.

With Edward Arnold, Shirley Ross, John Trent, Kitty Kelly, Weber and Fields, the Radio Rogues, William Frawley. Song: "Blossoms on Broadway" (lyrics, Leo Robin); plus songs by others.

EBB TIDE (1937), Paramount. Color. Directed by James Hogan. With Frances Farmer, Ray Milland, Oscar Homolka, Lloyd Nolan, Barry Fitzgerald. Songs: "Ebb Tide," "I Know What Aloha Means" (lyrics, Leo Robin).

SWING HIGH, SWING LOW (1937), Paramount. B&W. Directed by Mitchell Leisen. With Carole Lombard, Fred MacMurray, Dorothy Lamour, Charles Butterworth, Jean Dixon, Anthony Quinn, Harvey Stephens. Song: "If It Isn't Pain Then It Isn't Love" (lyrics, Leo Robin); plus songs by others. Soundtrack LP: excerpt included in *Hollywood Story,* Festival 214. Videocassette: Budget Video.

EASY LIVING (1937), Paramount. B&W. Directed by Mitchell Leisen. With Jean Arthur, Edward Arnold, Ray Milland, William Demarest, Franklin Pangborn, Mary Nash. Song: "Easy Living" (lyrics, Leo Robin).

SOULS AT SEA (1937), Paramount. B&W. Directed by Henry Hathaway. With Gary Cooper, George Raft, Frances Dee, Olympe Bradna, Robert Cummings, Henry Wilcoxon, Joseph Schildkraut, Harry Carey. Song: "Susie Sapple" (lyrics, Leo Robin).

THE BIG BROADCAST OF 1938 (1937), Paramount. B&W. Directed by Mitchell Leisen. With W. C. Fields, Martha Raye, Dorothy Lamour, Bob Hope, Shirley Ross, Leif Erickson, Ben Blue, Grace Bradley, Tito Guizar, Kirsten Flagstad, Shep Fields and his Orchestra. Songs: "You Took the Words Right Out of My Heart," "Mama, That Moon Is Here Again," "Thanks for the Memory," "Don't Tell a Secret to a Rose," "This Little Ripple Has Rhythm," "The Waltz Lives On" (lyrics, Leo Robin); plus songs and arias by others. Soundtrack LP: excerpts included in *The Classic Movie Musicals of Ralph Rainger,* Music Masters JJA-19811.

COCOANUT GROVE (1938), Paramount. B&W. Directed by Alfred Santell. With Fred MacMurray, Harriet Hilliard, Eve Arden, Ben Blue, Harry Owens. Songs: "The Waltz Lives On," "Love In Bloom" (lyrics, Leo Robin); plus songs by others.

TROPIC HOLIDAY (1938), Paramount. B&W. Directed by Theodore Reed. With Dorothy Lamour, Martha Raye, Ray Milland, Bob Burns, Tito Guizar, Binnie Barnes. Song: "Having Myself a Time" (lyrics, Leo Robin); plus songs by others.

GIVE ME A SAILOR (1938), Paramount. B&W. Directed by Elliott Nugent. With Bob Hope, Martha Raye, Betty Grable, Jack Whiting, Nana Bryant. Songs: "What Goes on Here in My Heart?," "The U.S.A. and You," "A Little Kiss at Twilight," "It Don't Make Sense" (lyrics, Leo Robin). Soundtrack LP: excerpt included in *The Classic Movie Musicals of Ralph Rainger,* Music Masters JJA-19811; also in *Martha Raye, Legends* 1000/5–6.

THE TEXANS (1938), Paramount. B&W. Directed by James Hogan. With Randolph Scott, Joan Bennett, May Robson, Walter Brennan, Robert Cummings, Harvey Stephens. Song: "Silver on the Sage" (lyrics, Leo Robin).

ARTISTS AND MODELS ABROAD (1938), Paramount. B&W. Directed by Mitchell Leisen. With Jack Benny, Joan Bennett, Mary Boland, Charley Grapewin, the Yacht Club Boys. Songs: "What Have You Got That Gets Me?," "You're Lovely Madame," "Do the Buckaroo" (lyrics, Leo Robin); plus songs by others.

ROMANCE IN THE DARK (1938), Paramount. B&W. Directed by H. C. Potter. With Gladys Swarthout, John Boles, John Barrymore, Claire Dodd, Fritz Feld, Curt Bois. Song: "Tonight We Love" (lyrics, Leo Robin); songs by others. Soundtrack LP: excerpt included in *The Classic Movie Musicals of Ralph Rainger,* Music Masters JJA-19811.

HER JUNGLE LOVE (1938), Paramount. B&W. Directed by George Archainbaud. With Dorothy Lamour, Ray Milland, Lynne Overman, Dorothy Howe (Virginia Vale), J. Carrol Naish. Songs: "Jungle Love," "Coffee and Kisses" (lyrics, Leo Robin); plus songs by others.

PARIS HONEYMOON (1939), Paramount. B&W. Directed by Frank Tuttle. With Bing Crosby, Franciska Gaal, Shirley Ross, Edward Everett Horton, Akim Tamiroff, Ben Blue. Songs: "I Have Eyes," "The Funny Old Hills," "The Maiden by the Brook," "Joobalai," "Work While You May" (lyrics, Leo Robin). Soundtrack LP: excerpts included in *The Classic Movie Musicals of Ralph Rainger,* Music Masters JJA-19811.

MAN ABOUT TOWN (1939), Paramount. B&W. Directed by Mark Sandrich. With Jack Benny, Dorothy Lamour, Edward Arnold, Binnie Barnes, Betty Grable, Eddie "Rochester" Anderson, Phil Harris, Monty Woolley. Song: "Bluebirds in the Moonlight" (lyrics, Leo Robin); also songs by others.

GULLIVER'S TRAVELS (1939), Max Fleischer for Paramount release. Color. Directed by Dave Fleischer. Animated cartoon feature, with the voices of Jessica Dragonette, Lanny Ross, others. Songs: "Faithful Forever," "Bluebirds in the Moonlight," "All's Well," "We're All Together Again," "I Hear a Dream" (lyrics, Leo Robin); plus songs by others. Videocassette: Republic; also, Media/Nostalgia Merchant;

Budget Video.

NEVER SAY DIE (1939), Paramount. B&W. Directed by Elliott Nugent. With Martha Raye, Bob Hope, Gale Sondergaard, Andy Devine, Monty Woolley, Sig Rumann. Song: "The Trala-la and Oom-pah-pah" (lyrics, Leo Robin). Soundtrack LP: excerpt included in *Martha Raye, Legends* 1000/5–6.

ONE THOUSAND DOLLARS A TOUCHDOWN (1939), Paramount. B&W. Directed by James Hogan. With Martha Raye, Joe E. Brown, Eric Blore, Susan Hayward, John Hartley, Joyce Matthews. Song: "Love With a Capital U" (lyrics, Leo Robin). Soundtrack LP: *The Classic Movie Musicals of Ralph Rainger,* Music Masters JJA-19811.

MOON OVER MIAMI (1941), Twentieth Century-Fox. Color. Directed by Walter Lang. With Betty Grable, Don Ameche, Carole Landis, Robert Cummings, Charlotte Greenwood, Cobina Wright Jr., Jack Haley. Songs: "Oh Me, Oh My, Miami," "You Started Something," "I've Got You All to Myself," "Is That Good?," "Loveliness and Love," "Kindergarten Conga," "Solitary Seminole," "What Can I Do for You?" (lyrics, Leo Robin). Soundtrack LP: Caliban 6001 (with *Coney Island*); and excerpts included in *The Movie Musicals of Ralph Rainger,* Music Masters JJA-19811.

CADET GIRL (1941), Twentieth Century-Fox. B&W. Directed by Ray McCarey. With Carole Landis, George Montgomery, John Shepperd, William Tracy, Janis Carter. Songs: "My Old Man Was an Army Man," "She's a Good Neighbor," "I'll Settle for You," "It Happened, It's Over, Let's Forget It," "It Won't Be Fun (But It's Got to Be Done)," "Uncle Sam Gets Around," "Making a Play for You" (lyrics, Leo Robin).

NEW YORK TOWN (1941), Paramount. B&W. Directed by Charles Vidor. With Mary Martin, Fred MacMurray, Robert Preston, Lynne Overman, Eric Blore. Song: "Love in Bloom" (lyrics, Leo Robin); plus songs by others.

TALL, DARK AND HANDSOME (1941), Twentieth Century-Fox. B&W. Directed by H. Bruce Humberstone. With Cesar Romero, Virginia Gilmore, Milton Berle, Charlotte Greenwood, Sheldon Leonard, Marion Martin. Songs: "Wishful Thinking," "Hello, Ma, I Done It Again," "I'm Alive and Kickin'" (lyrics, Leo Robin).

RISE AND SHINE (1941), Twentieth Century-Fox. B&W. Directed by Allan Dwan. With Jack Oakie, Linda Darnell, George Murphy, Walter Brennan, Ruth Donnelly, Milton Berle, Sheldon Leonard. Songs: "Men of Clayton," "I'm Making a Play for You," "I Want to

Be the Guy," "Heil to Bolenciewicz," "Central Two Two Oh Oh," "Get Thee Behind Me Clayton" (lyrics, Leo Robin).

A YANK IN THE R.A.F. (1941), Twentieth Century-Fox. B&W. Directed by Henry King. With Tyrone Power, Betty Grable, John Sutton, Reginald Gardiner, Morton Lowry, Bruce Lester. Songs: "Another Little Dream Won't Do Us Any Harm," "Hi-Ya Love" (lyrics, Leo Robin). Soundtrack LP: excerpt included in *The Classic Movie Musicals of Ralph Rainger,* Music Masters JJA-19811.

MY GAL SAL (1942), Twentieth Century-Fox. Color. Directed by Irving Cummings. With Rita Hayworth, Victor Mature, John Sutton, Carole Landis, James Gleason, Phil Silvers. Songs: "Oh, the Pity of It All," "Here You Are," "On the Gay White Way," "Midnight at the Masquerade," "Me and My Fella and a Big Umbrella" (lyrics, Leo Robin); plus songs by others. Soundtrack LP: excerpts included in *The Classic Movie Musicals of Ralph Rainger,* Music Masters JJA-19811; also, excerpts included in *Rita Hayworth,* Curtain Calls 100/2

FOOTLIGHT SERENADE (1942), Twentieth Century-Fox. B&W. Directed by Gregory Ratoff. With Betty Grable, John Payne, Victor Mature, Jane Wyman, James Gleason, Phil Silvers, June Lang, Cobina Wright Jr. Songs: "Are You Kidding?" "I Heard the Birdies Sing," "I'm Still Crazy About You," "Land on Your Feet," "Living High (on a Western Hill)," "I'll Be Marching to a Love Song" (lyrics, Leo Robin). Soundtrack LP: Caliban 6002 (with *Rose Washington Square*).

TALES OF MANHATTAN (1942), Twentieth Century-Fox. B&W. Directed by Julien Duvivier. With Charles Boyer, Rita Hayworth, Ginger Rogers, Henry Fonda, Charles Laughton, Edward G. Robinson, Ethel Waters, Paul Robeson, Eddie "Rochester" Anderson, Cesar Romero, Elsa Lanchester, George Sanders. Song: "Glory Day" (lyrics, Leo Robin); plus songs by others.

CONEY ISLAND (1943), Twentieth Century-Fox. Color. Directed by Walter Lang. With Betty Grable, Victor Mature, Cesar Romero, Charles Winninger, Phil Silvers. Songs: "Take It From There," "Beautiful Coney Island," "There's Danger in a Dance," "Lulu From Louisville," "Old Demon Rum" (lyrics, Leo Robin); plus songs by others. Soundtrack LP: Caliban 6001 (with *Moon Over Miami*).

RIDING HIGH (1943), Paramount. Color. Directed by George Marshall. With Dorothy Lamour, Dick Powell, Victor Mature, Cass Daley, Gil Lamb, Rod Cameron, Milt Britton and his Orchestra. Songs: "You're the Rainbow," "Get Your Man," "Whistling in the Dark" (lyrics, Leo Robin); "Injun Gal Heap Hep" (collaboration by Rainger, Joseph Lilley, Leo Robin). Soundtrack LP: excerpts included in *Dorothy Lamour,* Legends 1000/4.

COLT COMRADES (1943), United Artists. B&W. Directed by Lesley Selander. With William Boyd, Andy Clyde, Victor Jory, Bob Mitchum, George Reeves. Song: "Tonight We Ride" (lyrics, Leo Robin).

KEY LARGO (1946), Warner Brothers. B&W. Directed by John Huston. With Humphrey Bogart, Lauren Bacall, Edward G. Robinson, Lionel Barrymore, Claire Trevor. Song: "Moanin' Low" (lyrics, Howard Dietz). Videocassette and videodisc: CBS-Fox.

WITH A SONG IN MY HEART (1952), Twentieth Century-Fox. Color. Directed by Walter Lang. With Susan Hayward, Rory Calhoun, David Wayne, Thelma Ritter, Robert Wagner, Una Merkel. Song: "On the Gay White Way" (lyrics, Leo Robin); plus songs by others. Soundtrack LP: excerpts included in *Susan Hayward,* Legends 1000/2.

THE JOKER IS WILD (1957), Paramount. B&W. Directed by Charles Vidor. With Frank Sinatra, Jeanne Crain, Mitzi Gaynor, Eddie Albert, Jackie Coogan, Sophie Tucker, Beverly Garland. Song: "June in January" (lyrics, Leo Robin); plus songs by others.

BLUE HAWAII (1962), Paramount. Color. Directed by Norman Taurog. With Elvis Presley, Joan Blackman, Angela Lansbury, Iris Adrian, Roland Winters. Song: "Blue Hawaii" (lyrics, Leo Robin); plus songs by others. Soundtrack LP: RCA Victor AYLI-3683. Videocassette and videodisc: Key-CBS/Fox.

Richard Rodgers in the 1970s.

The two teams of songwriters who have most profoundly influenced American musicals in this century have had one thing in common: the composer, Richard Rodgers. First with Lorenz Hart as his lyricist (from about 1920 to 1943) and then with Oscar Hammerstein II (from 1943 to 1960), Rodgers not only composed hundreds of songs that remain among the most popular of all time, but also significantly shaped the direction as well as the quality of theater music—and, through it, movie musicals. As Leonard Bernstein once said: "He is, perhaps, the most imitated songwriter of our time. He has established new levels of taste, distinction, simplicity in the best sense, and inventiveness."

For nearly sixty years Rodgers produced an unequaled and seemingly boundless flow of melody—mostly for Broadway musicals. But the movie versions of those musicals, plus Rodgers's original work for some eighteen motion pictures, have reached many more millions of people. In fact, it is a Rodgers musical, *The Sound of Music,* that for more than a decade held the all-time box-office record for a movie musical.

Richard Charles Rodgers was born in Hammels Station, near Arverne, Long Island, New York, on June 28, 1902. His father, Dr. William Rodgers, a general practitioner of Alsatian Jewish parentage, had been born William Abrams in Missouri, but he changed his name to Rodgers while studying medicine at the City College of New York in the 1880s. According to writer-director Garson Kanin, the 1938 Hollywood film *A Man to Remember* (which Kanin directed) was partly inspired by Dr. Rodgers's career as a hard-working, idealistic neighborhood doctor.

Dick, as the family called him, grew up in New York City, in a brownstone on West 120th Street in which his father's office was on the ground floor. He began playing the piano by ear at about age six and took his first lessons from his mother, Mamie Rodgers, an accomplished amateur pianist.

When Rodgers was eight years old, he developed a severe infection of one of the fingers on his right hand. For a while, doctors feared that the finger might have to be amputated. But Dr. Rodgers found a bone surgeon who could perform a delicate operation that saved his son's finger. The operation, however, ended any thoughts Rodgers and his family may have had about a concert career as a pianist—although Dick continued to play the piano expertly and made a number of recordings of his music in later years with himself as the pianist.

Soon after the operation, Rodgers's mother took him to see one of his first Broadway musicals: Jerome Kern's *Very Good Eddie,* one of that composer's most popular Princess Theater musicals. Young Dick was so taken with the show that he went back to see it six times. He was soon playing its songs for his family and friends at every opportunity.

Rodgers was fourteen when he volunteered to write songs for a show at a summer camp he was attending in Maine. His older brother, Mortimer, provided the lyrics. The songs were clearly modeled after those in the Kern and Victor Herbert operettas he had seen on Broadway, but the compliments he received were encouraging. The following fall, through a club to which Mortimer belonged, the two Rodgers brothers again teamed up to write songs for an amateur production.

Meanwhile, Rodgers's musical interests took a new direction. While still a student at DeWitt Clinton High School, he discovered opera. He became so passionate about it that he bought a seventeen dollar season's subscription for a balcony seat at the Metropolitan Opera. He also began buying his own balcony tickets for the Carnegie Hall concerts of the New York Philharmonic. (Years later, he would become a member of the board of directors of the Philharmonic.)

But Rodgers's interest in musical comedy became dominant again when a Columbia classmate of his brother Mortimer introduced him to Lorenz "Larry" Hart. The New York–born Hart, then twenty-three, had dropped out of Columbia at the end of his junior year because he was more interested in shows than in his studies. He and Rodgers discovered they had a lot in common, despite a seven-year difference in their ages. Not only had they attended the same high school and the same summer camp, but they both loved the Princess Theater shows and had ambitions to write for shows of that type. Hart was outspoken about his ideas for improving the sophistication and intelligence levels of lyrics. Rodgers was impressed. They decided to try writing songs together.

In 1919, soon after Rodgers enrolled as a freshman at Columbia, a friend arranged for the young songwriters to meet Lew Fields, one of the stars of the comedy team of Weber and Fields (and father of lyricist-to-be Dorothy Fields). Fields liked the songs that Rodgers and Hart played for him. He arranged to put one of them, "Any Old Place With You," into one of his shows, *A Lonely Romeo*. Neither the show nor the song made much of an impression on audiences or the critics. But Fields decided to take another chance with the young team. When his *Poor Little Rich Girl* opened on Broadway in July of 1920, seven of its fifteen songs were by Rodgers and Hart. (The others were by Sigmund Romberg and Alex Gerber.) This time the reviews were modestly complimentary. But they led to no further Broadway offers.

For the next four years, Rodgers continued with his studies at Columbia and then at the Institute of Musical Art (later the Juilliard School). Hart, making the most of his being descended from the great German poet Heinrich Heine, earned money translating the lyrics of German operettas for various American productions. Meanwhile, much as Cole Porter had done a decade earlier, Rodgers and Hart continued to write songs for college shows, including one at Columbia titled *A Danish Yankee in King Tut's Court*.

Just when Rodgers despaired of ever doing another Broadway show and was preparing to take a job in the children's underwear business, Lew Fields's son Herbert came to the rescue of Rodgers and Hart. The three of them teamed up to write a musical comedy spoofing European operettas. With Lew Fields as the star, *Melody Man* —credited to Herbert Richard Lorenz, a collective pseudonym for Fields, Rodgers, and Hart—premiered on Broadway in May of 1924, after tryouts under other titles in Detroit, Cleveland, and Chicago. The reviews were not kind and the show folded after fifty-six performances. But one of its songs, "I'd Like to Poison Ivy," attracted enough attention for Rodgers and Hart to be invited to contribute songs for a fund-raising revue that the prestigious Theatre Guild was planning for two Sunday-evening-only performances at the Garrick Theater.

When the revue, *The Garrick Gaieties*, opened in May of 1925, all but two of the musical numbers were by Rodgers and Hart—and one of their songs, "Manhattan," quickly became a hit. The Theatre Guild kept extending the engagement until, after the eighth Sunday night, the Guild was able to secure the theater for a regular weeknight schedule. *The Garrick Gaieties* then ran for twenty-five weeks (211 performances).

Herbert Fields now had little difficulty finding backing for another show he would write with songs by Rodgers and Hart. *Dearest Enemy,* essentially a romantic operetta set during American Revolutionary days, opened to good reviews while *The Garrick Gaieties* was still running in the fall of 1925. Within three years, it was followed by four other Rodgers-Hart-Fields Broadway hits: *The Girl Friend* (1926), *Peggy-Ann* (1926), *A Connecticut Yankee* (1927), and *Present Arms* (1928). Much of the popularity of the shows clearly rested on their risqué dialogue and song lyrics. Hart, in particular, loved trying to get away with as much as he could in the way of sexual innuendo, if not blatant ribaldry. But his lyrics also came in for generous praise for their clever rhymes, literateness, and sophistication.

Rodgers's music, meanwhile, was praised for its lilting melodies and simplicity. One of the toughest critics of the day, George Jean Nathan, made this comment about *A Connecticut Yankee* for *Judge* magazine: "This Rodgers is to be congratulated for writing simple, spirited and lively music show tunes." Among the songs from these four shows that have gone on to become pop standards: "Here in My Arms," "The

Blue Room," "The Girl Friend," "Where's That Rainbow?" "Thou Swell," "My Heart Stood Still," and "You Took Advantage of Me."

For all of the team's success and the close personal friendship that grew between them during this period, Rodgers had serious problems working with Hart. One biographer has compared Hart with Shakespeare's Puck as "the eternal sophomore." Others agree he was a lazy worker, undisciplined, and sometimes irresponsible—in contrast to Rodgers, who was meticulous, well organized, and something of a work-aholic. Hart would rather party than work and, as his Broadway successes grew, he became well-known as a lavish party giver (even hiring Paul Whiteman's whole orchestra to provide the music for one party). He was also obsessed about his short height (five foot five) and his rapidly receding hairline—and, if only to prove that he could compete with the tallest and the fairest, he seemed to enjoy making a show of being constantly "on the make." Sometimes while walking down the street, as Rodgers once related, "you'd suddenly find yourself talking to yourself" as Hart took off after someone and disappeared. Yet some believe much of this was for "show" and that Hart's sexual frustrations and "dwarf" complex were at the root of his excessive drinking.

The conservative Rodgers, who some said looked and acted more like a banker than a songwriter, admitted on occasion that working with Hart was "a constant irritation." But most of the time he defended his partner, referring to Hart as "the sweetest little guy in the world—soft, generous, lovable." Yet Rodgers never denied that they fought continually over their work, particularly over Rodgers's insistence on editing some of Hart's more salacious lyrics and toning them down to what he felt would be acceptable without being square or prudish. Over the years, Rodgers also grew troubled by Hart's increasing tendency toward a self-pitying undercurrent in many lyrics, or what English critic Robert Cushman has called their "shrugged-off pain."

By 1929 Rodgers and Hart were vying with Cole Porter and the Gershwins as the brightest of the younger generation of Broadway's songwriting stars. So it wasn't surprising that Hollywood, in the first spurt of talkie picture making, would seek out Rodgers and Hart. Paramount got them first—as actors as well as songwriters. In 1929 they appeared in a two-reel short titled *Makers of Melody,* filmed at Paramount's Astoria (Long Island) studios. The short purported to tell how they had gone about writing such tunes as "Manhattan," "The Blue Room," and "The Girl Friend," with the script giving them ridiculously fictionalized lines about how inspiration "struck." That same year Rodgers and Hart also wrote three new songs to supplement the three Buddy DeSylva-Lew Brown-Ray Henderson songs that Paramount didn't dump in filming the '29 Broadway hit *Follow Thru.* None of Rodgers and Hart's new songs caught on.

Within the year, Rodgers and Hart were to find the scores of several of their own Broadway shows treated as cavalierly as *Follow Thru,* with the work of other songwriters replacing their own. In turning the only moderately successful 1929 Broadway production of *Spring Is Here* into a 1930 movie, First National dropped all but three of Rodgers and Hart's songs (as well as most of Fields's original book), though keeping and heavily promoting the show's big hit, "With a Song in My Heart." That same year, RKO dropped even more of the score of *Present Arms* in adapting it to the screen (partly in color) as *Leathernecking*—keeping only two songs, including

"You Took Advantage of Me." Similarly, Paramount's 1930 film version of the '29 *Heads Up!* kept just two songs of Rodgers and Hart's original eleven (including "A Ship Without a Sail"), with the dropped songs being replaced by melodramatic action rather than other songs (except for one interpolated song by the picture's director, Victor Schertzinger). None of these three movies did particularly well with either the critics or the public, and have long since faded from circulation.

But the same year that First National was mangling *Spring Is Here,* the studio offered Rodgers and Hart $50,000 to come to Hollywood to write songs for two original films. That was more money than they could hope to earn from two Broadway shows, especially with the Depression deepening. Their last Broadway musical up to that point, *Simple Simon* (produced by Florenz Ziegfeld, starring Ed Wynn and featuring Ruth Etting singing "Ten Cents a Dance"), had closed after a modest 135 performances, despite generally good reviews. So Rodgers and Hart headed west to Hollywood for the first time.

They did not travel by themselves—for in 1930 Rodgers had married a twenty-year-old sculptress, Dorothy Feiner, whom he had been courting for the previous four years. The Rodgers family had long known the Feiner family, but Dick began to think romantically about Dorothy only after they met on a transatlantic voyage on the S.S. *Majestic,* when Rodgers was returning from a London production of his *Lido Lady* in 1926. For their honeymoon the couple sailed back to England, where Rodgers and Hart worked on *Ever Green* (starring Jessie Matthews and her husband, Sonnie Hale). Then their extended honeymoon took them on their first trip to Hollywood.

Richard Rodgers's Major Movies and Their Songs

Rodgers and Hart's first original film musical, *The Hot Heiress,* didn't do so hot with either audiences or the critics. The Herbert Fields screenplay tells a slight, wisecracking story about a Manhattan heiress (Ona Munson) who falls in love with a handsome construction worker (Ben Lyon) but who runs into trouble trying to pass him off as an architect among her snooty friends. There's even a hint of a much-used Depression theme—about the rich and the poor finding common ground for the future —but it's not handled very imaginatively or cleverly. The wry songs ("You're the Cats," "Like Ordinary People Do") avoid most of the era's prevalent "moon-June-spoon" clichés and grow out of the story line, unlike those of most musicals of the period. But they never rise above the ordinary.

Part of the problem surely rests with the limited singing talents of the two leading performers, which could not have inspired Rodgers, in particular, to compose any of his usually wide-ranging melodies. Though Ben Lyon has a pleasant-enough singing voice, its range is small. Ona Munson's voice is even more restricted and not that attractive. In fact, the bland Munson is the weakest element in the picture as a whole, giving no evidence here of the talent she would later show as a fine character actress (Belle Watling in *Gone With the Wind,* Madam Gin Sling in *The Shanghai Gesture*). Perhaps *The Hot Heiress* might have worked with another leading lady, such as Constance Bennett, Vivienne Segal, or Lyon's own real-life wife, Bebe Daniels—all of them then under contract to First National/Warner Brothers.

Interestingly, in the opening scene of *The Hot Heiress,* Rodgers and Hart experiment with rhythmic dialogue (dialogue spoken in verse against a musical background). The rhythmic pulse is determined by the construction workers' rivets—the same rhythmic basis for the "New York Rhapsody" sequence in Gershwin's *Delicious*, a sequence Gershwin had originally planned to call "Rhapsody in Rivets." Since *The Hot Heiress* opened shortly before *Delicious* in 1931, I can't help but wonder whether Gershwin may have changed his title in order to downplay the probably coincidental similarity with the Rodgers and Hart sequence.

When *The Hot Heiress* flopped, First National bought back its contract for a second original Rodgers and Hart film musical. Back in New York, the team went to work writing a musical comedy satirizing some of the ways of Hollywood. *America's Sweetheart* opened to only so-so reviews in February of 1931, with Jack Whiting and Harriette Lake in the leads and with one of *The Hot Heiress*'s supporting players, Inez Courtney, in a featured role. Monty Woolley was the director. Only one of the show's songs, "I've Got Five Dollars," became even a moderate hit. But Harriette Lake was offered a movie contract (she had previously played two minor movie roles) and returned to Hollywood with a new name: Ann Sothern.

Rodgers and Hart also returned to Hollywood, this time with a two-picture contract from Paramount—and with a determination to prove they could do better than *The Hot Heiress*. Their first assignment was *Love Me Tonight*, with one of Paramount's biggest stars, Maurice Chevalier, reteamed with his co-star of the previous year's hit *One Hour With You*, Jeanette MacDonald. Rodgers later learned that he and Hart had been specifically requested by the film's director, Rouben Mamoulian, who had just completed the much-acclaimed *Dr. Jekyll and Mr. Hyde*. Mamoulian had seen some of their Broadway work and liked it.

The first thing that Rodgers and Hart did this time 'round in Hollywood, as Hart later wrote for the *New York Times,* "was to study pictures, not on the sound set but in the cutting room. Then, with Chevalier and Mamoulian, we developed for the first time dialogue with a sort of phony little half rhyme, with a little music under it, cut to the situation." Hart called the technique rhythmic conversation, and it is used in several parts of *Love Me Tonight*.

There are many other ingenious, innovative touches throughout the film—some visual, some aural, but all of them combining to turn a fairly trite operetta plot (about a princess who falls in love with a tailor masquerading as a baron at a ball) into something fresh and winning, and turning *Love Me Tonight* into one of Hollywood's classic musical comedies.

The film begins with shots of Paris at sunrise, as church bells toll softly in the distance. The bells give way to the rhythmic sounds of people beginning their daily work—a woman sweeping, a cobbler tapping nails into a heel, a street repairman picking at a cobblestone. Then, as the camera pans through an open window, we see Chevalier waking up and closing the window to shut out the noises, saying "Lovely

Jeanette MacDonald and Maurice Chevalier in Love Me Tonight *(1932), in which Richard Rodgers and Lorenz Hart experimented with what Hart called rhythmic conversation.*

summer morning, Paree, but you're much too noisy for me." He then goes directly into the verse of the lighthearted "Song of Paree," which, in turn, leads immediately into a second song, "How Are You?", as Chevalier greets his neighbors and fellow shopkeepers on his way to his tailor shop. Thus, for the first ten minutes of *Love Me Tonight,* music and sounds become the uninterrupted basis for the action.

Shortly afterward, Mamoulian cleverly uses only a few choruses of another song, "Isn't It Romantic?", to shift the focus of the story away from Chevalier, in order to introduce MacDonald as the princess. Chevalier begins the song, singing it to a customer in his tailor shop. The customer leaves, singing it to a taxi driver, who continues singing it as he drives a fare to the railroad station. Eventually, it reaches MacDonald, who overhears it as she stands at a window of her chateau. It's a marvelous sequence, made completely credible by the infectious lilt of Rodgers's melody and the wit of Hart's lyrics.

The way in which the waltz "Lover" is introduced may come as a jolt to those who know the song as a Rodgers and Hart romantic standard. MacDonald sings it not to Chevalier but to her horse, as she takes a solo buggy ride through the countryside. Hart's lyrics take on some cunning double-entendres as MacDonald's song to an imaginary lover is combined to her horse.

Scene after scene is peppered with dialogue that keeps *Love Me Tonight* closer in spirit to Rodgers and Hart's Broadway shows than any of their other '30s movies. In one of the film's most-often-quoted exchanges, Charles Ruggles rushes out of a room to get help for MacDonald, who has fainted. He spots Myrna Loy (playing MacDonald's nymphomaniac cousin) sitting alone on a divan and sputters to her: "Oh, Valentine, can you go for a doctor?" Loy pulls herself up to reply eagerly: "Certainly. Bring him in."

All the songs, moreover, fulfill some kind of plot function—although one, the bright and bouncy "Mimi," does so in an almost off-the-wall manner. Chevalier sings it to MacDonald right after her horse has run her carriage off the road. As Chevalier asks solicitously if she's all right, he utters: "You're a dream. Give me just a moment to sing to you, Mimi." MacDonald insists her name is not Mimi, that he must be mad. But Chevalier goes right ahead and sings "Mimi," with its sly references to love-making—to MacDonald's alternating delight and disquiet.

Love Me Tonight was no sooner released in August of 1932 than "Mimi" became a song hit, moving quickly onto the Top 10 list of the nation's hits and remaining there for several months. "Lover" took a bit longer to catch on, making the Top 10 in April of 1933 and lasting almost twice as long as "Mimi." "Isn't It Romantic?" never made the Top 10, but nonetheless has survived as a Rodgers and Hart standard. The title song, the most operetta-ish of the score, never caught on at all, despite considerable promotion by Paramount. Neither did another song of the same title with which it sometimes gets confused, composed by Victor Young with lyrics by Ned Washington and Bing Crosby, which came out in the spring of '32 (just a few months before the release of *Love Me Tonight*).

With *Love Me Tonight* both a critical and popular success, Rodgers's wife and their baby daughter, Mary, moved to Beverly Hills, prepared to stay a while. Hart and his widowed mother also moved in with the Rodgerses, until Hart eventually found a house of his own. Hart adapted more quickly to Hollywood's social life than did Rodgers, with some reports playing up his popularity with the movie colony's busy gay set.

For their second Paramount film, Rodgers and Hart were assigned *The Phantom President,* starring George M. Cohan in his movie debut—a dual role as an uncharismatic Presidential candidate and a more affable lookalike who's hired to pose as a campaign stand-in. Cohan was miffed that Paramount didn't want him to compose his own songs for the picture—he had, after all, written such hits as "Give My Regards to Broadway" and "Over There"—and he openly disdained Rodgers and Hart as little more than upstarts. Rodgers would later declare that making *The Phantom President* was an unhappy experience for all concerned because of Cohan's attitude. Neither Cohan nor director Norman Taurog, moreover, was as interested as Mamoulian had been in integrating music and dialogue. As a result, the best song in the picture, the ballad "Give Her a Kiss," is heard only on the radio as Cohan and leading lady Claudette Colbert ride in a car. The other songs are decidedly below par for Rodgers and Hart—with one of them, "Somebody Ought to Wave a Flag," even justifying some of Cohan's uncomplimentary comments about the team when the song is compared to Cohan's own classic, "You're a Grand Old Flag."

Released a month before the 1932 elections, *The Phantom President* proved to be vapid as political satire and irrelevant to any of that year's searing campaign issues. As Rodgers himself has said: "Even Hoover was more popular than that film." Cohan would never make another movie. (He also didn't do another musical on Broadway until 1937's *I'd Rather Be Right*—with, ironically, a score by Rodgers and Hart, which produced only one modest song hit, "Have You Met Miss Jones?", even though the show itself was a smash. Cohan and the songwriters got along no better in '37 than they had in '32. This time Cohan played a real President, Franklin D. Roosevelt, in a good-natured but sharp-edged spoof of FDR's administration that won bipartisan kudos for showing the world how the U.S. could openly poke fun at the President in power at a time when Fascist and Communist dictators were tightening censorship controls in other countries.)

Rodgers's and Hart's Hallelujah, I'm a Bum *presented Al Jolson in an offbeat role, with silent-film comic Harry Langdon (peering over Jolson's shoulder) and Edgar Connor (left) as pals.*

Before *The Phantom President* was released, Rodgers and Hart moved over to United Artists on a one-picture deal, to work with another egomaniacal star, Al Jolson. Although Jolson's *The Jazz Singer* had made history, his subsequent talkies, with similarly sentimental story lines and "Mammy"-like songs, had fared less and less well. Jolson felt a fresh approach was needed. Ben Hecht and S. N. Behrman came up with *Hallelujah, I'm a Bum,* a Depression-set satire about a New York hobo.

Scriptwriter Behrman was influential in getting Rodgers and Hart assigned to *Hallelujah, I'm a Bum.* Behrman and director Lewis Milestone (winner of the 1930 Academy Award for *All Quiet on the Western Front*) gave Rodgers and Hart the go-ahead for more extensive use of the rhythmic dialogue technique with which they had experimented in *Love Me Tonight.* As a result, more than three-quarters of *Hallelujah, I'm a Bum* has dialogue that is either sung or spoken in rhythmic cadences. There are only two complete songs in the usual Rodgers and Hart sense, the title song and "You Are Too Beautiful."

Hallelujah, I'm a Bum was a flop. Instead of providing Jolson's career with a shot in the arm, it put him further in decline. Although some critics praised the film's adventurousness and its attempt at something different, most audiences found the rhythmic dialogue tiresome and unappealing. The passage of the years has not altered that verdict. Rodgers's music rarely lets loose with an interesting melodic theme and, after the first twenty minutes or so, becomes monotonous. Particularly frustrating is one song that gets off to an appealing start right at the picture's beginning, "I've Gotta Get Back to New York," yet is never heard all the way through, although its theme is repeated later in a merry-go-round scene. Hart's lyrics and Behrman's screenplay do little to make the story itself very believable as it follows a happy-go-lucky hobo (Jolson), living in a Central Park shantytown, and his ill-fated love affair with an amnesia victim (Madge Evans), who turns out to be the mistress of the city's mayor (Frank Morgan)! Neither Hart nor Behrman contribute any real social or political bite to the tale, so that it ends up being a very bland commentary on the Depression's effect on its characters.

Jolson's performance must also be counted among the picture's weaknesses. He is heavy-handed with the Jolson bravura throughout, and in a kangaroo-court sequence it's hard to tell whether he's deliberately mocking the gushy sentimentality of his defense (which would be understandable) or just overdoing some bad acting (which seems more likely). But at least Jolson doesn't do a blackface sequence.

Rodgers and Hart played bit parts in *Hallelujah, I'm a Bum*—Rodgers as a photographer, Hart as a bank teller. Their footage is among the scenes that were cut in a general tightening-up of the movie for a 1940s reissue, retitled *Heart of New York*. The reissue is the version now in general TV circulation in the United States.

While *Hallelujah, I'm a Bum* was in production, United Artists learned that the title was unacceptable to the British, to whom "bum" means derrière. Not only was the picture retitled *Hallelujah, I'm a Tramp* for British release, but Jolson also had to film two separate versions of the title song (which he sings in two different places in the movie).

Before *Hallelujah, I'm a Bum* was completed in 1933 and its bad notices came in, MGM's young and mighty production chief Irving Thalberg let Rodgers and Hart know how impressed he was with *Love Me Tonight,* and offered them a contract to work on another original musical for Jeanette MacDonald, who had just been signed to a long-term MGM contract. Thalberg suggested a fantasy based on a Hungarian play by John Vaszary, about a roué who's bored with women until an angel comes flying through his window. Rodgers and Hart worked out a scenario-synopsis for *I Married an Angel* with Moss Hart (no relation to Lorenz Hart) and started writing some of the songs. But MGM chieftain Louis B. Mayer cancelled the project. With all the Hollywood studios facing increasing pressure from the Catholic Legion of Decency and other censorship groups, Mayer felt that a film about an angel who goes to bed with a man on earth would surely be asking for trouble. Rodgers shrewdly acquired the rights to the work he and Hart had started, and later used it as the basis for a 1938 hit Broadway musical with the same title.

While waiting for Thalberg and Mayer to decide between several other musical projects, Rodgers and Hart were asked to write a song for the finale of *Dancing Lady,* a lavish backstage musical (starring Joan Crawford and Clark Gable) with which MGM hoped to cash in on some of the success of Warner Brothers's *42nd Street.* Various teams of songwriters (including Jimmy McHugh and Dorothy Fields, Burton Lane and Harold Adamson, and MGM's resident songsmiths Nacio Herb Brown and Arthur Freed) had written songs for the picture, which also featured Fred Astaire in his movie debut. From Rodgers and Hart came the snappy, martial "That's the Rhythm of the Day." Thalberg assigned the song to a young baritone the studio had just signed, Nelson Eddy. It leads off the film's final production number, which MGM touted as bigger in the size of its sets and the number of dancers than any studio had done before. As usual, bigger did not mean better—especially in comparison with the more imaginative numbers Busby Berkeley was then turning out at Warner Brothers. The song was soon forgotten, and so also, for a while, was the baritone.

That same year, Rodgers and Hart were borrowed by independent producer Samuel Goldwyn to write a song for the American movie debut of a new European import that Goldwyn hoped he could turn into a new Garbo or Dietrich. She was the part-Swedish, part-Ukrainian Anna Sten. Despite one of the most lavish publicity campaigns attempted to that time, Sten failed to capture the American public—partly because her debut vehicle, *Nana,* based on Emile Zola's novel, was thoroughly white-washed by the '30s censors. For Sten's limited singing range, Rodgers and Hart wrote the uninspired, banal "That's Love." Song, picture, and Miss Sten all struck out.

Meanwhile, at the urging of producer Harry Rapf and producer-songwriter Howard Dietz, MGM planned a sequel to one of its first big musical hits, the all-star *Hollywood Revue of 1929.* This new edition would be called *Hollywood Revue of 1933* and would star Jean Harlow in a "framing" story involving a big party at which MGM musical and comedy stars would do guest spots. Rodgers and Hart were assigned to write the score. They went to work and wrote more than a dozen songs, including ballads, torch songs, comedy numbers, and novelty tunes with such MGM stars in mind as Harlow, Crawford, MacDonald, Marion Davies, and Jimmy Durante. Just before filming was to begin, Harlow was assigned to another picture and the script was altered to revolve around Durante instead. Filming went ahead with Durante while Rapf and Dietz tried to work out production plans around the availability of the studio's stars and directors. Then Rodgers and Hart were chagrined to learn that Rapf and Dietz had asked other songwriters to contribute songs as well.

With some of the studio's top stars yet to film their numbers, Louis B. Mayer decided to preview the acts that had already been filmed by Laurel and Hardy, Lupe Velez, Jack "Baron Munchausen" Pearl, Polly Moran, June Clyde, and newcomer Shirley Ross, as well as the completed "linking" footage with Durante. Mayer disliked what he saw. He ordered production stopped and told Rapf to patch up the existing footage as best he could and "let it go."

Retitled *Hollywood Party,* the movie was released in May of 1934 without any directoral credits, and with only three of Rodgers and Hart's songs included. Only one of them, the title song (sung by Frances Williams), is even halfway memorable. The others are essentially routine patter songs for Durante and Pearl. The picture itself is a decidedly uneven affair, with only three good sequences: an egg-breaking comedy routine with Laurel and Hardy and Lupe Velez; a takeoff on Tarzan movies with Durante playing "Schnarzan"; and a Disney cartoon sequence featuring Mickey Mouse (for which the rights have reverted to Disney, so that it is not in the current TV release version).

One of the songs cut from *Hollywood Party,* titled "Prayer," had been written for Jean Harlow to sing as a stenographer dreaming of becoming a movie star. When the studio asked Rodgers for something that could be used in a Cotton Club nightclub sequence in another 1934 release, *Manhattan Melodrama* (with Clark Gable, Myrna Loy, and William Powell), Hart simply wrote a new set of lyrics for "Prayer." Retitled "The Bad in Every Man," it's sung in the club sequence by Shirley Ross, wearing dark body makeup and a terrible-looking black wig—and it is reprised instrumentally in a prison scene later in the picture.

According to Rodgers biographer Frederick Nolan, when Rodgers and Hart approached MGM's music publisher, Jack Robbins, about publishing the song, he told them bluntly that it would be a waste of time—that the tune was okay but the lyrics just weren't commercial. Miffed, Hart shot back: "Commercial? I suppose it should be something corny like 'Blue Moon'?"—"Yeah," replied Robbins, " 'Blue Moon.' " Picking up the challenge, Hart came back a few days later with a new set of lyrics built around that title. "Blue Moon" became one of the few Rodgers and Hart songs ever published outside of a stage or film score, and it ended up in the Top Ten for nearly five months in late 1934. According to composer-producer Arthur Schwartz, Hart always hated "Blue Moon."

Discouraged by their experiences with *I Married an Angel* and *Hollywood Party,* and tiring of what Rodgers once called the "soft labor" of their life in California, the team determined to return to Broadway as soon as their MGM contract expired. But a trip back east proved equally discouraging in terms of the economics of getting a musical produced in New York. Moreover, Rodgers's family was about to be enlarged by the birth of daughter Linda in March of 1935. So Rodgers and Hart returned to Hollywood with a one-picture contract from Paramount, to write songs for *Mississippi,* a Herbert Fields adaptation of a Booth Tarkington Story, *The Fighting Coward,* previously filmed (without music) as *Magnolia.*

Mississippi (1935) is a genial if unexceptional mixture of musical romance for Bing Crosby and broad comedy and gags for W. C. Fields. Crosby plays a soft-spoken Philadelphia lad who joins a showboat troupe on the Mississippi in the 1880s and, under the tutelage of the boat's wily commodore (Fields), acquires a reputation as a dead shot and the nickname The Singing Killer. He also falls in love with two Southern belles (played by brunette Gail Patrick and blonde Joan Bennett). This time there is no rhythmic dialogue. The studio pressured Rodgers and Hart to stick to commercial song formulas that might produce one or two hits—and they did just that. Two Crosby-sung ballads quickly made radio's then-new *Your Hit Parade:* "It's Easy to Remember" and "Soon" (the latter not to be confused with a 1930 Gershwin song of the same title from *Strike Up the Band).* Another ballad, "Down by the River," also became moderately popular.

They weren't as lucky with their songs for *The Dancing Pirate* (1936). The independent Pioneer Pictures, financed by John Hay Whitney and releasing through RKO Radio, had created something of a stir in 1935 with the first three-strip Technicolor feature, *Becky Sharp.* Although the improved color process won favorable reviews, that picture, based on William Thackeray's novel *Vanity Fair,* had been too highbrow for most audience tastes. So Pioneer decided to film a simple adventure story for its second big Technicolor feature, and to dress it up with songs and dances.

The color designs of Robert Edmond Jones remain the most interesting element of *The Dancing Pirate*—a silly trifle about an early eighteenth-century Boston dance master (movie newcomer Charles Collins) who is shanghaied by pirates and ends up in a Mexican coastal town, where he wins the hand of the pirate leader's daughter (Steffi Duna). Of Rodgers and Hart's two songs for the film, "Are You My Love?" is an especially lovely, wistful ballad with an unmistakably Rodgers melody. But neither it nor the picture caught on—and Pioneer Pictures, in fact, went under when *The Dancing Pirate* flopped at the box office.

Meanwhile, a 1934 British-made film version of Rodgers and Hart's London show *Ever Green* was released in the United States, with Jessie Matthews repeating her

One of Bing Crosby's few costume pictures was Mississippi *(1935), with a score by Rodgers and Hart. In this scene, a chorus of Southern belles accompanies Crosby as he sings "It's Easy to Remember (And So Hard to Forget)."*

original role as a music-hall starlet who passes herself off as a sixty-year-old who's found the Fountain of Youth through cosmetology. Britian's filmmakers proved little different from Hollywood's, dumping most of Rodgers and Hart's score and substituting new songs (by Harry MacGregor Woods, best known for "When the Red, Red Robin Comes Bob-Bob-Bobbing Along"). They also altered the story considerably and changed the role of Matthews's real-life husband, Sonnie Hale, from suitor to old friend. (The suitor role went to younger Barry MacKay.) For some reason they also changed the title's spelling from *Ever Green* to *Evergreen*.

Only three of Rodgers and Hart's original songs survived the screen transfer, including the stage version's big hit, "Dancing on the Ceiling" (which Ziegfeld had cut from 1930's *Simple Simon* as "too fancy"). Matthews sings the song charmingly as she lounges in a filmy negligee, which billows appropriately as she then dances around her flat, including up and down its curved staircase. On the basis of *Evergreen*, RKO Radio wanted her as Astaire's partner for 1937's *A Damsel in Distress*, until they learned that she was taller than Astaire.

By 1936 the situation on Broadway had improved enough for Rodgers and Hart to move back to New York, making no secret of their mutual unhappiness working for the movies. From then on, Rodgers concentrated on composing for Broadway, with only occasional work for the movies. Yet over the years all but seven of the twenty-two musicals that Rodgers wrote for Broadway between 1936 and 1976 were turned into movies—several of them among the all-time most popular film musicals. Only a few, however, are even halfway faithful to the stage originals.

On Broadway, *On Your Toes* (1936) was a fresh, saucy, and sophisticated mixture of traditional and jazz ballet with musical-comedy songs—all built around a fairly routine romantic story line about a ballerina (Tamara Geva) and a jazz-loving music teacher (Ray Bolger). That story also marked the first time that Rodgers and Hart had written most of a show's book themselves (part was also written by the show's director, George Abbott). The two songwriters had come up with the idea for the story while in Hollywood and offered it to Fred Astaire. He turned it down, fearing the ballet background was too highbrow for his audiences. Ironically, a year after *On Your Toes* became a Broadway hit, Astaire would play a ballet dancer in the '37 Gershwin film *Shall We Dance,* which in part spoofs *On Your Toes.*

For the 1939 movie version of *On Your Toes,* starring Vera Zorina and Eddie Albert, the plot was considerably rewritten—and, in typical '30s-Hollywood fashion, most of the original songs were cut, with only three or four kept merely as background instrumentals. The result is a banally scripted, heavy-handed backstage comedy that's rarely funny. It comes to life only at the end with the "Slaughter on Tenth Avenue" ballet, adapted by George Balanchine from his Broadway choreography. The music for this ballet marked one of Rodgers's first successful efforts at a lengthy instrumental piece (about nine minutes), and it was soon picked up as a concert work by both pop and symphonic orchestras. Its lively rhythms and attractive melody have kept it a popular favorite ever since.

MGM's *Babes in Arms* (1939) was the first musical to be produced at that studio by Arthur Freed, who, over the following two decades, would produce some of the greatest of all movie musicals. *Babes in Arms* is not one of them. Any resemblance to Rodgers and Hart's Broadway show of 1937 is not in its musical numbers but in its story line—about a group of kids from down-on-their-luck vaudeville families who try to put on a show of their own. Thanks to spirited performances by a personable young cast headed by Mickey Rooney and Judy Garland, plus snappy direction by Busby Berkeley (his first MGM musical), the film version manages to make the most of the adolescent antics come across as modest fun, despite a commonplace script and the dumping of such great Rodgers and Hart songs as "My Funny Valentine," "Johnny One Note," "The Lady Is a Tramp," and "I Wish I Were in Love Again."

Only two of *Babes in Arms*'s Broadway songs are kept, at least in their entirety —with part of a third "The Lady Is a Tramp" showing up as the slyly appropriate instrumental background for a show-off gymnastic exercise by blonde hussy June Preisser (playing a spoiled former child star named Baby Rosalie). The wistful ballad "Where or When" is sung much too pretentiously during a rehearsal sequence by Betty Jaynes and Douglas MacPhail, accompanied by an amusingly screechy, off-key kids' orchestra. A seventeen-year-old Judy Garland, in her first movie after *The Wizard of Oz,* then starts to sing the song with a more appropriately intimate feeling, only to be interrupted after a few lines by plot-related dialogue. The title song gets robust treatment from baritone MacPhail as he marches through town to a bonfire with his showmates. Aside from the final "God's Country" (by Harold Arlen, Yip Harburg,

Vera Zorina (at left, on stage) in George Balanchine's restaging of his original Broadway ballet to Rodgers's "Slaughter on Tenth Avenue," for the 1939 film On Your Toes.

Mickey Rooney and Judy Garland in Babes in Arms *(1939). They got another chance to sing Rodgers and Hart songs cut from that film in 1948's* Words and Music.

and Roger Edens), none of the interpolated songs by other composers can hold a proverbial candle to the Rodgers and Hart songs they replace.

Universal's film version of *The Boys From Syracuse* (1940) doesn't add any songs by other songwriters, but it doesn't do too well by the four Rodgers and Hart songs from the Broadway production of 1938 that it keeps—nor, for that matter, by the two new songs Rodgers and Hart wrote especially for the movie. It also replaces the ribald wit and satire of George Abbott's original book, loosely based on Shakespeare's *A Comedy of Errors,* with broader comedy hijinks and anachronistic gags (such as Good Humor vendors in the plot's ancient Greek setting, trolley-car chariots, and so on), only some of which are funny.

Film technique, however, does make it possible for the two leading actors (Allan Jones, Joe Penner) to play two sets of twin brothers (four actors were used on Broadway, including Lorenz Hart's brother, Teddy). Theoretically, at least, that makes the mistaken-identity plot more believable. But even that advantage is undercut by the watered-down, lackluster script and by performances that are sometimes too broadly theatrical, without the saving grace of even a little self-spoofery.

Most of Rodgers and Hart's songs get just one short chorus in the movie *The Boys From Syracuse*. "Sing for Your Supper" comes off best, thanks to Martha Raye's spirited singing, with less mugging than usual and no screaming of the lyrics—proving that she is a much better straight singer than most of her movie comedies usually let her show. But soon after that, she's back to clowning her way through a heavily laundered version of "He and She" with Joe Penner, a nasal-voiced radio comedian who was not much of a singer. Allan Jones belts out "Falling in Love With Love" without much apparent regard for the cynical undercurrent of the lyrics behind Rodgers's lilting waltz melody. Jones also can't resist holding onto some of the high notes as if he were singing Puccini instead of Rodgers. Rosemary Lane is much too diffident with the delightfully sardonic "This Can't Be Love." As for the two new songs: "Who Are You?" is a pleasant but quickly forgettable romantic ballad (sung by Jones to Lane) and miles inferior to "You Have Cast Your Shadow on the Sea,"

With "Sing for Your Supper" in The Boys From Syracuse *(1940), Martha Raye shows herself to be a better straight singer than most of her comedies let her show. The same can't be said of comedian Joe Penner.*

Desi Arnaz (with bongo drum) leads the chorus, including Van Johnson (in his first movie role), through Rodgers's and Hart's "Spic and Spanish" in the film version of Too Many Girls *(1940).*

a song from the original show that was dropped for the movie. "The Greeks Have a Word for It" is a mediocre *hi-dee-ho*-style swinger, in which Raye gaily tosses off a few Hart-isms that relate Orpheus to the Orpheum vaudeville circuit and talk about Achilles getting the willies.

RKO Radio's *Too Many Girls,* also 1940, has the distinction of being the first Rodgers and Hart musical to be brought to the screen with some fidelity to its Broadway original (of just a year earlier)—including the same director (George Abbott), seven of the original cast members (Eddie Bracken, Desi Arnaz, Hal LeRoy, Ivy Scott, Libby Bennett, Van Johnson, Byron Shores), and six of the original twelve songs. It's too bad the original was so second-rate. Hollywood had already done more than enough collegiate musicals throughout the '30s, so it's surprising that the usually more inventive Rodgers and Hart would turn to that genre. But they did, and *Too Many Girls* is just as brainless as its predecessors, with its students doing little between football games except sing and dance.

But both the show and the movie were hits. Credit goes more to Abbott's zesty pacing and to a personable cast than to Rodgers and Hart's score. It was during their working on the Broadway version, in fact, that serious strains threatened to end the songwriting team. Hart's drinking became an increasing problem and he sometimes disappeared for days. In Hart's absence, Rodgers wrote some of the lyrics that are officially credited to Hart.

The film keeps the best of an uneven score, including two genially appealing ballads—the romantically dreamy "I Didn't Know What Time It Was," sung by Lucille Ball (dubbed by Trudi Erwin) to a crew-cut Richard Carlson, and "Love Never Went to College," engagingly sung by Frances Langford (and a much more attractive song than its scornful title suggests). Best of all is another ballad written especially for the film version, "You're Nearer." It's one of Rodgers and Hart's most sensitive and elegant love songs, and is sung wistfully by Ball/Erwin and later reprised by Langford in tandem with several other cast members. Only moderately catchy are the Latin rhythms (mostly conga) of "Spic and Spanish," which Desi Arnaz sings and then dances (well, half dances) with Ann Miller and later leads the whole cast in reprising for the noisy finale.

MGM's *I Married an Angel* (1942) is an unheavenly stinker. Whatever satisfaction Rodgers and Hart may have thought they'd take in having MGM finally film the musical that had been rejected in 1934 (and then turned into a successful Broadway show by the songwriters in 1938) must surely have died when they saw the insipid movie that resulted. The satiric, lighthearted charm of the original got lost in MGM's heavy-handed, plodding rewrite, as well in Jeanette MacDonald's alternately arch and prissy performance as the angel and Nelson Eddy's stilted portrayal of the noble roué she marries with the most earthbound of consequences.

Only four of the Broadway version's nine songs are kept intact—including the bouyant title song (which had made *Your Hit Parade* during the Broadway run) and the wistful "Spring Is Here (Why Doesn't My Heart Go Dancing?)," which also became a moderate hit. Two others turn up in new guises, with Hart's lyrics scrapped for silly new ones by Chet Forrest and Bob Wright: "Tira Lira La" (to the music of the Broadway version's showstopping "At the Roxy Music Hall") and "Little Worka-day World" (to the music originally for "Did You Ever Get Stung?"). Forrest and Wright also contributed lyrics to three forgettable songs composed by Herbert Stothart for the film, as well as English lyrics for some assorted selections by Bizet and Kreisler that MacDonald and Eddy sing. *I Married an Angel* was so soundly roasted by the critics and shunned by audiences that the team of MacDonald and Eddy, after eight films over a seven-year period, never again made another movie together.

The same year (1942), the team of Rodgers and Hart also ended up on the rocks, despite the success of one of their longest-running Broadway hits, *By Jupiter* (about ancient Greek warriors who invade a mythological Amazon kingdom—or, more correctly, queendom—where the women are the warriors and the men stay home in charge of household chores). Hart's continual drinking and general dissipation had led to his being hospitalized during part of the time that *By Jupiter* was being written. Rodgers realized that if he was to continue working in the theater, he would have to seek another collaborator—someone more reliable, more disciplined, and without Hart's increasingly troublesome personal problems.

As Dorothy Hart, wife of Larry's brother Teddy, once told an interviewer: "All partners sooner or later split up. The remarkable thing was not that [Dick and Larry] split up but that they ever stayed together for so long. Dick had lost his patience with Larry. I don't blame him. I can't. Larry didn't want to write anymore."

Rodgers first sought out Ira Gershwin, who had been working with a number of different composers since the death of his brother George. But Ira begged off. Rodgers turned next to Oscar Hammerstein II, whom he had known since they had written a song together in 1920 for a Columbia University varsity show. Since then, Hammerstein had written the lyrics for the classic *Show Boat* (with Kern), as well as operettas with Romberg, Friml, and Korngold. Rodgers told Hammerstein that he and Hart had been approached by the Theatre Guild (whose *The Garrick Gaieties* had really launched Rodgers and Hart's Broadway career) to turn Lynn Riggs's play *Green Grow the Lilacs* into a musical. But Hart, unlike Rodgers, wasn't interested. Hammerstein, in turn, reported that he and Kern had also been approached when it appeared that Rodgers and Hart would turn down the project—and that Kern, unlike Hammerstein, wasn't enthusiastic. Within a few weeks, Rodgers and Hammerstein had signed contracts to do the show together. After a difficult period finding financial backing and then serious preproduction problems, the musical opened on Broadway in March of 1943 with a new title: *Oklahoma!* The rest, as they say, is history—as *Oklahoma!* became the most distinctively American musical hit since *Show Boat.*

Even after the phenomenal success of *Oklahoma!*, Rodgers made several efforts to work again with Hart. One involved the 1943 all-star, wartime movie *Stage Door Canteen,* which paid tribute to Broadway performers who were then contributing their off-hour services to the celebrated New York servicemen's club run by the American Theater Wing. Rodgers and Hart reworked a lesser song from *By Jupiter,* "The Boy I Left Behind Me," into a special number for Ray Bolger to sing and dance. "The Girl I Love to Leave Behind" stands out (in a picture saturated with syrupy, sentimental numbers) for its sly digs at the man-eating girls whom some GIs are glad to escape when they join the service.

Much more substantive, however, was a proposal by Herbert Fields for a Broadway revival of 1927's *A Connecticut Yankee,* with revisions. Rodgers agreed to write additional songs if Hart would do the lyrics. As a further incentive to Hart, he and Fields agreed to enlarge the role of Morgan le Fay especially for Vivienne Segal, whom Hart adored and whom some considered to be his great, secret love (although Segal has always insisted their relationship was platonic). Hart agreed, Segal agreed, and the new version of *A Connecticut Yankee* opened in November of 1943.

On opening night Hart arrived drunk at the theater and finally had to be asked to leave when, from the back of the house, he began reciting the lyrics along with the performers. Contrary to the movie biography *Words and Music,* Hart did not wander the streets until he collapsed and died in a gutter. Instead, his sister-in-law Dorothy Hart had him taken to her home. The next morning, however, he had disappeared. A few days later he was found in a coma in his own apartment and rushed to a hospital. As Dorothy and Teddy Hart gathered outside his hospital room with Dick and Dorothy Rodgers, Larry Hart died on November 22, 1943. He was forty-eight. The cause of death was given as advanced pneumonia.

With Hart's passing, Rodgers's music moved in a new direction as he worked with the more openly sentimental, less acerbic Hammerstein. Although well-fashioned melodies had always been Rodgers's strong point, they were often overshadowed by the clever, witty rhyme schemes of Hart's lyrics. In some of their original movie work, moreover, Hart's preoccupation with rhythmic dialogue had tended to overwhelm Rodgers's melodic instincts. Hammerstein's operetta background led Rodgers away from wordplay to deeper melodic songs that caught the mood of a situation or an aspect of character. In effect, with Hammerstein, Rodgers stopped writing musical comedy and started composing musical plays.

Rodgers also found the tall, burly, even-tempered Hammerstein easier to work with. Ironically, in his years with Hammerstein, Rodgers himself acquired a reputation for sometimes being difficult to work with, stubborn in his positions and even haughty about his success. But the relationship with Hammerstein clicked emphatically. As Rodgers told an interviewer for the *Ladies Home Journal:* "What happened between Oscar and me was almost chemical. . . . [We] hit it off from the day we started discussing the show [*Oklahoma!*]. For one thing, I needed a little calm in my life after twenty-three hectic years. When Oscar would say I'll meet you at 2:30, he was *there* at 2:30. That had never happened to me before."

The difference between Rodgers-Hart and Rodgers-Hammerstein is sharply drawn in the first (and only) original movie musical the latter team wrote, Twentieth Century-Fox's *State Fair* (1945). Like *Oklahoma!*, it is filled from beginning to end with melody after melody of a warmly direct, sunny, unashamedly folksy type. In commissioning the score, producer Darryl F. Zanuck had told Rodgers and Hammerstein that he wanted the same kind of optimistic, homespun feeling that characterized *Oklahoma!*—and that is what he got. But in accepting the commission, Rodgers, still unhappy over his previous Hollywood experiences, insisted that his contract specifically exempt him from having to do any work *in* Hollywood itself. Yielding to the prestige that Rodgers and Hammerstein now enjoyed because of the phenomenal success of *Oklahoma!* (including a Pulitzer Prize), Zanuck reluctantly agreed. And so the songs for *State Fair,* set in Iowa and filmed in California, were written in New York, Connecticut, and Pennsylvania.

State Fair had originally been filmed in 1933 without songs, starring one of the era's most popular performers, Will Rogers, as an Iowa farmer who takes his family and his prize hog to the state fair. Although Charles Winninger (the original Cap'n Andy of Kern's and Hammerstein's *Show Boat*) is marvelous in the Rogers role, the musical version shifts the emphasis away from him to his children's romantic adventures at the fair. Jeanne Crain and Dick Haymes are the children, with Dana Andrews and Vivian Blaine as their respective fair-time romances—and it's they who figure in most of the musical numbers.

After the rousing, marchlike "Our State Fair" sets both a jolly and a homespun mood, Jeanne Crain (with her singing voice dubbed by Louanne Hogan) quickly shifts things into a much more typically intimate Rodgers and Hammerstein mood with the daydreaming ballad, "It Might As Well Be Spring." It's first sung melancholically by Crain/Hogan—despite a bright, sunlit background—and then, in a second chorus that's hardly ever heard outside the movie, with a romantically satiric verse in which she fantasizes about being romanced in turn by Ronald Colman, Charles Boyer, and Bing Crosby. A bit later there's still a third, openly mocking chorus in which Crain puts down her farmland boyfriend's vision of their "scientific" home life in the future. Within the six or seven minutes of the three choruses of the song, Rodgers and

Dick Haymes, Fay Bainter, Jeanne Crain, and Charles Winninger in the first version of Richard Rodgers's and Oscar Hammerstein's musical State Fair *(1945)—the only original musical that team ever wrote for the movies.*

In the 1962 remake of State Fair *Tom Ewell and Alice Faye are the parents, and Pamela Tiffin and Pat Boone their children.*

Hammerstein paint a marvelously warm, in-depth portrait of the lovesick daughter, and construct a framework for our caring what happens to her at the fair. "It Might As Well Be Spring" went on to become one of Rodgers's all-time great song hits, including seventeen weeks on radio's *Your Hit Parade* in 1945–46, and an Academy Award for Best Song.

Another ballad, "That's for Me," does much the same "character establishing" for Vivian Blaine and Dick Haymes after they meet at the fair—as well as underscoring the credibility of their love at first sight. "That's for Me" also went on to become a major song hit. "It's a Grand Night for Singing" never made *Your Hit Parade,* but it has become one of Rodgers and Hammerstein's best-known waltzes. It's not only the basis for one of *State Fair*'s most exhilarating sequences, as Haymes, Blaine, Crain, Andrews, William Marshall, and others pick up its cheery refrain, but it's also a 180-degree turn from the cynical bent that Hart's lyrics gave to some of Rodgers's earlier waltzes (such as "Falling in Love With Love" from *The Boys From Syracuse*).

With the smash success of *State Fair* added to their Broadway laurels for *Oklahoma!* and *Carousel,* Rodgers and Hammerstein were, by 1948, riding high. But Rodgers and Hart were not forgotten, and the former team became the subjects of the kind of flashy biographical tribute from Hollywood that Gershwin and Porter had received with *Rhapsody in Blue* and *Night and Day.* Ironically, the studio would be MGM, where Rodgers had been unhappiest in his Hollywood days. But thanks to producer Arthur Freed and his team of song and dance associates, MGM came through with some of the best treatments of Rodgers and Hart songs that the movies had done to that time—or have done since then. All of the songs, however, would be from their Broadway shows. Not a single song written *for* Hollywood is included.

Like the Gershwin and Porter biopics, *Words and Music* (1948) surrounds dozens of musical numbers with a heavily fictionalized story line that barely gets beneath the surface of Rodgers and Hart's professional lives and almost completely sidesteps the personal ones, especially on Hart's side. The casting of the diminutive, overbubbly Mickey Rooney as Hart and the clean-cut, somewhat stuffy Tom Drake as Rodgers doesn't help matters, not that the falsehoods and fabrications of the script ever give them a chance to create meaningful characterizations. Janet Leigh doesn't have much to do as Rodgers's wife, Dorothy, nor does Marshall Thompson as writer Herbert Fields.

Words and Music is just as cavalier as the earlier Gershwin and Porter biographies in presenting the movie's musical selections without much faithfulness to the original productions and out of correct chronological order. With two exceptions, no use is made of performers identified with Rodgers and Hart shows over the years—such as Ray Bolger, Vivienne Segal, Vera Zorina, Jimmy Durante, Victor Moore, Shirley Ross, Constance Moore, Marta Eggerth, and Van Johnson, even though several of them were under contract to MGM at the time. The exceptions were Gene Kelly and Ann Sothern. But Kelly does nothing from the Rodgers and Hart show that made him a star, *Pal Joey*—he performs a number from *On Your Toes,* in which he did not appear. Similarly, Ann Sothern's number in *Words and Music* is from *Peggy-Ann,* rather than something from the Rodgers and Hart show in which she did appear, 1931's *America's Sweetheart* (under her real name, Harriette Lake).

The stars who do most of the twenty-three musical numbers in *Words and Music* are an impressive lot, however, and some of those numbers, as staged by Robert Alton, are showstoppers indeed. Lena Horne sings as wickedly classy a version of "The Lady Is a Tramp" as you're ever likely to hear, with just the right mixture of wit and venom. She also does an exceptionally tender "Where or When." Judy Garland and Mickey Rooney make up for the deletion of "I Wish We Were in Love Again" from their '39 *Babes in Arms* by belting out arguably the definitive version of that lively duet. Garland promptly follows it with a knockout performance of "Johnny One Note" (also dropped from *Babes in Arms*). June Allyson cuts loose for a frothy song-and-dance version of "Thou Swell" with the Blackburn Twins, and even Perry Como shows more vitality than usual in "Blue Room" with Cyd Charisse and "Mountain Greenery" with Allyn Ann McLerie. Ann Sothern not only sings "Where's That Rainbow" delightfully, but also kicks up her heels snappily for a rare dance number.

Two dance numbers stand out in contrastingly highbrow and lowbrow ways. Cyd Charisse and Dee Turnell lead an elegantly lively sequence combining "On Your Toes," "This Can't Be Love," and "The Girl Friend" with easily the best toe-dancing to pop rhythms that anyone had done in the movies to that time, ending with a large corps of dancers spinning and kicking crisply in the best Radio City Music Hall fashion. The other number is a seven-minute jazz ballet danced by Gene Kelly and Vera-Ellen to "Slaughter on Tenth Avenue," completely rearranged musically (by Lennie Hayton) and choreographically (by Kelly) from the *On Your Toes* original. Though the original marked a Broadway milestone for the way it mixed ballet and jazz in a musical comedy, the movie version goes even further in terms of jazz dance and rhythms. It also goes well beyond Astaire's "Limehouse Blues" (in *Ziegfeld Follies,* '46) and Kelly's "Mack the Black" (in *The Pirate,* '48) in being a full-fledged, self-contained movie ballet. It proved that movie audiences would accept this style of dance number enthusiastically, and it paved the way for Kelly's *On the Town* and *An American in Paris.* Just as Agnes DeMille's ballets for *Oklahoma!* and *Carousel* had revolutionized Broadway dance, so Kelly's "Slaughter on Tenth Avenue" for *Words and Music* revolutionized movie dance. And in both cases it was to music by Richard Rodgers.

Studio bids for a movie version of *Oklahoma!* had begun soon after the Broadway opening in 1943. But Rodgers, mindful of how his earlier shows had been mistreated by Hollywood, was in no rush to make a deal—least of all while the Broadway production was still running. And run it did, for a record-breaking five years and nine weeks, or 2,212 performances. Even after the show closed in 1948, Rodgers and Hammerstein held off. There were English, Australian, and other overseas productions still going strong, as well as a touring U.S. company. It was not until the national company closed in Philadelphia in May of 1954 that they finally announced they would produce the movie version themselves, for release by Mike Todd's independent Magna Theatre Corporation.

That meant the movie version of *Oklahoma!* would also be filmed in Todd's then-new 70-milimeter widescreen process, Todd-AO, in contrast to the 35-milimeter square-screen standard. This was the period when Hollywood, facing increasing competition from television for an audience, was experimenting with all sorts of technological innovations, from CinemaScope and Cinerama to 3-D and stereophonic sound. Rodgers and Hammerstein felt that opening up the action of *Oklahoma!* to the real outdoors through the use of the Todd-AO photography and projection system would make *Okalahoma!* a really special movie event, as innovative cinematically as the original production had been theatrically.

Rodgers was unable to join Hammerstein on location during the summer of 1954 while *Oklahoma!* was being filmed (in typical Hollywood fashion, not in the state in which the action takes place, but in Arizona). Rodgers, in great pain, was suffering from cancer of the lower jaw. That fall he underwent surgery to remove his left jawbone and some glands in his neck. Stoic workhorse that he was, during the weeks of his recovery Rodgers spent his days attending rehearsals of the new Rodgers and Hammerstein Broadway show *Pipe Dream,* while sleeping nights at the hospital. And, of course, he kept in daily touch with the making of the film version of *Oklahoma!*

It premiered in October of 1955 to good but not extremely enthusiastic reviews. For all the hoopla about Todd-AO, the process was only a partial success. The stereo sound and the size of the screen were impressive, as was picture clarity in most scenes. But there was occasional lens distortion in long shots, and color matching from scene to scene was problematical. Most of these technical defects were corrected when Rodgers and Hammerstein arranged with Twentieth Century-Fox to re-release the film in CinemaScope in November of 1956—and it's that version that is in general circulation today (although for TV showings, of course, the width of the frame is cropped, as with all CinemaScope features).

In both Todd-AO and CinemaScope, the size of the production seemed at first to overwhelm the intimacy of the original. Also, what had been fresh, charming, and spirited on stage in 1943 was still charming and spirited, but no longer so fresh after a decade of stage productions, recordings, radio and TV performances of the songs, and even concert suites of the music. In particular, the dances of Agnes DeMille, which had been revolutionary in a musical play in 1943, now looked overly stylized, and even (in just a dozen years) dated.

Perhaps some of the disappointment with *Oklahoma!* in 1955 and 1956 involved both overexpectation and anticlimax. After all, *Oklahoma!* had become a musical institution, seen and heard by more people *before* the movie's release than any other American musical in history. In my own case, I had been in the audience in 1943 on the night of the very first performance of the pre-Broadway tryout in New Haven, when the show was called *Away We Go!* (a title that got changed just before the Broadway opening). I vividly recall the sunny spirit, warmth, and unexpected excitement of the unheralded production. At first, the movie version seemed to me bigger and louder but not necessarily better, or even as good. Moreover, the clean, wholesome, innocently American spirit that had been one of the show's strengths during the war years had come to seem, by the mid-'50s, closer to one of Hammerstein's lyrics about "the corn is as high as an elephant's eye." Yet my reseeing the picture several times on TV in recent years has modified those reactions. Perhaps we've become so accustomed in the '70s and '80s to superproductions of so many different types that the size and scope of the film version of *Oklahoma!* now takes a backseat to its characters and story—and, most important of all, to its incomparable score. Similarly, after so many hard-boiled and cynical "entertainments" in recent years, the wholesomeness and corniness of *Oklahoma!* now seems no more out of place than that of *E.T.*

From the opening song, "Oh, What a Beautiful Morning," *Oklahoma!* overflows with Rodgers melodies of the most glowing sort. They stem naturally from the story, which recounts a simple tale about two ranch hands in love with the same girl in the Oklahoma Indian Territories of the early 1900s (and focuses mainly on her indecision as to which one can take her to a box social). In quick succession, the songs "The Surrey

Gloria Graham, Charlotte Greenwood, Gordon MacRae, and Gene Nelson in the box social scene from the long-postponed and under-appreciated movie version of Rodgers's and Hammerstein's Oklahoma! *(1955).*

With the Fringe on Top," "Many a New Day," and "People Will Say We're in Love" move the slim story along smoothly, while giving us insights into the heroine (Shirley Jones) and the ranch hand she really loves (Gordon MacRae). A subsidiary romance between Ado Annie (Gloria Grahame) and her two suitors, Will (Gene Nelson) and Ali (Eddie Albert), is similarly told through such songs as "I Cain't Say No," "(Everything's Up-to-Date in) Kansas City," and "All 'er Nothin'." Moreover, all these performers, plus Charlotte Greenwood as Aunt Eller, are as near perfect as you could ask—and they do their own singing.

All in all, the lively way that director Fred Zinnemann blends the songs and dances with the more natural action one expects from movies (whatever the size of the screen) finally gives the film version of *Oklahoma!* many lasting satisfactions.

Within a year of the release of *Oklahoma!*, the second of Rodgers and Hammerstein's Broadway smashes, *Carousel,* was turned into a film by Twentieth Century-Fox. Once again the mid-'50s preoccupation with big-screen technology almost overpowered an essentially intimate, sentimental musical play. But at least there were few technical glitches this time, since Hollywood, by 1956, had three years' experience with CinemaScope and had fairly well mastered the advantages and limitations of the wide-screen format.

There are other problems with *Carousel,* however. Adapted for Broadway in 1944 from Ferenc Molnar's play *Liliom* (previously filmed as a straight drama in 1930, with Charles Farrell and Rose Hobart), the story's mixture of romantic tragedy and inspirational fantasy worked more naturally during the war years, when it had some relevance to thousands of families who had lost loved ones. But by 1956 the fantasy elements of the story (in which the dead hero is allowed to return to earth for a day to do a good deed for his family) merely seemed old-fashioned and overly sentimental.

The film's casting, moreover, is not as inspired as that of *Oklahoma!*, even though it includes the same two leads. Frank Sinatra began filming the role of the strutting

Gordon MacRae and Shirley Jones in Carousel *(1956), the first movie version of a Rodgers and Hammerstein hit musical to do badly at the box office despite a perennially popular score.*

carousel barker Billy Bigelow, but he quit the production after a few weeks and was replaced by Gordon MacRae, who is much too wholesome (and not so emotionally vulnerable) for the character. Shirley Jones is also too one-dimensionally innocent as the heroine Julie, and operatic contralto Claramae Turner (as Nettie) and tenor Robert Rounseville (as Mr. Snow), both with limited movie experience, seem to be performing mechanically.

Yet once again Rodgers's music proves irresistible, from the opening "Carousel Waltz," which is heard behind the opening titles and then in the carnival sequence that immediately follows. The romantic ballad "If I Loved You" is beautifully sung by Jones and MacRae—and beautifully photographed with apple-blossoms falling from above as their reflections shimmer in the water beside them. Billy's showstopping "Soliloquy" takes place as MacRae walks along the rocky Maine shore, and it is the film's best blending of the visual and the musical.

For "June Is Bustin' Out All Over," both the cameramen and the choreographer, Rod Alexander, let the dancers bust out all over the CinemaScope screen, leaping and spinning across the town's docks and onto the roof of a dockside restaurant with enormous energy, but with only moderately interesting choreography. Most disappointing of all is the stiff, static, almost recital-like camera treatment of "You'll Never

Walk Alone," one of Rodgers and Hammerstein's most moving musical tributes to faith in the brotherhood of man.

All in all, the film version of *Carousel* is better to listen to than to look at. It is also the only movie adaptation of a Rodgers and Hammerstein stage hit that didn't do well at the box office—reportedly losing more than $2 million for Twentieth Century-Fox.

That same studio fared much better with its 1956 filming of another Rodgers and Hammerstein musical, *The King and I.* In some ways, it marked a homecoming for Twentieth Century-Fox—for the musical is based on a best-selling novel, *Anna and the King of Siam,* that Fox had filmed as a straight drama in 1946 (with Irene Dunne and Rex Harrison in the leads) five years before Rodgers and Hammerstein turned it into a Broadway musical. The book recounts the tragicomic adventures of a mid-nineteenth-century English school teacher who is hired by the King of Siam to tutor his many children, and who helps modernize his feudal court in the process. The original Broadway production had been the most elaborate and expensive in sets and costumes of any Rodgers and Hammerstein production. The movie version not only surpasses it in those categories, but also proves to be a case where CinemaScope and the technical capabilities of Hollywood improve on the original. The film version of *The King and I* is easily the most visually stunning and exotic of all the Rodgers and Hammerstein movie musicals.

The King and I belongs first and foremost to Yul Brynner as the King, re-creating his Broadway role—and winning an Oscar for it. With his semi-Oriental features, shaved head, animal vitality, and commanding presence, Brynner dominates scene after scene with a dynamism that irrevocably identified him with the role—and the role with him. What's more, he has a strong and mellifluous singing voice. Although there were many (myself included) who were at first disappointed that the role of the schoolmistress did not go to a major singing actress, there is no denying the exceptionally fine performance of nonsinger Deborah Kerr in the role, and her expert lip-synching to the voice of Marni Nixon on the soundtrack. Kerr deservedly won an Oscar nomination for the performance (losing out to Ingrid Bergman for *Anastasia*). The onscreen chemistry between Kerr and Brynner is extraordinary, indicating that they could have been equally successful in a straight dramatic remake of *Anna and the King of Siam.*

In composing the score for *The King and I* in 1951, Rodgers had faced a special challenge: writing music that would suggest an Oriental atmosphere while not antagonizing Western ears. According to Rodgers, as quoted by biographer Deems Taylor in *Some Enchanted Evenings:* "It seems certain that a too-accurate reproduction of the sound of 1860 Siam would . . . drive an American audience howling into the streets." Aside from the occasional use of gongs and bells, Rodgers finally settled on keeping the music strictly Western and strictly tried-and-true Rodgers.

The music is perhaps *too* tried-and-true in places. "I Whistle a Happy Tune," which the schoolteacher sings to her young son as they arrive nervously in Siam, is little more than a perky variation on *Carousel*'s "You'll Never Walk Alone." "Something Wonderful," which the King's No. 1 wife (Terry Saunders in the movie) sings to explain her devotion to her abusive husband, similarly seems like a partial reworking of *Carousel*'s "What's the Use of Wondrin'?" "Getting to Know You," which the schoolteacher sings to the King's children, not only is the same song (with new lyrics)

The on-screen chemistry between Deborah Kerr and Yul Brynner in The King and I *(1956) remains extraordinary.*

that Rodgers had written as "Suddenly Lucky" for *South Pacific* (cut before the Broadway opening), but is also somewhat reminiscent melodically of Rodgers and Hart's 1925 "Manhattan."

But then come two Rodgers ballads of undeniably fresh charm, "Hello, Young Lovers" and "We Kiss in a Shadow"—the latter sung in the film by Rita Moreno and Carlos Riva (dubbed by Reuben Fuentes) as part of a romantic subplot. Best of all is the showstopping "Shall We Dance?", an exuberant polka that Brynner and Kerr turn into a genuine musical climax to celebrate the story's real meeting of East and West. The movie also includes a re-creation by choreographer Jerome Robbins of his original production's ingenious part-mime, part-ballet "The Little House of Uncle Thomas," a droll reinterpretation of *Uncle Tom's Cabin* from a Siamese viewpoint.

Sad to say, some of the visual splendors that movie audiences saw during the first few years of *The King and I*'s release have become a victim in recent years of a deterioration in the film's color (affecting even the original color negatives), caused by the instability of the color film and color-processing techniques in use at the time of the movie's making. Print quality for both theatrical and TV showings can now vary drastically, depending on the source of the print and the extent of deterioration. (The American Film Institute undertook a costly program in the early 1980s to try to preserve the best available prints of this and other movies that used the same color process in the '50s and '60s, and the film industry is taking steps to prevent similar problems with other films.)

The '50s Hollywood pattern of faithfulness to both the content and spirit of

Rodgers and Hammerstein's *Oklahoma!*, *Carousel,* and *The King and I* disappeared with Columbia's film version of Rodgers and Hart's *Pal Joey* in 1958. From the start, there were some who doubted that Hollywood's Production Code would ever be loosened enough for a major studio to touch the sharp, spicy, amoral musical version of John O'Hara's tale of an on-the-make heel of a nightclub entertainer and the rich, married lady who indulges him in her "little den of iniquity." Several times movie productions were announced, involving such performers as Gene Kelly, Gloria Swanson, James Cagney, Bebe Daniels, Marlon Brando, and Mae West—and were then aborted. Finally, in 1958, Columbia, in tandem with Frank Sinatra's Essex Productions, took the plunge. But the version that ended up on film is just a pale shadow of the original stage musical.

The Broadway production of 1940, starring Gene Kelly and Vivienne Segal, had been daring and radical—a complete departure from the goody-goody, make-believe world of most musical comedies. It presented a sharp-tongued, hard-edged portrait of an antihero and the woman he "uses," with scarcely any characters who might be called sympathetic in the traditional sense. In some ways, *Pal Joey* made the most risqué musicals of Cole Porter seem almost wholesome in comparison. Yet *Pal Joey* wasn't a "dirty" show as much as it was a candid, lifelike one that didn't flinch from depicting a certain type of adult situation with colloquial, sometimes sexually explicit dialogue and lyrics. It also had a healthy if sardonic sense of humor about itself and its characters.

Contrary to a legend that has built up over the years, the original 1940 production of *Pal Joey* was not a flop. Despite mixed reviews, it ran for 374 performances (longer than Rodgers and Hart's two previous shows, *The Boys From Syracuse* and *Too Many Girls*). But there's no denying it was controversial. As Rodgers himself later said: "I think that when *Pal Joey* was done originally, the theater-going public wasn't ready to meet people like that in a musical comedy." On another occasion, Rodgers said that "while Joey himself may have been fairly adolescent in his thinking and his morality, the show bearing his name certainly wore long pants and in many respects forced the musical theater to wear long pants for the first time."

Not everyone was prepared to accept it as such in 1940. The influential critic for the *New York Times,* Brooks Atkinson, for example, called the story "odious" and some of Hart's lyrics "scabrous." With specific reference to the song "Bewitched, Bothered and Bewildered." Atkinson wrote: "Although it is expertly done, can you draw sweet water from a foul well?"—a remark that deeply offended both Hart and Rodgers.

By 1952 theater audiences were more willing to accept *Pal Joey,* and a new production starring Vivienne Segal and Harold Lang became the most successful revival in Broadway history to that time, running for 542 performances. Even Brooks Atkinson joined the critics in hailing it this time as a landmark musical. The intervening twelve years, of course, had seen the displacement of the old-fashioned style of light musical comedy by a more serious and deeper form of musical play, with Rodgers and Hammerstein as the spearheads.

But Hollywood in 1958 was still a long way from being able to accept an unadulterated *Pal Joey.* The movie version is so watered down that, as the New York *Herald-Tribune* critic William K. Zinsser put it, it's "only a distant cousin" of the original. For unnecessary reasons, the locale is shifted from seamy Chicago to sunnier San Francisco. Not only is the leading lady changed from a married woman to a widow, but the entertainer she decides to "sponsor" is not as rotten to the core and even reforms at the end—in a complete reversal of the original story. As for the score, only six of the original show's fourteen songs are kept (with the lyrics of one of them changed to fit the San Francisco locale). In place of the dropped songs, four well-known Rodgers and Hart songs from other productions are interpolated ("I Didn't Know What Time It Was," "My Funny Valentine," "There's a Small Hotel," and "The Lady Is a Tramp").

Yet the film version of *Pal Joey* is not without its merits. First of all, the casting of the two leads is just about perfect. Even though the title character is made just a singer instead of a singer-dancer, Frank Sinatra brings to Joey the right blend of hipness, vulgarity, childishness, nastiness, and spunkiness—and he has rarely been in better vocal shape. As the gracefully aging widow, Rita Hayworth, at age thirty-nine, exudes both class and sexiness in an appropriately world-weary yet wise and witty way. The characterizations are among the best that Sinatra and Hayworth have ever done on the screen. The same cannot be said, however, of the dull performance by Kim Novak (then being groomed by Columbia as a rival to Marilyn Monroe) in the built-up role of the younger "mouse" who also falls for Joey.

Several of the film's musical numbers are memorably done. Of the original show's songs, "Bewitched, Bothered and Bewildered" has had its lyrics laundered considerably, though Hayworth manages to imply a lot more than she's actually mouthing (to the dubbed voice of Jo Ann Greer). What's more, she sings it in a remarkably sensual sequence that begins with her stretched out on a bed in a pose reminiscent of one of her most famous wartime *Life* magazine covers, and ends with a view of her in the shower, photographed through an only partly opaque shower curtain. For the mock striptease of "Zip" (which the movie, by making the widow an ex-showgirl, switches to Hayworth from a reporter character eliminated in the screenplay), Hayworth lets loose with some provocative, bawdy strutting, obviously designed to recall her similar and classic "Put the Blame on Mame" in *Gilda* (1946)—though it's not matched on the soundtrack by Greer's much-too-polite vocal.

Best of all is the interplay as Sinatra sings "The Lady Is a Tramp" to a first stunned and then amused Hayworth. It's the only one of the interpolated songs that really works in the *Pal Joey* context, although Sinatra also gives a few lines of "There's a Small Hotel" a *Joey*-ish inference far removed from the usual romantic implications of the song's lyrics—especially with the lines *Good night, sleep well* and *". . . a room for us to share, together."* As for Novak's version of "My Funny Valentine" (dubbed by Trudi Erwin), it's as lifeless as the rest of her performance.

For the 1958 film version of *South Pacific*, Rodgers and Hammerstein decided to take a second chance with the Todd-AO process, improved and refined since 1955's *Oklahoma!* This time the background and nature of the wartime story are better suited to the widescreen technique, and some of the lush Hawaiian locales chosen to represent the story's South Pacific islands are breathtakingly captured. But the production is sabotaged by arty cinematography and the pretentious overuse of color filters for such musical numbers as "Bali Hai," "Some Enchanted Evening," and "This Nearly Was Mine." The tints not only give the sequences a distractingly artificial look but also weaken rather than heighten their dramatic impact. Oscar Hammerstein hated the tints and, according to biographer Frederick Nolan, tried unsuccessfully to get Twentieth Century-Fox to eliminate them.

Rita Hayworth sings the mock striptease "Zip" in Pal Joey *(1958), in which she lets loose with some provocative, bawdy strutting patterned after her classic "Put the Blame on Mame" in* Gilda. *Frank Sinatra, as Joey, watches admiringly.*

Even more damaging are the heavy-handed direction of Joshua Logan (the original Broadway director) and the disappointing performances of Mitzi Gaynor and Rossano Brazzi in the leading roles (played on Broadway in 1949 by Mary Martin and Ezio Pinza—admittedly not an easy act to follow). What had been on Broadway a bright and breezy musical play with a meaningful point of view about brotherhood and interracial romance became a ponderous, overproduced, overpreachy movie. *South Pacific* is easily the least satisfying of all the movies made from Rodgers and Hammerstein stage hits.

It does include *all* of the original score, plus one song ("My Girl Back Home") dropped before the Broadway opening. Unfortunately, few of the songs are presented with much distinction. "Some Enchanted Evening" and "This Nearly Was Mine" come off best, thanks to Brazzi's excellent matching of the fervent, dubbed singing voice of Metropolitan Opera bass Giorgio Tozzi. But Gaynor's colorless singing voice and ingenue-ish acting (in a role that Doris Day desperately wanted and would have been ideal for) make "I'm Gonna Wash That Man Right Out of My Hair," "I'm in Love With a Wonderful Guy," and "Cockeyed Optimist" merely routine.

Mitzi Gaynor and Ray Walston clown their way through "Honey Bun" in South Pacific *(1958)—the least satisfying of all the movies made from Rodgers and Hammerstein stage hits.*

Juanita Hall re-creates the role of Bloody Mary that she played on Broadway and steals several scenes in the process, but the passing years had affected her voice enough for the stronger singing voice of Muriel Smith (who played the role in London) to be dubbed for her for "Bali Hai" and "Happy Talk." John Kerr (dubbed by Bill Lee) makes "Younger Than Springtime" a touching sequence, and Ray Walston (un-dubbed) gives some welcome spice to "There Is Nothin' Like a Dame" and "Honey Bun."

Soon after the release of *South Pacific,* Hammerstein was hospitalized with a stomach ailment. Following an operation and a month's recuperation, he appeared to be feeling well again and returned to work on the musical play *Flower Drum Song* with Rodgers. But a year later, while putting the finishing touches on *The Sound of Music* prior to its New Haven tryout, Hammerstein had to be rehospitalized. This time the doctors confirmed that he had a malignant cancer. Aside from his family, plus Rodgers and several close associates, few knew that he had only six months to a year to live. He tried to keep busy, even flying to London for its production of *Flower Drum Song* in 1960. But as his condition worsened, he retired to his farm in Doylestown, Pennsylvania, to prepare for the end in the surroundings he loved the best. He died there on August 23, 1960, just a month after his sixty-fifth birthday.

Hammerstein's final illness and death hit Rodgers particularly hard. Rodgers himself had battled cancer six years earlier and, now well again, wanted to continue work. But he felt that at age fifty-eight it would be difficult to find another partner with whom he could work as closely and as well as he had with Hammerstein. At first he accepted several strictly orchestral commissions, including the background score for a twenty-eight-part ABC-TV documentary on Winston Churchill, titled *The Valiant Years*—similar in style to the score he had written in 1952 for NBC's *Victory at Sea*. (Both scores won him Emmy Awards.)

In 1961 Rodgers kept his distance from the filming of *Flower Drum Song* after producer Ross Hunter and Universal-International acquired the rights. The show had been only a moderate hit on Broadway, but it had been close to Hammerstein's heart, and dealt with two recurring Hammerstein themes: the impact of Western ways on Oriental cultures and the need for people of different racial and cultural backgrounds to learn to get along with each other.

The movie version of *Flower Drum Song* is generally faithful to the spirit, content, irrelevancies, and overcuteness of the Broadway show. There is not so much a plot as a series of episodes depicting different aspects (some humorous) of the conflicts between young, Americanized Chinese living in San Francisco and their more traditional elders —with the main focus on two contrasting romances. What upset some critics about both the show and the movie was the casting of non-Chinese actors and actresses in most of the key roles. Of the six movie leads, only Nancy Kwan is at least part Chinese (she is also part English), while Miyoshi Umeka, James Shigeta, Jack Soo, and Reiko Sato are Japanese, and Juanita Hall is an American mulatto. Three key supporting players, however, are Chinese: Benson Fong, Victor Sen Yung, and Soo Yung. Almost all of the singing voices are dubbed.

Even less Chinese than the cast is Rodgers's music. Although he uses a few more Oriental bell and percussion effects than he did in *The King and I,* plus a quick rhythmic cadence for some songs that may strike some Occidental ears as "Chinese," Rodgers's score is ninety-five percent Broadway. The best-known song, "I Enjoy Being a Girl," sung in the movie by Nancy Kwan (dubbed by B. J. Baker), is an exuberant, brassy hymn to the things that pre-lib women were supposed to relish—such as stylish hairdos, talking on the telephone for hours, getting flowers, and being flattered by attractive men. Two lovely ballads also stand out: "Love Look Away," sung by Reiko Sato

Juanita Hall and Jack Soo kick up their heels in Flower Drum Song *(1961).*

(dubbed by Marilyn Horne before she went on to become an opera star), and "You Are Beautiful," sung by James Shigeta. The rest of the score, including the delicately roseate "A Hundred Million Miracles," sung by Miyoshi Umeki (repeating her Broadway role), and the rousing, swinging "Grant Avenue, San Francisco," sung by Kwan/Baker, is generally pleasant if not top-drawer Rodgers and Hammerstein.

In 1961 Rodgers also agreed to write five additional songs for Twentieth Century-Fox's CinemaScope remake of *State Fair*—acting as his own lyricist now that Hammerstein was gone. The remake turned out to be a disaster. It's bigger and flashier but almost completely lacking in the homespun charm, warmth, and verve of the 1945 version. Not only is director José Ferrer out of his element with this type of story, but he was also unable to get more than vapid performances out of Pamela Tiffin and Pat Boone as the two Frakes children who find romance at the fair, or to control the excesses of Ann-Margret's sex-kittenish performance as the band singer who falls for Boone.

Alice Faye came out of retirement to play her first mother role (with special billing, as Melissa), and promptly went back after the movie's release. The few sparks of life that the movie displays come from Bobby Darin as the newspaper reporter for whom Tiffin falls. It's one of the first roles in which the former teen idol and rock 'n' roll singer showed his adult depth as an actor with a Sinatra-like potential, before his death a decade later at age thirty-eight.

None of Rodgers's wonderful songs are done as well in the '62 version as they were in '45. Nor do any of Rodgers's new songs help much. "Young and Willing" (sung by Boone and Ann-Margret) sounds more like the verse to a song than a song itself, and Alice Faye's one solo, "Never Say No to a Man," is perfunctory in both words and music.

The same year that Fox's remake of *State Fair* flopped, so did MGM's film version of Rodgers and Hart's 1935 circus musical *Jumbo*. But *Jumbo* didn't deserve to flop—and it remains unjustly underrated among MGM's supermusicals of the '50s and early '60s. Perhaps movie audiences had had their fill of circus movies after Cecil B. DeMille's Oscar-winning *The Greatest Show on Earth* (1952), Carol Reed's *Trapeze* (1956), and Joseph Newman's *The Big Circus* (1959), among others. MGM's now-legendary Arthur Freed Unit had first planned to film *Jumbo* in the early '50s as a vehicle for Jimmy Durante, who had starred in the original Broadway production. But the project kept getting postponed until, in 1961, it was transferred to producers Joe Pasternak and Roger Edens. They got Busby Berkeley to come out of retirement to stage some of the big musical numbers in collaboration with director Charles Walters, in what turned out to be Berkeley's last movie work.

On Broadway, *Jumbo* had been famous (some might say notorious) for being one of the most lavish and expensive extravaganzas of the Depression '30s. It played at the cavernous Hippodrome (then the world's largest theater, and best known for expensive extravaganzas). It was part musical comedy, with Durante, Paul Whiteman's Orchestra, and a large cast of singers and dancers, and part circus performance, with clowns, jugglers, freaks, and hundreds of animals, including Jumbo the elephant. Although a popular show, it was so expensive to produce that it lost money for producer-showman Billy Rose. When Rose sold the film rights to MGM, he insisted (as he had for Twentieth Century-Fox's *Diamond Horseshoe* in 1945) that his name be included as part of the movie's title.

Doris Day and Jumbo the elephant in the much-underrated film version of Billy Rose's Jumbo *(1962)—one of the last of MGM's super-musicals of the 1950s and early '60s.*

Billy Rose's Jumbo keeps most of Rodgers and Hart's original score and also interpolates two Rodgers and Hart songs from other productions ("This Can't Be Love" from *The Boys From Syracuse* and "Why Can't I?" from *Spring Is Here*). If *Jumbo* were just these musical numbers and the circus acts, it would have more going for it than most musicals. The creaky story line (by Ben Hecht and Charles MacArthur, as adapted by Sidney Shelton) is a sawdust variation on *Romeo and Juliet* featuring two funding circus families. Doris Day and Stephen Boyd make attractive if stereotyped romantic leads, but it's Jimmy Durante and Martha Raye (as his longtime circus mate) who make the meanderings of the story bearable through the combination of comic bite and dramatic warmth that they give their moth-eaten roles.

Admid all the glitter and froth of *Jumbo,* two melancholy songs with heart-wrenching Hart lyrics about unrequited love stand out. "Little Girl Blue" is sung quietly yet touchingly by Doris Day, most of it in a cinematically effective voice-over as Day sits alone in a darkened circus ring and reflects on a setback in her romance with Boyd. The more bluesy "Why Can't I?" is done as a duet between Day and Raye, in which they achieve the rare feat of making the song disquietingly heart-sore but not so self-pitying as it sometimes becomes with other singers.

In a more upbeat mood are *Jumbo*'s two matchless Rodgers waltzes. "The Most Beautiful Girl in the World" is first set appropriately on a carousel, as Boyd sings to Day, and it later becomes a delightful wedding hymn for Durante to sing in his inimitable way to Raye. Best of all is "Over and Over," which swoops and soars as Day (and her double), plus the circus acrobats and trapeze artists, fly through the air to some incredibly "musical" camera work, in a sequence credited to Busby Berkeley.

Although *Billy Rose's Jumbo* flopped in 1962, three years later the equally well-produced, musically wonderful, and even more sentimentally old-fashioned *The Sound of Music* scored as one of the most successful movie musicals ever made. The Todd-AO production, released by Twentieth Century-Fox, won Academy Awards for Best Picture, Best Director (Robert Wise), Best Film Editing, and Best Sound. It produced more royalties for Richard Rodgers and the estate of Oscar Hammerstein II than any of their other history-making works.

It's become fashionable in some quarters to sneer loudly at the success of *The Sound of Music* and to dismiss the movie as just a sticky-sweet Cinderella tale with a syrupy score and some spectacular picture-postcard photography. Such judgments usually tell more about the people voicing them than about the film itself. When the original Broadway production was similarly criticized for being too saccharine in its focus on old-fashioned family values, Hammerstein, who often objected to writers who dwell on the ugly side of life, did not deny that the grim, the sordid, and the unlovely are very real, but he said that he wanted to show that such things are not *all* there are to life. To which Rodgers added: "Most of us feel that nature can have attractive manifestations, that children aren't necessarily monsters, and that deep affection between two people is nothing to be ashamed of."

There are faults with *The Sound of Music*—including a rather clichéd script based on the real-life story of Maria Von Trapp, a postulant nun who leaves the convent to become governess to seven children of an aristocratic Salzburg widower, whom she then marries and with whom she escapes to Switzerland as the Nazis move into Austria in 1938. But the movie's qualities are many and impressive, both cinematically and musically. Next to *The King and I, The Sound of Music* benefits most of all of Rodgers and Hammerstein's stage productions in being opened up by the movie cameras. The film begins with breathtaking aerial shots of the Austrian Alps, before the cameras soar down to the lone figure of Julie Andrews (as the errant nun) standing with outstretched arms as she sings the title song.

The songs that follow it are not only well integrated into the story but, on a few occasions ("Do Re Mi," "I Have Confidence in Me"), are also adroitly edited, so that a single song advances the story through multiple settings and situations—a technique that has since come to be fairly standard in movies but which was still innovative in 1965. In contrast, several other songs are presented with almost stark simplicity: the stirring secular hymn "Climb Every Mountain" (dubbed by Marjorie McKay for Peggy Wood in the role of the Mother Abbess), the nostalgic "Edelweis" (with Bill Lee dubbing Christopher Plummer's voice), and the romantic ballad "Something Good" (sung by Julie Andrews and Plummer/Lee in a beautifully understated sequence). There is also a cleverly staged and thoroughly delightful sequence in which Andrews and the children provide the voices for the Bil Baird Marionettes for "The Lonely Goatherd." All but three of the original fourteen Broadway songs are kept,

Julie Andrews, as the errant postulant nun in The Sound of Music, *meets with a mixture of disapproval and indulgence by her convent sisters, including Peggy Wood and Portia Nelson.*

with two new ones ("Something Good," "I Have Confidence in Me") written especially for the movie by Rodgers (both words and music).

Much of the success of *The Sound of Music* must be credited to Julie Andrews, who gives in it one of the all-time great movie musical performances—full of wide-eyed charm, spirit, spunkiness, and, yes, sugar-sweetness. She even manages not to be upstaged by any of the seven adorable kids with whom she must share many of her scenes. Ironically, Andrews made *The Sound of Music* just a year after she was passed over by Warner Brothers for the lead in the film version of the Broadway show that had first made her a star, *My Fair Lady.* As Rodgers had learned before her, you win some and you lose some, but you can still come out on top.

Since the release of *The Sound of Music,* no other Rodgers musical has been filmed, although Rodgers continued to write for Broadway—sometimes acting as his own lyricist (*No Strings,* 1962), sometimes collaborating with others (Stephen Sondheim for *Do I Hear a Waltz?,* 1965; Martin Charnin for *Two by Two,* 1971; Sheldon Harnick for *Rex,* 1976). For several years he also served as president and producing director of the Music Theater of Lincoln Center, set up to revive major American musicals as part of New York City's Lincoln Center for the Performing Arts. But production costs and other factors, including criticisms of Rodgers's allegedly autocratic administrative ways, doomed the project after a few seasons.

In 1969 Rodgers's health again became a problem after he suffered a heart attack. Then, in the early 1970s, his throat began giving him serious trouble. In August of 1974 his doctors insisted on an operation to remove a cancerous larynx. Rodgers made a game effort to learn esophageal speech, but he became less and less willing to make public appearances and, in effect, quietly retired. He died in New York on December 30, 1979, at the age of seventy-seven.

Rodgers's legacy of popular songs remains unequaled—if not in number then certainly in melodic quality. Even if he had never written another note after the death of Lorenz Hart in 1943, Richard Rodgers would rank as one of America's great songwriters. When you add his work after 1943 with Oscar Hammerstein II, he takes on a historical importance that few other songwriters have approached. Although Rodgers's original work for movies was limited and uneven in quality, the movie adaptations of his Broadway musicals have brought his songs to millions more than Broadway ever could—and enriched the history of movie musicals significantly in the process.

RICHARD RODGERS'S MOVIES AND SONGS ON TAPE AND DISC

MAKERS OF MELODY (1929), Paramount short subject. B&W. With Richard Rodgers, Lorenz Hart. Songs: "Manhattan," "The Blue Room," "The Girl Friend" (lyrics, Lorenz Hart).

FOLLOW THRU (1930), Paramount. B&W. Directed by Lawrence Schwab and Lloyd Corrigan. With Nancy Carroll, Buddy Rogers, Jack Haley, Zelma O'Neal, Thelma Todd, Eugene Pallette. Songs: "I'm Hard to Please," "Softer Than a Kitten," "It Never Happened Before" (lyrics, Lorenz Hart); plus songs by others.

SPRING IS HERE (1930), First National. B&W. Directed by John Francis Dillon. With Bernice Claire, Lawrence Gray, Alexander Gray, Inez Courtney, Louise Fazenda. Songs: "Yours Sincerely," "With a Song in My Heart," "Spring Is Here in Person," "Baby's Awake Now," "Rich Man, Poor Man" (lyrics, Lorenz Hart); plus songs by others. Soundtrack LP: excerpts included in *Rodgers and Hart in Hollywood, Vol. 1,* Music Masters JJA-19766.

LEATHERNECKING (1930), film version of *Present Arms*. Radio Pictures. B&W. Directed by Edward Cline. With Irene Dunne, Ken Murray, Lilyan Tashman, Ned Sparks, Benny Rubin, Eddie Foy Jr. Songs: "You Took Advantage of Me," "A Kiss for Cinderella" (lyrics, Lorenz Hart); plus songs by others.

HEADS UP (1930), Paramount. B&W. Directed by Victor Schertzinger. With Buddy Rogers, Helen Kane, Victor Moore, Margaret Breen, Gene Gowing, Preston Foster. Songs: "A Ship Without a Sail," "My Man Is on the Make" (lyrics, Lorenz Hart); plus songs by others. Soundtrack LP: excerpts included in *Rodgers and Hart in Hollywood, Vol. 1,* Music Masters JJA-19766.

THE HOT HEIRESS (1931), First National. B&W. Directed by Clarence Badger. With Ben Lyon, Ona Munson, Walter Pidgeon, Tom Dugan, Thelma Todd, Inez Courtney. Songs: "Like Ordinary People Do," "You're the Cats," "Nobody Loves a Riveter" (lyrics, Lorenz Hart). Soundtrack LP: included in *Rodgers and Hart in Hollywood, Vol. 1,* Music Masters JJA-19766.

THE PHANTOM PRESIDENT (1932), Paramount. B&W. Directed by Norman Taurog. With George M. Cohan, Claudette Colbert, Jimmy Durante, George Barbier, Sidney Toler. Songs: "Give Her a Kiss," "The Country Needs a Man," "Somebody Ought to Wave a Flag," "The Medicine Show," "The Convention" (lyrics, Lorenz Hart). Soundtrack LP: included in *Rodgers and Hart in Hollywood, Vol. 1,* Music Masters JJA-19766.

LOVE ME TONIGHT (1932), Paramount. B&W. Directed by Rouben Mamoulian. With Maurice Chevalier, Jeanette MacDonald, Charlie Ruggles, Charles Butterworth, Myrna Loy, C. Aubrey Smith, Elizabeth Patterson, Ethel Griffies, Blanche Frederici, George "Gabby" Hayes. Songs: "Lover," "Mimi," "Isn't It Romantic?," "Love Me Tonight," "The Poor Apache," "That's the Song of Paree," "A Woman Needs Something Like That," "The Son of a Gun Is Nothing But a Tailor" (lyrics, Lorenz Hart). Soundtrack LP: included in *Rodgers and Hart in Hollywood, Vol. 1,* Music Masters JJA-19766.

HALLELUJAH, I'M A BUM (1933), TV title: *Heart of New York.* United Artists. B&W. Directed by Lewis Milestone. With Al Jolson, Madge Evans, Frank Morgan, Harry Langdon, Chester Conklin, and (in bit roles) Richard Rodgers and Lorenz Hart. Songs: "I Gotta Get Back to New York," "My Pal Bumper," "Hallelujah, I'm a Bum," "Laying the Cornerstone," "Sleeping Beauty," "Dear June," "Bumper Found a Grand," "What Do You Want With Money?," "Kangaroo Court," "I'd Do It Again," "You Are Too Beautiful" (lyrics, Lorenz Hart). Soundtrack LP: included in *Rodgers and Hart in Hollywood, Vol. 1,* Music Masters JJA-19766.

DANCING LADY (1933), MGM. B&W. Directed by Robert Z. Leonard. With Joan Crawford, Clark Gable, Franchot Tone, May Robson, Ted Healy, Fred Astaire, Robert Benchley, Eunice Quedens (Eve Arden), Nelson Eddy, the Three Stooges. Song: "That's the Rhythm of the Day" (lyrics, Lorenz Hart); plus songs by others. Soundtrack LP: included in *Rodgers and Hart in Hollywood, Vol. 1*, Music Masters JJA-19766.

MANHATTAN MELODRAMA (1934), MGM. B&W. Directed by W. S. Van Dyke II. With Clark Gable, William Powell, Myrna Loy, Leo Carillo, Isabel Jewell, Mickey Rooney, Shirley Ross, Nat Pendleton. Song: "The Bad in Every Man" (lyrics, Lorenz Hart). Soundtrack LP: included in *Rodgers and Hart in Hollywood, Vol. 1*, Music Masters JJA-19766.

NANA (1934), Samuel Goldwyn for United Artists release. B&W. Directed by Dorothy Arzner. With Anna Sten, Phillips Holmes, Lionel Atwill, Richard Bennett, Muriel Kirkland. Song: "That's Love" (lyrics, Lorenz Hart).

HOLLYWOOD PARTY (1934), MGM. B&W and Color. Directed by Richard Boleslawski, Allan Dwan, Roy Rowland. With Stan Laurel, Oliver Hardy, Jimmy Durante, Polly Moran, Lupe Velez, Charles Butterworth, Frances Williams, Jack Pearl, Ted Healy and the Three Stooges, Eddie Quillan, Shirley Ross, Harry Barris, June Clyde. Songs: "Hello," "Hollywood Party," "Reincarnation" (lyrics, Lorenz Hart); plus songs by others. Soundtrack LP: included in *Rodgers and Hart in Hollywood, Vol. 1*, Music Masters JJA-19766; also 1982 studio recording, including 11 songs cut from film, Beginners Productions BRP-2 (British import).

MISSISSIPPI (1935), Paramount. B&W. Directed by Edward A. Sutherland. With Bing Crosby, W. C. Fields, Joan Bennett, Queenie Smith, Gail Patrick, Claude Gillingwater. Songs: "Soon," "Easy to Remember," "Roll Mississippi," "Down By the River" (lyrics, Lorenz Hart); plus songs by others. Soundtrack LP: included in *Rodgers and Hart in Hollywood, Vol. 1*, Music Masters JJA-19766.

EVERGREEN (1934), Gaumont British. B&W. Directed by Victor Saville. With Jessie Matthews, Sonnie Hale, Barry MacKay, Betty Balfour, Ivor MacLaren. Songs: "Dancing on the Ceiling," "Dear, Dear," "If I Give in to You" (lyrics, Lorenz Hart); plus songs by others. Studio recordings LP: included in *Jessie Matthews Selections from Ever Green and Evergreen*, Monmouth-Evergreen MES-7049 (withdrawn). Videocassette: Video Images (Video Yesteryear).

THE DANCING PIRATE (1936), Pioneer for RKO Radio release. Color. Directed by Lloyd Color. With Charles Collins, Frank Morgan, Steffi Duna, Luis Alberni, Victor Varconi, Jack LaRue. Songs: "Are You My Love?," "When You're Dancing the Waltz" (lyrics, Lorenz Hart).

HOLLYWOOD HOTEL (1937), Warner Brothers. B&W. Directed by Busby Berkeley. With Dick Powell, Rosemary Lane, Lola Lane, Benny Goodman and his Orchestra, Louella Parsons, Glenda Farrell, Hugh Herbert, Frances Langford, Jerry Cooper, Raymond Paige and his Orchestra, Johnny "Scat" Davis, Edgar Kennedy. Song: "Blue Moon" (lyrics, Lorenz Hart); plus songs by others.

FOOLS FOR SCANDAL (1938), Warner Brothers. B&W. Directed by Mervyn LeRoy. With Carole Lombard, Fernand Gravet, Ralph Bellamy, Allen Jenkins, Marie Wilson. Songs: "How Can You Forget?," "There's a Boy in Harlem" (lyrics, Lorenz Hart).

ON YOUR TOES (1939), Warner Brothers. B&W. Directed by Ray Enright. With Vera Zorina, Eddie Albert, Frank McHugh, James Gleason, Donald O'Connor, Gloria Dickson, Alan Hale, Leonid Kinsky. Songs (as background music only): "There's a Small Hotel," "On Your Toes," "Quiet Nights" (lyrics, Lorenz Hart). Music: "Slaughter on Tenth Avenue" and "Zenobia" ballets.

AT THE CIRCUS (1939), MGM. B&W. Directed by Mervyn LeRoy. With Groucho, Chico, and Harpo Marx, Kenny Baker, Florence Rice, Eve Arden, Margaret Dumont. Song: "Blue Moon" (lyrics, Lorenz Hart; but used as instrumental only); plus other songs. Videocassette: MGM/UA.

BABES IN ARMS (1939), MGM. B&W. Directed by Busby Berkeley. With Mickey Rooney, Judy Garland, Charles Winninger, June Preisser, Guy Kibbee, Grace Hayes, Betty Jaynes, Douglas MacPhail, Rand Brooks, Margaret Hamilton. Songs: "Babes in Arms," "Where or When" (lyrics, Lorenz Hart); plus songs by others. Soundtrack LP: Curtain Calls 100/6-7 (with *Babes on Broadway*). Videocassette: MGM/UA.

THE BOYS FROM SYRACUSE (1940), Universal. B&W. Directed by A. Edward Sutherland. With Allan Jones, Martha Raye, Joe Penner, Rosemary Lane, Irene Hervey, Charles Butterworth, Alan Mowbray, Eric Blore. Songs: "Sing for Your Supper," "He and She," "This Can't Be Love," "Falling in Love With Love," "Who Are You?," "The Greeks Have No Word for It" (lyrics, Lorenz Hart). Soundtrack LP: excerpts in *Martha Raye*, Legends 1000/5-6.

TOO MANY GIRLS (1940), RKO Radio. B&W. Directed by George Abbott. With Lucille Ball, Richard Carlson, Ann Miller, Eddie Bracken, Frances Langford, Desi Arnaz, Hal LeRoy, Libby Bennett, Van Johnson. Songs: "I Didn't Know What Time It Was," "Spic and Spanish," "Love Never Went to College," "'Cause We Got Cake," "You're Nearer," "Look Out" (lyrics, Lorenz Hart).

THEY MET IN ARGENTINA (1941), RKO Radio. B&W. Directed by Leslie Goodwins and Jack Hively. With Maureen O'Hara, James Ellison, Buddy Ebsen, Alberto Vila, Joseph Buloff, Robert Barrat. Songs: "You've Got the Best of Me," "North America Meets South America," "Amarillo," "Lolita," "Cutting the Cane," "Never Go to Argentina," "Simpatica" (lyrics, Lorenz Hart).

I MARRIED AN ANGEL (1942), MGM. B&W. Directed by W. S. Van Dyke II. With Jeanette MacDonald, Nelson Eddy, Edward Everett Horton, Binnie Barnes, Reginald Owen, Douglass Dumbrille, Anne Jeffreys, Janis Carter. Songs: "I Married an Angel," "Spring Is Here," "A Twinkle in Your Eye," "I'll Tell the Man in the Street" (lyrics, Lorenz Hart); "Little Workaday World," "May I Present the Girl?," "Tira Lira La" (lyrics, Bob Wright, Chet Forrest); plus songs and arias by others. Soundtrack LP: excerpts included in Pelican 103 (with *The New Moon*).

MOONLIGHT IN VERMONT (1943), Universal. B&W. Directed by Edward Lilley. With Gloria Jean, Ray Malone (Ray Lynn), George Dolenz, Sidney Miller, the Jivin' Jills and the Jivin' Jacks. Song: "Lover" (lyrics, Lorenz Hart); plus songs by others.

STAGE DOOR CANTEEN (1943), Sol Lesser Productions for United Artists release. B&W. Directed by Frank Borzage. With Cheryl Walker, William Terry, Lon McCallister, Ray Bolger, Ethel Merman, Gracie Fields, Lanny Ross, Peggy Lee, Trudi Erwin, Harry Babbitt, Kay Kyser and his Orchestra, Count Basie and his Orchestra, Benny Goodman and his Orchestra, Xavier Cugat and his Orchestra, Freddy Martin and his Orchestra, Guy Lombardo and his Orchestra; Katharine Hepburn, Alfred Lunt, Lynn Fontanne, Katharine Cornell, Judith Anderson, Helen Hayes, Tallulah Bankhead, Ethel Waters, Edgar Bergen, George Jessel, Harpo Marx, George Raft, Ed Wynn, Yehudi Menuhin, Paul Muni, Merle Oberon, Dorothy Fields, Ina Claire, Gypsy Rose Lee (Louise Hovick), Franklin Pangborn, other guest stars. Song: "The Girl I Love to Leave Behind" (lyrics, Lorenz Hart); plus songs by others. Soundtrack LP: Curtain Calls 100/11-12 (with *Hollywood Canteen*). Videocassette: Video Images; Discount Video.

HIGHER AND HIGHER (1944), RKO Radio. B&W. Directed by Tim Whelan. With Michele Morgan, Jack Haley, Frank Sinatra, Leon Errol, Marcy McGuire, Mel Tormé, Victor Borge, Mary Wickes, Paul and Grace Hartman, Dooley Wilson. Song: "Disgustingly Rich" (lyrics, Lorenz Hart); plus songs by others. Soundtrack LP: Hollywood Soundstage 411. Videocassette: Blackhawk.

MEET THE PEOPLE (1944), MGM. B&W. Directed by Charles Riesner. With Dick Powell, Lucille Ball, Bert Lahr, Virginia O'Brien, June Allyson, Rags Ragland, Vaughn Monroe and his Orchestra, Spike Jones and His City Slickers. Song: "I Like to Recognize the Tune" (lyrics, Lorenz Hart); plus songs by others.

THIS IS THE LIFE (1944), Universal. B&W. Directed by Felix Feist. With Donald O'Connor, Susanna Foster, Patric Knowles, Louise Albritton, Peggy Ryan, Ray Eberle and his Orchestra. Song: "With a Song in My Heart" (lyrics, Lorenz Hart); plus songs by others.

STATE FAIR (1945), Twentieth Century-Fox. Color. Directed by Walter Lang. With Jeanne Crain, Dana Andrews, Dick Haymes, Vivian Blaine, Charles Winninger, Fay Bainter, Frank McHugh, Percy Kilbride. Songs: "Our State Fair," "It Might As Well Be Spring," "That's for Me," "It's a Grand Night for Singing," "All I Owe Ioway," "Isn't It Kind of Fun?" (lyrics, Oscar Hammerstein II). Soundtrack LP: Classic International Filmusicals CIF-3009 (with *Centennial Summer*).

ISN'T IT ROMANTIC? (1948), Paramount. B&W. Directed by Norman Z. McLeod. With Veronica Lake, Mona Freeman, Mary Hatcher, Pearl Bailey, Billy De Wolfe, Patric Knowles, Roland Culver. Song: "Isn't It Romantic?" (lyrics, Lorenz Hart); plus songs by others.

WORDS AND MUSIC (1948), MGM. Color. Directed by Norman Taurog. With Mickey Rooney, Tom Drake, Ann Sothern, Perry Como, Betty Garrett, Janet Leigh, Marshall Thompson, Judy Garland, June Allyson, Lena Horne, Gene Kelly, Cyd Charisse, Vera-Ellen, Mel Tormé, Allyn Ann McLerie, Dee Turnell, the Blackburn Twins. Songs: "Manhattan," "There's a Small Hotel," "Way Out West (On West End Avenue)," "With a Song in My Heart," "Spring Is Here," "On Your Toes," "This Can't Be Love," "The Girl Friend," "Blue Room," "Mountain Greenery," "A Tree in the Park," "Where's That Rainbow?," "A Little Birdie Told Me So," "Thou Swell," "Someone Should Tell Them," "Where or When?," "The Lady Is a Tramp," "I Wish I Were in Love Again," "Johnny One Note," "My Heart Stood Still" (lyrics, Lorenz Hart); "Slaughter on Tenth Avenue" ballet. Soundtrack LP: MGM MS-580 (withdrawn). Videocassette: MGM/UA.

YOUNG MAN WITH A HORN (1950), Warner Brothers. B&W. Directed by Michael Curtiz. With Kirk Douglas, Lauren Bacall, Doris Day, Juano Hernandez, Mary Beth Hughes, Hoagy Carmichael. Song: "With a Song in My Heart" (lyrics, Lorenz Hart); plus songs by others.

MALAYA (1949), MGM. B&W. Directed by

Richard Thorpe. With Spencer Tracy, James Stewart, Valentina Cortese, Sydney Greenstreet, Lionel Barrymore. Song: "Blue Moon" (lyrics, Lorenz Hart); plus songs by others.

TWO TICKETS TO BROADWAY (1951), RKO Radio. Color. Directed by James V. Kern. With Janet Leigh, Ann Miller, Tony Martin, Gloria DeHaven, Eddie Bracken, Barbara Lawrence, Bob Crosby and his Orchestra, Smith and Dale. Song: "Manhattan" (lyrics, Lorenz Hart); plus songs by others. Videocassette: King of Video.

PAINTING THE CLOUDS WITH SUN-SHINE (1951), Warner Brothers. Color. Directed by David Butler. With Dennis Morgan, Virginia Mayo, Gene Nelson, Lucille Norman, Virginia Gibson, Tom Conway, Wallace Ford, S. Z. Sakall. Song: "With a Song in My Heart" (lyrics, Lorenz Hart).

WITH A SONG IN MY HEART (1952), Twentieth Century-Fox. Color. Directed by Walter Lang. With Susan Hayward, Rory Calhoun, David Wayne, Thelma Ritter, Una Merkel, Robert Wagner, Leif Erickson. Songs: "With a Song in My Heart," "Blue Moon" (lyrics, Lorenz Hart); plus songs by others. Soundtrack LP: excerpts included in *Susan Hayward, Legends* 1000/2; also, studio-recorded excerpts in *Jane Froman: With a Song in My Heart,* Capitol T-309 (withdrawn).

THE JAZZ SINGER (1953), Warner Brothers. Color. Directed by Michael Curtiz. With Danny Thomas, Peggy Lee, Mildred Dunnock, Eduard Franz. Song: "Lover" (lyrics, Lorenz Hart); plus songs by others.

TORCH SONG (1953), MGM. Color. Directed by Charles Walters. With Joan Crawford, Michael Wilding, Gig Young, Marjorie Rambeau, Dorothy Patrick, Eugene Loring, Benny Rubin. Song: "Blue Moon" (lyrics, Lorenz Hart); plus songs by others.

A STAR IS BORN (1954), Warner Brothers. Color. Directed by George Cukor. With Judy Garland, James Mason, Jack Carson, Charles Bickford, Tom Noonan, Amanda Blake. Song: "You Took Advantage of Me'" (lyrics, Lorenz Hart); plus songs by others. Soundtrack LP: CBS Special Products ACS-8740. Videocassette: Warner Home Video 11335A/B (restored version).

GENTLEMEN MARRY BRUNETTES (1955), Voyager for United Artists release. CinemaScope. Color. Directed by Richard Sale. With Jeanne Crain, Jane Russell, Scott Brady, Alan Young, Rudy Vallee, Guy Middleton. Songs: "My Funny Valentine," "Have You Met Miss Jones?" (lyrics, Lorenz Hart); plus songs by others. Soundtrack LP: Coral 57013 (withdrawn).

LOVE ME OR LEAVE ME (1955), MGM. Color. Directed by Charles Vidor. With James Cagney, Doris Day, Cameron Mitchell, Robert Keith. Song: "Ten Cents a Dance" (lyrics, Lorenz Hart); plus music by others. Soundtrack LP: CBS Special Products ACS-8773.

OKLAHOMA! (1955), Magna. Todd-AO and CinemaScope. Color. Directed by Fred Zinnemann. With Gordon MacRae, Shirley Jones, Charlotte Greenwood, Rod Steiger, Gene Nelson, Gloria Grahame, Eddie Albert, James Whitmore, Bambi Lynn, James Mitchell. Songs: "Oh, What a Beautiful Mornin'," "The Surrey With the Fringe on Top," "Kansas City," "I Cain't Say No," "Many a New Day," "People Will Say We're in Love," "Pore Jud Is Daid," "Out of My Dreams," "The Farmer and the Cowman," "All er Nothin'," "Oklahoma" (lyrics, Oscar Hammerstein II); "Laurey Makes Up Her Mind" ballet. Soundtrack LP: Capitol SWAO-005951. Videocassette and videodisc: CBS/Fox.

CAROUSEL (1956), Twentieth Century-Fox. CinemaScope. Color. Directed by Henry King. With Gordon MacRae, Shirley Jones, Cameron Mitchell, Barbara Ruick, Claramae Turner, Robert Rounseville, Audrey Christie, Gene Lockhart, Jacques d'Amboise, Susan Luckey. Songs: "If I Loved You," "Mister Snow," "June Is Bustin' Out All Over," "When the Children Are Asleep," "Soliloquy," "A Real Nice Clambake," "There's Nothin' So Bad for a Woman," "What's the Use of Wond'rin'," "You'll Never Walk Alone" (lyrics, Oscar Hammerstein II); "Carousel Waltz," "Louise's Ballet." Soundtrack LP: Capitol SW-00694.

THE KING AND I (1956), Twentieth Century-Fox. CinemaScope. Color. Directed by Walter Lang. With Deborah Kerr, Yul Brynner, Rita Moreno, Terry Saunders, Martin Benson, Carlos Rivas, Alan Mowbray, Gemze de Lappe. Songs: "I Whistle a Happy Tune," "Hello, Young Lovers," "A Puzzlement," "Getting to Know You," "We Kiss in a Shadow," "Something Wonderful," "I Have Dreamed," "The King's Song," "Shall We Dance?" (lyrics, Oscar Hammerstein II); "March of the Siamese Children," "The Small House of Uncle Thomas Ballet." Soundtrack LP: Capitol SW-00740. Videocassette and videodisc: CBS/Fox

THE EDDY DUCHIN STORY (1956), Columbia. Color. Directed by George Sidney. With Tyrone Power, Kim Novak, Victoria Shaw, James Whitmore, Larry Keating. Song: "Blue Room" (lyrics, Lorenz Hart); plus songs by others. LP: MCA VIM-7215 (featuring Carmen Cavallaro, who dubbed the soundtrack piano).

THIS COULD BE THE NIGHT (1957), MGM. CinemaScope. B&W. Directed by Robert Wise. With Jean Simmons, Paul Douglas, Tony Franciosa, Joan Blondell, ZaSu Pitts, Neile Adams, J. Carrol Naish, Murvyn Vye, Julie Wilson, Rafael Compos. Song: "Blue Moon" (lyrics, Lorenz Hart); plus songs by others. Soundtrack LP: MGM 3530 (withdrawn).

PAL JOEY (1957), Columbia. Color. Directed by George Sidney. With Frank Sinatra, Rita Hayworth, Kim Novak, Barbara Nichols, Bobby Sherwood, Elizabeth Patterson. Songs: "Bewitched, Bothered and Bewildered," "Zip," "Chicago (Great Big Town)," "That Terrific Rainbow," "Pal Joey," "The Lady Is a Tramp," "There's a Small Hotel," "My Funny Valentine," "I Didn't Know What Time It Was" (lyrics, Lorenz Hart). Soundtrack LP: Capitol W-912.

BEAU JAMES (1957), Paramount. Color. Directed by Melville Shavelson. With Bob Hope, Vera Miles, Alexis Smith, Paul Douglas, Darren McGavin, Jimmy Durante, George Jessel, Sammy Cahn. Song: "Manhattan" (lyrics, Lorenz Hart); plus songs by others.

SOUTH PACIFIC (1958), Magna for Twentieth Century-Fox release. Todd-AO and CinemaScope. Color. Directed by Joshua Logan. With Rossano Brazzi, Mitzi Gaynor, John Kerr, Ray Walston, Juanita Hall, France Nuyen. Songs: "Dites-moi," "A Cockeyed Optimist," "Twin Soliloquies," "Some Enchanted Evening," "Bloody Mary," "There Is Nothin' Like a Dame," "Bali Ha'i," "I'm Gonna Wash That Man Right Out of My Hair," "(I'm in Love With) A Wonderful Guy," "Younger Than Springtime," "This Is How It Feels," "Happy Talk," "My Girl Back Home," "You've Got to Be Taught," "This Nearly Was Mine," "Honey Bun" (lyrics, Oscar Hammerstein II). Soundtrack LP: RCA LOC-1032. Videocassette and videodisc: CBS/Fox.

PEPE (1960), Columbia. CinemaScope. Color. Directed by George Sidney. With Cantinflas, Shirley Jones, Dan Dailey, Edward G. Robinson, Maurice Chevalier, Bing Crosby, Frank Sinatra, Jimmy Durante, André Previn, Zsa Zsa Gabor, Debbie Reynolds, Bobby Darin, other guest stars. Song: "Mimi" (lyrics, Lorenz Hart); plus songs by others. Soundtrack LP: Colpix 507 (withdrawn).

FLOWER DRUM SONG (1961), Universal International. Color. Directed by Henry Koster. With Nancy Kwan, James Shigeta, Miyoshi Umeki, Juanita Hall, Benson Fong, Jack Soo. Songs: "A Hundred Million Miracles," "You

Are Beautiful," "I Enjoy Being a Girl," "I Am Going to Like It Here," "Chop Suey," "Don't Marry Me," "Grant Avenue," "Love Look Away," "Fan Tan Fannie," "Gliding Through My Memoree," "The Other Generation," "Sunday" (lyrics, Oscar Hammerstein II). Soundtrack LP: MCA 37089. Videocassette: MCA

STATE FAIR (1962), Twentieth Century-Fox. CinemaScope. Color. Directed by Jose Ferrer. With Pat Boone, Bobby Darin, Pamela Tiffin, Ann-Margret, Alice Faye, Tom Ewell, Wally Cox. Songs: "Our State Fair," "It Might As Well Be Spring," "That's for Me," "Isn't It Kinda Fun?," "It's a Grand Night for Singing" (lyrics by Oscar Hammerstein II), "More Than Just a Friend," "Willing and Eager," "Never Say No to a Man," "It's the Little Things in Texas," "This Isn't Heaven" (lyrics, Richard Rodgers). Soundtrack LP: Dot 29011 (withdrawn).

BILLY ROSE'S JUMBO (1962), MGM. Color. Directed by Charles Walters. With Doris Day, Stephen Boyd, Jimmy Durante, Martha Raye, Dean Jagger, Charles Watts. Songs: "Over and Over Again," "The Circus Is on Parade," "The Most Beautiful Girl in the World," "My Romance," "Little Girl Blue," "Why Can't I?," "This Can't Be Love" (lyrics, Lorenz Hart); plus songs by others. Soundtrack LP: CBS Special Products AOS-2260.

THE SOUND OF MUSIC (1965), Twentieth Century-Fox. Todd-AO. Color. Directed by Robert Wise. With Julie Andrews, Christopher Plummer, Eleanor Parker, Peggy Wood, Richard Haydn, Anna Lee, Portia Nelson, Marni Nixon, Doris Lloyd, the Bil Baird Marionettes. Songs: "The Sound of Music," "Maria," "My Favorite Things," "Do-Re-Mi," "Sixteen Going on Seventeen," "The Lonely Goatherd," "So Long, Farewell," "Climb Ev'ry Mountain," "Edelweis," "Preludium" (lyrics, Oscar Hammerstein II); "Something Good," "I Have Confidence in Me" (lyrics, Richard Rodgers). Soundtrack LP: RCA LSOD-2005. Videocassette and videodisc: CBS/Fox.

NEW YORK, NEW YORK (1977), United Artists. Color. Directed by Martin Scorsese. With Liza Minnelli, Robert DeNiro, Lionel Stander, Mary Kay Place, Barry Primus, Georgie Auld. Song: "Blue Moon" (lyrics, Lorenz Hart); plus songs by others. Soundtrack LP: Liberty LKBL-00750. Videocassette and videodisc: CBS/Fox (restored version).

Harry Warren (at the piano), with lyricist Al Dubin in the early 1930s.

HARRY WARREN

When the first recording of "Rose of the Rio Grande" was released in 1922 by Vincent Lopez's Orchestra, the record label neglected to include the name of the song's composer, Harry Warren. It was a kind of harbinger of Warren's future. Even though he would write hundreds of the most popular songs over the next thirty years—and would win three Academy Awards and have forty-two of his songs on *Your Hit Parade* between 1935 and 1950 (compared to Irving Berlin's thirty-three)—Harry Warren never became as well-known to the general public in his lifetime as Berlin, Kern, Gershwin, or Porter, in whose league he certainly was as a hit-maker.

Most of Warren's songs were written specifically for the movies. For ten years he was the No. 1 composer at Warner Brothers, during the heyday of the now-classic Busby Berkeley musicals. Later he moved over to Twentieth Century-Fox for five years, writing mostly for the hit musicals of Betty Grable and Alice Faye. Then it was MGM for another five years for Astaire, Garland, and Esther Williams pictures, and, finally, a decade of free-lancing, mostly at Paramount, for Bing Crosby, Martin and Lewis, and a few others.

With those credits, why hasn't Warren become better known? Some place much of the blame on Warren's own penchant for privacy, and on his refusal to engage in the personal publicity that some other songwriters actively cultivated. Some also cite the critical snobbism that long looked down on "strictly Hollywood" composers compared with those who concentrated on Broadway first and Hollywood second. Yet, ironically, Warren was always, at heart, a New Yorker—as his many songs attest.

Warren was born on December 24, 1893, in Brooklyn, New York, the youngest of the eleven children of Antonio and Rachel Guaragna. He was christened Salvatore by his Italian-born, Roman Catholic parents. But before Salvatore reached school age, his father, a bootmaker, legally changed the family name to Warren, to make it easier for his children to be absorbed into the American melting pot. At about the same time, Salvatore became Harry.

Warren always traced his interest in music back as far as he could remember, including singing in the choir of his church in Brooklyn. An average student, he quit school at age sixteen and took a number of odd jobs, mainly to get money to study music. He worked in a tin factory and in an insurance office, and also filled in for a while as a drummer in a traveling brass band organized by a relative in the Hudson Valley, north of New York City.

Then, in 1915, Warren got a job at the busy Vitagraph silent-film studios in the Flatbush section of Brooklyn—but not as a musician. He was hired as a property man and extra. Some months later, Warren was on the set of a film that was being shot with one of Vitagraph's biggest stars, Corinne Griffith. When she asked for mood music to help her prepare for a scene, Warren improvised at the piano. Both Griffith and the picture's director (Griffith's husband, Webster Campbell) liked what Warren played and arranged for his transfer out of the property department. They also helped him get incidental jobs as a pianist in Brooklyn movie and vaudeville houses. Warren later confessed that many of his improvised accompaniments at this time leaned heavily on Puccini, who was to remain his favorite composer and the strongest influence on his musical ideas.

Warren's love for Italian opera in general, and his ability to transcribe its themes for piano, also helped to win him the young lady he would marry in 1917, Josephine Wensler. Her father, an American of German family background, wasn't sure he wanted his daughter to marry an Italian—until Warren impressed him with his knowledge of opera and his ability to play selections from it on the Wensler's piano.

A few months after his marriage, the United States entered World War I and Warren joined the Navy Air Corps. He was stationed for most of the next year at an isolated base at Montauk, on the then-undeveloped eastern end of Long Island. Just to pass the time, Warren started writing songs. When the war ended, he used his former contacts at Vitagraph (whose activities were then in a slump) to help get him a job as a song plugger for a small music publisher, at twenty dollars a week.

Over the next few years, in addition to promoting the songs of others, Warren was able to get a few of his own published. But none of them made much of an impression on the public until he teamed up with Mort Dixon and Billy Rose in 1924. The songs they wrote together were mostly Warren's and Dixon's, but the ideas and titles were usually Rose's—and it was Rose's aggressive pushing of them with publishers and other song pluggers that got them heard. By 1927 Warren had moved on to the major publishing house of Remick and felt confident enough about his future as a songwriter to buy a small house in Forest Hills for his growing family (son Harry, Jr., and daughter Joan).

A year later, with the success of *The Jazz Singer,* New York songwriters were suddenly in demand by Hollywood studios jumping on the talkie bandwagon. Warner Brothers, moreover, made a daring move in purchasing (for ten million dollars) several New York music-publishing houses, including Remick. This assured the studio of rights to the works of some important songwriters—as well as all the profits from successful movie use of their material. As an employee of Remick, Warren was among the songwriters invited to go to Hollywood. He resisted until the stock market crash drastically unsettled the New York music scene, making the movies seem a more secure bet at the moment. Warren agreed to give Hollywood a try for a few months early in 1930.

His first assignment: to write additional songs for the film version of Rodgers and Hart's *Spring Is Here,* starring Bernice Claire (who also filmed Gershwin's *Song of the Flame* and Youmans's *No, No, Nanette* that same year). The show had been only a moderate success on Broadway, so Warner Brothers felt no qualms about dumping much of its book and all but three of its original songs. That left the studio room to create a few new song hits from which it hoped to profit directly.

As Warren later told biographer Tony Thomas, for his lively and authoritative *Harry Warren and the Hollywood Musical:* "I could never understand the business manipulations of the movie business. . . . I couldn't figure out why they would buy a movie musical, dump most of its songs, and ask us to write new ones. . . . It was just that the studios owned the publishing houses, which the public didn't seem to realize, just as they owned chains of theaters and radio stations."

With his work on *Spring Is Here* completed, Warren decided he didn't like California or most of the studio people with whom he had to deal. He also missed the excitement of New York and his friends there. So he headed back east, to work on a Broadway revue that Billy Rose was producing for his wife, singer-comedienne Fanny Brice. Titled *Corned Beef and Roses* (modesty was never one of Rose's virtues), the revue was roundly panned during its Philadelphia tryout. Rose shut down the show, completely reworked it, and opened in New York with a new title, *Sweet and Low.* Warren was only one of eleven composers who contributed songs to the revue. Among the others: Duke Ellington, Dana Suesse, and Vivian Ellis. But the show's two biggest song hits were Warren's—the rhythmically catchy "Just a Cheerful Little Earful" (lyrics by Ira Gershwin and Rose) and the romantic ballad "(Mm-mm-mm) Would You Like to Take a Walk?" (lyrics by Mort Dixon and Rose). At about the same time, a wistful ballad that Warren had composed a few years earlier with Edgar Leslie, "By the River Sainte-Marie," was reconsidered by a publisher who had previously rejected it as not jazzy enough—and it, too, quickly became a hit.

Meanwhile, Warner Brothers had released *Spring Is Here* and, although it didn't do too well at the box office, two of Warren's five songs for it (with lyrics by Sam Lewis and Joe Young) became moderately popular with dance bands and radio performers: "Crying for the Carolines" and "Absence Makes the Heart Grow Fonder." Warner Brothers invited Warren to come back to Hollywood to write more movie scores. He declined, in order to work on another Billy Rose revue, 1931's *Crazy Quilt* —actually a further reworking of *Sweet and Low,* with considerable new material and a new cast of performers supporting Fanny Brice. Rodgers and Hart contributed "Rest Room Rosie" for Brice, but it was overshadowed by the Warren-Dixon-Rose "I Found a Million Dollar Baby (in a Five and Ten Cent Store)," which Brice shared with comics Ted Healy and Phil Baker. It quickly became one of that Depression year's biggest hits, particularly after Bing Crosby recorded it.

Again Hollywood beckoned. Again Warren said no, in order to write his first complete Broadway score—for Ed Wynn's *The Laugh Parade* (with lyrics by Joe Young and Mort Dixon). Although the show ran for a healthy 231 performances, only one of its songs, "You're My Everything," became a popular hit.

By 1932, however, the Depression had hit Broadway hard. New shows just weren't materializing, with adequate financial backing harder and harder to find. So Warren agreed to write a song for Warner Brothers's *Crooner* (starring David Manners and Ann Dvorak), on the condition that he do so from New York. The picture, a hard-edged satire about a handsome college-band saxophonist who becomes an overnight singing idol only to meet an equally sudden downfall when success goes to his head, was widely recognized as a thinly veiled put-down of Broadway nightclub and radio singer–bandleader Rudy Vallee. Despite good critical reviews, Depression-worried audiences weren't in the mood for such put-downs, and the movie fared badly. Warren's song, "Three's a Crowd" (lyrics by Irving Kahal), died with it.

Warren was then approached by Warner producer Darryl F. Zanuck to collaborate on an entire film score with lyricist Al Dubin. Warren had gotten to know Dubin during his song-plugging days in the mid-'20s. They had even teamed up briefly to write a song with Billy Rose in 1926 ("Too Many Kisses") and another by themselves in 1928 ("Then Came the Dawn"). Neither song clicked with the public, and so Warren and Dubin had gone their separate ways—with Dubin eventually going west and establishing himself as Warner's top lyricist, with such early musicals as *Gold Diggers of Broadway* and *The Show of Shows*.

Zanuck's project attracted Warren because it would be a completely original movie musical, about young performers trying to get a break on Broadway. Its title: *42nd Street*. After accepting the assignment, Warren boarded a train for Hollywood, little realizing that this would not be just another short-term trip to the movie capital —that, in fact, the sensational success of *42nd Street* and its musical numbers would revitalize the whole genre of movie musicals and make Harry Warren, at age thirty-nine, the movies' hottest composer.

Harry Warren's Major Movies and Their Songs

After more than fifty years, *42nd Street* remains not only the archetypal '30s backstage musical, but also as brightly entertaining a film classic as you're likely to find. It is, of course, the movie that made Busby Berkeley as big a name as any star appearing on the screen, and established him as the creator of some of the most imaginative, distinctive, and purely cinematic production numbers Hollywood ever turned out. Behind most of those numbers for the rest of the decade would be the music of Harry Warren.

The screenplay surrounding the numbers in *42nd Street* is slight and fairly ordinary but down-to-earth and believable (in contrast to most musical-comedy plots of the era). It's also continually saucy and funny in the way that it catches backstage theater life along '30s Broadway (or, more accurately, in one of the 42nd Street theaters just off

42nd Street, the archetypal 1930s backstage musical, featured lively ensemble dancing that was to become one of the hallmarks of Busby Berkeley's production numbers.

Broadway)—even if some of the lines and situations have since become clichés from reuse in countless later movies.

When *42nd Street* was made, Warner Baxter and Bebe Daniels were its nominal stars. He was a 1929 Academy Award-winner (for *In Old Arizona*), she a veteran of major Douglas Fairbanks and Cecil B. DeMille pictures. Good as they are in their roles —he as a slave-driving Broadway director, she as a temperamental star who breaks her leg just before opening night—it's the newcomer "kids" who walk off with the picture. By today's standards, Ruby Keeler may not be the smoothest of actresses (or dancers), but her average girl-next-door qualities work perfectly for her role here as the chorine who goes on in the injured star's place. Dick Powell's verve as the show's singing "juvenile" mixes well with Keeler's gaucheries, and Ginger Rogers (still a year away from stardom as Fred Astaire's partner) has a choice supporting role as "Anytime Annie," of whom one chorine remarks: "She only said no once, and then she didn't hear the question."

There are only four songs in *42nd Street,* and only two of them get the full-fledged Busby Berkeley treatment. Even then, the numbers are fairly short, at least by later Berkeley standards. Three of the songs, however, became popular hits soon after the picture's release: "Forty-Second Street," "Shuffle Off to Buffalo," and "You're Getting to Be a Habit With Me." Each of them lasted eleven weeks on *Variety*'s Top 10 list in early 1933—with the title song rising to the No. 2 spot for two of those weeks and "Shuffle Off to Buffalo" holding down the No. 1 spot for four. Ironically, it's "You're Getting to Be a Habit With Me," which never rose above No. 4 in 1933, that has endured over the years as the film's most frequently performed song, although all three have remained firmly entrenched pop standards.

The unabashed optimism of these songs undoubtedly played a big role in their success, certainly in the Depression year in which the movie was released. Not only are Warren's melodies bright, cheerful, and easily likeable, but Dubin's catchy, essentially simple, and unaffected lyrics make them easily remembered. They are, in other words, middle-brow and fun. These were to remain the principal characteristics of most of the songs that Warren and Dubin would continue to write together for most of the next decade.

"You're Getting to Be a Habit With Me" gets perhaps the most casual treatment of the songs in *42nd Street.* Bebe Daniels sings it twice—once as she lounges atop a piano during a rehearsal scene, and later, complete with the verse, in a number in which she tries to make up her mind among a quartet of dance (and smooching) partners. Although Dubin's lyrics have obvious double entendres relating to drugs (and spurred a revival of the song among pop groups in the '60s and '70s), Warren always insisted that the underground drug culture among musicians in the '20s and '30s had not inspired the song. Instead, he said, the idea came from a secretary on the Warner lot who had remarked to Dubin one day that she was uncertain about a guy she was going around with, but that "he's getting to be a habit with me."

The mildly risqué "Shuffle Off to Buffalo" is the only song in the movie that's staged by Berkeley as it might realistically be sung and danced on a Broadway stage —with Ruby Keeler and Clarence Nordstrom as a honeymoon couple on a train headed for the upstate New York that was then the nearest train stop to Niagara Falls. Running counterpoint to the honeymooners' wide-eyed expression of bliss is a wise-

Warner Baxter, as a dying Broadway director, admonishes Ruby Keeler (second from left) during a rehearsal—little realizing she's the one who will save his show in 42nd Street. Among those in the chorus line: Ginger Rogers (fifth from right) and Una Merkel (fifth from left).

cracking second chorus, sung by Ginger Rogers and Una Merkel as a couple of gold diggers munching on a symbolic apple and banana in an upper berth.

Dick Powell woos blonde and beautiful Toby Wing with "Young and Healthy," a fairly routine "up" tune with an obvious message for Depression-stunned young people: that things aren't all that bad so long as you've got youth and health. It was perhaps too obvious, for it's the only song from *42nd Street* not to become a major hit. But there's nothing routine about Berkeley's staging of it. With this number, *42nd Street* moves into a new dimension, going well beyond what most theaters could ever achieve on an actual stage. Using three enormous revolving platforms and all sorts of unusual camera angles to record the pretty faces and legs of his chorines, Berkeley creates the constantly moving, kaleidoscopic patterns of human geometry that were to become his trademark.

But it's with the nearly six-minute finale that Berkeley completely explodes stage limitations cinematically, to present the movie's most revolutionary (for its time) production number. Once beyond a weak opening—as Ruby Keeler stridently sings the breezy title song and dances a brief tap solo atop a taxi roof—the number opens up into a fast-moving, multilevel tap ballet, mixing melodrama, deliberate farce, and lively ensemble dancing. It ends a bit anticlimactically as a cutout New York skyline (manipulated by the chorines) spreads apart to reveal Powell and Keeler atop a skyscraper waving dumbly into the camera (like the studio audiences of so many later-day TV shows). But in between its weak opening and ending, "42nd Street" heralds a significant new direction for non-highbrow movie choreography.

One other song makes a partial appearance in the film, "It Must Be June." It's used in a scene in which Harry Warren and Al Dubin, playing songwriters (what else?), interrupt a rehearsal to protest to the show's director that he's doing the song all wrong. Warren once commented, not entirely inaccurately, that in the brief walk-on he and Dubin look "like a couple of gangsters."

In some respects, Warren and Dubin were the Odd Couple of '30s songwriters. Warren was of medium height, trim, meticulous, and shy. Dubin was over six feet tall, of ample girth, and, according to Warren, "a little sloppy in the way he dressed." He also loved to eat and would sometimes disappear for hours, returning with the lyrics for a tune written on the back of a menu from a restaurant many miles from the studio.

42nd Street almost single-handedly ended the slump that had afflicted movie musicals at the box office in 1931 and 1932—a slump that can be blamed on too many unimaginative, stage-bound productions performed without zest or individual style. Zanuck's film proved that there was still a public for good musicals with good scores and good production numbers.

Nearly fifty years later, a stage production of the same title would prove the point all over again—when *42nd Street* opened on Broadway in 1980, at a time when Broadway musicals were in the doldrums. The show was still running in mid-1986. Broadway's *42nd Street,* of course, is a reverse example of the usual adaptation procedure, for this time Broadway took on a Hollywood original. The film's story was modified a bit, mostly to turn the show's director into the leading man who wins the newborn star at the end. All of Warren and Dubin's original songs for the movie were retained (except the partial "It Must Be June"), and nine Warren and Dubin songs from later movies were also added.

After the first preview of *42nd Street* late in 1932, Warner Brothers realized it had a hit and promptly went to work on a sequel: *Gold Diggers of 1933.* This time the focus of the backstage story is a quartet of chorines trying to help get a Broadway show produced despite the Depression. Warren and Dubin were again assigned to write songs and Busby Berkeley was again put in charge of the production numbers. Dick Powell and Ruby Keeler again copped the romantic leads, backed up this time by one of the studio's most popular young players, Joan Blondell, plus Warren William, Aline MacMahon, Ginger Rogers, Ned Sparks, and Guy Kibbee—most of them familiar faces among Warner's early-'30s contractees.

To almost everyone's surprise, considering the haste with which it was filmed plus the fact that Darryl F. Zanuck had left Warner in a contract dispute, *Gold Diggers of 1933* turned out even better in some respects than *42nd Street.* So, too, did Warren and Dubin's score and Berkeley's even more adventurous production numbers. From the opening number, in which a group of chorines led by Ginger Rogers (scantily clad in strategically-placed large replicas of silver dollars) warble the Depression-chasing "We're in the Money," the songs and their presentations are all audience grabbers. To underline the frolicsome spirit that is to follow, Ginger Rogers even sings one chorus in pig-latin.

"Pettin' in the Park" is perhaps the closest in spirit to the songs of *42nd Street,* especially to "Shuffle Off to Buffalo." The seven-and-a-half minute number that Berkeley devised to go with it was considered risqué and daring in its day, when public "petting" was landing people in jail in some cities as part of the morals crusade sweeping the country.

Left: Ginger Rogers in costume for the opening number, "We're in the Money," in Gold Diggers *of* 1933.

Below: The risqué "Pettin' in the Park" number from Gold Diggers of 1933 *took aim at local "anti-petting" ordinances in some U.S. cities of the early '30s.*

Ruby Keeler leads hoop-gowned dancers with neon-lighted violins through Warren's "The Shadow Waltz" in Gold Diggers of 1933.

For Warren's haunting "The Shadow Waltz," Berkeley comes up with a technical spectacular unlike any that the screen had previously seen in a musical number. In a beautifully photographed six-minute sequence, some sixty hoop-gowned dancers move up and down a vast array of ramps and then "play" neon-lighted violins through an ingenious series of Berkeley-style geometric patterns, all of them built around the song's shadow theme. The song itself remains one of the most enduring (and endearing) of pop waltzes written by any American composer. Like Richard Rodgers, Warren was to reveal a special fondness for waltzes throughout his career. Dick Powell gets to sing the song twice in the picture, both times much too matter-of-factly. But it still went on to become the only song from *Gold Diggers of 1933* to end up among *Variety*'s Top 10 hits following the picture's release.

The film's most extraordinary number is its eight-minute finale, "Remember My Forgotten Man," an unexpectedly serious yet touching and poignant piece of social comment—a reminder of the plight of thousands of unemployed war veterans reduced by the Depression to breadlines and handouts. Joan Blondell quietly recites the verse and first chorus before blues singer Etta Moten, perched in a tenement window, begins a full-throated wailing of the song, as Berkeley's cameras create a dramatic series of images of men marching off gamely to fight for Old Glory fifteen years earlier and now, cold and disheveled, having to wait in long lines for a cup of coffee. The sequence ends with more than a hundred soldiers marching across three enormous arches that would seemingly dwarf the stage of the Radio City Music Hall, as Blondell repeats the plea of the lyrics, this time with her singing voice dubbed by an unidentified singer. Just before the number begins, incidentally, that's Busby Berkeley himself knocking on a dressing room door and saying, "On stage for the 'Forgotten Man' number!"

In addition to their instant appeal, what stands out years later about Warren's songs for *Gold Diggers of 1933* is their adaptability to the varied pacings of Berkeley's increasingly longer production numbers. "Remember My Forgotten Man," for example, works effectively as both a slow blues and a forthright march. In less obvious fashion, "The Shadow Waltz" and "Pettin' in the Park" each go through at least seven instrumental or choral repeats without wearing out a listener's receptiveness to the tune. In this respect, Warren had few equals in Hollywood in the early '30s.

Yet Warren always went out of his way to make it clear that most of the ideas for these early successes came from Dubin, and that some of the ideas for Berkeley's production numbers also originated with Dubin. As Warren told Tony Thomas, "There was nothing in the script about a Shadow Waltz or a Forgotten Man. Those were Dubin's ideas, and he deserves the credit for them."

When *Gold Diggers of 1933* turned into another smash box-office hit for Warner Brothers, the studio offered Warren $1,500 a week to stay on. That was considerably more than he could hope to earn in New York. Warren agreed to stay, on the condition that his contract be on a yearly renewable basis.

Before he accepted the contract, however, Warren was approached by Eddie Cantor to write the songs for Cantor's next movie for independent producer Samuel Goldwyn. It is *Roman Scandals,* based on a script by two of Broadway's top writers, George S. Kaufman and Robert E. Sherwood. Busby Berkeley had charge of the production numbers, under a contract with Goldwyn that predated Berkeley's signing with Warner Brothers. (Berkeley's first movie, in fact, had been Cantor's New York–filmed *Whoopee* for Goldwyn in 1930.) With Dubin, Warren wrote four songs for *Roman Scandals,* a farce about a small-town history buff (Cantor) who dreams he is back in ancient Rome, where he spends most of his time trying to avoid being thrown to the lions by the corrupt emperor Valerius (Edward Arnold). Since the emperor bears a remarkable resemblance to a crooked politician in Cantor's modern hometown, the plot leans heavily on built-in parallels between past and present.

Roman Scandals is not only one of Cantor's funniest movies, with many topical '30s references to the Depression and the beginning of the Roosevelt New Deal, but also Cantor's most elaborate in terms of its musical numbers. Warren and Dubin's songs, however, come across as pale imitations of what they'd written for their Warner musicals the previous year—and this would be their first score not to produce a single song hit.

"Keep Young and Beautiful" is little more than a perky variation on *42nd Street*'s "Young and Healthy," and the torchy "No More Love" is reminiscent of both "I've Got to Sing a Torch Song" (from *Gold Diggers of 1933*) and "Too Many Tears" (cut from *42nd Street*). But Berkeley's staging of both numbers is memorable indeed. "No More Love" is plaintively sung by Ruth Etting, in one of her few feature films. (Many years later, Etting's life would be the subject of the dramatic film biography *Love Me or Leave Me,* with Doris Day and James Cagney.) Etting plays a deposed Roman courtesan who is sent to a slave market, where dozens of nude Berkeley chorines are decorously chained together, with some strategic placements of their long, flowing, blonde wigs their only defense against the Legion of Decency. This scene and its accompanying dances are the most erotic that Berkeley ever did for the screen— in the year before Hollywood's Production Code began clamping down rigorously on all the studios.

Before *Roman Scandals* could be released (it was held up, in part, because of litigation between producer Goldwyn and writers Kaufman and Sherwood), Warner Brothers rushed into production and release another backstage musical, *Footlight Parade* —with what was becoming virtually the studio's musical stock company: Joan Blondell, Dick Powell, Ruby Keeler, Frank McHugh, Guy Kibbee, and Ruth Donnelly. Berkeley was again in charge of the production numbers, but this time the songs were divided between Warren and Dubin and the team of Sammy Fain and Irving Kahal.

The plot premise of this one is more clever than most. James Cagney, in his first movie musical, plays a Broadway producer who comes up with an idea to help save the jobs of Depression-plagued musical performers fighting for survival as vaudeville dies and talking pictures take hold. His idea: to produce "live musical prologues" to tie in directly with whatever movie a theater is showing. Little matter that the spectacular numbers he produces (courtesy of Busby Berkeley) would never fit any normal theater stage and would cost more than any all-star cast of vaudeville headliners —they're great fun. The most outrageous is done to Fain and Kahal's "By a Waterfall," with a hundred chorines cavorting in seminude-looking rubber swimsuits in and around an eighty-foot pool surrounded by a gigantic, multilayered waterfall and dozens of fountains, as Dick Powell and Ruby Keeler sing the song's silly lyrics.

The numbers to the two Warren and Dubin songs in *Footlight Parade* are just not in the same league, nor are the songs themselves more than routine. "Honeymoon Hotel" is essentially a sequel in both music and lyrics to "Shuffle Off to Buffalo." Despite the presence of dozens of chorus girls parading around in nightgowns and lingerie, and the brief appearance of the same lasciviously smirking midget dressed up as an infant that Berkeley used in "Pettin' in the Park," the eight-minute "Honeymoon Hotel" number is almost squarely innocuous.

The other Dubin and Warren song, "Shanghai Lil," leans on a story line rather than a theme or situation. But it's a banal one, about an American sailor and a Chinese waif, that neither Dubin's clever rhyme schemes nor Berkeley's busy staging can enliven. The number is further doomed by Ruby Keeler's awkward performance as the Oriental of the song's title. Cagney, as the sailor, gives the number its only engaging moments, including a genially spirited tap dance (his only one in the movie).

Following *Footlight Parade,* Warren and Dubin were back on the Samuel Goldwyn lot, this time on a loan-out from Warner Brothers to the man who had teamed them for *42nd Street,* Darryl F. Zanuck. In 1934, after leaving Warner, Zanuck had formed his own production company, Twentieth Century Pictures, renting Goldwyn's

The slave-market scene in Roman Scandals (1933), in which Ruth Etting sings "No More Love."

Ruby Keeler, James Cagney (in his first movie musical), and Joan Blondell watch as stage manager Frank McHugh shows Blondell how he wants her to react to Dick Powell, as they rehearse a number in Footlight Parade *(1933).*

studios for filming and releasing through United Artists. Among Zanuck's first dozen productions: a musical, *Moulin Rouge,* with Constance Bennett, Franchot Tone, and Russ Columbo. With no songwriters under contract, Zanuck arranged with his old studio for the temporary services of Warren and Dubin, in a deal that profited Warner Brothers but brought no extra salary to the songwriters themselves. This would be but one of a number of financial and policy disagreements Warren would have with Warner Brothers over the years, despite his basic liking for the Warner production team and players he worked with.

Moulin Rouge is a silly romantic trifle about twin sisters, both played by Constance Bennett. Of the film's three songs, the one that became a popular hit was almost the antithesis of the upbeat numbers that Warren and Dubin had made their trademark in the Warner musicals. The nostalgically downbeat "The Boulevard of Broken Dreams" is in some ways the reverse side of the coin of "Remember My Forgotten Man"—replacing the male done wrong by economic conditions with a woman done wrong by her romantic dreams. Bennett, using her own pleasant singing voice, gives the song an appropriately sultry performance in a production number that's staged by Russell Markert, who would go on to become the most famous of Radio City Music Hall's stage directors. "The Boulevard of Broken Dreams" became not only Warren's first torch-song hit, but also the first of his songs in more than a year (and two hit-less pictures) to enter *Variety*'s Top 10 list.

One *Moulin Rouge* song that did not become a hit, "Coffee in the Morning, Kisses at Night," holds up as a most likeable song in the style of "You're Getting to Be a Habit with Me." It has also become a cinematic curio as one of the few numbers filmed by Russ Columbo before his death, at age twenty-six, in a shooting accident. At the time of *Moulin Rouge*'s release a few months earlier, the handsome Columbo was becoming a major rival to Bing Crosby on radio, and was moving from supporting film roles to starring ones (1934's *Wake Up and Dream*). Although his acting in *Moulin Rouge* is sometimes less than adequate, the same can be said of both Dick Powell's and Bing Crosby's in their first few musicals, too. Columbo's crooning of "Coffee in the Morning, Kisses at Night," in a sequence with Bennett and the Boswell Sisters, shows him to be vocally smoother than Powell but less ingratiating as a screen personality than either Powell or Crosby.

Long before TV's *Love Boat* and its imitators, Warner Brothers produced a slew of multistory comedies and melodramas built around a single locale (such as *Central Park, Union Depot,* and *Convention City*), in the manner of MGM's 1932 hit *Grand Hotel.* Their success led Warner–First National to extend the formula to a musical, *Wonder Bar.* The title and basic premise came from an unsuccessful 1931 Broadway show starring Al Jolson, which in turn had been based on a German musical called *Wunderbar.* Warner dumped both the German and Broadway scores (by Karl Farkas–Geza Herczeg and Robert Katscher–Irving Caesar, respectively) in favor of a new one by Warren and Dubin, and moved the club's locale from Berlin to Paris. But Jolson is kept as the focal point of the varied stories involving a missing diamond necklace, an attempted murder, and assorted romantic intrigues backstage and among the club's customers. It's all heavier stuff than the standard Warner musical of the period and, aside from Jolson and Dick Powell, it features primarily nonmusical players, led by Kay Francis, Dolores Del Rio, and Ricardo Cortez.

All of this inspired neither Warren and Dubin nor Busby Berkeley to more than so-so contributions, and Jolson's interpolation of the Russian folk song "Dark Eyes" at one point doesn't help either. Warren's "Don't Say Goodnight" is a pallid waltz in comparison with the earlier "The Shadow Waltz," and it's bogged down with some of Dubin's most strained lyrics. For a few brief moments, the number becomes visually breathtaking as a series of strategically placed octagonal mirrors create the impression that there are a thousand dancers instead of a hundred, performing as far as the eye can see.

Jolson's blackface finale, "Goin' to Heaven on a Mule," is as offensive a piece of racial claptrap as you're likely to see even from this unenlightened period of movie history. Apparently taking its cue from the then-recent Broadway production of *The Green Pastures* (which Warner was to film in 1936), the number finds Jolson being greeted at Heaven's gate, minstrel-style, by a blackface Saint Peter and Archangel Gabriel, and then being escorted to the Celestial Cabaret by some hundred "hi-dee-ho-ing" children dressed up as black angels. Stereotyped references abound—from picka-ninnies to mammies to watermelon and possum pie. The number is now understandably cut from some TV showings of the movie.

By 1934 Warren and Dubin were on a virtual assembly-line schedule, working on picture after picture at Warner Brothers–First National. The quality of the songs they turned out varied as sharply as the pictures themselves. Sometimes a major

Al Jolson is greeted in a blackface heaven by half of Central Casting in "Goin' to Heaven on a Mule," the finale of 1934's Wonder Bar.

production, such as *Wonder Bar,* produced no song hits, while a lesser production, such as that same year's *Twenty Million Sweethearts,* produced several.

The latter film is a modestly budgeted comedy with music (and no production numbers) that tells its lighthearted story against the background of network radio's early days. Dick Powell plays a singing waiter trying to make it on the airwaves. Ginger Rogers is the young radio actress he falls for, and top-billed Pat O'Brien is the fast-talking talent scout who almost wrecks more than their careers. Mixed in with the B-level romantic ups-and-downs are some amusing, satiric broadsides at kiddie shows and other radio programs of the era, as well as a running gag about the early-'30s song craze, "The Man on the Flying Trapeze" (words and music by Walter O'Keefe). The four Warren and Dubin songs for *Twenty Million Sweethearts* are modestly staged, mostly just sung in front of a standing radio mike by Powell, Rogers, and the Mills Brothers, with Ted Fio Rito's orchestra also on hand for several of the numbers. "I'll String Along With You," a ballad that again reflects the recurring Warren-Dubin theme of looking on the bright side of a situation, went on to eight weeks on *Variety*'s Top 10 list and has remained a pop standard through the years. The bubbly "(It's Getting) Fair and Warmer," another upbeat Depression-chaser, also got lots of radio and dance-band play but never really caught on.

Dames should have been called *Gold Diggers of 1934*—for it has the same style and the same trying-to-put-on-a-Broadway-show background as the '33 entry in that series. It also has virtually the same cast: Joan Blondell, Dick Powell, Ruby Keeler, Guy Kibbee, ZaSu Pitts, and Hugh Herbert. And, of course, Busby Berkeley is in charge of the production numbers. But this time there are songs from three teams of songwriters: Allie Wrubel and Mort Dixon, Sammy Fain and Irving Kahal, and Warren and Dubin. Berkeley chose to build all three of his big production numbers around the Warren and Dubin songs—to Warren's reported embarrassment, since all of the other songwriters were his friends.

The title song of *Dames* is a snappy, unabashed paean to the showgirls that had become the most essential ingredient of Berkeley's (and many others') musicals. Powell first sings it to a group of potential show backers who have been asking questions about the show's plot, its words and music, the director, and so on. As Powell keeps insisting that all that counts are the pretty girls who'll be in the show, the Berkeley girls begin making their entrances—including two who are enthusiastically introduced as "Miss Warren and Miss Dubin" (but never shown). In the lengthy (nine-and-a-half minutes) number that follows, there are more facial close-ups than usual in a Berkeley routine, as well as some of his most surrealistically ingenious patterns.

More traditional on the surface but almost as surrealistic as it goes along is "The Girl at the Ironing Board," set in the Gay '90s—which, startling as it may seem to some of us, was then nearer in time than the present day is to the year the movie was made. The marvelous Joan Blondell, given a chance to be more wistful than sassy, half-sings, half-speaks the lyrics as a lovesick laundress whose clothesline comes to life, marionette-style, to console her.

But the song in *Dames* that made the biggest impression on the public (including eighteen weeks on the Top Ten list), and is still one of Warren's best-loved ballads, is "I Only Have Eyes for You." If "Dames" is a tribute to showgirls generally, then

To Harry Warren's and Al Dubin's title song for Dames *(1934), Busby Berkeley created some of his most famous human-geometry dance patterns.*

"I Only Have Eyes for You," as staged by Berkeley in *Dames,* is a tribute to Ruby Keeler specifically. After Powell croons the song's romantic lyrics to Keeler as they ride on a spanking-clean New York subway, the photos of all the girls in the train's overhead ads keep turning into photos of Keeler. Before long, hundreds of Keeler look-alikes join Ruby herself in a series of liltingly genteel routines on several revolving stages and a small Ferris-wheel type of contraption. Curiously (or perhaps significantly) Berkeley never lets Keeler dance in the entire ten-minute sequence, other than a few graceful turns in formation with the other chorines. Nor does Keeler sing more than two or three lines of the song. This particular use of a performer whose limited abilities long divided critics and fans takes on added noteworthiness since *Dames* turned out to be the last movie in which Keeler and Berkeley worked together (although they remained lifelong friends).

Warren, however, continued to compose songs for several subsequent Keeler musicals, including the only one she ever made with then-husband Al Jolson: *Go Into Your Dance* (1935). The songs are the only saving grace of that fiasco, in which Jolson's abrasiveness and Keeler's gaucheries continually undercut whatever potential there is in the somewhat offbeat script—about a blacklisted Broadway star trying to make a comeback with a racketeer's money and getting involved in a near-murder in the process.

Warren and Dubin make a brief appearance in *Go Into Your Dance,* again playing themselves. Their scene comes during the rehearsal of a song by Helen Morgan, her only one in the picture. By 1935 Morgan's once-promising career had been reduced (partly by alcoholism) to occasional guest spots and minor movie roles. Reportedly at Jolson's request, she was given a few scenes in *Go Into Your Dance* as a gangster's mistress hoping to make a Broadway comeback. In one of those scenes, she sings "The Little Things You Used to Do," a gentle, nostalgic, and quickly forgotten torch song written for her by Warren and Dubin, who sit by the piano as she sings it. It's just no match for the two Kern songs Morgan would sing the following year in the classic '36 *Show Boat,* which show Morgan at her best.

Among the other songs in *Go Into Your Dance,* "She's a Latin from Manhattan" takes sly digs at the type of fictions Hollywood's publicity departments often perpetrated—although Warren proves considerably more adept at composing a song with rhumba and tango beats than Keeler is at dancing to them. "A Good Old-Fashioned Cocktail With a Good Old-Fashioned Girl," despite its unwieldy title, is a catchy put-down of die-hard attitudes about "nice people" and drinking (Prohibition having officially ended just two years earlier). "About a Quarter to Nine" is a typically bright and jaunty Warren and Dubin ballad that quickly went on to eight weeks on radio's then-new *Your Hit Parade.* In the film, Jolson (in white tie and tails) and Keeler (in white tap pants, jacket, and top hat) lead a singing and dancing chorus through an elegant if none-too-imaginative routine choreographed by Bobby Connolly, a recent Hollywood arrival from Broadway's Ziegfeld Follies and other shows. Midway through, the routine turns illogically (even for a Jolson movie), but briefly, into a tambourine-slapping minstrel-style number with the chorus still in evening clothes but in blackface. Jolson again dons blackface for the film's finale, in which he sings a reprise of "About a Quarter to Nine."

While *Go Into Your Dance* was still in production, Warren and Dubin were also

Al Jolson and his real-life wife at the time, Ruby Keeler, made their only film appearance together in Go Into Your Dance *(1935), with a score mostly by Warren and Dubin.*

assigned to write three songs for another *Gold Diggers* musical. This time Busby Berkeley, in addition to handling the production numbers, directs an entire picture— after years of pleading with Warner Brothers to let him do so. Except for the musical numbers, *Gold Diggers of 1935* falls pretty flat. A pedestrian script (about putting on a show at a swank resort) and a nonmusical leading lady are as much at fault as Berkeley's direction is. With Ruby Keeler busily at work on her picture with Jolson, Dick Powell was given nonsinging, nondancing Gloria Stuart to woo. She ends up being a pretty but passive participant in two of the numbers Powell sings to her: "I'm Going Shopping With You," a chipper and amusing piece of material about a shopping spree that helps advance the plotline, and "The Words Are in My Heart," a middling waltz that Berkeley gives a pictorially grandiose workout—involving some fifty white-gowned Berkeley girls "playing" fifty white pianos that are maneuvered in rhythmic patterns across a black stage by men wearing black coveralls under the piano shells.

But these numbers pale in comparison with the finale, "The Lullaby of Broadway." Over the years this has become Busby Berkeley's most famous single production number and the one he often cited as his personal favorite. It's really a self-contained music short, about a young woman (Winifred Shaw) caught up in the whirl of New York's nightlife, with unhappy results. One of its most memorable sections calls for more than a hundred dancers tapping in unison across a series of platforms and steps as far as the eye can see—in arguably the most exciting mass tap dance ever put on film. But it's the song itself that remains most memorable of all, as both its words and music capture the special flavor, glamour, and distinctiveness of The Great White Way.

Ever since their arrival in Hollywood, Warren and Dubin had argued frequently about the relative merits of New York and California—with Warren remaining perpetually homesick for New York. As Tony Thomas has recounted from conversations with Warren, the melody for "The Lullaby of Broadway" came first, with no direct inspiration from either Dubin or Berkeley. A few days later, Dubin produced his lyric, telling Warren that he had written it especially for him because the melody just seemed to say "New York." Warren was both touched and elated.

But Jack Warner didn't like the song when Warren first played it for him. He told Warren to tell Dubin to write a new lyric. Replied Warren: "I'll write you a new song, but I won't divorce this lyric from the melody." Then, Thomas has written, Warren played the song for Jolson on the set of *Go Into Your Dance*. Jolson liked it so much that he went to Jack Warner and said, "I gotta have that song in my picture!" When Berkeley heard this, he "put up such a stink" (Warren's words), insisting that the song had been written for *his* picture, that Warner finally yielded and gave

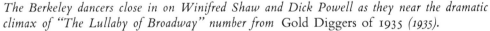

The Berkeley dancers close in on Winifred Shaw and Dick Powell as they near the dramatic climax of "The Lullaby of Broadway" number from Gold Diggers of 1935 *(1935).*

Berkeley the okay to use it in *Gold Diggers of 1935.* The song not only became the first Warren song to make the No. 1 spot on radio's *Your Hit Parade,* but it also won Warren his first Academy Award for Best Song (beating out Berlin's "Cheek to Cheek" from *Top Hat* and the Kern-Fields-McHugh "Lovely to Look At" from *Roberta*).

For Warren, 1935 turned out to be his busiest year in Hollywood. Writing exclusively with Al Dubin, he turned out twenty-seven songs for eight movies. A couple of them are long-forgotten title songs for nonmusical movies. Some are for modest-budget, run-of-the-mill musicals that Warner kept churning out with such contract players as Dick Powell and Joan Blondell *(Broadway Gondolier),* Powell and Ruby Keeler *(Shipmates Forever),* and unsuccessful movie newcomers Jane Froman and James Melton *(Stars Over Broadway).* Most of the songs for these pictures are likeable without being especially distinctive. But several made it to *Your Hit Parade:* the rakish ballad "Lulu's Back in Town" (from *Broadway Gondolier*), the patriotic rouser "Don't Give Up the Ship" (from *Shipmates Forever*), and the lovely "Where Am I (Am I in Heaven)?" (from *Stars Over Broadway*)—though for only a few weeks each, in comparison with "The Lullaby of Broadway" 's fourteen weeks.

Warner Brothers's workhorse schedule took an increasing toll on the quality of Warren and Dubin's output in 1936, with more and more songs sounding like mere variations on earlier hits. Their fifteen songs for six movies produced only one moderately popular hit, "I'll Sing You a Thousand Love Songs," from *Cain and Mabel.* Actually, that song's success was due more to the active promotion the studio gave it, at the insistence of the picture's backer, William Randolph Hearst. *Cain and Mabel* is one of four films that Hearst's Cosmopolitan Pictures produced at Warner Brothers, starring the powerful publisher's longtime lady friend, Marion Davies. Hearst arranged to borrow Clark Gable from MGM for *Cain and Mabel* and then hired choreographer Bobby Connolly to dress up the contrived story (about a prizefighter and a dancer) with several ultra-elaborate production numbers. "I'll Sing You a Thousand Love Songs" is thus set in a studio-built Venice that outstrips in elaborateness and gaudiness the one RKO Radio built a year earlier for the Astaire-Rogers *Top Hat.* Warren was only lukewarm about the song to begin with, so to keep it from having to be repeated too often in the eight-minute sequence, he arranged for interpolations of his earlier "The Shadow Waltz," as well as the well-known French song "L'Amour, Toujours, L'Amour." Despite mixed reviews, *Cain and Mabel* was a modest hit. However, Davies's subsequent Warner film, 1937's *Ever Since Eve,* flopped so badly that both she and Hearst retired permanently from filmmaking.

Two other '36 musicals with Warren and Dubin scores also drew mixed reviews: *Colleen* and *Gold Diggers of 1937. Colleen* reunited Joan Blondell, Dick Powell, and Ruby Keeler for the last time, in a lighthearted romp about an eccentric millionaire's dress shop. None of its four songs are more than routine, and Bobby Connolly's production numbers, while energetic, suffer from the very different dancing styles of Ruby Keeler and Paul Draper not blending too smoothly. The best musical moment comes with a spoof of ballroom dancers that Blondell and Jack Oakie do to "A Boulevardier from the Bronx."

Warner's efforts to keep its *Gold Diggers* series going faltered badly with *Gold Diggers of 1937,* despite its blend of familiar faces (Dick Powell and Joan Blondell, then recently married in private life) with some fresh faces (Broadway character comic

Victor Moore, dancer Lee Dixon, band singer Rosalind Marquis). There was even a blend of "old" and "new" songwriters: Warren and Dubin for two songs and Harold Arlen and E. Y. "Yip" Harburg for four. Only one song made *Your Hit Parade:* Warren and Dubin's typically breezy and optimistic "With Plenty of Money and You," sung right at the start of the picture and clearly patterned after "We're in the Money" from *Gold Diggers of 1933.*

The '37 *Gold Diggers*'s most spectacular number is staged by Busby Berkeley to Warren and Dubin's "All's Fair in Love and War." The idea for the number came from Dubin, who was having marital problems and suggested to Berkeley a battle of the sexes in terms of military maneuvers. Berkeley (then separated from his second wife) went to work planning an elaborate set of precision drills to Warren's marching song, with seventy flag- and drum-carrying chorines in shortie uniforms executing the drills on a shiny, reflecting black floor. The number remains one of Berkeley's most visually stunning, and shows how clever and imaginative he could be when rising production costs forced the studio to restrict drastically his budget in relation to earlier films. The number won an Academy Award nomination during one of the only two years that there was such an award for dance direction. (Berkeley lost to Seymour Felix for MGM's *The Great Ziegfeld.*)

After Warner's mid-'30s success with musicals set at West Point (*Flirtation Walk,* '34) and Annapolis (*Shipmates Forever,* '35), it came as no surprise when the studio followed them up with one about the Marines—and with the same star, Dick Powell. But the previous pictures' costar Ruby Keeler was replaced for *The Singing Marine* ('37) by a look-alike newcomer, Doris Weston. She had a better singing voice than Keeler, but turned out to be just as amateur an actress, without Keeler's compensating spunkiness. Warren hoped that the bittersweet ballad "I Know Now" would become the picture's big hit, but Weston's colorless rendition didn't help much, and the song went nowhere. It remained one of Warren's lifelong favorites among all his songs, however, and he even requested that it be included in the 1980 Broadway production of *42nd Street.* But it failed to make much of an impression there either, and got cut out of the original-cast recording for timing reasons. Soon after Warren died, producer David Merrick cut the song from the show itself.

The anthemlike "Song of the Marines" also became a popular addition to patriotically themed radio shows, together with Warren and Dubin's earlier "Don't Give Up the Ship" (which the Naval Academy had adopted as its official service song).

The Singing Marine also brought a crisis in the working relationship between Warren and Dubin. For the previous year Dubin had complained more and more about the number and declining quality of the pictures to which he and Warren were being assigned—and the constant studio pressure to produce profitable song hits. Dubin was also having marital problems. He would disappear for days, with no one having any idea where he was. Then he would turn up, well within a picture's production schedule, with his lyrics in hand.

In a 1983 memoir about Dubin, his daughter, Patricia Dubin McGuire, writes that, as a team, Warren and Dubin "were loyal to one another, accepted each other's faults, foibles, eccentricities, and peculiarities." In the memoir, titled *Lullaby of Broadway,* she adds that "neither of them ever spoke a bad word about the other and, although they did not meet much socially, they stood tight together against the injustices and

Joan Blondell and seventy Berkeley chorines tap out the message that "All's Fair in Love and War," from Gold Diggers of 1937 *(1936).*

inequities of the studio and quickly learned to defend themselves as best they could."

Matters came to a head, however, when Dubin failed to show up on the date Berkeley set for starting work on *The Singing Marine*'s biggest production number, "Night Over Shanghai." Warren, who had tried to be patient and open-minded about his partner's lapses, finally suggested that Johnny Mercer be invited to provide the missing lyrics. Warren had been instrumental in getting the studio to sign both Mercer and Richard Whiting that same year, in hopes of taking some of the pressure off Dubin and himself.

Mercer's quickly written, workmanlike lyrics for "Night Over Shanghai" did little more than reinforce the plot line of the number's somber story (a sort of Oriental sequel to "The Lullaby of Broadway"). Warren's haunting, Puccini-influenced theme was intended from the start as more of a mood piece than a song hit, and it is especially effective in the sections featuring classical harmonicist Larry Adler.

Dubin, meanwhile, agreed to check into the Mayo Clinic for a while for treatment of what his doctor said was too much food and alcohol. When he returned to the studio, he and Warren wrote an incidental song for Ann Sheridan to sing in the

Disembodied arms (an idea adapted from Jean Cocteau's surrealist French film Blood of a Poet*) are part of Busby Berkeley's staging of the Harry Warren-Johnny Mercer song "Night Over Shanghai," in 1937's* The Singing Marine.

prison melodrama *San Quentin* (1937), in which the studio's "Oomph Girl" played a nightclub singer. To their surprise, the song, "How Could You?," ended up on *Your Hit Parade*—but for only one week before being generally forgotten.

Tenors other than Dick Powell helped to make hits of two other Warren and Dubin songs during 1937, both from now-long-forgotten, minor musicals. For *Melody for Two,* Dubin added lyrics to a background theme Warren had written two years earlier for James Melton's first starring musical, *Stars Over Broadway.* The lyrics turned the theme into "September in the Rain," which Melton introduced in *Melody for Two* and started on its way to fourteen weeks on *Your Hit Parade.* Meanwhile, in *Mr. Dodd Takes the Air,* radio singer Kenny Baker introduced "Remember Me?", with Dubin's tongue-in-cheek lyrics nostalgically jabbing postwedding relationships.

The song caught the fancies of both newlyweds and long-married couples, and moved onto *Your Hit Parade* for eleven weeks. But the trivial *Mr. Dodd Takes the Air,* about a radio singer whose voice changes from baritone to tenor after a visit to a quack doctor, ended up mostly on the bottom half of double-feature programs at 1937 theaters —and then disappeared into the Warner vaults, rarely to reemerge like other '30s Warner musicals on TV.

Warren reteamed unexpectedly with Johnny Mercer late in 1937, after Richard Whiting suffered a fatal heart attack before completing the score for 1938's *Cowboy From Brooklyn.* One more song was needed—the title song, which, in effect, tells how a Brooklyn crooner (Dick Powell), influenced by the western movies he's seen as a kid, becomes a singing cowboy star on the radio. The song is strictly routine and is easily overshadowed by Whiting's "Ride, Tenderfoot, Ride" in the movie.

Not long after this, Warner Brothers, increasingly concerned about Dubin's health and erratic behavior, assigned the now-partnerless Mercer to work with Warren and Dubin on *Gold Diggers in Paris* (1938). Dubin reacted antagonistically, even though he personally liked Mercer and socialized more often with Mercer and his wife Ginger than he did with Warren and his wife Jo. Dubin and Mercer finally worked out an uneasy division of the lyric writing between them.

Of the six songs that Warren wrote for *Gold Diggers in Paris,* only one, "Daydreaming," with lyrics by Mercer, got much radio play. But it never reached the hit class. The picture itself did even less well, and marked the end of both the Warner *Gold Digger* series and Rudy Vallee's starring career in movies. (In the 1940s, he became a popular character comedian and supporting actor in many movies, most notably Preston Sturges's *The Palm Beach Story* and *The Beautiful Blonde From Bashful Bend.*)

By 1938 it was obvious to Warren that the heyday of the Warner Brothers musicals was ending, despite efforts to inject fresh faces on-screen and fresh talents behind the screen. Warren's four assignments that year *(Garden of the Moon, Hard to Get, Going Places,* and *Naughty But Nice)* all had scripts and production values that were strictly B-movie quality. Bette Davis had even gone on suspension rather than appear in *Garden of the Moon.* Sometimes in the past, good songs and imaginative production numbers had put over a picture with a second-rate script, but now the studio was increasingly tightening the budget on production numbers and relying on the mere presence of such popular bandleaders as Benny Goodman, Louis Armstrong, and Fred Waring to create musical excitement. Only two of Warren's 1938 songs became hits: the playfully cajoling "You Must Have Been a Beautiful Baby" (lyrics by Mercer), sung by Dick Powell to Olivia de Havilland in *Hard to Get;* and the jivey "Jeepers Creepers" (lyrics by Mercer), introduced in *Going Places* by "Satchmo" Armstrong. "Jeepers Creepers" also won an Oscar nomination for Best Song. (It lost to Ralph Rainger's and Leo Robin's "Thanks for the Memory" from *The Big Broadcast of 1938.)*

Al Dubin, unable to cope with his reduced status at the studio, asked for his release from his contract and it was granted. Later Warren would learn that part of Dubin's problems during the final period of their collaboration was drug addiction, dating from a prescription for morphine following a painful operation. Dubin had kept the extent of his addiction even from his family. From Hollywood, he returned to New York to write songs with Jimmy McHugh for a hit Broadway show, *Streets of Paris,* which introduced Carmen Miranda and Abbott and Costello. But the following years brought only intermittent work in both New York and Hollywood, plus a steady decline in Dubin's health. On February 8, 1945, Dubin collapsed on a New York street. When he died three days later, the autopsy showed the cause of death to be barbiturate poisoning.

Meanwhile, tragedy also struck Warren and his family, with the death in 1938, at age nineteen, of Warren's son, Harry Jr., from pneumonia. Warren and his wife took the death so hard that they sold their Beverly Hills home and took an apartment, uncertain how much longer they would stay in Hollywood. A year later, Warren and Warner Brothers mutually agreed not to renew their contract. That same year, 1939, also saw the departure from Warner of Busby Berkeley and of Dick Powell and his wife, Joan Blondell. An era in the history of movie musicals had indeed come to a close. But before his contract expired, Warner loaned Warren out to MGM for an Eleanor Powell musical, *Honolulu,* on which Warren worked with lyricist Gus Kahn, a longtime friend. Their three songs are all tuneful but unexceptional, including the romantic ballad "This Night Will Be Our Souvenir."

At that point, Warren was prepared to move back to New York, which he still deeply missed. But again enter Darryl F. Zanuck. He was now the kingpin at Twentieth Century-Fox and still a great admirer of Warren's. He also needed a songwriter to collaborate with the studio's No. 1 lyricist, Mack Gordon, who no longer wanted to work with longtime partner Harry Revel. When Gordon and Zanuck heard that Warren was leaving Warner Brothers, they lost no time in offering him a contract to work at Twentieth Century-Fox.

Warren's first Fox assignment, *Young People,* was not encouraging. Shirley Temple, who had been the studio's biggest money-maker for many years, was at an awkward age (twelve), between adorable muppet and attractive teenager. Her last two films had not done well at the box office. Zanuck hoped to reverse the trend with a musical that was essentially an update of some of Temple's earlier winners, in which she played the daughter of vaudevillians (this time, Jack Oakie and Charlotte Greenwood). There are even clips from some of Temple's earlier pictures worked into the story line. It didn't work. *Young People* became Temple's last Fox picture for some nine years. Warren's three songs, including the too self-consciously cute "I Wouldn't Take a Million (for a Girl Like You)," were soon forgotten along with the picture.

But then came *Down Argentine Way* (1940). It not only reversed Warren's fortunes but also shot both Betty Grable and Carmen Miranda to stardom. Its success convinced Zanuck that what was needed to revitalize movie musicals were touristic locales and Technicolor splendor—plus, of course, good songs. *Down Argentine Way* certainly has those ingredients, if only a so-so story line (but at least not another backstage story). Betty Grable plays an American who loves racehorses and Don Ameche plays an Argentine horse breeder whose father hates Grable's father. Grable and Ameche fall in love to one of Warren's most lilting romantic ballads, "Two Dreams Met." They also get to introduce the infectious, tango-inflected "Down Argentine Way," including a chorus sung in Spanish by Ameche. Both songs went on to *Your Hit Parade,* and "Down Argentine Way" even got an Oscar nomination (losing out to Ned Washington and Leigh Harline's "When You Wish Upon a Star" from Disney's *Pinocchio*).

There was a certain irony in Carmen Miranda's making her debut in a film with a Warren score, for the Broadway show that had brought the Brazilian singer-comedienne her movie contract was *Streets of Paris,* the first musical for which Al Dubin had written the lyrics after breaking with Warner Brothers and Warren. What's more, one of the songs Miranda sings in *Down Argentine Way* is her big hit from that show, McHugh and Dubin's "The South American Way"—or, as it comes out of

Twentieth Century-Fox found a formula in exotic locales and splashy Technicolor to turn its musicals into hits in the '40s. The first was Down Argentine Way, *in which Don Ameche and Betty Grable sang Warren's "Two Dreams Met."*

Miranda's English-mangling mouth "The Souse American Way." Miranda also sings two other non-Warren songs, in Portuguese. The movie nonchalantly glosses over the fact that she is singing samba-based songs in Portuguese in a movie with a Spanish locale —presuming, perhaps, that most viewers north of the Rio Grande wouldn't notice (or know) the difference.

Moviegoers certainly did notice Betty Grable. A veteran (at age twenty-four) of some twenty 1930s pictures, in which she moved from chorine walk-ons to minor roles in A features and a few B-musical leads, Grable had been signed by Zanuck after she scored a hit on Broadway in Cole Porter's *DuBarry Was a Lady* (1939). Soon afterward, Alice Faye, Fox's reigning musical queen and the star originally announced for *Down Argentine Way,* was hospitalized for an appendectomy. Grable was rushed into the part so as not to hold up production. The blonde, curvaceous Grable came across particularly well in Fox's Technicolor camerawork—and also as a more spirited performer and better dancer than Faye. For years afterward, Twentieth Century-Fox publicity tried to milk the impression that Faye and Grable were feuding rivals for each new Fox musical. But like so many other reported Hollywood feuds, this one had little basis in fact, with the two ladies actually getting along quite amicably offscreen and with plenty of Fox musicals during the war years to keep them both busy. Each star got to introduce quite a few Harry Warren songs—although it's Faye who sings the only Warren and Gordon song in the one film they made together, *Tin-Pan Alley* (1940). The song: the deliberately old-fashioned "You Say the Sweetest Things, Baby."

In an interview with pop and jazz critic Mort Goode, Warren once explained how he worked with Gordon on their early-'40s Fox musicals. "I worked during the day and would get the tunes," Warren said. "Then Mack would come around late in the afternoon, pick up the lead sheet, and go off to work with a piano player on the words. He'd call from time to time to ask what I thought. It made for long days."

The success of *Down Argentine Way* brought forth two other lushly Technicolored, Pan-American musicals: *That Night in Rio* (1941) with Alice Faye, Don Ameche, and Carmen Miranda; and *Weekend in Havana* (also 1941), with Faye, Miranda, John Payne, and Cesar Romero. Both musicals stand out for their splashy Technicolor hues —with deep blue skies and seas, and bright, rich, primary colors highlighted by imaginative use of whites in costumes and decor—and for the plentiful Latin beats on their soundtracks.

For the Rio musical, Warren (with Gordon as lyricist) composed one of his most elegant romantic ballads, "Boa Noite," or "Good Night," which both Faye and Ameche get to sing in different parts of the movie. But the song failed to register with audiences the way two catchy Warren and Gordon songs for Carmen Miranda did: "Chica, Chica, Boom, Chic" and "I Yi Yi Yi Yi (I Like You Very Much)." For the Havana musical, Warren and Gordon wrote "Tropical Magic," as seductive and romantic a rhumba as any movie has introduced—and sultrily sung by Faye against an appropriately moonlit setting.

In between these gaudy musical fiestas, Warren wrote the songs for a less lavish black-and-white musical that would turn out to be one of Fox's biggest wartime hits, *Sun Valley Serenade*. The picture also helped put the Idaho ski resort (in which a number of prominent Hollywood stars had financial investments) on the international map. Although ice-skating star Sonja Henie gets top billing in this film, her popularity was slipping seriously by '41, and it's the costarring presence of Glenn Miller and his Orchestra that brought in most of the customers to the theaters. Most of them also left singing Warren and Gordon's "Chattanooga Choo-Choo," "I Know Why (And So Do You)," and "It Happened in Sun Valley"—and Miller's best-selling recordings kept them all popular hits for many months afterward, with "Chattanooga Choo-Choo" making fourteen weeks on *Your Hit Parade*.

In this first of only two feature movies that he made before joining the Air Force and becoming one of World War II's most lamented Missing-in-Actions, Glenn Miller proves himself to be a somewhat stiff but competent actor. In addition to the picture's Warren-and-Gordon songs, the Miller orchestra performs two of its most famous instrumental hits, "In the Mood" (Andy Razaf and Joe Garland) and "Moonlight Serenade" (Glenn Miller and Mitchell Parrish). During these performances, and particularly during "The Chattanooga Choo-Choo," there are lots of good shots of the players that big band buffs will savor—including Miller sidemen who went on to become big names on their own after the war (Tex Beneke, Billy May, Hal McIntyre, and Ray McKinley). The "Chattanooga Choo-Choo" number is climaxed by a gravi-

For Sun Valley Serenade *(1941), the first feature movie with Glenn Miller's charts-leading orchestra, Warren wrote one of Miller's all-time bestselling hits, "Chattanooga Choo-Choo."*

ty-defying tap dance by the incredible Nicholas Brothers and, briefly, by a teenage Dorothy Dandridge. In true '40s-Hollywood fashion, nonsinging actress Lynn Bari has the role of the band's vocalist (her songs are dubbed by Pat Friday).

Sonja Henie and Glenn Miller also figured, separately, in Warren and Gordon's next two 1942 Fox assignments: *Iceland* and *Orchestra Wives*. The first is a lackluster wartime romance about an American marine (John Payne) and a Reykjavik skater (Henie), and is noteworthy only for the lovely ballad "There Will Never Be Another You." It's nicely sung by Joan Merrill, backed by Sammy Kaye's orchestra, which is also featured in the movie. Two other songs in *Iceland,* "Let's Bring New Glory to Old Glory" and "I Like a Military Tune," only prove that Warren was no Irving Berlin when it came to memorable patriotic pieces.

Orchestra Wives gives the Miller band a chance to swing out again to "Chattanooga Choo-Choo" and to introduce three new Warren and Gordon songs that quickly went on to *Your Hit Parade:* "Serenade in Blue," "At Last," and "I've Got a Gal in Kalamazoo." Once again Lynn Bari does lip-syncs for several of them, to Pat Friday's dubbed voice as the band vocalist. Overall, *Orchestra Wives* remains a fairly interesting if fictionalized behind-the-scenes view of the early-'40s big band era. Miller plays a bandleader whose road tours create domestic problems for his players. Real Millerites Tex Beneke, Ray Eberle, Bobby Hackett, and Billy May have roles as some of the band players, with studio contractees George Montgomery, Cesar Romero, and Jackie Gleason enacting others. Most of the soap-opera-ish story focused, however, on the wives, in line with the picture's title—with Carole Landis, Ann Rutherford, Mary Beth Hughes, and Virginia Gilmore injecting considerable nonmusical acerbity.

Lest our Canadian neighbors feel slighted by all of Fox's attention to Latin America, Betty Grable's next Technicolored extravaganza was set in the Canadian Rockies. *Springtime in the Rockies* (1942) not only became one of Grable's most popular wartime musicals, but also started her real-life romance with bandleader-trumpeter Harry James. (They were married soon after the movie's release.) James and his orchestra get to introduce most of the picture's Warren and Gordon tunes. But unlike the Glenn Miller movies, there is no substitution for the band's chief vocalist, and so the marvelous Helen Forrest gets to introduce the movie's big ballad, "I Had the Craziest Dream"—even though the first half of the song is staged with Forrest at a hefty distance from the camera, as if Fox were afraid audiences would find out too soon before the song's end that she wasn't "Hollywood-pretty." The song is later reprised for a delightful solo dance by the long-legged Charlotte Greenwood.

Springtime in the Rockies also gives additional mileage to "Chattanooga Choo-Choo." This time Carmen Miranda sings it—in a very funny version, in Portuguese. Miranda is also the spark plug for a colorful but prosaic finale blending samba and swing beats in "Pan-American Jubilee," a number that eventually involves the whole cast. Much more quietly impressive is a strictly instrumental bolero, Warren's "A Poem Set to Music," to which Grable does an elegant dance with Cesar Romero, one of the era's most underrated dancers as well as the possessor of great comic style behind his "Latin lover" image.

Alice Faye and Betty Grable both donned late-nineteenth-century costumes for two of Fox's biggest '43 hits—Faye for *Hello, Frisco, Hello* and Grable for *Sweet Rosie O'Grady*. Both pictures are burdened with tiresome "girl-loves-boy, girl-loses-boy, girl-again-loves-boy" stories, which lots of songs help make tolerable. Most of the songs in the Faye musical were old-timers by a dozen or more songwriters (including Irving Berlin, Richard Whiting, and Harry von Tilzer)—although not all their songs go back as far as the film's turn-of-the-century setting. Warren, in helping to select these songs, shrewdly used the title song (by Gene Buck and Louis Hirsch) in tandem with the one new romantic ballad that he and Gordon wrote for Faye to sing, "You'll Never Know (Just How Much I Love You)." It quickly became the picture's big song hit—tallying an exceptional twenty-five weeks on *Your Hit Parade* and winning that year's Academy Award for Best Song (Warren's second Oscar). Over the years, "You'll Never Know" also has become Warren's biggest sheet-music seller.

The romantic ballad that Warren and Gordon wrote for Grable's *Sweet Rosie O'Grady*, "My Heart Tells Me," also did exceptionally well that same year, making *Your Hit Parade* for nineteen weeks. Grable, then widely publicized as the Armed Forces' No. 1 "pin-up girl," even gets to sing it while partly (and discreetly) submerged in a bathtub. Throughout the picture, Grable also finds ways to get her famous legs out from underneath all those long 1880 costumes from time to time. Once again the score features some old-time songs (about six, including Maude Nugent's famous title tune), with Warren and Gordon contributing five fairish new ones in a style to match the period.

Cesar Romero and Betty Grable dance to Warren's instrumental bolero, "A Poem Set to Music," in 1942's Springtime in the Rockies, set in the Canadian Rockies.

Carmen Miranda's fractured English, colorful costumes, and fantastic headgear combined to make her a popular singer-comedienne in many '40s musicals. She introduced Warren's "I Yi Yi Yi I Like You Very Much," "Chica Boom Chic," and "The Lady in the Tutti-Frutti Hat," among other songs.

Alice Faye's last starring musical before she retired from the movies for nineteen years reunited Warren with Busby Berkeley for the director-choreographer's first musical in color: *The Gang's All Here* (1943). While only a modest hit on its initial release, the movie has become something of a cult classic since the 1960s, especially among college film buffs—for the almost psychedelic color designs of some of its production numbers, as well as for some sly sexual innuendos (in one case, actually blatantly phallic) that Berkeley managed to sneak past the Hays Office censors. And, in the finale, Berkeley lets loose with some of the most visually stunning of all the abstract, kaleidoscopic, geometric designs he ever attempted—this time executing them in spectacular color.

The film's insipid home-front wartime story, about a singer who falls in love with a soldier engaged to another girl, is another matter. Contrived and threadbare in its time, it has become badly dated with the passage of the years. But Berkeley interrupts it regularly enough for musical numbers—with more Warren songs, in fact, than are in any other Fox musical. With Mack Gordon involved on another project, Warren teamed for the first time with lyricist Leo Robin, for one of Robin's first projects following the death of his longtime collaborator Ralph Rainger.

Two ballads sung by Alice Faye especially stand out: the warmly lyrical "A Journey to a Star" and the romantic home-front anthem "No Love, No Nothin' (Until My Baby Comes Home)." The latter went on to fourteen weeks on *Your Hit Parade*. Carmen Miranda, garbed more colorfully than ever throughout *The Gang's All Here* in extravagant headgear and gowns (baring, as customary, her midriff), sings the Miranda number to end all Miranda numbers: "The Lady With the Tutti-Frutti Hat." Anyone who may have raised an eyebrow at Busby Berkeley's sly banana symbolism in the "Shuffle Off to Buffalo" sequence in 1933's *42nd Street* will surely be left gasping at what he does with bananas in this number ten years later. Titillating or even campy it may be, but it is also choreographically and visually extraordinary.

Miranda and a contingent of Berkeley girls also introduce "You'll Discover You're in New York," a breezily topical song about New York visitors coping with wartime prices and shortages. There are also two other lively Warren-Robin songs in which bandleader-clarinetist Benny Goodman, the era's "King of Swing," makes a passable stab at singing: "Minnie's in the Money" and "Paducah."

Warren's contract with Twentieth Century-Fox expired with *The Gang's All Here,* and he announced well in advance that he had no intention of renewing it—partly because of his irritation with what he called Fox's legal tricks, whereby the studio and its lawyers were able to keep half of the royalties coming to Warren for his songs. As Warren once bitterly complained: "They were hard people and I could never understand them. They would talk millions and yet they would haggle over a few cents' more royalties on copies of songs."

But then, in 1944, Warren's old New York collaborator, Billy Rose, specifically requested that Warren write the songs for a musical that Fox was preparing, built around Rose's popular New York nightclub, the Diamond Horseshoe. Warren agreed to a one-picture deal—and then took enormous delight in watching Twentieth Century-Fox get caught by some of Rose's own legal maneuverings. After paying Rose $76,000 for the picture's concept and the right to use the Diamond Horseshoe name for the picture's title, the studio discovered that Rose's terms included using his name as part of the title. Fox lawyers spent a year trying to get Rose to back down. He

Busby Berkeley's elaborate production number to "The Lady in the Tutti-Frutti Hat" in The Gang's All Here *(1943) has become a cult classic for the sexual innuendos that he managed to get past the Hays Office censors.*

refused to budge. Finally, a full year after filming had been completed, Fox released *Billy Rose's Diamond Horseshoe.*

Betty Grable stars in the lavish musical, playing a top entertainer at the club who falls in love with a young medical student and would-be singer (Dick Haymes). The better-than-average screenplay is an adaptation by screenwriter-director George Seaton of an old John Kenyon Nicholson play, *The Barker,* and it allows for plentiful musical interludes, of acts supposedly being staged at the club. Warren's songs, with Mack Gordon as lyricist, range from the nostalgic "Play Me an Old-Fashioned Melody," introduced by Beatrice Kay (a popular '40s radio specialist in Gay '90s songs), to Grable's very '40s "A Nickel's Worth of Jive" and the Latin-flavored "In Acapulco." But once again it's the romantic Warren and Gordon ballads that come off best—with two that went on to *Your Hit Parade:* "I Wish I Knew" (for fourteen weeks) and "The More I See You" (for twenty-three weeks).

While he was still at Fox, Warren was approached by MGM's Arthur Freed with an offer to work with him at Metro-Goldwyn-Mayer as soon as he was contractually free. Warren signed with MGM in 1944, with the understanding that he could first fulfill his commitment to *Billy Rose's Diamond Horseshoe*. He would later be frequently glowing in his comments about Freed as "the greatest producer of musicals because he was himself a songwriter."

MGM first put Warren to work in late 1944 on *Ziegfeld Follies,* one of the classiest Technicolor all-star musical revues that Hollywood has ever turned out. The picture is pegged to a minimal plot device, with ol' Florenz Ziegfeld (William Powell, who had played the Broadway showman in MGM's '36 blockbuster *The Great Ziegfeld*) looking down from heaven and wishing he could put on a show with the best talent then on the MGM lot. Then follows a series of sketches and musical numbers with Fred Astaire, Judy Garland, Lena Horne, Gene Kelly, Lucille Ball, Fanny Brice, Red Skelton, Esther Williams, Cyd Charisse, and Kathryn Grayson, among others. Producer Freed and director Vincente Minnelli spent more than two years filming, editing, revising, and trimming the lavish production—so that it wasn't released until after two subsequent Warren-MGM films, in 1946. Television usually titles the picture *Ziegfeld Follies of 1946.*

Warren's two numbers are not the best parts of *Ziegfeld Follies.* "This Heart of Mine" (lyrics by Arthur Freed) is a pleasant-enough romantic ballad that's sung by Fred Astaire as part of a long (twelve minutes), colorfully designed, but only intermittently interesting pop ballet (by Robert Alton), about a dapper jewel thief (Astaire) who woos his beautiful prey (Lucille Bremer) at a fancy dress ball—with ironic results. The operetta-ish "There's Beauty Everywhere" was originally planned for tenor James Melton, with whom Warren had worked several times at Warner Brothers. But then Freed decided to give the song to soprano Kathryn Grayson as part of an extravagant soap-bubble production number for the finale, and Melton was reassigned an aria from Verdi's opera *La Traviata* with soprano Marion Bell. But during filming of the finale with Grayson, the bubble-making machine went haywire. Because of wartime conditions, there was no way to repair or replace the imported machine. So the number is abruptly foreshortened without ever building to a visual or musical climax, ending with Grayson standing atop a huge pedestal as the picture's title *Ziegfeld Follies* lights up behind her. The ending is a considerable letdown after all the first-rate numbers that have preceded it, and Warren's vapid song must share part of the blame.

Warren's second score for MGM, for *Yolanda and the Thief* (1945), is also a disappointment. So is the picture itself—a whimsical, stylized musical fantasy that tries to do something different but ends up flying like the proverbial lead balloon. Fred Astaire plays a traveling con man who tries to bilk an inheritance out of a sheltered and devoutly Catholic Latin-American heiress (Lucille Bremer) by posing as her guardian angel. It's all splendidly photographed in Technicolor, but neither Vincente Minnelli's direction nor Warren's songs (lyrics by Arthur Freed) ever establishes the mischievously delicate air needed to bring off the plot's fancies. Matters are not helped by the beautiful but dull Bremer, whose singing of "Angel" and "This Is the Day for Love" was dubbed by Trudi Erwin. The "Coffee Time" carnival sequence offers a lively mixture of Latin American and jitterbug dance beats for Astaire and Bremer to dance to, but a sixteen-minute, Dali-esque "Dream Sequence" merely gives new dimension to the words arty and pretentious.

What "The Chattanooga Choo-Choo" had done for Warren's career at Fox, "On the Atchison, Topeka, and the Santa Fe" did for Warren at MGM in 1946. Warren and lyricist Johnny Mercer rode it to fourteen weeks on *Your Hit Parade* and then on to an Academy Award for Best Song (Warren's third). Robert Alton's spectacular staging of the song for *The Harvey Girls* has become a classic in itself—with its great "boom shot" of the train coming into town and then the jubilant celebration as the townspeople greet Judy Garland, Ray Bolger, and the other train passengers—all to Kay Thompson's alternately winsome and rousing vocal arrangement of the song. (The sequence is also one of the highlights of MGM's 1974 compilation feature, *That's Entertainment.*)

The popularity of "On the Atchison, Topeka and the Santa Fe" has tended to obscure the rest of Warren's outstanding score for *The Harvey Girls.* The movie—about how a group of intrepid waitresses for the Fred Harvey restaurant chain helped tame the Wild West—is spiritedly lighthearted and romantic, and the ten Warren-Mercer songs fit in more naturally to the story line than most previous Warren scores.

A hauntingly lovely ballad, "In the Valley (Where the Evening Sun Goes Down)," begins the picture against a bright blue sky, with Judy Garland singing on the back of a train as it takes a group of Harvey Girls westward. The scene and the song combine to symbolize the optimistic, pioneering spirit of not only the 1880 girls on the train but also of 1946 Americans moving into the new postwar era of a world many felt to have been radically changed by World War II. Just as Warren (with Dubin) had written some of the most "up" tunes of the Depression era, so he was now (with Mercer) putting a bright face on the adjustments many were coping with back

After arriving to Warren's "On the Atchison, Topeka & the Santa Fe," Judy Garland, as one of The Harvey Girls *(1946), helps tame a western town despite opposition from Stephen McNally (left) and Angela Lansbury (right).*

home after the war, especially involving the changing role of women. The movie's most memorable expression of that feeling comes with a gentle but outgoing waltz, "It's a Great Big World," which Garland, Virginia O'Brien, and Cyd Charisse (with Betty Russell dubbing for Charisse) sing to each other after being scared out of their wits by an attempt to force them to leave town.

Another happy excursion into Americana—this time set in turn-of-the-century Connecticut—followed with MGM's *Summer Holiday,* a heart-warming musical version of Eugene O'Neill's play *Ah, Wilderness!* (which had starred George M. Cohan on Broadway, and is much closer in spirit to Booth Tarkington than to standard O'Neill). MGM had first filmed the small-town-family comedy (without music) in 1935, with Mickey Rooney in a minor role in a cast headed by Lionel Barrymore as the father. This time Mickey Rooney starred as the son about to graduate from high school, with Walter Huston as the father, Gloria DeHaven as the girlfriend, and Frank Morgan as the boozy uncle. Rouben Mamoulian, who had staged *Oklahoma!* on Broadway just a few years earlier, directed and Arthur Freed produced. With Ralph Blane (lyricist for *Meet Me in St. Louis*), Warren composed what would remain his personal favorite among all his scores.

But *Summer Holiday* was not a hit, and it's rarely shown today—which is a shame, for it has more qualities and charms than some better-known (and much more frequently shown) "period musicals." And it got good reviews from most of the critics, and glowingly good ones from some.

Part of the picture's problem at the box office may have been that the public had reached a saturation point with Mickey Rooney's performances as a perennial teenager. By 1948 Rooney had already played Andy Hardy in fifteen movies in that series, plus similar teenage characters in musicals with Judy Garland. Now, at the age of twenty-seven, his boyish style and antics had seen their day with many former fans, particularly after several well-publicized real-life marriages and divorces. Yet, ironically, Rooney's performance in *Summer Holiday* is one of his all-time best, combining the energy and fun of his Andy Hardy with a more subtle and sensitive revealing of deeper character. (Following a three-year absence from the movies after *Summer Holiday,* Rooney would return in older roles as an increasingly respected character actor and comic.)

Another part of the problem with *Summer Holiday,* however, was MGM's own attitude about the film. After their first screenings, key studio executives found it long on charm and atmosphere but short on the razzmatazz they felt its musicals were best known for. While debates went on within the studio about how to release and promote it, the picture sat on the shelf for a year-and-a-half. Finally, the decision was made to cut some twenty minutes, including four of Warren's songs. Lost in the cutting were three songs that Warren had carefully worked out with lyricist Blane to bring out the inner character of the father, uncle, and girlfriend—"Spring Isn't Everything," "Never Again," and "Wish I Had a Braver Heart," respectively. All three songs are included in an LP recording of the original soundtrack that Warren's own publishing company (Four Jays Music) released in the 1970s. (Under his MGM contract, Warren retained the rights to all deleted material.) While none of them have the instant "hit" appeal of so many of Warren's best-known songs, they have genuine warmth and tenderness and character.

Of the five songs that remain, two stand out: a jaunty, romantic ballad "Afraid to Fall in Love," which Rooney and DeHaven sing in a beautifully photographed

Mickey Rooney takes Gloria DeHaven, Shirley Johns, Walter Huston, Selena Royle, and Butch Jenkins for a Sunday ride, as they all sing Harry Warren's and Ralph Blane's "Stanley Steamer" in 1948's Summer Holiday. *The score was Warren's personal favorite among all his movies.*

sequence (filmed at the Busch Gardens in Pasadena) and reprise at the end; and "The Stanley Steamer," a rollicking ensemble number that successfully transfers the catchy flavor of Warren's railroad song hits ("On the Atchison, Topeka and the Santa Fe" and "Chattanooga Choo-Choo") to the turn-of-the-century automobile of that name.

The failure of *Summer Holiday* disappointed Warren tremendously. For a while, he considered trying to do a stage version, but that idea was abandoned after another musical version of *Ah, Wilderness!* opened on Broadway in 1959: *Take Me Along,* with Walter Pidgeon and Jackie Gleason and songs by Bob Merrill.

Warren returned briefly to Warner Brothers in 1949, at the request of the head of its music department, Leo Forbstein, for a Technicolor remake of 1934's *Twenty Million Sweethearts,* now retitled *My Dream Is Yours.* In addition to five new songs written by Warren with Blane as lyricist, the picture uses Warren and Dubin's hit song from the earlier version, "I'll String Along With You," and also tosses in some later-'30s Warren tunes to which Warner still owned the rights ("Jeepers Creepers," "You Must Have Been a Beautiful Baby," and "With Plenty of Money and You"). The story underwent a major sex change, so that Doris Day (in her second movie musical) plays the singer who goes on to radio fame (Dick Powell played the part in the original). Much of the satiric edge of the original got lost this time 'round, and Warren's new songs fail to rival his older ones.

Warren's next MGM musical, *The Barkleys of Broadway,* was virtually guaranteed to be a hit, for it finally reunited Fred Astaire and Ginger Rogers after a screen separation of ten years—and did so for their first time together in Technicolor. Rogers was actually a last-minute substitution for Judy Garland, who had teamed with Astaire in the previous year's *Easter Parade*. *The Barkleys* was planned as a follow-up to that blockbuster Irving Berlin hit, focusing on the same dancing couple in a later period of their life. But early in production, Garland became too ill to continue. Rogers, whose career in nonmusicals was in the doldrums, agreed to step in.

Ironically, the book by Betty Comden and Adolph Green parallels certain aspects of the breakup of the Astaire-Rogers team ten years earlier, so that Rogers ends up spoofing herself—delightfully—in several scenes. In the dance numbers, however, she proves much less supple than in the old days and sometimes seems to be doing more gesturing than real dancing. Still, there's an undeniable magic to Astaire and Rogers's work together—especially in their stylishly elegant dance to Gershwin's "They Can't Take That Away From Me" and a joyously crisp and rhythmic rehearsal number (with echoes of the great rehearsal number in Kern's *Roberta* of 1935) to Warren's strictly instrumental "Bouncin' the Blues."

Six other Warren numbers, with lyrics by Ira Gershwin, spark the movie considerably, even if none of them went on to become popular hits and even though there's sometimes too long a wait for the drawn-out plot to take its course between them. "The Swing Trot" gets the picture off to a spirited start, showing behind the opening titles exactly what most of the audience came to see: Astaire and Rogers dancing together again. That's followed by a romantic ballad whose lyrics certainly sum up what was then many viewers' attitude about the Astaire-Rogers team: "You'd Be Hard to Replace."

"A Weekend in the Country" is a jaunty little ditty that Astaire, Rogers, and Oscar Levant sing as they stroll along a country road. It takes on additional interest for Warren's down-to-earth melodic simplicity in comparison to the more complex and more operatic approach of Stephen Sondheim for a later song of the same title (and much the same feeling) for *A Little Night Music*. The finale, "Manhattan Downbeat," finds Warren once again singing the musical praises of his favorite city, as Astaire and Rogers twirl and swirl much too briefly (two minutes) in a colorful number that I, for one, wish would go on as long as some of Busby Berkeley's old ones.

After losing roles to Ginger Rogers in *The Barkleys of Broadway* and to Betty Hutton in Irving Berlin's *Annie Get Your Gun,* Judy Garland finally held her health and temperament together long enough to make *Summer Stock* in 1950 with Gene Kelly. It would be her last MGM musical, and it's best known for the production number in which she sings Harold Arlen's "Get Happy." But most of the other songs in *Summer Stock* are by Warren, with lyrics mostly by Mack Gordon, who had just been dropped by Twentieth Century-Fox and was hired by MGM at Warren's request. Just as *Summer Stock*'s plot is merely a rehash of countless "Hey, kids, let's put on a show in the barn" predecessors, so Warren's score seems tired and uninspired, if never unappealing. Garland, looking a bit plumper than usual but in superb singing voice, makes the most of the bittersweet ballad "Friendly Star" and the carefree "If You Feel Like Singing Sing." She and Kelly also do a charming duet to "You, Wonderful You," for which Gordon's original lyrics were dumped and new ones by Saul Chaplin and Jack Brooks substituted after Warren had moved on to another assignment and no longer had a say in the matter. That action, plus the interpolation of Arlen's "Get

Ginger Rogers and Fred Astaire dance to "Manhattan Downbeat," another paean to Warren's favorite city, in The Barkleys of Broadway *(1949). It was the last number the duo ever danced together in the movies.*

Happy" and Chaplin's "All for You" in the finale, soured Warren on his relationship with MGM. After writing incidental songs for three Esther Williams "aquatic operas" and the full score for Fred Astaire's *The Belle of New York* (1952), Warren left MGM.

The Belle of New York is one of Astaire's weakest musicals, a part-fantasy about an early 1900s playboy who discovers he can walk on air after he falls in love with a mission evangelist (Vera-Ellen, whose singing voice was dubbed for this one by Anita Ellis). Astaire actually walks through much of the picture looking bored. Even Johnny Mercer's nimble lyrics, with one exception, can't raise Warren's songs for this one above the ordinary. The exception: "I Wanna Be a Dancing Man," an easy-going ballad whose lyrics sum up Astaire's whole legacy: *"Gonna leave my footsteps on the sands of time. . . ."*

Though Harry Warren had by then left much more than *his* footprints on the sands of time, he was not yet ready to retire when he left MGM at age sixty. So when Bing Crosby phoned him—"at six o'clock one morning," according to Warren—Crosby's invitation to write the score for *Just for You* got an eager *yes*. The 1952 Paramount film reteamed him with lyricist Leo Robin, and resulted in no fewer than

THE MELODY LINGERS ON

eleven songs, the most Warren had ever composed for a film other than the precut version of *Summer Holiday.*

Crosby plays a widowed Broadway songwriter-producer in *Just for You,* with the overly sentimental plot split between Crosby's problems over his neglected teenage children (played by Natalie Wood and Robert Arthur) and his on-again-off-again romance with a musical-comedy star (Jane Wyman). The zippy Crosby-Wyman duet to "Zing a Little Zong" helped spur that one on to *Your Hit Parade;* it also won an Academy Award nomination for Best Song (Dimitri Tiomkin and Ned Washington won for *High Noon*'s title song). Crosby also has a lot of fun with another Warren train song, "On the Ten-Ten from Ten-Ten-Tennessee," though this one is a pale sequel to "Chattanooga Choo-Choo" or "On the Atchison, Topeka and the Santa Fe." And since Latin beats had long been a staple among hit Crosby arrangements, Warren obliged Crosby's request for a possible successor with "I'll Si-Si You in Bahia." Although it provides one of the movie's liveliest production numbers, there weren't that many saying si-si to the song itself and it was soon forgotten.

Just for You turned out to be one of the last completely original nonrock movie musicals of the '50s, before adaptations of Broadway hits or remakes of old plays and movies as musicals began to dominate Hollywood's output. Warren stayed on at Paramount for the next few years, working without a long-term contract on a picture-to-picture basis, primarily contributing incidental songs to several Dean Martin and Jerry Lewis comedies, with Jack Brooks as lyricist. For one Martin and Lewis farce, *The Caddy,* Warren dug back to his (and Martin's) Italian family roots to write the joyful "That's Amore." It brought Warren his fourth Oscar nomination, but lost to Sammy Fain and Paul Francis Webster's "Secret Love" from *Calamity Jane.*

Warren's last Academy Award nomination came in 1957 for the title song for Leo McCarey's *An Affair to Remember.* (The winner that year was Jimmy Van Heusen and Sammy Cahn's "All the Way" from *The Joker Is Wild.*) The picture is a remake of a sentimental romantic drama that McCarey had first filmed in 1939 as *Love Affair* with Irene Dunne and Charles Boyer. This time it starred Deborah Kerr and Cary Grant, and was just as saccharine—and just as successful. Warren's openly sentimental title song, with lyrics by McCarey and Harold Adamson, is sung over the opening titles by Vic Damone, and then later in the movie ostensibly by Kerr but actually dubbed by Marni Nixon (who also dubbed Kerr's singing voice in Rodgers and Hammerstein's *The King and I.*) Warren also contributed several other incidental songs for Kerr /Nixon to sing in the course of the picture—none of them as memorable as that title song.

Warren continued to write incidental songs in the 1960s and 1970s, if only to prove to himself that he wasn't "written out." At the time of his death in Los Angeles on September 22, 1981, at age eighty-seven, Warren's old songs were—as they still are—being heard, sung, whistled, and hummed by millions throughout the land in testimony to the fact that no movie composer has come close to matching both his prolificacy and durability. More than those of any other composer, Warren's songs helped millions of Americans get through the hard Depression years of the '30s and the war-torn years of the '40s—and they still have much to say for all decades and all generations.

THE WOLF SONG (1929), Paramount. B&W. Directed by Victor Fleming. With Lupe Velez, Gary Cooper, Louis Wolheim, Russ Columbo. Song: "Mi Amado" (lyrics, Sam Lewis, Joe Young); plus songs by others.

SPRING IS HERE (1930), First National. B&W. Directed by John Francis Dillon. With Bernice Claire, Lawrence Gray, Alexander Gray, Inez Courtney, Frank Albertson, Louise Fazenda. Songs: "Cryin' for the Carolines," "Have a Little Faith in Me," "Absence Makes the Heart Grow Fonder," "Bad Baby," "How Shall I Tell?" (lyrics, Sam Lewis, Joe Young); plus songs by others. Soundtrack LP: *The Hollywood Years of Harry Warren,* Music Masters JJA-19791.

CROONER (1932), First National/Warner Brothers. B&W. Directed by Lloyd Bacon. With David Manners, Ann Dvorak, Eddie Nugent, Ken Murray, Guy Kibbee, Sheila Terry. Song: "Three's a Crowd" (lyrics, Al Dubin); plus songs by others.

FORTY-SECOND STREET (1933), Warner Brothers. B&W. Directed by Lloyd Bacon. With Warner Baxter, Bebe Daniels, George Brent, Ruby Keeler, Dick Powell, Ginger Rogers, Una Merkel, Ned Sparks, Clarence Nordstrom. Songs: "Forty-Second Street," "Shuffle Off to Buffalo," "You're Getting to Be a Habit With Me," "Young and Healthy," "It Must Be June" (lyrics, Al Dubin). Soundtrack LP: included in *The Classic Movie Musicals of Harry Warren,* Music Masters JJA-19793; also excerpts included in *Hooray for Hollywood,* United Artists LA361-H. Videocassette and videodisc: CBS/Fox.

GOLD DIGGERS OF 1933 (1933), Warner Brothers. B&W. Directed by Mervyn LeRoy. With Warren William, Joan Blondell, Ruby Keeler, Dick Powell, Ginger Rogers, Aline MacMahon, Ned Sparks, Guy Kibbee, Clarence Nordstrom. Songs: "We're in the Money (Gold Diggers' Song)," "Pettin' in the Park," "The Shadow Waltz," "I've Got to Sing a Torch Song," "Remember My Forgotten Man" (lyrics, Al Dubin). Soundtrack LP: included in *The Classic Movie Musicals of Harry Warren.* Music Masters JJA-19793. Videocassette: Key-CBS/Fox.

FOOTLIGHT PARADE (1933), Warner Brothers. B&W. Directed by Lloyd Bacon. With James Cagney, Joan Blondell, Ruby Keeler, Dick Powell, Ruth Donnelly, Frank McHugh, Hugh Herbert, Guy Kibbee, Claire Dodd. Songs: "Honeymoon Hotel," "Shanghai Lil" (lyrics, Al Dubin); plus songs by others.

Soundtrack LP: excerpt included in *The Hollywood Years of Harry Warren,* Music Masters JJA-19791; another excerpt included in *The Classic Movie Musicals of Harry Warren,* Music Masters JJA-19793. Videocassette: Key-CBS/Fox.

ROMAN SCANDALS (1933), Samuel Goldwyn for United Artists release. B&W. Directed by Frank Tuttle. With Eddie Cantor, Ruth Etting, Gloria Stuart, David Manners, Verree Teasdale, Edward Arnold, Alan Mowbray, Lucille Ball (in a bit role). Songs: "Keep Young and Beautiful," "No More Love," "Rome Wasn't Built in a Day," "Build a Little Home" (lyrics, Al Dubin); "Put a Tax on Love" (lyrics, L. Wolfe Gilbert). Soundtrack LP: Classic International Filmusicals CIF-3007, with *Kid Millions*).

MOULIN ROUGE (1934), Twentieth Century for United Artists release. B&W. Directed by Sidney Lanfield. With Constance Bennett, Franchot Tone, Tullio Carminati, Helen Westley, Russ Columbo, the Boswell Sisters. Songs: "The Boulevard of Broken Dreams," "Coffee in the Morning and Kisses at Night," "Song of Surrender" (lyrics, Al Dubin). Soundtrack LP: included in *The Films of Russ Columbo,* Golden Legends 2000/1.

WONDER BAR (1934), First National/Warner Brothers. B&W. Directed by Lloyd Bacon. With Al Jolson, Kay Francis, Dolores Del Rio, Dick Powell, Ricardo Cortez, Ruth Donnelly, Guy Kibbee, Hugh Herbert, Hal LeRoy, Louise Fazenda, Fifi D'Orsay. Songs: "Wonder Bar," "Why Do I Dream Those Dreams?," "Don't Say Goodnight," "Vive la France," "Goin' to Heaven on a Mule" (lyrics, Al Dubin); "Tango del Rio;" plus songs by others. Soundtrack LP: Soundstage 402 (with *Go Into Your Dance*); also, excerpt included in *Hooray for Hollywood,* United Artists LA361-H.

TWENTY MILLION SWEETHEARTS (1934), First National/Warner Brothers. B&W. Directed by Ray Enright. With Pat O'Brien, Dick Powell, Ginger Rogers, Allen Jenkins, Grant Mitchell, Joseph Cawthorne. Songs: "I'll String Along With You," "Fair and Warmer," "Out for No Good," "What Are Your Intentions?" (lyrics, Al Dubin); plus songs by others. Soundtrack LP: Milloball TMSM-34031 (with *Mammy.*)

DAMES (1934), Warner Brothers. B&W. Directed by Ray Enright. With Joan Blondell, Dick Powell, Ruby Keeler, ZaSu Pitts, Guy Kibbee, Hugh Herbert, Sammy Fain, Phil Regan. Songs: "Dames," "I Only Have Eyes for

You," "The Girl at the Ironing Board" (lyrics, Al Dubin); plus songs by others. Videocassette: Key-CBS/Fox.

SWEET MUSIC (1935), Warner Brothers. B&W. Directed by Alfred E. Green. With Rudy Vallee, Ann Dvorak, Alice White, Helen Morgan, Ned Sparks, Robert Armstrong, Al Shean. Song: "Sweet Music" (lyrics, Al Dubin); plus songs by others. Studio recording of song included in *Rudy Vallee: The Kid from Maine*, Unique 116.

LIVING ON VELVET (1935), First National/Warner Brothers. B&W. Directed by Frank Borzage. With Kay Francis, George Brent, Warren William, Maude Turner Gordon, Henry O'Neill, Edgar Kennedy. Song: "Living on Velvet" (lyrics, Al Dubin). Studio recording of song included in *Johnny Green, 1934–1937*, Music Masters JJA-19755.

IN CALIENTE (1935), First National/Warner Brothers. B&W. Directed by Lloyd Bacon. With Dolores Del Rio, Pat O'Brien, Leo Carillo, Glenda Farrell, Edward Everett Horton, Judy Canova, Winifred Shaw, Phil Regan. Song: "Muchacha" (lyrics, Al Dubin); plus songs by others. Soundtrack LP: included in *The Hollywood Years of Harry Warren*, Music Masters JJA-19791.

GOLD DIGGERS OF 1935 (1935), First National/Warner Brothers. B&W. Directed by Busby Berkeley. With Dick Powell, Adolphe Menjou, Gloria Stuart, Alice Brady, Glenda Farrell, Frank McHugh, Winifred Shaw, Hugh Herbert, Dorothy Dare. Songs: "The Lullaby of Broadway," "The Words Are in My Heart," "I'm Going Shopping With You" (lyrics, Al Dubin). Soundtrack LP: included in *The Classic Movie Musicals of Harry Warren, Vol. 2*, Music Masters JJA-19793.

GO INTO YOUR DANCE (1935), First National/Warner Brothers. B&W. Directed by Archie Mayo. With Al Jolson, Ruby Keeler, Glenda Farrell, Helen Morgan, Patsy Kelly, Barton MacLane. Songs: "Go Into Your Dance," "About a Quarter to Nine," "She's a Latin from Manhattan," "A Good Old-Fashioned Cocktail," "The Little Things You Used to Do," "Casino de Paree," "Mammy, I'll Sing About You" (lyrics, Al Dubin). Soundtrack LP: Soundstage 402 (with *Wonder Bar*); also, excerpt included in *The Golden Age of the Hollywood Stars*, United Artists USD-311 (withdrawn).

BROADWAY GONDOLIER (1935), Warner Brothers. B&W. Directed by Lloyd Bacon. With Dick Powell, Joan Blondell, Adolphe Menjou, Louise Fazenda, William Gargan, the Mills Brothers, Judy Canova, Joseph Sauers (Joe Sawyer). Songs: "Lulu's Back in Town," "Lonely Gondolier," "Outside of You," "You

Can Be Kissed," "The Rose in Her Hair," "The Pig and the Cow (The Dog and the Cat)," "Flagenheim's Odorless Cheese" (lyrics, Al Dubin). Soundtrack LP: excerpt included in *Hollywood Is on the Air*, Radiola AAB-1215/8; also, studio recordings of four songs included in *Dick Powell in Hollywood*, CBS Hall of Fame Series C2L-44.

SHIPMATES FOREVER (1935), Cosmopolitan/Warner Brothers. B&W. Directed by Frank Borzage. With Dick Powell, Ruby Keeler, Ross Alexander, Lewis Stone, Eddie Acuff, Dick Foran, John Arledge. Songs: "Shipmates Forever (Don't Give Up the Ship)," "I'd Rather Listen to Your Eyes," "I'd Love to Take Orders from You," "Do I Love My Teacher?" (lyrics, Al Dubin).

PAGE MISS GLORY (1935), Cosmopolitan/Warner Brothers. B&W. Directed by Mervyn LeRoy. With Marion Davies, Pat O'Brien, Dick Powell, Mary Astor, Frank McHugh, Patsy Kelly, Lyle Talbot, Allen Jenkins, Al Shean. Song: "Page Miss Glory" (lyrics, Al Dubin).

STARS OVER BROADWAY (1935), Warner Brothers. B&W. Directed by William Keighley. With Pat O'Brien, Jane Froman, James Melton, Jean Muir, Frank McHugh, Marie Wilson, Frank Fay, E. E. Clive. Songs: "Where Am I? (Am I in Heaven?)," "Broadway Cinderella," "You Let Me Down," "At Your Service, Madame" (lyrics, Al Dubin); plus songs and arias by others.

COLLEEN (1936), Warner Brothers. B&W. Directed by Alfred E. Green. With Dick Powell, Ruby Keeler, Joan Blondell, Jack Oakie, Hugh Herbert, Paul Draper, Louise Fazenda, Marie Wilson. Songs: "I Don't Have to Dream Again," "A Boulevardier From the Bronx," "An Evening With You," "You Gotta Know How to Dance" (lyrics, Al Dubin). Soundtrack LP: Caliban 6007 (with *Variety Girl*).

HEARTS DIVIDED (1936), Cosmopolitan/Warner Brothers. B&W. Directed by Frank Borzage. With Marion Davies, Dick Powell, Claude Rains, Charlie Ruggles, Edward Everett Horton, Arthur Treacher, Hattie McDaniel, the Hall Johnson Choir. Songs: "Two Hearts Divided," "My Kingdom for a Kiss"; plus songs by others. Studio recordings of songs included in *The Dick Powell Songbook*, Ace of Hearts E50 (English import).

CAIN AND MABEL (1936), Cosmopolitan/Warner Brothers. B&W. Directed by Lloyd Bacon. With Marion Davies, Clark Gable, Allen Jenkins, Roscoe Karns, Ruth Donnelly, Pert Kelton, Sammy White, David Carlyle. Songs: "I'll Sing You a Thousand Love Songs," "Coney Island" (lyrics, Al Dubin). Soundtrack LP: excerpt included in *The Hollywood Years of Harry Warren*, Music Masters JJA-19791.

SONS O' GUNS (1936), Warner Brothers. B&W. Directed by Lloyd Bacon. With Joe E. Brown, Joan Blondell, Beverly Roberts, Eric Blore, Winifred Shaw, Craig Reynolds. Songs: "For a Buck and a Quarter a Day," "In the Arms of an Army Man" (lyrics, Al Dubin).

SING ME A LOVE SONG (1936), Cosmopolitan/Warner Brothers. B&W. Directed by Ray Enright. With James Melton, Patricia Ellis, Hugh Herbert, ZaSu Pitts, Allen Jenkins, Ann Sheridan, Nat Pendleton. Songs: "The Least You Can Do for a Lady," "Summer Night," "The Little House That Love Built" (lyrics, Al Dubin); plus songs by others.

GOLD DIGGERS OF 1937 (1936), Warner Brothers. B&W. Directed by Lloyd Bacon. With Dick Powell, Joan Blondell, Victor Moore, Glenda Farrell, Lee Dixon, Osgood Perkins, Rosalind Marquis. Songs: "With Plenty of Money and You," "All's Fair in Love and War" (lyrics, Al Dubin); plus songs by others. Soundtrack LP: *The Classic Movie Musicals of Harry Warren, Vol. 2,* Music Masters JJA-19793; also, excerpt included in *Hooray for Hollywood,* United Artists LA-361-H.

MARKED WOMAN (1937), Warner Brothers. B&W. Directed by Lloyd Bacon. With Bette Davis, Humphrey Bogart, Lola Lane, Jane Bryan, Isabel Jewell, Rosalind Marquis, Eduardo Ciannelli, Mayo Methot. Song: "My Silver Dollar Man" (lyrics, Al Dubin); plus songs by others.

MELODY FOR TWO (1937), Warner Brothers. B&W. Directed by Louis King. With James Melton, Patricia Ellis, Marie Wilson, Winifred Shaw, Fred Keating, Dick Purcell. Songs: "September in the Rain," "Melody for Two" (lyrics, Al Dubin). Soundtrack LP: excerpt included in *The Hollywood Years of Harry Warren,* Music Masters JJA-19791.

STOLEN HOLIDAY (1937), Warner Brothers. B&W. Directed by Michael Curtiz. With Kay Francis, Claude Rains, Ian Hunter, Alison Skipworth, Alexander d'Arcy. Song: "Stolen Holiday" (lyrics, Al Dubin).

THE SINGING MARINE (1937), Warner Brothers. B&W. Directed by Ray Enright. With Dick Powell, Doris Weston, Lee Dixon, Jane Darwell, Hugh Herbert, Larry Adler, Allen Jenkins, Veda Ann Borg. Songs: "The Song of the Marines," "I Know Now," "The Lady Who Couldn't Be Kissed," "You Can't Run Away From Love Tonight," "'Cause My Baby Says It's So" (lyrics, Al Dubin); "Night Over Shanghai" (lyrics, Johnny Mercer). Studio recording of one song included in *The Dick Powell Songbook,* Ace of Hearts E50 (English import).

SAN QUENTIN (1937), Warner Brothers. B&W. Directed by Lloyd Bacon. With Pat O'Brien, Humphrey Bogart, Ann Sheridan, Veda Ann Borg, Barton MacLane. Song: "How Could You?" (lyric, Al Dubin).

MR. DODD TAKES THE AIR (1937), Warner Brothers. B&W. Directed by Alfred E. Green. With Kenny Baker, Jane Wyman, Alice Brady, Frank McHugh, Gertrude Michael, Henry O'Neill. Songs: "Remember Me?," "Here Comes the Sandman," "The Girl You Used to Be," "Am I in Love?" (lyrics, Al Dubin); plus songs by others.

COWBOY FROM BROOKLYN (1938), Warner Brothers. B&W. Directed by Lloyd Bacon. With Dick Powell, Pat O'Brien, Priscilla Lane, Ann Sheridan, Dick Foran, Ronald Reagan. Song: "Cowboy From Brooklyn" (lyrics, Johnny Mercer); plus songs by others.

JEZEBEL (1938), Warner Brothers. B&W. Directed by William Wyler. With Bette Davis, Henry Fonda, George Brent, Margaret Lindsay, Fay Bainter, Donald Crisp, Richard Cromwell. Song: "Jezebel" (lyrics, Johnny Mercer).

GOLD DIGGERS IN PARIS (1938), Warner Brothers. B&W. Directed by Ray Enright. With Rudy Vallee, Rosemary Lane, Hugh Herbert, Allen Jenkins, Gloria Dickson, Mabel Todd, Melville Cooper, the Schnickelfritz Band. Songs: "A Stranger in Paree," "I Wanna Go Back to Bali," "Put That in Writing," "The Latin Quarter" (lyrics, Al Dubin); "Daydreaming (All Night Long)," "My Adventure" (lyrics, Johnny Mercer); plus songs by others. Soundtrack LP: excerpt included in *The Hollywood Years of Harry Warren,* Music Masters JJA-19791.

GARDEN OF THE MOON (1938), Warner Brothers. B&W. Directed by Busby Berkeley. With Pat O'Brien, Margaret Lindsay, John Payne, Johnny "Scat" Davis, Mabel Todd, Jerry Colonna, Melville Cooper. Songs: "Garden of the Moon," "Confidentially," "The Lady on the Two-Cent Stamp," "Love Is Where You Find It," "The Girlfriend of the Whirling Dervish" (lyrics, Al Dubin, Johnny Mercer). Soundtrack LP: excerpt included in *The Hollywood Years of Harry Warren,* Music Masters JJA-19791.

HARD TO GET (1938), Warner Brothers. B&W. Directed by Ray Enright. With Dick Powell, Olivia de Havilland, Charles Winninger, Allen Jenkins, Bonita Granville, Penny Singleton, Grady Sutton. Songs: "You Must Have Been a Beautiful Baby" (lyrics, Johnny Mercer); "There's a Sunny Side to Every Situation" (lyrics, Al Dubin, Johnny Mercer).

GOING PLACES (1938), Warner Brothers. B&W. Directed by Ray Enright. With Dick Powell, Anita Louise, Allen Jenkins, Louis Armstrong, Maxine Sullivan, Ronald Reagan, Walter Catlett. Songs: "Jeepers Creepers," "Mutiny in the Nursery" (lyrics, Johnny Mercer); "Say It With a Kiss," "Oh, What a Horse Was Charlie" (lyrics, Al Dubin, Johnny Mercer). Soundtrack LP: Caliban 6010 (with *Lady Be Good*); also, excerpt included in *The Hollywood Years of Harry Warren*, Music Masters JJA-19791.

NAUGHTY BUT NICE (1939), Warner Brothers. B&W. Directed by Ray Enright. With Ann Sheridan, Dick Powell, Gale Page, Helen Broderick, Ronald Reagan, ZaSu Pitts, Jerry Colonna. Songs: "Hooray for Spinach," "I'm Happy About the Whole Thing," "In a Moment of Weakness," "Corn Pickin'," "I Don't Believe in Signs" (lyrics, Johnny Mercer); plus music by others.

HONOLULU (1939), MGM. B&W. Directed by Eddie Buzzell. With Eleanor Powell, Robert Young, George Burns, Gracie Allen, Rita Johnson, Ruth Hussey, Willie Fong, the King's Men with Ken Darby. Songs: "Honolulu," "This Night Will Be Our Souvenir," "The Leader Doesn't Like Music" (lyrics, Gus Kahn); plus songs by others. Soundtrack LP: excerpt included in *Hollywood Is on the Air*, Radiola AAB-1215/8.

WINGS OF THE NAVY (1939), Warner Brothers. B&W. Directed by Lloyd Bacon. With Olivia de Havilland, George Brent, John Payne, Frank McHugh. Song: "Wings Over the Navy" (lyrics, Johnny Mercer).

YOUNG PEOPLE (1940), Twentieth Century-Fox. B&W. Directed by Allan Dwan. With Shirley Temple, Jack Oakie, Charlotte Greenwood, Arleen Whelan, George Montgomery, Mae Marsh. Songs: "Young People," "I Wouldn't Take a Million," "Tra-la-la" (lyrics, Mack Gordon); plus songs by others. Soundtrack LP: excerpts included in *The Shirley Temple Songbook*, 20th-Fox 103-2 (withdrawn); another excerpt included in *The Hollywood Years of Harry Warren*, Music Masters JJA-19791.

DOWN ARGENTINE WAY (1940), Twentieth Century-Fox. Color. Directed by Irving Cummings. With Don Ameche, Betty Grable, Carmen Miranda, Charlotte Greenwood, J. Carrol Naish, the Nicholas Brothers, Six Hits and a Miss, Thomas and Catherine Dowling. Songs: "Down Argentine Way," "Two Dreams Met," "Sing to Your Senorita," "Nenita" (lyrics, Mack Gordon); plus songs by others. Soundtrack LP: Caliban 6003 (with *Tin Pan Alley*); also, Hollywood Soundstage HS-5013 (with Springtime In The Rockies).

TIN PAN ALLEY (1940), Twentieth Century-Fox. B&W. Directed by Walter Lang. With Alice Faye, Betty Grable, Jack Oakie, John Payne, Allen Jenkins, the Nicholas Brothers, Billy Gilbert. Song: "You Say the Sweetest Things, Baby" (lyrics, Mack Gordon); plus songs by others. Soundtrack LP: Soundtrak 110; also excerpts on Caliban 6003 (with *Down Argentine Way*).

THAT NIGHT IN RIO (1941), Twentieth Century-Fox. Color. Directed by Irving Cummings. With Alice Faye, Don Ameche, Carmen Miranda, S. Z. Sakall, J. Carrol Naish, Maria Montez, the Banda Da Lua. Songs: "Chica Boom Chic," "I Yi Yi Yi Yi (I Like You Very Much)," "Boa Noite," "The Baron Is in Conference," "They Met in Rio" (lyrics, Mack Gordon); plus songs by others. Soundtrack LP: Curtain Calls 100/14 (with *Weekend in Havana*).

THE GREAT AMERICAN BROADCAST (1941), Twentieth Century-Fox. B&W. Directed by Archie Mayo. With Alice Faye, Jack Oakie, John Payne, Cesar Romero, the Ink Spots, Mary Beth Hughes, James Newill, the Nicholas Brothers. Songs: "Where Are You?," "It's All in a Lifetime," "I Take to You," "Long Ago Last Night," "I've Got a Bone to Pick With You," "The Great American Broadcast" (lyrics, Mack Gordon); plus songs by others. Soundtrack LP: excerpts included in *Alice Faye and the Songs of Harry Warren*, Citadel 6004; also, excerpt in *The Hollywood Years of Harry Warren*, Music Masters JJA-19791, and in *Hollywood Is on the Air*, Radiola AAB-1215/8.

SUN VALLEY SERENADE (1941), Twentieth Century-Fox. B&W. Directed by H. Bruce Humberstone. With Sonja Henie, John Payne, Glenn Miller and his Orchestra, Lynn Bari, Joan Davis, Milton Berle, the Nicholas Brothers, Dorothy Dandridge. Songs: "Chattanooga Choo-Choo," "It Happened in Sun Valley," "I Know Why," "The Kiss Polka" (lyrics, Mack Gordon); plus songs by others. Soundtrack LP: excerpts included in *Glenn Miller and His Orchestra*, 20th-Fox 100-2.

WEEKEND IN HAVANA (1941), Twentieth Century-Fox. Color. Directed by Walter Lang. With Alice Faye, Carmen Miranda, John Payne, Cesar Romero, Cobina Wright Jr., Sheldon Leonard, Leonid Kinsky. Songs: "A Weekend in Havana," "Tropical Magic," "When I Love, I Love," "The Man With the Lollipop," "The Nango" (lyrics, Mack Gordon); plus songs by others. Soundtrack LP: Curtain Calls 100/14 (with *That Night in Rio*).

ORCHESTRA WIVES (1942), Twentieth Century-Fox. B&W. Directed by Archie Mayo. With Glenn Miller and his Orchestra, George Montgomery, Ann Rutherford, Cesar Romero, Lynn Bari, Carole Landis, Virginia Gilmore, Mary Beth Hughes, the Nicholas Brothers, Tamara Geva. Songs: "I've Got a Gal in Kalamazoo," "At Last," "People Like You and Me," "That's Sabotage," "Serenade in Blue" (lyrics, Mack Gordon); plus songs by others. Soundtrack LP: excerpts included in *Glenn Miller and His Orchestra*, 20th-Fox 100-2 (withdrawn).

ICELAND (1942), Twentieth Century-Fox.

B&W. Directed by H. Bruce Humberstone. With Sonja Henie, John Payne, Jack Oakie, Sammy Kaye and his Orchestra, Osa Massen, Felix Bressart, Joan Merrill. Songs: "There'll Never Be Another You," "You Can't Say No to a Soldier," "It's the Lover's Knot," "I Like a Military Tune," "Let's Bring New Glory to Old Glory" (lyrics, Mack Gordon).

SPRINGTIME IN THE ROCKIES (1942), Twentieth Century-Fox. Color. Directed by Irving Cummings. With Betty Grable, John Payne, Carmen Miranda, Cesar Romero, Charlotte Greenwood, Edward Everett Horton, Harry James and his Orchestra, Jackie Gleason, Helen Forrest. Songs: "I Had the Craziest Dream," "Pan-American Jubilee," "Run, Little Raindrop, Run," "I Like to Be Loved by You," "A Poem Set to Music," "Chattanooga Choo-Choo" (lyrics, Mack Gordon); plus songs by others. Soundtrack LP: Hollywood Soundstage HS-5013 (with *Down Argentine Way*); also Sandy Hook/Radiola SH-2090 (with *Sweet Rosie O'Grady*).

HELLO, FRISCO, HELLO (1943), Twentieth Century-Fox. Color. Directed by H. Bruce Humberstone. With Alice Faye, John Payne, Jack Oakie, Lynn Bari, June Havoc, Laird Cregar, Ward Bond. Songs: "You'll Never Know," "I Gotta Have You" (lyrics, Mack Gordon); plus songs by others. Soundtrack LP: Caliban 6005 (with *Spring Parade*); also, Sandy Hook SH-2070; also, Hollywood Soundstage HS-5005.

SWEET ROSIE O'GRADY (1943), Twentieth Century-Fox. Color. Directed by Irving Cummings. With Betty Grable, Robert Young, Adolphe Menjou, Reginald Gardiner, Virginia Grey, Phil Regan. Songs: "My Heart Tells Me," "My Sam," "The Wishing Waltz," "Get Your Police Gazette," "Going to the County Fair," "Where, Oh Where, Is the Groom?" (lyrics, Mack Gordon); plus songs by others. Soundtrack LP: Sandy Hook/Radiola SH-2090, with *Springtime in the Rockies;* also, excerpt included in *The Hollywood Years of Harry Warren,* Music Masters JJA-19791.

THE GANG'S ALL HERE (1943), Twentieth Century-Fox. Color. Directed by Busby Berkeley. With Alice Faye, Carmen Miranda, Phil Baker, Benny Goodman and his Orchestra, Charlotte Greenwood, James Ellison, Edward Everett Horton, Tony DeMarco, Sheila Ryan, and, in bit parts, Jeanne Crain, June Haver. Songs: "A Journey to a Star," "No Love, No Nothin'," "Minnie's in the Money," "Paducah," "You Discover You're in New York," "The Lady in the Tutti-Frutti Hat," "The Polka Dot Polka" (lyrics, Leo Robin); plus songs by others. Soundtrack LP: Classic International Filmusicals CIF-3003; also, excerpts included in *Alice Faye*

and the Songs of Harry Warren, Citadel 6004.

FOUR JILLS IN A JEEP (1944), Twentieth Century-Fox. B&W. Directed by William A. Seiter. With Kay Francis, Martha Raye, Carole Landis, Mitzi Mayfair, Dick Haymes, Phil Silvers, Jimmy Dorsey and his Orchestra; Betty Grable, Alice Faye, Carmen Miranda, George Jessel. Songs: "You'll Never Know," "No Love, No Nothin'," "I Yi Yi I Like You Very Much" (lyrics, Leo Robin); plus songs by others. Soundtrack LP: Hollywood Soundstage 407.

GREENWICH VILLAGE (1944), Twentieth Century-Fox. Color. Directed by Walter Lang. With Carmen Miranda, Don Ameche, William Bendix, Vivian Blaine, Tony and Sally DeMarco, the Four Step Brothers. Song: "I Like to Be Loved by You" (lyrics, Mack Gordon); plus songs by others.

SWING IN THE SADDLE (1944), Columbia. B&W. Directed by Lew Landers. With Jane Frazee, Jimmy Wakely, Nat King Cole Trio, Slim Summerville, Guinn "Big Boy" Williams, Sally Bliss. Song: "By the River Sainte Marie" (lyrics, Edgar Leslie); plus songs by others.

SWEET AND LOWDOWN (1944), Twentieth Century-Fox. B&W. Directed by Archie Mayo. With Benny Goodman and his Orchestra, Linda Darnell, Lynn Bari, Jack Oakie, James Cardwell, Allyn Joslyn, Dickie Moore. Song: "No Love, No Nothin'" (lyrics, Leo Robin); plus songs by others.

BILLY ROSE'S DIAMOND HORSESHOE (1945), Twentieth Century-Fox. Color. Directed by George Seaton. With Betty Grable, Dick Haymes, Phil Silvers, William Gaxton, Beatrice Kay, Carmen Cavallaro, Margaret Dumont. Songs: "The More I See You," "I Wish I Knew," "In Acapulco," "Mink Lament," "Play Me an Old-Fashioned Melody," "A Nickel's Worth of Jive" (lyrics, Mack Gordon); plus songs by others. Soundtrack LP: excerpts included in *The Hollywood Years of Harry Warren,* Music Masters JJA-19791; other excerpts included in *Betty Grable,* Curtain Calls 100/5.

ZIEGFELD FOLLIES OF 1946 (1944-45), MGM. Color. Directed by Vincente Minnelli. With William Powell, Fred Astaire, Judy Garland, Gene Kelly, Lena Horne, Esther Williams, Lucille Ball, Cyd Charisse, Fanny Brice, Kathryn Grayson, Lucille Bremer, Red Skelton, James Melton, Marion Bell. Songs: "This Heart of Mine," "There's Beauty Everywhere" (lyrics, Arthur Freed). Soundtrack LP: Curtain Calls 100/15-16. Videocassette: MGM/UA.

YOLANDA AND THE THIEF (1945), MGM. Color. Directed by Vincente Minnelli. With Fred Astaire, Lucille Bremer, Frank Morgan, Mildred Natwick, Leon Ames, Mary Nash. Songs: "Yolanda," "Angel," "Coffee Time,"

"This Is the Day for Love," "Will You Marry Me?" (lyrics, Arthur Freed); plus ballet music. Soundtrack LP: Hollywood Soundstage 5001 (with *You'll Never Get Rich*); also, excerpts included in *The Hollywood Years of Harry Warren*, Music Masters JJA-19791.

THE HARVEY GIRLS (1946), MGM. Color. Directed by George Sidney. With Judy Garland, Ray Bolger, John Hodiak, Angela Lansbury, Marjorie Main, Preston Foster, Virginia O'Brien, Cyd Charisse, Kenny Baker. Songs: "On the Atchison, Topeka and the Santa Fe," "It's a Great Big World," "Wait and See," "Waltz Your Partner Round and Round," "The Wild, Wild West," "In the Valley," "Oh, You Kid" (lyrics, Johnny Mercer). Soundtrack LP: Hollywood Soundstage 5002; also, three songs cut before release included in *Cut! Outtakes from Hollywood's Greatest Musicals*, Out Take 1.

THE JOLSON STORY (1946), Columbia. Color. Directed by Alfred E. Green. With Larry Parks, Evelyn Keyes, William Demarest, Bill Goodwin. Song: "About a Quarter to Nine" (lyrics, Al Dubin); plus songs by others. Soundtrack LP: Pelican 129.

MOTHER WORE TIGHTS (1947), Twentieth Century-Fox. Color. Directed by Walter Lang. With Betty Grable, Dan Dailey, Mona Freeman, Vanessa Brown, Connie Marshall, Veda Ann Borg, Senor Wences. Song: "Tra-la-la" (lyrics, Mack Gordon); plus songs by others.

SUMMER HOLIDAY (1948), MGM. Color. Directed by Rouben Mamoulian. With Mickey Rooney, Gloria DeHaven, Walter Huston, Marilyn Maxwell, Frank Morgan, Agnes Moorehead, Selena Royle, Butch Jenkins. Songs: "It's Our Home Town," "Afraid to Fall in Love," "The Stanley Steamer," "Independence Day," "Danville High," "The Weary Blues," "You're the Sweetest Kid I've Ever Known" (lyrics, Ralph Blane). Soundtrack LP: Four Jays HW-602 (also includes four deleted songs).

MY DREAM IS YOURS (1949), Warner Brothers. Color. Directed by Michael Curtiz. With Doris Day, Jack Carson, Lee Bowman, Adolphe Menjou, Eve Arden, Edgar Kennedy, S. Z. Sakall, Franklin Pangborn. Songs: "My Dream Is Yours," "Someone Like You," "Love Finds a Way," "Tick, Tick, Tick," "Freddie, Get Ready" (lyrics, Ralph Blane); "I'll String Along With You," "You Must Have Been a Beautiful Baby," "With Plenty of Money and You" (lyrics, Johnny Mercer); "Nagasaki" (lyrics, Mort Dixon); "Canadian Capers" (music, Henry Cohen, Gus Chandler, Bert White; lyrics, Ralph Blane, Warren). Soundtrack LP: Titania 501 (with *West Point Story*).

THE BARKLEYS OF BROADWAY (1949), MGM. Color. Directed by Charles Walters. With Fred Astaire, Ginger Rogers, Oscar Levant, Gale Robbins, Jacques Francois, Billie Burke, George Zucco. Songs: "Swing Trot," "Shoes With Wings On," "You'd Be Hard to Replace," "My One and Only Highland Fling," "A Weekend in the Country," "Bouncin' the Blues," "Manhattan Downbeat" (lyrics, Ira Gershwin); plus songs by others. Soundtrack LP: Soundtrak STK-116. Videocassette: MGM/UA.

JOLSON SINGS AGAIN (1949), Columbia. Color. Directed by Henry Levin. With Larry Parks, Barbara Hale, William Demarest, Bill Goodwin. Song: "About a Quarter to Nine" (lyrics, Al Dubin); plus songs by others.

YOUNG MAN WITH A HORN (1950), Warner Brothers. B&W. Directed by Michael Curtiz. With Kirk Douglas, Lauren Bacall, Doris Day, Juano Hernandez, Mary Beth Hughes, Hoagy Carmichael. Songs: "I Only Have Eyes for You," "The Lullaby of Broadway" (lyrics, Al Dubin); plus songs by others.

TEA FOR TWO (1950), Warner Brothers. Color. Directed by David Butler. With Doris Day, Gordon MacRae, Gene Nelson, Patrice Wymore, Eve Arden, Billy DeWolfe. Song: "I Only Have Eyes for You" (lyrics, Al Dubin); plus songs by others.

SUMMER STOCK (1950), MGM. Color. Directed by Charles Walters. With Judy Garland, Gene Kelly, Gloria DeHaven, Eddie Bracken, Carleton Carpenter, Marjorie Main. Songs: "If You Feel Like Singing, Sing," "Howdy Neighbor, Happy Harvest," "Friendly Star," "Dig, Dig, Dig for Your Supper," "Memory Island" (lyrics, Mack Gordon); "You, Wonderful You" (lyrics, Saul Chaplin, Jack Brooks); plus songs by others. Soundtrack LP: excerpts included in *The Hollywood Years of Harry Warren*, Music Masters JJA-19791; also in *The Judy Garland Story: The Star Years*, MGM 3989 (withdrawn); also in *Songs by Harry Warren*, Four Jays HW-601.

PAGAN LOVE SONG (1950), MGM. Color. Directed by Robert Alton. With Esther Williams, Howard Keel, Rita Moreno, Minna Gombell, Charles Mau. Songs: "The Sea of the Moon," "Singing in the Sun," "Tahiti," "The House of Singing Bamboo," "Why Is Love So Crazy?," "Etiquette," "Music on the Water" (lyrics, Arthur Freed); plus songs by others. Soundtrack LP: MGM 534 (now out of print), MGM 2-SES-43ST (with *The Pirate, Hit the Deck*); also, excerpt included in *The Hollywood Years of Harry Warren*, Music Masters JJA-19791.

LULLABY OF BROADWAY (1951), Warner Brothers. Color. Directed by Roy Del Ruth. With Doris Day, Gene Nelson, Gladys George, Billy DeWolfe, S. Z. Sakall, Anne Triola. Songs: "The Lullaby of Broadway," "You're Getting to Be a Habit with Me" (lyrics, Al Dubin); plus songs by others. Soundtrack LP: Caliban 6008.

TEXAS CARNIVAL (1951), MGM. Color. Directed by Charles Walters. With Esther Williams, Red Skelton, Howard Keel, Ann Miller, Keenan Wynn, Red Norvo Trio, Foy Willing and his Band. Songs: "It's Dynamite," "Whoa, Emma," "Young Folks Should Get Married," "Carnie's Pitch" (lyrics, Dorothy Fields); plus songs by others. Soundtrack LP: excerpt included in *The Hollywood Years of Harry Warren,* Music Masters JJA-19791.

PAINTING THE CLOUDS WITH SUNSHINE (1951). Warner Brothers. Color. Directed by David Butler. With Dennis Morgan, Virginia Mayo, Gene Nelson, Lucille Norman, Virginia Gibson, Tom Conway, Wallace Ford, S. Z. Sakall. Song: "You're My Everything" (lyrics, Mort Dixon); plus songs by others.

SHE'S WORKING HER WAY THROUGH COLLEGE (1952), Warner Brothers. Color. Directed by H. Bruce Humberstone. With Virginia Mayo, Ronald Reagan, Gene Nelson, Frank Lovejoy, Patrice Wymore. Song: "With Plenty of Money and You" (lyrics, Al Dubin); plus songs by others.

THE BELLE OF NEW YORK (1952), MGM. Color. Directed by Charles Walters. With Fred Astaire, Vera-Ellen, Marjorie Main, Keenan Wynn, Gale Robbins, Alice Pearce, Clinton Sundberg. Songs: "I Wanna Be a Dancing Man," "When I'm Out With the Belle of New York," "Bachelor Dinner Song," "Naughty But Nice," "Oops," "Seeing's Believing," "Thank You, Mr. Currier, Thank You, Mr. Ives," "Baby Doll" (lyrics, Johnny Mercer); plus song by others. Soundtrack LP: DRG/Stet DS-15004; also, excerpt included in *Songs by Harry Warren,* Four Jays HW-601.

SKIRTS AHOY! (1952), MGM. Color. Directed by Sidney Lanfield. With Esther Williams, Vivian Blaine, Joan Evans, Barry Sullivan, Keefe Brasselle, Dean Miller, Margalo Gilmore, Billy Eckstine, Debbie Reynolds, Bobby Van. Songs: "Hold Me Close to You," "What Good Is a Gal Without a Guy?," "I Got a Funny Feeling," "Hilda Matilda," "Glad to Have You Aboard," "What Makes a Wave?," "The Navy Waltz," "We Will Fight" (lyrics, Ralph Blane); plus songs by others.

JUST FOR YOU (1952), Paramount. Color. Directed by Elliot Nugent. With Bing Crosby, Jane Wyman, Ethel Barrymore, Natalie Wood, Cora Witherspoon, Robert Arthur. Songs: "Just for You," "Zing a Little Zong," "I'll Si-Si Ya in Bahia," "On the Ten-Ten from Ten-Ten-Tennessee," "He's Just Crazy for Me," "Checkin' My Heart," "The Maiden of Guadalupe," "The Live Oak Tree," "Call Me Tonight," "A Flight of Fancy," "Ol' Spring Fever" (lyrics, Leo Robin). Studio recording of some of the songs included in *Bing Crosby: Zing a Little Zong,* Decca 4259 (withdrawn).

THE JAZZ SINGER (1953), Warner Brothers. Color. Directed by Michael Curtiz. With Danny Thomas, Peggy Lee, Mildred Dunnock, Eduard Franz. Song: "I'll String Along With You" (lyrics, Al Dubin); plus songs by others.

THE CADDY (1953), Paramount. B&W. Directed by Norman Taurog. With Dean Martin, Jerry Lewis, Donna Reed, Fred Clark, Barbara Bates, Marshall Thompson, Marjorie Gateson. Songs: "That's Amore," "What Would You Do Without Me?," "It's a Whistlin' Kinda Mornin'," "The Gay Continental," "You're the Right One," "(It Takes a Lot of Little Likes to Make) One Big Love" (lyrics, Jack Brooks).

THE EDDIE CANTOR STORY (1953), Warner Brothers. Color. Directed by Alfred E. Green. With Keefe Brasselle, Marilyn Erskine, Aline MacMahon, Marie Windsor, Ann Doran, Hal March, Will Rogers Jr. Song: "You Must Have Been a Beautiful Baby" (lyrics, Johnny Mercer); plus songs by others.

THE GLENN MILLER STORY (1954), Universal. Color. Directed by Anthony Mann. With James Stewart, June Allyson, Charles Drake, George Tobias, Frances Langford, Count Basie, Gene Krupa, Ben Pollack, the Modernaires. Song: "Chattanooga Choo-Choo" (lyrics, Mack Gordon); plus songs by others. Soundtrack LP: MCA 1624.

ARTISTS AND MODELS (1955), Paramount. Color. Directed by Frank Tashlin. With Dean Martin, Jerry Lewis, Shirley MacLaine, Dorothy Malone, Anita Ekberg, Eva Gabor, George Winslow. Songs: "Inamorata," "When You Pretend," "The Lucky Song," "You Look So Familiar," "Bat Lady," "Artists and Models" (lyrics, Jack Brooks). Soundtrack LP: excerpt included in *The Singing Actors of Hollywood,* Capitol 2C-184.

MARTY (1955), United Artists. B&W. Directed by Delbert Mann. With Ernest Borgnine, Betsy Blair, Joe DeSantis, Esther Minciotti, Jerry Paris, Karen Steele. Song: "Hey, Marty" (lyrics, Paddy Chayefsky).

THE BIRDS AND THE BEES (1956), Paramount. Color. Directed by Norman Taurog. With George Gobel, Mitzi Gaynor, David Niven, Reginald Gardiner. Songs: "The Birds and the Bees," "La Parisienne" (lyrics, Mack David).

THE EDDY DUCHIN STORY (1957), Columbia. Color. Directed by George Sidney. With Tyrone Power, Kim Novak, Victoria Shaw, James Whitmore, Larry Keating. Song: "You're My Everything" (lyrics, Mort Dixon); plus songs by others. LP: MCA VIM-7215 (featuring Carmen Cavallaro, who dubbed the soundtrack).

THE JOKER IS WILD (1957), Paramount.

B&W. Directed by Charles Vidor. With Frank Sinatra, Mitzi Gaynor, Jeanne Crain, Eddie Albert, Beverly Garland, Jackie Coogan. Song: "I Love My Baby" (lyrics, Bud Green); plus songs by others.

SPRING REUNION (1957), Paramount. B&W. Directed by Robert Pirosh. With Betty Hutton, Dana Andrews, Jean Hagen, James Gleason, Laura LaPlante, George Chandler: Song: "Spring Reunion" (lyrics, Harold Adamson).

AN AFFAIR TO REMEMBER (1957), Twentieth Century-Fox. CinemaScope. Color. Directed by Leo McCarey. With Cary Grant, Deborah Kerr, Richard Denning, Cathleen Nesbitt, Robert Q. Lewis, Neva Patterson. Songs: "An Affair to Remember," "Tomorrow Land," "You Make It Easy to Be True," "The Tiny Scout" (lyrics, Harold Adamson, Leo McCarey). Soundtrack LP: Columbia CL-1013 (now out of print); excerpts included in *The Hollywood Years of Harry Warren*, Music Masters JJA-19791.

SEPARATE TABLES (1958), United Artists. B&W. Directed by Delbert Mann. With Burt Lancaster, Rita Hayworth, Deborah Kerr, David Niven, Wendy Hiller. Song: "Separate Tables" (lyrics, Harold Adamson).

THESE THOUSAND HILLS (1958), Twentieth Century-Fox. CinemaScope. Color. Directed by Richard Fleischer. With Don Murray, Richard Egan, Lee Remick, Stuart Whitman, Albert Dekker, Fuzzy Knight, Patricia Owens. Song: "These Thousand Hills" (lyrics, Harold Adamson).

ROCK-A-BYE BABY (1958), Paramount. Color. Directed by Frank Tashlin. With Jerry Lewis, Marilyn Maxwell, Salvatore Baccaloni, Connie Stevens, Reginald Gardiner. Songs: "Dormi, Dormi, Dormi!," "Love Is a Lonely Thing," "The White Virgin of the Nile," "The Land of La-La-La," "Why Can't He Care for Me?," "Rock-a-Bye Baby" (lyrics, Sammy Cahn).

CINDERFELLA (1960), Paramount. Color. Directed by Frank Tashlin. With Jerry Lewis, Ed Wynn, Judith Anderson, Anna Maria Alberghetti, Count Basie and his Orchestra, Henry Silva, Robert Hutton. Songs: "Somebody," "Let Me Be a People," "The Other Fella," "Turn It On" (lyrics, Jack Brooks), "The Princess Waltz" (collaboration with Walter Scharf). Studio recording of some of songs included in *Cinderfella*, Dot 38001 (discontinued).

THE LADIES' MAN (1961), Paramount. Color. Directed by Jerry Lewis. With Jerry Lewis, Helen Traubel, Jack Kruschen, Doodles Weaver, Pat Stanley, Harry James and his Orchestra. Songs: "He Doesn't Know," "Don't Go to Paris" (lyrics, Jack Brooks).

SATAN NEVER SLEEPS (1962), Twentieth Century-Fox. CinemaScope. Color. Directed by Leo McCarey. With William Holden, Clifton Webb, France Nuyen, Martin Benson, Edith Sharpe, Burt Kwouk. Song: "Satan Never Sleeps" (lyrics, Harold Adamson, Leo McCarey).

FUNNY LADY (1975), Columbia/Warner Brothers. Color. Directed by Herbert Ross. With Barbra Streisand, James Caan, Omar Sharif, Roddy McDowall, Carole Wells, Ben Vereen. Song: "I Found a Million Dollar Baby in a Five-and-Ten Cent Store" (lyrics, Mort Dixon); plus songs by others. Soundtrack LP: Arista 9004.

Richard Whiting on a movie set in the early 1930s.

Like that of George Gershwin, Richard Whiting's career as a Hollywood song-writer was lamentably short. But over a nine-year period, from 1929 to 1938, Whiting wrote song after song that became nationwide hits, and which are still pop standards. They include that jolly movieland anthem, "Hooray for Hollywood," such romantic ballads as "Too Marvelous for Words" and "Beyond the Blue Horizon," and Shirley Temple's most famous kiddie tune, "On the Good Ship Lollipop." And any number of songs that Whiting wrote before he went to Hollywood have continued to be used in movie after movie—including "She's Funny That Way," "Sleepy Time Gal," "You're an Old Smoothie," "Ain't We Got Fun," and "Eadie Was a Lady."

Whiting was born in Peoria, Illinois, on November 12th, 1891, but grew up in Detroit. Both of his parents played musical instruments, so it wasn't surprising that he began taking piano lessons at an early age and that music soon became his first love. While a student at a Los Angeles military academy, Whiting spent most of his nonstudy hours writing songs and playing piano for the academy's musical shows.

Encouraged by his classmates, he submitted three of his songs to the Remick publishing company soon after graduation. Remick offered Whiting fifty dollars for each of the songs—and also a job in its Detroit office. Whiting took the job, eventually becoming office manager. He also worked nights playing piano in a Detroit hotel.

Whiting's big dream at that time was to own a Steinway grand piano. So he offered Remick a deal. If they'd buy him the piano, he'd give them outright all the rights to his next song, "It's Tulip Time in Holland." Whiting was sure he'd gotten the best of the deal until two months later—when the song passed the million mark in sales. If he had taken the standard royalties, he would have had a house full of Steinway grands!

In 1915, two other Whiting songs, "And They Called It Dixieland" and "Mammy's Little Coal Black Rose," earned him about $30,000 in royalties, a whopping sum for a twenty-three-year-old fledgling songwriter in those days. If there was still any doubt in his mind that he could succeed as a songwriter, it disappeared in 1917 when "Till We Meet Again" became the biggest hit of the World War I years.

No one was more surprised by that one than Whiting. As his daughter, songstress Margaret Whiting, told me: "My father was a shy man who never took his success for granted. And what happened with 'Till We Meet Again' is straight out of a Doris Day movie." Whiting's original collaborator, Ray Egan, had written the lyrics to fit a little waltz that Whiting had composed, intending to enter it in a war-song contest at the Michigan Theater in Detroit. But Whiting thought the lyrics were too simple and the song not patriotically fervent enough to win the contest. So he threw the song in a wastepaper basket. Whiting's secretary, cleaning up after Whiting had left for the day, saw the manuscript in the wastebasket, pulled it out and decided to check with Jerome Remick himself whether or not it was meant to be discarded. Remick played it and said, "Let's not tell Richard." Remick then entered it in the contest. It won. Within a year, "Till We Meet Again" had sold more than five million copies of sheet music.

During the 1920s, Whiting not only kept turning out pop hits but also became a regular contributor to such Broadway shows as *George White's Scandals* and *Toot-Sweet*. Then, in 1928, partly at his wife's urging, Whiting moved from Detroit to New York and signed up with Max Dreyfus, head of the Chappell publishing firm. Just a few months later, Dreyfus convinced Whiting that he should try his hand at movies —many of which were then being made in New York, at the Astoria Studios on Long Island. Most of the movie companies in both New York and Hollywood were offering fantastic short-term deals for songwriters with hits to their name to help churn out the musicals that had become a box-office bonanza following Jolson's success with *The Jazz Singer*.

Whiting signed a contract with Paramount, together with a twenty-eight-year-old lyricist with whom Dreyfus teamed him: Leo Robin. But there was a hitch. Paramount wanted them to work out of Hollywood, not New York. Whiting agreed to go west but only for three months. Hollywood, however, would soon change his mind—and make him a permanent resident.

Richard Whiting's Major Movies and Their Songs

The first movie assignment for Whiting and Robin at Paramount was *Innocents of Paris,* starring the toast of Parisian music halls, Maurice Chevalier, in his first American feature film. At the time, virtually every movie, silent or talkie, had a song named after the girl in the picture. So Whiting and Robin promptly went to work writing such a song for *Innocents of Paris*—"Louise."

When Chevalier arrived in Hollywood, he liked "Louise" and several other songs when Whiting played them for him. But he hated the script that Paramount presented him for *Innocents of Paris.* Like many other stars of that era, Chevalier had been talked into signing a six-week contract to make "a moving picture" at a salary much higher than he could possibly earn in Paris—but without any idea of what the picture would be. Once shooting began, Chevalier became more and more unhappy with what he considered a stupid story about a Parisian junkman who poses as a mysterious prince. Paramount executives, meanwhile, grew more and more nervous about their Continental star walking out and returning to Paris. To counter Chevalier's discontent, Paramount agreed to add a music-hall sequence to the picture, in which Chevalier would sing several of the specialty numbers he had popularized in Paris, including "Valentine" and "Les Ananas" (literally "The Pineapples," and a French takeoff on "Yes, We Have No Bananas").

In his first American feature film, Innocents of Paris, *Maurice Chevalier introduced Richard Whiting's and Leo Robin's classic "Louise."*

By the third week of production, Paramount executives were convinced, after screening the daily rushes, that Chevalier's charm and magnetism would turn him into the talkies' first international superstar, whatever the picture. So they offered him a year's extension of his six-week contract at a salary close to half a million dollars. Chevalier accepted, convinced that when *Innocents of Paris* was released it would be such a bomb at the box office that the studio would have to pay him off even if it never wanted to make another picture with him. But Chevalier had underestimated the public acceptance of his talents just as much as Whiting had his own back in Detroit with the grand piano deal.

When *Innocents of Paris* was released in 1929, even Paramount was surprised at just how big a hit it turned out to be. Chevalier was flabbergasted. And it was not his interpolated Parisian songs that everyone left the theaters humming, but Whiting's "Louise." Paramount promptly extended the contracts of both Richard Whiting and Leo Robin.

In quick succession, Whiting was assigned to write songs for three Nancy Carroll movies, *Close Harmony, Dance of Life* and *Sweetie.* Carroll was a cute, dimpled, "dream-girl" type who had started out in silent comedies and dramas, but whose modest singing and dancing abilities carried her successfully into the first wave of musical talkies. She was, in fact, the first real star of movie musicals developed by the talkies themselves, without previously having been a star on Broadway or in Europe. But her limited musical talents—and the silliness of most of the musical vehicles in which Paramount cast her—caused a quick decline in her box-office appeal after 1931. Carroll fought to get more dramatic and straight-comedy roles, but too late. Within a few years, Carroll, not helped by widely publicized stories about her temperament, was a has-been, playing in B-movies at a lesser studio. As Paul L. Nemick writes in his perceptive survey, *The Films of Nancy Carroll,* "She often wondered what her screen career might have been had she not been sidetracked by the musical films."

Ironically, one of the first songs that Whiting and Robin wrote for Carroll to sing was "I Want to Go Places and Do Things" in *Close Harmony.* It did little for Carroll or for that routine movie about vaudeville troupers. In fact, only one song hit came out of Whiting's three '29 scores for Carroll pictures: "True Blue Lou," which is sung in *Dance of Life* not by Carroll but by Hal Skelly (who had starred in the Broadway version of the movie, under its original title, *Burlesque*). The song is a typically '20s blues lament of the "Frankie and Johnny" type. It has survived better than the picture itself, thanks to later recordings by Larry Carr, Tony Bennett and Frank Sinatra.

As with most studio contract songwriters of the period, Whiting was also assigned by Paramount to compose incidental songs for nonmusicals. These included two Mexican-flavored songs for the part-talkie '29 melodrama *The Wolf Song,* with Lupe Velez and Gary Cooper (who were then making headlines with a tempestuous off-screen romance), and the theme song for the leading female character ("Celia") of a Mary Brian tearjerker, *The Man I Love* (no relation to a later Ida Lupino movie and with no use of the Gershwin song of the same name). Cooper's singing voice in *The Wolf Man* was dubbed by Russ Columbo, then a member of Gus Arnheim's Cocoanut Grove Orchestra and soon to emerge as a major crooner rival to Bing Crosby.

Then came *Paramount on Parade,* the studio's part-Technicolor, all-star answer to

MGM's successful *Hollywood Revue of 1929*, Warner Brothers's *Show of Shows*, and Universal's *King of Jazz*. Virtually every performer under contract to Paramount was assigned to a musical number or comedy skit of varying length—with the direction of the sequences divided among Dorothy Arzner, Edmund Goulding, Ernst Lubitsch, Victor Schertzinger, Edward Sutherland, Frank Tuttle, and several others. Inevitably, the production was a hodgepodge of styles and there was decidedly variable quality from act to act. Whiting contributed one of the revue's best songs, and one of its worst.

The latter is "My Marine" (lyrics by Ray Egan), which dramatic actress Ruth Chatterton half speaks, half sings as a heavily-accented French streetwalker still pining over the American soldier who had promised to take her to Idaho after the war. Among the soldiers listening to her saga as dispiritedly as must most of the audience: Stuart Erwin and Fredric March. Much more memorable, though it never became a major song hit, is "All I Want Is Just One Kiss" (lyrics by Robin), which is first sung with considerable charm and spirit by Maurice Chevalier (in a sequence directed by Lubitsch), and then is amusingly mimicked by young Mitzi Green. The songs for the other numbers in *Paramount on Parade* were contributed by Sam Coslow, Wolfe Gilbert, Abel Baer, Elsie Janis, Jack King, and Victor Schertzinger—and are uneven at best.

The first really big hit that Whiting wrote for a Paramount picture was "Beyond the Blue Horizon," introduced by Jeanette MacDonald in 1930's *Monte Carlo*. The movie itself, as directed by Ernst Lubitsch, is a slight and silly romantic trifle about a down-on-her-luck Countess and the dapper Count she mistakes at the Monte Carlo gambling tables for a hairdresser. Lubitsch wanted as many of the songs as possible integrated into the picture's story line—and "Beyond the Blue Horizon" plays a key role in showing the Countess's determination to rise above her financial adversity. That, of course, was a theme with meaning in Depression America that went far beyond the characters of the movie.

Robin's lyrics convey that meaning perfectly. But it is Whiting's melody and the unique arrangement he worked out for it that turned the song into a classic. Jeanette MacDonald first sings the song on a train that's headed for Monte Carlo, with the train's chug-chug rhythm, the spins of the wheels and the click-click of the pistons setting the basic rhythm for the song. She recaps it to the same accompaniment for the finale in a duet with Jack Buchanan. Even the improbability of MacDonald's opening her compartment window so that farmers working in the fields can join in with her chirping as the train whizzes by—not to mention the fact that, in the process, she doesn't get a face-full of soot from the coal-driven engine—never undercuts the musical imaginativeness of the two scenes.

Soon after the movie's release, "Beyond the Blue Horizon" shot onto *Variety*'s Top Ten list of song hits and stayed there for a total of sixteen weeks. Moreover, many of the recordings of the song, not only in the '30s but in succeeding decades as well, kept the train rhythm of the original presentation in *Monte Carlo*, so irrevocably cross-identified had they become. MacDonald, incidentally, also sings a more straightforward—or is it straitlaced?—version of "Beyond the Blue Horizon" in a later movie, 1944's *Follow the Boys*, a multistar picture featuring some of the performers who had entertained American troops overseas during World War II. As did many other war era singers, she had to change a line of the lyrics, however—so that "rising sun" became "shining sun" (because of Japan's calling itself the Empire of the Rising Sun).

Monte Carlo contains several other good Whiting songs that never became hits but that work well within the context of the picture. "Give Me a Moment Please" is closer in style to the romantic operetta ballads of Romberg and Friml than to Whiting's usual pop style, but it has a lovely melody that both MacDonald and Buchanan sing fervently if also a bit pretentiously. "Always in All Ways" is a more up-tempo ballad that rises above its too-deliberately cute title to express melodically the growing affection between the Countess and the Count. The song is also used behind both the picture's opening and closing titles.

That same year, 1930, Whiting, working mostly with Leo Robin but also sometimes (as assigned by the studio) with George Marion, Jr., and Newell Chase, contributed songs to individual Maurice Chevalier and Jeanette MacDonald musicals. It was for Chevalier's *Playboy of Paris* that Whiting composed what his daughter Margaret says always remained his favorite song, "My Ideal." "He loved that one better than any other song he'd ever written," Margaret told me. "He always went back to it before he'd start writing another—as if he had written one thing that he really approved of. He'd say, 'I'll never turn out another one like it.' And then he'd sit down and write wonderful songs such as 'Too Marvelous for Words' or 'Can't Teach My Old Heart New Tricks.' But 'My Ideal' was special to him, and it's still my own favorite among all his songs."

Playboy of Paris, about a waiter who finds that inheriting a fortune doesn't solve his romantic problems (another fairly frequent Depression-era movie theme), was only a lukewarm success, but "My Ideal" quickly became a song hit, remaining on *Variety*'s Top 10 list for sixteen weeks in late 1930 and early 1931. (It would also return for seven weeks on radio's *Your Hit Parade* in 1944, following a recording of the song by Margaret Whiting—her very first.)

No comparable hit came out of the seven songs that Whiting wrote for Jeanette MacDonald's *Let's Go Native,* a disjointed variation on J. M. Barrie's *The Admirable Crichton,* about shipwrecked passengers on a tropical isle. Jack Oakie, James Hall, Kay Francis, and Skeets Gallagher head the cast. If Whiting's songs don't seem especially inspired, the screenplay and direction by Leo McCarey (one of his first talkie efforts) seem even less so. Throughout her life, MacDonald always preferred not to talk about this film, probably the worst she ever made.

Whiting had better luck with *Follow Thru,* another musical reteaming of Nancy Carroll and Buddy Rogers. For this all-Technicolor version of a 1929 Broadway hit, only some of the show's original songs by Lew Brown, B. G. de Sylva, and Ray Henderson were kept (including "Button Up Your Overcoat" and "Would You?"). Whiting, with George Marion, Jr., as lyricist, contributed the chipper "We'd Make a Peach of a Pair," which went on to become a moderate hit when popular radio crooner Russ Columbo recorded it. (A year later, Whiting would have an even bigger hit thanks to a Columbo recording, but of a song not from any movie: "Guilty." That one would also provide another major hit for Margaret Whiting when she revived it in 1947; it stayed thirteen weeks on *Your Hit Parade.*)

In 1931 Whiting was assigned to write the title tune and several other songs for *One Hour With You,* a remake of a 1924 Ernst Lubitsch silent comedy, *The Marriage Circle.* Lubitsch announced plans to star Maurice Chevalier in it with Kay Francis (with whom Chevalier was then romantically linked offscreen) and Carole Lombard (then

Buddy Rogers and Nancy Carroll tie the knot in 1930's Follow Thru, *for which Whiting and George Marion, Jr., wrote "We'd Make a Peach of a Pair."*

just a promising Paramount contractee). But production was delayed by a series of executive changes at Paramount that included Lubitsch becoming production chief for all of the studio's pictures. When shooting finally started, with George Cukor co-directing with Lubitsch, Francis and Lombard were busy on other pictures and were replaced by Jeanette MacDonald and Genevieve Tobin. With MacDonald's casting, more songs were added—not by Whiting but by Oscar Straus, whose operetta style better suited MacDonald. Straus's songs for *One Hour With You* (including "Only a Dream Kiss" and "We Will Always Be Sweethearts") are virtually forgotten today. Whiting's contributions might have met the same fate except for Eddie Cantor. He adopted the Whiting-Robin title song as the theme song for his popular radio show, and continued to use it not only as his radio theme throughout the '30s and '40s, but also as his TV show's theme in the '50s.

Before *One Hour With You* was completed, Whiting's Paramount contract expired at just about the same time that Leo Robin had to return to New York for personal family reasons. Whiting signed a new short-term contract with Fox Pictures. His first assignment there was *Adorable,* one of those romantic mythical-kingdom costumers that enjoyed a vogue in the '30s—this one with the studio's popular Janet Gaynor. Although best known for dramatic tearjerkers (she had won the first Academy Award for Best Actress in 1927) and even more limited musically than Nancy Carroll, Gaynor had also made two musicals, the successful *Sunny Side Up* (1929) and the less popular *Delicious* (1931), both of them with her frequent costar, Charles Farrell. But for *Adorable* she was teamed with French actor Henri Garat, making his Hollywood debut. Neither Garat nor any of Whiting's songs for the picture ("My Heart's Desire," "My First Love to Last,"and "Adorable,"all with lyrics by George Marion, Jr.) caught on with the public, and the picture itself fared weakly with critics and audiences. It

Monte Carlo *(1930) teamed Maurice Chevalier and Jeanette MacDonald with Genevieve Tobin and Charlie Ruggles, and introduced Whiting's classic "Beyond the Blue Horizon."*

would be the last musical that Gaynor would make before she retired from moviemaking in the early 1940s.

Whiting's second Fox picture fared little better, even though it reteamed him briefly with Leo Robin. *My Weakness* is a musical fantasy in which silent-film comedian Harry Langdon plays Cupid trying to steer a handsome young man (Lew Ayres) into a romance. The heroine, in her Hollywood debut, is Lilian Harvey, a petite English actress who had won international fame in the 1931 German musical *Congress Dances* (costarring with *Adorable*'s Henri Garat). But neither *My Weakness* nor Harvey's subsequent Fox picture *I Am Suzanne* (1934) found much favor with American audiences, and so Harvey returned to Europe where she made only a few more pictures before retiring in 1939. Whiting's songs for *My Weakness* ("How Do I Look?" "You Can Be Had, So Be Careful," and "Gather Lip Rouge While You May") are even more forgotten today.

But one of Whiting's biggest song hits was just around the corner—and in what, at the time, seemed like the most unlikely place: a Shirley Temple movie. By 1934, six-year-old Shirley had become one of the brightest box-office attractions in the country, stealing not only a number of movies in which she had been featured in support of Gary Cooper, Carole Lombard, Janet Gaynor, Charles Farrell, Ginger Rogers, Adolphe Menjou, and others, but also stealing the affections of the entire country with her singing, dancing, and acting. For her first starring movie, *Bright Eyes,* Whiting and lyricist Sidney Clare were assigned to write the songs.

As Margaret Whiting recalls, her father was getting nowhere coming up with something appropriate for a youngster to sing—a youngster close to his own daughter's age. "Then, one day I came in while he was working and I had this gigantic lollipop.

Bright Eyes *(1934) was six-year-old Shirley Temple's first starring movie, shown in a scene with Jane Withers.*

My father took one look at it and said, 'Margaret, get away from me with all that sticky stuff! You're going to get it all over the piano!' I started to leave and I heard him say, 'No—that's it! The lollipop!' So I guess you can say I inspired 'On the Good Ship Lollipop.'"

The song went on to become one of the most famous of all kiddie songs—and also found enough favor with adults to make *Variety*'s Top 10 list for six weeks after the release of *Bright Eyes.*

That same year, 1934, Richard Whiting also wrote what may be the first rock and roll song. It is not a song with the type of rock beat that came along in the 1950s to revolutionize pop music, but for 1934's *Transatlantic Merry-Go-Round,* starring Jack Benny and Nancy Carroll, Whiting wrote a lively novelty tune that's actually titled "Rock and Roll." Its lyrics, by Sidney Clare, refer to the rocking and rolling motions of the ocean liner on which most of the movie's action takes place. The song is sung first by Mitzi Green while the ship's passengers dance to it in the old-fashioned, cheek-to-cheek style. Then the Boswell Sisters get a chorus, as they sit in chintzy stage-prop rowboats with spangled oars, with eight chorines in sailor hats and satin bell-bottoms cavorting in a routine that spoofs Clare's lyrics. By today's standards, it's sheer camp—made notable only by the accident of what its title has come to mean in the history of music, something that neither Whiting nor Clare could have foreseen.

In the year before Fox merged with Darryl F. Zanuck's Twentieth Century Pictures to become Twentieth Century-Fox, Fox decided to test the talents and box-office appeal of nineteen-year-old Alice Faye in two B comedies with music, *She Learned About Sailors* and *365 Nights in Hollywood.* Whiting and Clare were assigned to both pictures. The results were encouraging enough for Faye to be signed to a

At the start of her career Alice Faye appeared in two musicals with Richard Whiting scores, She Learned About Sailors *and* 365 Nights in Hollywood *(both 1934).*

long-term contract that soon made her one of the top movie-musical stars of the '30s and '40s.

In *She Learned About Sailors* (costarring Lew Ayres), Faye sings Whiting and Clare's cheerfully come-hither "Here's the Key to My Heart," as she throws prop keys to some sailors in a somewhat sleazy waterfront cafe setting—managing to look (and sound) both innocent and knowing in the way of so many '30s heroines. In *365 Days in Hollywood* (costarring James Dunn), the Whiting-Clare "Yes to You" and "My Future Star" get more elaborate treatment as musical production numbers supposedly being filmed as part of the movie's hackneyed behind-the-Hollywood-cameras story (a switch, at least, on all the early '30s backstage-Broadway sagas).

The best of the trio is "(How I'd Love to Say) Yes to You," a likable ballad of the straightforward, sentimental, but not-too-gushy type for which Faye would become famous over the next decade—and she sings it with the deep-voiced languidness that was her trademark. The setting for the song is, at first, a glamorous ballroom, with Faye decked out in a sequined gown and an ostrich fan (for which Fox musicals, in particular, seemed to have had an oversupply). But the number soon moves, in dream-sequence fashion, to various places around the world, with Faye's costumes changing with each new location.

365 Days in Hollywood also includes a few scenes in which Whiting himself appears, including one as Faye's accompanist for a rehearsal of "Yes to Me." He even gets cast billing (fourteenth down the list) as Dick Whiting.

After several routine Fox assignments, Whiting went back to Paramount to work again with Leo Robin. But before leaving Fox, he contributed one song to another Alice Faye musical, *Sing, Baby, Sing.* The picture's story slyly spoofs (with lots of modifications to keep the lawyers at bay) the headline-making romance that actor John Barrymore was then carrying on cross-country with young actress-protégée Elaine Barrie. Adolphe Menjou hams it up as the boozy Barrymore figure, while Faye, in the role that did more than any previous one to make her a star, settles for singing most of the songs—except Whiting's.

His song, a beautifully dreamy ballad titled "When Did You Leave Heaven?," went instead to Tony Martin, making his movie debut in a small supporting role. Whiting's song enjoyed thirteen weeks on *Your Hit Parade,* where, in a rare triple play for songs from one movie, it was joined for part of that time by two of Faye's songs from *Sing, Baby, Sing:* "You Turned the Tables on Me" (by Louis Alter and Sydney Mitchell) and the title song (by Lew Pollack and Jack Yellen). Whiting even won an Oscar nomination (his only one) for this song, but lost to Jerome Kern and Dorothy Fields's "The Way You Look Tonight" from *Swing Time.*

Back at Paramount, his next two assignments would be on musicals that can most charitably be described as awful. *The Big Broadcast of 1936* is easily the weakest of the four in that series. Although the silly plot revolves around the romantic misadventures of a fictitious radio personality known as The Great Lochinvar (Jack Oakie), at least half the guest musical performers have little or no connection with radio—such as tap dancers Bill Robinson and the Nicholas Brothers, the Vienna Choir Boys, and Broadway's Ethel Merman. Merman's sole number, in fact, is patched together partly from one that was cut out of 1934's *We're Not Dressing:* "It's the Animal in Me" (by Harry Revel and Mack Gordon). Bing Crosby gets the movie's best song, "I Wished on the Moon" (by Ralph Rainger and Dorothy Parker). But one of the Whiting-Robin contributions, "Why Dream?," gets the most exposure throughout the movie. It's supposedly sung first by The Great Lochinvar's vocal stand-in, played by Henry Wadsworth—although Wadsworth himself is actually dubbed by Kenny Baker (who would soon become well-known as the singer on Jack Benny's radio program). It's indicative of the picture's problems when the on-camera dubber has to be dubbed.

Bad as that one may be, *Coronado,* set at the California resort of that name, is even worse. Paramount's attempts to develop youthful, fresh-faced counterparts to Warner Brothers's dancing-and-singing Ruby Keeler and Dick Powell foundered badly with this one—not so much because of Betty Burgess and Johnny Downs in the leads as because of the dumb, cliché-ridden, rich-boy-loves-poor-girl script and the overlong, unfunny footage given to the supporting comedians (Leon Errol, Jack Haley, Andy Devine).

Still, Whiting's score for *Coronado* has its pluses, even though it's not easy to discern them from the movie's routine presentations of the songs, including those featuring Eddy Duchin and his Orchestra. "Keep Your Fingers Crossed" is a catchy number with clever Sam Coslow lyrics built around popular superstitions. "How Do I Rate With You?" is also a bright and chipper Whiting-Coslow ballad that unfortunately died with *Coronado*—even though Tommy Dorsey's Orchestra recorded it as one of their first Bluebird 78-rpm record sides in 1935 and it still shows up in various Dorsey reissues and anthologies.

One of the 1930s' most popular comedy teams on radio, George Burns and Gracie Allen, had been featured in a number of Paramount musicals and comedies since 1932, always in supporting or "guest star" spots. In 1935 Paramount decided to test their audience "pull" as movie leads in *Here Comes Cookie*. The movie flopped with both critics and audiences. But it contains one funny song that Whiting and Robin wrote for Gracie: "The Vamp of the Pampas." The number drolly spoofs a Busby Berkeley production number, "The Lady in Red," that had been featured in an earlier 1935 Warner Brothers musical, *In Caliente*. Whiting's melody not only keeps the same Latin beat of "The Lady in Red" but also has a theme that's deliberately similar. The number is kept short (unlike Berkeley's) and is simply staged (again, unlike Berkeley's), with Gracie singing and dancing a few steps with eight guitar-strumming choristers. But it makes its comic points sharply and delightfully, especially if you're familiar with *In Caliente* and "The Lady in Red."

Bing Crosby in a western? Yes, and *Rhythm on the Range* (1936) turned out to be one of El Bingo's most popular '30s musicals. He costars in it with Frances Farmer, then being groomed for stardom by Paramount (and years away from the breakdowns that would shatter her career), and singer-comedienne Martha Raye, in her movie debut. Whiting and Robin wrote the title song and "I Can't Escape from You," an easy-going ballad with a slow-rocking rhythm. But they were not the hits that emerged from the picture. Instead, "Empty Saddles" (by Billy Hill and Keirn Brennan) and "I'm an Old Cowhand" (by Johnny Mercer) went on to *Your Hit Parade* and became 78-rpm recording best-sellers for Crosby, while Raye scored with Sam Coslow's "Mr. Paganini," which later became one of her most famous specialty numbers in her wartime troop shows.

The exasperating Hollywood habit of buying '30s Broadway hits and then filming them shorn of most of their original songs resulted in an emasculated Cole Porter score in Paramount's 1936 version of *Anything Goes*. Although Ethel Merman was, happily, cast in her original Broadway role as Reno Sweeney, only four of Porter's songs ended up being fully used in the screen version. Six new songs of unequal quality—and especially unequal to the dropped Porter songs—were furnished "to order" from Paramount's music department by various combinations of Hoagy Carmichael, Edward Hayman, Frederick Hollander, Leo Robin, and Richard Whiting. Whiting's contribution (with Robin lyrics) is a fairly innocuous up-tempo ballad for Bing Crosby, "Sailor Beware," designed to help Bing croon his way into the shipboard affections of the leading lady, Ida Lupino.

With his assignments from Paramount in '35 and '36 striking no popular sparks, Whiting decided to accept a bid from Warner Brothers to join their music department. The extravagant Warner's cycle of Busby Berkeley musicals, with scores mostly by Harry Warren and Al Dubin, was in decline at the box office, and fresh musical blood was being wooed. At Warners, Whiting would be teamed for the first time with Johnny Mercer, then in his late twenties and an unabashed admirer of Whiting's music. As Mercer once told author-producer Max Wilk: "Buddy Morris at Warners asked me who I'd like to work with, and I said 'I'd rather work with Dick Whiting than anybody.' One of my idols. He had a lot of quality, and he was an original. A dear fellow, too. Modest and sweet, and not at all pushy like a lot of New York writers."

In short order, the Whiting-Mercer team went to work on three Warner musicals in 1937—and each one produced *Your Hit Parade* song hits. The three musicals themselves were only marginal improvements on Whiting's recent Paramount and Fox assignments. But lively pacing, personable casts including many fresh faces, production gloss, and, most of all, the new vitality that working with Mercer inspired in Whiting's songs, made big differences in the final product.

Ready, Willing and Able was both the title of the first Whiting-Mercer collaboration and a summing-up of the new team's rarin'-to-go status at Warners. Unfortunately, only two-thirds of the title applied to the picture itself and only one-third to leading lady Ruby Keeler. She was particularly unable to carry a major musical without costar Dick Powell (with whom she'd been teamed in 1933's *42nd Street* and six subsequent musicals) or Al Jolson (her husband at that time and with whom she'd made 1936's *Go Into Your Dance*). Keeler's initial popularity as a tap dancer had waned with the emergence of the more versatile Eleanor Powell at MGM, and she was increasingly outclassed as a singer and actress by practically every other musical star in Hollywood. *Ready, Willing and Able* would mark the likeable but limited Keeler's last Warner's musical.

The picture's overcomplicated backstage plot, about a star-struck American girl who tries to pass herself off as a London star, didn't help matters. Neither did a real-life, behind-the-cameras tragedy. Warners had planned *Ready, Willing and Able* as a major "breakthrough" vehicle for handsome, curly-haired Ross Alexander, who had shown promise in a number of secondary roles. With Dick Powell on a loan-out to Twentieth Century-Fox for Irving Berlin's *On the Avenue,* Alexander was given the romantic lead opposite Keeler in *Ready, Willing and Able,* even though he couldn't sing (James Newell dubbed for him). But before the picture's release, Alexander committed suicide, under circumstances never explained publicly. Warners recut the movie to downplay Alexander's role and build up that of hoofer Lee Dixon, further confusing the plot.

Ready, Willing and Able's saving graces, however, are its songs and production numbers. The standout: "Too Marvelous for Words." The number is staged by Bobby Connolly in the spectacular Warner–Busby Berkeley manner, with Keeler, Dixon and dozens of chorines tap-dancing on the huge keys of an oversize typewriter, typing out some of the words from Mercer's lyrics. The song itself went on to six weeks on *Your Hit Parade* and has long been a pop standard.

Less successful commercially but undeserving of its obscurity is a song that Wini Shaw sings midway in the movie, "Sentimental and Melancholy." It's one of Whiting's rare attempts at an outright torch song, and is perfectly suited to Shaw's plaintive style, though not as memorable as "The Lullaby of Broadway" (by Warren and Dubin) that Shaw had introduced in *Gold Diggers of 1935.*

At first glance, Whiting's second Warner assignment may have seemed a step or two backward—another collegiate musical, *Varsity Show* (1937). But, once again, snappy pacing, a personable cast, good Whiting-Mercer songs, and a first-class production topped off by a Busby Berkeley–directed finale made a big difference. Dick Powell and Rosemary Lane get the movie's best romantic ballad, "You've Got Something There"—which is reprised as a dance in a later scene by the great black dance team of Buck and Bubbles. But it's Priscilla Lane, in her first movie and in a secondary role to her sister Rosemary, who puts over the movie's hit song, "Have You Got Any Castles, Baby?," which went on to eleven weeks on *Your Hit Parade.*

It's all too wonderful, and so I'll stick to words

Ruby Keeler and Lee Dixon tap on the keys of a giant typewriter to Whiting's and Johnny Mercer's "Too Marvelous for Words," in Ready, Willing, and Able *(1937).*

Varsity Show's finale is a mammoth college show sequence that, as directed by Busby Berkeley, probably wouldn't even fit into the Yale Bowl. It mixes a number of college songs arranged by Fred Waring (whose orchestra is featured throughout the picture) with reprises of most of the movie's earlier songs plus one new one: a typically up-tempo Whiting ballad, "Love Is on the Air Tonight." For all its topical references, the last one never caught on. But it did, indirectly, play a role in movie history, by providing the title for the minor B picture in which a young Warner contractee, Ronald Reagan, would make his movie debut that same year: *Love Is on the Air.*

The biggest Warner Brothers hit on which Whiting and Mercer would work in 1937 was *Hollywood Hotel,* pegged to a popular radio variety show of that name, hosted by the well-known Hollywood gossip columnist Louella Parsons. The movie's opening song has become virtually a movie-industry anthem: "Hooray for Hollywood."

"Hooray for Hollywood" gives *Hollywood Hotel* a spirited send-off as sung by Johnny "Scat" Davis and Frances Langford with Benny Goodman's Orchestra, as they head for the St. Louis airport in open roadsters to see Dick Powell off to Hollywood. It's delivered with the driving, swinging bounce that, by late '37, had made Goodman's orchestra the No. 1 dance band in the country, with Benny himself nicknamed "The King of Swing." The song is also reprised by Davis in the picture's finale, with Dick Powell and Rosemary Lane getting the song's last lines before the fade-out kiss.

One of Whiting's most romantic ballads, "Silhouetted in the Moonlight," is spotted in two places in *Hollywood Hotel*. The first time, it's sung as part of the budding romance between Powell and Lane, in a moonlit setting at an empty Hollywood Bowl. Powell, by 1937, had managed to overcome the pretentiousness that his crooning often conveyed in earlier musicals, and he had instead developed a casual and more subtle "I-know-this-is-corny-but-isn't-it-fun?" manner with even the most saccharine lyrics —which Mercer's border on here. The second go-round for the song comes as part of the movie's "big broadcast" finale, with the actual baritone of the *Hollywood Hotel* radio series, Jerry Cooper, singing it with Frances Langford, backed by Raymond Paige's on-camera orchestra. It's too bad that Powell and Langford couldn't have been teamed for at least one chorus, because they're the best singers of the four who do the song. Cooper's nasal baritone is ill-matched with Langford's cleanly elegant contralto,

The finale of 1937's Hollywood Hotel, *featuring Dick Powell (behind the microphone), with (from left) Jerry Cooper, Frances Langford, Johnny Davis, Lola and Rosemary Lane, Raymond Paige, Louella Parsons, Robert Paige, Mabel Todd, and Ted Healy.*

whereas the cutting edge of Lane's band-trained voice was stylistically better-suited to belting out Broadway songs than to blending with Powell's crooning style.

Hollywood Hotel also includes a number of functional, throwaway songs, such as "Sing, You Son of a Gun," "I'm Like a Fish Out of Water," and "I've Hitched My Wagon to a Star." But one other song literally got thrown away, cut from the film just before its release: "Can't Teach My Old Heart New Tricks." Margaret Whiting calls it her favorite of all the songs her father wrote with Mercer. "It's the most beautiful torch song my father wrote," she says, "with some of Johnny's best lyrics. Frances Langford was to sing it, but it was taken out of the picture. It's become sort of an underground classic." Margaret Whiting has recorded the song, and she reports it's been sung (but not recorded by) Bobby Short and Tony Bennett.

One further nonmusical note about *Hollywood Hotel.* TV showings sometimes advertise the picture as starring Ronald Reagan and it's listed among his standard film credits. But Reagan plays only a very minor role as a radio announcer who interviews celebrities arriving for a movie premiere. Curiously, this brief sequence has been deleted from the TV prints of *Hollywood Hotel* I've seen in recent years (probably for TV timing and not political reasons).

Whiting was at work on another Dick Powell musical, *Cowboy From Brooklyn,* when, unexpectedly and to the shock of his colleagues, he suffered a heart attack. He died on Feb. 10, 1938. He was forty-six.

Harry Warren, working with Mercer, completed the score for *Cowboy From Brooklyn,* a routine comedy with music, about a Brooklyn crooner (Dick Powell) who's turned into a singing cowboy star on radio by a talent scout (Pat O'Brien) and his sidekick (Ronald Reagan). There are a few attempts at spoofing the vogue of singing cowboys that hit the movies in the mid-'30s, but the script just isn't all that clever and the two leading ladies (Priscilla Lane and Ann Sheridan) have much too little to do. But one of Whiting's songs, "Ride, Tenderfoot, Ride," catches the easy, steady rhythm of a cantering horse in the best "pop Western" tradition and has gone on to become a cowboy standard.

Although none of Whiting's four Warner musicals with Johnny Mercer are '30s classics, each one produced a song hit that has become a pop standard. Obviously, the collaboration with lyricist Mercer had a stimulating effect on Whiting's creative juices—and it's tragic that death in his mid-forties cut short a talent that seemed on the verge of topping the already-impressive list of hits he'd written over the preceding decade. In a succession of assignments at different studios, Whiting had helped to set the standards for good songs in the first decade of movie musicals, even when the films themselves were run-of-the-mill or worse.

The title that Johnny Mercer gave to one of the last songs he and Whiting wrote together—one that's used instrumentally in a Benny Goodman segment in *Hollywood Hotel* and then vocally in *Cowboy From Brooklyn*—perhaps best sums up Whiting's legacy: "A Heartful of Music."

Richard Whiting was working on Cowboy from Brooklyn *(1938) when he suffered a heart attack and died. Harry Warren completed the film's score with Johnny Mercer. One of the songs Whiting had finished for Dick Powell, "Ride, Tenderfoot, Ride," went on to become a cowboy standard.*

INNOCENTS OF PARIS (1929), Paramount. B&W, Directed by Richard Wallace. With Maurice Chevalier, Sylvia Beecher, Russell Simpson, Margaret Livingston. Songs: "Louise," "It's a Habit of Mine," "On Top of the World Alone," "Wait Till You See Ma Cherie" (lyrics, Leo Robin); plus songs by others. LP: studio recordings of some of the songs included in *Maurice Chevalier: You Brought a New Kind of Love to Me,* Monmouth-Evergreen 7028 (withdrawn).

CLOSE HARMONY (1929), Paramount. B&W. Directed by John Cromwell and Edward Sutherland. With Nancy Carroll, Buddy Rogers, Skeets Gallagher, Jack Oakie. Songs: "All A-Twitter, All A-Whirl," "I Want to Go Places and Do Things," "She's So I Dunno" (lyrics, Leo Robin); plus songs by others.

DANCE OF LIFE (1929), Paramount. B&W and Color. Directed by John Cromwell and Edward Sutherland. With Nancy Carroll, Hal Skelly, Dorothy Revier, May Boley, Oscar Levant. Songs: "True Blue Lou," "Cuddlesome Baby," "King of Jazzmania," "Flippity Flop," "Ladies of the Dance" (lyrics, Leo Robin, Sam Coslow); plus songs by others. Soundtrack LP: excerpts included in *The Classic Movie Musicals of Richard A. Whiting,* Music Masters JJA-19806.

WHY BRING THAT UP? (1929), Paramount. B&W. Directed by George Abbott. With George Moran, Charles Mack, Evelyn Brent, Freeman S. Wood. Songs: "Do I Know What I'm Doing While in Love?" (lyrics, Leo Robin), "Shoo Shoo Boogie Boogie" (lyrics, Sam Coslow).

SWEETIE (1929), Paramount. B&W. Directed by Frank Tuttle. With Nancy Carroll, Jack Oakie, Helen Kane, Stuart Erwin, William Austin. Songs: "My Sweeter Than Sweet," "Bear Down, Pelham," "Alma Mammy," "Prep Step," "I Think You'll Like It" (lyrics, George Marion, Jr.); plus songs by others. Soundtrack LP: Caliban 6018 (with *Honey* and *Give My Regards to Broadway*).

POINTED HEELS (1929), Paramount, B&W. Directed by Edward Sutherland. With William Powell, Fay Wray, Helen Kane, Skeets Gallagher, Adrienne Dore. Song: "I Have to Have You" (lyrics, Leo Robin); plus songs by others.

THE MAN I LOVE (1929), Paramount. B&W. Directed by William Wellman. With Mary Brian, Richard Arlen, Jack Oakie, Olga Baclanova, Pat O'Malley. Song: "Celia" (lyrics, Leo Robin).

THE WOLF SONG (1929), Paramount. B&W. Directed by Victor Fleming. With Lupe Velez, Gary Cooper, Louis Wolheim. Songs:

"Mi Amado," "Yo Te Amo Means I Love You" (lyrics, Al Bryan).

WILD PARTY (1929), Paramount. B&W. Directed by Dorothy Arzner. With Clara Bow, Fredric March, Marceline Day, Jack Oakie, Joyce Compton. Song: "My Wild Party Girl" (lyrics, Leo Robin).

THE KIBITZER (1929), Paramount. B&W. Directed by Edward Sloman. With Mary Brian, Neil Hamilton, Harry Green. Song: "Just Wait and See Sweetheart" (lyrics, Leo Robin).

PARAMOUNT ON PARADE (1930). B&W and Color. Directed by Dorothy Arzner, Edmund Goulding, Ernst Lubitsch, Victor Schertzinger, Edward Sutherland, Frank Tuttle, others. With all-star cast including Maurice Chevalier, Clara Bow, Nancy Carroll, Ruth Chatterton, Fredric March, Lillian Roth, Buddy Rogers. Songs: "My Marine" (lyrics, Ray Egan); "All I Want Is Just One Girl" (lyrics, Leo Robin). Soundtrack LP: Caliban 6044 (retitled *Musical Movie Stars on Parade*); also, excerpt only, included in *The Classic Movie Musicals of Richard A. Whiting,* Music Masters JJA-19806.

SAFETY IN NUMBERS (1930), Paramount. B&W. Directed by Victor Schertzinger. With Buddy Rogers, Josephine Dunn, Kathryn Crawford, Carole Lombard, Roscoe Karns, Virginia Bruce. Songs: "My Future Just Passed," "Do You Play, Madame?," "The Pick-Up," "I'd Like to Be a Bee in Your Boudoir," "Business Girl," "You Appeal to Me," "Pepola" (lyrics, George Marion, Jr.). Soundtrack LP: excerpts only, included in *The Classic Movie Musicals of Richard A. Whiting,* Music Masters JJA-19806.

LET'S GO NATIVE (1930), Paramount. B&W. Directed by Leo McCarey. With Jack Oakie, Jeanette MacDonald, Skeets Gallagher, Kay Francis, David Newell, James Hall. Songs: "I've Got a Yen for You," "It Seems to Be Spring," "My Mad Moment," "Let's Go Native," "Pampa Rose," "Don't I Do" (lyrics, George Marion, Jr.).

MONTE CARLO (1930), Paramount. B&W. Directed by Ernst Lubitsch. With Jack Buchanan, Jeanette MacDonald, ZaSu Pitts, Claude Allister. Songs: "Give Me a Moment Please," "Always in All Ways," "Beyond the Blue Horizon," "Trimmin' the Women," "She'll Love Me and Like It," "Whatever It Is, It's Grand," "Day of Days," "Monsieur Beaucaire" (music-lyrics, Whiting, W. Franke Harling, Leo Robin). Soundtrack LP: excerpts included in *The Classic Movies of Richard A. Whiting,* Music Masters JJA-19806.

PLAYBOY OF PARIS (1930), Paramount.

B&W. Directed by Ludwig Berger. With Maurice Chevalier, Frances Dee, Stuart Erwin, O. P. Heggie, Cecil Cunningham. Songs: "My Ideal," "It's a Great Life If You Don't Weaken," "In the Heart of Old Paree," "Yvonne's Song" (music-lyrics, Whiting, Newell Chase, Leo Robin). Soundtrack LP: Caliban 6013 (with *The Way to Love*, others).

FOLLOW THRU (1930), Paramount. Color. Directed by Laurence Schwab and Lloyd Corrigan. With Nancy Carroll, Buddy Rogers, Jack Haley, Zelma O'Neal, Thelma Todd, Eugene Pallette. Song: "A Peach of a Pair" (lyrics, George Marion, Jr.); plus songs by others.

DANGEROUS PARADISE (1930), Paramount. B&W. Directed by William A. Wellman. With Nancy Carroll, Richard Arlen. Song: "Smiling Skies" (lyrics, Leo Robin).

DANGEROUS NAN MCGREW (1930), Paramount. B&W. Directed by Malcolm Saint Clair. With Helen Kane, Victor Moore, Stuart Erwin, Frank Morgan. Song: "Aw C'Mon, Whatta Ya Got to Lose?" (lyrics, Leo Robin); plus songs by others.

MONKEY BUSINESS (1931), Paramount. B&W. Directed by Norman Z. McLeod. With the Four Marx Brothers, Thelma Todd, Tom Kennedy, Ruth Hall. Song: "Blue Blazes" (lyrics, Leo Robin); plus songs by others. Videocassette: MCA.

DUDE RANCH (1931), Paramount. B&W. Directed by Frank Tuttle. With Jack Oakie, Stuart Erwin, Mitzi Green, June Collyer. Song: "Consolation" (lyrics, Leo Robin); plus songs by others.

BLONDE VENUS (1932), Paramount. B&W. Directed by Josef von Sternberg. With Marlene Dietrich, Herbert Marshall, Cary Grant, Dickie Moore. Song: "You So-and-So" (lyrics, Leo Robin); plus songs by others. Soundtrack LP: excerpt included in *The Classic Movie Musicals of Richard A. Whiting*, Music Masters JJA-19806.

ONE HOUR WITH YOU (1932), Paramount. B&W. Directed by Ernst Lubitsch and George Cukor. With Maurice Chevalier, Jeanette MacDonald, Genevieve Tobin, Roland Young, Donald Novis. Songs: "One Hour With You," "Three Times a Day," "(Now I Ask) What Would You Do?" (lyrics, Leo Robin); plus songs by others. Soundtrack LP: Ariel CMF-23 (with *The Love Parade*); also, excerpts included in *The Classic Movie Musicals of Richard A. Whiting*, Music Masters JJA-19806.

RED-HEADED WOMAN (1932), MGM. B&W. Directed by Jack Conway. With Jean Harlow, Chester Morris, Lewis Stone, Leila Hyams, Una Merkel. Song: "Red-Headed Woman" (lyrics, Ray Egan); plus songs by others.

ADORABLE (1933), Fox. B&W. Directed by William Dieterle. With Janet Gaynor, Henri Garat, C. Aubrey Smith, Blanche Frederici. Songs: "Adorable," "My Heart's Desire," "My First Love to Last," "I Loved You Wednesday," "It's All for the Best" (lyrics, George Marion, Jr.).

MY WEAKNESS (1933), Fox. B&W. Directed by David Butler. With Lilian Harvey, Lew Ayres, Harry Langdon, Charles Butterworth. Songs: "How Do I Look?," "Gather Lip Rouge," "You Can Be Had, So Be Careful" (lyrics, Leo Robin, Buddy DeSylva).

I LOVED YOU WEDNESDAY (1933), Fox. B&W. Directed by Henry King. With Warner Baxter, Elissa Landi, Laura Hope Crews, Victor Jory. Song: "It's All for the Best" (lyrics, George Marion, Jr.); plus songs by others.

TAKE A CHANCE (1933), Paramount. B&W. Directed by Laurence Schwab and Monte Brice. With James Dunn, Lillian Roth, Buddy Rogers, June Knight, Cliff Edwards. Songs: "Turn Out the Light," "Eadie Was a Lady" (music-lyrics: Whiting, Nacio Herb Brown, Buddy DeSylva); plus songs by others. Soundtrack LP: excerpt included in *Broadway Melody*, Music Masters JJA-19802.

BOTTOMS UP (1934), Fox. B&W. Directed by David Butler. With Spencer Tracy, Pat Patterson, John Boles, Thelma Todd, Sid Silvers. Song: "Waiting at the Gate for Katie" (lyrics, Gus Kahn); plus songs by others. Soundtrack LP: excerpt included in *The Classic Movie Musicals of Richard A. Whiting*, Music Masters JJA-19806.

TRANSATLANTIC MERRY-GO-ROUND (1934), Edward Small for United Artists release. B&W. Directed by Benjamin Stoloff. With Nancy Carroll, Gene Raymond, Jack Benny, Mitzi Green, Frank Parker, the Boswell Sisters, Jimmie Grier's Orchestra. Songs: "It Was Sweet of You," "Oh, Leo, It's Love," "Rock and Roll," "Moon Over Monte Carlo" (lyrics, Sidney Clare); plus songs by others. Soundtrack LP: excerpts only, included in *The Classic Movie Musicals of Richard A. Whiting*, Music Masters JJA-19806.

BRIGHT EYES (1934), Fox. B&W. Directed by David Butler. With Shirley Temple, James Dunn, Judith Allen, Jane Withers. Song: "On the Good Ship Lollipop" (lyrics, Sidney Clare); Soundtrack LP: included in *The Classic Movie Musicals of Richard A. Whiting*, Music Masters JJA-19806; also in *Shirley Temple's Hits from Her Original Soundtracks*, 20th-Fox 3006 (withdrawn).

SHE LEARNED ABOUT SAILORS (1934), Fox. B&W. Directed by George Marshall. With Alice Faye, Lew Ayres, Jack Durant, Frank Mitchell. Songs: "Here's the Key to My Heart," "She Learned About Sailors" (lyrics, Sidney Clare); plus songs by others. Soundtrack LP: excerpt only, in *The Classic Movie Musicals of Richard A. Whiting,* Music Masters JJA-19806; also, studio recording of song included in *Alice Faye in Hollywood (1934–1937),* CBS Special Products CL-3068.

365 NIGHTS IN HOLLYWOOD (1934), Fox. B&W. Directed by George Marshall. With Alice Faye, James Dunn, Jack Durant, Frank Mitchell, Dick Whiting. Songs: "Yes to You," "My Future Star" (lyrics, Sidney Clare); plus songs by others. LP: excerpt, included in *Alice Faye in Hollywood (1934–1937),* CBS Special Products CL-3068.

HANDY ANDY (1934), Fox. B&W. Directed by David Butler. With Will Rogers, Peggy Wood, Mary Carlisle. Song: "Roses in the Rain." (lyrics, Sidney Clare).

BACHELOR OF ARTS (1934), Fox. B&W. Directed by Louis King. With Anita Louise, Tom Brown, Arline Judge, Mae Marsh, Henry B. Walthall. Songs: "When the Last Year Rolls Around," "Phi Phi Phi"; plus songs by others.

CALL IT LUCK (1934), Fox. B&W. Directed by James Tinling. With Georgia Caine, Pat Patterson, Herbert Mundin. Songs: "I'll Bet on You" (lyrics, George Marion, Jr.); "A Merry Cheerio," "Drinking Song" (lyrics, Sidney Clare).

THE BIG BROADCAST OF 1936 (1935), Paramount. B&W. Directed by Norman Taurog. With Jack Oakie, George Burns, Gracie Allen, Lyda Roberti, Wendy Barrie, Bing Crosby, Ethel Merman, Bill Robinson, Ray Noble and his Orchestra, the Nicholas Brothers. Songs: "Miss Brown to You," "Through the Doorway Dreams I Saw You," "Armagura" (lyrics, Leo Robin); "Double Trouble," "Why Dream" (music-lyrics, Whiting, Ralph Rainger, Leo Robin); plus songs by others. Soundtrack LP: excerpt only, included in *The Classic Movie Musicals of Richard A. Whiting,* Music Masters JJA-19806.

HERE COMES COOKIE (1935), Paramount. B&W. Directed by William LeBaron. With Gracie Allen, George Burns, Betty Furness, George Barbier. Song: "Vamp of the Pampas" (lyrics, Leo Robin); plus songs by others.

CORONADO (1935), Paramount. B&W. Directed by Norman McLeod. With Betty Burgess, Johnny Downs, Jack Haley, Leon Errol, Alice White, Eddy Duchin and his Orchestra. Songs: "All's Well in Coronado By-the-Sea," "You Took My Breath Away," "How Do I Rate With You?," "Keep Your Fingers Crossed," "Midsummer Madness," "Down on the Beach at Oomph," "Mashed Potatoes" (lyrics, Sam Coslow); plus songs by others.

THE CRUSADES (1935), Paramount. B&W. Directed by Cecil B. DeMille. With Henry Wilcoxon, Loretta Young, Ian Keith, Katherine De-

Mille. Song: "Song of the Crusades" (collaboration with Rudolph Kopp; lyrics, Leo Robin).

ANYTHING GOES (1936), Paramount. B&W. Directed by Norman Taurog. With Bing Crosby, Ethel Merman, Charles Ruggles, Ida Lupino, Arthur Treacher. Song: "Sailor Beware" (lyrics, Leo Robin); plus songs by others. Soundtrack LP: included in *The Classic Movie Musicals of Richard A. Whiting,* Music Masters JJA-19806.

RHYTHM ON THE RANGE (1936), Paramount. B&W. Directed by Norman Taurog. With Bing Crosby, Frances Farmer, Martha Raye, Bob Burns. Songs: "I Can't Escape From You" (lyrics, Leo Robin); "Rhythm on the Range" (lyrics, Walter Bullock); plus songs by others.

SING, BABY, SING (1936), Twentieth Century-Fox. B&W. Directed by Sidney Lanfield. With Alice Faye, the Ritz Brothers, Adolphe Menjou, Patsy Kelly, Tony Martin, Ted Healy, Michael Whalen. Song: "When Did You Leave Heaven?" (lyrics, Walter Bullock); plus songs by others. Soundtrack LP: Caliban 6029 (with *Wabash Avenue*).

VARSITY SHOW (1937), Warner Brothers. B&W. Directed by William Keighley. With Dick Powell, Fred Waring and His Pennsylvanians, Rosemary Lane, Priscilla Lane, Ted Healy, Buck and Bubbles. Songs: "Have You Got Any Castles, Baby?," "We're Working Our Way Through College," "Old King Cole," "On With the Dance," "You've Got Something There," "Moonlight on the Campus," "Love Is on the Air Tonight," "Let That Be a Lesson to You," "When Your College Days Are Gone" (lyrics, Johnny Mercer).

READY, WILLING AND ABLE (1937), Warner Brothers. B&W. Directed by Ray Enright; production numbers directed by Bobby Connolly. With Ruby Keeler, Lee Dixon, Ross Alexander, Wini Shaw, Allen Kenkins, Louise Fazenda. Songs: "Too Marvelous for Words," "Sentimental and Melancholy," "Just a Quiet Evening," "Handy With Your Feet," "Ready, Willing and Able" (lyrics, Johnny Mercer). Soundtrack LP: excerpt only, included in *The Classic Movie Musicals of Richard A. Whiting,* Music Masters JJA-19806.

HOLLYWOOD HOTEL (1937), Warner Brothers. B&W. Directed by Busby Berkeley. With Dick Powell, Rosemary Lane, Lola Lane, Benny Goodman and his Orchestra, Louella Parsons, Glenda Farrell, Hugh Herbert, Frances Langford, Jerry Cooper, Raymond Paige and his Orchestra, Johnny "Scat" Davis, Edgar Kennedy. Songs: "Hooray for Hollywood," "Like a Fish Out of Water," "Let That Be a Lesson to You," "I've Hitched My Wagon to a Star," "Silhouetted in the Moonlight," "Sing You Son of a Gun" (lyrics, Johnny Mercer).

Soundtrack LP: EOH Records 99601; excerpts only, included in *Hooray for Hollywood,* United Artists LA361H, and *The Classic Movie Musicals of Richard A. Whiting,* Music Masters JJA-19806.

COWBOY FROM BROOKLYN (1938), Warner Brothers. B&W. Directed by Lloyd Bacon. With Dick Powell, Pat O'Brien, Priscilla Lane, Ann Sheridan, Dick Foran, Ronald Reagan. Songs: "Ride, Tenderfoot, Ride," "I'll Dream Tonight," "I've Got a Heartful of Music" (lyrics, Johnny Mercer); plus song by others.

RIDE, TENDERFOOT, RIDE (1940), Republic. B&W. Directed by Frank McDonald. With Gene Autry, Smiley Burnette, June Travis. Song: "Ride Tenderfoot, Ride" (lyrics, Johnny Mercer); plus songs by others.

SLEEPYTIME GAL (1942), Republic. B&W. Directed by Albert S. Rogell. With Judy Canova, Tom Brown, Ruth Terry, Elisha Cook Jr., Skinnay Ennis and his Orchestra. Song: "Sleepytime Gal" (collaboration with Ange Lorenzo, Joseph R. Alden); plus songs by others.

FOR ME AND MY GAL (1942), MGM. B&W. Directed by Busby Berkeley. With Judy Garland, Gene Kelly, George Murphy, Lucille Norman, Keenan Wynn, Richard Quine, Horace McNally. Song: "Till We Meet Again" (lyrics, Ray Egan); plus songs by others. Soundtrack LP: Soundtrak 107.

HELLO, FRISCO, HELLO (1943), Twentieth Century-Fox. Color. Directed by H. Bruce Humberstone. With Alice Faye, John Payne, Jack Oakie, June Havoc, Lynn Bari. Song: "It's Tulip Time in Holland" (lyrics, Dave Radford); plus songs by others.

NEVER A DULL MOMENT (1943), Universal. B&W. Directed by Edward Lilley. With the Ritz Brothers, Mary Beth Hughes, Frances Langford, Jack LaRue. Song: "Sleepytime Gal" (lyrics, Ray Egan, Joseph Alden); plus songs by others.

YOU CAN'T RATION LOVE (1944), Paramount. B&W. Directed by Lester Fuller. With Betty Rhodes, Johnny Johnston, Marie Wilson, Johnny "Scat" Davis, Marjorie Weaver, D'Artega and his All-Girl Orchestra. Song: "Louise" (lyrics, Leo Robin); plus songs by others.

SHINE ON HARVEST MOON (1944), Warner Brothers. B&W and Color. Directed by David Butler. With Ann Sheridan, Dennis Morgan, Irene Manning, Jack Carson, Marie Wilson, S. Z. Sakall. Song: "Breezin' Along With the Breeze" (lyrics, Haven Gillespie, Seymour B. Simons); plus songs by others.

FOLLOW THE BOYS (1944), Universal. B&W. Directed by Edward Sutherland. With George Raft, Vera Zorina, Grace McDonald, Regis Toomey; Dinah Shore, Jeanette MacDonald, Sophie Tucker, the Andrews Sisters, Marlene Dietrich, Orson Welles, Arthur Rubin-

stein, W. C. Fields, other guest stars. Song: "Beyond the Blue Horizon" (lyrics, Leo Robin, W. Franke Harling); plus songs by others.

EADIE WAS A LADY (1945), Columbia. B&W. Directed by Arthur Dreifuss. With Ann Miller, Joe Besser, William Wright, Marion Martin, Hal McIntyre and his Orchestra. Song: "Eadie Was a Lady" (music-lyrics, Whiting, Nacio Herb Brown, Buddy DeSylva); plus songs by others.

THE POSTMAN ALWAYS RINGS TWICE (1946), MGM. B&W. Directed by Tay Garnett. With Lana Turner, John Garfield, Hume Cronyn, Cecil Kellaway. Song: "She's Funny That Way" (lyrics, Neil Moret).

THE FABULOUS DORSEYS (1947), United Artists. B&W. Directed by Alfred E. Green. With Tommy and Jimmy Dorsey, Janet Blair, William Lundigan, Paul Whiteman, Bob Eberle, Helen O'Connell, Art Tatum, Henry Busse, Charlie Barnet. Song: "Waitin' at the Gate for Katie" (lyrics, Gus Kahn); plus songs by others. Videocassette: Republic.

APRIL SHOWERS (1948), Warner Brothers. Directed by James Kern. With Ann Sothern, Jack Carson, Robert Alda, S. Z. Sakall. Song: "It's Tulip Time in Holland" (lyrics, Dave Radford); plus songs by others.

YOU'RE MY EVERYTHING (1949), Twentieth Century-Fox. Color. Directed by Walter Lang. With Dan Dailey, Anne Baxter, Shari Robinson, Anne Revere, Buster Keaton. Song: "On the Good Ship Lollipop" (lyrics, Sidney Clare); plus songs by others.

YOUNG MAN WITH A HORN (1950), Warner Brothers. B&W. Directed by Michael Curtiz. With Kirk Douglas, Lauren Bacall, Doris Day, Hoagy Carmichael, Mary Beth Hughes, Nestor Paiva, Juano Hernandez. Song: "Too Marvelous for Words" (lyrics, Johnny Mercer); plus songs by others.

ON MOONLIGHT BAY (1951), Warner Brothers. Color. Directed by Roy Del Ruth. With Doris Day, Gordon MacRae, Jack Smith, Rosemary DeCamp, Leon Ames. Song: "Till We Meet Again" (lyrics, Ray Egan); plus songs by others.

MEET DANNY WILSON (1952), Universal International. B&W. Directed by Joseph Pevney. With Frank Sinatra, Shelley Winters, Alex Nichol. Song: "She's Funny That Way" (lyrics, Neil Moret); plus songs by others.

I'LL SEE YOU IN MY DREAMS (1952), Warner Brothers. Color. Directed by Michael Curtiz. With Doris Day, Danny Thomas, Frank Lovejoy, Patrice Wymore, Mary Wickes. Songs: "Ain't We Got Fun," "Ukelele Lady" (lyrics, Ray Egan); plus songs by others.

RAINBOW 'ROUND MY SHOULDER (1952), Columbia. Color. Directed by Richard

Quine. With Frankie Laine, Billy Daniels, Charlotte Austin, Ida Moore, Barbara Whiting. Song: "She's Funny That Way" (lyrics, Neil Moret); plus songs by others.

THE JAZZ SINGER (1953), Warner Brothers. Color. Directed by Michael Curtiz. With Danny Thomas, Peggy Lee, Mildred Dunnock, Eduard Franz. Song: "Breezin' Along With the Breeze" (lyrics, Seymour Simons, Haven Gillespie); plus songs by others.

BY THE LIGHT OF THE SILVERY MOON (1953), Warner Brothers. Color. Directed by David Butler. With Doris Day, Gordon MacRae, Leon Ames, Rosemary DeCamp, Mary Wickes. Song: "Ain't We Got Fun" (lyrics, Ray Egan); plus songs by others.

THE STOOGE (1953), Paramount. B&W. Directed by Norman Taurog. With Dean Martin, Jerry Lewis, Polly Bergen, Marion Marshall, Eddie Mayehoff. Song: "Louise" (lyrics, Leo Robin); plus songs by others.

THE EDDY DUCHIN STORY (1957), Columbia. Color. Directed by George Sidney. With Tyrone Power, Kim Novak, Victoria Shaw, James Whitmore, Larry Keating. Song: "Till We Meet Again" (lyrics, Ray Egan); plus

songs by others. LP: MCA VIM-7215 (featuring Carmen Cavallero, who dubbed the soundtrack piano).

THE HELEN MORGAN STORY (1958), Warner Brothers. B&W. Directed by Michael Curtiz. With Ann Blyth, Paul Newman, Richard Carlson, Alan King. Song: "Breezin' Along With the Breeze" (lyrics, Haven Gillespie, Seymour Simons); plus songs by others.

PEPE (1960), Columbia. Color. Directed by George Sidney. With Cantinflas, Shirley Jones, Edward G. Robinson, Ernie Kovacs, Matt Mattox, Sammy Davis Jr., Bing Crosby, Maurice Chevalier, Jimmy Durante, Andre Previn, Frank Sinatra, Debbie Reynolds, other guest stars. Song: "Hooray for Hollywood" (lyrics, Mercer); plus songs by others. Soundtrack LP: Colpix 507 (withdrawn).

THOROUGHLY MODERN MILLIE (1967), Universal. Color. Directed by George Roy Hill. With Julie Andrews, Mary Tyler Moore, Carol Channing, John Gavin, James Fox, Beatrice Lillie, Jack Soo. Song: "Japanese Sandman" (lyrics, Ray Egan); plus songs by others. Soundtrack LP: MCA DL-71500. Videocassette: MCA.

And Not To Be Forgotten: Nacio Herb Brown
Hoagy Carmichael
Frank Loesser
Arthur Schwartz
Jule Styne
James Van Heusen

Nacio Herb Brown

Frank Loesser

Arthur Schwartz

Jule Styne

James Van Heusen with Bing Crosby

*I*n addition to the ten great songwriting composers chronicled in the foregoing chapters, there are other musical giants who have contributed memorable songs to movies over the years. They even include a couple of my personal favorites, such as Arthur Schwartz and James Van Heusen, as well as some that I'm sure are favorites of others.

But I believe their work for the movies, in most cases, has not been as notable in overall quality, variety, scope, or historical significance as that of the foregoing ten. That is not to say, however, that some of their individual songs haven't been outstanding—and durable. In particular, the six composers discussed briefly in this last chapter cannot be overlooked—they are indeed great songwriters, and their songs grace many well-known movies still in circulation.

Nacio Herb Brown

Nacio Herb Brown (1896–1964) won his place among Hollywood's top composers partly by the luck of just being *in* Hollywood at the start of the talkie era and partly by the talent he showed for writing hit songs for some of the first major movie musicals.

Although born in Deming, New Mexico, he grew up primarily in Los Angeles where his father was county sheriff. Brown attended L.A.'s Musical Arts High School but then dropped out of the University of California to work as a piano accompanist for vaudevillian Alice Doll. A year later he gave that up to go into the custom-tailoring business, catering mostly to silent-movie stars. His business was such a success that he began investing its profits in Hollywood real estate. He continued to compose on the side, and prevailed upon area hotel bandleaders to play some of his music in exchange for custom-made suits.

MGM's production chief, Irving Thalberg, heard and liked some of Brown's songs and when MGM made the plunge into talkies he signed Brown for the studio's first all-sound musical, *The Broadway Melody* (1929). With Arthur Freed as lyricist, Brown composed six songs for that movie, three of which became hits: "You Were Meant for Me," "The Wedding of the Painted Doll," and "Broadway Melody." The picture itself broke attendance records nationwide for MGM and won the 1929 Academy Award for Best Picture.

Later that same year Brown and Freed wrote the songs "Singin' in the Rain" and "You Were Meant for Me" for MGM's *Hollywood Revue*. They became such smash hits that MGM convinced Brown to give up his other businesses and work full-time for the studio. For the rest of the decade, Brown and Freed turned out some of the '30s' most popular movie songs—including "Should I?" (from *Lord Byron of Broadway,*

Nacio Herb Brown's and Arthur Freed's "You Stepped Out of a Dream" was the appropriately-titled big production number of MGM's 1941 Ziegfeld Girl *with (in front, left to right) Lana Turner, Hedy Lamarr, and Judy Garland.*

1930), "Temptation" and "We'll Make Hay While the Sun Shines" (from *Going Hollywood,* 1933), "All I Do Is Dream of You" (from *Sadie McKee,* 1934), "Alone" (from *A Night at the Opera,* 1935), "Would You?" (from *San Francisco,* 1936), and "You Stepped Out of a Dream" (from *Ziegfeld Girl,* 1941), among others.

Broadway Melody of 1936 remains Brown's best '30s score—just as the movie itself is easily the best of MGM's *Broadway Melody* series. Like so many '30s musicals, the story line of this one (by Moss Hart, no less) stretches credibility about as far as it can. Yet the MGM production is mounted so handsomely, the songs are so good, and a well-chosen cast pitches in so spiritedly that you can't help but enjoy it. Eleanor Powell plays a stagestruck former small-town girlfriend of a big Broadway producer (Robert Taylor). When he refuses to give her a job, she and a wisecracking columnist (Jack Benny) plot revenge. They fool him into believing she's a French star, La Belle Arlette, fresh off the boat. Powell never was the subtlest of actresses and her French accent and disguise wouldn't fool even the densest backwoods producer, but she certainly could dance—and she tears up the soundstage for the "Broadway Rhythm" finale. Both

Kitty Carlisle and Allan Jones make it clear to opera impresario Sig Rumann that they want to be alone—mostly to sing Brown's and Freed's "Alone" in 1935's A Night at the Opera, *for which the songwriting team provided the musical interludes surrounding the Marx Brothers' hijinks.*

Powell and radio songstress Frances Langford get to sing one of the most memorable of all Brown-Freed ballads, "You Are My Lucky Star." But perhaps the biggest surprise comes with Robert Taylor's quite-decent singing (his own voice, too) of "I've Got a Feeling You're Fooling" with blonde vamp June Knight.

In the 1940s, as Freed became one of MGM's top producers, Brown returned to the real-estate business and moved for a time to Mexico. He continued to write an occasional movie score for MGM and Twentieth Century-Fox—including several with lyricist Leo Robin (for Sonja Henie's *Wintertime,* 1943, and Carmen Miranda's *Greenwich Village,* 1946), and one with Edward Heyman and Earl Brent (for Frank Sinatra's *The Kissing Bandit,* 1948). However, no major hits emerged from any of them.

Although Brown, in effect, had retired from writing for the movies by the end of the '40s, he will always be best remembered for the 1952 musical that recycled some of his late-'20s and early-'30s songs and took its title from one of them: MGM's *Singin' in the Rain.* This classic understandably heads quite a few critics' lists of all-time greatest movie musicals—and, for me, it vies with 1935's *Top Hat* for the No. 1 spot among originals in the genre. Lyricist-turned-producer Arthur Freed not only serves up some great songs (the cream of the Brown-Freed catalog) but also bright, lively orchestrations by Conrad Salinger and Skip Martin, terrific dances codirected by Gene Kelly and Stanley Donen, a clever, witty book by Betty Comden and Adolph Green that spoofs film musicals themselves, and a wonderful cast in peak form: Kelly, Donald O'Connor, Debbie Reynolds, Cyd Charisse, and the unforgettable Jean Hagen.

"Singin' in the Rain" has been featured in at least four major musicals since 1929, but no treatment has been more unique than Gene Kelly's puddle-prancing version in the 1952 musical to which it gave its name.

Fully sixty of *Singin' in the Rain*'s 103 minutes' running time are given over to musical numbers. The title number, of course, has become one of the most famous of all movie-musical numbers, as a love-happy Kelly sloshes and frolics his way through a downpour, singing and dancing his heart out. Kelly, O'Connor, and Reynolds also sing and dance "Good Mornin', Good Morning" with such sunny brio that they convert that fairly routine song (written for the first musical that Freed produced for MGM in 1939, the partly Rodgers and Hart *Babes in Arms*) into another of the picture's highlights. Also memorable is the warmly tender *pas de deux* that Kelly and Reynolds perform on an empty soundstage to "You Were Meant for Me." Brown's "Broadway Rhythm" and "Broadway Melody" also form the musical basis for the film's big, splashily colorful, deliberately hokey, fifteen-minute "Broadway Ballet," highlighted by as sultry a *pas de deux* as Kelly and Charisse ever danced.

Brown composed one new song with Freed for *Singin' in the Rain,* the rollicking "Make 'Em Laugh," which provides O'Connor with one of his all-time great song-and-dance routines. It turned out to be the last song the team would write together, and it came about only because Donen could not find anything else in the Brown-Freed catalog that he thought suitable for a sequence in which O'Connor tries to cheer up Kelly. When Donen asked for something on the order of Cole Porter's "Be a Clown" from *The Pirate* (1948), Freed and Brown took him literally and turned out a number that comes close to outright plagiarism of Porter's song—which at that time was not too well known, since *The Pirate* had not been all that successful in its original release. According to Hugh Fordin in his superb account of the Freed Unit in *The World of Entertainment,* Donen later admitted that "none of us had the courage to say to [Freed] it obviously works for the number but it's a stolen song, Arthur." Fordin also discreetly notes that "only a man of Cole Porter's tact and distinction would have chosen to ignore the existence of that song."

In any case, "Make 'Em Laugh" marks something of an inglorious finale, musically speaking, to Brown's impressive career as a pioneer songwriter for movie musicals. But the rest of *Singin' in the Rain* still assures him of a lasting place among Hollywood's top songwriters.

NACIO HERB BROWN'S MOVIES AND SONGS ON TAPE AND DISC

THE BROADWAY MELODY (1929), MGM. B&W. Directed by Harry Beaumont. With Bessie Love, Anita Paige, Charles King, James Burroughs. Songs: "You Were Meant for Me," "Broadway Melody," "The Wedding of the Painted Doll," "Love Boat," "Boy Friend" (lyrics, Arthur Freed); plus songs by others. Soundtrack LP: excerpts in Radiola BMPM-1929, with *Parisian Belle.*

HOLLYWOOD REVUE (1929), MGM. B&W. Directed by Charles F. Reisner. With Jack Benny, Marion Davies, Norma Shearer, John Gilbert, Joan Crawford, Marie Dressler, Polly Moran, Stan Laurel, Oliver Hardy, Bessie Love, Charles King, the Brox Sisters, Buster Keaton, Cliff Edwards. Songs: "Singin' in the Rain," "Tommy Atkins on Parade," "You Were Meant for Me" (lyrics, Arthur Freed); plus songs by others. Soundtrack LP: excerpts included in *The Classic Movie Musicals of Nacio Herb Brown (1929–39),* Music Masters JJA 19802.

MARIANNE (1929), MGM. B&W. Directed by Robert Z. Leonard. With Marion Davies, Lawrence Gray, Cliff Edwards, Oscar Shaw, Benny Rubin. Song: "Blondy" (lyrics, Arthur Freed); plus songs by others.

THE PAGAN (1929), MGM. B&W. Directed by W. S. Van Dyke. With Ramon Novarro, Renee Adoree, Dorothy Janis, Donald Crisp. Song: "Pagan Love Song" (lyrics, Arthur Freed).

UNTAMED (1929), MGM. B&W. Directed by Jack Conway. With Joan Crawford, Robert Montgomery, Ernest Torrence, John Miljan. Songs: "Chant of the Jungle" (lyrics, Arthur Freed); plus songs by others.

LORD BYRON OF BROADWAY (1929), MGM. B&W and Color. Directed by William Nigh and Harry Beaumont. With Ethelind Terry, Charles Kaley, Cliff Edwards, Gwen Lee. Songs: "Should I?," "A Bundle of Old Love Letters," "The Woman in the Shoe," "Only Love Is Real," "When I Met You" (lyrics, Arthur Freed); plus songs by others.

THE SHOW OF SHOWS (1929), Warner Brothers. B&W and Color. Directed by John Adolfi. With Frank Fay, Winnie Lightner, Beatrice Lillie, Louise Fazenda, Nick Lucas, Myrna Loy, Loretta Young, Sally Blane, Richard Barthelmess, Douglas Fairbanks Jr., John Barrymore, Noah Beery, Ben Turpin, Chester Conklin, other guest stars. Song: "You Were Meant for Me" (lyrics, Arthur Freed); plus songs by others.

MONTANA MOON (1930), MGM. B&W. Directed by Mal St. Clair. With Joan Crawford, Johnny Mack Brown, Cliff Edwards, Benny Rubin. Songs: "The Moon Is Low," "Happy Cowboy" (lyrics, Arthur Freed); plus songs by others.

GOOD NEWS (1930), MGM. B&W. Directed by Nick Grinde. With Bessie Love, Mary Lawlor, Stanley Smith, Cliff Edwards, Lola Lane, Dorothy McNulty, Al "Rubberlegs" Norman. Songs: "If You're Not Kissing Me," "Football" (lyrics, Arthur Freed); plus songs by others.

ONE HEAVENLY NIGHT (1930), Samuel Goldwyn-United Artists. B&W. Directed by George Fitzmaurice. With Evelyn Laye, John Boles, Lilyan Tashman, Leon Errol, Marion Lord. Song: "Heavenly Night" (lyrics, Edward Eliscu); plus songs by others.

A WOMAN COMMANDS (1932), MGM. B&W. Directed by Paul L. Stein. With Pola Negri, Basil Rathbone, Roland Young, H. B. Warner. Song: "Paradise" (lyrics, Gordon Clifford).

TAKE A CHANCE (1933), Paramount. B&W. Directed by Laurence Schwab and Monte Brice. With James Dunn, June Knight, Lillian Roth, Cliff Edwards, Charles "Buddy" Rogers. Songs: "Turn Out the Light," "Eadie Was a Lady" (collaboration: Richard Whiting, B. G. DeSylva, Brown); plus songs by others.

GOING HOLLYWOOD (1933), MGM. B&W. Directed by Raoul Walsh. With Marion Davies, Bing Crosby, Fifi D'Orsay, Patsy Kelly, Stuart Erwin, Ned Sparks. Songs: "Temptation," "We'll Make Hay While the Sun Shines," "Our Big Love Scene," "After Sundown," "Beautiful Girl," "Cinderella's Fella," "After Sundown" (lyrics, Arthur Freed); plus songs by others. Soundtrack LP: excerpts included in *The Classic Movie Musicals of Nacio Herb Brown (1929–39),* Music Masters JJA 19802; also, Caliban 6039 (with *Too Much Harmony* and *Best Foot Forward*); also, excerpt also included in *That's Entertainment,* MCA 2-11002.

DANCING LADY (1933), MGM. B&W. Directed by Robert Z. Leonard. With Joan Crawford, Clark Gable, Franchot Tone, May Robson, Winnie Lightner, Fred Astaire, Eunice Quedens (Eve Arden), Nelson Eddy, Robert Benchley. Song: "Hold Your Man" (lyrics, Arthur Freed); plus songs by others.

THE BARBARIAN (1933), MGM. B&W. Directed by Sam Wood. With Ramon Novarro, Myrna Loy, Reginald Denny, Edward Arnold, C. Aubrey Smith. Song: "Love Songs of the Nile" (lyrics, Arthur Freed).

STAGE MOTHER (1933), MGM. B&W. Directed by Charles R. Brabin. With Alice Brady, Maureen O'Sullivan, Franchot Tone, Phillips Holmes. Songs: "I'm Dancing on a Rainbow," "Beautiful Girl" (lyrics, Arthur Freed).

HOLD YOUR MAN (1933), MGM. B&W. Directed by Sam Wood. With Jean Harlow, Clark Gable, Dorothy Burgess, Stuart Erwin. Song: "Hold Your Man" (lyrics, Arthur Freed).

PEG O' MY HEART (1933), MGM. B&W. Directed by Robert Z. Leonard. With Marion Davies, Onslow Stevens, Alan Mowbray. Song: "I'll Remember Only You" (lyrics, Arthur Freed); plus songs by others.

HOLLYWOOD PARTY (1934), MGM. B&W and Color. Directed by Roy Rowland, others uncredited. With Jimmy Durante, Polly Moran, Stan Laurel, Oliver Hardy, Lupe Velez, Frances Williams, Shirley Ross, Ted Healy and the Three Stooges. Song: "Hot Chocolate Soldiers" (lyrics, Arthur Freed), for the Disney sequence removed when rights reverted to Disney; plus songs by others.

STUDENT TOUR (1934), MGM. B&W. Directed by Charles Reisner. With Jimmy Durante, Maxine Doyle, Charles Butterworth, Phil Regan, Florence McKinney, Betty Grable, Monte Blue, Herman Brix. Songs: "A New

Moon Is Over My Shoulder," "From Now On," "Fight 'Em," "The Carlo" (lyrics, Arthur Freed); plus songs by others.

HIDEOUT (1934), MGM. B&W. Directed by W. S. Van Dyke. With Robert Montgomery, Maureen O'Sullivan, Edward Arnold, Mickey Rooney. Song: "The Dream Was So Beautiful" (lyrics, Arthur Freed).

SADIE MCKEE (1934), MGM. B&W. Directed by Clarence Brown. With Joan Crawford, Franchot Tone, Gene Raymond, Edward Arnold, Gene Austin. Songs: "All I Do Is Dream of You," "Please Make Me Care" (lyrics, Arthur Freed); plus songs by others.

A NIGHT AT THE OPERA (1935), MGM. B&W. Directed by Dudley Murphy. With Groucho, Chico, and Harpo Marx, Kitty Carlisle, Allan Jones, Margaret Dumont, Sig Rumann, Walter Woolf King. Song: "Alone" (lyrics, Arthur Freed); plus songs and arias by others. Videocassette: MGM/UA.

CHINA SEAS (1935), MGM. B&W. Directed by Tay Garnett. With Jean Harlow, Clark Gable, Wallace Beery, Rosalind Russell, Lewis Stone, Robert Benchley. Song: "China Seas" (lyrics, Arthur Freed).

BROADWAY MELODY OF 1936 (1935), MGM. B&W. Directed by Roy Del Ruth. With Robert Taylor, Eleanor Powell, Jack Benny, Una Merkel, Frances Langford, June Knight, Sid Silvers. Songs: "You Are My Lucky Star," "Sing Before Breakfast," "I've Gotta Feelin' You're Foolin'," "On a Sunday Afternoon," "Broadway Rhythm" (lyrics, Arthur Freed). Soundtrack LP: excerpt included in *The Classic Movie Musicals of Nacio Herb Brown (1929–39),* Music Masters JJA 19802; except in *That's Entertainment, Part Two,* MCA MGI-5301.

AFTER THE THIN MAN (1936), MGM. B&W. Directed by W. S. Van Dyke. With William Powell, Myrna Loy, James Stewart, Elissa Landi, Joseph Calleia, Dorothy McNulty. Song: "Smoke Dreams" (lyrics, Arthur Freed); plus songs by others.

SAN FRANCISCO (1936), MGM. B&W. Directed by W. S. Van Dyke. With Clark Gable, Jeanette MacDonald, Spencer Tracy, Jack Holt, Shirley Ross. Song: "Would You?" (lyrics, Arthur Freed); plus songs and arias by others. Videocassette: MGM/UA.

THOROUGHBREDS DON'T CRY (1937), MGM. B&W. Directed by Alfred E. Green. With Mickey Rooney, Judy Garland, Sophie Tucker, Frankie Darro, C. Aubrey Smith. Songs: "Got a Pair of New Shoes," "Sun Showers" (lyrics, Arthur Freed).

BROADWAY MELODY OF 1938 (1937), MGM. B&W. Directed by Roy Del Ruth. With Robert Taylor, Eleanor Powell, George Murphy, Judy Garland, Sophie Tucker, Buddy Ebsen, Robert Benchley, Igor Gorin, Willie

Howard. Songs: "Broadway Rhythm," "I'm Feeling Like a Million," "Your Broadway and My Broadway," "Got a Pair of New Shoes," "Yours and Mine" (lyrics, Arthur Freed). Soundtrack LP: Motion Picture Tracks International MPT-3; also, excerpt included in *The Classic Movie Musicals of Nacio Herb Brown (1927–39)*, Music Masters JJA 19802; excerpt in *That's Entertainment*, MCA 2-11002.

BABES IN ARMS (1939), MGM. B&W. Directed by Busby Berkeley. With Mickey Rooney, Judy Garland, Charles Winninger, June Preisser, Guy Kibbee, Grace Hayes. Songs: "Broadway Rhythm," "Good Morning," "You Are My Lucky Star" (lyrics, Arthur Freed); plus songs by others. Soundtrack LP: Sandy Hook SH-2077; also, Curtain Calls 100/6-7 (with *Babes on Broadway*). Videocassette: MGM/UA.

ICE FOLLIES OF 1939 (1939), MGM. B&W. Directed by Rheinhold Schunzel. With Joan Crawford, James Stewart, Lew Ayres, Lional Stander. Song: "Something's Gotta Happen Soon" (lyrics, Arthur Freed); plus songs by others.

LITTLE NELLIE KELLY (1940), MGM. B&W. Directed by Norman Taurog. With Judy Garland, George Murphy, Charles Winninger, Douglas MacPhail. Song: "Singin' in the Rain" (lyrics, Arthur Freed); plus songs by others. Soundtrack LP: excerpt included in *That's Entertainment*, MCA 2-11002.

TWO GIRLS ON BROADWAY (1940), MGM. B&W. Directed by S. Sylvan Simon. With Lana Turner, Joan Blondell, George Murphy, Kent Taylor, Wallace Ford. Song: "My Wonderful One, Let's Dance" (collaboration: Brown, Arthur Freed, Roger Edens); plus songs by others.

HULLABALOO (1940), MGM. B&W. Directed by Edwin L. Marin. With Frank Morgan, Virginia Grey, Dan Dailey Jr., Billie Burke. Song: "You Were Meant for Me" (lyrics, Arthur Freed); plus songs by others.

ANDY HARDY MEETS DEBUTANTE (1940), MGM. B&W. Directed by George B. Seitz. With Mickey Rooney, Lewis Stone, Judy Garland, Ann Rutherford, Fay Holden, Cecilia Parker. Song: "Alone" (lyrics, Arthur Freed); plus songs by others.

ZIEGFELD GIRL (1941), MGM. B&W. Directed by Robert Z. Leonard. With James Stewart, Judy Garland, Hedy Lamarr, Lana Turner, Tony Martin, Charles Winninger, Jackie Cooper, Eve Arden, Al Shean, Edward Everett Horton. Song: "You Stepped Out of a Dream" (lyrics, Gus Kahn); plus songs by others.

BORN TO SING (1942), MGM. B&W. Directed by Edward Ludwig. With Virginia Weidler, Ray McDonald, Leo Gorcey, Rags Ragland, Douglas MacPhail, Darla Hood. Songs: "Alone," "You Are My Lucky Star" (lyr-

ics, Arthur Freed); plus songs by others.

PRESENTING LILY MARS (1943), MGM. B&W. Directed by Norman Taurog. With Judy Garland, Van Heflin, Richard Carlson, Fay Bainter, Martha Eggerth, Tommy Dorsey and his Orchestra, Bob Crosby and his Orchestra. Song: "Broadway Rhythm" (lyrics, Arthur Freed); plus songs by others. Soundtrack LP: Soundtrak STS-117.

THOUSANDS CHEER (1943), MGM. Color. Directed by George Sidney. With Kathryn Grayson, Gene Kelly, Mary Astor, John Boles; Mickey Rooney, Lena Horne, June Allyson, Gloria DeHaven, Virginia O'Brien, Eleanor Powell, Red Skelton, Judy Garland, Jose Iturbi, Lucille Ball, Ann Sothern, Kay Kyser and his Orchestra, Bob Crosby and his Orchestra, other guest stars. Song: "Should I?" (lyrics, Arthur Freed); plus songs by others. Soundtrack LP: Hollywood Soundstage HS-409. Videocassette: MGM/UA.

SWING FEVER (1943), MGM. B&W. Directed by Tim Whelan. With Kay Kyser, Marilyn Maxwell, Lena Horne, William Gargan, Tommy Dorsey, Harry James. Song: "One Girl and Two Boys" (lyrics, Arthur Freed); plus songs by others.

WINTERTIME (1943), Twentieth Century-Fox. B&W. Directed by John Braham. With Sonja Henie, Cornel Wilde, Jack Oakie, Carole Landis, Cesar Romero, Woody Herman and his Orchestra. Songs: "Wintertime," "Later Tonight," "I Like It Here," "All A-Twitter Over You," "Dancing in the Dawn" (lyrics, Leo Robin).

TWO GIRLS AND A SAILOR (1944), MGM. B&W. Directed by Richard Thorpe. With Van Johnson, June Allyson, Gloria DeHaven, Jimmy Durante, Jose Iturbi, Gracie Allen, Lena Horne, Ben Blue, Harry James and his Orchestra, Xavier Cugat and his Orchestra. Song: "My Wonderful One, Let's Dance" (collaboration: Brown, Arthur Freed, Roger Edens); plus songs by others.

GREENWICH VILLAGE (1944), Twentieth Century-Fox. Color. Directed by Walter Lang. With Carmen Miranda, Don Ameche, Vivian Blaine, William Bendix, Tony and Sally DeMarco. Songs: "Could It Be You?," "Give Me a Band and a Bandana," "It's All for Art's Sake," "It Goes to Your Toes," "Our Lucky Day," "Down to My Last Dream," "Oh, Brother!" "I Have to See You Privately," "You Make Me So Mad," "I've Been Smiling in My Sleep," "That Thing They Talk About," "Never Before" (lyrics, Leo Robin); plus songs by others.

MEET ME IN SAINT LOUIS (1944), MGM. Color. Directed by Vincente Minnelli. With Judy Garland, Margaret O'Brien, Mary Astor, Marjorie Main, Tom Drake, Leon Ames, Lucille

Bremer. Song: "You and Me" (lyrics, Arthur Freed); plus songs by others. Videocassette and videodisc: MGM/UA.

NIGHT CLUB GIRL (1944), Universal. B&W. Directed by Edward Cline. With Vivian Austin, Edward Norris, Judy Clark, Maxie Rosenbloom, the Delta Rhythm Boys. Song: "Pagan Love Song" (lyrics, Arthur Freed); plus songs by others.

HI BEAUTIFUL (1944), Universal. B&W. Directed by Leslie Goodwins. With Martha O'Driscoll, Noah Beery Jr., Hattie McDaniel, Walter Catlett. Song: "Singin' in the Rain" (lyrics, Arthur Freed); plus songs by others.

EADIE WAS A LADY (1945), Columbia. B&W. Directed by Arthur Dreifuss. With Ann Miller, Joe Besser, Jeff Donnell, William Wright, Hal McIntyre and his Orchestra. Song: "Eadie Was a Lady" (collaboration: Brown, Richard Whiting, Buddy DeSylva); plus songs by others.

HOLIDAY IN MEXICO (1946), MGM. Color. Directed by George Sidney. With Walter Pidgeon, Jane Powell, Ilona Massey, Roddy McDowall, Jose Iturbi, Xavier Cugat and his Orchestra, Ampara Iturbi, Linda Christian. Song: "You (So It's You)" (lyrics, Earl Brent); plus songs by others.

YOU WERE MEANT FOR ME (1948), Twentieth Century-Fox. Color. Directed by Lloyd Bacon. With Jeanne Crain, Dan Dailey, Oscar Levant, Barbara Lawrence, Harry Barris, Percy Kilbride. Song: "You Were Meant for Me" (lyrics, Arthur Freed); plus songs by others.

ON AN ISLAND WITH YOU (1948), MGM. Color. Directed by Richard Thorpe. With Esther Williams, Peter Lawford, Jimmy Durante, Cyd Charisse, Xavier Cugat and his Orchestra. Songs: "On an Island With You," "Buenos Noches, Buenos Aires," "Taking Miss Mary to the Ball," "If I Were You," "The Dog Song" (lyrics, Edward Heyman); plus songs by others.

THE KISSING BANDIT (1948), MGM. Color. Directed by Laszlo Benedek. With Kathryn Grayson, Frank Sinatra, Ann Miller, Ricardo Montalban, Cyd Charisse, Sono Osato, Mildred Natwick: Songs: "Love Is Where You Find It" (lyrics, Earl Brent); "If I Steal a Kiss," "Señorita," "Tomorrow Means Romance," "What's Wrong With Me?," "Siesta," "I Like You (Whip Dance)" (collaboration: Brown, Earl Brent, Edward Heyman).

A DATE WITH JUDY (1948), MGM. Color. Directed by Richard Thorpe. With Wallace Beery, Jane Powell, Elizabeth Taylor, Carmen Miranda, Robert Stack. Song: "Temptation" (lyrics, Arthur Freed); plus songs by others.

MALAYA (1949), MGM. B&W. Directed by Richard Thorpe. With Spencer Tracy, James Stewart, Valentina Cortesa, Lionel Barrymore, Sydney Greenstreet. Song: "Temptation" (lyrics,

Arthur Freed); plus songs by others.

THE BRIBE (1949), MGM. B&W. Directed by Robert Z. Leonard. With Robert Taylor, Ava Gardner, Charles Laughton, Vincent Price, John Hodiak. Song: "Situation Wanted" (lyrics, William Kantz).

THREE LITTLE WORDS (1950), MGM. Color. Directed by Richard Thorpe. With Fred Astaire, Red Skelton, Vera-Ellen, Arlene Dahl, Keenan Wynn, Debbie Reynolds, Gloria DeHaven, Gale Robbins, Phil Regan. Song: "You Are My Lucky Star" (lyrics, Arthur Freed); plus songs by others.

PAGAN LOVE SONG (1950), MGM. Color. Directed by Robert Alton. With Esther Williams, Howard Keel, Rita Moreno, Minna Gombell, Charles Mau. Song: "Pagan Love Song" (lyrics, Arthur Freed); plus songs by others. Videocassette: MGM/UA.

WITH A SONG IN MY HEART (1952), Twentieth Century-Fox. Color. Directed by Walter Lang. With Susan Hayward, Rory Calhoun, David Wayne, Thelma Ritter, Robert Wagner. Song: "I've Got a Feeling You're Fooling" (lyrics, Arthur Freed); plus songs by others.

SINGIN' IN THE RAIN (1952), MGM. Color. Directed by Gene Kelly and Stanley Donen. With Gene Kelly, Debbie Reynolds, Donald O'Connor, Jean Hagen, Millard Mitchell, Cyd Charisse. Songs: "Singin' in the Rain," "All I Do Is Dream of You," "You Were Meant for Me," "Would You?," "Should I?," "You Are My Lucky Star," "Good Morning, Good Morning," "I've Got a Feeling You're Fooling," "The Wedding of the Painted Doll," "Fit As a Fiddle and Ready for Love," "Make 'Em Laugh" (lyrics, Arthur Freed); plus songs by others. Soundtrack LP: MCA 39044; excerpts included in *That's Entertainment,* MCA 2-11002. Videocassette and videodisc: MGM/UA.

THE AFFAIRS OF DOBIE GILLIS (1953), MGM. B&W. Directed by Don Weis. With Debbie Reynolds, Bobby Van, Lurene Tuttle, Bob Fosse, Barbara Ruick, Hans Conreid. Song: "All I Do Is Dream of You" (lyrics, Arthur Freed); plus songs by others.

THE SEVEN HILLS OF ROME (1958), MGM. Color. Directed by Roy Rowland. With Mario Lanza, Peggie Castle, Maria Alassio, Renato Rascel. Song: "Temptation" (lyrics, Arthur Freed); plus songs by others.

THE FIVE PENNIES (1959), Paramount. Color. Directed by Melville Shavelson. With Danny Kaye, Barbara Bel Geddes, Tuesday Weld, Louis Armstrong, Bob Crosby, Shelly Manne, Bobby Troup, Ray Anthony. Song: "Paradise" (lyrics, Gordon Clifford); plus songs by others.

THE BOY FRIEND (1971), EMI-MGM. Color. Directed by Ken Russell. With Twiggy, Christopher Gable, Glenda Jackson, Max Adrian,

Georgina Hale, Tommy Tune. Songs: "All I Do Is Dream of You," "You Were Meant for Me" (lyrics, Arthur Freed); plus songs by others.
NEW YORK, NEW YORK (1977), United Artists. Color. Directed by Martin Scorsese.

With Robert DeNiro, Liza Minnelli, Lionel Stander, Mary Kay Place, Georgie Auld. Song: "You Are My Lucky Star" (lyrics, Arthur Freed); plus songs by others. Videocassette and disc: CBS/Fox (restored version).

Hoagy Carmichael

Although his biggest song hits were not written for the movies, Hoagy Carmichael spent a major part of the 1930s and 1940s under contract to Paramount Pictures as a songwriter, and then appeared as an actor as well as writing songs for a number of major hits of the '40s and '50s, including *To Have and Have Not* (1944), *The Best Years of Our Lives* (1946), *Canyon Passage* (1946), *Young Man With a Horn* (1950), and *Las Vegas Story* (1952).

Hoagland Howard Carmichael (1899–1981) was born in Bloomington, Indiana, and learned to play the piano as a youngster, mostly through his mother, the pianist in a local silent-movie theater. He dropped out of high school at age sixteen to take odd jobs, but four years later he went back to complete his schooling and then went on to the University of Indiana, intent on becoming a lawyer. Carmichael helped support himself by playing in jazz bands for college dances and private parties. He also began writing tunes for the bands. One of them, "Riverboat Shuffle," was heard and then recorded by Bix Beiderbecke's Wolverines and was soon afterward picked up and recorded by Paul Whiteman's Orchestra too.

Carmichael earned his law degree in 1926 and moved to Florida to begin his practice. But an invitation from Whiteman to be part of a recording of Carmichael's "Washboard Blues" permanently sidetracked his legal career. Whiteman had heard an amateur recording of the tune with Carmichael at the piano, and he wanted him to repeat the solo on the new recording. During rehearsals, Whiteman asked about a vocal and Hoagy obliged him by singing a chorus. As Carmichael expressed it in his autobiographical memoir, *The Star Dust Road:* "I did the number the best my wheezy voice would permit." Whiteman decided Carmichael should be both vocalist and pianist for the recording. But, just to be on the safe side, Whiteman privately assigned one of his band's new singers, a then-unknown Bing Crosby, to learn the song and be ready to step in if the recording didn't go well. Crosby never got to make that recording, and Carmichael's own twangy, raspy sound was soon on its way to becoming moderately famous. Crosby and Carmichael, meanwhile, became good friends and, later, frequent movie and radio collaborators.

For the rest of the '20s and the early '30s, Carmichael played piano and sang with the jazz orchestras of Don Redman and Jean Goldkette. He also composed such songs

as "Rockin' Chair," "Lazy River," "Georgia on My Mind," and his biggest hit of all, "Star Dust." Several times he sought Hollywood jobs, without success. Then, partly through Bing Crosby's intercession, he was hired by Paramount in 1935 to write a song for Crosby to interpolate into the film version of Cole Porter's *Anything Goes*. The song, "Moonburn" (with lyrics by Edward Heyman), is a casually perky ballad that Crosby sings as he flirts with a very young, blonde Ida Lupino, but it was soon forgotten after the picture's release.

A bigger impression resulted from the one song that Carmichael contributed to the 1936 Broadway revue *The Show Is On,* starring Beatrice Lillie and Bert Lahr. Carmichael's "Little Old Lady" managed to become the show's big song hit against competition within the show from songs by George and Ira Gershwin, Richard Rodgers and Lorenz Hart, Harold Arlen and Yip Harburg, and Vernon Duke and Ted Fetter. It led to Paramount's inviting Carmichael back to Hollywood. Over the next few years—working with such lyricists as Leo Robin, Frank Loesser, Sam Coslow, Ned Washington, and Stanley Adams—he wrote "Jubilee" for Mae West's *Every Day's a Holiday,* "Small Fry" for Crosby's *Sing You Sinners,* "The Nearness of You" for Gladys Swarthout's *Romance in the Dark,* "Two Sleepy People" for Bob Hope and Shirley Ross's *Thanks for the Memory,* and "Heart and Soul" for Hope and Ross's *Some Like It Hot,* among other wonderful songs. He also made his on-screen debut in Hal Roach's hit comedy *Topper,* playing and singing his own "Old Man Moon" in a saloon sequence with Cary Grant and Constance Bennett.

During the 1940s Carmichael increasingly combined acting with composing, usually playing droll, slow-speaking, Hoosier-type characters in movies and on radio and TV, and usually singing at least one of his own songs. Perhaps the quintessential

Carmichael is to be seen and heard in *To Have and Have Not* (1944), Howard Hawks's classic version of one of Ernest Hemingway's lesser adventure stories, rewritten and updated by William Faulkner and Jules Furthman to a World War II setting in Martinique. Carmichael plays a pianist in a grubby waterfront saloon, in which much of the action takes place. In addition to singing his own "Hong Kong Blues," he also accompanies Lauren Bacall (in her movie debut and her first teaming with Humphrey Bogart) as she sings his "How Little We Know" (lyrics by Johnny Mercer). Bacall's smoky-voiced purring of the song, incidentally, was dubbed by—of all people—a teenage Andy Williams.

Carmichael won an Academy Award nomination in 1946 for "Ol' Buttermilk Sky" from *Canyon Passage* (but lost to Harry Warren and Johnny Mercer's "On the Atchison, Topeka and Santa Fe" from *The Harvey Girls*). He won an Oscar five years later, for "In the Cool, Cool, Cool of the Evening" (lyrics by Mercer) from Bing Crosby's *Here Comes the Groom*.

In the 1960s and 1970s, TV involved most of Carmichael's time as a frequent guest star and also as a regular on such shows as the 1959–63 western series *Laramie* and the PBS children's series *Hoagy Carmichael's Music Shop.* These appearances, plus those in movies still shown regularly on television, have kept him, five years after his death, one of the best-loved composers of popular songs of the past fifty years, in or out of the movies.

Hoagy Carmichael (at piano) not only got a featured role in 1945's To Have and Have Not, *but got to accompany Lauren Bacall in his "How Little We Know." Know who dubbed her?*

ANYTHING GOES (1936), TV title: *Tops Is the Limit*. Paramount. B&W. Directed by Lewis Milestone. With Bing Crosby, Ethel Merman, Ida Lupino, Charles Ruggles, Arthur Treacher. Song: "Moonburn" (lyrics, Edward Heyman); plus songs by others.

I MET HIM IN PARIS (1937), Paramount. B&W. Directed by Wesley Ruggles. With Claudette Colbert, Melvyn Douglas, Robert Young, Lee Bowman, Mona Barrie. Song: "I Met Him in Paris" (lyrics, Helen Meinardi).

TOPPER (1937), MGM. B&W. Directed by Norman Z. McLeod. With Constance Bennett, Cary Grant, Roland Young, Billie Burke, Alan Mowbray, Hedda Hopper. Song: "Old Man Moon" (music-lyrics, Carmichael). Videocassette: Hal Roach Video (newly colorized version of '85).

EVERY DAY'S A HOLIDAY (1938), Paramount. B&W. Directed by Edward Sutherland. With Mae West, Edmund Lowe, Lloyd Nolan, Charles Butterworth, Charles Winninger, Chester Conklin, Herman Bing. Song: "Jubilee" (lyrics, Stanley Adams); plus songs by others.

COLLEGE SWING (1938), Paramount. B&W. Directed by Raoul Walsh. With George Burns, Gracie Allen, Martha Raye, Bob Hope, Ben Blue, Edward Everett Horton, Florence George, Betty Grable, Jackie Coogan, John Payne, Robert Cummings. Song: "College Swing" (lyrics, Frank Loesser); plus songs by others.

SING YOU SINNERS (1938), Paramount. B&W. Directed by Wesley Ruggles with Bing Crosby, Fred MacMurray, Donald O'Connor, Ellen Drew, Elizabeth Patterson. Song: "Small Fry" (lyrics, Frank Loesser); plus songs by others.

ROMANCE IN THE DARK (1938), Paramount. B&W. Directed by H. C. Potter. With Gladys Swarthout, John Boles, John Barrymore, Claire Dodd, Fritz Feld, Curt Bois. Song: "The Nearness of You" (lyrics, Ned Washington); plus songs by others.

MEN WITH WINGS (1938), Paramount. Color. Directed by William Wellman. With Fred MacMurray, Ray Milland, Louise Campbell, Virginia Weidler, Walter Abel, Andy Devine. Song: "Men With Wings" (lyrics, Frank Loesser).

SAY IT IN FRENCH (1938), Paramount. B&W. Directed by Andrew L. Stone. With Olympe Bradna, Ray Milland, Irene Hervey, Mary Carlisle, Janet Beecher. Song: "April in My Heart" (lyrics, Helen Meinardi).

THANKS FOR THE MEMORY (1938), Paramount. B&W. Directed by George Archainbaud. With Bob Hope, Shirley Ross, Charles Butterworth, Otto Kruger, Hedda Hopper, Laura Hope Crews, Eddie Anderson. Song: "Two Sleepy People" (lyrics, Frank Loesser); plus songs by others.

ST. LOUIS BLUES (1939), Paramount. B&W. Directed by Raoul Walsh. With Lloyd Nolan, Dorothy Lamour, Jessie Ralph, Tito Guizar, Maxine Sullivan, Matty Malneck and His Boys, the King's Men. Songs: "The Song in My Heart Is a Rhumba" (lyrics, Frank Loesser); "Kinda Lonesome" (lyrics, Leo Robin, Sam Coslow); plus songs by others.

SOME LIKE IT HOT (1939), Paramount. B&W. Directed George Archainbaud. With Bob Hope, Shirley Ross, Gene Krupa and his Orchestra, Bernard Nedell, Una Merkel. Song: "Heart and Soul" (lyrics, Frank Loesser); plus songs by others.

ROAD SHOW (1941), Hal Roach for United Artists release. B&W. Directed by Hal Roach. With Carole Landis, John Hubbard, Adolphe Menjou, Patsy Kelly, Willie Best, the Charioteers. Songs: "I Should Have Known You Years Ago" (music-lyrics, Carmichael); "Calliope Jane," "Slav Annie," "Yum-Yum" (lyrics, Stanley Adams).

MR. BUG GOES TO TOWN (1941), TV title: *Hoppity Goes to Town*. Max Fleischer for Paramount release. Color. Directed by Dave Fleischer. Animated cartoon feature. Songs: "We're the Couple in the Castle," "I'll Dance at Your Wedding," "Kat-y Did, Kat-y Didn't" (lyrics, Frank Loesser); plus songs by others. Videocassette: Republic/Spotlight.

HI, BUDDY (1943), Universal. B&W. Directed by Harold Young. With Harriet Hilliard, Dick Foran, Robert Paige, Marjorie Lord, Bobs Watson, Jennifer Holt. Song: "Star Dust" (lyrics, Mitchell Parrish); plus songs by others.

TRUE TO LIFE (1943), Paramount. B&W. Directed by George Marshall. With Mary Martin, Dick Powell, Franchot Tone, Victor Moore, William Demarest. Songs: "The Old Music Master," "There She Was," "Mister Pollyanna," "Sudsy Suds" (lyrics, Johnny Mercer). Studio LP by Carmichael: excerpt in *Hoagy Carmichael: The Star Dust Road*, Decca 8588 (withdrawn).

COWBOY CANTEEN (1944), Columbia. B&W. Directed by Lew Landers. With Charles Starrett, Jane Frazee, Tex Ritter, Barbara Allen (Vera Vague), the Mills Brothers, Jimmy Wakeley, Roy Acuff. Song: "Lazy River" (lyrics, Sidney Arodin); plus songs by others.

TO HAVE AND HAVE NOT (1944), Warner Brothers. B&W. Directed by Howard Hawks. With Humphrey Bogart, Lauren Bacall, Walter Brennan, Hoagy Carmichael, Marcel Dalio. Songs: "How Little We Know," "Hong Kong Blues" (lyrics, Johnny Mercer); plus songs by others. Studio recording by Carmichael included in *Hoagy Carmichael: The Star Dust Road,* Decca 8588 (withdrawn). Videocassette: CBS/Fox.

THE STORK CLUB (1945), Paramount. B&W. Directed by Hal Walker. With Betty Hutton, Barry Fitzgerald, Don DeFore, Robert Benchley, Andy Russell, Iris Adrian. Songs: "Doctor, Lawyer, Indian Chief," "Baltimore Oriole" (lyrics, Paul Francis Webster); plus songs by others. Studio recording by Carmichael included in *Hoagy Carmichael: The Star Dust Road,* Decca 8588 (withdrawn).

JOHNNY ANGEL (1945), RKO Radio. B&W. Directed by Edwin L. Marin. With George Raft, Claire Trevor, Signe Hasso, Hoagy Carmichael. Song: "Memphis in June" (lyrics, Paul Francis Webster).

CANYON PASSAGE (1946), Universal. Color. Directed by Jacques Tourneur. With Dana Andrews, Susan Hayward, Brian Donlevy, Ward Bond, Lloyd Bridges. Songs: "Rogue River Valley," "I'm Gonna Get Married in the Morning" (music-lyrics, Carmichael); "Ol' Buttermilk Sky" (lyrics, Jack Brooks). Studio recording by Carmichael included in *Hoagy Carmichael: The Star Dust Road,* Decca 8588 (withdrawn).

THE BEST YEARS OF OUR LIVES (1946), Samuel Goldwyn-RKO Radio. B&W. Directed by William Wyler. With Fredric March, Myrna Loy, Teresa Wright, Dana Andrews, Virginia Mayo, Harold Russell, Cathy O'Donnell, Hoagy Carmichael. Song: "Lazy River" (lyrics, Sidney Arodin). Videocassette: Embassy.

DARK PASSAGE (1947), Warner Brothers, B&W. Directed by Delmer Daves. With Humphrey Bogart, Lauren Bacall, Bruce Bennett, Agnes Moorehead. Song: "How Little We Know" (lyrics, Johnny Mercer). Videocassette: Key-CBS/Fox.

IVY (1947), Universal. B&W. Directed by Sam Wood. With Joan Fontaine, Patric Knowles, Herbert Marshall, Sir Cedric Hardwicke, Lucile Watson. Song: "Ivy" (music-lyrics, Carmichael).

NIGHT SONG (1947), RKO Radio. B&W. Directed by John Cromwell. With Merle Oberon, Dana Andrews, Ethel Barrymore, Hoagy Carmichael. Song: "Who Killed the Black Widder?" (lyrics, Fred Spielman, Janice Torres); plus songs by others.

HERE COMES THE GROOM (1951), Paramount. B&W. Directed by Frank Capra. With Bing Crosby, Jane Wyman, Alexis Smith, Franchot Tone, James Barton, Anna Maria Alberghetti, Louis Armstrong, Phil Harris. Song: "In the Cool, Cool, Cool of the Evening" (lyrics, Johnny Mercer); plus songs by others. Studio recording by Crosby, Wyman included in Bing Crosby: *Cool of the Evening,* Decca 4262 (withdrawn).

LAS VEGAS STORY (1952), RKO Radio. B&W. Directed by Robert Stevenson. With Jane Russell, Victor Mature, Vincent Price, Hoagy Carmichael, Brad Dexter. Songs: "I Get Along Without You Very Well," "The Monkey Song" (music-lyrics, Carmichael); plus songs by others. Videocassette: King of Video.

GENTLEMEN PREFER BLONDES (1953), Twentieth Century-Fox. Color. Directed by Howard Hawks. With Jane Russell, Marilyn Monroe, Charles Coburn, Tommy Noonan, Elliot Reid, George "Foghorn" Winslow. Songs: "Ain't There Anyone Here for Love?," "When Love Goes Wrong" (lyrics, Harold Adamson); plus songs by others. Soundtrack LP: MGM 208 (withdrawn); excerpts included in Stet-DRG SD-15005. Videocassette: CBS/Fox

THOSE REDHEADS FROM SEATTLE (1953), Paramount. Color. 3-D. Directed by Lewis R. Foster. With Rhonda Fleming, Gene Barry, Guy Mitchell, Agnes Moorehead, Teresa Brewer. Song: "I Guess It Was You All the Time" (lyrics, Johnny Mercer); plus songs by others.

TIMBERJACK (1955), Republic. B&W. Directed by Joseph Kane. With Vera Ralston, Sterling Hayden, Adolphe Menjou, David Brian, Hoagy Carmichael. Song: "Timberjack" (lyrics, Johnny Mercer).

THREE FOR THE SHOW (1955), Columbia. Color. CinemaScope. Directed by H. C. Potter. With Betty Grable, Jack Lemmon, Marge and Gower Champion, Myron McCormick. Song: "Down Boy" (lyrics, Harold Adamson); plus songs by others.

HEY BOY, HEY GIRL (1959), Columbia. B&W. Directed by David L. Rich. With Louis Prima, Keely Smith, Sam Butera and the Witnesses, Kim Charney. Song: "Lazy River" (lyrics, Sidney Arodin).

GIRLS! GIRLS! GIRLS! (1962), Paramount. Color. Panavision. Directed by Norman Taurog. With Elvis Presley, Stella Stevens, Jeremy Slate, Benson Fong, Robert Strauss, Guy Lee. Song: "The Nearness of You" (lyrics, Ned Washington); plus songs by others. Soundtrack LP: RCA LSP-2621. Videocassette: Key-CBS/Fox.

Frank Loesser

Like many songwriters, Frank Loesser (1910–1969) had a somewhat checkered Hollywood career. He first went to Hollywood in the 1930s as a lyricist for such composers as Hoagy Carmichael, Frederick Hollander, Burton Lane, Jimmy McHugh, and Victor Schertzinger. After leaving to serve as a private in the Army's Special Services Division during World War II, he returned as a composer-lyricist. He then went on to win his greatest fame as a Broadway composer-lyricist, with *Where's Charley?* (1948), *Guys and Dolls* (1950), *The Most Happy Fella* (1956), and *How to Succeed in Business Without Really Trying* (1961)—all of which, except for *The Most Happy Fella,* were then adapted by Hollywood, with varying degrees of success.

Overall, Loesser's Hollywood work was no match for what he achieved on Broadway. Still, quite a few of Loesser's movie songs brightened many fair-to-good pictures (though no really great ones), and some have survived as popular standards.

Frank Loesser's father was a piano teacher who had come to the United States from Germany in the 1880s, and his brother Arthur became a well-known concert pianist. In contrast to his father and brother, though, Loesser's main interest from his earliest years was popular music. By his own admission no scholar, he dropped out of City College of New York after one year and went to work in 1929 as a reporter for a small newspaper in New Rochelle, New York, and then for *Women's Wear Daily* in New York City. He also worked occasionally as a singer and pianist in local clubs and in a Berkshire Mountains resort, and began writing special lyrics for a few vaudevillians and for Lions Club shows.

In 1930 Loesser submitted a few of his lyrics to the Leo Feist publishing house, which signed him up at fifty dollars a week—not a bad salary in that Depression year. But a year later, only one of his lyrics had been considered good enough to be published: "In Love With the Memory of You," a now-forgotten song with music by a then-unknown young composer named William Schuman, who would soon go on to become a major classical composer and a top music administrator (including a period as president of the Juilliard School).

Someone at RKO Radio Pictures liked "In Love With the Memory of You" enough to offer Loesser a Hollywood contract. But after a year at RKO writing lyrics that never got used in any films, Loesser returned to New York. Once again he sang in small clubs and wrote material for vaudeville and radio performances. Then, in 1936, he wrote the lyrics for a Broadway revue, *The Illustrators Show,* with Irving Actman as composer. It closed after four performances—but not before Loesser was offered another Hollywood contract.

This time, some of his lyrics made it to the screen, beginning with the exotically romantic "The Moon of Manakoora" (music by Alfred Newman) for Samuel Goldwyn's popular South Seas adventure-drama *The Hurricane* (the first of its two film versions). In quick succession between 1937 and 1941 came such good songs from mostly forgettable movies as "You Can't Tell a Man by His Hat" from *Blossoms on Broadway* (music, Manning Sherwin), "Says My Heart" from *Cocoanut Grove* (music,

Burton Lane), "Small Fry" from *Sing You Sinners* (music, Hoagy Carmichael), "Fidgety Joe" from *Man About Town* (music, Matt Malneck), "Dolores" from *Las Vegas Nights* (music, Louis Alter), and "Drums in the Night" and "Say It (Over and Over Again)" from *Buck Benny Rides Again* (lyrics, Jimmy McHugh).

Along the way there were two major song hits written especially for Shirley Ross and Bob Hope. Both songs were follow-ups to the smash success that Ross and Hope had introducing Rainger and Robin's "Thanks for the Memory" in *The Big Broadcast of 1938:* "Two Sleepy People" (music by Hoagy Carmichael) for the B comedy that took its title from the earlier song hit, *Thanks for the Memory;* and "The Lady's in Love With You" (music by Burton Lane) from the '39 *Some Like It Hot* (retitled *Rhythm Romance* for its TV release, to avoid confusion with a later and unrelated Marilyn Monroe movie of the same name). Both songs made radio's *Your Hit Parade* for twelve weeks.

In 1940, Paramount, for the first time, let Loesser write both lyrics and music for the title song of a B comedy, *Seventeen,* based on the once-popular Booth Tarkington novel and starring Jackie Cooper and Betty Field. Then, only days after the Japanese bombing of Pearl Harbor and the U.S. entry into World War II in December of 1942, Loesser turned out both the music and lyrics for "Praise the Lord and Pass the Ammunition." It became the first major new song hit of the war years, selling more than two million records and more than one million copies of sheet music.

After joining the Army, Loesser wrote several other songs with war themes, including "Wacky for Khaki" and "What Do You Do in the Infantry?" (the latter eventually adopted as the Infantry's official song).

While he was in the Army, Loesser songs continued to appear in wartime movies. For '44's *Christmas Holiday,* a Somerset Maugham tearjerker in which Deanna Durbin shed her sweet-little-girl image to play a down-on-her-luck nightclub singer who unknowingly marries a psychopathic and presumably gay young killer (played by Gene Kelly), Loesser wrote both words and music for the plaintive "Spring Will Be a Little Late This Year." Other memorable Loesser songs from the war period include the lyrics for the Jimmy McHugh ballad, "Can't Get Out of This Mood" (sung by Ginny Simms in '42's *Seven Days Leave*) and the deliciously wry "Love Isn't Born, It's Made" (sung by Ann Sheridan in '43's *Thank Your Lucky Stars*, to music by Arthur Schwartz).

Back at Paramount after the war, Loesser was determined to work strictly as a composer-lyricist. He got off to a shaky start with three Betty Hutton pictures of varying quality: *The Perils of Pauline* (1947), in which Hutton introduced the manic "Poppa, Don't Preach to Me" and the lovely "I Wish I Didn't Love You So" (the latter an Oscar nominee); *Red, Hot and Blue* (1949), which took little more than the title and one of the stars (Bob Hope) of the original '36 Broadway show and dropped all of Cole Porter's original songs, replacing them with some of Loesser's most forgettable ("I Wake Up in the Morning Feeling Fine," "Where Are You Now That I Need You?", "That's Loyalty"); and *Let's Dance* (1950), arguably Fred Astaire's worst musical and his only (mis)teaming with Hutton, but introducing the agreeable ballad "Why Fight the Feeling?" and the cheerily fast-talking "Can't Stop Talkin' About Him."

Loesser won his only Academy Award in 1949 (out of three nominations as composer-lyricist and two as just lyricist). It was for the words and music of "Baby,

One of Frank Leosser's finest original film musicals—as both composer and lyricist—was 1952's Hans Christian Andersen, *starring Danny Kaye as the legendary Danish children's storyteller.*

It's Cold Outside" from *Neptune's Daughter,* one of MGM's splashier aquatic musical-comedies for swimming star Esther Williams. The song remains Loesser's brightest original contribution to the movies—a delightfully witty, catchy duet in which Williams tries to resist the romantic pleadings of Ricardo Montalban while Red Skelton does likewise with those of Betty Garrett.

The following year, with the smash Broadway success of *Guys and Dolls,* Loesser was finally recognized as a major composer as well as a top lyricist. When Samuel Goldwyn bought the show's film rights, he also signed Loesser to write the score for one of Goldwyn's most lavish original movie musicals, *Hans Christian Andersen* (1952), starring Danny Kaye. Although none of its songs became major hits, Loesser's score remains one of his finest—including "No Two People" (which squeezed in just one week on *Your Hit Parade*), "Inch Worm," "Wonderful, Wonderful Copenhagen," and, particularly, the romantic ballad "Anywhere I Wander."

For Goldwyn's spirited and colorful '55 movie version of *Guys and Dolls*—with Marlon Brando, Frank Sinatra, Jean Simmons, and Vivian Blaine heading the cast—Loesser wrote three new songs ("Adelaide," "Pet Me Poppa," and "A Woman in Love"). They would be the last original songs he would write for the movies. But none of them made as much of an impression as the carryovers from Broadway, including "Luck Be a Lady Tonight," "Take Back Your Mink," "If I Were a Bell," "Sit Down, You're Rockin' the Boat," and "Fugue for Tinhorns." These are all prime

Loesser's popular Broadway musical Guys and Dolls *got the lavish Samuel Goldwyn movie treatment in 1955, with Frank Sinatra, Vivian Blaine, Jean Simmons, and Marlon Brando starred. Loesser wrote three new songs for the film.*

How to Succeed in Business Without Really Trying *(1967) took the musical out of the theater backstage and plumped it right in the middle of modern offices—with just about as much resemblance to reality.*

Loesser and keep the movie version of *Guys and Dolls,* despite its stylistic unevenness and some questionable casting, mostly good if unbelievable fun.

Two other Loesser Broadway hits have fared less well in their movie versions. *Where's Charley?* (1952) has Ray Bolger repeating his Broadway role as an Oxford student who impersonates his aunt from Brazil ("where the nuts come from") in order to provide a needed chaperone for two of his classmates' dates. For all of Bolger's deft clowning and his inimitable way with Loesser's "Once in Love with Amy," it's a tepid version of that old chestnut, *Charley's Aunt* by Brandon Thomas. *How to Succeed in Business Without Really Trying* (1967) keeps the original Broadway leads, Robert Morse and Rudy Vallee, but much of the show's original bite, glow, and intimacy got lost somewhere in the transfer to the Panavision screen. Also lost: a couple of Loesser's best songs ("Paris Original," "Happy to Keep His Dinner Warm," and "Love From a Heart of Gold"). But the delightful "The Company Way," "Coffee Break," and "The Brotherhood of Man" are spiritedly done, as well as the show's big hit song, the at first slyly ironic and then romantic "I Believe in You."

Disappointingly, Loesser's finest stage work, *The Most Happy Fella,* has not yet been made into a movie, even though the Sidney Howard play on which it is based has been filmed three times as a straight drama—most notably in 1940 as *They Knew What They Wanted* with Charles Laughton and Carole Lombard.

FRANK LOESSER'S MOVIES AND SONGS ON TAPE AND DISC

THE HURRICANE (1937), Samuel Goldwyn for United Artists release. B&W. Directed by John Ford. With Dorothy Lamour, Jon Hall, Mary Astor, Raymond Massey, Thomas Mitchell, C. Aubrey Smith, John Carradine, Inez Courtney, Movita Castenada. Song: "The Moon of Manakoora" (music, Alfred Newman). Videocassette: Embassy.

VOGUES OF 1938 (1937), Walter Wanger for United Artists release. Color. Directed by Irving Cummings. With Warner Baxter, Joan Bennett, Helen Vinson, Mischa Auer, Alan Mowbray, Marjorie Gateson, Hedda Hopper, Jerome Cowan. Song: "Lovely One" (music, Manning Sherwin); plus songs by others. TV title: *Vogues.*

BLOSSOMS ON BROADWAY (1937), Paramount. B&W. Directed by Richard Wallace. With Edward Arnold, Shirley Ross, John Trent, Kitty Kelly, Weber and Fields, William Frawley, Rufe Davis, the Radio Rogues. Songs: "You Can't Tell a Man By His Hat," "No Ring on Her Finger," "Olympiad" (music, Manning Sherwin); plus songs by others.

FIGHT FOR YOUR LADY (1937), RKO Radio. B&W. Directed by Ben Stoloff. With John Boles, Ida Lupino, Jack Oakie, Margot Grahame, Erik Rhodes, Gordon Jones, Billy Gilbert, Maude Eburne. Song: "Blame It on the Danube" (music, Harry Akst).

COCOANUT GROVE (1938), Paramount. B&W. Directed by Alfred Santell. With Fred MacMurray, Harriet Hilliard, Ben Blue, the Yacht Club Boys, Eve Arden, Rufe Davis, Billy Lee, Harry Owens and his Orchestra. Songs: "Says My Heart" (music, Burton Lane); "Ten Easy Lessons" (music, Burton Lane; lyrics, "Jock" and Loesser); plus songs by others. Soundtrack LP: excerpt included in *Frank Loesser in Hollywood,* Music Masters JJA 19762.

COLLEGE SWING (1938), Paramount. B&W. Directed by Raoul Walsh. With George Burns, Gracie Allen, Martha Raye, Bob Hope, Ben Blue, Edward Everett Horton, Florence George, Betty Grable, Jackie Coogan, John Payne, Robert Cummings, Skinnay Ennis, Jerry Colonna, the Slate Brothers. Songs: "I Fall in Love With You Every Day," "What a Rhumba Does to Romance," "You're a Natural," "The

Old School Bell" (music, Manning Sherwin); "Moments Like This," "How'd'ja Like to Love Me?," "What Did Romeo Say to Juliet?" (music, Burton Lane); "College Swing" (music, Hoagy Carmichael). Soundtrack LP: excerpts included in *Frank Loesser in Hollywood,* Music Masters JJA 19762; excerpt also included in *Martha Raye,* Legends 1000/5-6.

SING YOU SINNERS (1938), Paramount. B&W. Directed by Wesley Ruggles. With Bing Crosby, Fred MacMurray, Donald O'Connor, Ellen Drew, Elizabeth Patterson, John Gallaudet, Irving Bacon. Song: "Small Fry" (music, Hoagy Carmichael); plus songs by others. Soundtrack LP: included in *Frank Loesser in Hollywood,* Music Masters JJA 19762.

THANKS FOR THE MEMORY (1938), Paramount. B&W. Directed by George Archainbaud. With Bob Hope, Shirley Ross, Charles Butterworth, Otto Kruger, Hedda Hopper, Roscoe Karns, Laura Hope Crews, Eddie "Rochester" Anderson, "Honey Chile" Wilder. Song: "Two Sleepy People" (music, Hoagy Carmichael). Soundtrack LP: included in *Frank Loesser in Hollywood,* Music Masters JJA 19762.

SPAWN OF THE NORTH (1938), Paramount. B&W. Directed by Henry Hathaway. With George Raft, Henry Fonda, Dorothy Lamour, John Barrymore, Akim Tamiroff, Louise Platt, Lynne Overman, Fuzzy Knight, Vladimir Sokoloff. Songs: "I Wish I Was the Willow," "I Like Hump-Backed Salmon" (music, Burton Lane).

MEN WITH WINGS (1938), Paramount. B&W. Directed by William A. Wellman. With Fred MacMurray, Ray Milland, Louise Campbell, Andy Devine, Lynne Overman, Walter Abel, Porter Hall, Donald O'Connor, Virginia Weidler. Song: "Men With Wings" (music, Hoagy Carmichael).

FRESHMAN YEAR (1938), Universal. B&W. Directed by Frank MacDonald. With William Lundigan, Constance Moore, Dixie Dunbar, Stanley Hughes, Ernest Truex, Frank Melton, Tommy Wonder, Alan Ladd, the Three Diamond Brothers, the Three Murtha Sisters. Song: "Chasin' You Around" (music, Irving Actman); plus songs by others.

STOLEN HEAVEN (1938), Paramount. B&W. Directed by Andrew L. Stone. With Olympe Bradna, Gene Raymond, Lewis Stone, Glenda Farrell, Douglas Dumbrille, Porter Hall. Song: "The Boys in the Band" (music, Manning Sherwin); plus song by others.

SAINT LOUIS BLUES (1939), Paramount. B&W. Directed by Raoul Walsh. With Lloyd Nolan, Dorothy Lamour, Jessie Ralph, Tito Guizar, Maxine Sullivan, William Frawley, Jerome Cowan, Matty Malneck and His Boys, the King's

Men. Songs: "Blue Nightfall" (music, Burton Lane); "The Song in My Heart Is a Rhumba" (music, Hoagy Carmichael); "I Go for That" (music, Matt Malneck); plus songs by others. Soundtrack LP: Caliban 6014 (with *Dames*); also, excerpts included in *Dorothy Lamour,* Legends 1000/4.

MAN ABOUT TOWN (1939), Paramount. B&W. Directed by Mark Sandrich. With Jack Benny, Dorothy Lamour, Edward Arnold, Binnie Barnes, Monty Woolley, Phil Harris, Betty Grable, Eddie "Rochester" Anderson, Isabel Jeans, E. E. Clive, Matty Malneck and His Orchestra. Songs: "Fidgety Joe" (music, Matt Malneck); "Strange Enchantment," "That Sentimental Sandwich" (music, Frederick Hollander). Soundtrack LP: excerpt included in *Betty Grable,* Star-Tone 219.

THE GRACIE ALLEN MURDER CASE (1939), Paramount. B&W. Directed by Alfred E. Green. With Gracie Allen, Warren William, Ellen Drew, Kent Taylor, Jed Prouty, Jerome Cowan, H. B. Warner, William Demarest. Song: "Snug As a Bug in a Rug" (music, Matt Malneck). Soundtrack LP: included in *Frank Loesser in Hollywood,* Music Masters JJA 19762.

CAFE SOCIETY (1939), Paramount. B&W. Directed by Edward H. Griffith. With Madeleine Carroll, Fred MacMurray, Shirley Ross, Jessie Ralph, Claude Gillingwater, Allyn Joslyn. Songs: "Kiss Me With Your Eyes" (music, Burton Lane); "Park Avenue Gimp" (music, Leo Shuken).

INVITATION TO HAPPINESS (1939), Paramount. B&W. Directed by Wesley Ruggles. With Irene Dunne, Fred MacMurray, Charles Ruggles, Billy Cook, William Collier Sr., Marion Martin. Song: "Invitation to Happiness" (music, Frederick Hollander).

ZAZA (1939), Paramount. B&W. Directed by George Cukor. With Claudette Colbert, Herbert Marshall, Bert Lahr, Helen Westley, Genevieve Tobin, Constance Collier, John Sutton, Rex O'Malley. Songs: "Forget Me," "Zaza," "Hello, My Darling" (music, Frederick Hollander); plus songs by others.

ISLAND OF LOST MEN (1939), Paramount. B&W. Directed by Kurt Neumann. With Anna May Wong, J. Carrol Naish, Eric Blore, Ernest Truex, Anthony Quinn, Broderick Crawford, Richard Loo. Song: "Music on the Shore" (music, Frederick Hollander).

HAWAIIAN NIGHTS (1939), Universal. B&W. Directed by Albert S. Rogell. With Johnny Downs, Mary Carlisle, Constance Moore, Eddie Quillan, Etienne Girardot, Princess Luana, Prince Leileni, Matty Malneck and His Orchestra, Sol Hoopi and His Hawaiian Band. Songs: "Hey, Good Lookin'!," "I Found

My Love," "Hawaii Sang Me to Sleep" (music, Matt Melneck); "Then I Wrote the Minuet in G" (music, Matt Malneck after Beethoven).

DESTRY RIDES AGAIN (1939), Universal. B&W. Directed by George Marshall. With James Stewart, Marlene Dietrich, Charles Winninger, Irene Hervey, Una Merkel, Mischa Auer, Brian Donlevy, Allen Jenkins, Billy Gilbert, Jack Carson. Songs: "(See What) The Boys in the Back Room (Will Have)," "You've Got That Look That Leaves Me Weak," "Li'l Joe the Wrangler" (music, Frederick Hollander). Soundtrack LP: excerpt included in *Frank Loesser in Hollywood,* Music Masters JJA 19762; studio recordings of songs by Marlene Dietrich on miscellaneous recordings over the years.

SOME LIKE IT HOT (1939), Paramount. B&W. Directed by George Archainbaud. With Bob Hope, Shirley Ross, Gene Krupa and his Orchestra, Una Merkel, Rufe Davis, Bernard Nedell, Bernadene Hayes. Songs: "The Lady's in Love With You" (music, Burton Lane); "Some Like It Hot" (music, Gene Krupa, Remo Biondi); "Heart and Soul" (music, Hoagy Carmichael); plus songs by others. Soundtrack LP: excerpts included in *Frank Loesser in Hollywood,* Music Masters JJA 19762.

BUCK BENNY RIDES AGAIN (1940), Paramount. B&W. Directed by Mark Sandrich. With Jack Benny, Ellen Drew, Eddie "Rochester" Anderson, Phil Harris, Andy Devine, Virginia Dale, Lillian Cornell, Dennis Day, Theresa Harris, Ward Bond, Kay Linaker. Songs: "Drums in the Night," "Say It Over and Over Again," "My, My," "My Kind of Country" (music, Jimmy McHugh).

JOHNNY APOLLO (1940), Twentieth Century-Fox. B&W. Directed by Henry Hathaway. With Tyrone Power, Dorothy Lamour, Lloyd Nolan, Edward Arnold, Charley Grapewin, Lionel Atwill, Fuzzy Knight. Songs: "Dancing for Nickels and Dimes" (music, Lionel Newman), "This Is the Beginning of the End" (music, Alfred Newman). Soundtrack LP: excerpts included in *Dorothy Lamour,* West Coast 14002, and in *Dorothy Lamour,* Legends 1000/4.

MOON OVER BURMA (1940), Paramount. B&W. Directed by Louis King. With Dorothy Lamour, Robert Preston, Preston Foster, Doris Nolan, Albert Basserman. Songs: "Moon Over Burma" (music, Frederick Hollander); "Mexican Magic" (music, Harry Revel). Soundtrack LP: excerpts included in *Dorothy Lamour,* West Coast 14002.

SEVEN SINNERS (1940), Universal. B&W. Directed by Tay Garnett. With Marlene Dietrich, John Wayne, Broderick Crawford, Oscar Homolka, Mischa Auer, Anna Lee, Albert Dekker, Billy Gilbert. Songs: "I've Fallen Over-

board," "I've Been in Love Before," "The Man's in the Navy" (music, Frederick Hollander).

SEVENTEEN (1940), Paramount. B&W. Directed by Louis King. With Jackie Cooper, Betty Field, Richard Denning, Otto Kruger, Peter Lind Hayes, Ann Shoemaker. Song: "Seventeen."

A NIGHT AT EARL CARROLL'S (1940), Paramount. B&W. Directed by Kurt Neumann. With Ken Murray, Rose Hobart, Elvia Allman, Russell Hicks, Blanche Stewart. Songs: "Li'l Boy Love" (music, Frederick Hollander), "I Wanna Make With the Happy Times" (music, Gertrude Niesen).

DANCING ON A DIME (1940), Paramount. B&W. Directed by Joseph Santley. With Grace McDonald, Robert Paige, Peter Lind Hayes, Virginia Dale, Frank Jenks, Eddie Quillan, Lillian Cornell, William Frawley. Songs: "Dancing on a Dime," "Mañana," "I Hear Music" (music, Burton Lane); "Loveable Sort of Person" (music, Victor Young). Soundtrack LP: excerpt included in *Frank Loesser in Hollywood,* Music Masters JJA 19762.

TYPHOON (1940), Paramount. B&W. Directed by Louis King. With Dorothy Lamour, Robert Preston, Lynne Overman, J. Carroll Naish, Chief Thundercloud, Jack Carson. Song: "Palms of Paradise" (music, Frederick Hollander).

NORTHWEST MOUNTED POLICE (1940), Paramount. Color. Directed by Cecil B. DeMille. With Gary Cooper, Madeleine Carroll, Paulette Goddard, Robert Preston, Preston Foster, Akim Tamiroff, George Bancroft, Lynne Overman, Lon Chaney Jr. Song: "Does the Moon Shine Through the Tall Pine?" (music, Victor Young).

THE FARMER'S DAUGHTER (1940), Paramount. B&W. Directed by James Hogan. With Martha Raye, Richard Denning, Charles Ruggles, Gertrude Michael, William Frawley. Song: "Jungle Jingle" (music, Frederick Hollander).

THE QUARTERBACK (1940), Paramount. B&W. Directed by H. Bruce Humberstone. With Wayne Morris, Virginia Dale, Edgar Kennedy, Lillian Cornell, Alan Mowbray, Jerome Cowan, William Frawley. Song: "Out With Your Chest (And Up With Your Chin)" (music, Matt Malneck); plus songs by others.

YOUTH WILL BE SERVED (1940), Twentieth Century-Fox. B&W. Directed by Otto Brower. With Jane Withers, Jane Darwell, Joe Brown Jr., Robert Conway, Elyse Knox, Charles Holland, Lillian Porter, Clara Blandick, John Qualen. Song: "Hot Catfish and Corn Dodgers" (music, Louis Alter).

LAS VEGAS NIGHTS (1941), Paramount.

THE MELODY LINGERS ON

B&W. Directed by Frank Murphy. With Tommy Dorsey and his Orchestra, Bert Wheeler, Constance Moore, Phil Regan, Lillian Cornell, Virginia Dale, Betty Brewer, Frank Sinatra, Jo Stafford and the Pied Pipers. Songs: "Dolores" (music, Louis Alter); "I've Gotta Ride," "Mary, Mary, Quite Contrary" (music, Burton Lane); plus songs by others.

SIS HOPKINS (1941), Republic. B&W. Directed by Joseph Santley. With Judy Canova, Bob Crosby, Charles Butterworth, Susan Hayward, Jerry Colonna, Elvia Allman, Katherine Alexander. Songs: "Cracker Barrel Country," "If You're in Love," "Well! Well!," "Look at You, Look at Me," "That Ain't Hay (It's the U.S.A.)" (music, Jule Styne). Soundtrack LP: excerpts included in *Frank Loesser in Hollywood,* Music Masters JJA 19762.

KISS THE BOYS GOODBYE (1941), Paramount. B&W. Directed by Victor Schertzinger. With Don Ameche, Mary Martin, Oscar Levant, Virginia Dale, Eddie "Rochester" Anderson, Barbara Allen (Vera Vague), Elizabeth Patterson, Raymond Walburn. Songs: "Kiss the Boys Goodbye," "I'll Never a Day Let Pass By," "Find Yourself a Melody," "Sand in My Shoes," "That's How I Got My Start" (music, Victor Schertzinger). Soundtrack LP: excerpts included in *Frank Loesser in Hollywood,* Music Masters JJA 19762.

ALOMA OF THE SOUTH SEAS (1941), Paramount. Color. Directed by Alfred Santell. With Dorothy Lamour, Jon Hall, Philip Reed, Lynne Overman, Katherine DeMille. Song: "The White Blossoms of Tah-ni" (music, Frederick Hollander).

MR. BUG GOES TO TOWN (1941), TV title: *Hoppity Goes to Town.* Max Fleischer for Paramount release. Color. Directed by Dave Fleischer. Animated cartoon feature. Songs: "We're the Couple in the Castle," "I'll Dance at Your Wedding," "Kat-y Did, Kat-y Didn't" (music, Hoagy Carmichael); "Boy, Oh, Boy" (music, Sam Timberg). Videocassette: Republic/ Spotlight.

GLAMOUR BOY (1941), Paramount. B&W. Directed by Ralph Murphy. With Jackie Cooper, Susanna Foster, Walter Abel. Songs: "Love Is Such an Old-Fashioned Thing," "The Magic of Magnolias" (music, Victor Schertzinger).

WORLD PREMIERE (1941), Paramount. B&W. Directed by Ted Tetzlaff. John Barrymore, Frances Farmer. Song: "Don't Cry Little Cloud" (music, Burton Lane).

CAUGHT IN THE DRAFT (1941), Paramount. B&W. Directed by David Butler. With Bob Hope, Dorothy Lamour, Eddie Bracken, Lynne Overman. Song: "Love Me As I Am"

(music, Louis Alter).

HOLD BACK THE DAWN (1941), Paramount. B&W. Directed by Mitchell Leisen. With Charles Boyer, Olivia de Havilland, Paulette Goddard, Walter Abel, Victor Francen, Rosemary DeCamp. Song: "My Boy, My Boy" (music-lyrics, Loesser-Berg-Spielman-Jacobson).

SAILORS ON LEAVE (1941), Republic. B&W. Directed by Herbert Dalmas. With William Lundigan, Shirley Ross. Song: "Since You" (music, Jule Styne).

THE FLEET'S IN (1942), Paramount. B&W. Directed by Victor Schertzinger. With William Holden, Dorothy Lamour, Betty Hutton, Eddie Bracken, Cass Daley, Betty Jane Rhodes, Jimmy Dorsey and his Orchestra, with Helen O'Connell, Bob Eberle. Song: "Tangerine" (music, Victor Schertzinger); plus songs by others.

TRUE TO THE ARMY (1942), Paramount. B&W. Directed by Albert S. Rogell. With Allan Jones, Judy Canova, Ann Miller, Jerry Colonna, Rod Cameron. Songs: "Need I Speak?," "Jitterbug's Lullaby," "In the Army," "Wacky for Khaki," "Spangles on My Tights" (music, Harold Spina); plus songs by others.

PRIORITIES ON PARADE (1942), Paramount. B&W. Directed by Albert S. Rogell. With Ann Miller, Johnny Johnston, Betty Rhodes, Barbara Allen (Vera Vague), Harry Barris, Eddie Quillan. Song: "You're in Love With Someone Else (But I'm in Love With You)" (music, Jule Styne); plus songs by others.

SWEATER GIRL (1942), Paramount. B&W. Directed by William Clemens. With Eddie Bracken, June Preisser, Betty Rhodes, Nils Asther, Kenneth Howell. Songs: "I Don't Want to Walk Without You," "I Said No," "Sweater Girl," "What Gives Out Now?" (music, Jule Styne); plus songs by others.

SEVEN DAYS LEAVE (1942), RKO Radio. B&W. Directed by Tim Whelan. With Lucille Ball, Victor Mature, Ginny Simms, Harold Peary, Peter Lind Hayes, Ralph Edwards, Arnold Stang, Freddy Martin and his Orchestra, Les Brown and his Orchestra. Songs: "Can't Get Out of This Mood," "Soft-Hearted," "Please, Won't You Leave My Girl Alone?," "I Get the Neck of the Chicken," "Puerto Rico," "You Speak My Language" (music, Jimmy McHugh).

BEYOND THE BLUE HORIZON (1942), Paramount. Color. Directed by Alfred Santell. With Dorothy Lamour, Richard Denning, Jack Haley, Patricia Morison, Walter Abel. Song: "Pagan Lullaby" (music, Jule Styne); plus songs by others. Soundtrack LP: Caliban 6033 (with *The Great Victor Herbert*).

REAP THE WILD WIND (1942), Paramount. Color. Directed by Cecil B. DeMille. With Ray Milland, John Wayne, Paulette Goddard, Robert Preston, Susan Hayward, Raymond Massey, Charles Bickford, Martha O'Driscoll, Hedda Hopper, Lynne Overman. Song: "Sea Chanty" (music, Victor Young).

THIS GUN FOR HIRE (1942), Paramount. B&W. Directed by Frank Tuttle. With Alan Ladd, Veronica Lake, Robert Preston, Laird Cregar, Pamela Blake. Songs: "Now You See It," "I've Got You" (music, Jacques Press).

TORTILLA FLAT (1942), MGM. B&W. Directed by Victor Fleming. With Spencer Tracy, Hedy Lamarr, John Garfield, Frank Morgan, Akim Tamiroff. Songs: "How I Love a Wedding," "Ai-Paisano" (music, Franz Waxman).

HAPPY GO LUCKY (1943), Paramount. B&W. Directed by Curtis Bernhardt. With Mary Martin, Dick Powell, Betty Hutton, Eddie Bracken, Rudy Vallee, Mabel Paige, Clem Bevans. Songs: "Happy Go Lucky," "Murder, He Says," "Let's Get Lost," "Sing a Tropical Song," "Fuddy-Duddy Watchmaker" (music, Jimmy McHugh). Soundtrack LP: excerpts included in *The Classic Movie Musicals of Jimmy McHugh,* Music Masters JJA-19825.

TORNADO (1943), Paramount. B&W. Directed by William Berke. With Chester Morris, Nancy Kelly, Marie McDonald. Song: "There Goes My Dream" (music, Frederick Hollander).

THANK YOUR LUCKY STARS (1943), Warner Brothers. B&W. Directed by David Butler. With Eddie Cantor, Joan Leslie, Dennis Morgan, Edward Everett Horton, S. Z. Sakall, Bette Davis, Ann Sheridan, Olivia de Havilland, Ida Lupino, Errol Flynn, John Garfield, Alexis Smith, Dinah Shore, Hattie McDaniel, Spike Jones and his Orchestra. Songs: "Love Isn't Born, It's Made," "They're Either Too Young or Too Old," "Goodnight, Good Neighbor," "How Sweet You Are," "I'm Ridin' for a Fall," "We're Staying Home Tonight," "The Dreamer," "No You, No Me," "Ice-Cold Katie," "That's What You Jolly-Well Get," "I'm Goin' North," "Thank Your Lucky Stars" (music, Arthur Schwartz). Soundtrack LP: Curtain Calls 100/8.

FOREST RANGERS (1943), Paramount. B&W. Directed by George Marshall. With Fred MacMurray, Paulette Goddard, Susan Hayward, Rod Cameron, Albert Dekker. Song: "Jingle, Jangle, Jingle" (music, Frederick Hollander).

SWING YOUR PARTNER (1943), Republic. B&W. Directed by Frank McDonald. With Judy Clark, Barbara Allen (Vera Vague), Roger Clark, Richard Lane, Esther Dale, Lulubelle and Scotty, the Tennessee Ramblers. Song: "Cracker Barrel County" (music, Jule Styne); plus songs by others.

YOU CAN'T RATION LOVE (1944), Paramount. B&W. Directed by Lester Fuller. With Johnny Johnston, Betty Rhodes, Marie Wilson, Marjorie Weaver. Song: "I Don't Want to Walk Without You" (music, Jule Styne); plus songs by others.

MOON OVER LAS VEGAS (1944), Universal. B&W. Directed by Jean Yarbrough. With Ann Gwynne, David Bruce, Lillian Cornell, Barbara Allen (Vera Vague), Lee Patrick, Joe Sawyer, Mantan Moreland, Gene Austin, Connie Haines, the Sportsmen. Song: "A Touch of Texas" (music, Jimmy McHugh); plus songs by others.

JAM SESSION (1944), Columbia. B&W. Directed by Charles Barton. With Ann Miller, Jess Barker, Alvino Rey and his Orchestra, Jan Garber and his Orchestra, Teddy Powell and his Orchestra, Glen Gray and his Casa Loma Orchestra, the Pied Pipers with Jo Stafford, Louis Armstrong and his Orchestra, Charlie Barnet and his Orchestra. Song: "Murder, He Says" (music, Jimmy McHugh); plus songs by others. Soundtrack LP: Hollywood Soundstage 5014 (with *Reveille with Beverly*).

CHRISTMAS HOLIDAY (1944), Universal. B&W. Directed by Robert Siodmak. With Deanna Durbin, Gene Kelly, Gladys George, Gale Sondergaard, Richard Whorf. Song: "Spring Will Be a Little Late This Year" (music-lyrics, Loesser); plus songs by others.

SEE HERE, PRIVATE HARGROVE (1944), MGM. B&W. Directed by Wesley Ruggles. With Robert Walker, Donna Reed, Keenan Wynn, Robert Benchley, Bob Crosby. Song: "In My Arms" (music, Ted Grouya).

HER LUCKY NIGHT (1945), Universal. B&W. Directed by Edward Lilley. With The Andrews Sisters, Noah Beery Jr., Martha O'Driscoll, Grady Sutton. Song: "Sing a Tropical Song" (music, Jimmy McHugh); plus songs by others.

DUFFY'S TAVERN (1945), Paramount. B&W. Directed by Hal Walker. With Ed Gardner, Victor Moore, Marjorie Reynolds, Barry Sullivan, Bing Crosby, Betty Hutton, Dorothy Lamour, Alan Ladd, Veronica Lake, Paulette Goddard, other guest stars. Song: "Leave Us Face It" (lyrics, Abe Burrows); plus songs by others.

THE PERILS OF PAULINE (1947), Paramount. B&W. Directed by George Marshall. With Betty Hutton, John Lund, Billy DeWolfe, William Demarest, Constance Collier. Songs: "Poppa Don't Preach to Me," "I Wish I Didn't Love You So," "The Sewing Machine," "Rumble Rumble Rumble" (music-lyrics, Loesser). Videocassette: Media.

VARIETY GIRL (1947), Paramount. B&W. Directed by Frank Butler. With Mary Hatcher, Olga San Juan, DeForest Kelley, William Demarest; Bing Crosby, Bob Hope, Robert Preston, Alan Ladd, Dorothy Lamour, Paulette Goddard, Barbara Stanwyck, Veronica Lake, William Holden, Ray Milland, Lizabeth Scott, Sonny Tufts, other guest stars. Songs: "Tallahassee," "Your Heart Calling Mine," "He Can Waltz," "I Must Have Been Madly in Love," "I Want My Money Back," "Impossible Things" (music-lyrics, Loesser); plus songs by others. Soundtrack LP: excerpts on Caliban 6007 (with *Colleen*).

MALAYA (1949), MGM. B&W. Directed by Richard Thorpe. With Spencer Tracy, James Stewart, Valentina Cortesa, Lionel Barrymore, John Hodiak, Sydney Greenstreet. Song: "Pagan Lullaby" (music, Jule Styne); plus songs by others.

NEPTUNE'S DAUGHTER (1949), MGM. Color. Directed by Edward Buzzell. With Esther Williams, Red Skelton, Betty Garrett, Ricardo Montalban, Keenan Wynn, Xavier Cugat and his Orchestra. Songs: "Baby, It's Cold Outside," My Heart Beats Faster," "I Love Those Men" (music-lyrics, Loesser). Soundtrack LP: excerpt included in *Celebrities*, Lion 70108 (withdrawn).

RED, HOT AND BLUE (1949), Paramount. B&W. Directed by John Farrow. With Betty Hutton, Victor Mature, June Havoc, William Demarest, William Talman. Songs: "(Where Are You) Now That I Need You?," "That's Loyalty," "Hamlet," "I Wake Up in the Morning Feeling Fine" (music-lyrics, Loesser).

ROSEANNA MCCOY (1949), RKO Radio. B&W. Directed by Irving Reis. With Joan Evans, Farley Granger, Charles Bickford, Raymond Massey, Richard Basehart, Aline MacMahon. Song: "Roseanna" (music-lyrics, Loesser).

LET'S DANCE (1950), Paramount. Color. Directed by Norman Z. McLeod. With Betty Hutton, Fred Astaire, Roland Young, Melville Cooper, Ruth Warrick, Lucille Watson, Barton MacLane. Songs: "Can't Stop Talking," "Oh Them Dudes," "Why Fight the Feeling?," "Tunnel of Love," "Hyacinth," "Jack and the Beanstalk" (music-lyrics, Loesser). Soundtrack LP: excerpts included in *Frank Loesser in Hollywood*, Music Masters JJA 19762.

THE FLAMING FEATHER (1951), Paramount. B&W. Directed by Ray Enright. With Sterling Hayden, Arleen Whelan, Forrest Tucker, Barbara Rush, Victor Jory. Song: "No Ring on Her Finger" (music, Manning Sherwin).

WITH A SONG IN MY HEART (1952), Twentieth Century-Fox. Color. Directed by Walter Lang. With Susan Hayward, Rory Calhoun, David Wayne, Thelma Ritter, Robert Wagner, Una Merkel. Song: "They're Either Too Young or Too Old" (music, Arthur Schwartz); plus songs by others. Soundtrack LP: included in *Susan Hayward*, Legends 1000/3.

WHERE'S CHARLEY? (1952), Warner Brothers. Color. Directed by David Butler. With Ray Bolger, Allyn McLerie, Robert Shackleton, Mary Germaine. Songs: "Once in Love With Amy," "Make a Miracle," "My Darling, My Darling," "At the Red Rose Cotillion," "Lovelier Than Ever," "The Years Before Us," "Better Get Out of Here," "Serenade With Asides," "The New Ashmolean Marching Society," "Where's Charley?"

HANS CHRISTIAN ANDERSEN (1952), Samuel Goldwyn for RKO Radio. Color. Directed by Charles Vidor. With Danny Kaye, Renee Jeanmaire, Farley Granger, Roland Petit, Erik Bruhn. Songs: "I'm Hans Christian Andersen," "Thumbalina," "Inchworm," "Wonderful Copenhagen," "Anywhere I Wander," "No Two People," "The King's New Clothes," "Dream Fantasy," "Wedding Fantasy" (music-lyrics, Loesser). LP: studio recording of excerpts narrated and sung by Frank Loesser, included in *Frank Loesser in Hollywood*, Music Masters JJA 19762. Videocassette: Embassy.

GUYS AND DOLLS (1955), Samuel Goldwyn for MGM release. Color. Directed by Joseph L. Mankiewicz. With Marlon Brando, Frank Sinatra, Jean Simmons, Vivian Blaine, Stubby Kaye, B. S. Pully, Sheldon Leonard, Veda Ann Borg. Songs: "A Woman in Love," "Adelaide," "Pet Me Poppa," "Luck Be a Lady," "Fugue for Tin Horns," "Follow the Fold," "The Oldest Established," "I'll Know," "Sit Down, You're Rockin' the Boat," "Sue Me," "Take Back Your Mink," "Guys and Dolls." Soundtrack LP: excerpts included in *Frank Loesser in Hollywood*, Music Masters JJA 19762. Videocassette and videodisc: CBS/Fox.

HOW TO SUCCEED IN BUSINESS WITHOUT REALLY TRYING (1967), Color. Mirisch-United Artists. Directed by David Swift. With Robert Morse, Rudy Vallee, Michelle Lee, Ruth Kobart, Maureen Arthur, Anthony Teague, Sammy Smith. Songs: "How to Succeed," "The Company Way," "Coffee Break," "A Secretary Is Not a Toy," "Grand Old Ivy," "The Brotherhood of Man," "Been a Long Day," "Finch's Frolic," "I Believe In You," "Paris Original" (instrumental only), "Rosemary." Soundtrack LP: conducted by Nelson Riddle, United Artists 5151 (withdrawn).

Arthur Schwartz

Of all the great composers who helped to shape the style of Broadway musicals in the 1930s, Arthur Schwartz (1900–1984) probably fared the least well in Hollywood. Only one of his Broadway hits, 1930's *The Band Wagon,* was later (much later) adapted into a movie hit—in fact, one of the all-time film-musical classics. But Schwartz's original movie scores, with one or two exceptions, remain among the least known with fans of movie musicals in general. Schwartz, ironically, was more successful as a producer of movie musicals by other composers—Kern's *Cover Girl* and Porter's *Night and Day*—than as the composer for *Under Your Spell, That Girl From Paris, Navy Blues, Cairo, Dangerous When Wet,* and other forgettables.

Schwartz's father was a lawyer who wanted his son to follow in his footsteps, even though young Arthur, from his earliest school years, was clearly more interested in music than in anything else. By age fourteen he had become a pianist at a Brooklyn, New York, theater that was showing silent films. In his later teens he began composing songs for shows at a summer camp, teaming for some of them with a then-unknown lyricist named Lorenz Hart. Schwartz continued to write songs for college and amateur productions while attending New York University and then Columbia University Law School.

From 1924 to 1928 Schwartz practiced law while writing songs in his spare time for vaudeville shows and off-Broadway revues. Lorenz Hart kept encouraging Schwartz to give up the law and concentrate full-time on songwriting—though not with Hart as lyricist, since he had already teamed himself with composer Richard Rodgers. Finally, in 1928, at a performance of a Broadway revue titled *Merry-Go-Round,* Schwartz found the collaborator he wanted when he heard the lyrics of Howard Dietz for the first time.

Dietz, a young publicist for MGM in its New York office, wrote songs strictly as a sideline. At first he was reluctant to work with a complete unknown, since he had just completed a score with one of Broadway's top names, Jerome Kern *(Dear Sir).* But Schwartz persisted, and Dietz finally agreed to write the lyrics for several Schwartz songs for a revue to be produced by a man they both knew, Tom Weatherly. That revue became one of 1929's biggest hits: *The Little Show,* starring Fred Allen, Libby Holman, and Clifton Webb. Included in its score was "I Guess I'll Have to Change My Plan," a song that Fred Astaire much later helped to popularize through several recordings. Schwartz and Dietz collaborated on a follow-up, *The Second Little Show* (1930), which flopped. Later that same year, a third revue, *Three's a Crowd,* also starring Allen, Holman, and Webb, was a hit—as was one of its songs, "Something to Remember You By."

The show that really established Schwartz and Dietz as major songwriters was 1930's *The Band Wagon.* It starred Fred and Adele Astaire (in their last show together), and included the song hits "Dancing in the Dark," "I Love Luisa," and "New Sun in the Sky." But subsequent Schwartz and Dietz shows—*Flying Colors* (1932), *Revenge With Music* (1934), *At Home Abroad* (1935), and *Between the Devil* (1937)—received mixed reviews, although their scores produced such hits as "Louisiana Hayride," "All

Together," "You and the Night and the Music," "A Shine on Your Shoes," "By Myself," and "I See Your Face Before Me," all of which eventually became popular standards. Because Dietz's MGM job involved frequent trips between New York and Hollywood, Schwartz once noted that "we worked on trains, planes, limousines, and once even in Garbo's dressing room."

Despite Dietz's Hollywood connections, the team of Schwartz and Dietz received few offers to work in movies. In fact, Dietz once commented sardonically that whenever an MGM picture didn't click at the box office, a studio official would blame it on chief publicist Dietz's being busy with his "sideline" career. Other studios, meanwhile, weren't eager to employ a part-time lyricist who held a major full-time job with another studio. Only a handful of Schwartz and Dietz's Broadway songs turned up in early '30s movies.

Finally, in 1935, the newly merged Twentieth Century-Fox (whose president was Joseph Schenck, brother of MGM president Nicholas Schenck) signed Schwartz and Dietz to write songs for *Under Your Spell*. It starred Metropolitan Opera baritone Lawrence Tibbett in an unoriginal tale about an overworked singer who tries to flee his managers and fans at a Mexican ranch. But after the box-office failure of Tibbett's *Metropolitan* upon its release in late 1935—the first movie, incidentally, to be released under the Twentieth Century-Fox logo—the studio lost interest in Tibbett. To meet contractual obligations, the studio went ahead with *Under Your Spell*, but reduced it to little more than a programmer for the bottom half of double-feature bills. The picture's three routine Schwartz-Dietz songs were soon forgotten with the film itself.

With the Depression limiting Broadway activity, Schwartz considered going back to law practice. But he was stayed from that when NBC offered a contract to compose the music for a thirty-nine-week radio series, *The Gibson Family*. The 1936 series, a situation comedy with music and songs, didn't click and was dropped by the sponsor (Proctor and Gamble) after its first season. Before its demise, Schwartz was asked if the weekly grind of such a series didn't take a lot out of him. His reply: "Yes, but it also takes a lot out of Bach, Beethoven, and Brahms."

In the late 1930s Schwartz moved to Hollywood with his wife and family, hoping to get involved as a producer as well as a songwriter. Assignments were slow in coming. With Johnny Mercer as lyricist, he wrote four forgettable songs for *Navy Blues* (1941), a feeble Warner Brothers comedy about sailors in Honolulu that completely wasted the talents of Ann Sheridan, Martha Raye, Jack Oakie, and Jackie Gleason, and, unintentionally, made clear why the U.S. Navy got caught napping at Pearl Harbor. Even less impressive was MGM's *Cairo* (1942), starring Jeanette MacDonald and Robert Young in a mixture of operetta and spy thriller that set back MacDonald's career so decisively that she didn't make another movie for five years. Having to sing Schwartz's bravely martial "Keep the Light Burning Bright in the Harbor" (with cliché-ridden lyrics by Yip Harburg) certainly didn't help her.

Much better are the songs Schwartz wrote with Frank Loesser (as lyricist) for Warner Brothers's *Thank Your Lucky Stars* (1944) and with Leo Robin for Warner's *The Time, the Place and the Girl* (1946). The first of these is also the best of the all-star revues that most of the Hollywood studios turned out during the war—potpourris of comedy skits and musical numbers featuring just about every star on the lot in unaccustomed and unexpected song-and-dance turns. For *Thank Your Lucky Stars,*

Warner Brothers' "Oomph Girl" of the late '30s and early '40s, Ann Sheridan, sang Arthur Schwartz's and Frank Loesser's "Love Isn't Born, It's Made" in the all-star Thank Your Lucky Stars *(1944).*

Schwartz and Loesser had to write songs for stars who were marginal singers at best, yet they came through with some memorable and durable numbers. "Love Isn't Born, It's Made" is especially delicious as sung knowingly but not licentiously by Ann Sheridan, then at the peak of her popularity as Warner's "Oomph Girl." A wartime lament about the quality of men left on the homefront, "They're Either Too Young or Too Old," is "sung" by Bette Davis with her distinctive sense of pitch and rhythm, and is climaxed with a jitterbug dance by the great lady. Olivia de Havilland and Ida Lupino, as a couple of hepcats, lunge zestily into "The Dreamer," and Hattie McDaniel, a then-recent Oscar winner (for her role as Scarlett O'Hara's Mammy in *Gone With the Wind*), kicks up her heels spiritedly for "Ice-Cold Katie," although the number itself is riddled with some unmistakable racial stereotypes.

The Time, the Place and the Girl of 1946 bears no relationship to the 1929 Warner musical of the same title, even though of all Warner's '40s musicals it's the closest in spirit to those of the early '30s. The plot is strictly old hat—about the problems of Dennis Morgan, Jack Carson, Janis Paige, Martha Vickers, and the ubiquitous S. Z. "Cuddles" Sakall in getting a Broadway show launched. But the Schwartz-Robin songs are so appealing and the dance sequences (by LeRoy Prinz) so enjoyable that you can endure everything, including Sakall's overdone mannerisms. "Through a Thousand Dreams" is a haunting ballad somewhat reminiscent of "Dancing in the Dark." "A Gal in Calico" proves (again) that Easterners can write winning Western songs, and

"(What Do You Do) On a Rainy Night in Rio?" does the same with a samba-flavored Latin tune.

At Warner Brothers, Schwartz was the producer of its Cole Porter biography, *Night and Day* (1946), a commercially successful but disappointing production (discussed in detail in the Cole Porter chapter, page 169). For Columbia, meanwhile, Schwartz also produced the 1944 musical hit *Cover Girl*, starring Rita Hayworth and Gene Kelly. In making him the movie's producer, Columbia's studio chief, Harry Cohn, expected Schwartz to provide the score. "There's a better man available," Schwartz told him, "and I'd like to hire him." With that, Schwartz hired his longtime idol Jerome Kern, teaming him for the first time with lyricist Ira Gershwin for a score that is now a film classic (and discussed in detail in the Kern chapter, page 109).

Schwartz returned to Broadway after the war as both a producer and composer for *Park Avenue* (a flop), with Ira Gershwin as lyricist, and *Inside U.S.A.* (a hit), with Dietz as lyricist. Subsequent shows included *A Tree Grows in Brooklyn* (1951) and *By the Beautiful Sea* (1954), both with Dorothy Fields as lyricist, and *The Gay Life* (1961) and *Jennie* (1963), both with Dietz. None of these has been turned into a movie. During the 1950s there were also critically mixed musical versions for TV of *High Tor* and *A Bell for Adano*, with Schwartz doubling as composer and producer. Neither one, regrettably, has been shown again on TV since the original airings.

The movie by which Schwartz will surely be remembered the longest and most fondly is MGM's *The Band Wagon* (1953)—easily one of the ten best movie musicals ever made. Except for some of its songs and the same star, Fred Astaire, it bears little resemblance to the 1930 Schwartz-Dietz Broadway hit of the same title. Betty Comden and Adolph Green's much-altered and updated screenplay is one of their funniest, crispest, and most literate, as it traces the efforts of a declining film star (Astaire) to launch a new Broadway career while running into more than the usual hindrances from his costar (Cyd Charisse) and an overly artistic director (Jack Buchanan, who, in part, slyly spoofs the movie's actual director, Vincente Minnelli). The songs represent the crème de la crème of the Schwartz and Dietz Broadway songbook. The highlights: A romantic Astaire-Charisse *pas de deux* in Central Park to "Dancing in the Dark"; Astaire's buck-and-winging solo to "A Shine on Your Shoes" (set in a 42nd Street game arcade); and the hilarious "Triplets," with Astaire, Buchanan, and Nanette Fabray unforgettably snarling their way in moppet costumes through a clever routine on their knees.

The Band Wagon is climaxed by the one new song that Schwartz and Dietz wrote especially for the movie, the rousing, quip-filled "That's Entertainment." Appropriately enough, that song became the theme and title of the two outstanding compilation features that MGM made in 1974 and 1976 paying tribute to its best musical numbers of the previous five decades. Perhaps that, more than anything else, assures Arthur Schwartz's place among the Hollywood immortals.

Left: Jack Carson, Janis Paige, Martha Vickers, and Dennis Morgan seek cover to Schwartz's and Robin's "On a Rainy Night in Rio," in 1947's The Time, the Place, and the Girl.

Below: Arthur Schwartz's and Howard Dietz's "Triplets," from The Band Wagon *(1953), brought Fred Astaire, Nanette Fabray, and Jack Buchanan to their knees for one of the 1950s' most memorable comic numbers.*

QUEEN HIGH (1930), Paramount. B&W. Directed by Fred Newmeyer. With Frank Morgan, Charles Ruggles, Ginger Rogers, Stanley Smith, Tom Brown, Betty Garde. Song: "I'm Afraid of You" (collaboration with Ralph Rainger, Edward Eliscu); plus songs by others.

FOLLOW THE LEADER (1930), Paramount. B&W. Directed by Norman Taurog. With Ed Wynn, Ginger Rogers, Ethel Merman, Lou Holtz, Stanley Smith. Song: "Just Laugh It Off" (collaboration with Ralph Rainger, E.Y. Harburg); plus songs by others.

SHE LOVES ME NOT (1934), Paramount. B&W. Directed by Elliott Nugent. With Bing Crosby, Miriam Hopkins, Kitty Carlisle, Henry Stephenson, Lynn Overman. Song: "After All, You're All I'm After" (lyrics, Edward Heyman); plus songs by others.

UNDER YOUR SPELL (1936), Twentieth Century-Fox. B&W. Directed by Otto Preminger. With Lawrence Tibbett, Wendy Barrie, Arthur Treacher, Berton Churchill, Jed Prouty, Claudia Coleman. Songs: "Under Your Spell," "Amigo," "My Little Mule Wagon" (lyrics, Howard Dietz).

THAT GIRL FROM PARIS (1937), RKO Radio. B&W. Directed by Leigh Jason. With Lily Pons, Gene Raymond, Jack Oakie, Mischa Auer, Frank Jenks, Lucille Ball, Herman Bing. Songs: "Seal It With a Kiss," "My Nephew From Nice," "Moonface," "Love and Learn," "The Call to Arms" (lyrics, Edward Heyman); plus songs and arias by others.

NAVY BLUES (1941), Warner Brothers. B&W. Directed by Lloyd Bacon. With Ann Sheridan, Martha Raye, Jack Oakie, Jack Haley, Jack Carson, Herbert Anderson, Jackie Gleason. Songs: "Navy Blues," "You're a Natural," "In Waikiki," "When Are We Going to Land Abroad?" (lyrics, Johnny Mercer). Soundtrack LP: excerpts included in *Ann Sheridan / Marlene Dietrich,* Marsher 201.

CAIRO (1942), MGM. B&W. Directed by W. S. Van Dyke II. With Jeanette MacDonald, Robert Young, Reginald Owen, Ethel Waters, Lionel Atwill, Mona Barrie, Dooley Wilson. Songs: "Cairo," "The Waltz Is Over," "Keep the Light Burning Bright" (lyrics, E. Y. Harburg); plus songs by others. Soundtrack LP: Sunbeam p-514; also, excerpts included in *The Music of Arthur Schwartz,* Music Masters JJA-19758.

ALL THROUGH THE NIGHT (1942), Warner Brothers. B&W. Directed by Vincent Sherman. With Humphrey Bogart, Kaaren Verne, Peter Lorre, Conrad Veidt, Judith Anderson, Frank McHugh, Jane Darwell, Phil Silvers, Jackie Gleason. Song: "All Through the Night" (lyrics, Johnny Mercer).

CROSSROADS (1942), MGM. Directed by Jack Conway. With William Powell, Hedy Lamarr, Basil Rathbone, Claire Trevor, Margaret Wycherly, Felix Bressart, Sig Ruman. Song: "Till You Return" (lyrics, Howard Dietz).

PRINCESS O'ROURKE (1943), Warner Brothers. B&W. Directed by Norman Krasna. With Olivia de Havilland, Robert Cummings, Charles Coburn, Jane Wyman, Jack Carson, Gladys Cooper, Harry Davenport. Song: "Honorable Moon" (lyrics, E. Y. Harburg).

THANK YOUR LUCKY STARS (1943), Warner Brothers. B&W. Directed by David Butler. With Eddie Cantor, Joan Leslie, Dennis Morgan, Edward Everett Horton, S. Z. Sakall, Bette Davis, Ann Sheridan, Olivia de Havilland, Ida Lupino, Errol Flynn, John Garfield, Alexis Smith, Dinah Shore, Hattie McDaniel, Spike Jones and his Orchestra, Alan Hale, Jack Carson, George Tobias. Songs: "Love Isn't Born, It's Made," "They're Either Too Young or Too Old," "Goodnight, Good Neighbor," "How Sweet You Are," "I'm Ridin' for a Fall," "We're Staying Home Tonight," "The Dreamer," "No You, No Me," "Ice-Cold Katie," "That's What You Jolly-Well Get," "I'm Goin' North," "Thank Your Lucky Stars" (lyrics, Frank Loesser). Soundtrack LP: Curtain Calls 100/8.

THE TIME, THE PLACE AND THE GIRL (1946), Warner Brothers. Color. Directed by David Butler. With Dennis Morgan, Martha Vickers, Janis Paige, Jack Carson, S. Z. Sakall, Florence Bates, Alan Hale, Donald Woods, Carmen Cavallaro and his Orchestra, the Condos Brothers. Songs: "Through a Thousand Dreams," "A Gal in Calico," "A Rainy Night in Rio," "Oh, But I Do," "A Solid Citizen of the Solid South," "I Happened to Walk Down First Street" (lyrics, Leo Robin). Soundtrack LP: Titania 511 (with *The Paleface*); also, studio recording of two of the songs as sung by the composer included in *From the Pen of Arthur Schwartz,* RCA LPL1-5121.

HER KIND OF MAN (1946), Warner Brothers. B&W. Directed by Frederick De Cordova. With Dane Clark, Janis Paige, Faye Emerson, Zachary Scott, George Tobias. Song: "Something to Remember You By" (lyrics, Howard Dietz); plus songs by others.

DANCING IN THE DARK (1949), Twentieth Century-Fox. Color. Directed by Irving Reis. With William Powell, Betsy Drake, Mark Stevens, Adolphe Menjou, Hope Emerson, Walter Catlett, Randy Stuart. Songs: "Dancing in the Dark," "I Love Luisa," "New Sun in the Sky," "Something to Remember You By" (lyrics, Howard Dietz).

EXCUSE MY DUST (1951), MGM. Color. Directed by Roy Rowland. With Red Skelton, Sally Forrest, MacDonald Carey, Monica Lewis, William Demarest, Jane Darwell. Songs: "Spring Has Sprung," "Lorelei Brown," "Get a Horse," "That's for Children," "Goin' Steady," "I'd Like to Take You Out Dreaming," "It Couldn't Happen to Two Nicer People" (lyrics, Dorothy Fields).

WITH A SONG IN MY HEART (1953), Twentieth Century-Fox. Color. Directed by Walter Lang. With Susan Hayward, Rory Calhoun, David Wayne, Thelma Ritter, Una Merkel, Robert Wagner, Leif Erickson. Song: "They're Either Too Young or Too Old" (lyrics, Frank Loesser); plus songs by others. Soundtrack LP: excerpts included in *Susan Hayward, Legends* 1000/3.

DANGEROUS WHEN WET (1953), MGM. Color. Directed by Charles Walters. With Esther Williams, Fernando Lamas, Charlotte Greenwood, Jack Carson, Denise Darcel, Barbara Whiting, William Demarest, Donna Corcoran. Songs: "I Got Out of Bed on the Right Side," "Ain't Nature Grand," "I Like Men," "In My Wildest Dreams," "Fifi," "Liquipep" (lyrics, Johnny Mercer).

THE BAND WAGON (1953), MGM. Color. Directed by Vincente Minnelli. With Fred Astaire, Cyd Charisse, Jack Buchanan, Nanette Fabray, Oscar Levant, James Mitchell, Leroy Daniels; Ava Gardner. Songs: "Dancing in the Dark," "By Myself," "A Shine on My Shoes," "New Sun in the Sky," "Louisiana Hayride," "I Guess I'll Have to Change My Plan," "I Love Luisa," "Triplets," "That's Entertainment," "High and Low," "You and the Night and the Music," "Something to Remember You By" (lyrics, Howard Dietz). Soundtrack LP: MCA 25015. Videocassette: MGM/UA.

TORCH SONG (1953), MGM. Color. Directed by Charles Walters. With Joan Crawford, Michael Wilding, Gig Young, Marjorie Rambeau, Dorothy Patrick, Eugene Loring, Benny Rubin. Song: "Two-Faced Woman" (lyrics, Howard Dietz); plus songs by others. Soundtrack LP: excerpt included in *Joan Crawford,* Curtain Calls 100/23.

YOU'RE NEVER TOO YOUNG (1955), Paramount. Color. Directed by Norman Taurog. With Dean Martin, Jerry Lewis, Diana Lynn, Raymond Burr, Nina Foch, Veda Ann Borg. Songs: "Simpatico," "Love Is All That Matters" (lyrics, Sammy Cahn).

I COULD GO ON SINGING (1963), Barbican for United Artists release. Color. Directed by Ronald Neame. With Judy Garland, Dirk Bogarde, Aline MacMahon, Gregory Phillips, Jack Klugman, Pauline Jameson. Song: "By Myself" (lyrics, Howard Dietz); plus songs by others. Soundtrack LP: Capitol SW1861.

Jule Styne

Like Frank Loesser, Jule Styne's career as a songwriter has been the reverse of those of his most famous colleagues. Instead of tallying up a series of hits on Broadway and Tin Pan Alley before going to Hollywood, Styne spent a decade writing for the movies *before* achieving his greatest successes on Broadway. Even though most of his movies were B programmers at lesser studios, Styne's songs won four Oscar nominations (out of an eventual six) before his first Broadway hit, 1947's *High Button Shoes*.

Jule Styne (1905–) was born Julius Kerwin Stein in London, England, of Ukrainian-Jewish parents. He came to the United States with his family just before the outbreak of World War I and grew up in Chicago. He was ten when he won a Silver Medal in a competition among child pianists, which brought engagements with the youth concerts of the Chicago Symphony Orchestra, the Saint Louis Symphony, and the Detroit Symphony. Short and chubby as a youngster, he was discouraged from pursuing a concert career as a pianist by the renowned Harold Bauer, who told Styne's parents that the size of his hand and the spread of his fingers would prevent him from ever becoming a great pianist. Styne turned increasingly to jazz, and in his early twenties he began playing piano and making arrangements for jazz combos in the Chicago area. By 1931 he had formed his own dance band, playing in area hotels and clubs.

In 1938 Styne went to Hollywood to work for Twentieth Century-Fox as an arranger and vocal coach for such performers as Alice Faye, Tony Martin, Joan Davis, and the Ritz Brothers. When a staff composer died suddenly, Styne convinced studio chief Darryl F. Zanuck to give him a chance as a composer. He was assigned the writing of incidental songs for such B movies as *Kentucky Moonshine, Hold That Coed,* and *Straight, Place and Show,* working mostly with lyricist Sidney Clare.

In 1940 Styne moved to Republic Studios, which until then specialized in low-budget westerns and serials but was moving toward occasional B comedies and musicals as well. As Styne once told an interviewer: "I swallowed my pride and did just about anything they asked me to do—orchestrations, conducting, playing the piano for Trigger. . . ."

For several years, in between writing incidental songs for such Gene Autry and Roy Rogers musicals as *Melody Ranch, Back in the Saddle,* and *Sheriff of Tombstone,* Styne wrote songs for many hour-long, forgettable programmers, including *Melody and Moonlight, Barnyard Follies, Sing, Dance, Plenty Hot, Rookies on Parade,* and three Judy Canova hillbilly musicals, *Sis Hopkins, Puddin' Head,* and *Sleepytime Gal* (working mostly with lyricists Sol Meyer, Ed Cherkose, and Herb Magidson). He also wrote the score for the more ambitious *Hit Parade of 1941* (including the Oscar-nominated "Who Am I?", with lyrics by Walter Bullock) and *Ice Capades Revue* (1942) starring Vera Hruba Ralston, the Czech skater whom Republic president Herbert Yates married and spent years trying unsuccessfully to turn into a major film star.

During most of the war years, Styne divided his time among Republic, Columbia, Universal, Paramount, and United Artists. Although still working mostly on lesser musicals at each studio, some of his songs became major hits. Among them: "I Don't Want to Walk Without You" from *Sweater Girl* (1942, lyrics by Frank Loesser), "(It Seems to Me) I've Heard That Song Before" from *Youth on Parade* (1942, lyrics by Sammy Cahn), "There Goes That Song Again" from *Carolina Blues* (1944, lyrics by Cahn), and another Oscar nominee, "I'll Walk Alone" from *Follow the Boys* (1944, lyrics by Cahn). He was much less successful with the new songs that he was asked to write to be interpolated into Paramount's film version of Cole Porter's *Let's Face It* ('43) and United Artists's version of Kurt Weill's *Knickerbocker Holiday* ('44).

Lyricist Cahn introduced Styne to the country's "hottest" young singer, Frank Sinatra, who was instrumental in getting both Styne and Cahn assigned to his second feature movie for RKO Radio, *Step Lively,* a musical adaptation of the Broadway comedy *Room Service* (previously filmed as a Marx Brothers farce). None of the songs became hits, although one, "As Long As There's Music," has survived as a favorite of some jazz performers. But Sinatra liked the score enough to request Styne and Cahn for his first MGM musical, *Anchors Aweigh* (1945). One of its songs brought Styne another Oscar nomination, for "I Fall in Love Too Easily."

Jule Styne's first Oscar nomination came for the song "Who Am I?," from the stylish if modestly-budgeted Hit Parade of 1941, *which featured Ann Miller (center) with such other performers as Frances Langford, Kenny Baker, and Borrah Minnevitch's Harmonica Rascals.*

Styne and Cahn were now in demand for occasional major musicals, such as Columbia's *Tonight and Every Night* with Rita Hayworth, and Paramount's *The Stork Club* with Betty Hutton (both 1945). But most of Styne's mid-'40s credits continued to be in the B category, including such now-forgotten titles as *Cinderella Jones, Earl Carroll's Sketchbook, Tars and Spars, The Sweetheart of Sigma Chi,* and *Casanova in Burlesque.* An attempt at a Broadway musical, *Glad to See You,* ended in failure when the show closed after its Boston tryout.

Then came the Broadway hit *High Button Shoes*—and the tide turned. That show was followed by a succession of major Broadway musicals: *Gentlemen Prefer Blondes* ('49), *Two on the Aisle* ('51), *Hazel Flagg* ('53), *Peter Pan* ('54), *Bells Are Ringing* ('56), *Say Darling* ('58), *Gypsy* ('59), *Do Re Mi* ('60), and *Funny Girl* ('64). Some of these were turned into hit movies. *Gentlemen Prefer Blondes* achieved more fame as a '53 film because of its knockout teaming of Marilyn Monroe and Jane Russell, even though only three of the original Styne-Robin songs were kept (including "Diamonds Are a Girl's Best Friend"). More faithful to the originals, at least musically, are Judy Holliday's *Bells Are Ringing* ('60), Rosalind Russell's *Gypsy* ('62), and Barbara Streisand's *Funny Girl* ('68), all of them essentially one-woman shows built around unforgettable characters. Each of these three also won Academy Award nominations in one music category or another, and Barbra Streisand won an Oscar as Best Actress for re-creating the *Funny Girl* role that had made her a Broadway star. Among the popular standards to come out of them: "Just in Time" and "The Party's Over" (from *Bells Are Ringing*—lyrics by Betty Comden and Adolph Green), "Some People" and "Everything's Coming Up Roses" (from *Gypsy*—lyrics by Stephen Sondheim), and "People" and "Don't Rain on My Parade" (from *Funny Girl*—lyrics by Bob Merrill).

In between most of his Broadway shows, Styne continued to write occasionally for movies, winning Oscar nominations in 1948 and 1949 for songs in two Doris Day musicals: "It's Magic" from *Romance on the High Seas,* and the title song from *It's a Great Feeling.* Then, in 1954, he finally copped an Oscar—ironically for the title song of a nonmusical, the romantic tearjerker *Three Coins in the Fountain,* one of the first and most popular of Twentieth Century-Fox's CinemaScope productions.

There were also songs for three relatively routine backstage movie musicals: *West Point Story* (1950) with James Cagney and Doris Day, *Meet Me After the Show* (1951) with Betty Grable and Rory Calhoun, and *Two Tickets to Broadway* (1951) with Janet Leigh, Tony Martin, and Ann Miller. A 1955 musical version of *My Sister Eileen*— with Betty Garrett, Janet Leigh, Jack Lemmon, and Bob Fosse—suffered in comparison with *Wonderful Town,* another musical version of the same story written two years

Frank Sinatra got second billing to Gene Kelly in 1945's Anchors Aweigh, *but got the best Jule Styne-Sammy Cahn songs, as well as Pamela Britton (right). Jose Iturbi looks on.*

Bob Fosse, Janet Leigh, Betty Garrett, and Tommy Rall made "Give Me a Band and My Baby" one of the highlights of the 1955 musical version of My Sister Eileen.

earlier for Broadway by Leonard Bernstein, Betty Comden, and Adolph Green. Most undistinguished of all was 1966's *What a Way to Go!,* for which Styne (with Comden and Green) provided the songs for the film's one extended musical sequence, with Gene Kelly and Shirley MacLaine.

Has Styne ever regretted abandoning his classical career for Broadway and Hollywood? Styne once put it this way to an interviewer from *Time* magazine: "Art is great. But who can sing Shostakovich?"

JULE STYNE'S MOVIES AND SONGS ON TAPE AND DISC

KENTUCKY MOONSHINE (1938), Twentieth Century-Fox. B&W. Directed by David Butler. With The Ritz Brothers, Tony Martin, Marjorie Weaver, Slim Summerville. Song: "Kentucky Opera" (lyrics, Sidney Clare); plus songs by others.

STRAIGHT, PLACE AND SHOW (1938), Twentieth Century-Fox. B&W. Directed by David Butler. With The Ritz Brothers, Ethel Merman, Richard Arlen, Phyllis Brooks. Song: "International Cowboys" (lyrics, Sid Kuller, Ray Golden); plus songs by others.

HOLD THAT COED (1938), Twentieth Century-Fox. B&W. Directed by George Marshall. With John Barrymore, George Murphy, Marjo-

rie Weaver, Joan Davis, Jack Haley, Johnny Downs. Song: "Limpy Dip" (lyrics, Sidney Clare, Nick Castle); plus songs by others.

PACK UP YOUR TROUBLES (1939), Twentieth Century-Fox. B&W. Directed by H. Bruce Humberstone. With Jane Withers, The Ritz Brothers, Lynn Bari, Joseph Schildkraut. Song: "Who'll Buy My Flowers?" (lyrics, Sidney Clare).

THE GIRL FROM HAVANA (1940), Republic. B&W. Directed by Lew Landers. With Dennis O'Keefe, Steffi Duna, Claire Carleton, Victor Jory. Songs: "The Girl from Havana," "Querida (Take Me Tonight)" (lyrics, George R. Brown).

SLIGHTLY HONORABLE (1940), United Artists. B&W. Directed by Tay Garnett. With Pat O'Brien, Edward Arnold, Broderick Crawford, Ruth Terry, Eve Arden, Evelyn Keyes. Song: "Cupid's After Me" (lyrics, George R. Brown).

MELODY RANCH (1940), Republic. B&W. Directed by Joseph Santley. With Gene Autry, Jimmy Durante, Ann Miller, Barbara Allen, Barton MacLane, Gabby Hayes. Songs: "Rodeo Rose," "Stake Your Dreams on Melody Ranch," "Torpedo Joe," "What Are Cowboys Made Of?" (lyrics, Eddy Cherokose). Videocassette: Blackhawk.

MELODY AND MOONLIGHT (1940), Republic. B&W. Directed by Joseph Santley. With Jane Frazee, Johnny Downs, Mary Lee, Jerry Colonna, Barbara Allen. Songs: "Melody and Moonlight," "Tahiti Honey," "Rooftop Serenade," "Top of the Mornin'," "I Close My Eyes" (lyrics, George R. Brown, Sol Meyer).

SING, DANCE, PLENTY HOT (1940), Republic. B&W. Directed by Lew Landers. With Johnny Downs, Ruth Terry, Barbara Allen, Billy Gilbert, Mary Lee. Songs: "When a Fella's Got a Girl," "I'm Just a Weakie," "What Fools These Mortals Be," "Too Toy," "Tequila," "What You Gonna Do When There Ain't No Swing?" (lyrics, George R. Brown, Sol Meyer).

BARNYARD FOLLIES (1940), Republic. B&W. Directed by Frank McDonald. With Mary Lee, Rufe Davis, June Storey, Joan Woodbury, Jed Prouty. Song: "Poppin' the Corn" (lyrics, Sol Meyer); plus songs by others.

HIT PARADE OF 1941 (1940), Republic. B&W. Directed by John H. Auer. With Kenny Baker, Frances Langford, Hugh Herbert, Patsy Kelly, Mary Boland, Phil Silvers, Ann Miller, Six Hits and a Miss, Borrah Minnevitch and his Harmonica Rascals. Songs: "Who Am I?," "In the Cool of the Evening," "Make Yourself at Home," "Swing Low, Sweet Rhythm" (lyrics, Walter Bullock); plus songs by others.

SIS HOPKINS (1941), Republic. B&W. Directed by Joseph Santley. With Judy Canova, Jerry Colonna, Bob Crosby, Susan Hayward, Charles Butterworth. Songs: "If You're in Love," "Cracker Barrel County," "Look at You, Look at Me," "Well! Well!," "It Ain't Hay (It's the U.S.A.)" (lyrics, Frank Loesser).

DOCTORS DON'T TELL (1941), Republic. B&W. Directed by Jacques Tourneur. With John Beal, Florence Rice, Ward Bond, Edward Norris. Songs: "Take My Heart," "Querida" (lyrics, Eddie Cherkose); "Lilly and Billy" (lyrics, Sol Meyer).

SAILORS ON LEAVE (1941), Republic. B&W. Directed by Herbert Dalmas. With William Lundigan, Shirley Ross. Song: "Since You" (lyrics, Frank Loesser).

ICE CAPADES (1941), Republic. B&W. Directed by Joseph Santley. With James Ellison, Dorothy Lewis, Jerry Colonna, Barbara Allen. Song: "Forever and Ever" (lyrics, George R. Brown); plus songs by others.

RIDIN' ON A RAINBOW (1941), Republic. B&W. Directed by Lew Landers. With Gene Autry, Smiley Burnette, Mary Lee, Carol Adams. Songs: "Hunky Dorey," "Sing a Song of Laughter," "I'm the One Who's Lonely," "What's Your Favorite Holiday?" (lyrics, Sol Meyer); plus songs by others. Videocassette: Blackhawk.

NEVADA CITY (1941), Republic. B&W. Directed by Joseph Kane. With Roy Rogers, Gabby Hayes, Sally Payne. Songs: "Prairie Serenade," "Lonely Hills" (lyrics, Sol Meyer, Eddie Cherkose); plus songs by others.

BACK IN THE SADDLE (1941), Republic. B&W. Directed by Lew Landers. With Gene Autry, Smiley Burnette, Mary Lee. Songs: "Where the River Meets the Range," "Swingin' Sam, the Cowboy Man" (lyrics, Sol Meyer); plus songs by others.

DOWN MEXICO WAY (1941), Republic. B&W. Directed by Joseph Santley. With Gene Autry, Smiley Burnett, Fay McKenzie, Sidney Blackmer. Song: "Down Mexico Way" (lyrics, Eddie Cherkose).

JESSE JAMES AT BAY (1941), Republic. B&W. Directed by Joseph Kane. With Roy Rogers, Gabby Hayes, Sally Payne. Song: "Just for You" (lyrics, Sol Meyer).

PALS OF THE PECOS (1941), Republic. B&W. Directed by Lester Orlebeck. With Bob Livingston, Bob Steele, Rufe Davis, June Johnson. Song: "Don Pedro Pistachio" (lyrics, Eddie Cherkose).

BAD MAN OF DEADWOOD (1941), Republic. B&W. Directed by Joseph Kane. With Roy Rogers, Gabby Hayes, Carol Adams. Song: "Joe O'Grady" (lyrics, Sol Meyer).

SHERIFF OF TOMBSTONE (1941), Republic. B&W. Directed by Joseph Kane. With Roy Rogers, Gabby Hayes, Elyse Knox, Sally Payne. Songs: "Ridin' on a Rocky Road," "Ya Should'a Seen Pete" (lyrics, Sol Meyer); plus songs by others.

THE SINGING HILLS (1941), Republic. B&W. Directed by Lew Landers. With Gene Autry, Smiley Burnette, Virginia Dale, Mary Lee. Song: "Tumbledown Shack in Havana" (lyrics, Sol Meyer, Eddie Cherkose); plus songs by others.

WEST OF THE CIMARRON (1941), Republic. B&W. Directed by Lester Orlebeck. With Bob Steele, Tom Tyler, Rufe Davis, Lois Collier. Song: "Wa-Wa-Watermelon" (lyrics, Sol Meyer).

ROOKIES ON PARADE (1941), Republic.

B&W. Directed by Joseph Santley. With Bob Crosby, Ruth Terry, Gertrude Niesen, Eddie Foy Jr., Marie Wilson, William Demarest. Song: "Rookies on Parade" (lyrics, Eddie Cherkose); plus songs by others.

ANGELS WITH BROKEN WINGS (1941), Republic. B&W. Directed by Donald Vorhaus. With Jane Frazee, Binnie Barnes, Leo Gorcey, Gilbert Roland, Mary Lee. Songs: "Bye-lo, Baby," "Where Do We Dream from Here?," "Three Little Wishes," "In Buenos Aires," "Has To Be" (lyrics, Eddie Cherkose).

PUDDIN' HEAD (1941), Republic. B&W. Directed by Joseph Santley. With Judy Canova, Francis Lederer, Astrid Allwyn, Slim Summerville, Eddie Foy Jr., The Sportsmen. Songs: "Puddin' Head," "Hey, Junior," "Manhattan Holiday," "You're Telling I?" (lyrics, Sol Meyer, Eddie Cherkose).

SUNSET ON THE DESERT (1942), Republic. B&W. Directed by Joseph Kane. With Roy Rogers, Gabby Hayes, Lynne Carver. Song: "Ridin' on a Rocky Road" (lyrics, Sol Meyer); plus songs by others.

HEART OF THE RIO GRANDE (1942), Republic. B&W. Directed by William Morgan. With Gene Autry, Smiley Burnette, Fay McKenzie. Song: "Rainbow in the Night" (lyrics, Sol Meyer); plus songs by others. Videocassette: Blackhawk.

YOUTH ON PARADE (1942), Republic. B&W. Directed by Albert S. Rogell. With John Hubbard, Martha O'Driscoll, Tom Brown, Ruth Terry, Bob Crosby, Lynn Merrick. Songs: "If It's Love," "You're So Good for Me," "(It Seems to Me) I've Heard That Song Before," "You Gotta Study, Buddy," "Cotcha Too Ta Mee" (lyrics, Sammy Cahn).

SHEPHERD OF THE OZARKS (1942), Republic. B&W. Directed by Frank McDonald. With The Weaver Brothers, June Weaver. Song: "Well! Well!" (lyrics, Frank Loesser); plus songs by others.

CALL OF THE CANYON (1942), Republic. B&W. Directed by Joseph Santley. With Gene Autry, Smiley Burnette, Ruth Terry. Song: "When It's Chilly Down in Chile" (lyrics, Sol Meyer); plus songs by others. Videocassette: Blackhawk.

SLEEPYTIME GAL (1942), Republic. B&W. Directed by Albert S. Rogell. With Judy Canova, Tom Brown, Ruth Terry, Skinnay Ennis and his Orchestra. Songs: "Barrelhouse Bessie," "I Don't Want Anybody at All," "When the Cat's Away" (lyrics, Herb Magidson); plus songs by others.

COWBOY SERENADE (1942), Republic. B&W. Directed by William Morgan. With Gene Autry, Smiley Burnette, Fay McKenzie. Song: "Tahiti Honey" (lyrics, George R.

Brown, Sol Meyer); plus songs by others.

ICE CAPADES REVUE (1942), TV title: *Rhythm Hits the Ice.* Republic. B&W. Directed by Bernard Vorhaus. Vera Hruba (Ralston), Ellen Drew, Richard Denning, Jerry Colonna, Barbara Allen. Songs: "The Guy With the Polka-Dot Tie" (lyrics, Sol Meyer); "Tequila" (lyrics, Sol Meyer, George R. Brown); plus songs by others.

HI NEIGHBOR (1942), Republic. B&W. Directed by Charles Lamont. With Jean Parker, John Archer, Janet Beecher. Song: "When a Fella's Got a Girl" (lyrics, Sol Meyer, George R. Brown); plus songs by others.

JOHNNY DOUGHBOY (1942), Republic. B&W. Directed by John F. Auer. With Jane Withers, Henry Wilcoxon, William Demarest, Bobby Breen. Songs: "Victory Caravan," "It Takes a Guy Like I," "Baby's a Big Girl Now," "All Done and All Through" (lyrics, Sammy Cahn); plus songs by others.

PRIORITIES ON PARADE (1942), Paramount. B&W. Directed by Albert S. Rogell. With Ann Miller, Johnny Johnston, Betty Rhodes, Barbara Allen (Vera Vague), Harry Barris. Songs: "You're in Love With Someone Else But I'm in Love With You" (lyrics, Frank Loesser); "I'd Like to Know You Better," "Here Comes Katrinka," "Cooperate With Your Air-Raid Warden," "Conchita Marquita Lolita Pepita Rosetta Juanita Lopez" (lyrics, Herb Magidson).

SWEATER GIRL (1942), Paramount. B&W. Directed by William Clemons. With Eddie Bracken, June Preisser, Betty Rhodes, Nils Asther, Kenneth Howell. Songs: "I Don't Want to Walk Without You," "I Said No," "Sweater Girl," "What Gives Out Now?" (lyrics, Frank Loesser); plus songs by others.

THE POWERS GIRL (1942), United Artists. B&W. Directed by Norman Z. McLeod. With George Murphy, Carole Landis, Anne Shirley, Dennis Day, Benny Goodman and his Orchestra. Songs: "Three Dreams," "The Lady Who Didn't Believe in Love," "Partners," "We're Looking for the Big Bad Wolf" (lyrics, Kim Gannon); plus songs by others.

HIT PARADE OF 1943 (1942), TV title: *Change of Heart.* Republic. B&W. Directed by Albert S. Rogell. With Susan Hayward, John Carroll, Gail Patrick, Eve Arden, Count Basie and his Orchestra, Freddy Martin and his Orchestra, Ray McKinley and his Orchestra. Songs: "A Change of Heart," "Take a Chance," "Who Took Me Home Last Night?," "Harlem Sandman," "Do These Old Eyes Deceive Me?," "That's How to Write a Song," "Tahm-Boom-Bah" (lyrics, Harold Adamson); plus songs by others.

TAHITI HONEY (1943), Republic. B&W.

Directed by John H. Auer. With Simone Simon, Dennis O'Keefe, Michael Whalen, Lionel Stander. Song: "Tahiti Honey" (lyrics, George H. Brown); plus songs by others.

SALUTE FOR THREE (1943), Paramount. B&W. Directed by Ralph Murphy. With MacDonald Carey, Betty Rhodes, Dona Drake, Cliff Edwards, Lorraine and Rognan. Songs: "I'd Do It for You," "Don't Worry," "Wha' D'Ya Do When It Rains?," "My Wife's a WAC," "Left, Right" (lyrics, Kim Gannon, Sol Meyer); plus songs by others.

HENRY ALDRICH SWINGS IT (1943), Paramount. B&W. Directed by Hugh Bennett. With Jimmy Lydon, Charles Smith, Mimi Chandler, John Litel. Song "Ding-Dong, Sing a Song" (lyrics, Kim Gannon).

SHANTYTOWN (1943), Republic. B&W. Directed by Joseph Santley. With Mary Lee, John Archer. Song: "On the Corner of Sunshine and Main" (lyrics, Kim Gannon).

THUMBS UP (1943), Republic. B&W. Directed by Joseph Santley. With Brenda Joyce, Douglas Heath, Gertrude Niesen, Elsa Lanchester, Queenie Leonard. Songs: "From Here On," "Love Is a Corny Thing," "Who Are the British?" (lyrics, Sammy Cahn); plus song by others.

SWING YOUR PARTNER (1943), Republic. B&W. Directed by Frank McDonald. With Judy Clark, Barbara Allen (Vera Vague), Roger Clark, Richard Lane, Esther Dale, Lullubelle and Scotty, the Tennessee Ramblers. Songs: "Cracker Barrel County" (lyrics, Frank Loesser); "In the Cool of the Evening" (lyrics, Walter Bullock); plus songs by others.

LARCENY WITH MUSIC (1943), Universal. B&W. Directed by Edward Lilley. Allan Jones, Kitty Carlisle, Leo Carillo, Lee Patrick, Alvino Rey and his Orchestra. Song: "For the Want of You" (lyrics, Eddie Cherkose); plus songs by others.

HERE COMES ELMER (1943), Universal. B&W. Directed by Joseph Santley. With Al Pearce, Dale Evans, Pinky Tomlin, Nat "King" Cole Trio, Jan Garber and his Orchestra. Song: "You're So Good to Me" (lyrics, Sammy Cahn); plus songs by others.

LET'S FACE IT (1943), Paramount. B&W. Directed by Sidney Lanfield. With Bob Hope, Betty Hutton, Eve Arden, ZaSu Pitts, Phyllis Povah, Dona Drake. Songs: "Who Did? I Did, Yes I Did," "Plain Jane Doe" (lyrics, Sammy Cahn); plus songs by other.

YOU CAN'T RATION LOVE (1944), Paramount. B&W. Directed by Lester Fuller. With Johnny Johnston, Betty Rhodes, Marie Wilson, Marjorie Weaver. Song: "I Don't Want to Walk Without You" (lyrics, Frank Loesser); plus songs by others.

CASANOVA IN BURLESQUE (1944), Republic. B&W. Directed by Leslie Goodwins.

With Joe E. Brown, June Havoc, Dale Evans, Marjorie Gateson. Song: "Who Took Me Home Last Night?" (lyrics, Harold Adamson); plus songs by others.

FOLLOW THE BOYS (1944), Universal. B&W. Directed by Edward Sutherland. With George Raft, Vera Zorina, Grace McDonald, Dinah Shore, Jeanette MacDonald, Sophie Tucker, the Andrews Sisters, Marlene Dietrich, Orson Welles, Arthur Rubinstein, W. C. Fields, other guest stars. Songs: "I'll Walk Alone," "A Better Day Is Coming" (lyrics, Sammy Cahn); plus songs by others.

KNICKERBOCKER HOLIDAY (1944), United Artists. B&W. Directed by Harry Joe Brown. With Nelson Eddy, Charles Coburn, Constance Dowling, Shelley Winter [sic]. Songs: "Zuyder Zee," "Love Has Made This Such a Lovely Day," "One More Smile" (lyrics, Sammy Cahn); plus songs by others.

JAM SESSION (1944), Columbia. B&W. Directed by Charles Barton. With Ann Miller, Jess Barker, Alvino Rey and his Orchestra, Jan Garber and his Orchestra, Teddy Powell and his Orchestra, Glen Gray and his Orchestra, the Pied Pipers with Jo Stafford, Louis Armstrong and his Orchestra, Charlie Barnet and his Orchestra. Song: "Victory Polka" (lyrics, Sammy Cahn); plus songs by others. Soundtrack LP: Hollywood Soundstage 5014 (with *Reveille with Beverly*).

ROSIE THE RIVETER (1944), Republic. B&W. Directed by Joseph Santley. With Jane Frazee, Frank Albertson, Barbara Allen (Vera Vague), Frank Jenks. Song: "I Don't Want Anyone at All" (lyrics, Herb Magidson); plus songs by others.

JANIE (1944), Warner Brothers. B&W. Directed by Michael Curtiz. With Joyce Reynolds, Edward Arnold, Ann Harding, Robert Hutton. Song: "Keep Your Powder Dry" (lyrics, Sammy Cahn); plus songs by others.

STEP LIVELY (1944), RKO Radio. B&W. Directed by Tim Whelan. With Frank Sinatra, George Murphy, Gloria DeHaven, Adolphe Menjou, Anne Jeffreys. Songs: "As Long As There's Music," "Come Out, Come Out, Wherever You Are," "Where Does Love Begin?," "And Then You Kissed Me," "Why Must There Be an Opening Song?," "Some Other Time," "Ask the Madam" (lyrics, Sammy Cahn). Soundtrack LP: Hollywood Soundstage 412. Videocassette: RKO Home Video.

CAROLINA BLUES (1944), Columbia. B&W. Directed by Leigh Jason. With Kay Kyser and his Orchestra, Ann Miller, Victor Moore, Georgia Carroll, Harold Nicholas. Songs: "There Goes That Song Again," "You Make Me Dream Too Much," "Poor Little Rhode Island" (lyrics, Sammy Cahn); "Thanks a Lot, Mr. Beebe" (lyrics, Cahn, Dudley Brooks).

TONIGHT AND EVERY NIGHT (1945),

Columbia. Color. Directed by Victor Saville. With Rita Hayworth, Janet Blair, Lee Bowman, Marc Platt, Florence Bates. Songs: "The Heart of a City," "Anywhere," "What Does an English Girl Think of a Yank?," "The Boy I Left Behind," "You Excite Me," "Tonight and Every Night" (lyrics, Sammy Cahn). Soundtrack LP: excerpts included in *Rita Hayworth,* Curtain Calls 100/22.

ANCHORS AWEIGH (1945), MGM. Color. Directed by George Sidney. With Gene Kelly, Frank Sinatra, Kathryn Grayson, Jose Iturbi, Rags Ragland, Pamela Britton. Songs: "What Makes the Sun Set?," "I Begged Her," "I Fall in Love Too Easily," "The Charm of You," "We Hate to Leave" (lyrics, Sammy Cahn); plus songs by others. Soundtrack LP: Curtain Calls 100/17.

TELL IT TO A STAR (1945), Republic. B&W. Directed by Frank McDonald. With Ruth Terry, Robert Livingston, Aurora Miranda, Alan Mowbray. Song: "You're So Good to Me" (lyrics, Sammy Cahn); plus songs by others.

STORK CLUB (1945), Paramount. B&W. Directed by Hal Walker. With Betty Hutton, Barry Fitzgerald, Don Defore, Andy Russell, Robert Benchley. Song: "Love Me" (lyrics, Sammy Cahn); plus songs by others.

TARS AND SPARS (1946), Columbia. B&W. Directed by Alfred E. Green. With Janet Blair, Alfred Drake, Sid Caesar, Marc Platt, Jeff Donnell. Songs: "I'm Glad I Waited for You," "Love Is a Merry-Go-Round," "Kiss Me Hello, Baby," "He's a Hero," "I Love Eggs," "Don't Call on Me," "When I Get to Town," "I Love Eggs," "I Have a Love in Every Port," "I Always Meant to Tell You," "After the War, Baby" (lyrics, Sammy Cahn).

EARL CARROLL'S SKETCH BOOK (1946), Republic. B&W. Directed by Albert S. Rogell. With Constance Moore, William Marshall, Edward Everett Horton, Barbara Allen (Vera Vague). Songs: "I've Never Forgotten," "The Lady With a Mop," "Oh, Henry," "What Makes You Beautiful, Beautiful?," "I Was Silly, I Was Headstrong, I Was Impetuous" (lyrics, Sammy Cahn); plus songs by others.

CINDERELLA JONES (1946), Warner Brothers. B&W. Directed by Busby Berkeley. With Joan Leslie, Robert Alda, Julie Bishop, Edward Everett Horton, Ruth Donnelly. Songs: "When the One You Love Simply Won't Love Back," "If You're Waitin', I'm Waitin' Too," "You Never Know Where You're Going 'Til You Get There," "Cinderella Jones" (lyrics, Sammy Cahn).

SWEETHEART OF SIGMA CHI (1946), Monogram. B&W. Directed by Jack Bernhard. With Elyse Knox, Phil Regan, Anne Gillis, David Holt, Tom Harmon, Frankie Carle and his Orchestra, Slim Gaillard Trio. Song: "(Give Me)

Five Minutes More" (lyrics, Sammy Cahn); plus songs by others.

IT HAPPENED IN BROOKLYN (1947), MGM. Color. Directed by Richard Whorf. With Frank Sinatra, Kathryn Grayson, Peter Lawford, Jimmy Durante, Gloria Grahame. Songs: "Time After Time," "The Brooklyn Bridge," "It's the Same Old Dream," "I Believe," "Whose Baby Are You?," "The Song's Gotta Come From the Heart" (lyrics, Sammy Cahn); plus songs by others. Soundtrack LP: Caliban 6006.

LADIES' MAN (1947), Paramount. B&W. Directed by William D. Russell. With Eddie Bracken, Cass Daley, Johnny Coy, Roberta Jonay, Spike Jones and His City Slickers. Songs: "I Gotta Girl (in North and South Dakota)," "What Am I Gonna Do About You?," "Always Out West," "I'm As Ready As I'll Ever Be" (lyrics, Sammy Cahn); plus songs by others.

GLAMOUR GIRL (1947), Columbia. B&W. Directed by Alfred Dreifuss. With Gene Krupa, Virginia Grey, Susan Reed, Jack Leonard. Song: "Anywhere" (lyrics, Sammy Cahn); plus songs by others.

TWO GUYS FROM TEXAS (1948), Warner Brothers. B&W. Directed by David Butler. With Dennis Morgan, Jack Carson, Dorothy Malone, Penny Edwards, Forrest Tucker. Songs: "Every Day I Love You Just a Little Bit More," "Hankerin'," "I Don't Care If It Rains All Night," "I Wanna Be a Cowboy in the Movies," "There's Music in the Land," "I Never Met a Texan" (lyrics, Sammy Cahn).

ROMANCE ON THE HIGH SEAS (1948), Warner Brothers. Color. Directed by Michael Curtiz. With Janis Paige, Jack Carson, Doris Day, Don Defore, Oscar Levant. Songs: "It's Magic," "It's You or No One," "I'm in Love," "Two Lovers Met in the Night," "Run, Run, Run," "The Tourist Trade," "Put 'Em in a Box, Tie 'Em With a Ribbon and Throw 'Em in the Deep Blue Sea" (lyrics, Sammy Cahn); Soundtrack: Caliban 6015, with *It's a Great Feeling.*

SONS OF ADVENTURE (1948), Republic. B&W. Directed by Yakima Cunutt. With Russell Hayden, Lynne Roberts. Song: "If It's Love" (lyrics, Sammy Cahn).

IT'S A GREAT FEELING (1949), Warner Brothers. Color. Directed by David Butler. With Dennis Morgan, Doris Day, Jack Carson; Danny Kaye, Errol Flynn, Gary Cooper, Patricia Neal, Eleanor Parker, Joan Crawford, Ronald Reagan, Jane Wyman, Edward G. Robinson, other guest stars. Songs: "It's a Great Feeling," "There's Nothing Rougher Than Love," "Give Me a Song With a Beautiful Melody," "Blame My Absent-Minded Heart," "That Was a Big Fat Lie," "Fiddle-dee-dee," "At the Cafe Rendezvous" (lyrics, Sammy Cahn). Soundtrack LP: Caliban 6015, with *Romance on the High Seas.*

WEST POINT STORY (1950), Warner Brothers. B&W. Directed by Roy Del Ruth. With James Cagney, Doris Day, Gordon MacRae, Virginia Mayo, Gene Nelson. Songs: "By the Kissing Rock," "Long Before I Knew You," "Military Polka," "You Love Me," "It Could Only Happen in Brooklyn," "Duty, Honor, Country and the Corps," "One Hundred Days to June" (lyrics, Sammy Cahn). Soundtrack LP: Titania 501, with *My Dream Is Yours*.

I'LL GET BY (1950), Twentieth Century-Fox. Color. Directed by Richard Sale. With June Haver, Gloria DeHaven, William Lundigan, Dennis Day, Harry James and his Orchestra, Thelma Ritter. Song: "It's Been a Long, Long Time" (lyrics, Sammy Cahn); plus songs by others.

MEET ME AFTER THE SHOW (1951), Twentieth Century-Fox. Color. Directed by Richard Sale. With Betty Grable, MacDonald Carey, Rory Calhoun, Eddie Albert. Songs: "Meet Me After the Show," "No-Talent Joe," "Bettin' on a Man," "I Feel Like Dancing," "Let Go of My Heart," "It's a Hot Night in Alaska" (lyrics, Leo Robin). Soundtrack LP: Caliban 6012.

STARLIFT (1951), Warner Brothers. B&W. Directed by Roy Del Ruth. With Janice Rule, Dick Wesson, Ron Hagerty; Doris Day, Gordon MacRae, Virginia Mayo, Gene Nelson, James Cagney, Gary Cooper, Lucille Norman, Phil Harris, Jane Wyman, Randolph Scott, Ruth Roman, Louella Parsons. Song: "It's Magic" (lyrics, Sammy Cahn); plus songs by others. Soundtrack LP: Titania 510 (with *Call Me Mister*).

TWO TICKETS TO BROADWAY (1951), RKO Radio. Color. Directed by Charles V. Kern. With Tony Martin, Janet Leigh, Gloria DeHaven, Eddie Bracken, Ann Miller, Bob Crosby and his Orchestra. Songs: "The Closer You Are," "Are You Just a Beautiful Dream?," "Baby, You Won't Be Sorry," "Big Chief Hole-in-the-Ground," "The Worry Bird," "Pelican Falls," "It Began in Yucatan," "Let's Do Something New," "That's the Tune" (lyrics, Leo Robin). Videocassette: King of Video.

DOUBLE DYNAMITE (1951), RKO Radio. B&W. Directed by Irving Cummings. With Jane Russell, Frank Sinatra, Groucho Marx, Don McGuire. Songs: "It's Only Money," "Kisses and Tears" (lyrics, Sammy Cahn). Studio 78-rpm recording by original stars: Columbia 38790 (withdrawn).

WITH A SONG IN MY HEART (1952), Twentieth Century-Fox. Color. Directed by Walter Lang. With Susan Hayward, Rory Calhoun, David Wayne, Thelma Ritter, Robert Wagner, Una Merkel. Song: "I'll Walk Alone" (lyrics, Sammy Cahn); plus songs by others. Soundtrack LP: excerpts included in *Susan Hay-*

ward, Legends 1000/3; also, studio-recorded excerpts in *Jane Froman: With a Song in My Heart,* Capitol T-309 (withdrawn).

MACAO (1952), RKO Radio. B&W. Directed by Josef von Sternberg. With Jane Russell, Robert Mitchum, William Bendix, Gloria Grahame, Brad Dexter. Songs: "You Kill Me," "Ocean Breeze," "Talk to Me Tomorrow" (lyrics, Leo Robin); plus songs by others.

GENTLEMEN PREFER BLONDES (1953), Twentieth Century-Fox. Color. Directed by Howard Hawks. With Jane Russell, Marilyn Monroe, Charles Coburn, Tommy Noonan, George "Foghorn" Winslow. Songs: "Bye, Bye, Baby," "Two Little Girls from Little Rock," "Diamonds Are a Girl's Best Friend" (lyrics, Leo Robin); plus songs by others. Soundtrack LP: excerpts included in DRG/Stet DS-15005. Videocassette: CBS/Fox.

THREE COINS IN THE FOUNTAIN (1954), Twentieth Century-Fox. Color. Directed by Jean Negulesco. With Clifton Webb, Dorothy McGuire, Jean Peters, Louis Jourdan, Rossano Brazzi. Song: "Three Coins in the Fountain" (lyrics, Sammy Cahn).

LIVING IT UP (1954), film version of Styne's *Hazel Flagg.* Paramount. Color. Directed by Norman Taurog. With Dean Martin, Jerry Lewis, Janet Leigh, Edward Arnold, Sheree North. Songs: "Every Street's a Boulevard in Old New York," "How Do I Speak to an Angel?," "Money Burns a Hole in My Pocket," "That's What I Like," "You're Gonna Dance With Me, Baby," "Champagne and Wedding Cake" (lyrics, Bob Hilliard). Soundtrack LP: Capitol EAP-1-533 (withdrawn).

MY SISTER EILEEN (1955), Columbia. Color. Directed by Richard Quine. With Janet Leigh, Betty Garrett, Jack Lemmon, Bob Fosse, Tommy Rall, Kurt Kasznar, Dick York. Songs: "Give Me a Band and My Baby," "There's Nothing Like Love," "As Soon As They See Eileen," "It's Bigger Than You and Me," "We're Great But No One Knows It," "This Is Greenwich Village," "Conga," "Competition Dance" (lyrics, Leo Robin).

BELLS ARE RINGING (1960), MGM. Color. Directed by Vincente Minnelli. With Judy Holliday, Dean Martin, Eddie Foy Jr., Jean Stapleton, Hal Linden, Fred Clark. Songs: "Just in Time," "The Party's Over," "I Met a Girl," "It's a Simple Little System," "Drop That Name," "It's a Perfect Relationship," "The Midas Touch," "I'm Going Back (to the Bonjour Tristesse Brassiere Company)," "Better Than a Dream," "Do It Yourself," "Mu-cha-cha" (lyrics, Betty Comden, Adolph Green). Soundtrack LP: Capitol SW-1435. Videocassette: MGM/UA.

GYPSY (1962), Warner Brothers. Color.

CinemaScope. Directed by Mervyn LeRoy. With Rosalind Russell, Natalie Wood, Karl Malden, Ann Jilliann, Paul Wallace, Faith Dane, Betty Bruce, Roxanne Arlen. Songs: "Some People," "Small World," "Everything's Coming Up Roses," "You Gotta Have a Gimmick," "Let Me Entertain You," "Together, Wherever We Go," "If Mama Was Married," "You'll Never Get Away From Me," "(Have an Egg Roll) Mr. Goldstone," "Little Lamb," "All I Need Is the Girl," "Rose's Turn" (lyrics, Stephen Sondheim). Soundtrack LP: Warner Brothers 1480.

FUNNY GIRL (1968), Columbia. Color. PanaVision 70. Directed by William Wyler. With Barbra Streisand, Omar Sharif, Walter Pidgeon, Kay Medford, Anne Francis. Songs: "People," "Don't Rain on My Parade," "His Love Makes Me Beautiful," "A Temporary Arrangement," "If a Girl Isn't Pretty," "You Are Woman, I Am Man," "Sadie, Sadie," "Funny Girl," "Roller Skate Rag," "I'm the Greatest Star" (lyrics, Bob Merrill); plus songs by others. Soundtrack LP: Columbia BOS-3220. Videocassette and videodisc: RCA/Columbia.

James Van Heusen

Among the top composers of the musicals of Hollywood's "golden age," James Van Heusen (1913–) was a latecomer, arriving in Hollywood in 1940. But he quickly set his mark with a string of Bing Crosby movie hits, including most of Crosby's phenomenally successful *Road* pictures with Bob Hope. Later, when he worked on films for Frank Sinatra, Marilyn Monroe, Julie Andrews, and others, Van Heusen extended his career more actively into the 1960s than did most of his "golden age" peers. He also copped more Oscar nominations for Best Song (fourteen) than any of the other composers in this book. (The runner-up: Harry Warren with eleven.)

Van Heusen was born Edward Chester Babcock in Syracuse, New York. His father was a successful building contractor and his mother traced her ancestry to Stephen Foster. Young Babcock began composing songs while in high school. After he got a job with a local radio station as a part-time announcer and then as a pianist and singer, he sometimes worked his own compositions into his programs. It was at this time that Babcock, at the station manager's urging, changed his name to James Van Heusen, taking the last name from a popular brand of shirt he'd seen advertised.

At Syracuse University, Van Heusen became friends with Jerry Arlen, who introduced him to his older brother, composer Harold Arlen. In 1933 the elder Arlen arranged for several of Van Heusen's songs to be used in one of the *Cotton Club Revues* in New York City. But Van Heusen found the competition from older, better-known composers hard to buck. He spent most of the next four years as a staff pianist for several New York publishing houses.

In 1939 Van Heusen's fortunes began to change. With Edward de Lange as lyricist, he wrote the songs for a swing version of Shakespeare's *A Midsummer Night's Dream,* titled *Swingin' the Dream.* The show flopped on Broadway, but one of its songs, "Darn That Dream," became a pop hit. By 1940 four Van Heusen songs were on *Your Hit Parade:* "Polka Dots and Moonbeams," "All This and Heaven Too," "Shake Down the Stars," and "Imagination." The last one teamed him with lyricist Johnny Burke, a Hollywood veteran who had written quite a few scores with composer James V. Monaco for Paramount musicals, including half a dozen that starred Bing Crosby.

When Burke returned to Hollywood in 1940 after a falling out with Monaco, Van Heusen went with him to write the songs for *Love Thy Neighbor,* a Paramount musical teaming radio "feuders" Jack Benny and Fred Allen. The leading lady was Mary Martin, fresh from her Broadway success in Cole Porter's *Leave It to Me*—and the addition of her hit song from that show, "My Heart Belongs to Daddy," ended up completely overshadowing Van Heusen's efforts in *Love Thy Neighbor.* Still, one Van Heusen ballad, the perky "Isn't That Just Like Love?," managed to become a modest hit, thanks to Martin's insinuating delivery of its perfectly straightforward lyrics and to a spirited reprise by The Merry Macs.

At Paramount, Van Heusen and Burke were assigned, at Bing Crosby's request, to the Crosby-Hope-Lamour *The Road to Zanzibar* (1941) and *The Road to Morocco* (1942), for which they wrote such lovely ballads as "It's Always You" and "Moonlight Becomes You," both of which went on to more than a dozen weeks on *Your Hit Parade.* Then for the Crosby-Lamour *Dixie* (1943), Van Heusen and Burke wrote one of Crosby's biggest wartime hits, "Sunday, Monday and Always" (eighteen weeks on *Your Hit Parade*). The following year they topped that (twenty weeks) with "Swinging on a Star" for Crosby's Oscar-winning *Going My Way.* Among the seven Academy Awards captured by *Going My Way* (including Best Picture) was one for Van Heusen and Burke for "Swinging on a Star"—beating out other nominated songs by Harold Arlen, Jerome Kern, Jimmy McHugh, James Monaco, and Jule Styne.

It soon became evident that Van Heusen had become Bing Crosby's favorite composer, with Crosby plugging Van Heusen songs on many of his weekly radio shows as well as introducing them in his movies. Between 1943 and 1964, Van Heusen would write songs for some twenty-three different Crosby productions, mostly with Johnny Burke or Sammy Cahn as lyricist. Among them: 1945's *The Bells of Saint Mary's* ("Aren't You Glad You're You?"), 1945's *The Road to Utopia* ("Put It There, Pal," "Welcome to My Dream"), 1947's *The Road to Rio* ("But Beautiful," "You Don't Have to Know the Language"), 1949's *A Connecticut Yankee in King Arthur's Court* ("Once and For Always"), 1950's *Mr. Music* ("Accidents Will Happen"), 1950's *Riding High* ("Sunshine Cake"), 1952's *The Road to Bali* ("Moonflower," "The Merry-Go-Runaround"), 1956's *Anything Goes* ("You Gotta Give the People Hope"), 1959's *Say One for Me* ("The Secret of Christmas"), 1960's *High Time* ("The Second Time Around"), and 1962's *The Road to Hong Kong* ("Warmer Than a Whisper"). Among the requirements that Crosby made to Van Heusen: that the songs not be too sophisticated or too sentimental.

Beginning in 1954 Van Heusen also became the principal composer for a string of Frank Sinatra movies that helped reestablish Sinatra as a major star after several lean years (a period that had ended with Sinatra's 1953 Oscar for *From Here to Eternity*). These films, all with Sammy Cahn as lyricist, include 1955's *The Tender Trap* ("Love Is the Tender Trap") and 1964's *Robin and the Seven Hoods* ("My Kind of Town"), as well as the memorable 1955 television production (also with Cahn) of Thornton Wilder's *Our Town,* which introduced "Love and Marriage" and "Look to Your Heart."

Along the way, Van Heusen picked up three more Oscars—for "All the Way," from Sinatra's *The Joker Is Wild* (1957); "High Hopes," from *A Hole in the Head* (1959); and "Call Me Irresponsible," from Jackie Gleason's *Papa's Delicate Condition*

For his first movie assignment, 1940's Love Thy Neighbor *(starring Jack Benny), James Van Heusen wrote "Isn't That Just Like Love?" for screen newcomer Mary Martin. He probably thought, "Isn't that just like Hollywood?" when the studio attired Martin in the shortie fur coat that had first won her attention in Broadway's* Leave It to Me, *and then let her upstage his songs by interpolating Cole Porter's "My Heart Belongs to Daddy" (from that Broadway show).*

(1963)—plus ten further Oscar nominations. He also won an Emmy for his *Our Town* score in 1955.

But there were some major disappointments as well. The songs that Van Heusen and Cahn wrote for 1958's *Paris Holiday* (with Bob Hope, French comedian Fernandel, and Anita Ekberg), 1960's *Let's Make Love* (with Marilyn Monroe and Yves Montand), and 1967's *Thoroughly Modern Millie* (with Julie Andrews, Mary Tyler Moore, and Carol Channing) did little to compensate for the basic weaknesses of these musicals and did even less to stem the declining popularity of musicals in general. Incidental songs for such nonmusical films as *A Pocketful of Miracles, Come Blow Your Horn, Oceans 11, Not As a Stranger, Johnny Cool,* and *Where Love Has Gone* were mostly routine. Several Broadway musicals (with Cahn) also met disappointing fates, including *Skyscraper* (1965) and *Carnival in Flanders* (1953), although the latter produced a song that has since gone on to be a cabaret classic, "Here's That Rainy Day."

Many of Van Heusen's biggest commercial hits have been perky, uplifting, sunny

*Van Heusen won the first of his four Oscars for "Swinging on a Star,"
introduced by Bing Crosby, Rise Stevens, and a chorus of kids in 1943's*
Going My Way. *Frank McHugh is at the left.*

tunes (such as "High Hopes," "Sunshine Cake," "Smile Right Back at the Sun,"
"Swinging on a Star," and "Put It There, Pal"). These have tended to overshadow his
splendid romantic ballads, which I find most regrettable—for Van Heusen's ballads are
arguably the most beautiful of any composer since Jerome Kern. Their blend of
elegance and romantic warmth is especially distinctive. And whether the lyricist is
Burke or Cahn, there's also an ever-present feeling of hope and optimism for the future,
a feeling that comes through the music as well as the lyrics—that after the rain there's
a rainbow.

Sooner or later there's bound to be a major rediscovery of Van Heusen's movie
ballads, proving them to be much more than cozy romantic interludes in some popular
but far-from-classic pictures. Maybe then the aforementioned "Isn't That Just Like
Love?," "Moonlight Becomes You," "Once and For Always," and "The Second Time
Around," as well as "Suddenly It's Spring" (*Lady in the Dark,* 1944), "Like Someone
in Love" (*Belle of the Yukon,* 1944), "As Long As I'm Dreaming" (*Welcome Stranger,*
1947), and "All My Tomorrows" (*A Hole in the Head,* 1959) will become the popular
standards they deserve to be.

The Andrews Sisters and Bing Crosby teamed for many hit recordings in the '40s, but appeared together in only one film, 1947's The Road to Rio, *in which they introduced Van Heusen's and Burke's "You Don't Have to Know the Language."*

VAN HEUSEN'S MOVIES AND SONGS ON TAPE AND DISC

LOVE THY NEIGHBOR (1940), Paramount. B&W. Directed by Mark Sandrich. With Jack Benny, Fred Allen, Mary Martin, Veree Teasdale, Eddie "Rochester" Anderson, Virginia Dale, Theresa Harris, the Merry Macs. Songs: "Do You Know Why?," "Dearest, Darest I?," "Isn't That Just Like Love?" (lyrics, Johnny Burke); plus songs by others.
THE ROAD TO ZANZIBAR (1941), Paramount. B&W. Directed by Victor Schertzinger. With Bing Crosby, Bob Hope, Dorothy Lamour, Una Merkel, Eric Blore. Songs: "It's Always You," "Birds of a Feather," "You Lucky People, You," "You're Dangerous," "African Etude," "On the Road to Zanzibar" (lyrics,

Johnny Burke). LP: studio recordings of songs included in *Bing Crosby: Only Forever,* Decca 4255 (withdrawn).
PLAYMATES (1941), RKO Radio. B&W. Directed by David Butler. With Kay Kyser, Lupe Velez, John Barrymore, Ginny Simms, Patsy Kelly, May Robson, Peter Lind Hayes, Harry Babbitt, Sully Mason, Ish Kabibble. Songs: "Humpty Dumpty Heart," "How Long Did I Dream?," "Thank Your Lucky Stars and Stripes," "Romeo Smith and Juliet Jones," "Que Chica" (lyrics, Johnny Burke). LP: studio recordings of songs by Kay Kyser Orchestra included in Columbia 36433 (withdrawn).
MY FAVORITE SPY (1942), RKO Radio.

B&W. Directed by Tay Garnett. With Kay Kyser, Ellen Drew, Jane Wyman, Robert Armstrong, William Demarest, Trudi Erwin, Harry Babbitt, Sully Mason, Ish Kabibble. Songs: "Just Plain Lonesome," "Got the Moon in My Pocket" (lyrics, Johnny Burke). LP: studio recordings of songs by Kay Kyser Orchestra included in Columbia 36575 (withdrawn).

THE ROAD TO MOROCCO (1942), Paramount. B&W. Directed by David Butler. With Bing Crosby, Bob Hope, Dorothy Lamour, Anthony Quinn, Donna Drake, Vladimir Sokoloff. Songs: "Aladdin's Daughter," "Constantly," "Moonlight Becomes You," "Ain't Got a Dime to My Name," "We're Off on the Road to Morocco" (lyrics, Johnny Burke). LP: studio recordings of songs included in *Bing Crosby: Swinging on a Star,* Decca 4257 (withdrawn).

DIXIE (1943), Paramount. Color. Directed by A. Edward Sutherland. With Bing Crosby, Dorothy Lamour, Marjorie Reynolds, Billy DeWolfe, Lynne Overman, Eddie Foy Jr., Louis DaPron. Songs: "Sunday, Monday and Always," "If You Please," "She's from Missouri," "Kinda Peculiar Brown," "A Horse That Knows His Way Back Home," "Miss Jemima Walks Home" (lyrics, Johnny Burke); plus songs by others.

LADY IN THE DARK (1944), Paramount. Color. Directed by Mitchell Leisen. With Ginger Rogers, Ray Milland, Victor Mature, Warner Baxter, Jon Hall, Mischa Auer. Song: "Suddenly It's Spring" (lyrics, Johnny Burke); plus songs by others. Soundtrack LP: Rogers version of song cut from final film, included in *Choice Cuts Vol. 1,* Choice Cuts ST 500/1.

TAKE IT BIG (1944), Paramount. B&W. Directed by Frank McDonald. With Jack Haley, Harriet Hilliard, Ozzie Nelson, Mary Beth Hughes, Arline Judge, Frank Forest, Fuzzy Knight. Song: "Sunday, Monday and Always" (lyrics, Johnny Burke); plus songs by others.

AND THE ANGELS SING (1944), Paramount. B&W. Directed by Claude Binyon. With Dorothy Lamour, Betty Hutton, Fred MacMurray, Diana Lynn, Eddie Foy Jr., Frank Albertson. Songs: "It Could Happen to You," "His Rocking Horse Ran Away," "The First One Hundred Years," "How Does Your Garden Grow?," "My Heart's Wrapped Up in Gingham," "Knocking on Your Own Front Door," "When Stanislaus Got Married," "Bluebirds in My Belfry" (lyrics, Johnny Burke). Soundtrack LP: excerpts included in *Dorothy Lamour,* Legends 1000/4.

GOING MY WAY (1944), Paramount. B&W. Directed by Leo McCarey. With Bing Crosby, Barry Fitzgerald, Rise Stevens, Jean Heather, Frank McHugh, James Brown, William Frawley. Songs: "Swinging on a Star," "Going My Way," "The Day After Forever" (lyrics, Johnny Burke); plus songs and arias by others. LP: studio recordings of songs included in *Bing Crosby: Swinging on a Star,* Decca 4257 (withdrawn).

THE ROAD TO UTOPIA (1944/46), Paramount. B&W. Directed by Hal Walker. With Bing Crosby, Bob Hope, Dorothy Lamour, Robert Benchley, Douglass Dumbrille, Hillary Brooke. Songs: "Put It There, Pal," "Welcome to My Dream," "Good-Time Charley," "It's Anybody's Spring," "Would You," "Personality" (lyrics, Johnny Burke). LP: studio recordings of songs included in Bing Crosby: *Accentuate the Positive,* Decca 4258 (withdrawn).

THE BELLE OF THE YUKON (1944), RKO Radio. B&W. Directed by William A. Seiter. With Randolph Scott, Gypsy Rose Lee, Dinah Shore, Bob Burns, Charles Winninger, Robert Armstrong, William Marshall. Songs: "Belle of the Yukon," "Every Girl Is Different," "Like Someone in Love," "Sleigh Ride in July" (lyrics, Johnny Burke); plus songs by others.

DUFFY'S TAVERN (1945), Paramount. B&W. Directed by Hal Walker. With Ed Gardner, Victor Moore, Marjorie Reynolds, Barry Sullivan; Bing Crosby, Betty Hutton, Dorothy Lamour, Alan Ladd, Veronica Lake, Paulette Goddard, Eddie Bracken, Cass Daley, Sonny Tufts, Barry Fitzgerald, Billy DeWolfe, Gary, Phillip, Dennis, and Lindsay Crosby. Songs: "Doin' It the Hard Way," "Swinging on a Star" (lyrics, Johnny Burke); plus songs by others.

THE BELLS OF SAINT MARY'S (1945), RKO Radio. B&W. Directed by Leo McCarey. With Bing Crosby, Ingrid Bergman, William Gargan, Henry Travers. Song: "Aren't You Glad You're You?" (lyrics, Johnny Burke); plus songs by others. LP: studio recording of song included in *Bing Crosby: Accentuate the Positive,* Decca 4258 (withdrawn).

THE GREAT JOHN L (1945), Bing Crosby for United Artists release. B&W. Directed by Frank Tuttle. With Greg McClure, Linda Darnell, Barbara Britton, Rory Calhoun, Otto Kruger. Songs: "A Friend of Yours," "A Perfect Gentleman" (lyrics, Johnny Burke).

CROSS MY HEART (1946), Paramount. B&W. Directed by John Berry. With Betty Hutton, Sonny Tufts, Rhys Williams, Ruth Donnelly. Songs: "That Little Dream Got Nowhere," "Love Is the Darndest Thing," "Does Baby Feel All Right?," "How Do You Do It?," "It Hasn't Been Chilly in Chile" (lyrics, Johnny Burke); plus songs by others.

MY HEART GOES CRAZY (1946), TV title: *London Town.* United Artists. B&W. Directed by Wesley Ruggles. With Greta Gynt, Syd Field, Petula Clark, Kay Kendall, Tessie O'Shea, Beryl Davis. Songs: "So Would I," "My Heart

Goes Crazy," "The 'Ampstead Way," "Anyway the Wind Blows," "Hyde Park on a Sunday," "You Can't Keep a Good Dreamer Down" (lyrics, Johnny Burke).

WELCOME STRANGER (1947), Paramount. B&W. Directed by Elliott Nugent. With Bing Crosby, Barry Fitzgerald, Joan Caulfield, Wanda Hendrix, Percy Kilbride, Elizabeth Patterson. Songs: "My Heart Is a Hobo," "As Long As I'm Dreaming," "Smile Right Back at the Sun," "Smack in the Middle of Maine," "Country Style" (lyrics, Johnny Burke). LP: studio recordings of songs included in *Bing Crosby: But Beautiful,* Decca 4260 (withdrawn).

VARIETY GIRL (1947), Paramount. B&W. Directed by George Marshall. With Mary Hatcher, Olga San Juan, DeForest Kelley, William Demarest; Bing Crosby, Bob Hope, Gary Cooper, Alan Ladd, Robert Preston, Dorothy Lamour, Pearl Bailey, Judy Canova, Spike Jones and his Orchestra, Cass Daley, Paulette Goddard, Barbara Stanwyck, Veronica Lake, Joan Caulfield, Ray Milland, Barry Fitzgerald, William Holden, Lizabeth Scott, Burt Lancaster, other guest stars. Song: "Harmony" (lyrics, Johnny Burke); plus songs by others. Soundtrack LP: Caliban 6007 (with *Colleen*).

MAGIC TOWN (1947), RKO Radio. B&W. Directed by William A. Wellman. With James Stewart, Jane Wyman, Kent Smith, Regis Toomey, Ned Sparks, Wallace Ford. Song: "My Book of Memory" (collaboration by Van Heusen, Edward Heyman, Johnny Burke); plus songs by others.

THE ROAD TO RIO (1947), Paramount. B&W. Directed by Norman Z. McLeod. With Bing Crosby, Bob Hope, Dorothy Lamour, Gale Sondergaard, the Andrews Sisters, Jerry Colonna. Songs: "But Beautiful," "You Don't Have to Know the Language," "Experience," "Apalachicola," "Cavaquinho" (lyrics, Johnny Burke); plus songs by others. LP: studio recordings of songs included in *Bing Crosby: But Beautiful,* Decca 4260 (withdrawn).

THE EMPEROR WALTZ (1948), Paramount. B&W. Directed by Billy Wilder. With Bing Crosby, Joan Fontaine, Roland Culver, Richard Haydn, Lucille Watson. Song: "Get Yourself a Phonograph" (lyrics, Johnny Burke); plus songs by others.

MYSTERY IN MEXICO (1948), RKO Radio. B&W. Directed by Robert Wise. With William Lundigan, Jacqueline White, Ricardo Cortez, Tony Barrat. Songs: "Something in Common," "At the Psychological Moment," "Rolling in Rainbows," "I Could Get Along With You."

A CONNECTICUT YANKEE IN KING ARTHUR'S COURT (1949), Paramount. Color. Directed by Tay Garnett. With Bing Crosby, Rhonda Fleming, William Bendix, Sir Cedric Hardwicke, Henry Wilcoxon, Virginia Field. Songs: "Once and For Always," "If You Stub Your Toe on the Moon," "Busy Doing Nothing," "When Is Sometime?," "Twixt Myself and Me" (lyrics, Johnny Burke). LP: studio recordings of songs included in *Bing Crosby: Sunshine Cake,* Decca 4261 (withdrawn).

TOP O' THE MORNING (1949), Paramount. B&W. Directed by David Miller. With Bing Crosby, Barry Fitzgerald, Ann Blyth, Eileen Crowe, Hume Cronyn. Songs: "Top o' the Morning," "You're in Love With Someone," "Oh, 'Tis Sweet to Think," "The Donovans" (lyrics, Johnny Burke); plus songs by others.

RIDING HIGH (1950), Paramount. B&W. Directed by Frank Capra. With Bing Crosby, Coleen Gray, Frances Gifford, Charles Bickford, William Demarest, Oliver Hardy, James Gleason. Songs: "Sunshine Cake," "Sure Thing," "The Horse Told Me," "Some Place on Anywhere Road" (lyrics, Johnny Burke); plus songs by others. LP: studio recordings of songs included in *Bing Crosby: Sunshine Cake,* Decca 4261 (withdrawn).

MR. MUSIC (1950), Paramount. B&W. Directed by Richard Haydn. With Bing Crosby, Nancy Olson, Ruth Hussey, Peggy Lee, Dorothy Kirsten, Charles Coburn, Marge and Gower Champion, the Merry Macs, Groucho Marx. Songs: "Mr. Music," "Life Is So Peculiar," "High on the List," "Accidents Will Happen," "And Then You'll Be Home," "Wouldn't It Be Funny?," "Once More the Blue and White," "Milady," "Wasn't I There?" (lyrics, Johnny Burke). LP: studio recordings of songs included in *Bing Crosby: In the Cool of Evening,* Decca 4262 (withdrawn).

THE ROAD TO BALI (1953), Paramount. Color. Directed by Hal Walker. With Bing Crosby, Bob Hope, Dorothy Lamour, Murvyn Vye; Bob Crosby, Jane Russell, Humphrey Bogart, Dean Martin, Jerry Lewis. Songs: "The Merry-Go-Runaround," "Hoot Mon," "Moonflower," "Chicago Style," "To See You" (lyrics, Johnny Burke); plus songs by others. Videocassette: Unicorn.

LITTLE BOY LOST (1953), Paramount. B&W. Directed by George Seaton. With Bing Crosby, Nicole Maurey, Claude Dauphin, Gabrielle Dorziat. Songs: "The Magic Window," "A Propos de Rien (If It's All the Same to You)" (lyrics, Johnny Burke); plus songs by others.

YOUNG AT HEART (1954), Warner Brothers. Color. Directed by Gordon Douglas. With Doris Day, Frank Sinatra, Ethel Barrymore, Dorothy Malone, Gig Young. Song: "You, My Love" (lyrics, Mack Gordon); plus songs by others. Soundtrack LP: Titania 500 (with *April in Paris*); also, studio recording by Day and Sinatra, Columbia CL-6339 (withdrawn).

THE TENDER TRAP (1955), MGM, Color. Directed by Charles Walters. With Frank Sinatra, Debbie Reynolds, David Wayne, Celeste Holm, Lola Albright, Carolyn Jones. Song: "(Love Is) The Tender Trap" (lyrics, Sammy Cahn). Soundtrack LP: excerpt included in *Girls and More Girls,* MGM-Lion 70118 (withdrawn).

NOT AS A STRANGER (1955), Stanley Kramer for United Artists release. Directed by Stanley Kramer. With Olivia De Havilland, Robert Mitchum, Frank Sinatra, Gloria Grahame, Broderick Crawford, Lee Marvin, Lon Chaney, Charles Bickford. Song: "Not as a Stranger" (lyrics, Buddy Kaye).

OUR TOWN (1955), NBC-TV. B&W. Directed by Valerie Bettis. With Frank Sinatra, Paul Newman, Eva Marie Saint, Paul Hartman, Ernest Truex. Songs: "Love and Marriage," "Grovers Corners," "The Impatient Years," "Look to Your Heart," "Our Town" (lyrics, Sammy Cahn). LP: studio recordings of songs included in *The Sinatra Touch,* Capitol DNFR-7630.

ANYTHING GOES (1956), Paramount. Color. Directed by Robert Lewis. With Bing Crosby, Mitzi Gaynor, Zizi Jeanmaire, Donald O'Connor, Phil Harris, Roland Petit. Songs: "You Can Bounce Right Back," "Ya Gotta Give the People Hope," "A Second-Hand Turban and a Crystal Ball" (lyrics, Sammy Cahn); plus songs by others. LP: studio recordings of songs included in *Bing Crosby: Anything Goes,* Decca 4264 (withdrawn).

PARDNERS (1956), Paramount. Color. Directed by Norman Taurog. With Dean Martin, Jerry Lewis, Lori Nelson, Agnes Moorehead, Jeff Morrow. Songs: "Pardners," "Buckskin Beauty," "Wind, the Wind," "The Test of Time," "Me 'n' You 'n' the Moon" (lyrics, Sammy Cahn).

THE JOKER IS WILD (1957), Paramount. B&W. Directed by Charles Vidor. With Frank Sinatra, Jeanne Crain, Mitzi Gaynor, Eddie Albert, Jackie Coogan, Sophie Tucker, Beverly Garland. Song: "All the Way" (lyrics, Sammy Cahn); plus songs by others. LP: studio recording of song included in *The Sinatra Touch,* Capitol DNFR-7630.

SOME CAME RUNNING (1958), MGM. Color. Directed by Vincente Minnelli. With Frank Sinatra, Dean Martin, Shirley MacLaine, Martha Hyer, Arthur Kennedy, Leora Dana. Song: "To Love and Be Loved" (lyrics, Sammy Cahn).

INDISCREET (1958), Warner Brothers. Color. Directed by Stanley Donen. With Cary Grant, Ingrid Bergman, Cecil Parker, Phyllis Calvert, Megs Jenkins. Song: "Indiscreet" (lyrics, Sammy Cahn).

PARIS HOLIDAY (1958), United Artists. Color. Directed by Gerd Oswald. With Bob Hope, Anita Ekberg, Martha Hyer, Fernandel, Preston Sturges. Songs: "Life Is for Lovin," "Nothing in Common," "Love Won't Let You Get Away" (lyrics, Sammy Cahn); plus songs by others. Soundtrack LP: United Artists UAL-40001 (withdrawn).

A HOLE IN THE HEAD (1959), United Artists. Color. Directed by Frank Capra. With Frank Sinatra, Eleanor Parker, Edward G. Robinson, Carolyn Jones, Thelma Ritter, Eddie Hodges, Keenan Wynn. Songs: "High Hopes," "All My Tomorrows" (lyrics, Sammy Cahn).

THEY CAME TO CORDURA (1959), Columbia. Color. Directed by Robert Rossen. With Gary Cooper, Rita Hayworth, Van Heflin, Tab Hunter, Michael Callan, Richard York, Richard Conte. Song: "They Came to Cordura" (lyrics, Sammy Cahn).

SAY ONE FOR ME (1959), Twentieth Century-Fox. Color. Directed by Frank Tashlin. With Bing Crosby, Debbie Reynolds, Robert Wagner, Ray Walston, Frank McHugh, Connie Gilchrist, Sebastian Cabot. Songs: "Say One for Me," "You Can't Love 'em All," "The Secret of Christmas," "You're Starting to Get to Me," "I Couldn't Care Less," "The Girl Most Likely to Succeed," "Tico-Tico Choo-Choo," "The Night That Rock 'n' Roll Died, Almost" (lyrics, Sammy Cahn). Soundtrack LP: Columbia CS-8147 (withdrawn).

CAREER (1959), Paramount. B&W. Directed by Joseph Anthony. With Dean Martin, Anthony Franciosa, Shirley MacLaine, Carolyn Jones, Joan Blackman. Song: "(Love Is a) Career" (lyrics, Sammy Cahn).

THIS EARTH IS MINE (1959), Universal. Color. Directed by Henry King. With Rock Hudson, Jean Simmons, Dorothy McGuire, Claude Rains, Kent Smith, Anna Lee. Song: "This Earth Is Mine" (lyrics, Sammy Cahn).

JOURNEY TO THE CENTER OF THE EARTH (1959), Twentieth Century-Fox. Color. Directed by Henry Levin. With James Mason, Pat Boone, Arlene Dahl, Diane Baker. Songs: "My Love Is Like a Red, Red Rose," "The Faithful Heart" (lyrics, Sammy Cahn).

NIGHT OF THE QUARTER MOON (1959), MGM. B&W. Directed by Hugo Haas. With Julie London, John Drew Barrymore, Agnes Moorehead, Nat King Cole, Dean Jones, James Edwards, Anna Kashfi, Jackie Coogan. Song: "Night of the Quarter Moon" (lyrics, Sammy Cahn).

HOLIDAY FOR LOVERS (1959), Twentieth

Century-Fox. Color. Directed by Henry Levin. With Clifton Webb, Jane Wyman, Jill Saint John, Carol Lynley, Paul Henreid, Gary Crosby, Jose Greco. Song: "Holiday for Lovers" (lyrics, Sammy Cahn).

HIGH TIME (1960), Twentieth Century-Fox. Color. Directed by Blake Edwards. With Bing Crosby, Nicole Maury, Tuesday Weld, Fabian, Richard Beymer, Gavin McLeod. Songs: "The Second Time Around," "Nobody's Perfect," "Go, Go, Go," "Lovely Lady," "Showmanship" (lyrics, Sammy Cahn); plus songs by others.

WAKE ME WHEN IT'S OVER (1960), ABC-TV. Color. Directed by Mervyn LeRoy. With Dick Shawn, Ernie Kovacs, Margo Moore, Jack Warden. Song: "Wake Me When It's Over" (lyrics, Sammy Cahn).

WHO WAS THAT LADY? (1960), Columbia. B&W. Directed by George Sidney. With Tony Curtis, Dean Martin, Janet Leigh, James Whitmore, Barbara Nichols. Song: "Who Was That Lady?" (lyrics, Sammy Cahn).

THE WORLD OF SUZIE WONG (1960), Paramount. Color. Directed by Richard Quine. With William Holden, Nancy Kwan, Michael Wilding, Sylvia Syms, Laurence Naismith. Song: "Suzie Wong" (lyrics, Sammy Cahn).

LET'S MAKE LOVE (1960), Twentieth Century-Fox. Color. Directed by George Cukor. With Marilyn Monroe, Yves Montand, Tony Randall, Frankie Vaughan, David Burns; Bing Crosby, Gene Kelly, Milton Berle. Songs: "Let's Make Love," "Incurably Romantic," "You With the Crazy Eyes," "Sing Me a Song That Sells," "Specialization" (lyrics, Sammy Cahn); plus songs by others. Soundtrack LP: CBS Special Products ACS 8327.

OCEANS 11 (1960), Warner Brothers. Color. Directed by Lewis Milestone. With Frank Sinatra, Dean Martin, Sammy Davis Jr., Angie Dickinson, Peter Lawford, Joey Bishop, Cesar Romero, Richard Conte, Patrice Wymore, Akim Tamiroff. Songs: "Ain't That a Kick in the Head?," "Ec-o Eleven" (lyrics, Sammy Cahn). LP: studio recordings of songs by Sammy Davis Jr., Verve 10219 (withdrawn).

A POCKETFUL OF MIRACLES (1961), United Artists. Color. Directed by Frank Capra. With Glenn Ford, Bette Davis, Peter Falk, Hope Lang, Edward Everett Horton, Ann-Margret, Thomas Mitchell. Song: "A Pocketful of Miracles" (lyrics, Sammy Cahn).

BOYS' NIGHT OUT (1962), MGM. Color. Directed by Michael Gordon. With Kim Novak, James Garner, Tony Randall, Janet Blair, Howard Duff, Patti Page, Zsa Zsa Gabor. Songs: "The Boys' Night Out," "Cathy" (lyrics, Sammy Cahn).

THE ROAD TO HONG KONG (1962),

United Artists. B&W. Directed by Norman Panama. With Bob Hope, Bing Crosby, Joan Collins, Dorothy Lamour, Peter Sellers, Robert Morley, Jerry Colonna; Frank Sinatra, Dean Martin, David Niven. Songs: "Warmer Than a Whisper," "Teamwork," "Let's Not Be Sensible," "The Only Way to Travel," "The Road to Hong Kong" (lyrics, Sammy Cahn). Soundtrack LP: Liberty 17002.

PAPA'S DELICATE CONDITION (1963), Paramount. Color. Directed by George Marshall. With Jackie Gleason, Glynis Johns, Charles Ruggles, Elisha Cook. Song: "Call Me Irresponsible" (lyrics, Sammy Cahn).

COME BLOW YOUR HORN (1963), Paramount. Color. Directed by Bud Yorkin. With Frank Sinatra, Lee J. Cobb, Molly Picon, Jill Saint John, Barbara Rush, Tony Bill, Dean Martin. Song: "Come Blow Your Horn" (lyrics, Sammy Cahn).

UNDER THE YUM-YUM TREE (1963), Columbia. Color. Directed by David Swift. With Jack Lemmon, Carol Lynley, Edie Adams, Imogene Coca, Dean Jones, Paul Lynde. Song: "Under the Yum-Yum Tree' (lyrics, Sammy Cahn).

FOUR FOR TEXAS (1963), Warner Brothers. Color. Directed by Robert Aldrich. With Frank Sinatra, Dean Martin, Anita Ekberg, Ursula Andress, Charles Bronson, the Three Stooges. Song: "Four for Texas" (lyrics, Sammy Cahn).

MY SIX LOVES (1963), Paramount. Color. Directed by Gower Champion. With Debbie Reynolds, Cliff Robertson, David Janssen, Eileen Heckart, Alice Pearce, Jim Backus. Songs: "My Six Loves," "It's a Darn Good Thing" (lyrics, Sammy Cahn).

JOHNNY COOL (1963), United Artists. B&W. Directed by William Asher. With Henry Silva, Elizabeth Montgomery, Wanda Hendrix, Sammy Davis Jr., Telly Savalas, Joey Bishop, Jim Backus. Song: "The Ballad of Johnny Cool" (lyrics, Sammy Cahn).

ROBIN AND THE SEVEN HOODS (1964), Warner Brothers. Color. Directed by Gordon Douglas. With Frank Sinatra, Dean Martin, Sammy Davis Jr., Bing Crosby, Peter Falk, Barbara Rush, Allen Jenkins, Jack LaRue, Edward G. Robinson. Songs: "My Kind of Town," "Style," "Don't Be a Do-Badder," "Any Man Who Loves His Mother," "Mr. Booze," "All for One," "Charlotte Couldn't Charleston," "Give Praise," "I Like to Lead When I Dance" (lyrics, Sammy Cahn). Soundtrack LP: Reprise FS-2021 (withdrawn).

WHERE LOVE HAS GONE (1964), Paramount. Color. Directed by Edward Dmytryk. With Susan Hayward, Bette Davis, Michael Connors, Joey Heatherton, Jane Greer. Song:

"Where Love Has Gone" (lyrics, Sammy Cahn).
THE PLEASURE SEEKERS (1964), Twentieth Century-Fox. Color. Directed by Jean Negulesco. With Ann-Margret, Anthony Franciosa, Carol Lynley, Gene Tierney, Gardner McKay, Brian Keith. Songs: "Everything Makes Music When You're in Love," "Costa del Sol" (lyrics, Sammy Cahn). Soundtrack LP: RCA LSO-1101.

HONEYMOON HOTEL (1964), MGM. Color. Directed by Henry Levin. With Robert Goulet, Jill Saint John, Nancy Kwan, Robert Morse, Elsa Lanchester, Keenan Wynn. Song: "Honeymoon Hotel" (lyrics, Sammy Cahn).

THE SECOND BEST SECRET AGENT IN THE WHOLE WIDE WORLD (1965), Avco-Embassy. Color. Directed by Lindsay Shonteff. With Tom Adams, Peter Bull, Veronica Hurst, Karel Stepanek. Song: "The Second Best Secret Agent in the Whole Wide World" (lyrics, Sammy Cahn).

THOROUGHLY MODERN MILLIE (1967), Universal. Color. Directed by George Roy Hill. With Julie Andrews, Mary Tyler Moore, Carol Channing, John Gavin, James Fox, Beatrice Lillie, Jack Soo. Songs: "Thoroughly Modern Millie," "The Tapioca," "Jimmy" (lyrics, Sammy Cahn); plus songs by others. Soundtrack LP: MCA 71500. Videocassette: MCA.

STAR! (1968), Twentieth Century-Fox. Color. Todd-AO. Directed by Robert Wise. With Julie Andrews, Daniel Massey, Michael Craig, Richard Crenna, Robert Reed, Beryl Reid. Song: "Star!" (lyrics, Sammy Cahn); plus songs by others. Soundtrack LP: Twentieth Century-Fox 5102 (withdrawn).

THE GREAT BANK ROBBERY (1969), Warner Brothers. Color. Directed by Hy Averback. With Kim Novak, Zero Mostel, Clint Walker, Akim Tamiroff, Claude Akins, Larry Storch. Songs: "Rainbow Rider," "Heaven Helps Him Who Helps Himself" (lyrics, Sammy Cahn).

Academy Award Nominations/Winners

(This list includes only the songwriters in this book. Winners are marked with an asterisk.)

1934
Ralph Rainger and Leo Robin, "Love in Bloom" from *She Loves Me Not*

1935
Irving Berlin, "Cheek to Cheek" from *Top Hat*
Jerome Kern, Dorothy Fields, and Jimmy McHugh, "Lovely to Look At" from *Roberta*
*Harry Warren and Al Dubin, "Lullaby of Broadway" from *Gold Diggers of 1935*

1936
*Jerome Kern and Dorothy Fields, "The Way You Look Tonight" from *Swing Time*
Cole Porter, "I've Got You Under My Skin" from *Born to Dance*
Richard Whiting and Walter Bullock, "When Did You Leave Heaven?" from *Sing, Baby, Sing*

1937
George Gershwin and Ira Gershwin, "They Can't Take That Away From Me" from *Shall We Dance*

Harry Warren and Al Dubin, "Remember Me" from *Mr. Dodd Takes the Air*

1938
Irving Berlin, "Change Partners" from *Carefree*
Irving Berlin, "Now It Can Be Told" from *Alexander's Ragtime Band*
Harry Warren and Johnny Mercer, "Jeepers Creepers" from *Going Places*
Jimmy McHugh and Harold Adamson, "My Own" from *That Certain Age*
*Ralph Rainger and Leo Robin, "Thanks for the Memory" from *The Big Broadcast of 1938*

1939
*Harold Arlen and E.Y. Harburg, "Over the Rainbow" from *The Wizard of Oz*
Irving Berlin, "I Poured My Heart Into a Song" from *Second Fiddle*
Ralph Rainger and Leo Robin, "Faithful Forever" from *Gulliver's Travels*

1940
Jimmy McHugh and Johnny Mercer, "I'd Know You Anywhere" from *You'll Find Out*
Jule Styne and Walter Bullock, "Who Am I?" from *Hit Parade of 1941*
Harry Warren and Mack Gordon, "Down Argentine Way" from *Down Argentine Way*

1941
Harold Arlen and Johnny Mercer, "Blues in the Night" from *Blues in the Night*
*Jerome Kern and Oscar Hammerstein II, "The Last Time I Saw Paris" from *Lady Be Good*
Frank Loesser (lyrics) and Lou Alter, "Dolores" from *Las Vegas Nights*
Cole Porter, "Since I Kissed My Baby Goodbye" from *You'll Never Get Rich*
Harry Warren and Mack Gordon, "Chattanooga Choo-Choo" from *Sun Valley Serenade*

1942
*Irving Berlin, "White Christmas" from *Holiday Inn*
Jerome Kern and Johnny Mercer, "Dearly Beloved" from *You Were Never Lovelier*
Jule Styne and Sammy Cahn, "It Seems I Heard That Song Before" from *Youth on Parade*
Harry Warren and Mack Gordon, "I've Got a Gal in Kalamazoo" from *Orchestra Wives*

1943
Harold Arlen and E. Y. Harburg, "Happiness Is Just a Thing Call Joe" from *Cabin in the Sky*
Harold Arlen and Johnny Mercer, "Black Magic" from *Star-Spangled Rhythm*
Harold Arlen and Johnny Mercer, "My Shining Hour" from *The Sky's the Limit*
Jimmy McHugh and Herb Magidson, "Say a Prayer for the Boys Over There" from *Hers to Hold*
Cole Porter, "You'd Be So Nice to Come Home To" from *Something to Shout About*
Arthur Schwartz and Frank Loesser, "They're Either Too Young or Too Old" from *Thank Your Lucky Stars*
*Harry Warren and Mack Gordon, "You'll Never Know" from *Hello, Frisco, Hello*
Jule Styne and Harold Adamson, "Change of Heart" from *Hit Parade of 1943*

1944
Harold Arlen and Ted Koehler, "Now I Know" from *Up in Arms*
Jerome Kern and Ira Gershwin, "Long Ago and Far Away" from *Cover Girl*
Jimmy McHugh and Harold Adamson, "I Couldn't Sleep a Wink Last Night" from *Higher and Higher*

Jule Styne and Sammy Cahn, "I'll Walk Alone" from *Follow the Boys*
*James Van Heusen and Johnny Burke, "Swinging on a Star" from *Going My Way*

1945
Harold Arlen and Johnny Mercer, "Accentuate the Positive" from *Here Come the Waves*
Jerome Kern and E. Y. Harburg, "More and More" from *Can't Help Singing*
Jule Styne and Sammy Cahn, "Anywhere" from *Tonight and Every Night*
Jule Styne and Sammy Cahn, "I Fall in Love Too Easily" from *Anchors Aweigh*
*Richard Rodgers and Oscar Hammerstein II, "It Might As Well Be Spring" from *State Fair*
James Van Heusen and Johnny Burke, "Aren't You Glad You're You?" from *The Bells of St. Mary's*

James Van Heusen and Johnny Burke, "Sleighride in July" from *Belle of the Yukon*

1946
Irving Berlin, "You Keep Coming Back Like a Song" from *Blue Skies*
Hoagy Carmichael and Jack Brooks, "Old Buttermilk Sky" from *Canyon Passage*
Jerome Kern and Oscar Hammerstein II, "All Through the Day" from *Centennial Summer*
*Harry Warren and Johnny Mercer, "On the Atchison, Topeka and Sante Fe" from *The Harvey Girls*

1947
Frank Loesser, "I Wish I Didn't Love You So" from *The Perils of Pauline*
Arthur Schwartz and Leo Robin, "A Gal in Calico" from *The Time, the Place and the Girl*

1948
Harold Arlen and Leo Robin, "For Every Man There's a Woman" from *Casbah*
Jule Styne and Sammy Cahn, "It's Magic" from *Romance on the High Seas*

1949
*Frank Loesser, "Baby, It's Cold Outside" from *Neptune's Daughter*
Jule Styne and Sammy Cahn, "It's a Great Feeling" from *It's a Great Feeling*

1951
*Hoagy Carmichael and Johnny Mercer, "In the Cool, Cool, Cool of the Evening" from *Here Comes the Groom*

1952
Frank Loesser, "Thumbelina" from *Hans Christian Andersen*
Harry Warren and Leo Robin, "Zing a Little Zong" from *Just for You*

1953
Harry Warren and Jack Brooks, "That's Amore" from *The Caddy*

1954
Harold Arlen and Ira Gershwin, "The Man That Got Away" from *A Star Is Born*
Irving Berlin, "Count Your Blessings Instead of Sheep" from *White Christmas*
*Jule Styne and Sammy Cahn, "Three Coins in the Fountain" from *Three Coins in the Fountain*

1955
James Van Heusen and Sammy Cahn, "(Love Is) The Tender Trap" from *The Tender Trap*

1956
Cole Porter, "True Love" from *High Society*

1957
*James Van Heusen and Sammy Cahn, "All the Way" from *The Joker Is Wild*
Harry Warren, Harold Adamson and Leo McCarey, "An Affair to Remember" from *An Affair to Remember*

1958
James Van Heusen and Sammy Cahn, "To Love and Be Loved" from *Some Came Running*

1959
*James Van Heusen and Sammy Cahn, "High Hopes" from *A Hole in the Head*

1960
James Van Heusen and Sammy Cahn, "The Second Time Around" from *High Time*

1961
James Van Heusen and Sammy Cahn, "A Pocketful of Miracles" from *A Pocketful of Miracles*

1963
*James Van Heusen and Sammy Cahn, "Call Me Irresponsible" from *Papa's Delicate Condition*

1964
James Van Heusen and Sammy Cahn, "My Kind of Town" from *Robin and the Seven Hoods*
James Van Heusen and Sammy Cahn, "Where Love Has Gone" from *Where Love Has Gone*

1967
James Van Heusen and Sammy Cahn, "Thoroughly Modern Millie" from *Thoroughly Modern Millie*

1968
James Van Heusen and Sammy Cahn, "Star!" from *Star!*

Bibliography

For Further Reference & Reading About the Composers, the Movies, the
Performers, and Related Background

Books

ALTMAN, RICK, ed. *Genre: The Musical*. London: Routledge & Kegan Paul, in association with the British Film Institute, 1981.

ASTAIRE, FRED. *Steps in Time*. New York: Harper & Brothers, 1959.

AYLESWORTH, THOMAS G. *Broadway to Hollywood*. New York: Gallery Books/W. H. Smith Publishers Inc., 1985.

BARNES, KEN. *The Crosby Years*. New York: St. Martin's Press, 1980.

BAUER, BARBARA. *Bing Crosby*. New York: Pyramid, 1977.

BAVAR, MICHAEL. *Mae West*. New York: Pyramid, 1975.

BERGMAN, ANDREW. *We're in the Money: Depression America and Its Films*. New York: Harper & Row, 1971.

BOARDMAN, GERALD. *Jerome Kern: His Life and Music*. New York/London: Oxford University Press, 1980.

BOGLE, DONALD. *Toms, Coons, Mulattoes, Mammies, and Bucks: An Interpretive History of Blacks in American Films*. New York: Viking Press, 1973.

BROOKS, ELSTON. *I've Heard Those Songs Before: The Weekly Top Ten Tunes for the Last 50 Years*. New York: Morrow Quill Paperbacks, 1981.

BURTON, JACK, ed., *The Blue Book of Hollywood Musicals*. Watkins Glen, New York: Century House, 1953.

CAHN, SAMMY. *I Should Care: The Sammy Cahn Story*. New York: Arbor House, 1974.

CARMICHAEL, HOAGY. *The Stardust Road*. Bloomington, Indiana: Indiana University Press, 1946/1983.

CASPER, JOSEPH ANDREW. *Vincente Minnelli and The Film Musical*. New York: A. S. Barnes, 1977.

CASTANZA, PHILIP. *The Films of Jeanette MacDonald and Nelson Eddy*. Secaucus, New Jersey: Citadel Press, 1976.

CLAGHORN, CHARLES EUGENE. *Bibliographical Dictionary of American Music*. West Nyack, New York: Parker Publishing Co., 1973.

COHEN, DANIEL. *Musicals*. New York: Gallery Books/Bison, 1984.

COSLOW, SAM. *Cocktails for Two: The Many Lives of Great Songwriter Sam Coslow*. New Rochelle, New York: Arlington House, 1977.

CRAIG, WARREN. *The Great Songwriters of Hollywood*. New York/San Diego: A.S. Barnes & Co., 1980.

CROCE, ARLENE. *The Fred Astaire and Ginger Rogers Book*. New York: Galahad Books, 1972.

CROWTHER, BOSLEY. *The Lion's Share: The Story of an Entertainment Empire* (MGM). New York: E.P. Dutton & Co., 1957.

CURTIS, JAMES. *James Whale*. Metuchen, New Jersey/London: Scarecrow Press, 1982.

DACHS, DAVID. *Anything Goes: The World of Popular Music*. Indianapolis, Indiana/New York: Bobbs-Merrill, 1964.

DAHL, DAVID, and KEHOE, BARRY. *Young Judy*. New York: Mason/Charter, 1973.

DICKENS, HOMER. *The Films of Ginger Rogers*. Secaucus, New Jersey: Citadel Press, 1975.

DICKENS, HOMER. *The Films of Marlene Dietrich*. New York: Citadel Press, 1968.

DIETZ, HOWARD. *Dancing in the Dark*. New York: Quadrangle/The New York Times Book Co., 1974.

DI ORIO, AL, JR. *Little Girl Lost: The Life and Hard Times of Judy Garland*. New Rochelle, New York: Arlington House, 1973.

DOOLEY, ROGER. *From Scarface to Scarlett: American Films in the 1930s*. New York: Harcourt Brace Jovanovich, 1981.

EAMES, JOHN DOUGLAS. *The MGM Story*. New York: Crown Publishers, 1975.

EAMES, JOHN DOUGLAS. *The Paramount Story*. New York: Crown, 1985.

EDWARDS, ANNE. *Judy Garland: A Biography*. New York: Simon and Schuster, 1975.

EELS, GEORGE. *Hedda and Louella*. New York: G. P. Putnam, 1972.

EVERSON, WILLIAM K. *Claudette Colbert*. New York: Pyramid, 1976.

EWEN, DAVID. *American Composers Today*. New York: H.W. Wilson Co., 1949.

EWEN, DAVID. *Composers Since 1900: A Biographical and Critical Guide*. New York: H.W. Wilson Co., 1969.

EWEN, DAVID. *History of Popular Music*. New York: Barnes and Noble, 1961.

EWEN, DAVID. *A Journey to Greatness: The Life and Music of George Gershwin*. New York: Henry Holt and Co., 1956.

EWEN, DAVID. *Popular American Composers: From Revolutionary Times to the Present*. New York: H.W. Wilson Co., 1962.

FEUER, JANE. *The Hollywood Musical*. Bloomington, Indiana: Indiana University Press, 1982.

FINCH, CHRISTOPHER. *Rainbow: The Stormy Life of Judy Garland*. New York: Grosset and Dunlap, 1975.

FITZGERALD, MICHAEL G. *Universal Pictures: A Panoramic History*. Westport, Connecticut: Arlington House, 1977.

FORDIN, HUGH. *The World of Entertainment: Hollywood's Greatest Musicals* (MGM's Freed Unit). New York: Avon Books, 1975.

FOX, ROY. *Hollywood, Mayfair and All That Jazz*. London: Leslie Frewin, 1975.

FRANK, GEROLD. *Judy*. New York: Harper and Row, 1975.

FREEDLAND, MICHAEL. *Irving Berlin*. New York: Stein and Day, 1974.

GREEN, ABEL, and LAURIE, JOE, JR. *Show Biz from Vaude to Video*. New York: Henry Holt and Co., 1951.

GREEN, BENNY. *Fred Astaire*. New York: Exeter Books, 1979.

GREEN, STANLEY. *Encyclopedia of the Musical Film*. New York/London: Oxford University Press, 1981.

GREEN, STANLEY. *Ring Bells! Sing Songs! Broadway Musicals of the 1930s*. New York: Galahad Books, 1971.

GREEN, STANLEY. *The Rodgers and Hammerstein Story*. New York: The John Day Co., 1963.

GREEN, STANLEY. *The World of Musical Comedy*. New York: A.S. Barnes and Co., 1980; DaCapo Press, 1984.

GREEN, STANLEY, and GOLDBLATT, BURT. *Starring Fred Astaire*. New York: Dodd, Mead and Company, 1973.

HALLIWELL, LESLIE. *Halliwell's Filmgoer's Companion*. New York: Charles Scribner's Sons, 1980.

HARMETZ, ALJEAN. *The Making of The Wizard of Oz*. New York: Proscenium, 1977; Limelight Editions, 1984.

HARVEY, STEPHEN. *Fred Astaire*. New York: Pyramid, 1975.

HASKINS, JIM. *The Cotton Club*. New York: New American Library, 1977/1984.

HIRSCHHORN, CLIVE. *The Hollywood Musical*. New York: Crown Publishers, 1981.

HIRSCHHORN, CLIVE. *The Universal Story*. New York: Crown Publishers, 1983.

HIRSCHHORN, CLIVE. *The Warner Bros. Story*. New York: Crown Publishers, 1979.

JABLONSKI, EDWARD. *The Encyclopedia of American Music*. Garden City, New York: Doubleday and Co., 1981.

JABLONSKI, EDWARD. *Harold Arlen: Happy With the Blues*. Garden City, New York: Doubleday and Co., 1961; DeCapo Press, 1986.

JABLONSKI, EDWARD, and STEWART, LAWRENCE D. *The Gershwin Years*. Garden City, New York: Doubleday and Co., 1958/1973.

JEWELL, RICHARD B., and HARBIN, VERNON. *The RKO Story*. New York: Arlington House, 1982.

JUNEAU, JAMES. *Judy Garland*. New York: Pyramid, 1974.

KASS, JUDITH. *Ava Gardner*. New York: Pyramid, 1977.

KIMBALL, ROBERT, and SIMON, ALFRED. *The Gershwins*. New York: Bonanza Books, 1973.

KOBAL, JOHN. *Gotta Sing Gotta Dance: A Pictorial History of Film Musicals*. London/New York: Hamlyn, 1971.

KOBAL, JOHN. *People Will Talk.* New York: Alfred A. Knopf, 1986.

KOBAL, JOHN. *Rita Hayworth: Portrait of a Love Goddess.* New York: W. W. Norton/Berkley, 1978/1983.

KREUGER, MILES, ed. *The Movie Musical: From Vitaphone to 42nd Street.* New York: Dover, 1975.

KREUGER, MILES. *Show Boat: The Story of a Classic American Musical.* New York/London: Oxford University Press, 1977.

LASKY, BETTY. *RKO: The Biggest Little Major of Them All.* Englewood Cliffs, New Jersey: Prentice-Hall, 1984.

LEWINE, RICHARD, and SIMON, ALFRED. *Songs of the Theater.* New York: H.W. Wilson Co., 1984.

MALTIN, LEONARD. *The Great Movie Shorts.* New York: Bonanza Books, 1972.

MALTIN, LEONARD. *Movie Comedy Teams.* New York: Signet/Plume/New American Library, 1970/1985.

MARX, SAMUEL, and CLAYTON, JAN. *Rodgers and Hart: Bewitched, Bothered and Bedevilled.* New York: G.P. Putnam's Sons, 1976.

McCLELLAND, DOUG. *The Golden Age of "B" Movies.* Nashville, Tennessee: Charter House, 1978.

McGILLIGAN, PATRICK. *Ginger Rogers.* New York: Pyramid, 1975.

McGUIRE, PATRICIA DUBIN. *Lullaby of Broadway: The Life and Times of Al Dubin.* Secaucus, New Jersey: Citadel Press, 1983.

MERMAN, ETHEL, with EELS, GEORGE. *Merman, An Autobiography.* New York: Simon and Schuster, 1978.

MEYER, JOHN. *Heartbreaker* (Judy Garland). Garden City, New York: Doubleday and Co., 1983.

MINNELLI, VINCENTE, with ARCE, HECTOR. *I Remember It Well.* London: Angus and Robertson, 1974.

MORDDEN, ETHAN. *Broadway Babies: The People Who Made the American Musical.* New York/London: Oxford University Press, 1983.

MORDDEN, ETHAN. *The Hollywood Musical.* New York: St. Martin's Press, 1981.

MORDDEN, ETHAN. *Movie Star: A Look at the Women Who Made Hollywood.* New York: St. Martin's Press, 1983.

MORELLA, JOE, and EPSTEIN, EDWARD. *Judy.* New York: Citadel Press, 1969.

MOSHIER, W. FRANKLIN. *The Alice Faye Movie Book.* Harrisburg, Pennsylvania: A&W Visual Library/Stackpole Books, 1974.

NEMECK, PAUL L. *The Films of Nancy Carroll.* New York: Lyle Stuart, 1969.

NOBLE, PETER. *The Negro in Films.* London: Skelton Robinson, 1946.

NOLAN, FREDERICK. *The Sound of Their Music: The Story of Rodgers and Hammerstein.* New York: Walker and Co., 1978.

O'CONNOR, JIM. *Ann Miller, Tops in Taps.* New York: Franklin Watts, 1981.

PARISH, JAMES ROBERT. *The Jeanette MacDonald Story.* New York: Mason/Charter, 1976.

PARISH, JAMES ROBERT. *Paramount Pretties.* New York: Castle Books, 1972.

PARISH, JAMES ROBERT, and LEONARD, WILLIAM T. *Hollywood Players—The Thirties.* Carlstadt, New Jersey: Rainbow Books, 1977.

PEARY, GERALD. *Rita Hayworth.* New York: Pyramid, 1976.

PIKE, BOB, and MARTIN, DAVE. *The Genius of Busby Berkeley.* Reseda, California: CFS Books, 1973.

QUIRK, LAWRENCE J. *Claudette Colbert: An Illustrated Biography.* New York: Crown, 1985.

RAGAN, DAVID. *Who's Who in Hollywood, 1900–1976.* New Rochelle, New York: Arlington House, 1976.

RAYMOND, JACK. *Show Music on Record, From the 1890s to the 1980s.* New York: Frederick Ungar, 1982.

Richard Rodgers Fact Book (with Supplement). New York: Lynn Farnol Group Inc., 1968.

RINGGOLD, GENE. *The Films of Rita Hayworth.* Secaucus, New Jersey: Citadel Press, 1974.

RINGGOLD, GENE, and BODEEN, DeWITT. *Chevalier: The Films and Career of Maurice Chevalier.* Secaucus, New Jersey: Citadel Press, 1973.

SARRIS, ANDREW. *The American Cinema: Directors and Directions, 1929–1968.* New York: E.P. Dutton & Co., 1968.

SCHLOSSHEIMER, MICHAEL. *The Films You Don't See on Television.* New York: Vantage Press, 1979.

SCHWARTZ, CHARLES. *Cole Porter: A Biography.* New York: Dial Press, 1977.

SCHWARTZ, CHARLES. *Gershwin: His Life and Music.* New York: DaCapo Press, 1979.

SENNETT, TED. *Lunatics and Lovers.* New Rochelle, New York: Arlington House, 1973.

SENNETT, TED. *Warner Brothers Presents.* Secaucus, New Jersey: Castle Books, 1971.

SHALE, RICHARD, ed. *Academy Awards.* New York: Frederick Ungar, 1982.

SHEPHERD, DONALD, and SLATZER, ROBERT F. *Bing Crosby, The Hollow Man.* New York: St. Martin's Press, 1981.

SHIPMAN, DAVID. *The Great Movie Stars: The Golden Years.* New York: Bonanza Books, 1970.

SKLAR, ROBERT. *Movie-Made America, A Cultural History of American Movies.* New York: Random House, 1975.

SPRINGER, JOHN. *All Talking! All Singing! All Dancing!* New York: Citadel Press, 1966.

STERN, LEE EDWARD. *Jeanette MacDonald.* New York: Pyramid, 1977.

STERN, LEE EDWARD. *The Movie Musical.* New York: Pyramid, 1974.

TAPER, BERNARD. *Balanchine.* New York: Macmillan, 1974.

TAYLOR, DEEMS. *Some Enchanted Evenings: The Story of Rodgers and Hammerstein.* New York: Harper and Brothers, 1953.

THOMAS, LAWRENCE B. *The MGM Years.* New York: Columbia House/Arlington House, 1971.

THOMAS, TONY. *Astaire, The Man, the Dancer.* New York: St. Martin's Press, 1984.

THOMAS, TONY. *Harry Warren and the Hollywood Musical.* Secaucus, New Jersey: Citadel Press, NJ, 1975.

THOMAS, TONY. *Music for the Movies.* New York: A.S. Barnes and Co., 1973.

THOMAS, TONY. *Song and Dance Man: The Films of Gene Kelly.* Secaucus, New Jersey: Citadel Press, 1974.

THOMAS, TONY, and SOLOMON, AUBREY. *The Films of 20th Century-Fox.* Secaucus, New Jersey: Citadel Press, 1979.

THOMAS, TONY, and TERRY, JIM. *The Busby Berkeley Book.* New York: New York Graphic Society, 1973.

THOMPSON, CHARLES. *Bing.* New York: David McKay Co., 1976.

THOMSON, DAVID. *A Biographical Dictionary of Film.* New York: William Morrow and Co., 1981.

TOPPER, SUZANNE. *Astaire and Rogers.* New York: Leisure Books/Nordon Publications, 1976.

TYLER, DON. *Hit Parade, 1920–1955.* New York: William Morrow/Quill, 1985.

VALLANCE, TOM. *The American Musical.* New York: A.S. Barnes and Co., 1970.

VALLEE, RUDY. *Vagabond Dreams Come True.* New York: E.P. Dutton, 1930.

VERMILYE, JERRY. *The Films of the Thirties.* Secaucus, New Jersey: Citadel Press, 1982.

WHITE, MARK. *'You Must Remember This . . .': Popular Songwriters 1900–1980.* New York: Charles Scribner's Sons, 1985.

WILK, MAX. *They're Playing Our Song.* New York: Atheneum, 1973.

WILDER, ALEC. *American Popular Song.* Oxford, London, New York: Oxford University Press, 1972.

Articles

AUSTER, AL. "Gotta Sing! Gotta Dance! New Theory and Criticism on the Musical." *Cineaste* (Vol. XII, No. 4), 1983.

CARR, LARRY. "Musical Ghosts of the Stars." *Movie Digest,* 1973.

CUSHMAN, ROBERT. "Rodgers and Hart." *Sight and Sound,* Summer 1982.

DYER, RICHARD. "The Musical: Entertainment and Utopia." *Movie* (No. 24), 1977.

HARRIS, DALE. "Fred Astaire: Incarnation of Youthfulness, Energy and Optimism." *High Fidelity,* April 1974.

HARRIS, DALE. "I Just Dance" (Fred Astaire). *Ballet News,* 1982.

KOBAL, JOHN. "Eleanor Powell Talking to John Kobal." *Focus on Film* (No. 19), Autumn 1974.

KREUGER, MILES. "The Birth of the American Film Musical." *High Fidelity,* July 1972.

KREUGER, MILES. "Dubbers to the Stars, or Whose Was That Voice I Heard You Singing With?" *High Fidelity,* July 1972; follow-up readers' letters, October 1972.

LEDERER, JOSEPH. "Fred Astaire Remembers Gershwin, Porter, Berlin, Kerns and Youmans." *After Dark,* October 1973.

MARTIN, DAVID. "An Interview with Busby Berkeley." *Screen Facts* (No. 10), 1965.

ROSENBERG, DEENA. "Arlen and the Art of the Show Song." *New York Times* Arts & Leisure section, February 27, 1977.

Index

Boldface type indicates whole chapter is devoted to that composer. *Italics* refers to a photograph on the page. Index covers only principal text (not the listings of films or songs).

Adamson, Harold, 127, 131–135, 138, 140, 142, 200, 220, 292, 374–375

Adios Argentina, 156–157, 169

Alda, Robert, 73 *(73)*

Alexander's Ragtime Band, 37–38, *39*

Allen, Fred, 137, 162, 188, 347, 364

Allen, Gracie, 67–68 *(67),* 109, 190, 194, 311

Allyson, June, 71, 114, 233

Ameche, Don, 29 *(29), 39,* 168, 187, 202, 203, 278, *279,* 280

American in Paris, An, 75–76, *76, 77*

Anchors Aweigh, 354, *356*

Anderson, Eddie ("Rochester"), 12, 13–15, 137 *(137)*

Andrews, Julie, 246, *247,* 363, 365

Andrews Sisters, 163, *367*

Annie Get Your Gun, 45–47 *(46)*

Anything Goes, 157–158, 174–175, *177,* 312, 333

Arden, Eve, *109,* 115, 168, 170

Arlen, Harold, **1–28,** 80, 110, 134, 205, 224, 274, 290, 363, 364, 373–375

Armstrong, Louis ("Satchmo"), 3, 7, 15, 176, 201, 277

Artists and Models, 7

Astaire, Fred, xi, 16, *17,* 20, 29, 32–39 *(33, 34, 36),* 42–43, 44–45 *(45),* 48, *55,* 62–68 *(64, 66, 67),* 69, 73, 76–78 *(78),* 79, 80, 93–98 *(94, 95),* 107–109 *(108),* 110, 115, 118, 127, 155–156, 158, 163–166 *(165),* 170, 172, 179–180, *181,* 202, 224, 233, 253, 258, 273, 286, 289–291 *(291),* 338, 347, 350, *351*

At Long Last Love, 181–182 *(182)*

Babes in Arms, 10, 224–226 *(225)*

Bacall, Lauren, 334

Baker, Kenny, 10, 68–70, 128, 276, 311

Balanchine, George, 69, 224

Ball, Lucille, 35, 94, *104,* 138, 167, 228, 286

Band Wagon, The, 347, 350, *351*

Barkleys of Broadway, The, 81, 289–290, *291*

Battle of Paris, The, 154–155

Belle of New York, The, 291

Bennett, Constance, 112, 216, 266

Bennett, Joan, 197, 222

Benny, Jack, 12, 137, 162, 194, 197, 309, 325, 364, *365*

Berkeley, Busby, xi, 6, 32, 38, 46, 70–73, 113, 156, 195, 220, 224, 244, 253, 258–265, 268–275, 278, 284–285, 290, 312, 313, 314

Berlin, Irving, 12, **29–51,** 56, 68, 69, 124, 169, 176, 200, 253, 282, 290, 373–375

Billy Rose's Diamond Horseshoe, 284

Big Broadcast, The (1932), 189–190

Big Broadcast of 1936, 197, 311

Big Broadcast of 1938, 198–200, 388

Blaine, Vivian, 140, 141, 230, 232, 339, *340*

Blane, Ralph, 20, 71, 288, 289

Blonde Venus, 190–192 *(191)*

Blondell, Joan, 6–7, 260, 262, 264, *265,* 268, 273, 278

Blossoms on Broadway, 198–199, 337

Blue Skies, 44

Blues in the Night, 10–11

Bogdanovich, Peter, 182

Bolero, 195–196

Bolger, Ray, 4, 8, *9,* 106, 160, 224, 229, 232, 287, 341

Bolton, Guy, 87, 113, 160

Bordman, Gerald, 94, 106–107, 110

Born to Dance, 158–160 *(159)*

Boswell Sisters, 18, 190, 266, 309
Boys from Syracuse, The, 226–227 *(226)*
Breen, Bobby, 130
Bremer, Lucille, 113, 115, 286
Brice, Fanny, 189, 255–256, 286
Bright Eyes, 308–309 *(309)*
Broadway Melody of 1936, 325–326
Broadway Melody of 1940, 163–165 *(164)*
Broadway Rhythm, 106
Brooks, Jack, 290, 292, 374
Brown, Lew, 5, 214, 304
Brown, Nacio Herb, 198, 220, **324–332**
Brynner, Yul, 237–238 *(238)*
Buchanan, Jack, 305, 350 *(350)*
Buck Benny Rides Again, 137 *(137)*
Burke, Johnny, 17, 140, 364–365, 374
Burns, George, 67–68 *(67),* 109, 190, 194, 312

Cabin in the Sky, 13–15 *(14)*
Caesar, Irving, 56, 124, 266
Cagney, James, 16, 239, 264, *265,* 356
Cahn, Sammy, 175, 292, 354–355, 364, 366, 373–375
Cain and Mabel, 273
Cairo, 13, 348
Call Me Madam, 47–48 *(48),* 49
Calloway, Cab, 102, 190, 194, 201
Can-Can, 180–181, *182*
Can't Help Singing, 110–111
Cantor, Eddie, 5, 11, 130, 263–264, 307
Carefree, 38
Carlisle, Kitty, 194, 195, *326*
Carmichael, Hoagy, 69, 157, 200, 312, **332–336** *(334),* 337, 338, 374
Caron, Leslie, 75, *77*
Carousel, 235–237 *(236)*
Carroll, Nancy, 304, 306, *307,* 308
Casbah, 18–19
Cat and the Fiddle, The, 91–92
Centennial Summer, 111–112 *(111)*
Champion, Marge and Gower, 116, 118
Chaplin, Saul, 174, 290–291
Charisse, Cyd, 179, 233, 286, 288, 326–327, 350
Chevalier, Maurice, 35, 180, 187, 192, 201, 216–218 *(217),* 303–308 *(303, 308)*
Churchill, Frank, 135, 201
Clare, Sidney, 308–310
Clooney, Rosemary, 48–49
Cohan, George M., 31, 69, 218, 288
Colbert, Claudette, 192, 193, 218
Columbo, Russ, 99, 266, 304, 306
Comden, Betty, 290, 326, 350, 356–357
Como, Perry, 140, 141, 195, 233
Connolly, Bobby, 163, 270, 273, 313

Cornell, Lillian, 137
Coronado, 311
Coslow, Sam, 190, 305, 312
Cover Girl, 109–110 *(109),* 350
Cowboy from Brooklyn, 316, *317*
Crawford, Joan, 127, *129,* 220, 221
Croce, Arlene, 98, 156
Crosby, Bing, xi, 12, 18, 21, 29, 32, 41–43, 44, 48–49, 60, 101, 138, 140, 157–158, 174, 175, *176, 177,* 187, 189–190, *191,* 194–195, 197, 200, 222, *223,* 230, 253, 256, 266, 291–292, 304, 312, 332–333, 363–366 *(366),* 367

Dames, 268–270 *(269)*
Damsel in Distress, A, 66–68 *(67),* 223
Dancing Lady, 127, *129,* 220
Dancing Pirate, The, 222
Dandridge, Dorothy, 79, 281
Daniels, Bebe, 216, 239, 258
Darin, Bobby, 244
Davies, Marion, 56, 221, 273
Davis, Bette, 277, 349
Day, Doris, 241, 245–246, 356
DeHaven, Gloria, 106, 142, 288, *289*
DeHavilland, Olivia, 277, 349
Delicious, 61–62
Dell, Dorothy, 195
DeSylva, Buddy, 56–57, 127, 214, 306
Dietrich, Marlene, 174, *175,* 187, 190, *191,* 192, 193, 197–198, 221
Dietz, Howard, 188–189, 221, 347–348, 350
Dimples, 128–130 *(130)*
Disney, Walt, 135, 138, 201, 221
Dixon, Lee, *6, 7,* 313, *314*
Dixon, Mort, 254, 255, 256, 268
Donen, Stanley, 76, 326–328
Dorsey, Tommy, 71, *72,* 167, 311
Down Argentine Way, 278–280 *(279)*
DuBarry Was a Lady, 167
Dubin, Al, 6, 124, 126, 136, 256–277, 278–279, 287, 289, 312, 313, 373
Duke, Vernon, 5, 13, 69, 333
Dunham, Katherine, 12, 13, 15–16, 19
Dunne, Irene, 91 *(91),* 93, 99–100 *(100),* 101, 103–104 *(104),* 113, 115, 116, 237, 292
Durante, Jimmy, 59, 155, 160, 170, 221, 232, 244–246
Durbin, Deanna, 110–111, 134–135, *136,* 138, 200, 338

Easter Parade, 44–45 *(45)*
Eddy, Nelson, 8, 95, 113, 127, 160–162, 220, 228
Edens, Roger, 10, 70, 71, 76, 78, 117, 163, 224, 244

Egan, Ray, 302, 305
Ellington, Duke, 3, 59, 125, 255
Ellis, Anita, 291
Erwin, Trudi, 228, 240, 286
Etting, Ruth, 2, 215, 264
Evergreen, 222–223
Every Night at Eight, 127–128, *129*

Fain, Sammy, 264, 268, 292
Faye, Alice, xi, 29 *(29)*, 37–38, *39*, 127, 128,
    129, 132–134 *(133)*, 140, 203, *231*, 244, 253,
    279–280, 282–285, 309–311 *(310)*, 354
Fields, Dorothy, 20, 94–97, 101, 103, 125–212,
    220, 311, 350, 373
Fields, Herbert, 103, 213, 222, 229, 232
Fields, Lew, 56, 86, 94, 125, 126, 212, 213
Fleischer, Max and Dave, 201
Fletcher, Bob, 156–157
Flower Drum Song, 243–244 *(243)*
Follow the Fleet, 33–36 *(34, 36)*
Follow Thru, 306, *307*
Fontaine, Joan, 66–68
Footlight Parade, 264 *(265)*
Footlight Serenade, 204–205 *(204)*
Forrest, Chet, 228
Forty-Second Street, 220, 257–260 *(257)*, 274
Fosse, Bob, *173*, 174, 356, *357*
Four Jills in a Jeep, 140–141
Freed, Arthur, xi, 13, 70, 71, 76, 113, *171*, 220,
    232, 244, 285–286, 324–325, 326–328
Friday, Pat, 281
Froman, Jane, 273
Funny Face, 67, 76–78 *(78, 79)*
Funny Girl, 355, 356

Gable, Clark, 41 *(41)*, 50, *127*, *129*, 220, 221,
    273
Gage, Ben, 204
Gang's All Here, The, 284, *285*
Gardiner, Ava, 116
Garland, Judy, xi, 1, 8–10 *(9)*, 19, 20 *(20)*,
    21–24 *(22, 23)*, 29, 44–46 *(45)*, 70–71, *72*,
    80, 114, 115, 116, *171*, *173*, 193, 224, *225*,
    233, 253, 286–288 *(287)*, 289, 290, *325*
Garrett, Betty, 339, 356, *357*
Gay Divorcee, The, 155–156
Gaynor, Janet, 61–62 *(62)*, 307, 308
Gaynor, Mitzi, 49, 175, *177*, 178, 179, 241, *242*
Gentlemen Prefer Blondes, 202, 355
Gershe, Leonard, 23, 78
Gershwin, George, 3, 8, **55–80**, 106, 113, 115,
    126, 143, 155, 158, 160, 169, 187, 196, 214,
    216, 232, 253, 290, 301, 333, 374
Gershwin, Ira, 1, 4, 21–24, 55 *(55)*, 58–59,

62–70, 71, 73, 76, 106, 109, 197, 229, 255,
    290, 333, 350, 374–376
Gill, Florence, 129, 133
Girl Crazy, 70–72 *(72)*
Give Me a Sailor, 200
Go Into Your Dance, 270 *(271)*
Goddard, Paulette, 11–12 *(12)*, 68
Going My Way, 364, *366*
Gold Diggers of 1933, 260–263 *(261, 262)*
Gold Diggers of 1935, 271–273 *(272)*
Gold Diggers of 1937, 6 *(6)*, 273–274, *275*
Goldwyn Follies, 68–70, 75
Goldwyn, Samuel, 5, 69–70, 78, 221, 263
Goodman, Benny, 39, 166, 277, 315
Gordon, Mack, 17, 138, 278, 280–284, 290,
    311, 373–374
Grable, Betty, xi, 35, 74, 140, 167, 187, 200,
    202–204 *(203, 204)*, 253, 278–279 *(279)*, 282,
    283, 285, 356
Grant, Cary, 101, *102*, 169–170, *171*, 176, 195,
    292
Grant, Gogi, 142
Grayson, Kathryn, 11, 13, 115–116, 118 *(118)*,
    172, 173, 286
Green, Adolph, 290, 326, 350, 356, 357
Green, Johnny, 75, 189
Green, Mitzi, 71, 305, 309
Greenwood, Charlotte, 127, 235, 278
Greer, Jo Ann, 240
Guétary, Georges, 75, *76*
Gulliver's Travels, 201
Guys and Dolls, 339–341 *(340)*

Haber, Ron, 21–22
Haley, Jack, 8, *9*, 140, 311
Haley, Jack, Jr., 9
Hall, Juanita, 242, 243
Hallelujah, I'm a Bum, 219–220 *(219)*
Hammerstein, Dorothy, xi
Hammerstein, Oscar II, 61, 63, 70, 87–92,
    95–96, 99, 104–106, 110, 112, 127, 134, 135,
    211, 229–243, 246, 248, 373–374
Hans Christian Andersen, 339 *(339)*
Harbach, Otto, 61, 90, 93, 95, 104
Harburg, E.Y. ("Yip"), 5–6, 8, 10, 12, 13–16,
    19, 23–24, 110, 112, 134, 224, 274, 333, 373,
    374
Harlow, Jean, 96, 127, 221
Hart, Dorothy, 228–229
Hart, Lorenz, 10, 64, 71, 92, 107, 139, 140,
    192, 202, 211, 212–230, 239, 240, 244, 245,
    248, 255, 256, 327, 333, 347
Hart, Moss, 220, 325
Hart, Teddy, 226, 228, 229
Harvey Girls, The, 286–288 *(287)*

Haymes, Dick, 74, 140, 167, 230, *231*, 232
Hayworth, Rita, 107–110 *(108, 109)*, 165–166 *(165)*, 203, 240, *241*, 350, 355
Henderson, Ray, 214, 306
Henie, Sonja, 39–40, 128, 200, 280, 281, 326
Hepburn, Audrey, 77–78, *79*
Hepburn, Katharine, 174, 176
Here Is My Heart, 195
Heyman, Edward, 326, 33
High Society, 176–178 *(177, 178)*
High, Wide and Handsome, 103
Higher and Higher, 139–140, *141*, 200
Hildegarde, 106
Hilliard, Harriet, 35
Hit Parade of 1941, 354, *355*
Hoctor, Harriet, 59, 64 *(64)*
Hogan, Louanne, 73, 112, 230
Holiday Inn, 42, 44
Holliday, Judy, 355
Hollywood Hotel, 314–316 *(315)*
Hollywood Party, 221–222
Holman, Libby, 74, 162, 188–189, 347
Hope, Bob, 155, 160, 168, 199–201, 333 *(333)*, 338, 363, 364, 365
Horne, Lena, 3, 13–16 *(14, 15)*, 106, 113–114, 116, 142, 166, *168*, 232, 286
Horne, Marilyn, 244
Hot Heiress, The, 215–216
How to Succeed in Business Without Really Trying, *340*, 341
Hutton, Betty, 9, 11, 46 *(46)*, 71, 139, 166, 168, 290, 338, 355

I Dream Too Much, 96, *97*
I Married an Angel, 220, 228
Innocents of Paris, 303–304
International House, 193–194

Jablonski, Edward, 3, 4, 5, 8, 23, 24, 65
James, Harry, 282
Jeanmaire, Zizi (Renee), 175, *177*
Johnson, Van, 114, 227 *(227)*, 232
Jolson, Al, 5, 30, 31, 69, 73, 219–220 *(219)*, 266–267 *(267)*, 270, *271*, 272, 313
Jones, Allan, 99–100, *101*, 105, 113, 226, *326*
Jones, Shirley, 235–236 *(236)*
Joy of Living, 103–104 *(104)*
Jumbo, 244–246 *(245)*
Just for You, 292

Kahn, Gus, 4, 130, 278
Kaye, Danny, 17, 48–49, 168, 170, 339 *(339)*
Keel, Howard, 115, 118, 172, *173*, 174

Keeler, Ruby, 59, 66, 258–261, *259, 262*, 268, 270, 271 *(271)*, 273, 274, 311, 313, *314*
Kelly, Gene, xi, 44, 69, 74–76, *77*, 79, *80*, 109–110 *(109)*, 115, 162, 167, 171–172, *173*, 178, 232, 233, 239, 286, 290, 326–327 *(327)*, 338, 350, *356*, 357
Kelly, Grace, 21, 109–110, 176, *177*, 239
Kendall, Kay, 178–179
Kern, Jerome, 8, 10, 56, 63, 69, 70, **85–122**, 124, 153, 164, 197, 205, 212, 229, 253, 290, 311, 347, 350, 364, 366, 373–374
Kerr, Deborah, 237–238, 292
King and I, The, 135, 237–238 *(238)*
King of Burlesque, 128
King of Jazz, 58, 59–61 *(60)*
Kiss Me Kate, 172–174 *(173)*
Knef, Hildegard, 179
Koehler, Ted, 2–5, 7, 17, 128
Kostelanetz, André, 103
Krueger, Miles, 100, 115
Kyser, Kay, 137–138, *139*

Lady Be Good, 70, 106
Lahr, Bert, 4, 8, *9*, 125, 127, 134, 167, 170, 333
Lake, Harriette, 216, 232
Lake, Veronica, 11–12 *(12)*, 18
Lamour, Dorothy, 11–12 *(12)*, 103, 364
Lane, Burton, 7, 127, 220, 337, 338
Lane, Priscilla, 10, 313, 316
Lane, Rosemary, 226, 313, 315
Langford, Frances, 127, 128, *129*, 159, 197, 228, 315, 316, 326
LaPlante, Laura, 89
Lawrence, Gertrude, 73, 90, 126, 154–155
Lee, Bill, 242, 246
Leisen, Mitchell, 198–199
Les Girls, 178–179
Leslie, Joan, 16, *17*, 73
Let's Face It, 168
Let's Fall in Love, 4
Let's Sing Again, 130
Levant, Oscar, 69, 73, 74, 75, 290
Lewis, Jerry, 253, 292
Lillie, Beatrice, 154, 333
Little Miss Marker, 195
Loesser, Frank, 16, 137, 138, 139, 198, 200, 333, **337–346**, 354, 373, 374
Logan, Ella, 68, 131
Lombard, Carole, 195–198 *(196)*, 306, 308, 341
Long, Avon, 112
Lorre, Peter, 138, 179, *180*
Love Me Tonight, 216–218 *(217)*
Love Thy Neighbor, 162–163, *164*, 364, *365*
Lovely to Look At, 118 *(118)*

Loy, Myrna, 217, 221
Lunceford, Jimmie, 10, 39
Lupino, Ida, 157, 304, 312, 333, 349
Lyon, Ben, 215–216

MacDonald, Jeanette, 13, 91–92, 95, 113,
    216–218 *(217)*, 220, 221, 228, 305–307, 348
MacLaine, Shirley, 180, *182*, 357
MacRae, Gordon, 235–236 *(236)*
Mad About Music, 134–135
Magidson, Herb, 126, 138, 156, 354, 374
Makers of Melody, 214
Mamoulian, Rouben, 78, 216–218, 288
Marion, George, Jr., 306, 307
Martin, Dean, 253, 292
Martin, Hugh, 71
Martin, Mary, 11, 41–42, 139, 162–163, *164,*
    170, 364, *365*
Martin, Tony, 18–19, 113, *114,* 311, 354, 356
Matthews, Jessie, 66, 215, 222–223
Mayer, Louis B., 92, 113, 160–161, 170–171,
    220, 221
McDaniel, Hattie, 99, 100, 349
McGuire, Patricia Dubin, 274–275
McHugh, Jimmy, **123–150,** 200, 220, 277, 279,
    337, 338, 364, 373–374
Mears, Martha, 11, 42
Melton, James, 96, 273, 276, 286
Mercer, Johnny, 10–12, 16–17, 18, 107,
    137–138, 165, 200, 275, 277, 286–288, 291,
    312–316, 334, 348, 373–374
Mercer, Mabel, 105, 125
Merman, Ethel, 3, 5, 29, 38, 47–51 *(48),* 73,
    157, 158, 160, 166, 167, 170, 201, 311, 312
Merrill, Joan, 281
Miller, Ann, 45, 118 *(118), 173,* 174, 228, 354,
    356
Miller, Buzz, 175
Miller, Glenn, 280–281 *(281)*
Miller, Marilyn, 87, 90, 114, 160
Mills Brothers, 190
Minnelli, Vincente, xi, 7–8, 13–15, 20, 114,
    171, 286, 350
Miranda, Carmen, 136, 140–142, 277–280, 282,
    283, 285, 326
Mississippi, 222 *(223)*
Monaco, James V., 364, 365
Monroe, Marilyn, 50–51 *(50),* 240, 338, 355,
    363
Monte Carlo, 305–306
Moon Over Miami, 202–203 *(203)*
Moore, Constance, 18, 232
Moore, Grace, 4, 96, 101–102 *(102)*
Moore, Victor, 6, 11, 72, 157, 232, 274

Moran, Peggy, 105 *(105),* 136
Mordden, Ethan, 60, 158
Morgan, Dennis, 349, 351
Morgan, Frank, 46, 91, 128, 160, 162, 288
Morgan, Helen, 88, 89, 91, 98–101 *(100),* 114,
    116, 142, 270
Moten, Etta, 263
Moulin Rouge, 266
Murphy, George, 43 *(43),* 106, 131, 132, 163,
    164
Music in the Air, 92–93
My Dream Is Yours, 289
My Gal Sal, 203–204

Neagle, Anna, 38, 106
Nicholas Brothers, 2, 15, 171, 311
Niesen, Gertrude, 131, *133*
Night and Day, 162, 169–170, *171,* 350
Night at the Opera, A, 326
Nixon, Marni, 237, 292
Nolan, Frederick, 221–222, 241
Novarro, Ramon, 91–92

O'Brien, Virginia, 70, 114 *(114),* 166, 167, 288
O'Connor, Donald, 47–51 *(49),* 132, 174–175,
    177, 326–327
Oklahoma!, 106–107, 110, 229–230, 233–235
    (235)
On the Avenue, 36–37
On Your Toes, 64, 224, *225*
One Hour With You, 306–307
One Night in the Tropics, 104–105 *(105)*
Orchestra Wives, 281–282
Out of This World, 18

Paige, Janis, 180, *181,* 349, *351*
Pal Joey, 239–240, *241*
Pan, Hermes, 38–39, 174, 181
Panama Hattie, 166, *167*
Paris Honeymoon, 200
Parker, Dorothy, 197, 311
Parrish, Mitchell, 280
Parsons, Louella, 143, 314
Payne, John, 280, 281
Phantom President, The, 218
The Pirate, 170–172, *173*
Pons, Lily, 69, 96, *97*
Porgy and Bess, 63, 78–79
Porter, Cole, 16, 43, 50, 51, 69, 107, 115, 140,
    143, **151–186,** 213, 214, 232, 239, 253, 327,
    328, 338, 347, 350, 354, 364, 373–374
Porter, Linda Lee Thomas, 153, 162, 169, 170,
    178, 181
Powell, Dick, 6–7, 11, 37, 139, 258–262, 264,

Powell (*continued*)
265, 266, 268, 270–271, 273, 274, 275, 278,
311, 313, 315, 316
Powell, Eleanor, 70, 158–159 *(159)*, 160–165
(161, 164), 169, 170, 278, 313, 325
Powell, Jane, 142
Power, Tyrone, *29,* 37–38, 39–40 *(39),* 128
Presley, Elvis, 21, 176

Raft, George, 127, *129,* 142, 194, 195, *196,* 197
Rainger, Constance, 196
Rainger, Ralph, 112, 135, **187–210,** 277, 284,
311, 338, 373
Rall, Tommy, 174, *357*
Ralston, Vera Hruba, 354
Randell, Ron, 172
Ravel, Maurice, 172, 195–196
Ray, Leah, 192
Raye, Martha, 7, 140, 187, 197, 201–202, *226,*
227, 245–246, 312, 348
Ready, Willing and Able, 313, *314*
Reagan, Ronald, 314, 316
Revel, Harry, 130, 278, 311
Reynolds, Debbie, 326–327
Reynolds, Marjorie, 11, 42
Rhapsody in Blue, 56, 72–74, *75*
Richman, Harry, 31, 126
Road series, 364, *367*
Robbins, Jack, 221–222
Robbins, Jerome, 107, 238
Roberta, 93–95 *(94, 95),* 118, 127
Roberti, Lyda, 3, 94
Robeson, Paul, 98–100, 113, 117
Robin, Leo, 7, 18–19, 112, 135, 157, 189, 190,
192, 194–195, 197, 198–201, 202, 205, 277,
284, 291, 302, 304–308, 311–312, 326, 333,
338, 348, 373–374
Robinson, Bill, 15–16, 98, 142, 311
Rodgers, Dorothy Feiner, 215, 229, 232
Rodgers, Richard, 10, 17, 20, 64, 69, 71, 92,
107, 110, 134, 135, 139, 140, 151, 192, 202,
211–252, 255, 256, 262, 327, 333, 347, 374
Rogers, Buddy, 306, *307*
Rogers, Ginger, 29, 32–39 *(33, 36),* 63–65, *66,*
73, 79–90, 93–98 *(94, 95),* 118, 156, 166,
202, 258, 260, *261,* 268, 273, 289–290, *291,*
308
Rogers, Roy, 157, 354
Roman Scandals, 263–264, *265*
Romero, Cesar, 280, 282, *283*
Rooney, Mickey, 10, 70, 71, 224, *225,* 232,
233, 288, 289
Rosalie, 160–162 *(161)*
Rose, Billy, 189, 244, 254–256

Rose Marie, Baby, 193–194
Ross, Shirley, 197–198, *199,* 200, 221, 232,
333, 338
Rumba, 196 *(196)*
Russell, Betty, 288
Russell, Jane, 355

Salinger, Conrad, 75, 326
Sax, Sam, 154
Schertzinger, Victor, 4, 7, 215, 305, 337
Schwartz, Arthur, 13, 169–170, 188, 205, 222,
347–353, 374
Schwartz, Charles, 61, 153, 160, 170
Second Fiddle, 39
Segal, Vivienne, 56, 73, 92, 216, 229, 232, 239
Sennett, Mack, 190
Shall We Dance, 63–66 *(64, 66),* 79
Shaw, Artie, 163
Shaw, Winifred, 91, 92 *(92),* 272 *(272),* 313
She Done Him Wrong, 192–193 *(193)*
She Loves Me Not, 194–195
Shepherd, Cybill, 182 *(182)*
Sheridan, Ann, 275–276, 316, 338, 348, 349
(349)
Sherwin, Manning, 198, 337
Shocking Miss Pilgrim, The, 74–75
Shore, Dinah, 17, 114, 115
Show Boat, 87–88, 89, 98–101 *(100, 101),*
113–114 *(114),* 115–118 *(117)*
Sidney, George, 115, 174
Silk Stockings, 179–180 *(180, 181)*
Simms, Ginny, 106, 137–138, *139,* 170, 338
Sinatra, Frank, xi, 18, 115, 140, *141,* 176, *177,*
178, 180, 195, 235, 240, *241,* 304, 339, *340,*
356, 363, 364
Sing, Baby, Sing, 311
Singin' in the Rain, 327–328 *(327)*
Singing Marine, The, 274–275
Skelton, Red, 118, 167, 169, 286, 339
Skelly, Hal, 304
Sky's the Limit, The, 16–17 *(17)*
Smith, Alexis, 72, *73,* 169
Smith, Kate, 42–43, 190
Some Like It Hot, 333, 338
Something to Shout About, 169
Sondheim, Stephen, 247, 290, 356
Sothern, Ann, 4, 70, 106, 166, *167,* 216, 232
Sound of Music, The, 92, 211, 246–247 *(247)*
South Pacific, 240–242 *(242)*
Springtime in the Rockies, 282, *283*
Stage Fright, 174, *175*
Stage Struck, 7
Star Is Born, A, 1, 21–23 *(22, 23),* 80
Star-Spangled Rhythm, 11–12 *(12)*

State Fair, 230–232 *(231),* 244
Sten, Anna, 221
Stewart, James, 158, *159*
Stokowski, Leopold, 69, 134, 197
Stormy Weather, 15–16 *(15)*
Streisand, Barbra, 355–356
Strike Me Pink, 5
Styne, Jule, 202, 205, **353–363,** 364
Summer Holiday, 288–289 *(289)*
Summer Stock, 19–20 *(20)*
Sun Valley Serenade, 280–281 *(281)*
Sunny, 90, 106
Swanson, Gloria, 92, 239
Swarthout, Gladys, 96, 197, 333
Sweet Adeline, 90–91 *(91)*
Swift, Kay, 74
Swing High, Swing Low, 198
Swing Time, 96–98

Taranda, Anya (Mrs. Harold Arlen), 3, 4, 5, 24
Taylor, Robert, 325–326
Temple, Shirley, 8, 15, 128, 130 *(130),* 134, 193, 301, 308–309 *(309)*
Thalberg, Irving, 220, 324
Thanks for the Memory, 200, 333 *(333),* 338
Thank Your Lucky Stars, 348–349 *(349)*
That Certain Age, 135, *136*
That Night in Rio, 280
There's No Business Like Show Business, 49–51 *(50)*
This Is the Army, 42–43 *(43)*
Thomas, Tony, 255, 263, 273
Thompson, Kay, 77–78 *(78),* 287
Tibbett, Lawrence, 5, 19, 127, 348
Till the Clouds Roll By, 85, 113–115 *(114)*
Time, the Place, and the Girl, The, 349–350, *351*
To Have and Have Not, 333–334 *(334)*
Todd, Mabel, 11
Too Many Girls, 227–228 *(227)*
Top Hat, 32–33 *(33), 34,* 35, 45
Top of the Town, 131–132 *(132), 133*
Torch Singer, 192
Transatlantic Merry-Go-Round, 309
Tracy, Arthur, 190
Twenty Million Sweethearts, 268, 289

Valentino, Rudolph, 125
Vallee, Rudy, 40, 139, 256, 277, 341
Van Heusen, James, 17, 110, 140, 175, 292, **363–372,** 374–375
Varsity Show, 313–314
Velez, Lupe, 127, 221, 304

Vera-Ellen, 47–49, 233
Verrill, Virginia, 70, 96

Waikiki Wedding, 197
Walker, Robert, 85, 113
Waller, Fats, 15–16, 128
Walters, Charles, 19, 71, 176, 244
Warfield, William, 117
Waring, Fred, 155, 277, 314
Warner, Jack, 272
Warren, Annette, 116
Warren, Harry, 6, 17, 136, 138, 187, 198, 200, 202, 205, **253–300,** 312, 313, 316, 334, 373–374
Washington, Ned, 218, 292
Waters, Ethel, 3, 13–15 *(14)*
Webb, Clifton, 162, 188, 347
Webster, Paul Francis, 292
Weekend in Havana, 198, 354
Weill, Kurt, 198, 354
Welch, Elisabeth, 125, 155
West, Mae, 127, 187, 192–193 *(193),* 239, 333
Weston, Doris, 274
When You're in Love, 101–102 *(102)*
White Christmas, 48–49
White, George, 2, 57, 74, 75, 127, 302
Whiteman, Paul, 57–58, 59–61 *(60),* 73, 192, 214, 244, 332
Whiting, Jack, 90, 130, 201, 216
Whiting, Margaret, 302, 306, 308–309, 316
Whiting, Richard, 31, 112, 187, 190, 198, 277, 282, **301–322,** 373
Whitney, John Hay, 222
Whorf, Richard, 113, 157
Wieck, Dorothea, 194
Wilder, Alec, xi
Wilk, Max, 312
Williams, Andy, 335
Williams, Esther, 253, 286, 291, 339
Williams, Frances, 3, 221
Wilson, John S., 58, 63, 80
Winninger, Charles, 98, 106, 117, 230, *231*
Wizard of Oz, The, 1, 8–9 *(9),* 13, 19, 104
Wodehouse, P.G., 86–88
Wonder Bar, 266–267 *(267)*
Woolley, Monty, 152, 154, 155, 169, 170, *171*
Words and Music, 232–233
Wright, Bob, 228
Wrubel, Allie, 268
Wyman, Jane, 170, *204,* 292
Wynn, Nan, 107, 203

Yellen, Jack, 3, 61
Yolanda and the Thief, 286

You and Me, 198
You Were Never Lovelier, 107–108 *(108)*
You'll Find Out, 137–138, *139*
You'll Never Get Rich, 165–166 *(165)*
Youmans, Vincent, 2, 156
You're a Sweetheart, 132–134 *(133)*

Zanuck, Darryl F., 36–37, 128, 156, 202, 203, 230, 256, 260, 264–265, 278, 309, 354
Ziegfeld, Florenz, 30, 58, 87–89, 98, 223, 286
Ziegfeld Follies (1946), 79, *80,* 286
Ziegfeld Girl, 325 *(325)*
Zorina, Vera, 11, 68–69, 142, 224, *225,* 232